THEOLOGICAL LITERACY
for the
TWENTY-FIRST CENTURY

THEOLOGICAL LITERACY
for the
TWENTY-FIRST CENTURY

Edited by

Rodney L. Petersen

with

Nancy M. Rourke

WILLIAM B. EERDMANS PUBLISHING COMPANY
GRAND RAPIDS, MICHIGAN / CAMBRIDGE, U.K.

© 2002 Wm. B. Eerdmans Publishing Co.

Wm. B. Eerdmans Publishing Co.
255 Jefferson Ave. S.E., Grand Rapids, Michigan 49503 /
P.O. Box 163, Cambridge CB3 9PU U.K.
www.eerdmans.com

Printed in the United States of America

06 05 04 03 02   7 6 5 4 3 2 1

Library of Congress Cataloging-in-Publication Data

Theological literacy for the twenty-first century /
edited by Rodney L. Petersen, with Nancy M. Rourke.
p.   cm.
Includes bibliographical references.
ISBN 0-8028-4964-4 (pbk.: alk. paper)
1. Theology — Study and teaching.
I. Petersen, Rodney Lawrence.
II. Rourke, Nancy M.

BV4022.T47   2002
230′.01 — dc21
2002023823

Chapter 11 is based on material from *Rhetoric and Ethic: The Politics of Biblical Studies* by Elisabeth Schüssler Fiorenza © 1999 Augsburg Fortress (www.augsburgfortress.org).

Contents

Contents

Acknowledgments

The publication of this volume comes on the occasion of the thirty-fifth anniversary of the Boston Theological Institute (BTI). Some of the chapters in this volume originated at the thirtieth anniversary of the BTI. Others have been collected since that time.

The Boston Theological Institute is composed of at least three different patterns of theological education: that which occurs in university divinity schools, in schools of theology, and in seminaries. Each of these three types of schools offers a different shape to theological literacy. It is also important to note that one of the schools is Greek Orthodox, three are related to the Roman Catholic Church, and five are historically Protestant but with different degrees of relation to contemporary definitions and understandings about the way in which religion should be practiced. The different identities of the authors of this volume are detailed in the descriptions of the contributors.

In addition to the authors whose chapters make up the contents of this book, a word of thanks is in order to others as well. Robert C. Neville, Nancy D. Richardson, and Donald J. Dietrich helped to recommend authors and gave initial encouragement on behalf of the Board of Trustees of the BTI. Thanks to a grant from the Wabash Center and its director, Raymond B. Williams, the initial work done on this volume also led to the formation of two certificate programs across the breadth of the BTI schools. Other individuals who contributed to this volume include Forrest Clingerman, whose work as editor of the *BTI Newsletter* led to the production of a booklet entitled *Theological Literacy* that was used as the basis for a questionnaire and further work through the *Padare* at the Eighth Assembly of the World Council of Churches meeting in Harare in 1998. Further assistance was given by Chance Hunter. Thanks to the unstinting efforts of Nancy M. Rourke and Michael Campos, this volume has been brought to completion. Thanks also go to Lynne Bundesen for editorial assistance and to Tiffany Puett for work on the index.

Acknowledgments

I would be remiss if I did not also offer a word of appreciation to the late George H. Williams. His work on the history of religion at Harvard University and in New England has helped to guide this author's own respect and appreciation for the different patterns of Christian expression that have enlivened the Christian movement not only diachronically and across a vast terrain, but also synchronically in our own space and time. He had planned to write the foreword to this volume.

Foreword

RODNEY L. PETERSEN

This book is an invitation to a conversation, a conversation about what it means to be theologically literate. It is a conversation like many we enter into — stimulating, vexing, sometimes discouraging, at times encouraging, but always worthwhile. It is a conversation that we all have been part of for a long time, yet it will continue for a long time as well. It is one that marks us as eminently human.

This collection of essays presents a compendium of different perspectives by leading theological educators who write from their fields on what constitutes theological literacy in the twenty-first century. In order to lend coherence to a diversity of expression, this book is structured around points that have shaped a traditional curriculum in theological education. The context for this book, the Boston Theological Institute (BTI), is a consortium of theology schools.[1] Each school has its own tradition, educational methodology, goals, and constituency. Each has approached the social and pedagogical challenges of the past quarter century differently, setting its own trajectory for the future. One of the common denominators that serves this consortium well, of which this book is representative, is a commitment to conversation — and to conversation as constitutive of theological literacy toward the renewal of the churches and of the human community.[2]

The nature of renewal is a question that finds its way into the churches

---

1. Rodney L. Petersen, *Christianity and Civil Society: Theological Education for Public Life* (Maryknoll, N.Y.: Orbis Books, 1995). Written on the occasion of the twenty-fifth anniversary of the BTI, this work notes the identities of the different schools. Boston, as the social location for these schools, is well described by Thomas H. O'Conner in *The Hub: Boston Past and Present* (Boston: Northeastern University Press, 2001), pp. 276-98. His point is that Yankee, Irish, and Italian pasts have given way to a more complex present with additional African American, Hispanic American, Asian American, and other population groups.

2. See the BTI Mission Statement as outlined in the yearly catalogue.

as they struggle with change.[3] When churches, frequently conceived by the state as faith communities, work for conversion and transformation in individual lives and in the communities they seek to serve, institutions of higher learning can foster the theological literacy necessary for understanding what conversion means and how effective change can take place in social policy and organizational development appropriate to the social complexities of the twenty-first century.[4] Renewal in the schools is closely related to renewal in the communities out of which they have come or now seek to serve. We have found through the course of the twentieth century that religion is like sexuality in that it appears to be constitutive of our identity as individuals and societies. Just as some forms of sexuality can be abusive and destructive, so too not all religion is constructive. Philosophers of suspicion and our own foibles aside, religion appears to be an essential component of who we are and what we seek to be.[5] Religion matters.[6]

3. Change in light of the essence of the church is a subject taken up by Hans Küng in his book, *Christianity: Essence, History, and Future* (New York: Continuum, 1995). Noting significant growth in certain population and social sectors but decline in the Protestant mainline, Donald Miller writes, "If Christianity is going to survive, it must continually reinvent itself, adapting its message to the members of each generation, along with their culture and the geographical setting," in his *Reinventing American Protestantism* (Berkeley: University of California Press, 1997), p. 18. Küng develops trajectories that are helpful in plotting directions for evolving models of church life, practice, and ministry. C. Peter Wagner has taken such thinking into the domain of church growth, arguing that social change requires new forms of church organization and life; see *Churchquake: How the New Apostolic Reformation Is Shaking Up the Church as We Know It* (Ventura, Calif.: Regal, 1999).

4. Books include such differing perspectives as Conrad Cherry, *Hastening toward Zion: Universities, Divinity Schools, and American Protestantism* (Indianapolis: Indiana University Press, 1995), and George Marsden, *The Soul of the American University: From Protestant Establishment to Established Nonbelief* (New York: Oxford University Press, 1994); similarly, James Tunstead Burtchaell, *The Dying of the Light: The Disengagement of Colleges and Universities from Their Christian Churches* (Grand Rapids: Eerdmans, 1998).

5. Hans Küng, *Freud and the Problem of God* (New Haven: Yale University Press, 1990). See also Samuel Preus, *Explaining Religion: Criticism and Theory from Bodin to Freud* (New Haven: Yale University Press, 1987); Freud outlines his perspective on religion most succinctly in "The Question of a *Weltanschauung*," in *New Introductory Lectures on Psycho-Analysis*, trans. and ed. James Strachey (New York: Norton, 1965), pp. 195-225. Here he scores religion negatively for its inability to give what it offers: information, protection, and direction. Instead, Freud posits his scientific worldview as more honest and better able to provide these. The exchange of letters between Reformed pastor Oskar Pfister and Freud on these points is revealing, in *Psychoanalysis and Faith*, ed. Ernst L. Freud (New York: Basic Books, 1964); also, Oskar Pfister, "The Illusion of a Future," *Imago* 14, no. 2/3 (1928).

6. William Scott Green and Jacob Neusner, eds., *The Religion Factor: An Introduction to How Religion Matters* (Louisville: Westminster John Knox, 1996). Houston Smith describes the

Theological literacy begins with theology. Theology is the discipline that makes sense of the issues that shape our conception of religion. One need for theology comes when we feel a call that may seem distant to others.[7] Abraham's call was different from that of Lot. How did he and, insofar as this is thought to be relevant to us, how do we make sense of this? What about when one sees the need for reform and another appears not to notice injustice? Apparent pain and distress also call for theology, often referred to as theodicy or the vindication of the goodness of God in the face of suffering. How is it that we make sense of a belief that goodness is more basic than evil, a key belief for warding off depression and nihilism? Still again, when we believe we understand the ways of God but encounter different conceptions of God articulated with different theologies and definitions of salvation, how do we reconcile such differences? Election or national identity, restorative justice, an affirmation of goodness in the face of suffering and trauma, the encounter of different religions — each of these areas that mark the opening of the twenty-first century calls for theological literacy. André Malraux, the French minister of culture from the last century, wrote that the twenty-first century will be religious or it will not be at all. Theology is the science of religion, a systematic way of thinking about our most fundamental assumptions.

This conversation about theological literacy occurs in the context of academic disciplines that have morphed in shape and expanded in size. Whereas at one time persons training for the priesthood or ministry had only to take courses in four or five defined core areas, additions to the curriculum today include topics as diverse as computer programming, genetics, business administration, cultural studies, world religions, and social conflict analysis. And this question about what constitutes theological literacy occurs in the context of the changing place in American public culture of university divinity schools, schools of theology, and seminaries.[8] This change is part of a

---

need to make sense of things, "minds require eco-niches as much as organisms do," in *Why Religion Matters* (San Francisco: Harper Collins, 2001), p. 26.

7. Richard Grigg, *Theology as a Way of Thinking* (Atlanta: Scholars Press, 1990).

8. The need for conversation about religion and American public culture is the point of Martin Marty's two-volume set, *Politics, Religion, and the Common Good* (San Francisco: Jossey-Bass, 2000) and *Education, Religion, and the Common Good* (San Francisco: Jossey-Bass, 2000). Kenneth O. Gangel asks how to deliver a theological education that works. See his article, "Delivering Theological Education That Works," *Theological Education* 34, no. 1 (autumn 1997): 1-9. Accreditation standards for theological schools, as established by the Association of Theological Schools in the U.S.A. and Canada, are laid out by Daniel O. Aleshire, "The ATS Quality and Accreditation Project," *Theological Education* 30, no. 2 (spring 1994): 5-16. See additional articles in this and later volumes. Structural adjustments in theological education is a topic taken

larger structural transformation affecting all our universities, colleges, and institutes of learning.[9]

Changes in academic disciplines and in the structures of our schools, important as they are in themselves, also reflect a more fundamental revaluation of the core assumptions that have shaped our culture. Pedagogical change and cultural revaluation both affect what we mean by theological literacy. They are both a part of the debate over what constitutes general literacy in our society today. Stimulated by the revolution in information technology, much as that earlier period of humanism and Renaissance developed in relation to the new methodologies of printing in the fifteenth century, some argue optimistically that literacy is not just reading and following directions, but is found in the ability to write and to think, which is more pronounced in America today than ever in our history.[10] Other educators, like E. D. Hirsch, argue that literacy is related to a core of knowledge that permits wide social interaction, of which our children are being deprived in contemporary society.[11] Coming at the question differently, educators Theodore and Nancy Sizer argue for the role played by students and teachers in creating an environment where respect for learning and for each other exists.[12] Each of these positions has its analogue in theological education: those who celebrate interreligious diversity and recognition, those who lament the loss of core biblical understanding in our culture, and others, as in this book, who value the importance of respectful dialogue about things that matter most.[13]

---

up in Barbara G. Wheeler and Edward Farley, eds., *Shifting Boundaries: Contextual Approaches to the Structure of Theological Education* (Louisville: Westminster John Knox, 1991).

9. Neil Postman, *Technopoly: The Surrender of Culture to Technology* (New York: Vintage Books, 1993), observes how new technologies implemented widely in society bring a culture into crisis. This might be seen as further reflection on Émile Durkheim's argument concerning the relation between how work is done and the nature of social and cultural organization, including religion. Durkheim's sense of the sacred is picked up by Marcel Gauchet, who describes in this light, paradoxically, the development of human political and psychological autonomy. See his *The Disenchantment of the World: A Political History of Religion*, trans. Oscar Burge (Princeton: Princeton University Press, 1997). Issues of the *Chronicle of Higher Education* report on educational practice and pedagogy. An analysis of its treatment of religion would offer insight into social theory.

10. Leon Botstein, *Jefferson's Children: Education and the Promise of American Culture* (New York: Doubleday, 1997). Writing as president of Bard College, Botstein is critical of cultural pessimists who, he believes, are damaging American society.

11. E. D. Hirsch, Jr., *Cultural Literacy: What Every American Needs to Know* (New York: Vintage Books, 1988). He includes a list of 5,000 items he believes every high school senior should know.

12. Theodore R. Sizer and Nancy Faust Sizer, *Students Are Watching: Schools and the Moral Contract* (Boston: Beacon Press, 2000).

13. The value of finding a common language for the common good is a supposition that might be taken from Robert Bellah's collaborative work (with Richard Madsen, William M.

With the apparent tendency among some to abandon the Western tradition, central to our understanding of liberal thought and democratic values, the question about what to put in its place has emerged. This is viewed most sharply in the theological schools.[14] If this question has received no little discussion in our colleges and universities, it is debated as heatedly or more so in the politics of contemporary religion and theology departments, even in schools that have retained their church or religious affiliation.[15] To the extent that the "Western tradition" is code language for Christian values and understanding, open hostility may even result.[16] In this atmosphere a religious fundamentalism of the left and of the right often closes off the possibility of conversation, something that this volume contends is basic to theological literacy.[17] Each of the communities that values theological literacy within the orbit of Christian reflection struggles with these issues through a paradigm that puts culture in relation to church in a variety of configurations.[18] Orthodoxy has been particularly challenged by significant global and political change in its heartland, from eastern Europe across the Levant. This has had its effect upon Orthodoxy in North America.[19] Roman

---

Sullivan, Ann Swidler, and Steven M. Tipton), *Habits of the Heart: Individualism and Commitment in American Life* (Berkeley and Los Angeles: University of California Press, 1985). Bellah's comment about the coequal participation of church, sect, and mysticism, each playing a role in shaping American public culture, might be extended to all religious partners (p. 246).

14. Cornell W. Clayton, "Politics and Liberal Education," *Chronicle of Higher Education*, 8 April 1992, p. B1-2. Jaroslav Pelikan's own defense has been that of the academic calling in which teaching and scholarship are joined toward humane ends; see his *The Idea of the University: A Reexamination* (New Haven: Yale University Press, 1992).

15. Donald Wiebe, "Theology and the Academic Study of Religion in Protestant America," in *The Politics of Religious Studies: The Continuing Conflict with Theology in the Academy*, ed. Donald Wiebe (New York: St. Martin's Press, 1999), pp. 69-90. See Stephen Toulmin, "Theology in the Context of the University," and Ronald F. Thiemann, "The Future of an Illusion: An Inquiry into the Contrast between Theological and Religious Studies," *Theological Education* 26, no. 2 (spring 1990): 51-65, 66-85.

16. George M. Marsden, *The Outrageous Idea of Christian Scholarship* (New York: Oxford University Press, 1998). Marsden argues that universities have virtually established "nonbelief" as their creed, that Christians are not welcome under the umbrella of diversity, and that rather than threaten the modern university they have much to offer.

17. Robert K. Merton writes of social structure and anomie with implications for society in *Social Theory and Social Structure*, enlarged ed. (New York: Free Press, 1968), pp. 175-214; for observations with direct bearing on this discussion, but not only for Christianity, see Martin Marty and R. Scott Appleby, eds., *Fundamentalisms Observed*, Fundamentalism Project, vol. 1 (Chicago: University of Chicago Press, 1991), and later volumes.

18. The classic formulation is that of H. Richard Niebuhr, *Christ and Culture* (New York: Harper and Row, 1951). Niebuhr finds the following typologies: Christ against culture, of culture, above culture, in paradoxical relationship with culture, and the transformer of culture.

19. Stanley Harakas, "Orthodoxy in America: Continuity, Discontinuity, Newness," in

Catholic theological education has undergone continual reshaping in the American context, related to models of seventeenth-century reform, the exigencies of Vatican II, and the experience of plurality and otherness in the new century.[20] And Protestant theology, once confident in its ability to educate its own and to shape higher education in the United States, finds itself in internal division between a deepening commitment to a descriptive rather than normative approach to theology on the one hand, and on the other, to a fear that the future will be lost through a lack of integrity or will.[21]

These topics, and others, have been subject to discussion in the Association of Theological Schools in the U.S.A. and Canada (ATS), the accrediting body for schools of theology and seminaries in North America. A considerable amount of reflection has found its way into its publications. One issue invites past ATS presidents to share their thoughts and observations on the direction of theological education. Vincent Cushing considers the pastoral situation of

---

Orthodox Perspectives on Pastoral Praxis, ed. Theodore Stylianopoulos (Brookline, Mass.: Holy Cross Orthodox Press, 1988), pp. 13-29. Harakas lifts up the importance of "witness" instead of polarities of world-negating and affirming tendencies. More recently, see Daniel Ciobotea, "Is Academic Theology the Only Theology in the Church? Towards a Larger and Deeper Definition of Theology," in *Resources for Spiritual Formation in Theological Education,* ed. Samuel Amirtham and Robin Pryor (Geneva: World Council of Churches, 1989), pp. 23-36, and Petros Vassiliadis, "A Response to Konrad Raiser," in *Towards Viable Theological Education: Ecumenical Imperative, Catalyst of Renewal,* ed. John Pobee (Geneva: World Council of Churches Publications, 1997).

20. Joseph M. O'Keefe, S.J., *Catholic Education at the Turn of the New Century* (New York: Garland, 1997), and Katarina Schuth, *Seminaries, Theologates, and the Future of Church Ministry* (Collegeville, Minn.: Liturgical Press, 1999). Schuth details how formation for ministry is occurring in Catholic seminaries. While progress is noted, curricular concerns continue for multicultural studies, ecumenism, and collaboration (p. 236). Ever since the promulgation of the apostolic constitution *Ex Corde Ecclesiae* (ECE, "From the Heart of the Church"), this issue has loomed ever larger for Catholic universities and schools of theology. Issued by Pope John Paul II in 1990, this document was meant to articulate the relationship between higher education, faith, Christian culture, and the Roman Catholic Church. Respecting seminary formation, two documents by John Paul II remain central: *Pastores Dabo Vobis: Postsynodal Apostolic Exhortation on the Formation of Priests in the Circumstances of the Present Day,* in *Origins* 21 (16 April 1992), and *Program of Priestly Formation,* 4th ed. (National Conference of Catholic Bishops, 1993).

21. Jackson W. Carroll, Barbara G. Wheeler, Daniel O. Aleshire, and Penny Long Marler, *Being There: Culture and Formation in Two Theological Schools* (New York: Oxford University Press, 1997), pp. 269-79. Background to this discussion can be found in W. Clark Gilpin, "The Seminary Ideal in American Protestant Ministerial Education, 1700-1808," *Theological Education* 20, no. 2 (spring 1984): 85-106, and Glenn T. Miller, "Professionals and Pedagogues: A Survey of Theological Education," in *Altered Landscapes: Christianity in America, 1935-1985,* ed. David Lotz (Grand Rapids: Eerdmans, 1989), pp. 189-208. Authors such as Hauerwas, Lindbeck, Noll, Wells, and others have been a part of this discussion.

the local church and, for Roman Catholics, asks about the effects arising from more laypeople preparing for professional ministry than men studying for the ordained ministry. C. Douglas Jay notes the religiously diverse contexts in which ministry will occur in the twenty-first century. He addresses the importance of dealing with religious pluralism. Barbara Brown Zikmund comments positively on the advances in diversity of student bodies and ecumenical relationships, but shares her concern about such factors as rising costs, shape of the curriculum, significant new technologies, and impact of religious pluralism. Russell H. Dilday asks about how first-rate scholarship, spiritual formation, and faith and character development will balance the theoretical and practical concerns of church management and leadership. James L. Waits and Judith A. Berling add to the above the need for integrating a global perspective. And Luder Whitlock reflects on the ways large churches and megachurches "compete" with seminaries in training pastoral leadership.[22] A growing number of books have followed similar themes as schools charged with the end of theological literacy have worked to find the way ahead.[23]

Literacy is a function of measurable standards. By the third generation of Christians, we clearly see emerging catechetical schools at Alexandria and Antioch for the training of church leadership. By the time Jerome worked to bring together an early Bible, a canon or basis for literacy in the church had emerged. Jerome even reports being accused in a nightmare of remaining in love with the pagan canon of literature, particularly the works of Cicero, all appropriate to a passing dispensation. Living now in the dispensation of Christ, his canon was to be the prophets of Israel, the Gospels, and Paul.[24] To be literate was to know and to be shaped by the canon appropriate to the new dispensation. Boethius brought into this a curriculum based on the new canon but drawn from the pedagogy of Hellenism. Literacy in the medieval period was built around the trivium and quadrivium, the former consisting of grammar, rhetoric, and dialectic, the latter of music, arithmetic, geometry, and astronomy.

---

22. The issue of *Theological Education*, published by the ATS, vol. 36, no. 2 (spring 2000), focuses on these reflections from former ATS presidents on the future of theological education in the twenty-first century. On the last point, models of education have been established in megachurches like Willow Creek and Saddleback. These challenge denominational agencies and seminaries. Michael S. Hamilton, "Willow Creek's Place in History," *Christianity Today*, 13 November 2000, pp. 63-68.

23. Historian David Steinmetz writes that theological education may not be necessary for the church, but it has an "instrumental" role to play, belonging to the *"bene esse"* rather than *"esse"* of the church, in "The Protestant Minister and the Teaching Office of the Church," *Theological Education* 19, no. 2 (spring 1983): 58.

24. J. N. D. Kelly, *Jerome: His Life, Writings, and Controversies* (New York: Harper and Row, 1975), pp. 42-43 (Letter 22.29-30).

Derived in the fifth century[25] and extending from Alcuin's (ca. 735-804) day through the medieval period, these seven liberal arts constituted the propaedeutic to the study of theology. This is what it meant to be literate, and it constituted the foundation of theological literacy in western Europe. The Renaissance and then emergent humanism were both shaped around what it meant to be literate. From the Enlightenment into the twentieth century, this classical heritage became the foundation for an array of academic disciplines, based upon expanding humanist assumptions largely derivative of the authority of reason and experience as perceived by the individual or growing community of scholars. Literacy has always involved a given set of skills derivative of these arts.[26] As we now stand looking over this history from the opening years of the twenty-first century, we recognize more clearly ways in which language, culture, and human perspective have shaped this understanding.[27] We also know that something basic and intuitive can be lost under the weight of human learning.

Literacy in the church has meant absorbing this array of understanding as Scripture, tradition, reason, and experience have come to shape the ways we articulate faith. Instruction in these arts has been normally done in schools, but with an end in view. Education, to bring up or lead forth, implies a shared or accepted conception of fullness or maturation and the vision and skills needed to advance such a conception. In this sense education happens in the context of communities that profess shared values and believe that such values need to be passed on to others in the same generation or intergenerationally. Education is never neutral. Training means to become formed into something. It might even be fairly asked whether and how one can even be educated apart from a group.[28]

25. Attributed to Martianus Capella, who developed this categorization on the basis of Roman historian Marcus Terentius Varro.

26. Werner Jaeger, *Early Christianity and Greek Paideia* (Cambridge: Harvard University Press, 1960). Sylvan Barnet and Hugo Bedau summarize a contemporary way of defining literacy as the ability to: (1) summarize an argument accurately; (2) locate the thesis of an argument; (3) locate the assumptions, stated and unstated; (4) analyze and evaluate the strengths of the evidence and the soundness of the reasoning supporting the thesis; (5) analyze, evaluate, and account for discrepancies among various readings. See their *Critical Reading and Writing: A Brief Guide to Argument* (Boston: St. Martin's Press, Bedford Books, 1996), p. v.

27. Such diffuse ideas are represented by academic postmodernism, a loosely structured constellation of disciplines like cultural studies, feminist studies, gay and lesbian studies, science studies, and postcolonial theory. Drawing both from the works of French thinkers like Jacques Derrida, Michel Foucault, Julia Kristeva, and others, and the German Frankfurt School, a unifying theme is that of an emancipatory political end. On the political implications of postmodernism, see Mark Lilla, "The Politics of Jacques Derrida," *New York Review of Books,* 25 June 1998, pp. 36-41.

28. The assumption that education happens in community and in relation to general or

For some schools, particularly university divinity schools, a decisive question is whether an inclusive ethical vocabulary which permits different ontologies or worldviews to coexist can be developed, such as can occur in civil society under participatory democracy.[29] This point is particularly pertinent in light of growing debate over whether a value-free education is possible.[30] Indeed, schools probably have never functioned in a fully value-free environment.[31] It is hard to imagine what this environment would look like. This is not to say that we should not try to devise an ethical vocabulary in as inclusive a way as possible. Rather, such a vocabulary recognizes that there is always an array of ontologies embedded beneath the surface of language. Catherine Larrère makes this point as she discerns overtones of the irrational in rhetoric that gives primacy to cultural is-

communal ideas of maturation or fullness can be traced from Cicero's book *De legibus,* written first as a letter to his son Marcus, to present educational theorists. See discussion in Derek Bok, *Universities and the Future of America* (Durham, N.C.: Duke University Press, 1990); and see work pursued by the Derek Bok Center, Harvard University, Cambridge, Mass. Neil Postman suggests the current crisis in our educational system derives from a failure to provide students with clear goals, instead offering the false "gods" of economic utility, consumerism, ethnic separatism, and resentment, in *The End of Education: Redefining the Value of School* (New York: Knopf, 1996). Following on Postman's argument, this provides schools of theology a unique opportunity in society in North America. Author Brian V. Street distinguishes between "autonomous" and "ideological" models of literacy, implying group consciousness in the latter, in *Literacy in Theory and in Practice* (Cambridge: Cambridge University Press, 1984), pp. 2-3.

29. Hans Küng, *Global Responsibility: In Search of a New World Ethic* (New York: Continuum, 1993). Many are working in this area; see Joseph Runzo, ed., *Ethics, Religion, and the Good Society: New Directions in a Pluralistic World* (Philadelphia: Westminster John Knox, 1992).

30. Peter Madsen argues that such is not possible and never has been the case. Furthermore, in light of the environmental crisis, universities should function with environmental responsibilities in the social space between social atomism and the social whole; see his "What Can Universities and Professional Schools Do to Save the Environment?" in *Earth Summit Ethics* (Albany: State University of New York Press, 1996), ed. J. Baird Callicott and Fernando J. R. da Rocha, pp. 71-91.

31. See the concluding chapter in this volume. George H. Williams summarizes five themes inherent in the foundation of Harvard College, drawn from its past: (1) the autonomy of the university with respect to church and state, but an autonomy grounded in a religious epistemology; (2) a christological theme as definitive of the relative autonomy of the university and the professor (of particular interest in the light of contemporary debate over issues of tenure); (3) the transferential theme from Old to New World and implied religious motifs; (4) the paradisaic theme with its romantic implications in university life; and (5) the idea that the university is the scene of a special kind of "spiritual warfare." See his *Paradise and Wilderness in Christian Thought: The Biblical Experience of the Desert in the History of Christianity and the Paradise Theme in the Theological Idea of the University* (New York: Harper and Brothers, 1962), pp. 156-57. George Marsden enlarges the scope of this with respect to the secularization of colleges and universities in the United States in his *The Soul of the American University.*

sues over those of nature.[32] Different patterns of education have emerged even in the history of the church, where one might assume the ontology of Christianity would demand similar patterns. While similarities exist, cultural differences have shaped practices and perspectives differently.[33] A shared or accepted conception of fullness or maturation raises the question of to whom we listen. The answer, simply, is that we listen to one another. We listen to our neighbor, to the ones who have been put in the neighbor's place for us.

The quality of our relationship with our neighbor is assumed in Christian theology to be a mirror of that between us and God, or ultimate reality. Christianity assumes a deep need for neighbor, a need that is symmetrical to our need for God. This is seen in the structure of the Ten Commandments and in their dominical summary (Matt. 22:36-40). Writing about this relationship, the theologian Karl Barth includes the forgiveness of neighbor as a central feature of his material on "The Praise of God."[34] He argues that in Christian theology the neighbor is not the abstract "other" but God in our own image facing us in the other. He adds, "In the biblical sense of the concept my neighbor is not each of my fellow-men as such . . . as such consists of mere individuals. . . . My neighbor is an event, which takes place in the existence of a definite man definitely marked off from all other men. My neighbor is my fellow-man acting toward me as a benefactor."[35] Further, taking up the biblical challenge to "love my neighbor as I love myself," Barth writes that to love my neighbor means accepting the future that is shaped by the reality of my neighbor. We are, in fact, given to one another in order to benefit from each other, to find the restoration that is only possible because of each other, and to find our respective identities through each other.[36]

The structure of this book grows out of this last point, i.e., how we learn to listen to one another. We will parallel Augustine's *On Christian Doctrine*,[37] a book that modeled early theological education, particularly for the Latin Western

32. Catherine Larrère, "Ethics, Politics, Science, and the Environment: Concerning the Natural Contract," in *Earth Summit Ethics*, pp. 115-38.

33. For example, the schools within the one consortium in Boston represent widely different histories; see Petersen, *Christianity and Civil Society*. The ways in which the differences in religious cultures can shape different conceptions of the meaning of literacy are considered from the perspectives of gender, class, and global location by Lucretia Bailey Yaghjian, "Writing Practice and Pedagogy across the Curriculum: Teaching Writing in a Theological Context," *Theological Education* 33, no. 2 (spring 1997): 48-50.

34. Karl Barth, *Church Dogmatics*, ed. G. W. Bromiley and T. F. Torrance, trans. G. T. Thomson and H. Knight (Edinburgh: T. & T. Clark, 1970 ed.), II.2. #18.3 (pp. 401ff.).

35. Barth, pp. 419-20.

36. Barth, p. 430.

37. Augustine, *On Christian Doctrine (De doctrina Christiana)*, trans. D. W. Robertson, Jr. (Indianapolis: Bobbs-Merrill Educational Publishing, 1958 and after).

Church. Each section of our book is prefaced by introductory material that orients the reader to the chapters of the section around reflections on Augustine's early pattern for what we might call theological literacy. The prefaces are designed to tie together articles that move in significant and, at times, different directions.

Begun circa 396 at about the time Augustine became bishop of Hippo in North Africa, but completed many years later, *On Christian Doctrine* is among the most important books of this influential thinker in the Christian church. It has often been called "the fundamental plan of Christian culture." While *On Christian Doctrine* is an introduction and interpretation of the Bible, it might also be called the basis of a new philosophy and inheritor of the best of the ancient philosophical tradition in the West. Augustine did not fare as well among Orthodox theologians and churchmen. Insofar as theological education was concerned, the school of Alexandria under Clement and the earlier theological work of Origen, a student of Plotinus, shaped a curriculum that was deeply marked by Hellenism. The work of Justin Martyr,[38] the *Catechetical Homilies* of Cyril of Jerusalem and others formed a tradition that was both older than Augustine and arose independent of his ascendance in the West. If never as fully structured in some ways as that of the West, it was an education oriented more to the mystery of God's essence and the relative ineffable nature of God's energies than would be true in the West after the rise of Scholasticism.

On Christian Doctrine exerted a tremendous influence on Western culture, forming the basis of work by Cassiodorus, helping to shape early Scholasticism in Hugh of St. Victor and Peter Lombard. Endorsed by persons as diverse as John Wycliffe and Erasmus several centuries later, *On Christian Doctrine* has continued to provide basic ordering principles for theological education into the contemporary period. There is a certain logic here. Augustine proposes two things necessary in the treatment of the Scriptures: a way of discovering and a way of teaching.[39] This is similar to Jaroslav Pelikan's contemporary university as a place of scholarship and teaching. Augustine then spends three-quarters of the book discussing, first, what is really real. What is it that lies behind the signs that we use in language to talk about things, and ultimately about God? In our volume we will survey the topic with opening chapters on subjects that shape the study of theology today. Second, Augustine reflects on the context or history of those signs particularly as they come to us through media like institutions. Here we will consider this primarily as an opportunity to talk about the history of the church and churches. Third,

---

38. Demetrios Trakatellis, "Sharing with You the Words: Justin Martyr, a Man of Dialogue," in *The Contentious Triangle: Church, State, and University. A Festschrift in Honor of Professor George H. Williams*, ed. Calvin Pater and Rodney Petersen, Sixteenth Century Essays and Studies, vol. 51 (Kirksville, Mo.: Thomas Jefferson Press, 1999), pp. 71-80.

39. Augustine, *On Christian Doctrine*, prologue and bk. 4 (pp. 3-7 and 117).

his discussion turns to the interpretation of signs, or hermeneutics. We will do the same. Finally, Augustine discusses teaching, or rhetoric. In our fourth section of chapters we will do the same. A variety of chapters will touch on different ways in which we work to foster a way of teaching, through pastoral care, youth education, spiritual formation, and other means. This book concludes with two chapters on the nature of theological literacy with respect to the church and university.

In the prologue to *On Christian Doctrine*, Augustine writes that some of his detractors were critical of the book because they did not understand it, others who were not helped by it assumed that no one will be helped by it, and still others believed that any book that offers assistance into how to read Scripture is useless since divine assistance comes directly from the Holy Spirit. In his reply, Augustine is critical of those who think they do not need assistance from anyone else in the reading of Scripture. He begins by writing that all of us have at least learned the alphabet from one another. And those things that can be learned from others should be learned without pride or envy. Nevertheless, he adds, even Paul, who was taught by a divine and heavenly voice, was sent to another human for additional instruction (Acts 9:10-22). And Cornelius, whose prayers were heard by an angel, was sent to Peter for instruction (Acts 10:23-43). Philip was sent to instruct the Ethiopian eunuch (Acts 8:26-40). Though taught by God, Moses listened to the counsel of his father-in-law (Exod. 18:17-27). "For Moses knew that, from whatever mind true counsel might proceed, it should not be attributed to that mind but to Him who is the truth, immutable God."[40] In other words, if we presume that God speaks to us, we must also conclude that God can speak to others, even to our neighbor. In this way Augustine lays a foundation for listening to one another, for conversation.

It is on this note, on the value of conversation, that our chapters begin. In his opening article, "On Theological Education: A Reflection," David Tracy writes of our being "inheritors" of an ancient conversation, a conversation with the classics of all cultures. The impulse toward inclusiveness in Christianity and the value Christianity places upon particularity in relation to global pluralism evokes the value of conversation.[41] Education frees us to enter into the play that this conversation affords. It is this game of conversation that allows our traditions and identities to develop and enlarge. It is a conversation in which the questions and responses play a dominant role. It is one that calls us into dialogue with every culture and tradition. It is a conversation in theology. And

40. Augustine, *On Christian Doctrine*, prologue (p. 6).
41. Mary Elizabeth Mullino Moore, "Theological Education by Conversation: Particularity and Pluralism," *Theological Education* 33, no. 1 (autumn 1996): 31-47. She values conversation with God, with the communion of saints, with other religious traditions, and with the whole of creation. See her book, *Covenant and Call: Mission of the Future Church* (Nashville: Discipleship Resources, 2000).

here is something that immediately presses upon us in thinking of Tracy's point: How can we, and in what ways do we, let go of our own rules in order to enter into the game of the conversation? What criteria must another person meet before we are willing to listen to him or her?

This is all the more challenging in that this is a conversation in which theological reflection is challenged by what Tracy writes are the three "fatal modern separations," that of feeling from thought, form from content, and theory from practice. Tracy spends most of his time on the latter two, the "least healed" in contemporary experience. The effect of this has been the evisceration of meaningful life. Its restoration requires a conversation with all partners in the dialogue. Theological education is uniquely capable of fostering this healing. As Tracy writes, "Of all the disciplines, theology is that one where action and thought, academy and church, faith and reason, the community of inquiry and the community of commitment and faith are most explicitly and systematically brought together." Several of the chapters in this book draw upon these observations toward the end of personal and communal renewal.

Each of us stands to benefit through the conjoining of points of view. Conversation, listening to one another, good reading — all enable us to escape the illusions of perception and particularity without losing the privilege of individuality and particularity.[42] Through conversation I can expand my horizon so that I can take in yours, and through such confluence we see a larger and broader picture. This is valuable not only for understanding but also for issues of community justice and the salvation of the body of Christ (1 Cor. 12:12-31). We come once again to how we think of our neighbor. Barth is clear about drawing us to those aspects of Christian theology that ask me to love my neighbor as I love myself. In this light, we might ask about what it means for us to be people of different races, yet brothers and sisters. Miroslav Volf puts this question forward from his background in southeast Europe: What does it mean to love *cetnik* and *ustashe*?[43] What, might we add, about Afrikaner and Bantu?[44] How about Jew and Palestinian?[45] Miami and Cuba?[46]

---

42. C. S. Lewis, *An Experiment in Criticism* (New York: Cambridge University Press, 1961), pp. 137-41.

43. A question that Jürgen Moltmann asked Miroslav Volf; in Volf, *Exclusion and Embrace: A Theological Exploration of Identity, Otherness, and Reconciliation* (Nashville: Abingdon, 1996), p. 9.

44. Wilhelm Verwoerd, *My Winds of Change* (Randburg: Ravan Press, 1997). Verwoerd rejects the Grand Apartheid of his forebears as established in 1948 in South Africa.

45. An Israeli journalist for *Ha'aretz*, Amira Hass, details the grief and humiliation of the Palestinians in Gaza in *Drinking the Sea at Gaza: Days and Nights in a Land under Siege* (New York: Henry Holt, Metropolitan Books, 1999).

46. Louis A. Perez, Jr., *On Becoming Cuban: Identity, Nationality, and Culture* (Chapel

David Tracy recalls the task that was outlined in Augustine's prologue as the Christian movement was carried out of the Mediterranean basin and into wider areas of Europe. Andrew Walls reminds us that in the twenty-first century we face significant structural adjustments in the study and practice of Christianity, indeed of all religion.[47] Theological education in the seminaries, schools of theology, and university divinity schools has addressed this by taking up the challenge of globalization.[48] As the "battle in Seattle" over the World Trade Organization in April 1999, and further confrontations at the World Bank and International Monetary Fund in Washington, D.C., and at Switzerland's Davos Forum, in Quebec in 2001, and elsewhere have reminded us, apart from sensitivity and justice, globalization can also be as destructive as it is enhancing.[49] Terrorism and global violence since the galvanizing experiences in New York City, Washington, D.C., and elsewhere throughout our world since September 11, 2001, have underscored this point. In such light as this, Max Stackhouse writes of the need for "a profound public vision" that enables creative engagement with the new social and political realities that we now encounter.[50] This reality is marked by a massive southward shift of the center of gravity of the Christian world, but one that is also reflected in every urban center in the north. Globalization, whether considered from an international or parochial perspective, is frequently also an urban phenomenon.[51] The rapidity

---

Hill: University of North Carolina Press, 1999). Perez writes about the wider effects of Cuba's effort under Castro to repudiate the blandishments of American culture.

47. Andrew Walls, *The Missionary Movement in Christian History: Studies in the Transmission of Faith* (Maryknoll, N.Y.: Orbis Books, 1996); see James M. Phillips and Robert T. Coote, eds., *Toward the Twenty-first Century in Christian Mission* (Grand Rapids: Eerdmans, 1993).

48. *Theological Education* 35, no. 2 (spring 1999), entitled "Incarnating Globalization in ATS Schools: Issues, Experiences, Understandings, Challenges," takes up the issue of globalization and relates it to many different aspects of theological education.

49. Richard A. Falk reviews the development of human rights during the twentieth century and assesses their implications for the coming years in *Human Rights Horizons: The Pursuit of Justice in a Globalizing World* (New York: Routledge, 2000); and see William K. Tabb, *Amoral Elephant: Globalization and the Struggle for Social Justice in the Twenty-first Century* (New York: Monthly Review Press, 2001).

50. Max Stackhouse, "If Globalization Is True, What Shall We Do? Toward a Theology of Ministry," *Theological Education* 35, no. 2 (spring 1999): 158.

51. This point is made by Viv Grigg, "Sorry! The Frontier Moved," in *Planting and Growing Urban Churches: From Dream to Reality,* ed. Harvie M. Conn (Grand Rapids: Baker, 1997), pp. 150-63. See also Robert V. Kemper, "Theological Education for Urban Ministry: A Survey of U.S. Seminaries," *Theological Education* 34, no. 1 (autumn 1997): 51-72, and Efraín Agosto, "The Gifts of Urban Theological Education: A Personal and Professional Reflection," *Theological Education* 33, no. 1 (1996): 103. Both articles provide helpful bibliography on urban

of contemporary social change requires us to acknowledge the occasional and local character of theology (John Pobee), that theology arises out of situations that actually happen, not merely from broad general principles, while being tested in light of universal axioms (José Míguez Bonino and Gustavo Gutiérrez). This may imply new models for church and mission.[52]

Protestantism, long shaped in the twentieth century by sectarian ideas and the relativism of idealism and mysticism; Catholicism, with deep commitments to early and medieval Christian formulation but more susceptible to the same trends affecting Protestantism since Vatican II; and Orthodoxy, facing a world of new social freedoms after 1989, will discover fresh religious coherence in light of the cultural transitions that are presently occurring. The only positive response to the structural changes being experienced by schools of theology is a theological literacy that is ecumenical and seeks to be a catalyst of renewal for the churches and society.[53] Such social change calls us more clearly to the "indigenizing" and "pilgrim" principles evident since Abraham left Ur of the Chaldees and present in the realities of the refugee and immigrant experience that is so much a part of our contemporary reality. The conversation required of us demands an honesty that has been elusive since Abraham's first encounter with Abimelech (Gen. 20–21). It is in quest of such forthrightness that our conversation must begin.

---

ministry, and see Eldin Villafañe, *Seek the Peace of the City: Reflections on Urban Ministry* (Grand Rapids: Eerdmans, 1995).

52. The idea of different "models" of the church was raised up by Avery Dulles and has been appropriated elsewhere. Donal Dorr stresses the need for new models for mission in a world without inherited boundaries, characterized by pluralism, one in which Western civilization is no longer identified with the Christian message and in which human liberation and development are considered integral to human liberation. See his *Mission in Today's World* (Maryknoll, N.Y.: Orbis Books, 2000). In this light, see the concerns raised by Steve Brouwer, Paul Gifford, and Susan Rose in *Exporting the American Gospel: Global Christian Fundamentalism* (New York: Routledge, 1996), and Christopher Duraisingh, "Ministerial Formation for Mission: Implications for Theological Education," *International Review of Mission* 81, no. 321 (January 1992): 33-45.

53. The results of the Oslo global consultation on "Ecumenical Theological Education: Its Viability Today," 5-10 August 1996, move in this direction. See issues of *Ministerial Formation,* published by the Programme on Ecumenical Theological Education of the World Council of Churches, and Pobee, *Towards Viable Theological Education.* The latter includes six Bible studies centered on theological education as it involved Abraham, Jonah, the Servant of Yahweh, Jesus, and the disciples of the early church.

PART I

THEOLOGY:
WHAT IS THE REAL THING?

RODNEY L. PETERSEN

"What do we mean when we say God?" This is a question asked by former priest and Haitian president Jean-Bertrand Aristide.[1] It has a different resonance for one growing up in Cite Soleil, Port-au-Prince's largest slum, than for one living in Palm Beach, Florida, USA. But if "God" means "God," then the term has the same referent whether one is impoverished or wealthy.[2]

Theology is the conscience of the church. It deals with the real thing, whatever our social status, race, or gender might be. It is a tool for learning and an instrument of understanding, not the merit badge of the privileged and learned. Everyone can become theologically literate in some sense, because everyone is a theologian as he or she tries to find his or her place in the world and make sense of it. Catholic and ecumenical in scope, evangelical and pastoral in intent, theology is shaped not only by Scripture and church tradition but also by levels of human organization and technological assumption that shape our experiences and ways of reasoning.

Sometimes theological literacy is more easily understood in the abstract than in actuality. Often we do not know what we mean to say until we start to say it.[3] Much is hidden under the language of theology, as philosophers of sus-

1. Jean-Bertrand Aristide, *Eyes of the Heart: Seeking a Path for the Poor in the Age of Globalization* (Monroe, Maine: Common Courage Press, 2000), p. 63.
2. John H. Yoder observes that "The world of the twenty-first century will not be able to back away from having become one world." The implications of this for theology are discussed by Yoder and others in *The Future of Theology: Essays in Honor of Jürgen Moltmann*, ed. Miroslav Volf, Carmen Krieg, and Thomas Kucharz (Grand Rapids: Eerdmans, 1996). The citation is from Yoder, "Is There Such a Thing as Being Ready for Another Millennium?" p. 66.
3. A point made about writing by Thomas Merton, *The Sign of Jonas* (New York: Doubleday Image Books, 1956), pp. 178-79. He writes, "The main reason why I can't write it is

1

picion have taught us. Theology easily becomes ideology when the mystery of its referent is lost or our hope is invested in that which is less than ultimately real.[4] Theological literacy is, in the first place, learning to give a reason for the hope that is in us (1 Pet. 3:15). It can mean more than this. It can also mean learning to think theologically, which implies a more self-conscious effort at theological reasoning. The apostle Paul offers an example of this in his letter to the Corinthians when he offers warnings from Israel's history as applicable to disciples of Jesus (1 Cor. 10), or in his letter to the Galatians when he suggests rules for interpretation of Scripture (Gal. 4:21-31). In both cases, whether straightforward or more self-conscious, theological literacy is learning to discern and discuss what is the real thing in life.[5]

Theological reflection on what is really most important in life happens through language. Augustine is one of the first Christian theologians to stress the value of language. Especially helpful in this regard are his works *On the Teacher* (A.D. 389) and *On the Trinity* (A.D. 399-419), as well as *On Christian Doctrine* (A.D. 396). Each was written during a different period of his life. The general conclusion he reaches in *On the Teacher* is that human teachers teach us the meaning of words or signs. However, only the internal teacher, Christ dwelling in the mind, can teach us more. By at once displaying to the mind the reality to be known and providing the language for its understanding, we are taken to deeper spiritual truth. In doxological fashion, Augustine writes that Christ is the source both of the objects encountered and of the light that illuminates them for our understanding.[6]

Later in life, with a community dependent on him, Augustine takes up

---

that I don't know it. I don't know precisely what I mean to say, and therefore when I start to write I find I am working out theology as I go."

4. Two tendencies in theology have been to orient theological thinking either in relation to a vertical and transcendent or to a horizontal and immanent dimension. Particular social concerns often become a flash point for division, as happened before the Fifth Assembly of the World Council of Churches at Nairobi. See *The Nature of the Church and the Role of Theology: Papers from a Consultation between the World Council of Churches and the Reformed Ecumenical Synod, Geneva 1975* (Geneva: World Council of Churches Publications, 1976). Helpful perspective is offered in Hans Küng and David Tracy, *Paradigm Change in Theology* (New York: Crossroad, 1991).

5. *Confessing the One Faith,* Faith and Order Paper No. 153 (Geneva: WCC Publications, 1991).

6. See R. A. Markus, "St. Augustine on Signs," in *Augustine: A Collection of Critical Essays,* ed. R. A. Markus (Garden City, N.Y.: Doubleday, 1972), pp. 61-85, reprinted from *Phronesis* 2 (1957): 60-83. See Augustine, *De magistro* 11.3.8, as cited by Markus, p. 71. If Augustine in *On the Teacher* appears to stress an interior truth that may to some degree denigrate the use of signs or written words, by the time he has begun his work as a bishop we find a fresh reevaluation of the use of signs.

the question of what can be known through language, or signs, once again. In *On Christian Doctrine* they are said to carry us to divine things. Writing about the language of the Bible, signs and what they signify, he picks up where he left off in *On the Teacher*,[7] stressing the triadic nature of signification: there is the object for which the sign stands, the sign itself, and the interpreter. Each is subject to analysis, as our authors in this section will emphasize for our day.[8] The need for interpretation as an aid to theological literacy has spawned schools throughout the church's history. One might say that what one cannot agree on in worship is taken up for debate in newly founded schools, with many of the modern universities even of our era dating to the first Scholasticism of the twelfth century, a point that one finds stressed with new polemics as universities in North America come under growing scrutiny.[9] S. Mark Heim reminds us in this section that theological education, in an effort to foster theological literacy, has taken certain conversation partners for granted: the university, certain academic disciplines, and a kind of cultural propriety. But these are increasingly subject to suspicion as we become more aware of our own prejudices and prejudgments, something Catholic Blaise Pascal, Anglican William Law, and Quaker John Woolman warned against in different strands of our own culture in the early modern era. What is referred to as postmodernism is frequently only a more contemporary form of their argument.

Each of the articles in this section draws us back to the fundamental nature of theological literacy, asking of some aspect of theology, "What is the real thing" about which theology seeks to communicate? Who is our conversation partner? With whom are we trying to communicate when we want to be considered theologically literate? Ourselves? Our neighbor? Our community?

7. Augustine, *De magistro* 1.2.2; Markus, pp. 73-75; Augustine, *De doctrina Christiana* 11.1.1.9.

8. Augustine tells us there were two classes of signs in his day: natural and conventional. Conventional are those that humans use to disclose their minds to others. The only reason we have for making and giving signs is to indicate to another what is going on in the mind of the sign maker. Words are the most important of all signs. Scripture was at first given in one language, then many. Scripture "signs" to us what is the will of God as revealed to those who received prophetic inspiration. And in reading it, he tells us, we are to seek nothing more than to find out the thought and will of those by whom it was written, and through these to find out what is the will of God. There is a need for an interpreter of Scripture precisely because it has been written by persons who have signified things differently out of different life circumstances. Later still in life, Augustine will return to the mystery of language in works dealing with the mystery of God and nature of lying and truth telling. The topic is especially important because of his belief that personality is at the heart of things, not impersonality.

9. James Tunstead Burtchaell, *The Dying of the Light: The Disengagement of Colleges and Universities from Their Christian Churches* (Grand Rapids: Eerdmans, 1998).

What does it mean, Alkiviadis Calivas asks in the opening chapter of this section, "Theology and Theologians: An Orthodox Perspective," to say theology is the conscience of the church? This question is answered by the community of faith when it sings the *credo*. Some say, "no creed but the Bible," but Paul sang a *credo* as he wrote to the church at Philippi (Phil. 2:4-19). Theology is twined with the life and health of parish life. The nature of this relationship reflects the quality of seminary life. Calivas reminds us that theology and theological literacy begin with an affirmation of the transcendent. This is Augustine's understanding of personality at the heart of things. Apart from the act of praise even in the face of mystery, the theological enterprise quickly becomes arid, and its language, hence the meaning of literacy, empty. One might say that even the "God is Dead" theology which came in the latter third of the last century found its grounding in the apophatic theological tradition (Basil the Great and Gregory of Nyssa), that the essence of God is beyond knowing and that his works, or energies, are subject to the nature of revelation. This tradition has been long recognized among the Orthodox as being together with cataphatic theology (a distinction noted by Pseudo-Dionysius), the knowledge of God as he has revealed himself, as constituting another way to speak of the mystery of transcendence.[10] Theology is, in this sense, a gift of the Holy Spirit.[11]

It is, second, everything that can be said of the triune God. Calivas writes that its language is doxological and mystagogical. Its task is to ascertain and acknowledge the mystery of the living God and to bear witness to God in word and deed. Its goal is to propagate and sustain faith. Toward this end theological literacy is essential to the church. Without it the church becomes prisoner to the world. This poisons and obscures the absolute demands of the truth. Theology, and literacy in theology, preserves the identity of the message and prompts progress into the meaning of the mystery of salvation. Toward this end theology must be dynamic and creative, an aspect of the ceaseless growth in human understanding and appropriation of the changeless truth of salvation. Theological literacy knows how to avoid the extremes of pietistic conservatism and academic scientism. Theological literacy is essential for the defense of the truth. Its aim is a personal and relational union with ultimate personality, or God, not merely abstract knowledge. Theological literacy, grounded in scholarship and faith commitment, has a pastoral and existential end. Its intention is to lead to communion with the life of God. The theologian, with illumined intellect and vigilant

---

10. Gordon Kaufman, *In Face of Mystery: A Constructive Theology* (Cambridge: Harvard University Press, 1993).

11. This is implied in Augustine. It is even stronger in his near contemporaries, the Cappadocian Fathers. See Jaroslav Pelikan, *The Spirit of Eastern Christendom (600-1700)* (Chicago: University of Chicago Press, 1984).

soul, avoids holding on to a world that once was but is not (antiquarianism) and imagining a world that can never be (futurism). Good theology creates good praxis in such areas as modern science, ecological practice, and ideological understanding because it fosters responsible discipleship. It places high value on ecumenical activities that challenge the horizons within which universal themes are encapsulated in particular communal understandings. It is a way of being in the world. Becoming theologically literate is also a means to an end, becoming socialized into a community with a distinct way of looking at the world with the ability to articulate the nature of that participation.[12]

In his chapter, "On the Complexity of Theological Literacy," Robert C. Neville stresses the role of theology in promoting an inquiry into truth.[13] Conscious of different ways of doing theology, he refers to theological literacy as "a tool for learning, not a merit badge for having learned."[14] Here Neville outlines four loci of complexity in theological literacy: identity, expression, truth, and engagement.[15] Each of these four points bears pastoral implications. Theological identity is difficult today in part because we have become so much more sensitive to the many families of "indigenizations." Theological identity today has to be built out of all the traditions that claim Christianity, including those condemned by others. This can have implications for the ways religion is drawn into conflict.[16] The complexity of identity underscores the importance of Tracy's call to conversation in order to find community. We have also become

12. Clifford Geertz, *Local Knowledge: Further Essays in Interpretive Anthropology* (New York: Basic Books, 1983), p. 155.

13. See Neville's *A Theology Primer* (Albany: State University of New York Press, 1991), a book that clarifies many of Neville's different strains of thought.

14. Hans Frei, *Types of Christian Theology,* ed. George Hunsinger and William C. Placher (New Haven: Yale University Press, 1992). Frei notes five types of theology with representative figures for each: (1) theology as a philosophical discipline (Gordon Kaufman), (2) theology as a philosophical scheme foundational for Christian religion (David Tracy), (3) theology as academic enterprise and Christian self-description (Friedrich Schleiermacher), (4) theology as specific and critical Christian self-description (Karl Barth), and (5) theology as internal to religion (D. Z. Phillips). See chap. 4.

15. J. Harley Chapman and Nancy K. Frankenberry, eds., *Interpreting Neville* (Albany: State University of New York Press, 1999). The authors highlight four aspects of Neville's theology: a methodological and constitutive dialectical approach that reaches into his sense of ontology, a speculative pragmatism derivative of the importance of critical judgment, a comparative approach to theology that casts Christian theology into a place of critical assessment with respect to other world religions, and an engagement with issues of contemporary culture. Each of these four points can be seen in Neville's chapter in this book.

16. Donna Hicks, "Issues of Identity and Protracted Conflict," in *Forgiveness and Reconciliation: Religion, Public Policy, and Conflict Transformation,* ed. Raymond Helmick, S.J., and Rodney L. Petersen (Philadelphia: Templeton Foundation Press, 2001), pp. 129-49.

more aware of the complexities of theological expression as we have learned that symbols may mean different things to different persons and to different cultures in different stages of maturation. We are coming to terms with our own limitations in engagement with God and knowing how to express this, a statement that reflects Neville's dialectical approach to theology and qualified logical syntactical approach to language.

How we express theology brings us to what it is we are learning to make reference, the complexities of theological truth in the midst of which Neville identifies three kinds of reference: "iconicity," or ways by which theology mirrors the way reality really is; "indexical," or in what ways theology engages us and shapes our behavior; and "conventional," or the ways we use language in interpretation and engagement.[17] The ability to discern what is really at stake in theological judgment or interpretation and the imagination and determination to remain open and vulnerable to correction shape our understanding of theological literacy. This leads, finally, to the complexities of theological engagement, not merely knowing about theological matters but becoming more religious, more thoughtful and holy, particularly in areas that shape our engagement with life in the twenty-first century, areas shaped by the discussion of religion with the sciences, our environmental responsibilities, our encounter with other religious traditions,[18] and ways of living justly with all peoples.[19]

All this about building community and literacy is defined by its social and linguistic context. Literacy for the context of life in the twenty-first century means knowing how to navigate the conventions of identity, cultural meaning,

17. See Neville's *The Truth of Broken Symbols* (Albany: State University of New York Press, 1996). The distinction is made between religious language as signs of transcendence (symbolic instrumentalism) and as symbols embedded in religious forms of life (linguistic pragmatism) as directed by the work of Charles Peirce or Ludwig Wittgenstein.

18. See Neville's *Behind the Masks of God: An Essay toward Comparative Theology* (Albany: State University Press of New York, 1991). Neville asserts the importance of working from the following four themes: a broad theology of creation *ex nihilo*, the affirmation of public theology, the value of a history-of-religions approach to any theological formulation, and an empirical base and scope in the philosophy of religion. See also Neville's earlier book, *The Tao and the Daimon* (Albany: State University of New York Press, 1983), for comparative purposes.

19. See Neville's *The High Road around Modernism* (Albany: State University Press of New York, 1992). Taking cues from Peirce and Whitehead, Neville offers a dynamic reconstruction of American philosophy as a cultural force by first reviving the tradition of covenant theology and its implications for the relationship between power and religion. In other words, power is derivative of acknowledged universal public responsibility, not of conflict. Second, Neville suggests a more open conception of deity, less shaped by anthropocentric narcissism. He also suggests the defects of market and class as adequate categories for a just social order and the weakness of representative democracy as presently construed.

perspectives on the nature of truth, and rhetoric important to the complexities of contemporary life.[20]

S. Mark Heim defines levels of literacy in his chapter, "Renewing Ways of Life: The Shape of Theological Education." Recognizing the internal and external challenges in the twenty-first century for faith-based communities, Heim marks out the threshold of education and formation that allows a person to participate in a concrete religious community and to interpret a pluralistic world religiously and responsibly from an acknowledged particular faith standpoint. In a more detailed way his work on the meaning of salvation and the nature of religious ends has helped to do this.[21] Bernard Lonergan considers the dissonance between religious difference and particularity, writing that the foundation of a renewed theology is "reflection on the ongoing process of conversation." Explaining that "just as the scientist studies the scientific method to gain new truth, so the theologian must reflect on the process of conversation in order to understand religious truth."[22]

Pastoral in intent, Heim suggests two meanings to theological literacy. First, literacy implies an acquisition of the basic tools needed to access and produce written information. However, it also implies familiarity with a fundamental body of knowledge, to use the tools to grasp the content that should be known. Furthermore, he writes, "practical literacy" implies the basic skills that allow one to be a member of a church and follower of Christ, knowing about the tradition and how to participate.[23] At another level, "leadership literacy" involves higher education and draws one to many of the challenges arising from the European Enlightenment and theology's traditional engagement with this shaping influence in our ways of reasoning and understanding experience. Both forms of literacy have a critical side and look to the horizon of Christian faith defined by our own appropriation of Christian identity, the ways we understand mission, and how we are becoming formed as persons. Changes in

---

20. Michael A. K. Halliday and Rugaiya Hasan, *Context and Text: Aspects of Language in a Social-Semiotic Perspective* (Oxford: Oxford University Press, 1985), and David Bartholmae, "Inventing the University," in *When a Writer Can't Write: Studies in Writer's Block and Other Composing-Process Problems,* ed. Mike Rose (New York: Guildford Press, 1985), pp. 134-65.

21. S. Mark Heim, *Salvations: Truth and Difference in Religion* (Maryknoll, N.Y.: Orbis Books, 1995) and *The Depth of the Riches: A Trinitarian Theology of Religious Ends* (Grand Rapids: Eerdmans, 2000). See also Dennis L. Okholm and Timothy R. Phillips, eds., *Four Views on Salvation in a Pluralistic World* (Grand Rapids: Zondervan, 1996).

22. Bernard Lonergan, "Theology in Its New Context," in *A Second Collection,* ed. W. Ryan and W. Tyrell (Philadelphia: Westminster, 1983), p. 67.

23. S. Mark Heim, *Grounds for Understanding: Ecumenical Resources for Responses to Religious Pluralism* (Grand Rapids: Eerdmans, 1998). The different theological approaches that Christian denominations bring to the issue of religious pluralism are surveyed.

church and culture have made this older division of labor between practical and leadership literacy obsolescent. Throughout the twentieth century many churches saw changes in patterns of instruction, the decline of church-related colleges or universities, and a reassessment of theological education. Theological education had taken certain conversation "partners" for granted, but these partners have increasingly been subject to postmodern suspicion. Through such shifts in understanding and assumption, the structure given to theological education by such "partners" has given way like the collapse of a wall against which theological studies have often leaned.

The pastoral and critical aspects of theological literacy are acknowledged by Heim. This hybrid nature comes from its having been bred for practical and critical formation. Two programs that are central to a renewed theological literacy are, first, the nurture of sapiential theology, i.e., an engaged knowing that connects the whole person with God. Second, there is the need for an articulation of new horizons of universality — new areas for crucial struggle in this new century (in addition to critical fields of the past). These include two internal horizons, ecumenism and global Christianity or "representative Christianity." Also included are three external horizons (in addition to the literary-historical and philosophical horizons). These are science, world religions, and the struggle for economic, political, and social justice.

These last points are similar to concerns raised by Calivas and Neville. They draw us to our final paper in this section, the chapter by Anne Foerst and Rodney Petersen, "Identity, Formation, Dignity: The Impacts of Artificial Intelligence upon Jewish and Christian Understandings of Personhood."[24] This discussion is a part of the larger dialogue between religion and science that has grown anew in the last quarter century.[25] It raises the question of whether the-

---

24. The interdisciplinary nature of the question of personhood draws us to a biocultural paradigm for the person as an embodied and rational being. See papers presented on this topic in Niels Henrik Gregersen, Willem B. Drees, and Ulf Görman, eds., *The Human Person in Science and Theology* (Grand Rapids: Eerdmans, 2000). The question posed by contemporary debate for the nature of the soul is taken up in discussion in Warren S. Bensen, Nancey Murphey, and H. Newton Malony, eds., *Whatever Happened to the Soul? Scientific and Theological Portraits of Human Nature* (Minneapolis: Fortress, 1998).

25. Such models for dialogue as postfoundational epistemology, critical realism, scientific naturalism, nonintegrative pragmatism, complementarity, and contextual coherence are raised up by Niels Henrik Gregersen and J. Wentzel van Huyssteen, eds., *Rethinking Theology and Science: Six Models for the Current Dialogue* (Grand Rapids: Eerdmans, 1998). Ted Peters identifies four "dead ends" in the science and religion dialogue: (1) scientism (sometimes called secular humanism), which argues that science provides all the knowledge we need to know; (2) ecclesiastical authoritarianism; (3) scientific creationism; and (4) a "two-language" theory whereby it is argued that science speaks with an objective and public language while religion

ology is a "science" and what we mean by this term.[26] It includes the impacts of artificial intelligence and cognitive science upon how we think about ourselves and how we think about ourselves as embedded in nature.[27] Whether in this domain, in conversation about the mapping of the human genome, or in the distant realm of cosmology with its bearing upon religious identity and worldview, developments in the sciences have become a new arena once again for theological reflection.[28] Questions of human identity, "What is man?" or "What is woman?" are at the center of theological and philosophical concern. Philosophy becomes anthropology, and we are drawn to some of the oldest reflection about human identity.[29] Yet, why should this be a problem? Who does

---

speaks with an existential and personal language. He offers helpful criticism on each of these positions in Peters, ed., *Cosmos as Creation* (Nashville: Abingdon, 1989), pp. 13-19. In his opinion the dialogue between science and theology requires a deepening understanding of the theological implications of scientific knowledge around four themes: (1) a recognition that the world of nature is dynamic and changing, (2) the need for a doctrine of continuing creation *(creatio continua)* to complement the traditional idea of creation out of nothing *(creatio ex nihilo)*, (3) the interpretation of Scripture in light of current scientific knowledge, and (4) a sense of wonder and speculation about the place of humanity in the cosmos or God's creation. In North America the following centers and foundations are among those helping to deepen the science-religion dialogue: the Templeton Foundation, the Center for Theology and the Natural Sciences (Berkeley), the Chicago Center for Religion and Science, the Center for Theological Inquiry, the Faith and Science Exchange (Boston Theological Institute), and the Institute for Religion in an Age of Science.

26. In making his case for theology as a science in dialogue with the natural sciences, Pannenberg offers a careful analysis of the terms *Naturwissenschaften* and *Geisteswissenschaften* in *Theology and the Philosophy of Science*, trans. F. McDonagh (Philadelphia: Westminster, 1976), p. 72; more fully in his *Systematic Theology* (Grand Rapids: Eerdmans, 1991). See also the early work of David Tracy, *Blessed Rage for Order* (New York: Seabury, 1975), and Bernard Lonergan, *Insight: A Study of Human Understanding* (New York: Philosophical Society, 1958).

27. Stephen Toulmin describes different paradigms through which Christian theology has worked in history in its effort to understand nature and its larger cosmology, in "Religion and the Idea of Nature," in *Religion, Science, and Public Policy*, ed. Frank T. Birtel (New York: Crossroad, 1987), pp. 67-78.

28. Davies writes that the success of mathematics in describing nature points to a deep link between the human mind and the organization of the world, in *The Mind of God: The Scientific Basis for a Rational World* (New York: Simon & Schuster, 1992), pp. 140-60. John F. Haught, *Science and Religion*, (Mahwah, N.J.: Paulist Press, 1996), pp. 27-46. As for what is meant by "God," see Alister Hardy, *The Spiritual Nature of Man* (Oxford: Clarendon, 1979), p. 1. See John Barrow and Frank Tipler, *The Anthropic Cosmological Principle* (Oxford: Clarendon, 1986), and compare John Polkinghorne, *Science and Creation* (London: SPCK, 1988).

29. Hans U. von Balthasar, "Philosophy has become anthropology; not as though there were a reality outside men, but in the sense that all natural reality is oriented to man." See his *Die Gottesfrage des heutigen Menschen* (Vienna: Herold, 1956), p. 46. For classic reflection about theological anthropology, see David H. Kelsey, "Human Being," in *Christian Theology: An Intro-*

not know what we are? The question appears abstract until we begin to move down a ladder of abstraction. When it is posed, questions of identity, formation, and the nature of dignity come to the fore. Questions of human identity have a reflex effect upon human rights and justice.

The challenge for theological identity comes not only from the content of what is learned, but also from the organization of work and ways of structuring life dictated by technology.[30] Both are points taken up in this chapter. If contemporary life is increasingly shaped by artificial intelligence (AI), this will have an effect on how we understand theological literacy.

Through reference to the *Star Trek* series, Foerst and Petersen ask us to consider issues of identity, formation, and dignity in light of the impacts of AI upon our inherited conception of what it means to be a person. Not only does AI attempt to understand humans in an entirely mechanistic and functionalist way, but it also threatens to build humanlike creatures based on these models and thus reinforce the belief in their accuracy. Our thinking about personhood shapes patterns of education, character formation, the way human dignity is conceived and practiced — or violated — in contemporary society, and our understanding of the health and integrity of the person. The nature of the person together with the implications drawn from our understanding has been a topic of central concern to Pope John Paul II. Working in the last third of the twentieth century with the Commission on Higher Education at the Polish National Conference of Catholic Bishops, Cardinal Karol Wojtyla wrote, "in the heart of the matter lies not cosmology or a philosophy of nature, but philosophical anthropology and ethics: the most important and fundamental dispute on man."[31]

In this chapter the authors first summarize aspects of a theology of personhood, exploring the foundation of theological anthropology as it has guided the West out of the Jewish and Christian sources of reflection. They

---

duction to Its Tradition and Tasks, ed. Peter C. Hodgson and Robert H. King (Philadelphia: Fortress, 1985), pp. 167-93; Philip J. Hefner, "The Creation," in *Christian Dogmatics,* ed. Carl E. Braaten and Robert Jenson, 2 vols. (Philadelphia: Fortress, 1984), pp. 269-362; and G. C. Berkouwer, *Man: The Image of God* (Grand Rapids: Eerdmans, 1962).

30. The work of Émile Durkheim has continued to shape reflection into the twenty-first century in this area.

31. As cited by Andrew N. Woznicki, *A Christian Humanism: Karol Wojtyla's Existential Personalism* (New Britain, Conn.: Mariel Publications, 1980), p. ix. In his context, Woznicki notes Wojtyla's realization of the implications of Karl Marx's eleven theses on Ludwig Feuerbach, namely, the principle of priority of changing reality over speculative interpretation. Wojtyla foresaw anthropological, not cosmological, issues as central to the debate between Marxist and Christian philosophers. Insofar as Marxism has been replaced by functional, utilitarian, or merely secular assumptions, Wojtyla's argument still applies.

then review salient points arising from the challenge of research in artificial intelligence and conclude with reflections on some of the implications of this discussion for the concepts of human dignity, the formation of the self, and identity or personhood. The authors draw heavily from work on a theology of personhood developed by John D. Zizioulas in his retrieval of an Orthodox, or early Byzantine, understanding of the person.[32] This parallels Karol Wojtyla's (John Paul II) ontological neo-Thomism, grounding personhood in existential metaphysics, with a phenomenological description of "person" in terms of conscious acts through which one experiences substantial subjectivity. Early Christian theology was forced to derive a new metaphor for Being with anthropological implications for human self-understanding because of the cosmological revolution of which it was a part. As with Judaism, early Christian theology was drawn to conceive of God, not the world, as being absolute. The biblical doctrine of *creatio ex nihilo* obliged theology to trace ontology back to God, not the world, grounding the person, as also Thomas does, not in necessity as a product of nature or even nurture, but in a form of freedom derivative of divinity.[33]

In conclusion, theological literacy asks us to deal with what is finally real. In relation to metaphysics, this has often been to ground theology in the energies or will of God while acknowledging the greater mystery of Being. In relation to logic, this has meant a line of argument or search for what is substantial and enduring. In relation to politics, this has meant accommodation to human needs and cultural patterns. Each of these three domains, ontology, epistemology, and ethics, calls us to a realism of presentation whereby they are one with the presumed content. Each reflects not only a search for certitude but also a desire for authenticity. This search for what is real lies at the heart of anthropology.[34] In his

---

32. John D. Zizioulas, *Being as Communion: Studies in Personhood and the Church* (Crestwood, N.Y.: St. Vladimir's Seminary Press, 1997).

33. Vladimir Lossky's *kenotic* aspect of personhood draws out an important definition of the understanding of the person. Cp. Kallistos Ware, "'In the Image and Likeness': The Uniqueness of the Human Person," in Chirban, ed., *Personhood*, (Westport, Conn.: Greenwood, 1996), pp. 1-13.

34. By the mid-twentieth century, anthropology appeared dominated by the new psychoanalysis of Sigmund Freud, for whom modern science appeared able to provide the universal recipe, not just for the study of inanimate nature, but for rational inquires of all kinds. Freud articulated this most succinctly in "The Question of a Weltanschauung," found in *Sigmund Freud: New Introductory Lectures on Psycho-Analysis*, trans. and ed. James Strachey (New York: W. W. Norton, 1964). See Hans Küng on the repression of religiousness in psychology, *Freud and the Problem of God* (New Haven: Yale University Press, 1990); and the discussion of Freud, Freud's "scientism," and his continuing religious quest in Armand Nicholi, Jr., M.D., *The Question of God: C. S. Lewis and Sigmund Freud Debate God, Love, Sex, and the Meaning of Life* (New York: Simon & Schuster Free Press, 2002).

first encyclical as John Paul II, Karol Wojtyla quoted Augustine, "You have made us for yourself, Lord, and our heart is restless until it rests in you." Commenting, John Paul II writes: "In this creative restlessness, beats and pulsates what is most deeply human — search for truth, the insatiable need for the good, hunger for freedom, nostalgia for the beautiful and the voice of conscience."[35]

Good theology, reflective of theological literacy, brings this search close to us, makes it palpable and vivid, through narrative and story. This is why we resonate with C. S. Lewis's *Chronicles of Narnia*, J. R. R. Tolkien's *Lord of the Rings*. It is what makes Fyodor Dostoyevsky's *Brothers Karamazov* and the parables of Jesus current literature for theological literacy. Theological literacy is known by its fruit. It is that which takes us to a deeper engagement with life, rather than escapism. It is realistic fiction, not egoistic or even disinterested castle building and divertissements.[36]

---

35. As cited by Woznicki, p. 62.

36. C. S. Lewis, *An Experiment in Criticism* (New York: Cambridge University Press, 1961), pp. 67-69.

CHAPTER ONE

On Theological Education:
A Reflection

DAVID TRACY

As civilized beings, we are the inheritors, neither of an inquiry about ourselves and the world, nor of an accumulating body of information, but of a conversation, begun in the primeval forests and extended and made more articulate in the course of centuries. It is a conversation which goes on both in public and within each of ourselves. Education, properly speaking, is an initiation into the skill and partnership of this conversation in which we learn to recognize the voices, to distinguish the proper occasions of utterance, and in which we acquire the intellectual and moral habits appropriate to conversation.

MICHAEL OAKESHOTT

Indeed, an ability to enter the conversation with our own classics and (as contemporary multiculturalists justly teach) the classics of all cultures is, in fact, the heart of the very process of becoming educated. To become educated is to be freed to enter the conversation of all the living and the dead; to enter that conversation independently and critically, to be sure, but nonetheless to enter. The community of inquiry is nothing other than this centuries-long conversation. An education frees us to join that community of inquiry — the academy in all its forms — by entering that conversation. The coherence of education is, at bottom, the coherence of genuine conversation.

But what is a conversation as distinct from mere good feeling or from debate, confrontation, or dispensing information? Both Wittgenstein and Gadamer are correct, I believe, to insist that a conversation is really a peculiar kind of game. To call a conversation a game, I realize, may not seem a suffi-

13

ciently serious way to describe the very serious demands of an education into the community of inquiry. Yet it is true nonetheless. For every game is nothing other than a phenomenon that demands that we let go of our usual fears and controls. By letting go, we learn to play in order to discover some new possibility. When we really play the game, we free ourselves from the usual self-consciousness and move into the to-and-fro movement of the game itself. Is there anything worse for a drama than a self-conscious actor? Is there anything more fatal for a conversation than someone who cannot listen, cannot allow opinions to be tested, cannot allow the "to-and-fro movement" of the questions simply as they come, cannot permit the subject matter to take over?

For a genuine conversation, a true dialogue, is (as Plato knew) a singularly serious game where the subject matter, the questions and responses, are allowed to take over. We finally do let go. We finally allow ourselves to think. When we converse, we join the age-old tradition of the dialogue. We join ourselves to that conversation which is the community of inquiry, the academy. The basic coherence of a good education is the coherence provided by all genuine inquiry — as conversation.

To think clearly, sharply, critically at all is a rare achievement. It is also one of the surest ways of allowing future citizens of both society and a religious community to remain open to new experience — indeed, to all the unpredictable, undeducible experiences that the opening century is sure to offer. To learn to think, moreover, by thinking in conversation both with a great tradition (as all the religious traditions surely are) and (in principle) in any genuine university, with all cultural and religious traditions, is to discover that every tradition lives as *traditio* and not mere *tradita* only because each generation can rethink and retrieve the tradition in an ever changing situation. Every great religious tradition lives by welcoming a genuine critical community of inquiry. In any religious tradition, the university is precisely one of the singular places where that freedom to enter the critical conversation occurs.

What I have said thus far is true of any genuine community of inquiry. The question, therefore, recurs: Can a community of inquiry and a community of commitment and faith be united? Every community lives through the ideals articulated in its classics. In a sense the academic community of inquiry in the West still lives through the power of the great Socratic ideal — classically expressed in the famous saying, "The unreflective life is not worth living." All communities of commitment and faith add to that classic Socratic ideal of the Western community of inquiry the equally important thought in the Buddhist proverb: "And the unlived life is not worth reflecting upon."

This addition is, of course, no minor one. For all thought exists finally for the sake of action and commitment. It is true that mere action without thought is blind. It is equally true that all thought not somehow directed to action, concern, or commitment may be ultimately empty. The ancients still have much to teach us on the coherence of a true education as uniting a vision of life and a way of life.

Of all the disciplines, theology is that one where action and thought, academy and church, faith and reason, the community of inquiry and the community of commitment and faith are most explicitly and systematically brought together. Many students come to a university in a religious tradition, among many other reasons, in the hope of finding some basic if rough educational coherence: a community that unites thought and action to help one find some coherent way to both a "reflective life" and an ethically and religiously informed "lived life."

As Simone Weil insisted, a life of inquiry has its own demands — the demands of what Bernard Lonergan nicely called "the pure, detached, disinterested, unrestricted desire to know." A genuine university must possess free inquiry to breathe as a true community of inquiry. At the same time, the *eros* of all inquiry, as Augustine reminded the Platonists of his day, is itself driven by our commitments, our faiths, our loves. To know the truth of Augustine's great insight — *amor meus, pondus meum* — is to know what ultimately drives the life of reflection in a community of inquiry united to a community of moral and religious commitment: our ideals, our hopes, our loves.

A part of our difficulty in addressing the issues of contemporary theological education squarely as educators — whether faculty or students — is the failure to consider how the three great separations of modern Western culture have damaged our ability to reflect on education and its relationship to culture itself. The opening century will attempt to heal these fatal modern separations. These three fatal separations are:

- the separation of feeling and thought
- the separation of form and content
- the separation of theory and practice

All three of these peculiarly modern separations are related to one another. Moreover, each is based on an originally helpful distinction that became, in modernity, a separation. Recall, for a moment, the original distinctions and then their later, modern separations as a part of the larger contemporary attempts to render them again as distinctions, not separations.

The modern separations contrast sharply with the relative ease with which either the ancients (recall again the work of Pierre Hadot) or the medievals (see the work of Jean Le Clerq on the monastic schools and Marie-

Dominique Chénu on the scholastics) were able to develop (in their distinct contexts and schools) valuable distinctions, not separations: the distinctions of feeling and thought, form and content, practice and theory.

I will not discuss in this essay the first of these distinctions-become-separations, namely, feeling and thought. In the interests of space, it seems best to concentrate on the other two separations. For the fact is that in much of contemporary culture (including popular culture), this first separation of feeling and thought has been the most "healed" — i.e., rendered into a useful distinction, not separation, again. Consider the many discussions of experience (both personal and communal) as a "source" of contemporary theology. One may note especially the now widely accepted practice of the new contextual theologies around the globe: a practice of sustained critical reflection on a people's or culture's experience, sustained attempts to keep hope alive in the struggle for love and justice, sustained solidarity of all Christian communities with the new communities in our now global setting, expressing, in both academic and nonacademic forms, their important new visions of reality. These new contextual theologies (especially but not solely liberation, political, and feminist-womanist-*mujerista* theologies) do not hesitate to relate intrinsically, even as they distinguish but never separate, "feeling" and "thought," "experience" and "reflection," "witness" and "critique."

There is need for further discussion of this first separation, but for the moment I will discuss the other two, less healed distinctions-become-separations in modernity: practice and theory, and form and content. Regarding the distinction between practice and theory: indeed, theory itself as a distinct practice was a natural distinction (never separation) to all the ancient and medieval schools, including the great Scholastics. This distinction, rendered a separation in the fourteenth-century nominalist crisis and in most of modern neo-Scholasticism, was a distinction-not-separation in early modernity for the great Renaissance humanists (e.g., Erasmus, Colet, Ficino) as well as the great sixteenth-century reformers (Luther, Calvin, Loyola, Teresa, Las Casas).

The third distinction — between form and content — was crucial in the reflection of all the ancients even if often set aside by so many modern intellectuals in the ever more specialized university. As the least reflected upon of the three separations in modern thought, form and content deserves the closest, or at least the first, interpretation of the challenge of the future for theological education.

As Hans Urs von Balthasar argued, on theological grounds, for Christian theology, and Louis Dupré argued for Western philosophy and Henri Marrou for Western education, no interpreter can understand the Western intellectual tradition without focusing on the phenomenon of form in that tradition from its beginning to its present crisis, which can now be seen as a crisis of form. Indeed, the central ideal of Western thought from its beginning in Greece (or even before classical Greece, as argued by Mircea Eliade in his studies of archaic religious manifestations) was the idea of the real as, in essence, its appearance in form and availability to all education-as-formation in and through the many forms disclosive of Form itself. As Dupré interprets this centrality of form (the principal leitmotif of his fine study of modernity, *The Passage to Modernity*), form grounds the ancient and medieval ontotheological synthesis. For the ancients the essence of the real and our knowledge of it consists ultimately of form. Form, moreover, shows forth the real in harmonious appearance: whether in sensuous image as in Greek sculpture; in mathematics as in Pythagoras; in the forms of tragedy which render some aesthetic harmony even to chaos and strife; above all, through the ancient philosophical turn to reflective form in the soul or mind. The real appears in an orderly way and thus becomes (even in tragedy) harmonious appearance. This aesthetic, i.e., form-focused, understanding of the real provided the ultimate grounding for any harmonious synthesis of the cosmic, the divine, and the human realms among the ancients. It is a difficult thought to comprehend for us heirs of the fragmentation of all syntheses. It is even more difficult for us as inheritors of a hermeneutics of suspicion that every form may merely mask indeterminacy and every appearance or manifestation may always already hide a strife involving both disclosure and concealment.

Nevertheless, both critics and proponents of classical, medieval, and much modern thought (from Bruno to Hegel) cannot grasp Western thought without dwelling on the central principle of form. For the premoderns, what appears or manifests itself through form is not our subjective construction but the very showing forth, through form, of the real. Is an education formation to the objectively real not mere subjective delight? For the Greeks real being begins with intelligible form, i.e., with a multiplicity, chaos, strife rendered somehow orderly and harmonious through form. Education is a formation by introduction to the forms of the real in the great symbols, narratives, rituals, doctrines, and theories of a great tradition. The Jewish and Christian thinkers accepted the centrality of form but could not accept the necessity of form in Greek and Roman thought. The Greek gods need the form principle; indeed, the form is divine and the divine is form for the Greeks. For the Jew, Christian, and Muslim, God creates form. But as long as God is not understood exclusively as a purely transcendent will, and as long as God's actions are not read exclusively through efficient causality, form survives, indeed prevails: now through the creator God's formal, immanent causality. For Christian thought, as an intellectual and spiritual function moreover, the doctrine of the Word grounded this reality of form in the central Christian doctrines of Christology and Trinity.

This principle of reality manifested *as real* in and through harmonious form in-form-ed the Western philosophical ontotheological tradition from Plato through Hegel. For Plato, with his constant rethinking of "form," especially in *Parmenides,* form in some manner resided within the appearing objects of which it constituted the intelligible essence. As determining factor of that intelligibility (and thereby reality), form also surpassed the objects. In all Greek philosophy (including Aristotle, despite his famous critique of Plato on form), being is defined in terms of form. Moreover, form's dependence is to be understood primarily, not exclusively, in terms of participation. The same is also true, it might be added, of archaic and Greek religion as manifestation (Eliade) or, as Hegel nicely named Greek religion, the religion of beauty. The same centrality of form, as von Balthasar so brilliantly shows, is true of any form of Christianity faithful to the incarnational principle and to a properly theological understanding of Word as Logos, i.e., as manifestation in and through form, as Dante shows so well. Indeed, even as late as Hegel, all content attains its truth in and through form.

In Christian theology, for example, the new forms of theological education — the new narratives of peoples, the forms of all cultures in a multicultural world church — are the most recent development of new forms to render the content of the form principle itself in Christian theology and philosophy. The opening century will surely see more of these new forms. In that sense, formation, in and through the many forms disclosive of true content, shows how education *as* formation is a necessary intellectual and, at the very same time, spiritual practice in any true education. To undo the separation of form and content is also to help undo the separation of practice and theory.

A major difficulty for modern Westerners in reading the texts of the ancients and medievals in Western culture as well as the texts of other great cultures (e.g., not only classical but also contemporary Buddhist texts in east Asian, south Asian, and now even Western forms) is the habitual belief of some Western philosophers and even theologians that theory should be separate from practices, especially practices as specific as an ancient thinker meant by the phrase "spiritual exercises." Education, in that modern reading, will not involve what the ancients and medievals named formation. The ancients (and the monastic medieval schools and even several of the Scholastics) would have found such a separation of theory and practical exercises not merely strange but self-destructive for true education *(educare)*. Philosophy, as is well known, was for the ancients, above all, a love of wisdom, an attempt at a unity of thought and a way of life. The philosopher as philosopher (or theologian as theologian) was unclassifiable in ordinary life; she or he lived nowhere in ordinary life as ordinary life is usually understood. The unclassifiable character of the philosopher-sage determined, as Pierre Hadot maintains and Michel Foucault insisted in his last works on the self, all the major philosophical schools as well as all noninstitutionalized philosophic movements (skepticism, cynicism) of the entire Hellenistic period from the third century B.C.E. (when the "sorting out" of the schools as schools occurred) to the third century C.E. (when the classic Neoplatonic synthesis of Aristotelian and Stoic schools with Platonism was achieved).

Such exercises for philosophy (thus the word) were understood by all the ancient schools as analogous to the exercises employed by an athlete for the body as well as analogous to the application of a medical cure. In contemporary post-Freudian culture, one could expand the analogy (as both Bernard Lonergan and Martha Nussbaum do) to the exercises needed to appropriate one's feelings in therapy. Among the ancients, such exercises included intellectual exercises: recall the use of mathematics to help the exercitant to move from the realm of the sensible to the realm of the intelligible in Pythagoras and Plato (and Lonergan's *Insight*). These exercises also encompassed more obviously spiritual exercises, including the use of images, of memory training (as Frances Yates shows for the Renaissance humanists), of reflection on the basic doctrines or beliefs of the school (see Karl Rahner), as well as exercises above all of increasing one's attentiveness, or awareness or awakeness. Through all such exercises the exercitant can clarify her or his relationship to the ultimate norm, for example, a Stoic's exercise of attention to one's personal relationship to the Logos pervading the entire cosmos.

In contemporary culture, we can further expand the range of exercises (beyond the ancients and medievals) to allow a greater awareness of one's embodied participation in nature and in the whole of one's ethical response to all others and the different, especially the oppressed and marginalized and even nonhuman others, as Buddhism and an ecological consciousness alike teach and as this century will surely demand. Among the ancients, in sum, all reflection on the relationship between theory and practice must be understood from the perspective of such exercises. Even on the very limited basis of this summary of analysis of ancient "spiritual exercises" and ancient theory, it is clear that the need to rethink the *relationship* of education and exercises corresponds to the ancient insistence on the role of intellectual exercises for personal intellectual self-appropriation.

In the present and future, we need above all more attentiveness to the practices we are either already actively engaged in, as teachers and students, or passively engaged by. We need to be attentive to the ethical import of our most everyday practices. For example, our ordinary human interactions as colleagues, teachers, and students are often our best opportunity for both self-delusion and for spotting those self-delusions as we feel, through the very attractions and confusions of our interaction with others, the magnetic pull of the Good, and thereby of God. Moreover, as Iris Murdoch justly insists, art can, at times, free us to consider the possibility that "(a) pure transcendent value, a steady visible enduring higher good, . . . perhaps provides for many people, in an unreligious age without prayer or sacraments, their clearest *experience* of something grasped as separate and precious and beneficial and held quietly and unpossessively in the attention. Good art which we love can seem holy, and attending to it can be like praying. Our relation to such art though 'probably never' entirely pure is markedly unselfish" (Murdoch, *The Fire and the Sun*).

But it is not only love and beauty which are signals of the presence of our attraction to the Good. As the ancients insisted, intellectual practices function this way as well. Mathematics and dialectic direct our attention out of ourselves by their demand that we acknowledge something more, by intellectually entering a world of pure intelligibility. Indeed, learning anything really well — and genuine, painstaking work of scholarship or any careful attention to learning another language well, for example — can take us immediately out of ourselves to a different kind of call and demand. That call is to a sense of objectivity, as our paying virtuous attention to particular realities outside ourselves. Moreover, as Simone Weil suggests, explicitly spiritual exercises are also available to anyone. Above all, we can cultivate moments of tact, silence, and attentiveness to the world outside ourselves as ways of decreasing our natural egoism. We can learn to pay attention in nature and in scientific inquiry to the image of certain necessities as lay to nature. Such careful attentiveness to nature can help exhibit the futility of selfish purposes. We can learn to pay attention to other cultures and the many cultures within our world. Such attention in many postmodern works on language (e.g., Derrida and Kristeva) can promote as well an attentiveness to the Void: that unavoidable reality which can open suddenly in and through our very language use.

My hope for the reunion of theory and exercises in the theological education of the twenty-first century is not focused upon a typically Kantian abrupt call to duty for the will. Instead, my hope is the same as Plato's in the first Western academy: a slow shift of our attachments, a painstaking education of desire — an education like that which Plato foresaw as our best, perhaps our only, hope for both living and thinking well. Even metaphysics and the most abstract theology serve not only an intellectual but a spiritual purpose: another great barrier against our natural egoism; another form to sharpen our attention.

The devastating separation of spirituality from theology and philosophy in our ideas of a proper education must be undone. As a small part of that larger enterprise, I have suggested that we too must face and heal the separations modernity has bequeathed us and postmodernity and the demands of the twenty-first century are happily undoing: the separation of feeling and thought, form and content, practice and theory. Feeling discloses thought; it does not distract from it. Form renders content; it is not merely a pleasant "aesthetic" addition to content. And practices linked to both feeling and form are the key to that peculiar practice we all, both students and teachers, presume to hear as our calling: education as formation; education as a set of exercises heuristically guided by what my own teacher, Bernard Lonergan, did not hesitate to name the transcendental precepts: "Be attentive, be intelligent, be reasonable, be responsible, be loving and, if necessary, change."

Theological education in this century is especially promising for the healing of these separations. For the community of faith, the church, is that community where, despite its faults, even sins, God's Word is yet preached, God's sacraments are made present anew, God's people attempt to live out in action and commitment a life of faith working through love and justice. In the community of faith each person individually, and the whole people as a community, attempt (now well, now poorly) to make God's own story — the story of God's pure, unbounded love for all creation disclosed in the story of the people Israel and that Jesus who is the Christ — become our story as well. The life of the mind cannot live alone. As Aristotle insisted, only gods and beasts can do that. Rather, to think is to converse with the classics, to join the community of inquiry of the living and the dead. It is to acknowledge that we too can and must become part of that conversation. In truth, we *are* that conversation.

Nor does the life of faith live alone. We live that life because past communities of faith passed it on to us. Christians know the decisive narrative of Jesus of Nazareth because our tradition has seen fit to pass along, to hand over, this healing, transforming, gracious possibility to us. As my historical colleague, Martin Marty, has written: "Christianity is always one generation away from extinction." The healing power of faith comes to us because others have passed it on. We know Christ Jesus because long-extinct communities and too easily forgotten generations have allowed us to hear this judging and healing Word.

Some have suggested, with a sense of resignation, perhaps even quiet despair, that even the future is not what it used to be. Yet the truth is: it never was. For at the heart of the Jewish and Christian revolution of consciousness is the insistence that the future cannot be a mere *telos* — a working out of what already is. The future, for the Christian gospel, is *adventum* — that which is to come, the new, the unexpected, judgment and threat, gift and promise from God and God's disclosure in history. To expect and try to prepare for the unexpected is not a simple ideal. But it is the heart of a theological education in both the community of inquiry and the community of faith. Both coherence and re-lationship await upon it for any genuine theological education in the Catholic tradition in the opening global and multicultural century.

CHAPTER TWO

Theology and Theologians:
An Orthodox Perspective

ALKIVIADIS C. CALIVAS

As a priest and theologian, I am often asked by people to explain the nature, scope, and purpose of my work. "What do theologians do," they ask, "and what is theology?" Or they may pose the question differently: "How does one become a theologian, and how does what theologians do benefit the church and relate to the concerns of ordinary people burdened with the cares, the challenges, and the changing realities of contemporary society?" In this essay I shall endeavor to address these and similar questions by reflecting on the nature, task, and mission of theology from an Orthodox perspective.[1]

Theology Is the Gift of the Holy Spirit to the Church

The church is in the world for its renewal and salvation. In every age and place the church addresses the world's ills and problems by declaring and affirming God's plan for the universe, i.e., its ultimate transfiguration and glorification. The church is in the world as servant, in order to introduce people into the new life in Christ through the proclamation of the gospel and the ministry of the sacraments, motivating people to seek the truth and to pursue holiness through prayer, ascesis, and the practice of virtue. This vital task and activity of the church is first of all theological.

---

1. For a detailed bibliography on the nature and task of Orthodox theology, see my article "Orthodox Theology and Theologians: Reflections on the Nature, Task and Mission of the Theological Enterprise," *Greek Orthodox Theological Review* 37, no. 3-4 (1992): 275-307. Material in this essay is based on this article.

The church is the "pillar and bulwark of the truth" (1 Tim. 3:15). She is vested with the ultimate authority to discern and proclaim the truth. Therefore, as with worship, evangelism, and philanthropy, doing theology is an activity constitutive of the church. Theology belongs to the church, because she alone is the authentic depository of the apostolic kerygma (2 Pet. 1:16-21). Authentic theology always bears an ecclesial character. It is practiced in, by, and for the church. In the words of Ioannis Karmiris, theology is "a handmaid and servant of the Church, (her) thought and consciousness, a perfect gift of the Holy Spirit to the Church in which he dwells."[2]

The knowledge of the mystery of the triune God and of his divine economy, which constitute the subject of theology, does not originate with human beings. It is not attained immediately through human faculties, though the human intellect is intimately involved in the process (2 Pet. 1:21). Authentic theology is learned from the Holy Spirit. It is the Spirit who searches everything, even the depths of God, and alone apprehends the thoughts of God (1 Cor. 2:10-11). The Holy Spirit entrusts the truth to those in whom he dwells (2 Tim. 1:14). Through the Spirit people taste the goodness of the word of God and the powers of the age to come (Heb. 5:4-5), and are empowered to preach the good news (1 Pet. 1:12). We come to the knowledge of God through the grace of the Holy Spirit. He guides us into all the truth (John 16:13). Through the Spirit we recognize Christ the Son of God, and through Christ we are elevated to the knowledge of the Father (Matt. 11:27). Finally, it is the Holy Spirit who constitutes the church as the body of Christ and makes it the living presence of the Truth.

The Meaning and Task of Theology

Theology, according to Vladimir Lossky, means everything that can be said of the triune God, considered in himself and in his redemptive economy, through which he reveals himself in creating the world and in the incarnation of his Son.[3] At the center of the first mystery, which is related to God's inmost nature, is the doctrine of the Holy Trinity. At the center of the second mystery, which is related to God's redemptive economy, is Jesus Christ, the incarnate Son and Word of God. Theology, therefore, includes all that can be said of God and of

2. Ioannis Karmiris, "Contemporary Orthodox Theology and Its Tasks," *St. Vladimir's Theological Quarterly* 13, no. 1 and 2 (1969): 12, 13.

3. Vladimir Lossky, *The Image and Likeness of God* (Crestwood, N.Y.: Saint Vladimir's Seminary Press, 1974), p. 15. I am indebted to Professor Lossky for this perceptive and succinct summary of the content of Orthodox theology.

his divine economy, which includes the response of humankind to his transforming and sanctifying presence in the world. It is important, however, to understand clearly, as Father John Romanides has pointed out, "that the partial knowability of the divine actions and energies and the absolute and radical unknowability and incommunicability of the divine essence is not a result of philosophical or theological speculation . . . but of the personal experience of revelation and participation in the uncreated glory of God."[4]

We cannot begin to fathom the mystery of the living God apart from the economy in which he reveals himself. This economy, Lossky says, includes the creation of the cosmos; the establishment of the covenants; the incarnation, life, death, resurrection, and glorification of Jesus Christ; and the descent of the Holy Spirit. It also includes the establishment of the church, Christ's second glorious coming, and the future age of God's kingdom, which is both a present reality and a future realization.

Included in the economy is the human factor as well, because God accomplishes salvation in cooperation with humanity. Theology is also concerned with the human condition and with humanity's response to and appropriation and celebration of God's acts in history.

In his relation to the world, God works through the finite condition of human existence. Divine revelation is encoded and transmitted through the medium of human language. Hence the human intellect is indispensable to the appropriation of the truth of salvation. However, knowledge of this truth cannot be limited only to this form of understanding. The emotions and the senses are also called to experience the content of theology and to be brought into contact with divinity. It is even possible, through holiness of life, to have an experience of God that surpasses the faculties of understanding and perception. This is what we call mystical knowledge. It comes through the purification and illumination of the mind and heart by the Holy Spirit and presupposes both the knowledge and the practice of the Orthodox faith.

Though human language is finite, it is nevertheless the principal vehicle for both the transmission and the reception of divine revelation. Language, therefore, is a crucial component of the theological enterprise. It necessitates a

---

4. John S. Romanides, "Critical Examination of the Applications of Theology," in *Proces — Verbaux du Deuxième Congrès de Théologie Orthodoxe,* ed. Savas Agourides (Athens: Theological School of the University of Athens, 1978), p. 427. Father Romanides explains that the whole doctrine of the Holy Trinity can be reduced schematically to two simple statements: "(1) What is common in the Holy Trinity, i.e., essence, will, energy and power, is common to and identical in all Three Hypostases. (2) What is Hypostatic, or hypostatic property, or manner of existence, is radically individual and incommunicable and belongs to One person or Hypostasis only" (p. 430).

constant effort on the part of those who do theology for the church — theologians, priests, bishops, and synods — to strive for the most precise and accurate formulations of the divine truths, free from errors and distortions. Thus, one of the goals of Orthodox theology has always been to discern and understand rightly the eternal truths of divine revelation and to articulate and formulate them correctly through proper and adequate expressions and definitions, albeit through the narrow limits of human language. That said, it is equally important to note that "revelation itself transcends words and concepts although it inspires those participating in divine glory to express accurately and unerringly what is inexpressible in words and concepts."[5]

These expressions and definitions are intended to lead to the glory of God. Therefore the language of authentic theology is ultimately doxological and mystagogical; that is to say, it expresses the adoration of God. This means that theology is inextricably bound to worship. Metropolitan John Zizioulas emphasized this point when he observed that "the dogmas of the Church are not logical propositions to be tested and approved by the minds of individual believers, but doxological statements to be part of the worship and the life of the communities. The Creed is not there for theologians to study, but for communities to sing."[6]

The worshiping community, gathered together in the communion of the Holy Spirit, constitutes a unique theological witness. Grace, life, and teaching flow from the liturgical assembly. The worshiping community is always the primary place for the reception as well as the transmission of the vision that is believed, pondered, and formulated by the church. As Constantine Skouteris put it, "the one and only rock upon which theology, as a doxological event, can be based is the ecclesiastical body. It is within the Church, this continued Pentecost, that our mind . . . can be illuminated and transformed into a theological mind."[7] Theology is both taught and learned in the church, and especially in the context of her worship, in which faithful people encounter the living God.

Essentially, the task of theology, according to Father Georges Florovsky, is none other than "to ascertain and to acknowledge the mystery of the living

---

5. Romanides, p. 427.

6. Metropolitan John Zizioulas, "The Church as Communion," *St. Vladimir's Theological Quarterly* 38, no. 1 (1994): 12.

7. Constantine Skouteris, "Doxology, the Language of Orthodoxy," *Greek Orthodox Theological Review* 38, no. 1-4 (1993): 156. See also Stylianos Papadopoulos, *Theology and Language* (in Greek) (Tertios: Katerini, 1988), and Emmanuel Clapsis, "Naming God: An Orthodox View," in *Rightly Teaching the Word of Your Truth*, ed. N. M. Vaporis (Brookline, Mass.: Holy Cross Orthodox Press, 1995).

God, and to bear witness to it in word and deed."[8] The basic goal of theology is to propagate and sustain "the faith which was once delivered to the saints" (Jude 3). Looking outwardly toward the world, the function of theology is to convert the world through the projection and witness of the Orthodox faith. Looking inwardly toward the church, its aim is to instruct, edify, guide, nourish, illumine, and transform the faithful and to make church life conform to its essential mission and purposes through the explanation of the content of the Orthodox faith.

Critical Theological Reflection Is Essential to the Church

The real, practical, everyday life of the church must have theological substance. Without serious theological witness and criticism, according to Father Alexander Schmemann, the church "becomes a prisoner of her empirical needs and the pragmatic spirit of this world which poisons and obscures the absolute demands of the Truth."[9] The church needs theology. It is her conscience. Without vibrant and meaningful theological work, the church is neither worthy nor capable of fulfilling her saving mission in the world.

Critical theological reflection is essential to the church because, on the one hand, it helps preserve the identity of her message, while on the other hand it prompts continuous progress into the inexhaustible meaning of the mystery of salvation. Moreover, theology, as an act of the Holy Spirit, evaluates and judges continually the institutional life of the church in accordance with the truths of the faith, liberating it from sin and all other external pressures and influences that would compromise the church's nature, ethos, purpose, and mission.

Unquestionably, theology is committed to serve the church. However, this relationship is neither one of subservience nor one of servility. Theology can never become the instrument of special interests or the tool of blind partisan advocates. Theology is about truth — objective, constant truth, the entry into the unapproachable glory of God. It is the struggle to distinguish the tradition of the church from all alien accretions and to continuously formulate that tradition in the idiom of the modern world. Like tradition, theology is not only a protective and conservative principle, it is also a principle of regeneration and of growth in the perception of the one constant Truth.

8. Georges Florovsky, "St. Gregory Palamas and the Tradition of the Fathers," in vol. 1 of his collected works, *Bible, Church, Tradition: An Eastern Orthodox View* (Belmont, Mass.: Nordland Publishing, 1972), p. 108.

9. Alexander Schmemann, "Theology and Eucharist," *St. Vladimir's Theological Quarterly* 5, no. 4 (1961): 12.

Theology Is Dynamic and Creative

Authentic theology is dynamic and "ever-youthful," to use the phrase of Saint Irenaeus. It is cognizant of the inexhaustible mysterious character of the Christian faith and of the infinite complexity of its meanings. It reinterprets the dogmatic definitions, the liturgical expressions, and the canonical formulations of the church in relation to the present needs of the church and the perennial human quest for meanings. It does all this while remaining faithful to the uninterrupted historical and theological life of the church.

Theological creativity is not a departure from tradition. It constitutes, rather, the very manifestation of the true character of tradition. For, as Father Florovsky has observed correctly, "tradition is the continuity of the abiding presence of the Holy Spirit in the Church, the continuity of divine guidance and illumination."[10] Thus, to quote Father Dumitru Staniloae, "Orthodox theology does not make earlier formulations obsolete when it moves forward to new ones, but remains in continuity with them, the former being in fact a new explanation of the latter, a new step forward in the perception of the divine mystery, which had also been correctly perceived by the previous formulae."[11]

The conceptual elaboration of the living faith of the church is at the heart of the theological endeavor. This activity, however, is neither a continuous development of the truth nor a new revelation. It is rather a ceaseless growth in the human understanding and appropriation of the one, constant, changeless truth of salvation. Though this truth is constant — for Pentecost cannot be improved upon — the experience of it is dynamic and variable.[12] The elaboration of the truth is intended not only to preserve but also to explain and interpret the teachings of the church in each generation.

Keeping the faith whole and unadulterated does not mean that theology remains static or aloof from the demands and problems of each age. For sure, the church is never in need of new theologies that break with tradition, but unquestionably, as Father John Meyendorff has pointed out, "the Church needs theology to solve the problems of each age, not to repeat ancient solutions to ancient problems."[13] Static theology is unrelated to the needs and concerns of the church in a given time and place. It is a dead theology. As ignorance of and indifference to the past are both inappropriate and unacceptable, so also is the

10. Florovsky, "St. Gregory Palamas," p. 106.

11. Dumitru Staniloae, *Theology and the Church* (Crestwood, N.Y.: Saint Vladimir's Seminary Press, 1980), p. 214.

12. See, for example, Romanides, p. 432.

13. John Meyendorff, "Orthodox Theology Today," *St. Vladimir's Theological Quarterly* 13, no. 1 and 2 (1969): 77.

avoidance of creative movement, development, and progress in theological work. After all, as Ioannis Karmiris has stated, the Fathers "did not exhaust all the contents of the faith nor did they solve all the problems of theology, but they left it up to us to find a field of independent creative action and to continue their task, always of course, in their spirit."[14]

Doing theology in the patristic spirit and mode means we must avoid the extremes of pietistic conservatism on the one hand and academic scientism on the other. Orthodox theology is essentially experiential and nonspeculative. It is always God-centered, incarnational, prophetic, and pastoral. It is also demanding and self-critical.[15] In the words of Father Theodore Stylianopoulos, the practice of authentic theology "takes into account a greater balance between faith and reason, mystical cognition and scholarship, individual and faith community, Church and culture, according to the testimony of the Church fathers."[16]

Theological Literacy Is Essential for the Defense of the Truth

Theology tells the story of God and of his redemptive activity in creation. Since our God, however, is not the God of philosophers, the God of speculation and of theories, he cannot be reduced to abstract categories and formulas. He is known by grace. Theology, therefore, is more than the accumulation of data and the formulation of propositions. The ultimate aim of all theological thought is to confer union with God and to bring about the transfiguration of the human being through his penetration into the divine. Orthodox theology is first and always a means, "a unity of knowledge subserving an end that transcends all knowledge. This ultimate end is union with God or deification, the θέωσις of the Greek Fathers."[17]

Truth must be sought in personal and relational terms rather than in abstract concepts. Truth is the gift of the Holy Spirit to the church. The church possesses the truth and with it the gift of infallibility. Life in the church is life in

---

14. Karmiris, "Contemporary Orthodox Theology," p. 20.

15. See, for example, Petros Vassiliades, "Greek Theology in the Making — Trends and Facts in the 80s and Vision for the 90s," *St. Vladimir's Theological Quarterly* 35, no. 1 (1991): 33-52.

16. Theodore G. Stylianopoulos, *The New Testament — An Orthodox Perspective* (Brookline, Mass.: Holy Cross Orthodox Press, 1997), pp. 184-85.

17. Vladimir Lossky, *The Mystical Theology of the Eastern Orthodox Church* (London: J. Clarke, 1957), p. 9. See also Jaroslav Pelikan, *The Spirit of Eastern Orthodox Christendom* (Chicago: University of Chicago Press, 1974), pp. 16-22.

the truth; that is to say, life in Christ, who is himself the Truth. Truth is a person, Jesus Christ. It is his living presence in the church, his body, that preserves her free from error. The triune God himself, who alone is infallible, through his mysterious presence in the church, leads her in the way of truth. This is why the whole church is gifted with infallibility.[18]

Every Orthodox Christian, inasmuch as he shares in the life of the church, is vested with the responsibility to defend the truth (cf. Acts 15:22-28). For this reason clergy and laity alike must struggle to grow in genuine piety and strive to achieve a level of theological literacy, in order to discern more clearly the workings of the Holy Spirit, who lives in the church and guides her into all the truth. In the broadest sense, then, theology must be pursued and practiced by the whole body of the church in its life and struggles.

The church is a unity of persons, who fulfill their personal being in relationship with other beings and recognize in each member of the faith community his unique personal qualifications as well as his unique place, function, role, and vocation. Hence the individual members of the church, each in his own particular order, are graced with differing but complementary gifts or charisms.

The teaching function is an essential ministry of the church. Theologians and teachers are entrusted, by vocation and training, to practice theology for the church. It is their task to reflect upon, analyze, and teach the received tradition, in order to illumine, edify, and nourish the people of God with the truths of the faith. Although for the most part in the history of the church theologians have been clergy, especially bishops and presbyters, monastics as well as laypeople have practiced and continue to practice theology for the church.

The authority of the teaching ministry is vested primarily in the episcopate[19] and especially in local and ecumenical synods.[20] The episcopate is

18. See Bishop Kallistos Ware, "The Ecumenical Councils and the Conscience of the Church," *Kanon: Jahrbuch der Gesellschaft für das Recht der Ostkirchen* 2 (1974): 228-33.

19. See Thomas Hopko, "Ministry and the Unity of the Church: An Eastern Orthodox View," *St. Vladimir's Theological Quarterly* 34, no. 4 (1990): 269-79; Thomas FitzGerald, "Conciliarity, Primacy and the Episcopacy," *St. Vladimir's Theological Quarterly* 38, no. 1 (1994): 17-43.

20. See, for example, John Zizioulas, "Episkope and Episcopate in Ecumenical Perspectives," *Faith and Order Paper 102,* pp. 30-42; Archbishop Peter, "Authority in the Church," *St. Vladimir's Theological Quarterly* 39, no. 4 (1995): 325-37; Lewis Patsavos, *Primacy and Conciliarity* (Brookline, Mass.: Holy Cross Orthodox Press, 1995); Bishop Maximos Aghiorgoussis, "Theological and Historical Aspects of Conciliarity: Some Propositions for Discussion," *Greek Orthodox Theological Review* 24, no. 1 (1979): 5-19; J. Meyendorff, N. Afanasieff, A. Schmemann, and N. Kouloumzine, *The Primacy of Peter in the Orthodox Church* (London: Faith Press, 1963).

central among the orders and ministries of the church. Its primary role is to ensure the unity of the church and to proclaim and safeguard doctrinal truth. The episcopate gathered in synod is the organ through which the truths of the faith are examined, formulated, and expounded. However, the authority of the episcopate and the synods is not absolute but relative. The decisions of the synods become absolute only when the whole body of the church receives them.[21] This basic principle was noted by the patriarchs of the East in a statement issued in 1848 in response to Pope Pius IX, who called for the union of the churches. The statement, in part, reads as follows: "Among us, neither Patriarchs nor Synods have ever been able to introduce novelties, because the defender of the religion is the body of the Church; that is to say, the people which want its religion to remain eternally unchanged and of like form to that of the Fathers."[22]

The whole people — clergy and laity together, who constitute the common or general conscience of the church — act as the bearer of infallibility, protecting the church from doctrinal distortions and innovations.[23] Were it otherwise, the whole body of the church would be subordinate to one group of her members. The final authority rests upon the conscience of the whole church guided by the Holy Spirit. This said, however, it is equally important to make certain distinctions. The laity are neither the arbiters nor the official public teachers of the faith. Their task is to acknowledge and receive the truth and safeguard the faith from innovations and distortions. It is the responsibility chiefly of the bishops, either singly or corporately, to proclaim and define the truth, which has been present always in the conscience (συνείδησις) of the church.

The power to discern between truth and falsehood is not given solely to the hierarchy in isolation, but to the whole people, who are engaged actively in the life of the church. To be more precise, as Bishop Kallistos Ware tells it, "God, ever present in his Church, speaks both through councils of bishops and through the People of God as a whole. The members of God's people, in virtue of the Spirit that dwells within them, recognize the truth that has been proclaimed by the episcopate through the power of the same indwelling Spirit."[24]

21. See Metropolitan John Zizioulas, "The Church as Communion," *St. Vladimir's Theological Quarterly* 38, no. 1 (1994): 12.

22. Ioannis Karmiris, Τά Δογματικά καί Συμβολικά Μνημεῖα τῆς Ὀρθοδόξου Καθολικῆς Ἐκκλησίας (Athens, 1953), p. 920.

23. Father Theodore Stylianopoulos *(The New Testament)* underscores this point well when he writes that access to the knowledge of God is available to all. "For otherwise, not only would the faithful be deprived of their role of guardians of the faith but also the Church would be cut off from communication with the world to which it is charged to preach the gospel meaningfully" (p. 184).

24. Ware, "The Ecumenical Councils," p. 228.

As stewards of the one true faith, Orthodox Christians must always be vigilant, so that they may neither grieve nor quench the Spirit (Eph. 4:30; 1 Thess. 5:19). Rather, they should pursue the truth with all diligence. Hence, they must always guard against two temptations which, when carried to extremes, have tragic consequences for the church. Father Schmemann characterized these temptations as isolation and indifference.[25] The former attacks those theologians who alienate themselves from the real life of the church. The latter afflicts those people, clergy and laity alike, who avoid personal responsibility and engagement in the substantive issues of church life.

It happens sometimes that theologians are absorbed by their individual interests and become involved with esoteric controversies that fail to touch the real life of people and fail to relate to the real needs and problems of the church. On the other side of the issue are the clergy and the laity who regard theological scholarship with suspicion and believe that the problems of the church can be resolved without recourse to theology.

Clearly, when the church is deprived of vibrant and properly focused theological work or when the people cease to appreciate theology, the church faces the danger of losing the perspectives of her life. Without sound scholarship and critical research, theology becomes seriously handicapped and could deteriorate gradually into uncritical, repetitive, and sterile pietistic formulations. On the other hand, a theology that is not grounded spiritually carries no conviction. When theology does not flow out of the church's life, it runs the risk of being irrelevant and susceptible to erroneous interpretations of the faith.

Theological Scholarship and Faith Commitment

The perennial message of the gospel is reflected in the life and the structures of the church. It is kept alive and summarized in her creeds, dogmas, canons, and liturgy, which constitute, in part, the apostolic tradition. The kerygma of the apostles has been properly articulated and developed into a consistent body of correlated testimonies, the dogmas of the Fathers.[26] These testimonies are embedded in the church's rule of faith, rule of prayer, and rule of practice. It is the task of theology to critically examine these rules, to understand them, and to promulgate them. This task is accomplished especially through the academic disciplines of theology that have developed over the course of time.

---

25. Schmemann, p. 11.

26. See Georges Florovsky, *Aspects of Church History* (Belmont, Mass.: Nordland Publishing, 1975), p. 16.

The academic approach to theological work enables theologians to acquire a broader, more comprehensive knowledge of their field of study, in order to prosecute better and more thoroughly their task and mission. However, it is possible to overemphasize the academic approach to the detriment of theology's mission. A preoccupation with methodologies and questions of epistemology can lead to sterile intellectualism, while the obsession with obscure, minute historical details can render the discipline lifeless and make its subject matter irrelevant. Doing theology in this manner is unproductive. It obscures the message and leads to an overrationalization of the religious experience. The cautionary words of Father Nicholas Afanasieff are an appropriate reminder: "logic by itself is no proof of the truth."[27]

Orthodox theology is not sterile intellectualism but pastoral and existential. The record of Scripture and tradition is apprehended and understood correctly only within the context of the living faith of the church. The final intention and aim of all theology is to lead both the theologian and the people to communion with the life of God. The purpose for which theology is exercised on behalf of the church is to orient correctly the eucharistic assemblies of the church, in order to make truth into communion and life.[28]

Whatever intellectual abilities and other competencies, gifts, and talents theologians bring to their task, none is more vital than a prayerful commitment to God and devotion to the church. As Father Florovsky noted, "no one profits by the Gospels unless he be first in love with Christ. For Christ is not a text but a living person, and he abides in his body, the Church."[29]

According to the tradition of the church, an illumined intellect, a vigilant soul, silence before God, and purity of heart constitute the personal presuppositions for doing theology. For the Christian in general and the theologian in particular, the saying of Evagrios Pontikos is especially pertinent: "If you are a theologian, you will pray in truth; and if you pray in truth, you are a theologian."[30]

The Theologian Must Avoid Two Extremes

In doing theology, the theologian must avoid two extreme tendencies, both of which are related to history and heedlessly lend themselves to the obfuscation

---

27. Nicholas Afanasieff, "The Church Which Presides in Love," in *The Primacy of Peter in the Orthodox Church*, p. 64.

28. See John Zizioulas, *Being as Communion — Studies in Personhood and the Church* (Crestwood, N.Y.: Saint Vladimir's Seminary Press, 1985), pp. 116-17.

29. Georges Florovsky, "The Lost Scriptural Mind," in *Bible, Church, Tradition*, p. 14.

30. Evagrios Pontikos, Περί Προσευχής, Patrologia Graeca 79:1180B.

of the living tradition of the church. Let me speak to these tendencies briefly from the perspective of the discipline of liturgics. There are those, for example, who uncritically would have the church hold on to a world that once was or may have been, but no longer is. They revel in aspects of the liturgical tradition that are no longer meaningful or relevant. Resisting change, they would have the church retain these practices as if they represented the very core of the tradition.

On the opposite side of the *antiquarians* stand the *futurists* (my terms). The futurists conceive of a world that is not and perhaps can never be. They seek to impose it on others with unrestrained enthusiasm. They think of creativity as radical departure and immediate change, conceived mostly in their imagination — or some committee's imagination — apart from the realities, experiences, and possibilities of the faith community. They are not mindful of the fact that the success of any meaningful and lasting reform is closely related to the realm of possibilities, which is carefully guarded and tenaciously retained as an essential characteristic both by history and by humankind.

The theologian, on the one hand, must be careful not to be overcome with nostalgia in the face of changing cultural realities and lament the passing away of old patterns in church life. On the other hand, the theologian should not be an indifferent observer nor an uncritical participant in the evolving process of history. The theologian must be conscious of the fact that the historical process is not void of meaning, without constructive value. He is obliged to remind himself and the faith community that history is part of revelation.

Reflection and Application

Doing theology well requires both reflection and application. It is not enough simply to speak about the church as the body of Christ. James Cone reminds us that we must also say and do much about this body's relation to broken human bodies in society.[31] Authentic theology must be concerned and involved with the problems and ills that afflict humanity by analyzing and challenging the philosophical foundations and the socioeconomic structures and systems that produce injustices and devalue human life. Metropolitan (now Archbishop) Demetrios Trakatelis observes correctly that the task of the theologizing church is "to stand up for humanity and proclaim redemption in uncompromising faithfulness to God. The Church is the Church of God, and theology is the voice

---

31. James H. Cone, "The Servant Church," in *The Pastor as Servant,* ed. E. E. Shelp and R. H. Sunderland (New York: Pilgrim Press, 1986), pp. 61-80.

expressing God's immutable, dynamic and redeeming love for suffering humanity."[32]

Good theology must create good praxis. It is not enough to transmit the word faithfully. It is equally important to challenge the root causes of human misery and to confront and judge every historical situation with the searing truth of the gospel. "If the Church is to be truly apostolic," says Metropolitan John Zizioulas, "she must be both historically and eschatologically oriented; she must both transmit history and judge history by placing it in the light of the *eschata*."[33]

The church does not draw her identity from what she is but from what she will be. She reflects the future, the final stage of things. The theological endeavor therefore, as reflection and praxis, must be guided by the eschatological vision. Theology must help people to see and think differently, to abandon the false values and the untruths of the fallen world, and to become transparent of Christ Jesus.

Nowhere is the effectual power of theology more apparent than in the local parish and in the lives of its individual members. It is in these fundamental contexts that theology plays itself out. A parish that is organized in a manner that unites the faithful dynamically, makes Christian truths live in the hearts of people, and integrates these truths into life and acts upon them in concrete ways signifies that the theological activities of the seminary and of the parish are well focused, vibrant, and effective. However, where the secular mode of living and doing business has crept into the church, where spiritual identities have been blurred and compromised, and where individual and parish activities have become ambiguous, both the parish and the seminary are obliged to reconsider their agenda, redirect their priorities, and revitalize the theological enterprise.

While she is in the world, the church must raise up faithful persons who can be models of faith and courage, of humility and love, of prayer and godly action, of vision and of illumined leadership in transforming society. She must raise up men and women who participate in the will and plan of God for their lives and for their times. In other words, the *church-in-mission* seeks to make her people a *people-in-mission,* that is to say, a people who are aflame in the Spirit and who reflect like mirrors the brightness of the Lord.

In response to the imperatives of the gospel, the church must seek to influence the powers that shape the present and form the future. One way — the

---

32. Metropolitan Demetrios Trakatelis, "Theology in Encounters," *Greek Orthodox Theological Review* 32, no. 1 (1987): 36.

33. Zizioulas, *Being as Communion*, p. 181.

most significant way — of doing this is to bring the insights of her theological tradition into all manner and level of discussions that deal with the nature, the meaning, the purpose, and the future of human life and of all existence. The church must become for the world an "unlimited reserve . . . of authentic life that makes possible all the good and lasting creations of history."[34]

The unprecedented achievements of modern science have added greatly to our knowledge of the cosmos and have raised to new and unparalleled heights the quality of our biological existence. Progressing into the twenty-first century, scientists promise us an even greater expansion of human capabilities. Human beings both design and manage the scientific process. At every stage of the process people have at their disposal a wide range of possibilities to give form and shape to nature. Who is to help determine and develop the principles of choice by which the scientific process is guided and its ends and purposes defined? How are these purposes related to the ultimate destiny of humanity and the cosmos? Certainly Orthodox theology must play a significant role in this crucial debate. In the dialogue with the scientific world, theology has to bring clarity of purpose to the scientific process, in order that the aspirations, desires, pursuits, and activities of human beings are of the highest order, endued with ultimate meanings and moral content.

The ecological crisis is another example. The care of the material world — both animate and inanimate — cannot be left to scientists, environmentalists, sociologists, economists, and politicians. The integrity of creation and the protection of the environment are, first of all, theological issues and concerns. Philip Sherrard reminds us that a basic cause of today's ecological crisis is the loss of the full significance of the "relationship of interdependence, interpenetration, and reciprocity between God, man, and creation."[35]

The protection of the material world has theological as well as social and scientific implications. How we view, understand, and use the natural environment says much about our beliefs, motivations, and priorities, as persons, as

---

34. Olivier Clement, *The Roots of Christian Mysticism* (New York: New City Press, 1995), p. 287.

35. Philip Sherrard, *Christianity — Lineaments of a Sacred Tradition* (Brookline, Mass.: Holy Cross Orthodox Press, 1998), p. 243. See also Philip Sherrard, *The Eclipse of Man and Nature: An Inquiry into the Origins and Consequences of Modern Science* (West Stockbridge, Mass.: Lindisfarne Press, 1987), which is also published under the title *The Rape of Man and Man and Nature;* Stanley S. Harakas, "The Integrity of Creation: Ethical Issues," in *Justice, Peace, and the Integrity of Creation,* ed. Gennadios Limouris (Geneva: WCC Publications, 1990); Metropolitan John Zizioulas, "Preserving God's Creation — Three Lectures on Theology and Ecology," *King's Theological Review* 12, no. 1 and 2 (1989) and 13, no. 1 (1990); Bishop Kallistos Ware, "The Value of the Material Creation," *Sobornost* 6, no. 3 (1971): 154-65.

churches, and as societies. Father Stanley Harakas, for example, makes the point that a theology that distinguishes sharply between human life and the rest of nature and that spiritualizes salvation as unconnected with the created world unwittingly allows for the indiscriminate assault on creation.[36] The world is God's gift of life. His glory is diffused everywhere. It fills the vast expanses of the cosmos as well as every form of life and existence. It is precisely for this reason that we must not abuse the natural creation, this gift of life. It exists by the will of God for the appropriate use of human beings. Because God loves the world, humanity, in imitation of his providential concern, is duty-bound to care for it and protect it.

We can hardly talk about effective theological work without taking into account the prevailing theories that influence people in the way they think about themselves, about the world they live in, and about the meaning and purpose of their existence. The pressures of the secular world — where the media repeatedly mock the gospel, challenge church authority, and strip people of personal worth and dignity — have a way of weakening the faith community. These pressures make it all the more difficult for Christian families to communicate the faith and the ethos of the church to the next generation. There is, therefore, an increasing urgency to confront and forestall the corrosive powers of secularity. Theology must evaluate the defects as well as the merits of modern ideologies so that its critique of the baneful consequences of secular humanism may be powerful and plausible.

The Value of Ecumenical Activities

The ecumenical dialogues, once lively and hopeful, appear to be in a state of fatigue. The once urgent quest for Christian unity seems to have waned. Churches are retreating into isolation and theologians are less inclined to press forward the search for doctrinal reconciliation. Failures, frustrations, and contradictions within the ecumenical movement have dampened the enthusiasm of many. Legitimate concerns about methodologies, goals, and purposes have become a source of irritation. Yet, as real and as vexing as these problems may be, we must not abandon the cause of Christian unity. The Orthodox especially should mount new initiatives, propose new methodologies, and bring greater clarity to the purpose and goals of the ecumenical endeavor.

We must recognize the contributions and be mindful of the fruits that the ecumenical movement has produced. For example, friction among Christians

---

36. Harakas, pp. 70-71.

has been reduced, prejudices have been overcome, pastoral initiatives have been undertaken, succor has been provided to deprived persons and communities, theological education has been supported, common Christian witness has been strengthened, the theological dialogues have been advanced, and important convergence documents have been produced.

Orthodox participation in the ecumenical movement is essential because we believe that Christian unity is an inescapable imperative. Because truth matters greatly, we are bound to speak it in love (Eph. 4:15). Therefore, regardless of the fact that theological presuppositions, conceptual language, and spiritual traditions may differ — and sometimes significantly — it is nonetheless our duty to engage other Christians and even people of other religions or of no faith in earnest dialogue, precisely for the sake of the truth. Only then can we overcome what Metropolitan John Zizioulas terms "spiritual terrorism against ecumenism," which often paralyzes church leaders who fear the criticism of those within the church who identify Orthodoxy with negativity and polemic.[37]

The division of Christians is a scandal and a tragedy, the crucial vexing problem of Christian history. Theologians especially have a sacred duty to advance the cause of unity for the sake of the gospel and our common Christian ancestry. Father Florovsky spoke of the Orthodox Church's special role in the task to restore the broken unity of Christians. He wrote in one of his essays, "In the accomplishment of this task the Orthodox Church has a special function. She is the living embodiment of an uninterrupted tradition in thought and in worship. She stands not for a certain, peculiar tradition, but for the Tradition of the undivided Church." We have no choice but to continue to be a creative and dynamic force against estrangement and autonomous existence.

---

37. Metropolitan John Zizioulas, "The Self-Understanding of the Orthodox and Their Participation in the Ecumenical Movement," in *The Ecumenical Movement of the Churches and the World Council of Churches,* ed. George Lemopoulos (Geneva: WCC Publications, 1996), p. 46.

CHAPTER THREE

On the Complexity of Theological Literacy

ROBERT CUMMINGS NEVILLE

Much as some people want a simple faith, and theological educators want a manageable curriculum, the reality of our time is that theological literacy is so complex that it can't be neatly boxed. "Theological literacy" here means what religious leaders and intellectuals need to know in order to understand and become cognitively competent in the resources of their traditions and of their society, and in order to avoid the kind of stupid mistakes that come from not understanding what someone in their position ought to understand.[1] There are many other kinds of stupid mistakes, as well as honest mistakes. But even if one worries only about those mistakes that come from not knowing something that should be known by anyone in that position, the complexity of contemporary theological literacy is extraordinary. Theological literacy as a virtue applies especially to religious leaders trained in seminary, ordained and nonordained, but it also applies to those who rise to leadership and intellectual life through other routes.

Four loci of complexity will be explored here: the complexities of theological identity, theological expression, theological truth, and theological engagement. The discussion will be couched in terms of theological literacy for Christian leaders and intellectuals, though the points apply for leaders and thinkers in other religious traditions as well, with some obvious translations.

The generic reason for the complexity in each locus of theological literacy is that in our time an unusually large, or newly large, number of perspectives need to be brought into one's own perspective of theological life. Complexity here in its most abstract sense means embracing many perspectives into one with respect, deference, and fairness of judgment.[2]

1. To be sure, there are many other kinds of competence than cognitive ones, and religious leaders need more than theological literacy. But literacy is the topic here.
2. The peculiar kind of complexity that consists in the problem of constructing a perspective that is capable of embracing other perspectives fairly and with deference is not a new

39

The Complexity of Theological Identity

The good-old-days myth had it that one became literate in one's theological heritage or identity by mastering a trajectory of historical development. For most of the schools in the Boston Theological Institute, that trajectory started in Jerusalem and passed through Antioch, Constantinople/Athens, Rome, and Berlin before arriving in Boston. For some of us, the trajectory went pretty straight from the centers of Orthodoxy to Boston. For others, there were important detours through Geneva, Amsterdam, or Canterbury. For others, the Catholic Berlin was different from the Protestant Berlin. But for all, until at least the middle of the twentieth century, theological identity could be studied through the historical trajectory leading from Jerusalem down some singular path to the Boston situation.

Then the feminists raised the consciousness of literate theologians to the point of understanding that the theological expressions of any version of that Jerusalem-Europe-Boston trajectory had left out the voices of women except in marginal instances. Sometimes neglected women's voices could be uncovered and brought to attention along that trajectory. Yet the very fact of systematic neglect of women shakes the authority of the historical literature of that trajectory. We don't even know whether women would have said the exact same things that men said. Who we have been, we who got to Boston through that trajectory, and what we are now as the result of that, is deeply problematic, and the problem cannot be addressed without incorporating the perspectives of women. Even where we cannot find neglected but articulate women's theological perspectives in that historical trajectory, at least we need to incorporate the perspectives of contemporary women on that history. There are many such perspectives.

---

theme for Christianity, nor a marginal one. It lies at the heart of Jesus' controversial fellowship which included women, sinners, untouchables, the too rich and the too poor, and occasional Romans, Samaritans, and Canaanites. The institutionalization of such social inclusiveness was a deep issue for the nascent Christian Way, and was addressed in the first Jerusalem council in the matter of accepting Greek and other non-Jewish cultures in matters of cuisine and circumcision. Vapid tolerance of many perspectives is not enough. There has to be the construction of an inclusive perspective that concretely integrates the others without reducing them to something they are not. Concrete integration need not mean univocal agreement. It can also mean agreeing to disagree and still getting on cooperatively with other intellectual or practical work of the community. Confucians would point out that one of the chief values of social ritual is that it allows people who are very different to be themselves while dancing together in a larger enterprise. I have studied these issues in *Normative Cultures* (Albany: State University of New York Press, 1995), pt. 2. On the crucial difference between integrating things within a strict order and deference to them, interpreted as part of the Christian covenant, see my *A Theology Primer* (Albany: State University of New York Press, 1991), chaps. 5–6.

Meanwhile, liberation theologies have been arguing that theological identity is contextual. Part of that is a call for the legitimation of theological identity in the special contexts of Latin American, Korean, African, African American, and other communities, the gospel indigenized for each. The other side of that, however, is that the European trajectory of Christian identity needs itself to be regarded as but one more indigenization of the gospel, or one family of such indigenizations; only one among others.

Think what that means for the patristic period of European Christianity, which we at the Boston end of the trajectory regard as defining orthodoxy. It cannot be normative orthodoxy in any universal and essential sense for Christianity, but only for the indigenization of Christianity in the European theater. What bearing does it have on trajectories of Christian development that never had to be contextualized relative to Greek philosophy? Nestorian Christianity, for instance, was condemned as a heresy (at the Third Ecumenical Council, at Ephesus, in 431 C.E.), so it no longer has a legitimate place within Euro-American orthodox Christianity. Yet surely that condemnation stuck through the political battles of the next fifty years, including Chalcedon, because most of the Nestorians lived in Persia and hence were not responsible to the Roman emperor, indeed were patriotically in opposition to the Roman Empire.[3] Re-

---

3. The 431 Council at Ephesus was convened and concluded by Cyril with his Alexandrian contingent and his allies from Rome before the Antiochene supporters of Nestorius could arrive. When the latter did arrive, they held their own council, rejecting the anathemas against Nestorius and excommunicating Cyril; but that council simply didn't "take" in the battle for defining orthodoxy. One large reason, I'm sure, was the geopolitical one, that most of the Nestorians did not live within the Roman Empire. The Council of Chalcedon in 451 attempted to balance the interests of the Alexandrian school of Cyril with those of Rome and of the Antiochene school of Theodore and Nestorius, though it did not remove the condemnation of the Nestorians. The parochial blindness of the European trajectory of contextualized Christianity is innocently expressed by John H. Leith, editor of *Creeds of the Churches* (New York: Anchor, 1963), when he writes on pp. 34-35:

> The Christological settlement at Chalcedon illustrates the catholicity of the theology of the ancient church. Three major schools of theology had been involved in the Christological controversies and were represented at Chalcedon: Alexandria, Antioch, and Western Christianity. The final result could have been produced by none of these schools of thought alone. Chalcedon was truly catholic in the very great degree in which it was the result of the shared theological wisdom of the Church. . . . In spite of all the nontheological factors involved in the Christological controversies, the Church devoted its theological gifts to the problem with a singleness of interest that is hard to duplicate and with a catholicity that helped to keep the discussion in balance.

Compare this self-congratulatory assessment of Chalcedon with the lament of Samuel Hugh Moffett, in his chapter, "The Great Schism," in *A History of Christianity in Asia* (San Francisco: Harper, 1992), on pp. 169-70:

viewing the arguments today of Theodore of Mopsuestia, the chief Nestorian theologian, and Nestorius, compared to those of Cyril of Alexandria, their chief opponent, one finds no decisive advantage to the latter that would justify anathema and condemnation. Had the patristic councils been run under the auspices of the Persian monarchs rather than the Roman, the Nestorians likely would have been in rather than out.

Now it was the Nestorians who went to China and converted so many and grew such large Christian communities that some historians claim there were more Christians in China during the Tang Dynasty than were in Europe (the European population was very small compared to the Chinese). Even allowing for exaggeration and speculative census records, it might well be said that the first millennium of Christianity belonged to Asia rather than Europe, and that it was Nestorian.

Of course, the Nestorian wave of Asian Christianity was exterminated whereas the European development not only continued to the present but sent its own mission to Asia, and, most important, led to us Boston Christians — Orthodox, Roman Catholic, and Protestant, but not Nestorian.[4] Suppose that Chinese Nestorian Christianity had flourished into our own time, like Coptic Christianity but with the vast force of Chinese numbers. Would we not see the European trajectory of Christianity as merely the way Christianity was contex-

---

What finally divided the early church, East from West, Asia from Europe, was neither war nor persecution but the blight of a violent theological controversy that raged through the Mediterranean world in the second quarter of the fifth century. It came to be called the Nestorian controversy, and how much of it was theological and how much political is still being debated, but it irreversibly split the church not only east and west but also north and south and cracked it into so many pieces that it was never the same again. Out of it came an ill-fitting name for the church in non-Roman Asia, "Nestorian."

Leith does not even notice that anything is missing when the Nestorian Christianity of non-Roman Asia is lost to the European church because, for him, only the European trajectory counts as Christian. In point of fact, many of Cyril's Alexandrian supporters were dissatisfied with Chalcedon and became Monophysites, yet another heresy from the standpoint of the European indigenization. Many of the Monophysites moved to Islam for theological reasons when that opportunity arose in subsequent centuries.

4. Actually, because the distinguishing mark of Nestorianism was insistence on the human nature of Jesus and the point that human salvation is made possible because Jesus as human was united to God, in contrast to the Alexandrian claim that it's Christ's divine nature that saves us, Nestorianism is a practical if unnamed presence within at least Protestantism. Luther could find no heresy in Nestorius (Moffett, p. 26). The whole concern for the historical Jesus and the Christ of faith is intelligible in Nestorian terms but not in Alexandrian ones. Even the most orthodox of contemporary Christologists, who insist on the divine nature as well as human nature of Christ, as Theodore and Nestorius did, are Nestorian in spirit as they emphasize solidarity with the historical person of Jesus.

tualized in west Asia, its European peninsula, and Western colonies? Would not Chinese Nestorianism be attractive as a contemporary resource for theological identity, not only for Chinese Americans but for all of us? Would we not have to see the definition of Christian orthodoxy in the patristic period as merely one, now distant and somewhat alien, contextualization of the gospel? Would we not have to regard as hopelessly naive and parochial the claims by theologians or authorities to speak what "the Church always and everywhere has believed," and mean by that the outcome of the patristic discussions?[5]

Theological identity today cannot be the construction and affirmation of a single historical trajectory. Rather, it has to be built out of a fair consideration of all the traditions that claim Christianity, including those condemned by others. Theological identity today requires an extremely complex perspective that is able to weigh internally all those other perspectives. Of course, this is not to say that all are equally valid, only that all need to be understood and weighed. Theological identity is not merely the acknowledgment and adoption of a history, but the dialectical construction of a complex historical identity that allows for discernment and criticism of the historical paths that have led to our place and for the appreciation of other paths that need to be acknowledged and grafted into our own identity.

So theological literacy about identity requires a far broader understanding of Christian histories than that of one's denomination. This is bad news for a theological school curriculum that is already overfull. But as our Asian students want a knowledge of Nestorian Christianity, and our black students want a full background in Coptic Christianity, and the Indians want the traditions of Thomas, those pressures will have to be registered in the curriculum. The argument is that all students need a good understanding of all the ways that have been Christian in order to take responsibility for their own theological identity.

---

5. See, for instance, Thomas C. Oden's *The Living God: Systematic Theology: Volume One* (San Francisco: Harper and Row, 1987), which says in the preface, pp. ix-x:

> My basic purpose is to set forth an ordered view of the faith of the Christian community upon which there has generally been substantial agreement between the traditions of East and West, including Catholic, Protestant, and Orthodox. My purpose is not to present the views of a particular branch of modern Christian teaching, such as Roman Catholic or Baptist or Episcopal. Rather it is to listen single-mindedly for the voice of that deeper, ecumenical consensus that has been gratefully celebrated as received teaching by believers of vastly different cultural settings — whether African or European, Eastern or Western, sixth or sixteenth century.

How could he possibly write like this while still missing the Nestorians, Indians, and other Syrian-rite churches, and the Copts?

The Complexities of Theological Expression

Christian church life has to live with the full range of expressions from the most popular to the most sophisticated. Isolated congregations might limit themselves to some version of popular Christianity, and theologians at professional meetings might deal only with tempered abstractions. But church life itself embraces all those contexts, and no congregation can safely remain isolated for long. Even the new churches in the Third World, whose expressions come from new appropriations of popular Christianity shaped by popular traditional religions, will soon engage the perspectives of other Christian traditions, including the elite ones. And every young pastor soon learns that the same sermon will be heard by people who think of God as the Big Guy in the Sky and those who believe in the Ground of Being (If That), though what they hear is very different.

Christianity, like most of the other world religions, has a range of expressions for God that runs from very anthropomorphic images to abstract principles such as love, the act of *esse,* and even the ultimate negations of apophatic theology. Indeed, all the religions confess that the ultimate is beyond any finite description but then go on to provide a host of expressions that allow the ultimate to be engaged. Moreover, religions fix the center of their liturgical and meditative symbology at different places on the spectrum from anthropomorphic to abstract principle. Both the Chinese Confucian and the Jewish Christian traditions arose out of very anthropomorphic worship of a head sky god, and both developed less anthropomorphic language along the way so that, by the time of Thomas Aquinas, who defined God as the act of *esse* or "to be," the Neo-Confucians defined the ultimate as "Principle" or "Principle and Material Force." But the center of Confucian symbology, its basic texts and symbols, reflects a strong criticism of the anthropomorphic origins, whereas the Christian, especially Protestant, symbology centers on the rather anthropomorphic language of the Bible. Though recognizing similarly broad spectra of expressions, religions take their main expressions from some particular place on the spectrum.

A very crucial part of theological literacy is knowing the appropriate range and context for the use of religious symbols and other expressions, in liturgy, preaching, and the other conversations of Christian life. Few people would be fooled by the expression "God is the rock of my salvation" to believe that geology is the best way to know God. But serious questions need to be raised about what is really heard when God is described as a warrior or a king. To say God or Jesus is "Lord" has some obvious applications, but how far should the relation between Christians and Christ be defined by political meta-

44

phors? Feminists rightly have argued that calling God "Father" can easily be extended beyond appropriate ranges and contexts so as to entail false consequences — for Jesus that phrase seems to have been a deliberate substitute for "King" when considering the head of the kingdom of God. The problem with inappropriate extensions and contexts for theological and symbolic expressions is that the bad consequences shape our engagements with God just as much as the good ones, and often unconsciously.

Probably any Christian symbol or expression has or once had some legitimate and powerful appropriate extension and context. Otherwise it would not have lasted. But most also have had historic misuses. Even worse, in a contemporary congregation or Christian conversation, the same symbol will be heard appropriately by some and inappropriately by others. Theological literacy requires understanding just how those felicitous and infelicitous hearings work so that Christian leadership can be responsible.

This means that the use and interpretation of Christian expressions, for God and other religiously important things such as sin, redemption, and ecclesial life, must be multiperspectival. There are at least three generic kinds of perspectives that literacy about theological expressions needs to include.[6] One is distinctions of culture; symbols mean different things in different cultures, and some cultures find it difficult to register certain symbols in any meaningful way. Thus theological literacy requires knowing the background cultures and semiotic systems of the people engaged in mutual expression. Another kind of perspective has to do with stage of life; symbols mean things to children that they do not mean to adults, and vice versa. Theological literacy requires knowing how to talk with people at different stages in their cognitive, psychological, and spiritual development. A third kind of perspective has to do with the different states of soul of the people involved in the conversation of expression. Troubled people hear things differently from those who are at peace, those strong in faith can take meat while those weak in faith need milk. Theological literacy about expressions thus requires spiritual discernment.

The greatest difficulty in theological literacy of expression is not that of learning enough comparative cultures and semiotics, enough developmental psychology and forms of spiritual discernment, although this is hard enough in a crowded curriculum. The greatest difficulty is that each supposedly literate

---

6. These distinctions are analyzed in detail in my *The Truth of Broken Symbols* (Albany: State University of New York Press, 1996), chaps. 2 and 5. They arise from what I call "secondary reference" in contrast to primary reference. The primary referent is the reality referred to, and the secondary is the character of the interpreter for whom the symbol at hand works to refer to that reality. Whether the symbol actually can refer depends on the culture, stage of life, and state of soul of the interpreters.

person has his or her own specific congeries of perspectives. A person from a Protestant evangelical culture, for instance, might know in principle that God is not the Big Guy in the Sky, and might understand how expressions such as "act of *esse*" or "ground of being" have been developed to do justice to the transcendence of God over our limited imaginations. But such a person might, really deep down, so exclusively and strongly engage God with the anthropomorphic symbols that having to learn about their limited range and context would destroy the person's faith. Conversely, a person from a liberal Protestant culture might be so aware of the limitations of anthropomorphic language as never to be able to admit that there are legitimate uses and contexts for them.

Theological literacy of expression thus includes coming to terms with the peculiar limitations of one's own engagements with God, the kinds of symbols that "work" for one, and the kinds that "work" for others. Insofar as theological literacy is for the church as a fairly wide community and not just for oneself, it requires not only difficult knowledge of others in their cultures, stages, and states of soul but also a kind of humbling relativization of oneself. It requires accepting and becoming adept at the practice of communication with people who genuinely engage the ultimate differently from oneself, even if using the same symbols.

The Complexities of Theological Truth

Implicit in the previous discussion is the controversial problematic of theological truth. Why is theological identity a problem? If theological identity were merely a factual matter, a historian or sociologist could tell you who you are theologically and what you believe, just as a medical scientist can describe your genetic makeup. The approach to theology through church history has a weakness for this temptation. Moreover, given the existential quality of religious faith, it is tempting to reduce truth to will. That is, the historian or sociologist can say, "This is the profile of *X* (Protestant, Catholic, Orthodox, Methodist, African American, feminist, evangelical, late modern, whatever) Christian belief, and if you do not believe it you are not a genuine *X* Christian." That failure to be a genuine *X* Christian itself might seem to be a mere fact, and in some sense it is.

But to the contrary, very few thinking or literate religious people believe things only because that goes with the label they have adopted, or because that is what their religious community believes, to which they belong for reasons other than belief. Rather, even acknowledging that beliefs are shaped by the historical and intellectual experience of a community, people believe their beliefs are true, or at least closer to the truth than other beliefs or other expressions of beliefs, and they want to be corrected if they are wrong. Many religious leaders take part in the community's internal dialogue to determine just what the truth is and how to express it. In point of fact, few if any religious leaders and intellectuals believe that everything their community has advocated should be believed. Traditions of belief are too fluid and subject to shifts in meaning relative to shifts in context for that to be possible. Religious communities usually have the intellectual structure they do in the form of an ongoing dialogue, debate, or even argument with internal factions and external intellectual and other alternatives. Even when made subtle by the intricacies of shifts in interpretation, even when surrounded by issues of loyalty, solidarity, and continuity, even when theology is understood to be the intellectual expression of the grammar of a community's practice, theology is still inquiry into the truth of the matter at hand. It seeks interpretations that can be affirmed as true, not merely faithful to a previous interpretation. Theology seeks continuities that are valid and that might require restoration or reformation, not mere repetitions. It seeks articulations of the underlying grammar of practices of church life that truly embody how a community ought to live before God. Theology is not history or sociology defining what some group in fact believes, but is inquiry into the truth of what they ought to believe so far as that can be determined. So much for the complications of truth in matters of theological identity.

The discussion above of complexity of theological expressions also has presupposed the problematic of literacy regarding theological truth. The primary function of expressions is not communication but engagement with the realities to which the expressions refer. This point is the great contribution of pragmatic semiotics.[7] Our engagements with life, with the environment, with nature and one another, with what is ultimate and divine in reality are all shaped by our symbolic systems or our semiotics. We do not engage anything except by interpreting it to be something in some respect. "That is red in respect of color, a barn in respect to a kind of building, by the road in respect of place, and Farmer Brown's in respect of ownership." Because of the semiotic requirement for engagement, we engage things in the terms of a semiotic community; our symbols always have some public shaping, like a language. Thus symbols are learned through communication, and communities conjointly engage realities through communicative behavior. Engagement is the primary function of symbols and symbolic behavior. Symbolic expressions are true to

7. See my *The Truth of Broken Symbols*, chaps. 1–2. See also the discussion of pragmatism in my *The Highroad around Modernism* (Albany: State University of New York Press, 1992), introduction and chap. 1.

the extent and in the senses that they carry over what is important in the realities into the engagements with them.[8] They are false either when they block engagement or when they carry over something that is not important.

Religious symbols and expressions are important for their capacity to engage people truly with religious realities. In a secular society traditional religious expressions might simply fail to engage people at all. At least that complaint is often made. This is a failure of the imaginative quality of religious expressions. But in any society, the question can be asked of particular symbols in particular interpretive contexts whether they carry over what is really important or something else, that is, whether they are true. Some contemporary Christian theologians describe God as "for us."[9] In what sense is that true? Does it mean that God is for us and against our enemies or those we want to displace, as the Israelites thought about God and the Canaanite problem? Or does it mean that God is for everybody, including us? Is there content to our interest for which God is? Or does God being "for us" mean only that God is our creator just as God is "for" the space dust, supernovas, and deep-space neutrinos which God also creates? The question here is not merely the meaning of the phrase "God for us," but whether there is something in God's reality that is picked up and carried into the interpreters' understanding when the interpretive symbol "for us" is used. Some people have believed that God is indeed partial and bellicose, while others have believed that God cannot be that, but is love, or is indifferent. They cannot all be right except insofar as they might interpret God in different respects.

Properly to frame a question of truth, it is necessary to specify the context of interpretation, the respect in which the reality is being interpreted, and the various meaning systems that are contained within the symbols and semiotic codes through which the interpretation engages the reality.[10] This is extremely complicated. It means getting clear ·about the symbol systems being used, which is exhausting by itself. It means determining what is really being referred to when religious language is so often elliptical. It means identifying the respect

---

8. The definition of truth as carryover of value or importance is defended at length in my *Recovery of the Measure* (Albany: State University of New York Press, 1989), chaps. 3–4, and applied to the truth of religious and theological symbols in *The Truth of Broken Symbols*, chap. 7.

9. For instance, Catherine Mowry LaCugna in *God for Us: The Trinity and Christian Life* (San Francisco: Harper, 1991).

10. This "theory of interpretation" derives from Charles Peirce's semiotics. Most of his important texts are in *The Collected Papers of Charles Sanders Peirce*, vol. 2, ed. Charles Hartshorne and Paul Weiss (Cambridge: Harvard University Press, 1932). For fine analyses directed at religious interpretation, see Robert S. Corrington's *An Introduction to C. S. Peirce* (Lanham, Md.: Rowman and Littlefield, 1993) and Michael L. Raposa's *Peirce's Philosophy of Religion* (Bloomington: Indiana University Press, 1989).

in which the reality — God or some related matter — is being interpreted. And it means understanding the various theoretical and practical contexts of interpretation as they bear upon how the interpretation genuinely engages its object and whether that engagement is true. Because this is all so complicated, and we are now aware of so many pitfalls of misunderstanding, theology tends to fall into the black hole of hermeneutics. It is so hard to get straight on what is meant that we sometimes never get around to whether what is meant is true.

But suppose we find, after exhausting hermeneutical investigation, that some of our founding theological ancestors were, say, anti-Semitic. Even after making allowances for context, how "everyone" in those days talked, suppose we find that their theologies give strong place to the assertion that the covenant of the Jews with God as they engaged God is invalid, wrong, and a perverse displacement of the Christian truth. Suppose we find this in Luther, Aquinas, and Athanasius. And suppose that we have persuasive independent grounds for saying that this anti-Semitism is mistaken, indeed wicked. Although interpretation is always what Peirce called a "triadic relation" (in which an interpreter takes a sign to stand for an object in a certain respect), truth itself is a dyadic relation: the sign either gets the object right or it does not. Complicate and make ambiguous the interpretive situation as you will, limit the respect in which the reality is being interpreted as you will, it still is the case that the assertion gets the reality right or it does not. It either carries what is important in the reality over into the interpreter in the respect in which the assertion is made, or it does not.[11] The falsity of anti-Semitic Christian theology, in the suppositions of this example, is very important and has enormous practical consequences for how Christians should live before God.

The philosopher Whitehead once remarked that it is more important for a proposition to be interesting than for it to be true. The point is especially well taken for theology. Our theological interest ought to be to interpret God and related matters in those respects that are most important for us, that is, most interesting. Most Christian theologians would push this a step further and say that what is most important for us is what is most important in God and in God-related matters, so that we are defined in our real interests by what is most important in the ultimate as it might be revealed to us. Trivial truths about God are not important, however true. Of course, it takes a theology to make a case for what is most interesting or important in the ultimate, and that case needs to

---

11. As the Aristotelian tradition has put it so well, a true judgment says of what is that it is and of what is not that it is not. Although the Aristotelian tradition believed that what is carried over from the object to the interpreter is form, and the position defended here believes it is value or importance, the point is that judgments are true or not.

be a true one. We might well concede that it is better to be wrong about something important in the divine than right about something trivial; at least we would be in touch with something important, even if we have it wrong. But it is better yet to be right about what is divinely important. Expressions should be genuinely engaged and also true.

Part of the complexity of theological truth stems from the fact that there are three kinds of references, and most theological affirmations or assumptions involve all the ways of referring. One kind of reference is iconicity, where the religious symbol, or system of symbols, or theological position, is taken to mirror the way reality is.[12] Or put the other way, in iconic reference reality is taken to be the way the symbolic system says. Myths and narratives of origin are taken to be iconic of reality. So are scientific theories, especially on positivistic accounts. Theology in the form of doctrines and propositions is at least iconic.

Another kind of reference, however, is indexical. An index connects the interpreter causally to the object engaged. Indexical reference orients behavior, picks up on what is important and shapes an appropriate interpretive response. Insofar as religious truth has to do with the value in the religious reality being carried over into the interpreter in the respects being interpreted, indexical reference is what leads to religious actualization, realization, increased holiness. Knowing with indexical reference is to be engaged so as to be more attuned with the reality interpreted. Theological expressions of paradoxes, parables, and other forms of indirect speech are obvious indexical references, pointing out things otherwise unnoticed with iconic maps. But the maps themselves also causally orient behavior when reality is engaged through them, and so might be indexical as well as iconic. Whereas one might learn a system of symbols for iconic reference, one must acquire the capacity to use symbols indexically.

A third form of reference is conventional. Conventional signs are like language, arbitrary in form, neither mapping reality in one-to-one fashion nor causally orienting interpreters to the referent. No iconic or indexical reference could be talked about or even noticed if it did not have some conventional element that related it to other symbols in the semiotic system. Indeed, the connection of religious symbols with one another and with the rest of life comes from the conventions of culture. Conventions are constantly being altered, either by being made more specific or less specific, or by just being changed. Thus conventional reference is in constant, though usually slow, flux. Only by means of the conventions that encode religion with the rest of life is it possible for the symbolic maps and transformative indexical experiences to be turned into a

12. The distinction among the three kinds of references is from Peirce, and is analyzed along with his texts in my *The Truth of Broken Symbols*, introduction and chap. 2.

way of life. The Christian Way is a whole way to live before God, related to but different from the Jewish, Buddhist, and other religious ways. Indeed, there are many Christian Ways, as many as there are indigenizations of the gospel. The most potent meaning of "indigenization" is that it is the embodying of the Gospels in the conventions of the culture at hand, transforming the reception of divine grace in Christ into a Christian Way.

Theological literacy is complex regarding truth for all forms mentioned here, and doubtless more. The contextualization of interpretation is enormously complex, and is hard to press beyond hermeneutics. The existential reality of engagement is equally complex, and not to be read off theological expressions considered by themselves. The identification and sorting of the interweaving of iconic, indexical, and conventional reference in interpretation is mind-boggling in its complexity. And yet all these complexities must be in hand before adequate formulations of questions of theological truth are possible.

Given these complexities, it is easy to see why fideism is so tempting in theological life. Fideism abandons truth's role to engage us with reality and treats truth as a property attached to claims by will. A fideistic way of life might engage a person or community with some degree of validity by accident. But it obscures the issues of truth regarding the validity of the engagement. Theology as genuine inquiry into truth is the only way to be vulnerable to correction with regard to Ways we have of living before God.

Theological literacy therefore requires two things. One is the enormous sophistication required to tell what is actually at stake in a theological judgment or interpretation. The other is the imagination and determination to make the inquiry open and vulnerable to correction. Here the context of theological education often works against the truth, for so much of theological education is the handing down of tradition and the acquisition of competency in the tradition. How hard it is to make the truth-status of that tradition genuinely open to correction! Yet, anytime we encounter a serious alternative to our tradition's assumptions, it is incumbent to ask which is closer to the truth, the more subtle, the more expressive of what is really important. Theological literacy requires being able to ask the question of truth about the important topics. Validity of practice depends on that.

Complexities of Theological Engagement

Readers who have gotten this far know that "engagement" is not an innocent term. Theological literacy means not just "knowing about" theological matters, but becoming more religious. That is, theological literacy allows us to be more

51

direct and sophisticated, more nuanced and less blundering, in our engagement with life in its religious dimension, especially with God. For Christians theological literacy helps us engage God in Jesus Christ. It is the means by which we become more filled with God, both in cognitive senses and in practical senses that derive from cognitive orientation. It is a condition for leadership in religious communities where the aim of leadership is better engagement with God.

All the classical issues of engagement through traditions and their symbols, set in enduring contexts of society, are complex enough, as indicated above. But there are four areas in which our own time makes matters even more complex, areas in which the religious traditions of Christianity, not only the Jerusalem-Europe-Boston trajectory tradition but the rest as well, have not yet worked out what they need to know and do. These areas are religion-and-science, ecology or how to inhabit the environment, the encounter of the world's religions, and justice. Everyone is aware of these areas, and so they can be treated briefly.

The challenge of modern science to Christianity and other traditional religions is the most enduring of these areas, recognized already in the seventeenth century and addressed by such theological geniuses as Descartes, Leibniz, Hume, Kant, and Hegel, and in our own century by figures such as Charles Peirce and Alfred North Whitehead. The challenge is at least twofold, theoretical and practical.

The theoretical challenge is that the universe described by modern (especially late modern) science is vastly different from that described by biblical cultures, and hence is different from what is embodied in the biblical symbols in terms of which most Christians understand their faith. Some of the issues are matters of translating metaphors. But others are serious concerns for truth: for instance, how important can Jesus Christ be on a cosmic scale when he is defined in terms of a selection of cultures on tiny planet Earth? Are the cosmic claims often made for Jesus Christ, then, a diversion from something else more important about him? Can God be conceived to have subjective intentionality regarding the cosmos of expanding galaxies and atomic bonds? Whereas the earth might be a garden, or even a kingdom, and hence support personifications of God as provident gardener and righteous king, the cosmos does not. What gives? As scientific conceptions of the cosmos change, so do the conditions for framing that question.

The practical challenge to religion from science is how to weigh the new possibilities presented by technology in spiritual and moral perspectives. Medical technologies alone offer more problems than most religious leaders can address. But theological literacy requires that they do.

The ecological disasters of the 1970s alerted the theological world to the fact that Christianity's assumed ways of inhabiting its environment need to be questioned. The questioning quickly demonstrated that the crude assumptions that the environment is to be used for human purposes are not subtle enough, even for the sustaining of human life and society. How then are we to conceive of nature? What does it mean for us to inhabit a created world? What does Christianity have to say about this? These are questions on which there is no consensus within Christianity or among other world religions. Yet surely it is a central theological question: how to be at home in the universe! Theological literacy in this area means not only knowing the relevant science but also having the poetic imagination to raise the question of how to be at home.

The encounter of Christianity with other world religions is nothing new. Christianity arose during the encounter of Second Temple Judaism with the other religions of the Hellenistic world. The magnificent theological contributions of Thomas Aquinas were much shaped by his dialogue with Islam. What makes our time different is that all the world religions are involved, that the encounters are on local school boards and across the backyard fence instead of through arduous travel or the reports of intermediaries, and the Internet makes communication global and speedy. Moreover, late modern cultures are generally multicultural rather than homogenous in representing a religion. Thus all religions are somewhat dislocated from their traditional senses of dominating a culture, save perhaps Islam in some places.

An obvious and crucial part of theological literacy is having a theology of world religions. Such a theology cannot be derived from Christian sources alone but needs to be based on a thorough understanding of the other religions, especially when they are represented among coworkers, neighbors, and children. The European scholarly community has vastly increased the careful translations of the major texts of other religions, and there are now dialogue projects of many years' duration in which religious practices are shared. The study of world religions in depth now needs to be a part of Christian education, a large part of theological education.

The final new area of theological engagement that needs mention here is justice, and that in several senses, beginning with distributive justice. Christianity, like most of the other world religions, has traditional teachings on distributive justice, but they are generally limited to the scale of a kingdom or nation dominated by a single government. In the last 150 years the social sciences have provided the tools for understanding the causal contours of economic distribution, and they are global, not national. Because we understand many of the causal properties of inequalities of wealth, of economic domination and oppression, and of the means to overcome poverty, we can do something about that on a worldwide scale. Because we can do something about that, we ought to, an imperative that had no force when people did not understand economic causation very well. But what to do? Christianity has no carefully developed wisdom on this, and neither the Marxist nor pure capitalist moral sensibility has much religious depth. In fact, neither connects economic causation with effects on the spirit. Theological literacy requires serious reflection on global distributive justice.

Distributive justice is frequently contrasted with retributive justice, punishing people or groups in due proportion to their crimes. Retributive justice helps bring equanimity to the victims of injustice, if any are left, and as Hegel pointed out, it serves to demonstrate the humanity of the perpetrators, who are treated as responsible agents. Retributive justice is also effective sometimes in stopping a cycle of injustice in which the victim becomes a perpetrator in order to get even. War crimes trials, for instance, are a means to say enough is enough. Yet retributive justice does not sit easily with Christianity, which affirms that God is the only legitimate retributive judge. And what agency is the administrator of retributive justice — the victors in war? In classical legal theory, the state administers justice; but there is no world state, and many crimes are transnational — another conundrum in which theological literacy is required.

A third kind of justice is entering the legal and theological discussion, called "restorative justice." Retribution against the perpetrator has limited effectiveness in stopping a cycle of unjust violence when the perpetrators are representatives of larger groups or structures. The South African models of restorative justice that bring together the communities of both victims and perpetrators for mutual accusation, understanding, and confession are more promising than retribution for healing the wounds of systemic crime and injustice. Surely the role of Christianity is to press for healing and restoration, a form of justice that has wide application when the injustice is less between individuals and more between groups. This is a practical arena in which saving grace might be brought to situations of suffering, and Christians need to be theologically literate about how this works in order to make a contribution.

In sum, theological literacy requires much knowledge about the world ostensibly outside of religious topics, including science, our habitation, world religions, and all the conditions of justice. To theological educators such as myself, this seems a daunting task, especially when conjoined to the other aspects of theological literacy discussed earlier. We have to admit that even our best efforts produce only reasonably literate religious leaders. Moreover, so much of literacy is not learning something already known but attaining the skills and spirit of inquiry so as to learn it for the first time. Literacy is a tool for learning, not a merit badge for having learned.

The first step in responding to the difficulties of theological literacy is acknowledging and identifying its complexities.

CHAPTER FOUR

Renewing Ways of Life:
The Shape of Theological Education

S. MARK HEIM

Religious traditions recognize various categories for religious adepts. On the one hand are saints and holy persons who exhibit the fullness of particular religious ideals. On the other hand are priests, scholars, or ritual experts who have the skills and knowledge to carry out certain essential religious tasks. Sometimes these categories merge in one office or in the specific case of one person. Religious traditions also typically have threshold standards for initiation as a full, if beginning, member of the community. In all these cases, "knowing about" the religion (knowing *that* certain things are the case) may be a significant factor. But this is usually subordinate to and always integrated with a "knowing how" to practice the tradition's pattern of life, a realization or actualization. It has been characteristic of theological literacy in the recent Western context that it has stressed a heavy dose of "knowing about," presuming but not always connected with "knowing how." It becomes possible to view an exemplary practitioner of a religious tradition as illiterate about that same tradition, and to accept a person as literate and expert regarding a tradition of which he or she is in no way a practitioner, exemplary or otherwise.

There are certainly things that it may be wise and useful to know about religions that one does not practice. If the reasons for seeking this knowledge are not themselves religious, then I would not call the aim theological literacy but rather general cultural knowledge. On the other hand, there can be deeply religious reasons for seeking such knowledge.[1] In that case, even rather abstract

---

1. To take a simple example, this is the case for Islam in relation to Christianity and Judaism and for Christianity in relation to Judaism. The religious tradition internally commends the significance of knowledge of the substance of specific other traditions. This could be the case as

"knowledge about" various religions may at the same time be part of "knowing how" to practice one's own faith, just as rather abstract knowledge about elements of one's own tradition can figure in such practice. I understand "theological literacy" to be the threshold education/formation that allows a person to participate in a concrete religious community and to interpret a pluralistic world religiously and responsibly from an acknowledged particular faith standpoint.

The key question for theological literacy in our current situation revolves around the integration of these two dimensions, "knowing about" and "knowing how." I write as a Christian, an ordained minister, a teacher in a freestanding, denominationally related Protestant seminary whose mission is to train women and men for ordained and lay leadership in Christian churches. In what follows I focus on Christian theological literacy, though there are obvious connections with other cases. I will first offer some reflections on the current context for theological education and then indicate what I regard as the framework around which our perceptions of competence and literacy will and should increasingly be formed.

Types of Theological Literacy

"Literacy" ordinarily has two meanings. It can mean the mastery of the most basic *tools* which are necessary to access and produce written information. Alternatively it can mean familiarity with a fundamental body of knowledge, the use of the tools in question to grasp certain *content* that should be known by "any educated person." In our culture, literacy of the first type is an agreed universal goal, though there is some argument over whether modern aids (from computer spell checkers to calculators) have reduced the number of skills and the level of expertise essential for such basic competence. We have seen a sharp controversy over literacy of the second type, over the very idea of a "canon" of knowledge, as well as over what belongs in it.[2]

As part of the Western cultural tradition, Christian theology is implicated

---

well if a faith has certain intrinsic beliefs or practices that provide an impetus to find at least certain kinds of significance in other religions.

2. See, for instance, Harold Bloom, *The Western Canon: The Books and School of the Ages,* 1st ed. (New York: Harcourt Brace, 1994); W. B. Carnochan, *The Battleground of the Curriculum: Liberal Education and American Experience* (Stanford: Stanford University Press, 1993); William Casement, *The Great Canon Controversy: The Battle of the Books in Higher Education* (New Brunswick, N.J., and London: Transaction Pub., 1996); Henry Louis Gates, *Loose Canons: Notes on the Culture Wars* (New York: Oxford University Press, 1992).

in both these traditions of literacy. On the first score, the Bible has been both means and end of many movements for basic literacy (including the first Sunday schools). On the second score, the Bible and Christian texts have been central elements in the canon that defined liberal education. A pluralistic society like the United States, with some questions about basic literacy (for instance, whether literacy is to be expected in one common language or in one of several different ones) and in clear disarray over any canon of knowledge, impels the church to reflect on the standards of "literacy" necessary for its own life. The church cannot presume (if it ever rightly could) that cultural answers are adequate for its purpose.

When I speak of Christian literacy, I do not limit its meaning to — or even necessarily include in its meaning — the visual reading of written or printed texts. I think of literacy on two levels. We might call the first "practical literacy." It indicates the threshold of basic skills and information that allows one to be a member of the church and a follower of Christ. Through most of Christian history for most Christian people, this has not involved literacy of the written word, or at least not a very large measure of it. The second level is what I might call "leadership literacy," and involves the threshold of skills and information one would hope to have available within any Christian congregation or community, though not characteristic of every member. Even this need not necessarily include classical literacy, though normally it should. In most of what follows, it is leadership literacy that is in view. We should note also that this is not identical with what "every educated person should know" about Christianity or the theological enterprise. For that general cultural knowledge, it is probably more important to grasp the elements of practical Christian literacy.

The default setting for theological leadership literacy for most of this century had two dimensions. The first dimension was the practical literacy we have just described. Practical literacy was ordinarily gained by participation in or association with churches, though a good facsimile might also be acquired at one remove through more general diffusion in public or private schools, colleges, or civic organizations. It required its own mix of "knowing about" the tradition and "knowing how" to participate in it. This involved familiarity with a stock of biblical stories and references, with terminology and references from the Christian tradition, with hymnody and the conventions of public and private prayer or worship, and with certain moral expectations that were at once ecclesial and social. The distinctive second dimension added to this basis was critical literacy. Critical literacy ordinarily was a feature of higher education. It involved awareness both of the challenges to Christian tradition arising from Enlightenment rationalism, historical study, and science and of the various strategies of interpretation that responded to these challenges. Critical literacy has its own mix of "knowing about" and "knowing how."

It is important to note that both forms of literacy have a critical side and look toward the universal horizon of Christian faith. To think of "what everyone ought to know" about a subject is to pose the question of what might be of universal significance or importance in it. Though enclosed within Christian tradition, practical literacy involves several critical perspectives. It brings the core elements of tradition as a critical source over against the conventions and assumptions of the immediate cultural and historical context. It also brings the voices of interpretation within that tradition which span many centuries, races, and cultures. It brings a missional impulse, a desire to share the minimal requisites of faith with all people in the conviction that God's action and revelation take place for their sake. Perhaps most important, it involves a formation process oriented toward producing people who belong to particular cultures but are not entirely defined by them. Critical literacy corresponds in part to a reflexive or apologetic impulse. If Christianity is to make good its universal claim, it must engage the dominant *standards* for universality in a particular context. In the West over recent centuries, this means engaging Enlightenment philosophy, historical consciousness, and scientific method. This essentially defined the critical literacy we mentioned.

A person was Christianly literate who knew what constituted a Christian profession of faith, understood how one would be expected to behave in consistency with that profession, and was familiar in general terms with the reasons educated persons would give for discarding such faith and in equally general terms with the counterarguments or reformulations that offered a response. You were literate if you knew how to go about being a Christian (in most of the proximate steps) if you were to choose to do so, and if you knew enough about reasons not to do so that your choice could be called an informed one. In terms of higher education, both in colleges and seminaries, what we have called practical literacy was for the most part presumed already to have been acquired in churches or in the culture. The focus of literacy fell heavily on what I have called critical literacy (and this was true even where the primary task of theological education was conceived as *resistance* to the common conclusions of such critical study).

Changes in church and in culture have made this older assumed division of labor obsolescent. We have seen a series of significant works recently reviewing the process of decline of church-related colleges and universities as cradles of committed theological literacy in either the practical or critical mode.[3]

3. James Tunstead Burtchaell, *The Dying of the Light: The Disengagement of Colleges and*

Matching these, there has been a series of works reassessing the nature of seminary theological education.[4] These books address a number of issues. But we might compress the dilemma they describe in this way. Seminaries are squeezed between the challenge to provide a kind of practical literacy they did not have to organize themselves to provide in the past and the uncertainty that increasingly saps confidence in the agenda of critical literacy they have presumed as their primary task (and which largely dictates their current organization and standards).

Theological disciplines took certain conversation partners to provide the test for the universal intent of the theological enterprise. These were the literary-historical-critical methods of the modern humanities and social sciences, the critical analysis of modern philosophical systems, and (to a lesser extent) the disciplines of modern science. Without this engagement, theology could not rightly make a claim to contribute something to human literacy, to be a discipline in which everyone ought to have a basic grounding. The dramatic development has been that these — the grounds upon which Christianity particularity tried to vindicate its universality — have become themselves fields of factionalized particularity. Literary theory in particular, but the humanities and social sciences generally (including history), increasingly bear the mark of a postmodern suspicion of objectivity or nonlocal perspectives. Even the hard sciences, though for the most part unruffled in their inner practice, are subject to aggressive interpretation in these terms by those in other disciplines.[5]

We have the ironic spectacle of theological disciplines, which have conscientiously tried to engage with the "objective" norms of their secular counterparts, being instructed by new developments in those disciplines about the contextual and cultural character of all perspectives, about the "scandal of

---

Universities from Their Christian Churches (Grand Rapids: Eerdmans, 1998); George M. Marsden, *The Soul of the American University: From Protestant Establishment to Established Nonbelief* (New York: Oxford University Press, 1994); George M. Marsden and Bradley J. Longfield, eds., *The Secularization of the Academy* (New York: Oxford University Press, 1992).

4. Max L. Stackhouse, *Apologia: Contextualization, Globalization, and Mission in Theological Education* (Grand Rapids: Eerdmans, 1988); David H. Kelsey, *To Understand God Truly: What's Theological about a Theological School* (Louisville: Westminster John Knox, 1992); David H. Kelsey, *Between Athens and Berlin: The Theological Education Debate* (Grand Rapids: Eerdmans, 1993); Edward Farley, *Theologia: The Fragmentation and Unity of Theological Education* (Philadelphia: Fortress, 1983); Edward Farley, *The Fragility of Knowledge: Theological Education in the Church and the University* (Philadelphia: Fortress, 1988).

5. A good compressed picture of this discussion is presented in the response to physicist Alan Sokal's successful hoax submission to the journal *Social Text*. For instance, see Stanley Fish, "Professor Sokal's Bad Joke," *New York Times,* 21 May 1996, p. 23; Alan D. Sokal, "A Physicist Experiments with Cultural Studies," *Lingua Franca* (May/June 1996): 62-64.

particularity." On this point the structure given to the theological curriculum by an opposition with which it had grown familiar suddenly gave way, like the collapse of a wall you are leaning against.[6] The cutting edge of secular disciplines has changed in a way that leaves traditionally modern theological education somewhat marooned. This is notably true at the heart of theological education: biblical studies. The critical-historical skills and conclusions which have defined literacy as understood in old-line theological schools are neither the burning concern of many (probably most) of their entering students nor (increasingly) the exclusive paradigm of the biblical disciplines themselves.[7]

In some respects these trends reflect a new hospitality to the particular, even confessional knowledge involved in theological education. But they threaten another kind of constraint, the relegation of such knowledge to cultural and private parochialism, as an instrument for identity that deserves no public status. This irony is reflected in Pope John Paul II's most recent encyclical, *Fides et Ratio,* which expresses concern over the withering of belief in and search for ultimate, objective truth in philosophy and other fields of inquiry.[8] Theological education must struggle with standards for universal truth that appear to exclude faith. But it struggles also with the absence of such standards or disinterest in the aspiration they represent. In the current context, theological education can certainly endorse the realization that all knowledge is *engaged* knowledge. Its task is to recover this integral feature of its own tradition while also reconfiguring the constellation of conversation partners which represent the challenge and check of a universal horizon.

Theological Literacy for Christian Leaders

Theological literacy has been defined by a seminary curriculum that is a hybrid animal, bred for both practical and critical formation. The earlier strata of the curriculum were laid down for assimilation of the content of Bible and tradition, spiritual formation in the practice of the life they constituted, and training in the means by which such instruction and formation was to be carried out in

6. This is the dynamic pointed out in relation to the social sciences in John Milbank, *Theology and Social Theory: Beyond Secular Reason,* Signposts in Theology, 1st paperback ed. (Oxford and Cambridge, Mass.: Basil Blackwell, 1993).

7. See, for example, Jon D. Levenson, "The Bible: Unexamined Commitments of Criticism," *First Things* 30 (1993): 24-33; Jon D. Levenson, *The Hebrew Bible, the Old Testament, and Historical Criticism: Jews and Christians in Biblical Studies* (Louisville: Westminster John Knox, 1993).

8. Pope John Paul II, "Fides et Ratio," *Origins* 28, no. 19 (1981): 317-48.

the life of the church. This involved a significant critical component, both in addressing internal church arguments and in addressing intellectual and practical challenges that confronted the church. The next strata of the curriculum involved basic literacy in several different ways of reading the content of the curriculum just described. This meant teaching how the Bible, Christian tradition, Christian practice, and faith could be read from historical, literary, sociological, and psychological perspectives, for instance. An adequately religious person could not be literate in faith without a rudimentary ability to apply these kinds of analyses to the phenomena of his or her own faith. As we have already suggested, this approach tends to take religious faith itself as a kind of given. But an inverse question has increasingly arisen (both in seminaries and in religious studies) with regard to persons who can externally apply all these modes of critical analysis to religious phenomena but do not have firsthand knowledge through participation in such phenomena. What rudimentary level of religious practice is required to make an adequately critical person religiously literate?

One implication of this situation is that theological literacy cannot be effectively defined in terms of the traditional departmental divisions of our seminaries and graduate schools.[9] There are two programs that are crucial to a renewed literacy. The first is the nurture of what Ellen Charry calls sapiential theology, an engaged knowing that connects the whole person with God, forming and reforming our character.[10] This focus responds both to the decline in concrete theological literacy and to the interest (personal and intellectual) in religious faith as formative practice. The second program is the articulation of new horizons of universality, the designation of disciplines and contexts within which Christian faith will have its crucial struggles for both vitality and validity in the next century. This involves a reconfiguration of the elements taken to constitute the primary critical component of theological knowledge. Together, these two programs outline a new shape for education.

Theological education needs to reconnect with its own tradition of

9. Ellen Charry, speaking of reading classical Christian texts, has written: "As I worked through the texts, the divisions of the modern theological curriculum began making less and less sense to me. I could no longer distinguish apologetics from catechesis, or spirituality from ethics or pastoral theology. And I no longer understood systematic or dogmatic theology apart from all of these. In the older texts, evangelism, catechesis, moral exhortation, dogmatic exegesis, pastoral care and apologetics were all happening at the same time because the authors were speaking to a whole person. Our neat divisions simply didn't work." Ellen T. Charry, *By the Renewing of Your Minds: The Pastoral Function of Christian Doctrine* (New York: Oxford University Press, 1997), p. viii.

10. Charry, p. 4.

sapiential theology. The curriculum as it exists is usually experienced to specify a division between "practical" or applied subjects (of which "spirituality" is one among many) and "academic" or more critical disciplines (of which ethics, e.g., is one among many). But if we see each of these studies as facets of the same transformative process, this tension is relaxed. Primary religious sources clearly contemplate some definitive insight or fundamental transformation in the lives of practitioners who use them. Students of religion today at all levels are dissatisfied with the disconnection between these sources and modes of inquiry that neither engage this assumption nor foster its exploration. This issue may be particularly sharp in confessional contexts (like seminaries), but it is present in other contexts as well.

An illustration of the shift I am describing would be the recovery of what Paul Griffiths calls "religious reading."[11] In a fascinating review of Buddhist and Christian traditions, Griffiths points out that the great texts of each have characteristically been stored and deployed primarily in memory and speech. This has been true in periods that knew and used limited numbers of written texts as well as in those periods before they were available. Religious "reading" necessarily involves a certain contemplative internalization of these texts. Memory and speech are not just primitive technologies for functions that are completely taken over by print and sight. They are particularly congruent modalities for the interaction believers seek with these texts. As words, narratives and meanings are incorporated into our very being by becoming part of our memories, regular habits of our physical speech and constituent forms for our perception, so our characters are to be thoroughly transformed by our engagement with these religious texts. Griffiths argues very persuasively that the texts themselves and the formative commentaries that interpret them "expect" to be read in this manner, a manner which does not entirely preclude critical analysis of other types but which can in no way be replaced by it.

He suggests that a "consumerist" treatment of texts has increasingly eclipsed this approach even within our religious communities themselves. Renewal of religious reading in this sense is a task for serious theological education, as Charry suggests. Griffiths adds the observation that such reading deserves a place in the university and within the bounds of religious studies. Without familiarity with and training in this discipline, we cannot attain even a basic literacy. We cannot answer the question, "What were people doing when they were using these texts?" There are severe limits to the expertise we can assert in relation to religious texts without becoming or understanding the

---

11. Paul J. Griffiths, *Religious Reading: The Place of Reading in the Practice of Religion* (New York: Oxford University Press, 1999).

kind of religious readers those texts expect. There is an interesting convergence here between the requirements of "committed" and "objective" study. Since in the broadest terms (as Griffiths's examples of Buddhism and Christianity indicate) this principle applies to all the major religious traditions, and poses a quandary for all modern study of religion, it also represents a point of interreligious commonality. To develop a sapiential understanding of one's own particular tradition is a very profound asset in the faithful interpretation of others, an asset more common in the confessional as opposed to the "disinterested" scholar.

The second program I suggested has to do with the conversation partners or modes of analysis to which theological study should give special standing, as providing critical standards to test the universality of its confession. We have already indicated the disciplines that have held pride of place in recent centuries, including literary study, history, the social sciences, and modern philosophy. The center of gravity will and should shift toward a number of other studies.

Horizons of Theological Leadership for the Twenty-first Century

These critical horizons are both internal to Christianity and external. I will begin with the internal ones. The first of these is the horizon of ecumenism. In one sense this is an old horizon, as old as the council at Jerusalem in Acts 15. But the modern ecumenical movement, coincident with globalizing trends in economy, technology, and culture, has made it increasingly impossible for Christian churches to live in effective isolation from each other. At the same time, distinctly new parties to ecumenism have arisen, most notably Pentecostal churches and indigenous churches (especially in Africa). In the variegated world environment, if the Christian church is to hope to have any coordinated impact as the unique resource it is — the single largest and most universal human organization — it must be able to find ways of realizing its own ostensible and professed unity. At the same time, if individual Christians or groups are to be honest witnesses to their non-Christian neighbors, they must be able to give a true account not just of their peculiar denomination but of some general picture of Christians in their diversity.

Both of the considerations I have just mentioned, the collective impact of the Christian church in the world and the accurate description of it to others, have an external orientation. But I would put special emphasis on an internal concern that seems to me a matter of deep concern, particularly at the level of individual Christian congregations and in areas where only one or two Christian denominations may be predominant. It is crucial that those who inquire into Christian faith and those who seek to grow deeply into it should have access to the full range and depth of its resources. In one sense the vicissitudes of mission and history have advanced this end in a rough way, "transplanting" Eastern Orthodoxy to the United States and Pentecostalism to Russia, and making these ways of being Christian available in both places. But I have in mind something much more intentional. It seems to me that no clergyperson or church leader, at least, is "literate" who does not have some basic sense of the strengths and visions of the Christian faith and life as it is displayed in various major strands of the church. The most crucial dimension of this knowledge is not historical or abstract but directly practical. It has to do with spiritual diagnostics. Christian leaders unable to direct others in basic terms to the devotional exercises, liturgical options, theological developments, or communal practices that may be the most fruitful for their own growth in Christ are guilty of a certain kind of pastoral malpractice. They lack a skill one can reasonably expect them to have. The person who appears in a Baptist congregation may have need of the spirituality of the *Philocalia* from Orthodox tradition. A Roman Catholic may have need of the biblical exegesis of John Wesley (or the hymnody of Charles Wesley). A good example of this cross-fertilization is found in the work of Roberta Bondi, who has demonstrated the way the writings of the Desert Fathers might become a significant feature in the spirituality of many feminist Protestants.[12] Literacy requires a basic familiarity with the horizon of Christian diversity, across time and traditions.

The second internal horizon is global Christianity. Basic literacy requires some knowledge of what we might call "representative Christianity." Critics and adherents alike tend to assume that this is European Christianity. Andrew Walls has imagined a professor of comparative interplanetary religions who makes time-travel visits to earth every few centuries on a grant to study Christianity.[13] On strict scientific grounds, where should she visit to take a representative sample? Walls suggests she might visit Jerusalem in the first century, Anatolia or Egypt in the fourth century, England in the nineteenth century, and Nigeria in the twentieth. He points out that Christianity has been marked by serial expansion, unlike religious traditions like Hinduism or Islam that remain dominant in and centered on their culture of origin. Europe has been one pass-

---

12. Roberta C. Bondi, *To Love as God Loves: Conversations with the Early Church* (Philadelphia: Fortress, 1987); Roberta C. Bondi, *To Pray and to Love: Conversations on Prayer with the Early Church* (Minneapolis: Fortress, 1991).

13. Andrew F. Walls, "The Gospel as Prisoner and Liberator of Culture," in *The Missionary Movement in Christian History: Studies in the Transmission of Faith* (Maryknoll, N.Y.: Orbis Books, 1996), pp. 3-15.

ing phase in that serial pilgrimage. It was only many centuries into Christian history that Europe became an arguably representative (though never exclusive) site. This is a status it (and North America as well) has now definitively lost. Representative Christianity is African, Latin American, and Asian and will become dramatically more so.

This has profound implications for education in and about Christianity. European and North American Christianity will become, like North African or Syrian Christianity, important loci in the story of what the church has been, but very limited determinations of what the church currently is. Basic literacy requires recognition of this fact (itself rare) and some rudimentary information about the character of the faith that most Christians practice. What "we call third-world theology is too much an 'echo' of western theologies, [but] there is another kind, 'namely, that which is being continuously produced in the languages of the churches of the Third world — in the form of preaching, catechesis, song, story, and drama.'"[14] Our educational institutions, church-related or not, are not very well equipped to provide this. In seminaries this is because such information is not readily available in library resources, does not figure in the doctoral formation of teachers in the various disciplines (Bible, theology, etc.), and (where it exists) is often segregated into courses about mission. In religious studies programs these factors are frequently augmented by a dogmatic conviction that in non-Western societies Christianity is an alien intrusion and that study should be concentrated on more "authentic" cultural traditions even if they are numerically less significant than Christianity. Thus one often finds that more serious scholarship on this topic must be sought in political science, economics, or area studies departments. This poses a key challenge for theological education, since the resources to educate about world Christianity cannot be developed unless teachers and institutions are willing to work "outside the box" of traditional guilds and rewards. The ethnic-minority Christian churches of the United States (Hispanic, Asian, African) in many cases represent very different dynamics from those that may characterize churches on other continents, but they are also crucial links to world Christianity.

If ecumenism and world Christianity represent two internal horizons of theological literacy, there are three external horizons that are of crucial importance. The first is the primary holdover from those critical disciplines that shaped the existing theological curriculum. Science is one of the universal horizons of modernity that will continue to be with us, and in even more powerful terms. Although critical literary-historical study, philosophy, and science were

14. George R. Hunsberger, *Bearing the Witness of the Spirit: Lesslie Newbigin's Theology of Cultural Plurality* (Grand Rapids: Eerdmans, 1998), p. 262.

the three avenues to "critical literacy" in religion, the first two have had a far more pervasive impact in theological education than the third. In fact, in the study of religion it is the social and not the natural sciences that have been most vociferous to claim the mantle of science. With a few exceptions (like the doctrine of creation), specific scientific material and theory has not become integral to theological education. This is changing, in part because of the confusion in the other disciplines and in part because of a renewed, explicit interest in the relation of religion and science.[15]

Science increasingly takes a more direct role in many of the social disciplines that have been closely associated with theological education. Examples would be greater emphasis on neurophysiological perspectives in relation to psychological issues and the increasing application of evolutionary psychology in discussing personal and social ethics. Contemporary scientific discussions of the origin of the universe and the origin of life manifest a new openness to theological considerations. But the primary venue for interaction promises to rest in the understanding of our own humanity, through issues like artificial intelligence and biological technology. This is an area where religious literacy must have a scientific dimension because of the ever expanding roster of practical and pastoral issues that will require concrete response in the life of the church. Within this broad area, investigation of the relation between faith, health, and spirituality is a specific frontier that will receive increasing attention. On all these fronts, theological literacy will be tested less by familiarity with theories from the humanities and social sciences and more with understanding of relevant work in scientific fields themselves.

A second external horizon of universality is constituted by the world religions. Mission and evangelism were once unifying themes of theological education and compelling vocations that helped to define the nature of effective literacy — knowing enough about the faith to pass it on to others. But today these are points of division among and within the churches, which differ over the nature and practice of relation with other religious traditions. The religions are a horizon of universality analogous to that which critical-historical study once provided: one is not religiously literate if adherence to Christianity exists in ignorance of alternative faiths and their criticisms of Christianity. Much of theological education is ill equipped to address this concern, because the missiological studies that addressed these issues have disappeared as part of the curriculum and have not been replaced with any coherent study of world religious traditions. The scope of this study is daunting, because of the number

---

15. For the Boston area, this is reflected in, and partly stimulated by, the many initiatives of the Templeton Foundation.

and depth of the traditions and because of the limited resources and curricular space. Nevertheless, this is a key critical standard for future education.

The third horizon of universality is constituted by the struggle for economic, political, and social justice. Competing analyses of and prescriptions for justice make this horizon a rather indistinct boundary. But widely shared basic standards for survival and human dignity increasingly figure as religious norms. Religious practices, beliefs, and imagery are adopted or rejected on the basis of their (supposed) effect on personal and social morality. Probably the key area here is economics, standing as it does on the controverted border between science and philosophy. As I suggested in discussing science above, the use of justice as a theological norm will require increasing sophistication with empirical as opposed to abstract arguments or, alternatively, will develop more explicitly theological rationales for justice as something other than a maximization of empirical benefits.

*　　*　　*

This sketch of the future shape of theological literacy presents its own tension, between the recovery of sapiential spiritual formation in a tradition and engagement with these new critical horizons. Such a tension will always be a feature of theological education. But I am convinced that what I have described is not an opposition. The internal horizons of ecumenism and world Christianity provide the richest resources for engaging the questions that arise on the external horizons. And the attainment of religious formation, in the deepest sense, is the distinctive contribution to the human project we can seek from this study.

CHAPTER FIVE

Identity, Formation, Dignity: The Impacts of Artificial Intelligence upon Jewish and Christian Understandings of Personhood

ANNE FOERST AND RODNEY L. PETERSEN

Most people in the United States today have seen some parts of *Star Trek* and are familiar with the star of *The Next Generation:* Commander Data. Data is an android, and Gene Roddenberry, the creator of *Star Trek,* often toys with the question of whether Data is a machine or a person. In one episode (No. 39, "The Measure of a Man"), this question is brought to a peak: Star Fleet wants to disassemble Data to analyze how he functions. Star Fleet wants to build more like him to arm every ship with an android. It turns out to be less than safe for him since he is not well enough understood to guarantee that the engineers will be able to put him back together correctly. After learning this, Data rejects the notion and resigns as Star Fleet officer. The question now is asked: Can he even resign? Does he have the same rights as other Star Fleet officers? Is he allowed to pursue his own agenda? Or is Data a machine and, as such, a piece of property of Star Fleet that has to accept its decisions?

The arguments in this episode go back and forth until the judge finally declares the questions asked to be "metaphysical" and more for philosophers or saints than for her as a judge. She boils down the whole discussion to whether or not Data has a soul. She finally decides that even if Data is a machine, he should have the right to explore by himself whether or not he has a soul. With this decision, he is not property but a person with the right to decide. At the end Data formally refuses to be disassembled and stays with Star Fleet.

The concepts introduced in this show to define what it means to be human are "intelligence," "self-awareness," "consciousness," and — by the judge — the "soul." Each of these terms is ambiguous and not well defined. Debate over their meaning is a part of theological literacy today and shapes our

68

thought and practice in civil society. What, for instance, does it mean to be intelligent? Is intelligence the capability to play chess, or does intelligence mean to survive in various environments? What is self-awareness? Is it the ability to recognize yourself in the mirror? If so, then self-awareness is nothing uniquely human but most primates share this ability with us.[1] How about consciousness? This term is so widely used that a precise definition for it is difficult. The same is true for the soul; some people just define it as that which makes us special, some understand it as the Spirit of God in us, some identify it with the mind (another spongy term). These terms, as presented in the *Star Trek* show, are not sufficiently defined to answer unambiguously what it means to be a person.

There are other, more scientifically sound categories for the definition of personhood. One way to define a person is by her/his body, made of genes and cells. Every set of genes is unique and stays identical during the whole life. Genes are a constant that certainly determine the way a person becomes. However, genes alone do not define a person sufficiently. A large part of who we are was determined by our upbringing and cultural context.[2] Also, we share up to 98 percent of our genetic code with chimpanzees, which, along with the variations among human individuals, does not make our genetic code unambiguously human. Finally, every cell has a lifetime of approximately seven years and is then exchanged. That means that within our lifetime our cells are exchanged at least eight times completely. Even if our genes present a constant, our cells do not.

Another embodied concept of personhood lies in the definition of a person as a unit separated from the rest of her environment. A person, one might argue, is distinctively herself, and the boundaries between herself and others and/or her environment are unambiguous. But are they really? The invention of eyeglasses was in a way the first cyborg technology, and this changes the human bodily experience fundamentally. Organ transplants challenge the identification of personhood with traditional boundaries: if I get another person's heart (in mythical language the seat of the soul), is not the anima of the other person a part of me? How about if I change my looks through cosmetic surgery? Will my personality change since the reaction of other people toward me will be different? New technology can add more and more technical parts to the human body until the boundaries among people and between people and their nonhuman environment become confused.

1. See Marc Hauser, *The Evolution of Communication* (Cambridge: MIT Press, 1996).
2. See the discussion of various theories in Steven Pinker, *How the Mind Works* (New York: Norton, 1997).

That means that the bodily features of humankind are not sufficient to determine what it means to be a person. Commander Data does not have genes, but he has many other features of humankind or analogies to them so that he would pass a test for personhood based on these features. Another concept which is often introduced in the context of personhood is "character." We grow up, our character is formed and developed, our memory changes and reinforces or modifies the character. Since we don't know which characteristics of a person are added by genes and how much they depend on culture and education, the nature of character is ambiguous. We cannot clearly define what elements of a person's character actually belong to a person herself and what belongs to culture or to certain genetic specifics. It seems that all the ways to define personhood in an empirical way are ultimately unsatisfying, and the concepts of "identity," "formation," and "dignity" have to be defined in a different way.

Artificial intelligence (AI) and the cognitive sciences present humans as biological systems which can be solely defined by their mechanisms and functions and suggest that soon it will be possible to rebuild the human machinery (and actualize Commander Data). Thus they add to the definitions described above another empirical aspect to our understanding of personhood by defining personhood and consciousness as emergent properties, created out of the interplay of multiple subsystems within the human organism and the interaction between various human systems and subsystems. Marvin Minsky, one of the founders of AI, actually dubs humans "meat-machines" and says that even "though people still consider it degrading to be regarded as machines," he hopes his book "will make them entertain, instead, the thought of how wonderful it is to be machines with such marvelous powers."[3]

AI challenges our basic understandings of personhood and the assumptions pertaining to concepts of dignity, formation, and identity in a much more profound way than genetics or evolutionary theories have ever done. Not only does AI attempt to understand humans in an entirely mechanistic and functionalist way, it also threatens to build humanlike creatures based on these models and thus reinforce the belief in their accuracy. Already the mechanistic and functionalistic assumptions which guide AI and cognitive science research influence current perceptions of humankind, as formed in part from ancient Greek, Jewish, and Christian sources of revelation and wisdom. Scientific progress in understanding human intelligence and its emotional and bodily basis and engineering advances in building intelligent machines mandate penetrating questions about the nature of human identity and its relationship to religious faith and its

3. Marvin Minsky, *The Society of Mind* (New York: Simon & Schuster, 1986), p. 323.

assumptions.[4] For example, what are the main lines in a theology of personhood, exploring the foundation of theological anthropology, as it has guided the West in Jewish and Christian sources of reflection? Second, what are the salient points arising from the challenge of research in artificial intelligence, particularly if one posits a strong relationship between AI research and philosophy? And what are the implications of this discussion for the concepts of human dignity, the formation of the self, and identity or personhood? Such thinking will determine how we conceive of personhood and human wholeness in society.[5]

The Theology of Personhood

More than at any other time, the question "What is man?" or "What is woman?" is currently at the center of theological and philosophical concern. Yet, why should this be a problem? Who does not know what we are? The question appears abstract until we begin to move down a ladder of abstraction. When it is posed, questions such as identity, formation, and the nature of dignity come to the fore. Soon philosophy becomes anthropology and we are drawn to some of the oldest reflection about human identity.[6] Humanity draws meaning and a metaphor for identity from connection with the circumference of the world, reminding us of Joseph Weizenbaum's statement, "The computer is a powerful new metaphor for helping us to understand many aspects of the world." The computer is the thought tool for most philosophers of mind who try to under-

4. Christopher Kaiser, "How Can a Theological Understanding Enrich Artificial Intelligence Work?" *Asbury Theological Journal* 44, no. 2 (1989): 61-67. The significance of the relation between AI and issues concerning the deep meaning of mind, as opposed to brain, is raised by Robert Penrose, *The Emperor's New Mind: Concerning Computers, Minds, and the Laws of Physics* (New York: Oxford University Press, 1989), pp. 16-17. See also Leroy S. Rouner, ed., *Is There a Human Nature?* (Notre Dame, Ind.: University of Notre Dame Press, 1997).

5. We will take up the issues raised by R. J. Russell, extending and applying them to the concepts raised in the conference in May 1998. See Russell's article, "Theological Implications of Artificial Intelligence," in *The Science and Theology of Information,* ed. Christopher Wassermann, Richard Kirby, and Bernard Rordorf (Geneva: Labor et Fides, 1992), pp. 245-57. Note will also be made in this article of the Durham Conference in March 1998.

6. Hans Urs von Balthasar wrote, "Philosophy has become anthropology; not as though there were a reality outside men, but in the sense that all natural reality is oriented to man." See his *Die Gottesfrage des heutigen Menschen* (Vienna: Herold, 1956), p. 46. For classic reflection about theological anthropology, see David H. Kelsey, "Human Being," in *Christian Theology: An Introduction to Its Tradition and Tasks,* ed. Peter C. Hodgson and Robert H. King (Philadelphia: W. Fortress, 1985), pp. 167-93; Philip J. Hefner, "The Creation," in *Christian Dogmatics,* ed. Carl E. Braaten and Robert W. Jenson, 2 vols. (Philadelphia: Fortress, 1984), pp. 269-362; and G. C. Berkouwer, *Man: The Image of God* (Grand Rapids: Eerdmans, 1962).

stand how cognition works. The computer has for the last fifty years been the most powerful metaphor for self-understanding. Sentences like "I couldn't store it" or "I couldn't process this" indicate how deeply such metaphors influence our speech and the interpretation of our cognitive abilities. Weizenbaum continues his statement, saying the computer "enslaves the mind that has no other metaphors and few other resources to call on."[7]

Judaistic, Hellenistic, and Early Christian Concepts of Personhood

One source for our metaphor for self-understanding emerges in early Semitic culture, in Judaism. In Judaism that circumference, most broadly speaking, was God. Hence the tradition speaks of humanity in the image of God.[8] While differences pertain, there are important lines of similarity between Jewish and Christian ideas of personhood.[9] There is not a great deal of speculation about the nature of the person in early Judaism, but one does find thought about the nature of immortality from which one can infer back to the nature of the person as created in God's image. Where Yahweh reigns, life will prevail. This is especially evident in the Psalms and Prophets. The life that Yahweh possesses is the source of life for his followers. That a person can transcend death is inferred from the possibility and modes of resurrection. Later prophetic tradition (Hosea and Jeremiah), seen particularly in the vision of Ezekiel's animation of dry bones (in chap. 37), offers one a sense of immortality, and so the transcending value of the person. Additionally, the poem of the Servant of Yahweh (Isa. 53) and ideas of the resurrection of a righteous people (Dan. 12) draw us to the hope grounded in the power and justice of God, not to an innately immortal soul. A more mystical orientation based on the oneness of personal identity with God and grounded in faith can be discerned (Job 19).[10]

The slim speculation in early Hebrew thought on personhood generally followed the line that death is the end of life. The "spirit" which makes man a

7. Joseph Weizenbaum, *Computer Power and Human Reason* (New York: W. H. Freeman, 1976), p. 277.

8. H. Gunkel, *Genesis* (1902), pp. 90-95. Gunkel argues that the idea of "image of God" plays a more systematic role in Christian dogmatics than in ancient Judaism.

9. Harry Austryn Wolfson, *The Philosophy of the Church Fathers*, 3d ed. (Cambridge: Harvard University Press, 1970), pp. 73-96.

10. Wolfson, *Philosophy*, pp. 156-59; see his sources, particularly W. D. Davies, *Paul and Rabbinic Judaism*, 4th ed. (Philadelphia: Fortress, 1981), pp. 158-63.

living being (Gen. 2:7), lost at death, is not an anthropological reality but a gift of God which returns to God at death (Eccles. 12:7). However, death is never outside the control of God. It is either the punishment for and cause of sin or the sign of humanity's finiteness. It is not another "power," implying a cosmic dualism and some force on the person in his/her relationship with God. The concept of sheol reflects the strong weight that the Jewish tradition places upon relationship with God. Living in sheol means life without such a relationship with God — a major threat to one's existence (e.g., Ps. 6 or 16).

The ancient belief in either the end of existence at death or in an afterlife in shadowy sheol gives way to an increased interest in the status of the dead and speculation on the nature of the person. In postexilic Israel the dead appear to be thought of with greater individuality, and the sleep of the dead associated with triumph over death in resurrection. The word "soul" in English represents almost exclusively the Hebrew term *nephesh,* although it carries overtones of philosophical Greek (Platonism). In the Hebrew Bible it does not imply an immortal soul but is essentially the life principle of the self as subject to appetite, emotion, and volition.[11] *Nephesh* always exists in some form or manifestation without which it would not exist (Gen. 2:7). The Hebrew could speak of "flesh" as we might say "body," but *nephesh* usually meant a psychophysical entity: one does not have a body but one is an animated body. *Nephesh,* as "self" or "person," generally implies embodied existence.[12]

The Person in Early Christian Thought

Greek philosophical thought was formative for Jewish and early Christian perceptions.[13] Early debate in Origen and his contemporaries drew upon the Greek term *psyche* (meaning soul, or breath of life; a departed spirit or ghost; seat of the will, desires, passions) as it appeared in the New Testament, where it

11. To express volition or the organization of the soul, the word "heart" is often used and occasionally coupled with "soul." In the prophetic tradition the heart is often the chief seat of intelligence with an emphasis on practical rather than theoretical thinking.

12. Some texts mention a shadowy world of sheol with the implication of a nondynamic existence. Death is the opposite of life *(nephesh). Nephesh* does not continue to exist independently of the body, but dies with it.

13. Wolfson, *Philosophy,* pp. 73-96. See also in Wolfson, *The Philosophy of the Church Fathers: Faith, Trinity, Incarnation,* pp. 364ff. Five types of physical union of body and soul discerned in Aristotle and Stoicism as outlined in the minds of the early Church Fathers are: (1) an aggregate union, (2) a *tertium quid* capable of dissolution into its parts, (3) a mixture, capable of dissolution, but not a *tertium quid,* (4) a union of confusion, (5) a union of predominance (p. 385).

was used to translate *nephesh* but also carried additional meanings.[14] Paul sometimes uses *soma* (body) and *pneuma* (spirit; breath, *inspiration*), which imply further psychological distinctions. Paul, in particular, often used *pneuma* to express the invasive Spirit of God as fundamental ideas for human identity were wrestled with in the documents that became the Christian New Testament.[15]

Further, in late Judaism and early Christian thinking, shaped by Hellenistic (frequently Platonic) thought, reference is made to the preexistence of the soul, its immortality, as being burdened by a body, and the reservation of souls after death for judgment. In general, the term *psyche,* as found in the New Testament, continues the old Greek sense of "vitality" or "life." When a contrast is intended, *psyche* is opposed to the soul or spirit of flesh so as to heighten a distinction (made by Paul) between "spiritual" perception, granted by the Spirit, and natural perception. The trichotomy of spirit, soul, and body (1 Thess. 5:23) probably does not mean three entities to the personality, but the totality of the person in need of redemption.[16] Early church authors divide into two camps about the fate of the body/soul at death in a way not dissimilar from early Judaism. The *nephesh/psyche* is restored with the body at resurrection (with no consciousness until that time), or it goes to be with God (in later thinking by way of degrees of proximity through purgation) until the resurrection at the Last Judgment, when it is rejoined to the body.

A further evolution in the Western concept of the person emerged in the context of the trinitarian discussions of the early church.[17] This resulted in an identification of the person with the being of man/woman and carried with it further ramifications for relating "freedom," "cosmos," and Being.[18] This "ontological revolution" grew out of a change in cosmology, the way in which one viewed the person against the circumference of meaning. It is related to an understanding of humankind with the being of humanity, i.e., with the nature of

14. See in Berkouwer, pp. 67-118, the distinction between made in the "image" or "likeness" of God.

15. Krister Stendahl, "Selfhood in the Image of God," in *Selves, People, and Persons* (Notre Dame, Ind.: University of Notre Dame Press, 1972).

16. Cp. Deut. 6:5: "Love the Lord with all your heart, soul, and strength."

17. This cultural understanding is developed by John D. Zizioulas in his retrieval of an Orthodox, or early Byzantine, understanding of the person. John D. Zizioulas, *Being as Communion: Studies in Personhood and the Church* (Crestwood, N.Y.: St. Vladimir's Seminary Press, 1997).

18. These ideas are explored in *Personhood: Orthodox Christianity and the Connection between Body, Mind, and Soul,* ed. John T. Chirban (Westport, Conn.: Bergin & Garvey, 1996), a book reflecting the Ninth Annual Conference of the Orthodox Christian Association of Medicine, Psychology, and Religion held at Holy Cross Greek Orthodox School of Theology.

permanent and enduring existence. We continue to use the terms of this revolution today, often without realizing it, and in ignorance of the precise ways in which terms were developed and used to define an understanding of human identity in this formative period of Western culture. The word "person" was taken from ancient Greek philosophical categories *(persona/prosopon)* and was infused with a new meaning in order to express an understanding of personhood reflective of the trinitarian God, or ultimate Being (an interesting juxtaposition to the computer metaphors mentioned earlier).[19]

Other options existed for understanding human identity (and hence dignity and formation) and would continue to influence the philosophical and theological tradition in the evolution of understanding.[20] Indeed, a misconception or one-sided development of this "ontological revolution" would lead to a dualism in Western thought between body and soul.[21] We cannot walk down all of the paths of what is an intricate history of theological and philosophical discussion. However, Zizioulas's argument concerning the nature of God in early Christian theology and the assumptions developed for understanding personhood help to frame the discussion in the West and provide for a helpful theological retrieval today in relation to AI research. Indeed, it offers a way to redress an inherited dualism even as it works to clarify a source from which that dualism came.

The concept of the person in historical particularity and ontological content was birthed in the attempt by Christian theology to give ontological expression to its faith in the triune God. This shaped Western philosophical anthropology into the contemporary period. In attempting to express the nature of the being of God who is one and three, the particular concern of the Greek apolo-

19. Zizioulas, pp. 27-65. Referring to the limits of Platonic and Aristotelian thinking, Zizioulas argues that "in Platonic thought the person is a concept which is ontologically impossible, because the soul, which ensures man's continuity, is not united permanently with the concrete, 'individual' man: it lives eternally but it can be united with another concrete body and can constitute another 'individuality,' e.g., by reincarnation. With Aristotle, on the other hand, the person proves to be a logically impossible concept precisely because the soul is indissolubly united with the concrete and 'individual': a man is a concrete individuality; he endures, however, only for as long as his psychosomatic union endures — death dissolves the concrete 'individuality' completely and definitively" (p. 28).

20. For example, the later Racovian [Unitarian] Catechism (1605) equates man's identity with dominion, or lordship. In the past century Karl Barth argued for an analogy between God and man grounded in that of communitarian relation, not being. Old Testament theologian W. Eichrodt finds the image of God anchored in man's spiritual superiority, an idea challenged by colleague Gerhard von Rad, who argues that the whole man/woman is made in the image of God, an idea generally in line with contemporary theology.

21. See Berkouwer, pp. 76-118. See this idea as explored in Charles Taylor, *Sources of the Self: The Making of the Modern Identity* (Cambridge: Harvard University Press, 1989), especially the chapter "Descartes's Disengaged Reason," pp. 143-58.

gists was to avoid tritheism or Sabellianism. The difficulty confronting theology was the necessity to emphasize the distinctiveness of the Father, Son, and Holy Spirit without destroying the notion of the one God. Therefore, a category was needed to affirm the concrete existence of the Father, Son, and Holy Spirit. The useful term from Greek philosophy was *hypostasis*. While its exact meaning is not always easily discernible, in Christian usage it often carried the meaning of "common principle": the spiritual stuff or substance of the Godhead. It also had the sense of "individual existence." In terms of the identity of *hypostasis* and person, Zizioulas argues that the Cappadocians, perhaps basing their views on the reflection of Hippolytus, affirmed their unity: as *hypostases*, the Father, Son, and Holy Spirit are concrete individual beings and not simply appearances of the one God.[22]

However, the conception of *hypostasis* alone was insufficient to describe the nature of ultimate Being. It left open the charge of tritheism. For while it identified the Father, Son, and Holy Spirit with the divine substance, maintaining their distinctiveness, something more was needed in order to affirm that Christianity continued to participate in Jewish monotheism; in other words, that the Father, Son, and Holy Spirit constitute the one God, not three gods. According to Zizioulas, an answer was found to describe the perceived reality of Being by uniting the concepts of *prosopon* and *hypostasis*, two terms that had never had any relation to each other.

Zizioulas gives us a history of the meaning of the concept of *prosopon* in antiquity and in late antiquity. *Hypostasis* had ontological content in that it was defined in relation to *ousia* (nature), meaning that it is real, permanent, and lasting. *Prosopon (persona)* in Greek and Roman thought lacked ontological content. In Greek thought it was understood as "mask" and was frequently used in the theater where one strove in dramatic form to rise up against rational and moral necessity. Through the struggle depicted in the *Tragedies* one learns "a certain taste of freedom, a certain specific '*hypostasis*,' a certain identity, which the rational and moral harmony of the world in which he lives denies him." Man's freedom is circumscribed and therefore is not freedom.[23] Furthermore, while skirting etymological debate, Zizioulas concludes that in Roman thought the term *persona* carried with it connotations of one's social or legal relationships, not in any sense an ontology of the person. One derived one's sense of selfhood from the group, or ultimately the state, to which even in his rebellion man seeks to return in order to find identity.[24]

---

22. Zizioulas, pp. 36-38.
23. Zizioulas, pp. 31-33.
24. Zizioulas, pp. 31-35.

Early Christian theology was forced to derive a new metaphor for Being because of the cosmological revolution of which it was a part. As with Judaism, early Christian theology was drawn to conceive of God, not the world, as being absolute. The biblical doctrine of *creatio ex nihilo* obliged theology to trace ontology back to God, not the world. Hence the world was seen to have been created not out of necessity but as a product of the freedom of God. "The being of the world became free from necessity."[25] Furthermore, the being of God became identified with the person through the person of Jesus, effected through the course of the trinitarian debates, an event for the Christian community every bit as radical as the exodus experience had been for Israel. Ultimate Being, or this God, was not to be defined, as was the case in Greek philosophy, with one divine substance. Rather, the being of God consists in the *hypostasis,* that is, in the person of the Father. Zizioulas writes, "The one God is not the one substance but the Father, who is the 'cause' both of the generation of the Son and of the procession of the Spirit. Consequently, the ontological 'principle' of God is traced back, once again, to the person." He notes, in conclusion, that we identify God not with ontological necessity but with personal freedom in that this means that God, as Father and not as substance, perpetually confirms through "being" his *free* will to exist.[26]

The ontological revolution underscored by Zizioulas becomes defined in the identification of *prosopon* with *hypostasis.* This identification was for Basil of Caesarea the most adequate way to both express the distinctiveness of the Father, Son, and Holy Spirit and yet consider their inseparable unity, or *koinonia.* As persons, the three are real ontological beings (i.e., hypostatic) and exist only by virtue of their relation to one another. Further, this identification leads us to an ontology of personhood, or a relational ontology, which Zizioulas argues is a unique product of the Greek Fathers' interpretation of the revelation of Christ and becomes determinative of early Christian creedal expression.[27]

We cannot go further into Zizioulas's argument at this point except to say that God the Father as *aitia,* or cause, supports a relational ontology in two

---

25. Zizioulas, p. 39.

26. More precisely, "And it is precisely his trinitarian existence that constitutes this confirmation: the Father out of love — that is, freely — begets the Son and brings forth the Spirit. Thus God as person — as the *hypostasis* of the Father — makes the one divine substance to be that which it is: the one God" (Zizioulas, p. 40).

27. In our conference, see the paper by Aristotle Papanikolaou, "Orthodox Theological Understandings of Personhood" (May 1998). Papanikolaou draws attention to arguments concerning an implicit subordinationism in Zizioulas's *monarchia* of the Father for which Papanikolaou finds redress in Vladimir Lossky's kenotic aspect of personhood. Cp. Kallistos Ware, "'In the Image and Likeness': The Uniqueness of the Human Person," in *Personhood,* pp. 1-13.

ways. First, it links the unity of God to the person of the Father rather than to the divine *ousia,* or nature: the one God is the Father, and not the one substance. The latter is the direction in which Augustine and medieval Scholasticism tended, laying the foundation for dualism in the West. The Cappadocian Fathers evinced the priority of personal categories over substantial categories. They stressed the place of relationship rather than a spiritual substance as separate from concrete manifestation. Second, God's trinitarian existence is the result of a person, not the necessity of substance, i.e., derivative of the freedom and love of the Father. Divine being owes its being to freedom, not to impersonal substance, i.e., not to nature in some abstract or objective sense.[28]

Grounded in this relational understanding of Being, anthropology takes a definite turn. Rather than locked in finitude and fate as a derivative of a closed cosmological order, personal existence becomes expressed by *hypostasis* and *ekstasis.* For personal existence to be authentic, the "hypo-static" and the "ek-static" have to coincide. The former refers to love, as generated in and reflective of trinitarian Being, and the latter to freedom, implying the ability to operate apart from fate. As Zizioulas defines it, the anthropological significance of this means that personal existence is one of love and freedom.[29]

The Father, in begetting the Son and the Spirit, gives out of love the divine nature for their own identity but possesses the fullness of this nature in communion with the other persons. Thus hypostatic existence implies a relational existence, in which persons in communion with others possess the fullness of nature uniquely, and in so possessing, share what is common with other persons. The uniqueness of personal existence is not an isolated existence, but is constituted in relationship with other persons. Hypostatic existence is one in which particularity and community converge through love. Picking up on similar patristic tendencies, Karl Barth adds that we do not know ourselves in isolation from others, but yet we are uniquely individual, a point that has become central to contemporary theological efforts to deal with inclusion and exclusivity in social and ethnic conflict.[30] Accordingly, the second aspect of personal existence is its "ek-static" character. *Ekstasis,* for Zizioulas, is defined ultimately in

28. Zizioulas, pp. 44-49.

29. Zizioulas, pp. 44-46. Zizioulas cites the importance of Heidegger as independent of the Greek philosophical tradition in liberating ontology from an absolute "ontism" and from philosophical rationalism, citing E. Levinas, *Totalité et Infini: Essai sur l'Extériorité,* 4th ed. (Norwell, Mass.: Kluwer Academic Publishers, 1971), p. 45.

30. Karl Barth, *Church Dogmatics,* ed. G. W. Bromiley and T. F. Torrance, trans. G. T. Thomson and H. Knight (Edinburgh: T. & T. Clark, 1970), II.2 #18.3 (pp. 401ff.), and see the application of these ideas in Miroslav Volf, *Inclusion and Embrace: A Theological Exploration of Identity, Otherness, and Reconciliation* (Nashville: Abingdon, 1996).

terms of freedom. "Ek-static" existence is free existence, freedom from the given whether by nature or social nurture. As Zizioulas puts it, God is not subject to the necessity of existing according to the defined qualities of divine nature. In begetting the Son and the Spirit, the Father manifests an "ek-static" transcendence from the necessity of divine nature and a freedom to constitute divine existence in a trinitarian way, i.e., as a loving communion of persons.[31]

Effects of the Inherited Conceptions of Personhood upon Formation and Dignity

The interrelationship of personhood, formation, and dignity through patterns of philosophical and theological speculation in the West is a story in its own right with implications for politics, and it shapes ethics along the way.[32] Augustine provides a common point of departure for anthropological speculation in the West, albeit in a direction toward a dualism of body and soul in distinction from his Cappadocian near contemporaries.[33] Augustine is often interpreted as locating the experience of God *(ek-stasis)* in pure reason, proceeding out of the body and thereby attaining a vision of God in patterns shaped by Neoplatonic thinking. By comparison, it might be said that in Gregory Palamas and the Orthodox tradition one attains *theosis* through participation in the divine energies. This is relational of the whole person, not merely participatory through intellectual experience.[34]

By the time of the Council of Florence in 1439, the Latin Church had declared as canonical the belief in purgatory and the presupposition that the souls of the dead are conscious and are therefore capable of pain or joy even prior to the resurrection of their bodies. This defined the reality of a disembodied existence. However, the problem was hardly settled there. It reemerged and became a topic at the Fifth Lateran Council (1512-17) in the face of humanist interest and developments in the new medical schools. Almost as a first round in a de-

---

31. Zizioulas, pp. 44-46.

32. See George H. Williams, *The Radical Reformation,* Sixteenth Century Essays and Studies XV (Kirksville, Mo.: Sixteenth Century Journal Publishers, 1992), pp. 63-72. See also the rich bibliography in Sarah Coakley, ed., *Religion and the Body* (Cambridge: Cambridge University Press, 1997).

33. Rodney Petersen, "To Behold and Inhabit the Blessed Country: Revelation, Inspiration, Scripture and Infallibility . . . ," *Trinity Journal,* n.s., 7, no. 2 (fall 1986): 28-81.

34. George Papademetriou, "Saint Augustine in the Greek Orthodox Tradition," in *Agape and Diakonia: Essays in Memory of Bishop Gerasimos of Abydos,* ed. Peter A. Chambras (Brookline, Mass.: Holy Cross Greek Orthodox School of Theology, 1998). See also Vladimir Lossky, "The Procession of the Holy Spirit in Orthodox Trinitarian Doctrine," in *The Image and Likeness of God* (Crestwood, N.Y.: St. Vladimir's Seminary Press, 1974).

bate reflected in current discussions concerning replacement of body parts, genetic counseling, and the implications of mapping the human genome, the council dealt with the problem of natural immortality in relation to competing views of personal identity.[35]

The social significance of such a dualistic understanding of personal identity, or personhood, for conceptions of formation and dignity has yet to be tracked. One area of importance for the fifteenth and sixteenth centuries was in the debate over the identity of peoples newly discovered by Europeans in what came to be called the Americas. Debate turned on whether the natives possessed the power of reason and the ability to acknowledge God as understood by the Europeans. For some, the natives participated in a kind of prelapsarian state of innocence, while for others they were mere brutes — a debate not completely unlike that surrounding Commander Data. Finally, in a papal bull promulgated in 1537, Pope Paul III declared the natives of the Americas to be "true men" capable of reason and of receiving grace. Clearly, one's conception of personal identity affects how one proceeds with formation and accords dignity.

Zizioulas's retrieval of the relation between Cappadocian theology and anthropology enables us to grasp something of the more nuanced debate over our inherited ideas of personhood. However, this retrieval does not diminish the value for the Western philosophical tradition even if interpreted as giving rise to forms of philosophical dualism when negatively viewed. In this way it has been permitted to us to perceive through empirical analysis and the emergence of modern science an understanding of particularity.[36] It is the work of contemporary Christian ecumenical theology to find an appropriate rapprochement between this retrieval of Orthodox theology, with its emphasis upon a relational understanding of personhood, and the Western intellectual tradition with its current disengaged instrumentalism and a postmodernist protest against such.[37] Contemporary reflection upon embodied AI and work in the cognitive sciences should aid in this development.

35. Williams, p. 67 and passim. See the relevant portion of *Apostolici regiminis* (p. 67). Williams summarizes five different views of survival after death. These illustrate different conceptions of embodiment: (1) natural immortality, (2) contingent immortality, (3) the unconsciousness of the soul after death (psychosomnolence), (4) the death of the soul with the body (thnetopsychism), and (5) the absorption of the rational into the universal Intellect.

36. While in need of contemporary redress, the ability to observe self-consciously is certainly an aspect of this dualism. See Charles Taylor, pp. 159-76. Also note in his conclusion the three areas of tension he finds in modernity reflective of this dualism (pp. 498-99).

37. See the reflections of Michael Welker on the value of a nonreductionist faith, delivered at the Seventh European Conference on Science and Theology of the European Society for the Study of Science and Theology, March 1998, "The Autonomous Person of European Modernity," and his book, *Creation and Reality* (Minneapolis: Fortress, 1998).

The Challenge of Artificial Intelligence

The Nature of AI Research and Its Relation to Philosophy

The beginning of the modern artificial intelligence research program is generally regarded as 1956, when Marvin Minsky, Claude Shannon, Ray Solomonoff,
all from MIT, and researchers from other schools, gathered together in a work-
shop held on the campus of Dartmouth University. They crafted a statement
known as the "physical system hypothesis" that ever since has remained a cor-
nerstone of AI research: Every aspect of learning or any other feature of intelligence can in principle be so precisely described that a machine can be made to
simulate it.[38] This hypothesis was later published in the groundbreaking book,
Human Problem Solving.[39] This represented the first thorough attempt to explain such complex rational features of human cognition as learning and general problem solving entirely with computer models.

The assumption was that human intelligence is essentially the ability to
process symbols, and that this symbol-processing power can, in principle, be
replicated by the arrays of switches inside a digital computer. In the years following the Dartmouth conference, Carnegie-Mellon University, MIT and its
Lincoln Laboratory, and to a lesser extent Stanford and IBM emerged as the
leading centers of AI research.[40]

Even if the symbol system hypothesis has been widely applied in several
areas of AI, it is far from universally accepted. It is, therefore, not sufficient as a
definition for what AI really is. The best attempt at a definition reads like this:
"AI is that part of computer science and electrical engineering which attempts
to build machines which are capable of performing functions for which we
usually presume intelligence to be necessary." However, one can still see the ambiguity of this definition, largely flowing from the words "intelligence" and "intuitive," which are not defined at all. It is common today to define AI by its engineering and scientific goals.[41] Researchers for the engineering goal attempt to
build intelligent machines and concentrate on the tasks and behaviors they
want to achieve. Under the scientific goal, on the other hand, it is the declared
aim of researchers to understand how human intelligence works. It is the latter

38. Cited in Daniel Crevier, *AI: The Tumultuous History of the Search for Artificial Intelligence* (New York: Basic Books, 1993), p. 48.

39. Allan Newell and Herbert Simon, *Human Problem Solving* (Englewood Cliffs, N.J.:
Prentice-Hall, 1972).

40. Newell and Simon, p. 51.

41. Patrick H. Winston, *Artificial Intelligence*, 3rd ed. (Reading, Mass.: Addison-Wesley,
1992), pp. 5ff.

goal that is most germane to this paper because here the anthropological assumptions are the most prevalent.

Under the goal of scientific understanding, AI describes part of the reality of human intelligence in terms of theories, hypotheses, and working models. It is, however, the special object of research which leads to a subject-object problem because cognition is the research object and, at the same time, is used to understand it. This paradox is closely related to Descartes's problem on how to keep the *res cogitans* separated from the *res extensa* when the *res cognitans* becomes an object of research. But besides this paradox emerging out of the circle between *res cogitans* and cognition becoming a part of the *res extensa*, there is another problem. After decades of thorough research in the history and philosophy of science, we know today how many subjective elements scientists integrate into their research. The more closely the object of research comes to one's own self-understanding, the more one's own personal intuition and the scientific theories become intertwined. Consequently, in AI and the cognitive sciences, more than in any other scientific discipline, the boundaries between the scientist, her personal sense of who she is and how she works, her professional convictions, and scientific statements about human cognition are blurred.[42]

In the group of research areas which are working under constraints caused by this problem, AI plays a special role. It seems more appropriate to understand AI as cognition technology; as such, it complements cognitive science and scientifically verifies or falsifies theories and hypotheses about human intelligence.[43] In this role AI constructs working models about intelligent features which are not only used for verification of psychological theories but which also can be used for experimenting; as such, they complement and enrich empirical data since one can perform experiments on models which could never be performed on humans.[44]

---

42. Philosopher Clark Glymour claims that "artificial intelligence is philosophical explication turned into computer programs." See Glymour in "Artificial Intelligence in Philosophy," in *Aspects of Artificial Intelligence*, ed. James H. Fetzer (Dordrecht: Kluwer Academic Publications, 1988), pp. 195-207. Though Glymour is critical of arguments raised by Dreyfus and Searle, Glymour draws distinctions between the work of AI and the details of a philosophy of mind.

43. Francisco Varela, *Kognitionswissenschaft — Kognitionstechnik: Eine Skizze aktueller Perspektiven* (Frankfurt am Main: Suhrkamp, 1993).

44. Psychologists and neuroscientists rely mainly on the observation of brain-damaged people to find out the function of certain brain parts, to formulate theories on learning, etc.; see, for instance, the work of Oliver Sacks, *An Anthropologist on Mars* (New York: Vintage Books, 1995) and *The Man Who Mistook His Wife for a Hat and Other Clinical Tales* (New York: Summit Books, 1985).

AI, more than the cognitive sciences, has to assume that one can actually gain insights about human intelligence by building intelligent machines — an assumption which reflects the intuitive understanding of what it means to be human shared by most AI researchers (but not necessarily by all cognitive scientists). But AI researchers not only have to assume that human minds and machines can in principle be compared, an assumption most obviously stated in the hypothesis behind symbolic systems; they also work under engineering constraints. They have to build useful, reliable, and functioning machines and are therefore forced to choose only those theories of cognition that can be simulated or rebuilt.[45]

This raises the question of the relation between philosophy and AI research. How closely is philosophy tied to AI? This is a question raised by R. J. Russell in his philosophical critique of AI.[46] The philosophical issues raised by AI research were given sustained attention by Hubert Dreyfus and John Searle a number of years ago. Dreyfus lays out four assumptions underlying AI which he rejects on philosophical grounds. After contending that AI research fails to deliver on its promise of replicating human cognition, he summarizes four types of behavior he believes are beyond simulation by digital computers: fringe consciousness, ambiguity tolerance, essential/inessential discrimination, and perspicuous grouping. He then identifies four assumptions he believes guides AI research: biological, psychological, epistemological, and ontological assumptions, each of which he rejects.[47] Dreyfus adds that for AI research to make any headway, it must stress the role of the body in intelligent behavior. If computers are to take on the characteristics of human intelligence, the path to be followed must be that of embodiment. In his critique of AI, Dreyfus distinguishes persons from machines by pointing out that it is not "a detached, universal, immaterial soul but an involved, situated, material body . . . [which] . . . cannot be reproduced by a heuristically programmed digital computer."[48]

45. Anne Foerst, "Why Theologians Build Androids," *Insights: The Magazine of the Chicago Center for Religion and Science* 9 (August 1997): 1-7.

46. Russell, pp. 245-60.

47. I am following Russell here (p. 247): (1) Based upon neurological evidence, it is no longer assumed that the brain functions like a digital computer. (2) He rejects the reductionist assumptions underlying cognitive simulation that the mind must function like a digital computer. (3) The epistemological argument in AI research that machines can reproduce fully and similarly human intelligent behavior through formalized rules is an unwarranted assumption. (4) To assume that the world is composed solely of apparently independent, unambiguous, and interacting elements discerned in discrete empirical data is an ontological assumption following from an unwarranted mechanistic deduction.

48. Hubert L. Dreyfus, *What Computers Can't Do: The Limits of Artificial Intelligence*, rev. ed. (New York: Harper Colophon Books, 1979), pp. 236-37. See also Hubert L. Dreyfus and Stu-

Critique of AI

Dreyfus's points (that embodiment overcomes the infinite regress of determining which data are relevant, of formalizing the rules for processing data, and the input/output problem of processing external facts by these rules) represent an acknowledgment of the advances made over earlier forms of AI research. It actually fits with the criticism that several AI researchers have formulated against the system symbol hypothesis; these researchers have now formed a new camp within the AI community.

Currently AI research can be roughly categorized in three different camps. We might first cite classical AI (or GOFAI for "good, old-fashioned AI"), which usually works with classical, serial machines to model human thought processes. Even though the architectures of human wetware and computer hardware are fundamentally different, it is assumed within this camp that the human thought processes can be abstracted from the system on which they are running.[49] This approach toward artificially intelligent systems is usually used in applications which are well defined, such as medical expert systems and natural language processors, and the capabilities of these systems are quite impressive — but only within their limits. None of these systems would actually pass the Turing Test. If a researcher claims that this approach is actually sufficient to rebuild and understand human intelligence, the critique of Searle is somewhat valid.

We might next cite connectionism. This models the human brain and the interconnection of neurons. It holds that the parallel architecture of the human brain is crucial for intelligent processes and vast learning capacities. This camp within AI is often dubbed the "subsymbolic paradigm," as it agrees substantially with many basic assumptions of a classical AI approach but bases the abstract features of classical AI on parallel architectures.

Finally, embodied AI builds creatures in real environments and models the system architecture of biological systems and their interaction with their environments. Under the scientific goal, all camps model human functions, and if the behaviors of the computer system or the robot and the human system are similar, it is assumed that the functional description of the respective human feature is correct. But apart from this very basic anthropological assumption, which is in accordance with the biological and the cognitive sciences, the first two AI camps and the third differ fundamentally. Instead of assuming that

---

art E. Dreyfus, *Mind over Machine: The Power of Human Intuition and Expertise in the Era of the Computer* (New York: Free Press, 1986).

49. Newell and Simon, p. 796.

one can abstract intelligence from the hardware on which it is implemented, embodied AI researchers hold that intelligence cannot be out of the body and its complex interaction with the environment. The way we think depends crucially on the functions and capabilities of our bodies and the way our bodies are shaped.[50]

In the opening pages of this paper we mentioned cyborg technology and the way it changes our perception. The field of evolutionary epistemology supports this point of view by studying the development of various perception systems during evolution and to what extent different perceptions lead to different forms of intelligence. The whole field of constructivism studies not only the way our perceptions influence our thought, but also how concepts in our mind about the nature of the universe influence what we actually perceive. The work of Oliver Sacks demonstrates how much our perception of reality is shaped by our brains. We all together create a concept of the world around us and constantly reaffirm it with our own perceptions and those of others. An intelligent system, in the view of embodied AI, needs a body and a close connection to the world by sensors and actuators. Embodied AI researchers, therefore, do not program disembodied computers but build autonomous robots who can navigate around and explore their environment. While classical AI works with internal world models and with plans within those world models, then translating them into the real world, embodied AI lets its systems constantly renew their contact with the real world. As Rodney Brooks, the founder of the embodied AI camp, states: "To build a system that is intelligent it is necessary to have its representations grounded in the physical world. . . . The key observation is that the world is its own best model. It is always exactly up to date. It always contains every detail there is to be known. The trick is to sense it appropriately and often enough."[51]

The human-machine compatibility is held in all three camps of AI, but embodied AI includes embodiment, action in and interaction with the real world — "situatedness," as it is often called. This is translated into robust autonomous robots with a distributed architecture where every subsystem interacts with its local environment, which includes other subsystems as well as the environment. Complex capabilities are constructed through feedback loops and learning capabilities. The system as such is not determined any more since it is far too complex and too connected with its environment. Researchers, of course, can always analyze the system itself in a given moment in time and space and un-

50. Mark Johnson, *The Body in the Mind* (Chicago: University of Chicago Press, 1990).
51. Rodney A. Brooks, "Elephants Don't Play Chess," *Robotics and Autonomous Systems* 6 (1990): 3-15.

derstand how it is changed by its interaction and by what clues and hints from its surroundings it learns certain activities. But as soon as the system is again in its world, it enters a complex space which is irreproducible and irreducible. The concept of embeddedness is actually an analogue to the understanding of intelligence as described in the first, theological part of this paper.

Of course, one cannot just stop here. One has to look a little into the critique which has been offered. John Searle, one of the most prominent critics of AI, questions the whole field. For him, it is questionable whether the key to thinking can be captured by a computer program; that even if thinking were simulated so well as to pass the Turing Test, such simulation is not really thinking but only syntactical manipulation. Meaning, for Searle, is found instead in "mental content" or a "semantic framework." He writes: "computer programs are neither constitutive nor sufficient for minds."[52]

Searle argues that the clue to human knowing which distinguishes it from computer syntax is that the brain "does not merely instantiate a formal pattern or program . . . but it *causes* mental events by virtue of specific neurobiological processes." Thinking is more than computation.[53] Commenting on Searle's work, Russell writes, "What makes semantics more than syntactics is related to the 'bottom-up' causal power of brains to *produce* mental states. Hence, a computer program can never, in principle, be a 'mind' since mental activity necessarily involves the possibility of physical effects." Or, as Searle puts it, "The way that human brains actually produce mental phenomena cannot be solely by virtue of running a computer."[54]

Instead of using this kind of argument, we would like to ask how AI and especially its embodied camp can become attractive to theology. One reason is that it is a way of learning to deal more directly with the precise nature of our humanity. James Ashbrook and Carol Rausch Albright provide a fruitful path for reflection, arguing that an understanding of our humanity begins with such distinctions as brain and mind. Research here provides the threshold for coming to understand ways in which we are materially, biologically constrained creatures who are yet able to find meaning beyond the material.[55] Such meaning is often

52. In *Scientific American*, January 1990.

53. One might draw upon hierarchy in ways of knowing denoted by Augustine in *De Genesi ad litteram* (The literal meaning of Genesis), trans. J. H. Taylor, S.J. (New York: Newman Press, 1982), bk. 1, chaps. 19–21 (pp. 42-45); and cp. his work in bks. 2 and 3 of *De doctrina Christiana* (On Christian doctrine).

54. Russell, p. 250.

55. James B. Ashbrook and Carol Rausch Albright, *The Humanizing Brain: Where Religion and Neuroscience Meet* (Cleveland: Pilgrim Press, 1997). See Foerst, "Why Theologians Build Androids," pp. 33-37.

sought in the liminal fields of "complexity" and "chaos" studies today, pressing the syntactic-semantic division pointed out by Searle. While there is little consensus on the meaning of such terms as "complexity," researchers like Peter Coveney and Roger Highfield provide a lucid account of several stimulating lines of research. For example, they illustrate techniques of complexity that have yielded surprising results on the subject of artificial life (e.g., in the 1950s von Neumann analyzed computer-generated organisms, or automata, that were capable of creating copies of themselves).[56] This work has been continued by researchers like John Holland, demonstrating how computers can learn to cope with complexity in software settings by imitating how living creatures cope with the real world.[57] However, it is precisely at this point that George Johnson alerts us to a parallelism between science and religion, as both are guided by heuristic lines of faith.[58] Yet the really interesting point that draws us back to Ashbrook and Albright's argument here is the way in which the dominance of science (apart from its instrumental value) over religion proceeds from its democratic accessibility.

What has been said above draws us to the line of consciousness, a topic that we cannot probe deeply here. Through his pattern of "reverse-engineering," Daniel Dennett draws us to reflect upon the liminality of all fields of study in his critique of "unitary consciousness."[59] Critical of earlier theorists like Penrose, Dennett alerts us to life in a nondualistic world through habitation, salience, and the material root of consciousness. Owen Flanagan made this clear in his argument for "constructive naturalism," i.e., that consciousness is a natural phenomenon. Its nature, forms, roles, and origins can be realized by blending insights from sciences as diverse as psychology, cognitive science, neuroscience, and evolutionary biology.[60] Such a reductionary hypothesis about the collapse of the mind and body distinction need not give rise to either fatalism or determinism following the logic of both embodied AI and relational theology as seen in the retrieval of trinitarian thinking discerned in the work of Zizioulas.[61] Indeed,

---

56. Peter Coveney and Roger Highfield, *Frontiers of Complexity: The Search for Order in a Chaotic World* (New York: Ballantine Books, Fawcett Columbine, 1995).

57. John Holland, *Hidden Order: How Adaptation Builds on Complexity* (Reading, Mass.: Addison-Wesley, Helix Books, 1995); and see Stuart Kaufman, *At Home in the Universe: The Search for the Laws of Self-Organization and Complexity* (New York: Oxford University Press, 1995).

58. George Johnson, *Fire in the Mind: Science, Faith, and the Search for Order* (New York: Knopf, 1996). Johnson alerts us to the question of whether we have been oversold on the viability of "self-organized criticality."

59. Daniel C. Dennett, *Brainchildren: Essays on Designing Minds* (Cambridge: MIT Press, 1998).

60. Owen Flanagan, *Consciousness Reconsidered* (Cambridge: MIT Press, 1998).

61. See the remarks made by Mary Midgley in "Consciousness, Fatalism and Science,"

such a path augurs well for the project described by Brian Cantwell Smith, understanding between naive realism and pure constructivism, particularly as we are focusing upon artificial intelligence and cognitive science.[62] By drawing upon a more relational understanding of Being and an embodied understanding of the third AI camp, we can avoid the agnosticism of dualism and the determinism associated with reductionism.[63]

Dignity, Formation, and Identity

As we have seen through these remarks, concepts of identity, or personhood, formation, and dignity are difficult to locate in a purely empirical realm. The theological "take" on identity is closely bound up with embodiment and social interaction as well as the interaction between the person and God.[64] Especially the first feature is not empirical but embedded in a body of Christian story and its articulation through faith and creed. In classical AI, on the other hand, many attempts have been made to identify intelligence with personhood, and both with functional mechanisms which can be remodeled in a computer. Only recently has a change in the understanding of intelligence in the cognitive sciences and embodied AI brought social interaction and the interaction of humans with their nonhuman environment into focus for researchers who are attempting to rebuild and understand human cognition.

Identity

The same shift happened at the beginning of this century in pedagogy and in those parts of psychology which are more closely related to the humanities than connected with the clinical psychologies. Under the influence of Sigmund

---

delivered at the Seventh European Conference on Science and Theology of the European Society for the Study of Science and Theology, March 1998. She appears to evince an unwarranted fatalism and agnosticism in her remarks.

62. Brian Cantwell Smith, *On the Origin of Objects* (Cambridge: MIT Press, 1998).

63. The latter often poses a problem for those who seek to defend a separate realm for meaning, as in Malcolm Jeeves, *Mind Fields: Reflections on the Science of Mind and Brain* (Grand Rapids: Baker, 1994). Possible integration is dealt with more deftly in *Human Nature at the Millennium: Reflections on the Integration of Psychology and Christianity* (Grand Rapids: Baker, 1997).

64. This perspective is elaborated upon by Philip Hefner in his remarks on *imago Dei*, delivered at the Seventh European Conference on Science and Theology of the European Society for the Study of Science and Theology, March 1998. He helpfully grounds identity in relationships, drawing upon the theology of Paul Tillich.

Freud, people began to rethink the concept of personhood and attempted to define identity as emerging out of complex interactions between the ego and one's environment.[65] Many authors have adapted this idea and have thus transported it into the broader public. The Swiss author Max Frisch (1911-91) devoted his whole work to the problem of the relationship between the society and the individual. He focused especially on the destructive power of images, created by society about a person, and the identification with or rejection of these images. He often describes people who are confronted with a stereotype of prejudices against themselves and are destroyed by them or by the attempt to fulfill expectations. In this we are confronted existentially with the question of the center of our personhood.

The author Bertolt Brecht (1898-1956) reacted to Frisch's work with one story within the collection *Stories of Mr. Keuner.* Mr. Keuner is asked, "What do you do if you love a person?" "I make an image," he said, "and attempt to make it similar." "What? The image?" "No," says Mr. Keuner, "the person."[66] In his later years Brecht put forth a different perspective on the way in which we create images. He described the positive power of it. If someone has created an image with tenderness and affection and thus painted a very positive picture of the person, she might actually discover abilities and aspects of her personality which she was not aware of before. In this way an image of another person has a productive power.[67]

Formation

The psychologist Erik Erikson was the first who developed a scientifically sound perspective on this understanding of identity.[68] Every person, in his opinion, constructs her personality and character during childhood and adolescence. This construction is constantly revisited and modified, a process which is centered around a few basic questions. A young person might see herself in the light of her past and ask: "Who was I as a child (or as an adolescent)?" A person also might see herself in the light of the upcoming future: "What am I about to become?" Both, the definition of identity in the light of one's past and the one by the likelihood of future developments, are constructs

65. Sigmund Freud, *An Outline of Psycho-Analysis* (New York: Norton, 1969; first published in 1940). His discussion of the psychical apparatus appears on pp. 13-16.

66. Translation from *Geschichten von Herrn Keuner,* supplied by Anne Foerst.

67. From the perspective of the Christian story, the image of Christ plays this role, and it does so self-consciously in the theology of Paul (e.g., Col. 1:15-23).

68. Erik Erikson, *Identity and the Life Cycle* (New York: Norton, 1980; 1st ed., 1959).

of each person herself and usually lead to major memory shifts and changes in the way we remember. Such a process then reinforces the image already drawn. The shifts in memory and the constantly modified self-image are bound together by a need for coherence and identity and a construct motivated by another question: "Can I recognize and/or construct some continuity in my character formation which makes sense out of my various life stages and puts them together?" All of this has a special cogency for religious traditions that are self-conscious in their efforts to provide formation into a particular model of personhood.[69]

The community to which a person belongs adds a further aspect of character formation. The community has constantly to ask, "Is this person an integral part of our community?" and to evaluate whether or not he or she shares that community's values, morals, and constructs about reality. Since the community itself consists of people who all themselves are constantly in the process of character formation, this definition of a person and of a group is very dynamic and cannot be reduced to a static, empirical model. Every person has to reconcile her own conception of herself constantly with the community's recognition of herself. At the same time, every person has to constantly create an image which describes the dynamic development of every character formation in a meaningful way and not as solely arbitrary. Erikson's dynamic model of character formation and identity fits with some interpretations of *imago Dei,* that God has created humans in God's image.

Dignity

Finally, the concept of dignity is located in this interaction; a concept of humanity which is not based on special skills and features, but on humanity itself and a relationship with God. Dignity is assigned to us by God. It is also assigned to us by the community in which we live; we assign it to ourselves and to our neighbors. The rejection of all definitions of dignity with empirical features has a strong ethical component. If the assignment of dignity to a person depends on his or her features, then if any definition of dignity or personhood fails to include these features, one loses a basic right to be treated as human. History shows many dramatic examples of the mistreatment of humans because of ar-

---

69. For example, to continue with Orthodox Christianity, see John T. Chirban, "Developmental Stages in Eastern Orthodox Christianity," in *Transformation of Consciousness: Conventional and Contemplative Perspectives and Development,* ed. Ken Wilbur, Jack Engler, and Daniel P. Brown (Boston: Shambala, 1986).

bitrary categories established by religion, race, or some other limiting factor. The AI debate draws us down the ladder of abstraction to the place where we are required to wrestle more fundamentally with the nature of our identity and dignity.

An interactive model of dignity in the theological realm is usually identified with the *imago Dei*, the concept that God has made humans in God's image.[70] Martin Luther defined the *imago Dei* in the context of Genesis 2:7; humans share with animals bodily existence while the *imago Dei* distinguishes them from animals because it is an expression of God's consolation to humans — it describes the relationship between God and humans. The *imago Dei*, then, cannot be identified with certain skills and abilities but is a promise of God to start and maintain a relationship with humans. In humankind God has created beings he can talk to, beings who listen to him and answer him.[71] In the *imago Dei*, God assigns dignity and intrinsic value to each of us. This definition is not empirical but depends on the faith of a person who accepts this definition. What speaks for it is that it is in accordance with both the definition of personal identity through relationship by Erikson, and the apostolic understanding of personhood, and embodied AI.

Conclusion

We can finally conclude that a majority of the body of Christian stories, many modern psychologists, and the newest camp of AI agree that a person can never be seen as a closed system, but can only be understood within his or her social context. Intelligence, interaction, language, fantasy, emotions, consciousness, and all the other features which are dear to us ultimately depend on a system's interaction with other systems and its surroundings in an immediate way, and not mediated by abstraction, reduction, or internal world models. Embedded-

70. For example, these texts: "Then God said, 'Let us make humankind in our image, according to our likeness; and let them have dominion over the fish in the sea, and over the birds of the air, and over the cattle, and over all the wild animals of the earth, and over every creeping thing that creeps upon the earth.' So God created humankind in his image, in the image of God he created them; as male and female he created them" (Gen. 1:26-27); "Whoever sheds the blood of a human, by a human shall that person's blood be shed; for in his own image God made humankind" (Gen. 9:6), are the only parts in the Hebrew Scriptures in which the *imago Dei* is mentioned; later in the New Testament some theologians, especially Paul, refer to this concept. An unequivocal definition is never found. Throughout Judeo-Christian history, various theories have been given, as indicated in the opening pages of this paper. Many of these are challenged both from within the tradition as well as in a parallel way from embodied AI.

71. Claus Westermann, *I Mose*, Vil. 1 (Neukirchen: Neukirchen-Vluyn, 1986), p. 22.

ness in a real world environment is crucial for the development of artificial and human systems.

This understanding of "system" is much more complex than any classical dualistic model, even though it is remarkable that theology and AI both end up with a relational concept. There are, of course, differences in Christianity. Relationships ultimately depend on a person's community with others and with God. That means that even if social community is crucial, it is made possible by the assignment of dignity to humankind by God. Only when we accept this dignity in us and in others will we be able to construct and live in community.

AI, on the other hand, has an entirely naturalist approach. For scientific reasons a concept of God cannot be introduced into AI research. If AI researchers were to introduce some metaphysical concept of dignity into their concept of humanity, they would repeat the argumentation of Searle. Additionally, any research would have to be stopped at the moment it reaches this metaphysical and supernatural element in the human system. For the sake of their research, they have to approach the human system from a naturalistic framework. But since they are now beginning to accept the irreducibility of the human system, they just recognize the limits of the scientific method with regard to complexity and interaction. To return to our first illustration, this complexity leaves enough room for theological reasoning about dignity and personhood, and in the end the whole community will decide whether or not they will accept Commander Data as person and make him part of the human community.

PART II

THEOLOGY AND
INSTITUTIONAL EXPRESSION

RODNEY L. PETERSEN

At its best, theological literacy is borne by the church, promoted by structures of ecclesial organization, and supported by church-related and other schools.[1] Yet one of the most noteworthy historical features as related to all churches throughout the modern period has been an alienation toward the church as an institution. In this very alienation one can note the remarkable way new religious forms and institutions inspired by Jesus and engendered by the Spirit have continued to be birthed and evolve.[2] Although the opening of the twenty-first century is marked by religious institutional alienation in many places,[3] it is also shaped by the growth of the Christian movement worldwide — African Initiated Churches, Pentecostalism with a local flair, Uniting Churches, and many of the older ecclesial communities as well — and particularly in the Two-Thirds World. Through this flowering of faith, there is every expectation that Christianity will once again be the religion of the underclass, as was the case at

1. A division in teaching methods and curricula exists at points between those whose primary aim is pastoral ministry in its various forms and an academic approach to religion; this division is set in its larger framework by Donald Wiebe, ed., *The Politics of Religious Studies: The Continuing Conflict with Theology in the Academy* (New York: St. Martin's Press, 1999); see on this topic the articles collected in *Theological Education* 26, no. 2 (spring 1990).

2. Studies in Faith and Order have focused on the person and work of the Holy Spirit and the emerging orders of the churches. For background, see Meredith B. Handspicker, "Faith and Order 1948-1968," in *A History of the Ecumenical Movement*, ed. Harold E. Fey, vol. 2 (1948-68) (Geneva: World Council of Churches, 1970), pp. 147-70.

3. Peter Berger presents a helpful context for what has become a wide field of literature. See his *A Rumor of Angels: Modern Society and the Rediscovery of the Supernatural* (New York: Anchor Books, 1990); Scotty McLennan writes a helpful guide for those seeking to connect spirituality and religion: *Finding Your Religion* (San Francisco: Harper Collins, 1999).

its inception, rather than of the world's elite. It is fair to ask how these changes will affect theological literacy.

The chapters in this section are organized around the nature of the church as expressed institutionally. Institutions, the nature of the contemporary church and the churches through history, might be conceived of as the conventional "signs" or agencies through which we express our faith.[4] Such concerns are taken up by Augustine in the second book, or section, of *On Christian Doctrine*, the structure of which we are using for our considerations in this volume on theological literacy in the twenty-first century. This section deals primarily with the church broadly conceived. The church, all ecclesial communities, is shaped today by at least four factors: the reality of institutional alienation and its implications, the democratization of all persons and roles in society, the fact of religious pluralism and the particularity of religious understanding, and the valuing of all cultures with a view toward equal human rights. Our last section acknowledged that theological literacy begins with the quest for what is real in the deepest sense of this term. Here we are concerned with how we express our understanding of this reality, particularly in the church but also in all our communal relationships.[5] It is clear that with respect to theological literacy, the church must consider the public character of theological education. It takes on an institutional expression, whether evangelical and Pentecostal, Roman Catholic, Protestant, or Orthodox in form.[6]

Raymond Helmick, S.J., begins this section with his chapter, "Where Catholicism Has Been, and Where It Is Going," a survey of a range of historical and pastoral concerns with application to all Christian churches. He traces the church's sense of itself and its mission, addressing the significance of the church as sacramental sign.[7] He develops a threefold typology of church in relation to

---

4. Augustine, *On Christian Doctrine*, bk. 2, pp. 34-78: "Conventional signs are those which living creatures show to one another for the purpose of conveying, in so far as they are able, the motion of their spirits or something which they have sensed or understood. . . . We propose to consider and to discuss this class of signs in so far as men are concerned with it, for even signs given by God and contained in the Holy Scriptures are of this type also, since they were presented to us by men who wrote them" (2.2).

5. This is the starting point for M. Scott Peck's understanding of civility: *A World Waiting to Be Born: Civility Rediscovered* (New York: Bantam Books, 1993). See his reference and consideration of the work of Martin Buber for this point (p. 44); Martin Buber, *I and Thou*, trans. Walter Kaufmann (New York: Scribner, 1970).

6. See chapters devoted to the public character of theological education as taken up by these different denominational expressions in the issue of ATS devoted to this topic, *Theological Education* 37, no. 1 (autumn 2000).

7. Edward J. Kilmartin, S.J., *The Eucharist in the West: History and Theology*, ed. Robert J. Daly, S.J. (Collegeville, Minn.: Liturgical Press, 1998).

the state: the paradigmatic, pragmatic, and parabolic roles of the church. Helmick traces the medieval evolution of a culture of guilt, an authoritarian ecclesial posturing, and the mystification of its cultus.[8] Noting the value and excesses of the Protestant and successive Catholic reforms, he champions the work of the Second Vatican Council (1962-65). Several points from his chapter are worth noting here: the convergence of Protestants and Catholics in the area of religious symbolism and sacramental practice as opening new possibilities for addressing controversies that have separated the churches in the West;[9] with the healing of the churches will come a deeper reflection on the nature of alienation and a culture of guilt, an unfortunate heritage of medieval Christianity.[10] And finally, Helmick writes, a continuing question in light of Christian conscience is when and whether it is ever appropriate for the church to exercise power instrumentally.[11] This last point recognizes a trajectory of Catholic social doctrine in this century from sparring with the problem of the state to a focus on the nature of humanity, created and redeemed by Christ. John Paul II, for all his social and political significance touching on the fall of Communism, has identified the main question for society, as well as the church, to be that of

8. Thomas Bokenkotter writes of the "unmaking" of Christendom in this period, in *A Concise History of the Catholic Church*, revised and expanded ed. (New York: Doubleday Image Books, 1990), pp. 153-230. It might be said that Garry Wills carries this picture of the Roman Catholic Church into the contemporary period in *Papal Sin: Structures of Deceit* (New York: Doubleday, 2000). Since Vatican II the Roman Catholic Church has sought to emphasize the use of "the people of God" as indicative of its now greater emphasis upon the human and communal side of the church, rather than on institutional and hierarchical aspects; see in the Dogmatic Constitution on the Church *(Lumen Gentium)*, chap. 2, *The Documents of Vatican II*, ed. Walter M. Abbott, S.J. (St. Louis: Herder and Herder, 1966), pp. 14-24. See Richard P. McBrian, *Report on the Church: Catholicism after Vatican II* (San Francisco: Harper San Francisco, 1990).

9. Cheslyn Jones, Geoffrey Wainwright, Edward Yarnold, S.J., and Paul Bradshaw, eds., *The Study of Liturgy* (New York: Oxford University Press, 1992), pp. 66-67. The modern and contemporary period is discussed with the recovery of the paschal mystery, the trinitarian structure of worship, and liturgy as the "work of the people." Additional reflection from a contemporary ecumenical perspective is offered in Thomas F. Best and Dagmar Heller, eds., *So We Believe, So We Pray* (Geneva: World Council of Churches, 1995).

10. See the analysis of medieval theology and a retributive concept of justice in James C. Russell, *The Germanization of Early Medieval Christianity: A Sociohistorical Approach to Religious Transformation* (New York: Oxford University Press, 1994). I owe this reference to Fr. Raymond Helmick, S.J. Thomas Bokenkotter details a recovery of progressive politics in Catholicism in *Church and Revolution: Catholics in the Struggle for Democracy and Social Justice* (New York: Doubleday Image Books, 1998).

11. A question raised by Helmick in "Does Religion Fuel or Heal in Conflicts?" in *Forgiveness and Reconciliation: Religion, Public Policy, and Conflict Transformation*, ed. Raymond Helmick, S.J., and Rodney Petersen (Philadelphia: Templeton Foundation Press, 2001). See additional articles in this volume.

quid sit homo, "What is human?" not *quid sit Caesar*[12] — the question that ended our last section.

Alienation is not only a phenomenon experienced by churches. It is also expressed with respect to government, or social structure,[13] and higher education, or at least the educational establishment.[14] These three institutions — church, state, and academy — each represents an agency in society that exists to protect, adjudicate, and guide in one way or another. As in old Israel, the authority of priest, ruler, and prophet was acknowledged with an anointing with respect for the leadership that was expected. When that leadership failed, the nation was thrown into one form of alienation and distress or another. Perhaps this is instructive for today of the high holiness attached to these offices. Such recognition has formed a part of Christian consciousness and theological literacy investing in the earliest theology of the church Jesus as priest, prophet, and king.[15]

Issues of institutional identity and alienation are taken up differently in the article by Alice Mathews, "The Theological Is Also Personal: The 'Place' of

12. One might remark here on the value of *Evangelium Vitae* (1995), with its recognition of a contradiction between human rights and the political tendency not to choose between different moral opinions. In recognizing the problem of the power of the state to threaten individual freedom, contemporary societies have tended to shift sovereignty from the state to the individual. This privatization of morality can serve to undermine human rights, adding to the necessity of the churches grappling with the question of the truth about humanity. See Karol Wojtyla/Pope John Paul II, *Toward a Philosophy of Praxis,* an anthology edited by Alfred Bloch and George T. Czuczka (New York: Crossroad, 1981); George H. Williams, *The Mind of John Paul II: Origins of His Thought and Action* (New York: Seabury Press, 1981), pp. 264-79; and Williams, "John Paul II's Concepts of Church, State, and Society," *Journal of Church and State* 24, no. 3 (1982): 463-96.

13. Robert K. Merton calls attention to "mal-integration" between cultural understanding and structural expectations that results in a breakdown in norms, and subsequent anomie, in *Social Theory and Social Structure,* enlarged ed. (New York: Free Press, 1968), p. 217 and passim.

14. Lynn Nell Rhodes and Nancy D. Richardson explore the challenge to theological education of social implications that require transformative practice in *Mending Severed Connections: Theological Education for Communal Transformation* (San Francisco: San Francisco Networks Ministries, 1991). See their review of literature, "Education as a Resource for Liberating Moral Energy," pp. 9-21.

15. George H. Williams, "*Translatio Studii:* The Puritans' Conception of Their First University in New England, 1636," in Festschrift für Heinrich Bornkamm, *Archiv für Reformationsgeschichte,* vol. 52, no. ½ (1966), pp. 152-81. For inspiration in this, see Ernst Kantorowicz, *King's Two Bodies: A Study in Mediaeval Political Theology* (Princeton: Princeton University Press, 1957). Kantorowicz demonstrates how the early modern Western monarchies gradually began to develop a "political theology," a theme picked up by Williams and given christological significance for church, state, and academy in Puritan New England.

Evangelical Protestant Women in the Church," again with applicability to all churches. In this chapter the nature of theological literacy is connected by Mathews with the idea of identity (theological and religious). Mathews sketches a history for all women toward a democratization of service for Christ in and through the church.[16] Beginning with what she understands to be Jesus' affirmation of women and the New Testament portrayal of women teaching and evangelizing throughout the Roman Empire, she tells the story of the increasing marginalization of women in church leadership into the contemporary period. While historians and sociologists have documented the many cultural and religious strands that have contributed to this socialization, Mathews contends that the question of women's "place" in the Christian church will remain unresolved unless the theological and sociological underpinnings of the matter are more fully addressed.

Mathews writes about how women cope with the question of their "place" in the church. Drawing upon research that analyzes the relationship of doctrine to creed,[17] she asks whether the issue is of a creedal or doctrinal nature. If the latter, the debate is somewhat more ephemeral than if the former. An analogous issue might be that of race,[18] a point contended negatively by Orthodox and Roman Catholic leadership and by many evangelical church leaders. Dissatisfaction is extended to church authority, further questioning of social conventions, and experiments with alternative religious expressions. These are often the norm for women unable to acquiesce with prevailing theory respecting their role as church leaders.

16. Gilbert G. Bilezikian's work has been widely influential; see *Beyond Sex Roles: What the Bible Says about a Woman's Place in Church and Family* (Grand Rapids: Baker, 1985); see also Aída Besançon Spencer, *Beyond the Curse: Women Called to Ministry* (Peabody, Mass.: Hendrickson, 1985); and for contrast see her study, *The Goddess Revival* (Grand Rapids: Baker, 1995).

17. She draws on Samuel P. Huntington, *American Politics: The Promise of Disharmony* (Cambridge: Harvard University Press, Belknap Press, 1981), pp. 64ff., and Max Stackhouse, *Creeds, Society, and Human Rights: A Study in Three Cultures* (Grand Rapids: Eerdmans, 1984), p. 2. See also Ann Belford Ulanov, who writes of women constructing a sense of self-understanding in *Receiving Woman: Studies in the Psychology and Theology of the Feminine* (Philadelphia: Westminster, 1981).

18. John W. De Gruchy and Charles Villa-Vicencio, *Apartheid Is a Heresy* (Grand Rapids: Eerdmans, 1983). The question is, Is there a parallel gender argument to that of race? Most Christian exegetes today understand apartheid, or the separateness of the races, to be not just error but heresy. See the Belhar Confession of 1982 adopted by the Synod of the Dutch Reformed Mission Church, Cape Town, South Africa, in G. D. Cloete and D. J. Smit, *A Moment of Truth: The Confession of the Dutch Reformed Mission Church* (Grand Rapids: Eerdmans, 1984), pp. 1-6. The exegesis by Willem Vorster and Douglas Bax in De Gruchy and Villa-Vicencio is helpful.

Such disillusioned disengagement is often one aspect of a wider institutional alienation. Mathews contends that the slur of "secular humanism" is often applied by detractors of women leaders to feminists who are working through such alienation. When one senses a call from God, this frustration in the face of limited opportunities promotes disengagement.[19] Mathews drives her point home by making reference to the story of French Protestant Madeleine Blocher-Saillens, pastor of the largest Baptist church in France. Blocher-Saillens countered criticism of her effective church leadership with the argument that if women, one-half of the human race, are immobilized in their witness and work, then the archenemy of God has succeeded in cutting at least in half any efforts to reclaim humanity and the earth for God;[20] it is part of a genuine war against women. Mathews continues by discussing the other adjustments that women are sometimes willing to make: defiance within compliance, defecting in place, or even leaving traditional Christianity behind.[21] In this light Mathews understands many women having moved toward women-led forms of religious expression, for example, wicca or witchcraft as articulated by Starhawk, Goldenberg, and others,[22] or a "thealogy" rooted in the Goddess and the mystical experiences that spring from the earth or nature.[23]

The separations which Tracy draws in the beginning of this book become focused on civil society in the chapter by William Everett, "Public Works: Bridging the Gap between Theology and Public Ethics." Everett proposes a pattern for the church as it interfaces with other institutions and nourishes civic culture. In doing so, he describes a frequently acknowledged separation between theological memory and public discourse that reflects the cultural alienation raised by Helmick and others.[24]

19. Mathews uses Carol Christ's analysis of the options open to women who question the gap between the promise and reality of service within the church: (1) to stay in the tradition and keep silent, (2) to leave the tradition, or (3) to confront the tradition (*Laughter of Aphrodite*, [San Francisco: Harper and Row, 1987], p. 29).

20. Madam A. Blocher-Saillens, *Libéree par Christ pour Son Service* (Paris, 18eme: Les Bons Semeurs, diffusion évangelique, 1961).

21. Carol P. Christ and Judith Plaskow, eds., *Womanspirit Rising: A Feminist Reader in Religion* (San Francisco: Harper and Row, 1979).

22. *Womanspirit Rising*, chapter by Starhawk, "Witchcraft and Women's Culture," pp. 259-68; Naomi R. Goldenberg, *Changing of the Gods* (Boston: Beacon Press, 1979), pp. 85-114.

23. Christ, *Laughter of Aphrodite*; also see Christine Downing, *The Goddess: Mythological Images of the Feminine* (New York: Crossroad, 1984), and Nelle Morton, *The Journey Is Home* (Boston: Beacon Press, 1986).

24. For example, the Center for the Study of Values in Public Life, Harvard Divinity School. See the *Center Newsletter*. See Martin Marty with Jonathan Moore, *Politics, Religion, and the Common Good* (San Francisco: Jossey-Bass, 2000).

For fifteen hundred years, Everett reminds us, Europeans carried on their political, cultural, and ethical disputes in religious and theological language. Questions of authority were traced back to God with theories of "just war" that called upon a level of theological literacy.[25] Successive events that countered this association with increasing disengagement, the Peace of Westphalia (1648), the English Civil War (1647-60), the American and French Revolutions, and the disestablishment of religion all allowed religion to stay public if it supported the existing political or economic order. Everett writes that we are now experiencing a reaction against this division from those who would impose a new governmental orthodoxy. He asks, "What is the kind of 'literacy' that can guide us in recovering from the amnesia effected by the well-intentioned effort at separation?" His own proposal is to find bridges between religious and public policy discourse that allow for separation and conversation.

Everett proposes that we see how bridges function in the creation and shaping of civil society. We might also explore the role of theological concepts and symbols in vitalization and transformation of political culture. Finally, we might see in language the power to open up societies and culture to the mysterious transcendence of the divine purpose and power. The image of crossing bridges supports the integrity of the two vocabularies. This method acknowledges the life of civil society and its governance to be a valid part of creation as found in natural law theory and in classical Protestantism. It refuses to collapse the language of civil society into that of religious discourse. Toward this end, Everett suggests four concepts to guide our thinking about theological literacy in public life: covenant, assembly, household, and nature. Each can operate as a bridge concept between transcendence and its power to shape and transform culture and religious difference. They provide ways toward a common language of civility and vision in society.[26] For exam-

25. Michael Walzer, *Just and Unjust Wars: A Moral Argument with Historical Illustrations* (New York: Basic Books, 1992). The important role of religion in justifying the political order and its institutions is discussed in David Little, *Religion, Order, and Law: A Study in Pre-Revolutionary England* (New York: Harper and Row, 1969); with reference to Max Weber, pp. 6-32.

26. Hans Küng, *Global Responsibility: In Search of a New World Ethic* (New York: Continuum, 1993). The value of finding a common language for the common good is a supposition that might be taken from Robert Bellah's collaborative work (with Richard Madsen, William M. Sullivan, Ann Swidler, and Steven M. Tipton), *Habits of the Heart: Individualism and Commitment in American Life* (Berkeley and Los Angeles: University of California Press, 1985). Bellah's comment about the coequal participation of church, sect, and mysticism each playing a role in shaping American public culture might be extended to all religious partners (p. 246). Miroslav Volf offers a trinitarian vision of the church in the church as "gathered community," to counter tendencies toward individualism in Protestant ecclesiology, in *After Our Likeness: The Church as the Image of the Trinity* (Grand Rapids: Eerdmans, 1998).

ple, the idea of nature has come in the last third of the twentieth century to operate as such.[27] The idea of covenant, central to questions of identity as formed through a sense of revelation and election, could do so.[28] One might contend that religious illiteracy is the problem.[29] Marc Gopin and Abdulaziz Sachedina, from within their own Jewish and Muslim traditions, would appear to write from this perspective.[30] Each of these four bridges is rich with implications for theological education in a time of interreligious diversity and recognition.

The last article in this section takes us to what it means to be church in a different way. In "Christian Scholarship and the Demographic Transformation of the Church," historian Andrew Walls begins keying into our theme by noting that Christian scholarship follows and is derived from Christian mission.[31] This

27. Hans Küng and Karl-Josef Kuschel, eds., *A Global Ethic: The Declaration of the Parliament of the World's Religions* (New York: Continuum, 1993). The literature is legion: see Holmes Rolston III, "Environmental Ethics: Values in and Duties to the Natural World," in *Ecology, Economics, Ethics: The Broken World,* ed. F. Herbert Bormann (New Haven: Yale University Press, 1991), pp. 73-98, and a survey of the literature in Donald B. Conroy and Rodney Petersen, eds., *Earth at Risk: An Environmental Dialogue between Religion and Science* (Amherst, N.Y.: Humanity Books, 2000).

28. Everett argues that the idea of covenant and its derivative symbol of federal republic bears within itself the means for a renewal of church-state dialogue, in *God's Federal Republic* (Mahwah, N.J.: Paulist, 1988). Covenant is a central metaphor for Reformed Christianity; see Charles S. McCoy and J. Wayne Baker, *Fountainhead of Federalism: Heinrich Bullinger and the Covenantal Tradition with a Translation of "De testamento seu foedere Dei unico et aeterno"* (1534) (Louisville: Westminster John Knox, 1991).

29. R. Scott Appleby notes the shifting perspective on religion's public impact from that of its role as instigator of violence and consequent public marginalization to a recognition today of its more complicated, and often positive, public role. He notes the value of a new breed of religious peacemakers and contends that religion can hold the key to achieving and sustaining reconciliation and peace in Appleby, *The Ambivalence of the Sacred: Religion, Violence, and Reconciliation* (New York: Rowman and Littlefield, 2000). Constructive arguments in this direction are made by Elise Boulding, *Cultures of Peace: The Hidden Side of History* (New York: Syracuse University Press, 2000); Walter Wink, ed., *Peace Is the Way: Writings on Nonviolence from the Fellowship of Reconciliation* (Maryknoll, N.Y.: Orbis Books, 2000); and Helmick and Petersen, *Forgiveness and Reconciliation.*

30. Marc Gopin, *Between Eden and Armageddon: The Future of World Religions, Violence, and Peacemaking* (New York: Oxford University Press, 2000), and Abdulaziz Sachedina, *The Islamic Roots of Democratic Pluralism* (New York: Oxford University Press, 2001). Each author is able sympathetically to enter into the center of his faith tradition and find the basis for peacemaking.

31. Andrew Walls, *The Missionary Movement in Christian History: Studies in the Transmission of Faith* (Maryknoll, N.Y.: Orbis Books, 1996). Dana L. Robert draws attention to the fact that the International Missionary Council foresaw in 1938 that the future of world Christianity rests with the non-Western churches, in "Shifting Southward: Global Christianity Since 1945," *International Bulletin of Missionary Research* 24, no. 2 (April 2000): 50-57.

draws us to a consideration of globalization with its implication that people throughout the world are now drawn into a common horizon. Theological literacy, taught in the first "seminaries" or catechetical schools of Alexandria and Antioch, was at the heart of the transition and translation of Christian faith as it crossed its first cultural frontier, that from a Palestinian Jewish world to the world of Hellenism. This must be so today as well. Toward this end Walls outlines what he means: engendering new life in classical philosophy, defining new branches of learning, drawing into the orbit of universal scholarship wider circles of human experience, the construction of libraries and amassing the results of learning, linguistics and the work of translation that draws us into the deep translation and understanding of culture. Walls connects his argument about the challenge mission offers to our sense of identity, ways in which it opens us to the other, with the sedimentary residue of such encounters, which is scholarship and the realization of a more dynamic meaning of theological literacy.

Theological literacy for the twenty-first century for Walls means recognizing that Europe and North America are no longer the "Christian heartland." The North Atlantic world is now being replaced in this by Africa, Latin America, and some parts of Asia. This demographic shift is similar, Walls argues, to what happened to Christianity in the late second century as it moved out of the Jewish and into the Hellenistic world. Walls uses three formative Christian thinkers, Paul, Justin, and Origen, to outline a three-stage model for conceptualizing the way Christianity moves into new cultures throughout the world: (1) by borrowing from the inheritance (Paul), (2) by critiquing the inheritance for purposes of acceptance or rejection (Justin), and (3) by reconfiguring and reconciling with the inheritance (Origen). The theological task for the twenty-first century is to foster leadership in the cultures of Africa, Latin America, and Asia. This will have implications for the intellectual framework within which theology is practiced. Insights from Africa and elsewhere will enlarge our vision of theology, challenge our conception of individual and social pathology, and deepen our perspective on salvation.[32] The ingredients in this process will include things as prosaic as a genuine sharing of library resources made possible with contemporary technology. Walls lifts us out of a static world of privilege

32. *Ministerial Formation*, a publication of the Ecumenical Theological Education Programme, Unit I, Unity and Renewal, is helpful in presenting issues that foster and encourage critical ecumenical consciousness and global reflection. Additional aspects of theological education are taken up by the Oxford Centre for Mission Studies. An example of global Christian theological work is in Aída Besançon Spencer and William David Spencer, eds., *The Global God: Multicultural Evangelical Views of God* (Grand Rapids: Baker, 1998). See Alice Frazer Evans, Robert A. Evans, and David A. Roozen, eds., *The Globalization of Theological Education* (Maryknoll, N.Y.: Orbis Books, 1993).

and gives us a sense of the dynamism of the Spirit in history. He gives us a vision for theological literacy as practiced on the margins, in places of transition, under threat of execution, imprisonment, and torture. This he calls "evangelistic theology — scholarship in mission, made necessary by mission."

The church of the twenty-first century will be shaped on the cusp of the challenges framed by the themes picked up in these four chapters, by the way institutional alienation is handled, by democratization in the church, by modes of accommodation between particular religious affirmation and a recognition of pluralism in public life, and by globalization which implies that the horizon of pastoral care and public prophetic injunction includes all humanity. Churches, as with other identity movements, can quickly find themselves divided between different forms of prophetic vision. Orthodox churches wrestle with new social conditions, particularly in eastern Europe but also in North America, and wonder whether now is the time for an Orthodox council in the face of changing social conditions and ecclesial realities.[33] Roman Catholic churches continue to wrestle with the legacy of Vatican II and such documents as *Ut Unum Sint,* with its call for a participatory hierarchy and ecumenical thrust while also struggling with an older heritage that understands Rome alone as defining the church.[34]

New patterns of engagement are opening up for Christian churches.[35]

33. Stanley Harakas, "Orthodoxy in America: Continuity, Discontinuity, Newness," in *Orthodox Perspectives on Pastoral Praxis,* ed. Theodore Stylianopoulos (Brookline, Mass.: Holy Cross Orthodox Press, 1988), pp. 13-30. Emmanuel Clapsis considers a range of topics, indicative of Orthodox engagement with often divisive issues, in *Orthodoxy in Conversation: Orthodox Ecumenical Engagements* (Geneva: World Council of Churches Press, 2000).

34. *Dominus Jesus* finds the unity and uniqueness of the Roman Catholic Church in the unity and uniqueness of Christ, an argument that is similar to that of the Russian Orthodox Church in "Basic Principles of the Russian Orthodox Church toward the Other Christian Confessions," Jubilee Bishops' Committee of the Russian Orthodox Church, 14 August 2000 (http://www.russian-orthodox-church.org.ru/s2000e13.html). On *Dominus Jesus,* see Congregation for the Doctrine of the Faith, "*Dominus Jesus:* On the Unicity and Salvific Universality of Jesus Christ and the Church," *Origins* 30, no. 14 (14 September 2000): 4. Within Protestantism, a counterpart to the arguments of the Russian Orthodox Church and Roman Congregation for the Doctrine of the Faith is found in David F. Wells, *No Place for Truth; or, Whatever Happened to Evangelical Theology?* (Grand Rapids: Eerdmans, 1993). Such division highlights the value of ecumenical discussion, particularly among groups understood to have been given to deep division; see Charles Colson and Richard John Neuhaus, eds., *Evangelicals and Catholics Together: Toward a Common Mission* (Dallas: Word, 1995).

35. One of the more important documents that has been remanded to the churches by the World Council of Churches for study and discussion is *The Nature and Purpose of the Church,* Faith and Order Paper no. 181 (Geneva: World Council of Churches, 1998). This document summarizes what the churches can now say together and lays out areas that require further analysis and resolution. G. R. Evans grounds current discussion in underlying issues but

Even as this is occurring, some evangelical and Pentecostal churches define themselves in opposition to older forms of Protestantism in patterns that replicate division within Catholicism and Orthodoxy.[36] The impasse over a mutually acceptable understanding and affirmation of each other's ministry across different Christian churches bears within itself these tensions.[37] Such internal division in the Christian religion, or movement, affects the engagement of churches with culture and truncates mission. Churches cannot withdraw from engagement. When they do, a narrowing of mission, or sectarianism, results that causes destructive conflict by belittling or demonizing rival groups and reinforces the boundaries between them. This often results in justifying or enabling the domination of rival groups. When churches behave in this fashion, they increase the level of alienation and foster their own sense of self-privilege, rather than reducing it.[38] Nor can churches place an unbridled confidence in the efficacy of power, a point raised by Helmick. This ends in alienation and promotes cynicism. A judicious use of politics stands between the lures of sectarianism and the blandishments of power that allows for boundaries without domination, but promotes conversation.[39] Both sectarianism and domination

---

finds the concept of "communion" to be hopeful as a guide forward, in *The Church and the Churches: Toward an Ecumenical Ecclesiology* (Cambridge: Cambridge University Press, 1994).

36. Christian Smith argues that American evangelicalism thrives because of its oppositional approach to American culture, in *American Evangelicalism: Embattled and Thriving* (Chicago: University of Chicago Press, 1998). A turning point for evangelicalism and an appropriation of a conservative agenda, in distinction from an earlier liberative agenda, is seen by some to have come with the urban revival of 1857-58; see Kathryn Theresa Long, *The Revival of 1857-58* (New York: Oxford University Press, 1998). Donald W. Dayton and Robert K. Johnston point out the difficulties of discussion here because of the differences that exist in the American evangelical community in their edited collection, *The Variety of American Evangelicalism* (Downers Grove, Ill.: InterVarsity, 1991).

37. The value of the Faith and Order work of the World Council of Churches is underscored here, particularly the document *Baptism, Eucharist, and Ministry,* Faith and Order Paper no. 111 (Geneva: World Council of Churches, 1982). A helpful overview is found in Günter Gassmann, *Documentary History of Faith and Order, 1963-1993,* Faith and Order Paper no. 159 (Geneva: World Council of Churches, 1993), and Michael Kinnamon and Brian E. Cope, eds., *The Ecumenical Movement: An Anthology of Key Texts and Voices* (Grand Rapids: Eerdmans, 1997).

38. Trevor Williams and Alan Falconer, eds., *Sectarianism* (Dublin: Dominican Publications, 1995); and see Alan Falconer and Joseph Lichty, eds., *Reconciling Memories* (Dublin: Columbia Press, 1998).

39. Paul Hiebert's analysis of the term "Christian" draws upon the mathematical categories of "bounded sets," "fuzzy sets," and "centered sets" as he seeks to bring clarity to the meaning of the term. Opting for the latter category, he writes that a line of demarcation exists but the focus should be on "reaffirming the center" and not on "maintaining the boundary." See his article, "The Category 'Christian' in the Mission Task," *International Review of Mission* 72 (1983): 421-27, 424.

in matters religious lead to two dangerous forms of reductionist thinking. Either religion and politics are treated as completely separate entities, and so we miss their cultural interrelationship, or the role of religion as a part of the "ecology" of conflict is lost in a sense of self-absorption. The impulse in Christianity must be to serve the alienated, marginalized, and disenfranchised — not simply out of a politics of human rights, but because the love of God in Christ reaches to all persons.[40] Where this is done, we are standing on the cusp of mission. Where forgiveness is found, human empathy mirrors the suffering of God in Christ, moving ultimately to liberation.[41] When Christians move forward in mission, they are able to find the way through politics. The attempt to deal with the rupture in Christian unity through the development of the denominational ideal can be a legitimate recognition of cultural difference, but it is not a solution to finding the unity of the body of Christ.[42]

Leadership in the church comes through the magisterium, or through the ministry however it may be organized, but it also comes through the prophetic office of the church. This has been often regularized in the teaching ministry.[43] Among a variety of issues that divided the Latin Church and led to different visions of reform in the sixteenth century was whether the church was best led by its pastors or its teachers, if such a division can or even should

40. One might even now talk about a phenomenology of redemption; see René Girard, *I See Satan Fall Like Lightning*, translated with a foreword by James G. Williams (Maryknoll, N.Y.: Orbis Books, 2001). The concept of the "other" as objectified and different from me, and subject to scapegoating in Girard's sense, is raised in Miroslav Volf, *Exclusion and Embrace: A Theological Exploration of Identity, Otherness, and Reconciliation* (Nashville: Abingdon, 1996).

41. Paul Lehmann was one of the first theologians to take up the concept of "forgiveness" as a subject for study in the modern period; see his *Forgiveness: Decisive Issue in Protestant Thought* (New York: Harper and Brothers, 1940). Recent literature is summarized by different authors in Helmick and Petersen, *Forgiveness and Reconciliation.*

42. Philip Schaff (1819-93) held aloft the denominational ideal in his day while nevertheless seeking Christian unity, in *The Principle of Protestantism*, translated from the German by John W. Nevin (Philadelphia: United Church Press, 1844/1964). More recently Diane Kessler and Michael Kinnamon have written of the role of churches in relation to the goal of Christian unity, in *Councils of Churches and the Ecumenical Vision* (Geneva: World Council of Churches Publications, 2000).

43. However, general agreement exists among Orthodox, Roman Catholics, and Protestants that the apostolic ministry, as depicted in the New Testament, will do for later generations what the apostles did for theirs. The traditionalism of the patristic period reminds us that "Christianity is not something we can construct for ourselves . . . but a faith shaped by real occurrences reported and interpreted by trustworthy witnesses." See Avery Dulles, "The Magisterium in History: A Theological Perspective," *Theological Education* 19, no. 2 (spring 1983): 11. Different patterns can be found in Dulles, *Models of the Church*, rev. ed. (New York: Doubleday, 1987).

be tolerated.[44] As Avery Dulles reminds us, the term "magisterium" in its current sense dates only from the nineteenth century. Each of the other persons and offices, including that of emperor and representative assembly, was seen to have some responsibility for the church's doctrine and oversight.[45] As we approach the area of ministry, we would do well to pay attention to church discussions in relation to the document commended to the churches for study by the World Council of Churches, *The Nature and Purpose of the Church.*[46] Leadership comes from learning to triangulate holiness (priesthood), governance (statecraft), and education (prophecy).

In the face of the alienation we have encountered and the demographic changes through which the church is going, we might remind ourselves that while literacy involves translating the symbols of Christian faith anew for every generation, without the tradition we would not have a heritage to modernize. It also requires good rhetoric, a resonance between the Word we bear and ourselves,[47] and a sense for ambiguity, or the dialectic to which we are called when faced with difference. The valuable features of the patristic model of representation, influential upon Vatican II among Roman Catholics, that fostered unity from the consensus of the body of churches and their teachers underwent a mutation in the medieval period of western Europe as the study of theology became separated from the pastoral work of the church.[48] Rhetoric took the place of dia-

44. See the articles in *Theological Education* 19, no. 2 (spring 1983).

45. Dulles, "The Magisterium in History," p. 7. He notes that three problems for our theme emerge out of the New Testament and early church period: (1) What is the permanent significance of the preeminence accorded to Peter and the Twelve in the New Testament? (2) How did teaching authority operate in the local church? and (3) What provision was made for the preservation of pure doctrine as the apostolic generation died out (p. 8)?

46. *The Nature and Purpose of the Church: A Stage on the Way to a Common Statement,* Faith and Order Paper no. 181 (Geneva: World Council of Churches Publications, 1998).

47. It also reaches out into the domain of ethics as we wrestle with the degree to which gospel holiness must be modeled in church leadership. Here again there is wide berth for the emergence of alienation. What precisely constitutes the nature of that holiness is frequently contested. Daniel Taylor asks whether intolerance is the only sin left to us in society today, in "Are You Tolerant? (Should You Be?)" *Christianity Today,* 11 January 1999, pp. 43-52. He concludes with (1) the importance of resisting anger (James 1:19-20) and (2) the value of taking time to listen to the stories that others have to offer. Issues of ethics and church unity, good resonance, are taken up in Thomas F. Best and Martin Robra, eds., *Ecclesiology and Ethics: Ecumenical Ethical Engagement, Moral Formation, and the Nature of the Church* (Geneva: World Council of Churches Publications, 1997).

48. In its own quiet way the work of liturgical renewal across all Christian divisions, with its emphasis upon Trinity, symbolic embodiment in the Eucharist, and worship *(leitourgia)* as the work of the people, has had the most startling and far-reaching effect in promoting Christian unity. See Part One, "Theology and Rite," in *The Study of Liturgy,* pp. 3-60.

lectic, and dialectic was internalized at the place of rhetoric. This division, and confusion, in the heart of the church's leadership, between that of the pastor and that of the teacher, might represent a tension many feel today between knowledge and the need for knowledge to be connected with a moral sensibility. Human solicitude, whether psychological or deeply pastoral, must be seen to participate in what is true. At the same time, churches that function as viable and intentional faith communities can be places where knowledge and understanding is applied in ways that are truly humane, sensitive, and liberating.[49] Two questions informed by Dulles's discussion are: (1) How might the academic community and church leadership work together more fully? and (2) How might decisions made by churches be more inclusive and representational?

Institutional alienation, democratization, the challenges of particularity and pluralism, and globalization are topics that not only challenge churches and Christian identity today, but also other social identities. Each of the four challenges raised up in the chapters of this section can foster attitudes of victim and oppressor. Churches and Christian leadership can take a lead in fostering forgiveness in the context of new patterns of restorative justice. They can encourage conversation about how to move forward as individuals and social groups. Such thinking has been central to the political settlement in South Africa as that country has made the effort to move from an apartheid government to becoming fully a democracy. In this process, "no future without forgiveness" is the way it has been put by Archbishop Desmond Tutu.[50] "If forgiveness is the basal conception of Evangelical Christianity, it is impossible that it can express the relation of men to God and Christ without at the same time including a peculiar attitude of the believer to the world founded upon that relation."[51] In calling Christians "ministers of reconciliation" (2 Cor. 5:18), Paul did not mean for this work to be limited to a particular church, denomination, or ecclesial community.

49. Stephen A. Macchia, *Becoming a Healthy Church: Ten Characteristics* (Grand Rapids: Baker, 1999). In addition to an emphasis on God's word and prayer, the author lists nine common indicators of a healthy church, without denominational distinction, as developed through research, extensive surveys, and reflection. See also Paul Wilkes, *Excellent Protestant Congregations: The Guide to the Best* (Louisville: Westminster John Knox, 2001) and *Excellent Catholic Parishes: The Guide to Best Places and Practices* (New York: Paulist, 2001).

50. Desmond Tutu, *No Future without Forgiveness* (New York: Doubleday, 1999).

51. Albrecht Ritschl, *Justification and Reconciliation,* Mackintosh translation (Edinburgh, 1902), p. 30, as cited in Lehmann, p. 171. Martha Minow writes as a legal scholar of the implications of forgiveness without justice and of vengeance without mercy, in *Between Vengeance and Forgiveness: Facing History after Genocide and Mass Violence* (Boston: Beacon Press, 1998). Issues of impunity remind us of the difficult politics, at an interpersonal level as well as that of the engagement of social groups, that often surround naive efforts at reconciliation; see Charles Harper, ed., *Impunity: An Ethical Perspective* (Geneva: World Council of Churches Publications, 1996).

Sometimes the work of reconciliation will take place within and among churches. It may often take place outside of church structures, by persons working in voluntary associations, in nongovernmental agencies, and through other corporate bodies.[52] This is sometimes called "Track II diplomacy."[53] Churches and other voluntary societies have been instrumental as they have worked in the space between the state and the family in promoting civil society that fosters human and humane values.[54] Persons like Olga Botcharova and David Steele have fostered seminars throughout troubled regions of the world that have sought to break the cycle of violence and promote a new understanding of community among deeply alienated persons and social settings.[55] This is par-

52. The work of James Luther Adams has celebrated the work of voluntary associations. See his work in *Voluntary Associations: Socio-cultural Analyses and Theological Interpretation,* ed. J. Ronald Engel (Chicago: Association Press, 1986), and *Voluntary Associations: A Study of Groups in Free Societies: Essays in Honor of James Luther Adams,* ed. D. R. Robertson (Richmond: John Knox, 1966). While it might be said that voluntary movements are birthed in the church, Ruth Rouse completes the circle by writing of ways in which they contributed to the ecumenical movement: "Voluntary Movements and the Changing Ecumenical Climate," in *A History of the Ecumenical Movement, 1517-1948,* ed. Ruth Rouse and Stephen Charles Neill, vol. 1 (Geneva: World Council of Churches, 1986).

53. The term "Track II diplomacy" was coined by Joseph Montville of the Center for Strategic and International Studies for those forms of diplomacy that occur apart from or outside regular government "Track I" channels, specifically the work of religious organizations and other NGOs. See his edited publication, *The Psychodynamics of International Relationships,* vol. 2 (Lexington, Mass.: D. C. Heath and Co., 1991). Reports on the work of churches in the domain of human rights are summarized in *Human Rights and the Churches: New Challenges* (Geneva: World Council of Churches Publications, 1998). The question of rights, and whose rights, is raised in a series of penetrating articles in *The Cultures of Globalization,* ed. Fredric Jameson and Masao Miyoshi (Durham, N.C.: Duke University Press, 1998). Ted Robert Gurr, writing as director of the Minorities at Risk project at the University of Maryland, tells about human rights efforts and the work global NGOs have contributed toward policies that favor pluralism and accommodation, in *Peoples versus States: Minorities at Risk in the New Century* (Washington, D.C.: U.S. Institute of Peace, 2000).

54. While the work of the churches in the political realm is difficult to assess, George Weigel argues that John Paul II had more to do with bringing the Cold War to a peaceful conclusion than all the feverish braggadocio of Ronald Reagan's military buildup and Star Wars. Weigel draws attention to John Paul II's interposition in such troubled spots of the world as Nicaragua in 1983, Czechoslovakia in 1986, Paraguay in 1988, Cuba in 1998. Lamentably, a private initiative to the former Yugoslavia failed in 1994 to end the slaughter. See *Witness to Hope: The Biography of Pope John Paul II* (New York: Harper Books, 1999). A perspective that assesses Reagan's role more generously is that of Frances Fitzgerald, *Way Out There in the Blue: Reagan, Star Wars, and the End of the Cold War* (New York: Simon & Schuster, 2000).

55. Olga Botcharova, "Implementation of Track II Diplomacy: Developing a Model of Forgiveness," in *Forgiveness and Reconciliation.* Such thinking was first carried into public policy in the contemporary period by Donald W. Shriver, Jr., in *An Ethic for Enemies: Forgiveness in*

ticularly valuable in light of a resurgent politics of identity in contrast with a prevailing politics of interest into the contemporary period.[56] In his work to promote communal and socially responsible patterns of thinking, the sociologist Robert N. Bellah has sought to counter rampant individualism by reminding us of the languages of communal engagement, of republican values, and of the Bible. Such issues have surfaced in much of the contemporary discussion about civility in society.[57] However, reconciliation is more than civility. Learning to forgive means learning to live on the interface between victims and oppressors. In promoting forgiveness one may need to realize that degrees of forgiveness are possible, both within ourselves and among others.[58] The idea of degrees of forgiveness might find a parallel concept in degrees of community along the way toward the stages of community building, an idea developed by psychiatrist M. Scott Peck.[59]

Politics (New York: Oxford University Press, 1995); additional examples are in Chester Crocker and Fen Osler Hampson with Pamela Aall, eds., *Managing Global Chaos: Sources of and Responses to International Conflict* (Washington, D.C.: U.S. Institute of Peace, 1996).

56. Jonathan Sacks writes of ways in which a politics of interest, perhaps the heart of secularization, has given way to a politics of identity in the contemporary world, in "Judaism and Politics in the Modern World." See this and additional essays in Peter Berger, ed., *The Desecularization of the World: Resurgent Religion and World Politics* (Grand Rapids: Eerdmans, 1999), pp. 51-63. The reality of such a shift in politics is fraught with a political precariousness that invites displacement, difference, and contention, but also reaches to the heart of civil politics and democracy as pointed out by Jean Bethke Elshtain, *Democracy on Trial* (New York: Basic Books, 1995). See Karen Armstrong, *Jerusalem: One City, Three Faiths* (New York: Ballantine Books, 1996); and with particular poignancy, Naim Ateek, *Justice and Only Justice: A Palestinian Theology of Liberation* (Maryknoll, N.Y.: Orbis Books, 1997). Issues in the politics of dialogue are raised by John Witte, Jr., and Richard C. Martin, *Sharing the Book: Religious Perspectives on the Rights and Wrongs of Proselytism* (Maryknoll, N.Y.: Orbis Books, 1999).

57. M. Scott Peck cites the work of Robert N. Bellah and others in his own work, *A World Waiting to Be Born*. See Bellah et al., *Habits of the Heart*. In this light Stephen L. Carter argues that American society has created political and legal structures that force religiously devout people to act as if their faith and values do not matter, in *The Culture of Disbelief: How American Law and Politics Trivialize Religious Devotion* (New York: Basic Books, 1993).

58. See Beverly Flanigan, "Forgivers and the Unforgivable," in *Exploring Forgiveness*, ed. Robert D. Enright and Joanna North (Madison: University of Wisconsin Press, 1998), pp. 100-101. She cites the work of Michelle Killough Nelson (1992), who considers three types of forgiveness: detached forgiveness — a reduction in negative effect toward the offender but no restoration of the relationship; limited forgiveness — a reduction in negative effect toward the offender and partial restoration of and decreased emotional investment in the relationship; and complete forgiveness — total cessation of negative effect toward the offender and full restoration and growth of the relationship.

59. M. Scott Peck, *The Different Drum: Community Making and Peace* (New York: Simon & Schuster, 1987), see chap. 5.

In considering the role of churches, other faith communities, and voluntary societies in fostering reconciliation, it might be noted that the principle of foundation for churches lies in forgiveness. Over the last millennium the church has been defined primarily in terms of Matthew 16:16-19, with its language of stability (rock), defensiveness (gates of hell shall not prevail), and exercise of power (control of the keys; binding and loosing). In the new millennium, a gospel of forgiveness could envision new patterns of church and community that might open the way through the division of Orthodoxy and Catholicism, heal the internal split in the Latin Church between Protestants and Roman Catholics, and find the means to move beyond the institutional alienation subsequent to the Enlightenment. While the formal principle of the church's foundation might be grounded in either the dominical command of Jesus or Petrine confession (Matt. 16:18-19), the material principle must certainly be our willingness to extend and work for forgiveness as an expression of theological literacy (John 20:23).[60] To participate in this way in the humanity of one another is to overcome alienation.

> If you forgive anyone his sins, they are forgiven;
> if you do not forgive them, they are not forgiven.

---

60. In assessing the historical concerns and ethico-psychological principles of classic liberal theology as inherited from the Enlightenment through the theology of Albrecht Ritschl, and that of the suprahistorical concerns of Karl Barth, Paul Lehmann concludes that Protestantism, and in a certain way the Christian movement generally, will prosper to the extent it is able to learn from the dialectic provided by these two theologians in the reaffirmation of the Christian doctrine of forgiveness. See Lehmann, p. 195.

CHAPTER SIX

Where Catholicism Has Been, and Where It Is Going

RAYMOND G. HELMICK, S.J.

Before the 1960s brought the Second Vatican Council, people commonly thought of the Catholic Church as an unchanging monolith, whether they were looking from inside or outside. Catholics themselves had an impression of normality: things were as they were in Catholic life, it seemed, because they had always been so, and that would not change.

The years since the council have changed that outlook. Some older Catholics, used to the old ways, think the church has had a shipwreck. More of us are rather relieved to see the various changes and read them as progress. These divergent perceptions have generated, especially within the American Catholic community, angry rejections of one another as opposing factions, each supported by elements in the American and Roman hierarchy.[1]

But when we look for the table of contents of these changes, it hardly compares with the profound shifts that have occurred in Christian life and perception in the more distant past. That makes it worth our while to compare this new horizon of the postconciliar period with some of the earlier great watersheds.

For people experienced in the preconciliar church, as also for those among a new generation whose first concern is for stability, the most obvious transformation is that the Mass is now said in English or other vernacular lan-

---

1. In this regard, see the Common Ground program initiated by Joseph Cardinal Bernardin, then archbishop of Chicago, before his death in 1998.

This article is a revision of an occasional paper titled "Changeable/Unchangeable in Catholic Experience: A Longer Look," written for my course on sacraments and ministry in the Theology Department of Boston College, 1996.

guages. This is an enormous change for those whose understanding of sacred mystery was attached primarily to the remoteness of Latin; a change at which they find themselves seriously disoriented. Traditionalist dissident groups look for a return to Latin, the most aggrieved among them demanding a full restoration of the accustomed liturgical forms established in 1571 by the *Missale Romanum* of Pope Pius V. Even schismatic movements have grown up in the cause of such a reversal of course.

Clergy, once expected to be formidable and authoritarian, have in many cases become more approachable. For most of us, that counts on the positive side. On the more alarming side, large numbers have left the priesthood and the religious life. The reasons for this are little understood, and there even seems to be some deliberate hiding from inquiry into the reasons for it, as if that might produce some unwanted challenge to church discipline.

Church attendance has dropped significantly. Moreover, for many in the younger generation, who did not know the preconciliar church, none of these issues has much urgency. Deference to bishops and clergy, who have in some highly publicized cases disgraced themselves, is notably curtailed. Particularly in moral matters, people take church teaching far more critically than was the practice thirty years ago.

Looked at more generously, the church seems more welcoming and forgiving than previously. Ecumenical interest in other Christians, in their thinking and the prospect of some eventual reconciliation with them, is rather new to Catholic experience. Respectful interest in other religions, Judaism especially, but with some glimmerings of courtesy toward Islam and even further, gives an aura of openness to the church that it did not have before.

Yet even these are negative signs for some people, for whom the church stands in the role of bastion against a world gone sour with self-indulgence and the decay of standards. Many of these, the saddest cases of all, want their Christian faith to function, altogether unfittingly, as an instrument of their anger at all the world.

All these are merely surface manifestations. They deal only with the ways the church has moved off the very rigid Counter-Reformation patterns that were established in the sixteenth century through the Council of Trent and tightened up still more by Vatican Council I of 1869-70. That is in fact the image of the Catholic Church that occupied people's minds up to the time of Vatican Council II. It gives no way of assessing the far more sweeping changes, structural and conceptual, that the church has experienced in the longer reach of her history.

But in fact, these superficial things indicate something more important. The new sense of fluidity that presently marks Catholics' experience relates to the fact that a highly institutionalized life-form shifted. With that, an abyss opened under the certainty people had that their institution carried all the answers within itself. Doubtless that means that the church had become far too structured and fossilized. That was the sense of Pope John XXIII when, in 1959, he announced the convening of the council. He spoke of opening up the windows of the church, and clearly felt that the institution itself needed this, even for its own survival.

The winds have been strong since. That the Catholic public and even their leadership have become so divided leaves the church somewhat adrift for the moment in the fulfillment of its mission.

This paper will consequently try, by a few rapid and rather impressionistic excursions through the whole two millennia of Christian history, to relate that present sense of mutability and provisionality in the Catholic world to a fuller sense of the Christian experience. Some transitions from earlier in that history affected the church far more significantly, for good or ill, and may well give us essential indications about the direction things will likely go in the future. I find myself rather resistant to sharing the excitement about the new millennium, conscious that if we date things from the birth of Jesus the millennium already passed some years ago. But the millennium can serve as a marker as we try to assess how faithful we have been to the gospel message and make our plans, so far as it is in our power, to better do the things that are constitutive of church.

The Church's Sense of Itself and Its Mission

For the early Christian community of the first centuries, what we would call a *sacrament* (the effective sign — i.e., a sign that actually brings about what it signifies — of God's presence and action in the world), was *their community of faith itself and its life.*

Prior even to this, *the primary sign of God's presence and action in human life and history* ("sacrament" in our language, though they did not use that word) *was Christ himself,* the Word become flesh, Son of God incarnate. The Christian community was the sign of God's presence and action in the world because its life of faith showed, to all the rest of the world that did not share it, that the kingdom of God was already present among them. This meant that every aspect of the Christians' life, individually and corporately, was a sign in this sense. Faith in God's presence and action permeated all they did. It was their vocation to manifest it in everything. The Pauline Epistles expressed this in the image of the church as the body of Christ.

112

They had, of course, particular moments and practices in their lives that specially manifested God's presence and action among them, primarily the Eucharist, the sharing of Christ's body and blood as food and drink that they habitually practiced whenever they met together as an assembly. But this was not thought of in terms of its being separate from the rest of the actions of their life, but rather as a sign of what the rest of their life actually meant.

Above all, they did not think of themselves as having periods of time that were irrelevant to their life as witnesses of faith, or contrary to it. They were a holy people, "the saints," always witnesses to this presence and action of God in the world. Their attitude can be summed up as one of *sacramentality* (i.e., a sense that their life was "sacrament," even though the term "sacrament" is itself a later coinage).[2]

As time went on, this understanding of the whole of life as witness of faith faded. Being a member of the Christian community was no longer a constant risk of life itself and counter to the culture of the society the Christians lived in, but was instead an easy way of being a member of the general culture and of getting ahead in the world. Other things then seemed equally or more important, and the religious or faith-charged moments of life were understood as being something different from the rest. "Going to church" took the place of "being church" (faith community, living its witness in all things). Hence the particular moments or rituals of that part of life that was set apart as "in church" came to be explained and understood as "sacraments," ritual procedures that were the signs, as distinct from other elements of people's lives, of God's presence and action in the world.

This was a gradual process, but sometime in the Middle Ages (say, quite arbitrarily, by A.D. 1000) the concept of *sacramental rite*, an isolated moment in the person's or community's life that carried the burden of religious expression, took the place of that earlier sense of the sacramentality of the whole of the church's life of faith. The rest of life was about other things, and religion was now about these ritual actions that took place in church. The familiar definitions of sacraments, their matter and form, etc., accommodated themselves to this outlook. These particular actions were sacraments; those others were not.

That meant a practical secularization of most of life, a far vaster change in

---

2. For this expression and the discussion of the progression over a long range of the church's history, from sacramentality to ritualism, and more recently an effort to recover the outlook of sacramentality, I am indebted to Raymond Vaillancourt, *Toward a Renewal of Sacramental Theology* (Collegeville, Minn.: Liturgical Press, 1979), pp. 11-27; this work is a translation by Matthew J. O'Connell of *Vers un renouveau de la théologie sacramentaire*. My attention was brought to this book by Patricia Smith, R.S.M., *Teaching Sacraments* (Wilmington, Del.: Michael Glazier, 1987), pp. 17-35.

Christian consciousness than any of the things we have seen change more recently. But since it happened so gradually, it was hardly noticed. There remained a residual sense that religious faith ought, somehow, to occupy more of a person's life than this, and various stratagems were tried to give it that importance in some alternative way. I have always had a suspicion that this is part of the reason for the strong development of hierarchical ranking in the Christian community, the substitution of submission to authority for the pervasiveness of faith. But we will see that more sharply in another context a bit further on.

It is only in quite recent times, in the context of Vatican Council II (1962-65), that this enormous earlier transformation has been recognized as such. Some conscious effort (far from complete!) has been made to recover the early church's sense of itself as sign to the rest of the world, in everything that the faith community is and does, of the presence and action of God in human life and history. We may tend nowadays to spend less of our lives thinking deliberately of faith and religion than many other generations have done, but we can yet let our faith conviction permeate our lives, individual and corporate, in such a way that they express the sense of *the church as sacramental sign.*

As one way of summarizing, then, this long-range view of the church's history, we may divide it into three periods:

1. a period of *sacramentality,* the sense of the entire life of the Christian faith community as essentially sign of God's presence and action in the world, to which it was countercultural;
2. a period of the *sacramental rite,* replacing that earlier sense of sacramentality of the whole of life, from some point in the Middle Ages; and
3. a new period, recently initiated, of an attempted return to sources, in which we find a renewed quest for a sense of *the church as sacramental sign.*

The Church's Sense of Its Role in the World

If we read our way into the dialogue that today begins to take place between Christians and Muslims, we soon hear about one great supposed difference: that for Christians church and state are separate, while for Muslims religious and civil society are one. I have never believed that this dichotomy has been as clear or as absolute as that observation indicates, but it is true that in its beginnings the Islamic faith community, gathered about the Prophet Muhammad in Medina and then in Mecca, did simultaneously govern civil society. The Christian community, in contrast, was, for its first three centuries, an outsider group, barely if at all tolerated by the Roman imperial state, alien and marginalized to its culture.

For as long as (and to the extent that) this was true, the Christian community had neither power in nor responsibility for the state. The Christians were not all, as they are sometimes presented, the poor and enslaved, fringe citizens in Roman society. Prominent people, even some members of the senatorial class and imperial family, came into it from early on. But it was not until the opening years of the fourth century that the weight of the Christian community was such that the power class of the empire felt they had need of it.

Diocletian (emperor from A.D. 284, retired 305, died 313) was the last who believed he could get rid of the Christians by a renewal of the sporadic persecution that had been waged against them by authority. He tried harder, massacring more Christians, in the early 300s, than any of his predecessors, having to proceed often against his own trusted officers. He rather proved that it was a losing tactic. He had also tried to rationalize the administration of the vast territory of the empire by dividing it into eastern and western spheres, he ruling from the East and appointing a secondary emperor of the West to rule from Rome, each of them with a subordinate who was titled "Caesar."

At Diocletian's retirement, this administrative division resulted in rivalry among these four officers and eventually war for the succession. Constantine, Trier-born son of the Caesar Constantius Chlorus, who had ruled in northwestern Europe, the eventual winner, was first proclaimed Caesar by the legions in Britain in 306. He established his power in the Province of Gaul in 307, in Germany in 310, crossing the Alps into Italy in 312, and in 313 defeating his Western rival, Maxentius, at the battle of the Milvian Bridge outside Rome.[3]

According to legend, Constantine had a vision, seeing in the sun, as he first crossed the Alps, a luminous cross with the words *"In hoc signo vinces"* (in this sign you will conquer), and consequently took the Christian cross as the standard of his legions, subsequently professing himself a Christian.

It didn't work quite like that. But having defeated Maxentius, Constantine issued, in 313, the Edict of Milan, granting equal rights to Christianity and all other religions in the empire, much to the outrage of the emperor of the East, Licinius, who renewed the persecution of Christians in his region. It took ten more years of war before Constantine defeated Licinius, had him strangled in 323, and set up his new capital, as ruler of the whole empire, far in the East at Constantinople, which he caused to be built, beginning in 325, on the site of the ancient city of Byzantium. Like Diocletian before him, Constantine divided the

---

3. A helpful treatment of the whole context can be found in Timothy David Barnes, *The New Empire of Diocletian and Constantine* (Cambridge: Harvard University Press, 1982).

empire administratively, leaving weak subordinates to govern in the West, the prelude to the eventual collapse of the western part of the empire before the assault of the barbarian invaders.

By the time Constantine had consolidated his hold on the whole empire, the general religious toleration announced by the Edict of Milan had receded to the point that the old polytheistic tradition got as little tolerance as Constantine could manage to give it, and Christianity was to be the official religion of the state. The Christianity of the empire, however, was to be at the service of the state, a pillar of public order and support for the emperor, who did not himself take the trouble to be baptized until on his deathbed in 337. His new capital, the "new Rome," got a patriarch of its own, and while Constantine built sumptuous basilicas in Rome at the tombs of the apostles Peter and Paul (the Church of Byzantium/Constantinople claimed foundation by the apostle Andrew), Constantine never paid any special regard to a bishop of Rome. In 325, the same year he began building Constantinople, he convened all the bishops who could conveniently be assembled (i.e., mostly those from the eastern parts of the empire) to his summer palace at Nicaea for what became known as the First Ecumenical Council. The emperor presided, not in a church but in the audience hall of his palace, and had no hesitation about telling the bishops what they should decide.[4]

All this made a tremendous difference in what it meant to be a Christian. Where before it had been risk, something one undertook only out of deep conviction and that involved everything in one's life, now it was the smart thing to do, one of the conditions of worldly advancement. The emperor needed the bishops and the community they could vouch for. The bishops understood that they had attained their position of privilege for reasons other than the advancement of Christian faith, but chose nonetheless to give unqualified adulation to the emperor and treat him and his intervention on their behalf as the direct act of God, while giving him the assent and moral support he sought from them. It was politic.

We can describe this as the Constantinian order in the church. Church and state were to be two parallel bodies, reflective of one another: the state commanding the obedience of the subjects, the church supporting its demands and providing the moral context within which the state would act. The administrative structures of the Roman state, such as dioceses and vicariates, were ex-

---

4. The obsequious treatment of Constantine by the bishops of his time is clearly shown in *The Ecclesiastical History* by his contemporary and servant, Eusebius, bishop of Caesarea, of which the most current translation is by C. F. Cruse, new updated ed. (Peabody, Mass.: Hendrickson, 1998).

actly duplicated in the church, and remain even now. The *role* of the church was to be the *paradigm to the state.* For more than a thousand years this *paradigmatic role of the church,* the Constantinian pattern, remained the norm, and in some odd places we find vestiges of it even today. The Anglican Church, for instance, still has its bishops appointed by royal decree, actually the choice of the prime minister. Acts of state, particularly the ceremonial ones like the coronation of monarchs or royal weddings and funerals, are done under its aegis, even though its actual power in civil matters is as much reduced to figurehead as that of the monarchy itself.

Eventually Constantine himself overstepped his bounds, and in his assumption that he was entitled to dictate to the bishops became sponsor of the Arian heresy (denial of the divinity of Christ). It was the church in the West, in regions where the emperor's influence was weaker, that mounted the principal resistance to this heterodox teaching, to the outrage of Constantine and his successors. Bishops more directly under imperial control tended to conform, but as the Western Church and its papal leadership took up the slack of providing order and stability in the city of Rome and in Italy through the time of barbarian incursions, the rivalry of emperor and pope for control each of the other — caesaropapism and papalo-caesarism — was added to the normative condition of things. This had eventually, after much tragic conflict, its political advantage for Western culture, as the ability of the community to play off one authority against the other taught us all to keep both authorities accountable to the rest of us.[5]

The conflicts of church and empire, church and state, brought about an incidental change of empires, as papal interventions established the Carolingian empire and later the Holy Roman Empire of the German nation. Emperors made and broke popes in the tenth and eleventh centuries, but the popes demonstrated, in the twelfth and thirteenth centuries, their ability to depose or otherwise control emperors and kings.[6] And then, with the Holy Ro-

5. The Eastern Church of course had a different experience. Church and empire clashed at times but habitually resolved their quarrels. Church tended eventually to identify with ethnicity, and expected that emperors or their successor authorities in the state would, among other things, have decisive influence on the choice of bishops. This, under the name of Lay Investiture, was the very crux of the conflict between popes and emperors in the West.

6. The best commentary on the growth of papal power and its contests with medieval empire continues to be that of Walter Ullmann (1910-83), among his works *The Carolingian Renaissance and the Idea of Kingship* (London: Methuen, 1969); *The Growth of Papal Government in the Middle Ages: A Study in the Ideological Relation of Clerical to Lay Power* (London: Methuen, 1955; 2nd ed., 1962); *Law and Jurisdiction in the Middle Ages* (London: Variorum Reprints, 1988); and *Medieval Papalism: The Political Theories of Medieval Canonists* (London: Methuen, 1945).

man Empire reduced to a wreck of itself, fortunes were reversed. The kings of France and, to a lesser extent, of England were able to bring the church and the popes to heel. The ability of the church to exercise powers parallel to and paradigmatic of the state was made more and more a shadow of what had once been until, in the era of Napoleon, it was evident that the paradigmatic role of the church was at an end.

However much the Constantinian order may have compromised the very faith of the church throughout its long course, the bishops and other authorities who had grown so used to it saw its demise as a sad event: the deprivation of their accustomed institutional position. They instituted a rearguard action to preserve as much of the old order as they could. If the church could no longer parallel all the powers of the state, they would preserve and institutionalize those they could, most especially their control of *marriage,* of *education,* and of *the caring services of society* (hospitals, charity, etc.). As a substitute for the no longer feasible paradigmatic role, we can describe this as a *PRAGMATIC ROLE OF THE CHURCH.*

It was heavily contested by the power of the state, and always exercised with regret for the paradigmatic role that had been lost; both church and state authorities saw it as second best. We can see it in what Germans call *Kulturpolitik,* the administration of these cultural areas of family, school, and welfare, with church and state competing for control. Especially the nineteenth-century *Kulturkampf* was a concerted effort of the Bismarckian state to wrest control of these functions from the churches, particularly from the Catholic Church.[7] We can see it as well in Nazi campaigns against the churches, in the repressive antichurch activities of the Communist states, and even in a good deal of current American policy of creating obstacles to church control over schools or hospitals.

What substitute remains to us if these two long-traditional models for the church's role in society, paradigmatic and pragmatic, have both so failed? If, again, we look to the original experience of Christian community in the early centuries, we will not find it useful or historically true to pretend we live in a time other than our own, when Christians were without a recognized role or responsibility in society. But we can usefully look to the way in which their faith convictions as such, the living out of their faith, rather than institutionalized power, determined the role of Christian community in society.

If our emphasis as church were consistently on the building up of active

---

7. For a recent treatment, see Ronald J. Ross, *The Failure of Bismarck's Kulturkampf: Catholicism and State Power in Imperial Germany, 1871-1887* (Washington, D.C.: Catholic University of America Press, 1998).

faith commitment, i.e., basically catechetical, we could expect the presence of a Christian community to influence, in organic and pervasive ways, the free corporate decisions of the society. A useful descriptive term for such a manner of church activity in society's concern is the mathematical figure of the parabola, the plane curve generated by a point moving so that its distance from a fixed point is equal to its distance from a fixed line, the curve widening out between parallel lines without ever touching them. Thus our *third* model of the church's activity in society is the *PARABOLIC ROLE OF THE CHURCH*.[8]

There is no way to claim that such a procedure is accomplished fact in the church of our own time, only a rather far-out aspiration. That there is a hankering still for the full Constantinian paradigmatic model can be seen in a couple of extraordinarily instructive episodes of recent history.

Since the publication in the 1960s of Rolf Hochhuth's play, *Der Stellvertreter* ("The Deputy," or "The Vicar [of Christ]"), the complaint has frequently been made that Pope Pius XII, during World War II, failed to act decisively enough against the Nazi holocaust of the Jews. Much has been said and written for and against this charge. We can properly ask: Where were the Catholics of Germany that they needed to be ordered by the pope to resist the Holocaust? Was their faith not internalized enough to lead them to this without a papal order?

During the Vietnam War, Catholics had a large role in the antiwar movement in the United States, and many of them complained that the U.S. Catholic bishops did not plainly condemn the war as unjust and prohibit participation in it or payment of taxes that would be spent in prosecuting it. Had the bishops done that, quite probably they might have ended the war. Simultaneously they would have brought to ruin the democratic structure of the United States with its separation of church and state. Given the dire consequences of any such action, we can again ask: Where were the consciences of U.S. Catholics? Could they not reject an unjust war without the bishops commanding them to do so?[9]

---

8. These terms for the roles of church in society — "paradigmatic" for the Constantinian model, "pragmatic" for the familiar fallback position, "parabolic" for the more faithful model recommended here — are not my own, but come from a teacher, Argentinian Methodist professor José Míguez Bonino, whom I felt privileged to hear when I was in graduate studies at Union Theological Seminary in the late 1960s. Míguez Bonino uses them extensively in his many works, but I have reflected on them over so many years as to have made my own use of them.

9. Another fascinating instance of the enduring Constantinian concept of church-state interdependence is chronicled in David Steele's lucid account of the church role in the 1989-90 transition in East Germany: "At the Front Lines of the Revolution: East Germany's Churches Give Sanctuary and Succor to the Purveyors of Change," in *Religion, the Missing Dimension of Statecraft*, ed. Douglas Johnston and Cynthia Sampson (Oxford: Oxford University Press, 1994),

At issue in both these instances, of course, is the question of instrumental use of the structures of church. Even where Christian conscience has immediate responsibility to act, as in these cases, we need to question the use of the institution as instrument of power.

We have seen, then, three models of the church's sense of its role in the world, once again reflecting an enormous range of change in the church's self-understanding over the course of its history:

1. the *paradigmatic* role of the long Constantinian era;
2. the *pragmatic* role that sought to supply for the failure of the Constantinian system; and
3. the *parabolic* role, based on early church experience and now simply a hope.

The Church's Way of Looking at Its Own Members

We have had to hear a great deal in recent years, simply because the thought is new to us, that "the church" is the entire community of faith, with all its members, not merely the clergy or hierarchy. It is anomalous that this should be a new idea to us, since this is one of the most fundamental teachings of the New Testament, but we continue to need reminding of it. Our press and media have generally not caught on to this yet, except occasionally. When reporters want to know "What has the church to say about . . ." whatever issue, they still understand it to mean what the bishops have to say on it, or what is in a papal document. It seldom occurs to them yet to ask, in any other form, what is the belief of the church community on the subject (unless, of course, they are anxious to set up a conflict between official teaching and lay response), or what "the faith" accepted (on principle) by the community has to teach about it.

---

pp. 199-252. The Evangelische Kirche in Germany had already experienced Nazi efforts to control it as a state church and established the Confessing Church as an antidote. Faced with Communist determination to make the church an instrument for its own purposes, the German Protestants crafted a repertory of fine distinctions ranging from the "church *within* socialism" to a "church *for* socialism," to a concept of church as "guardian office" or voice of conscience against abuse of power by the state, to a "church for others" that would focus on support for disenfranchised individuals, and a "critical solidarity" of church with state. This latter was still unacceptable to the state, because it seemed to imply that socialism could somehow be improved. (See p. 123, with nn. 24 and 25, pp. 145-46.) Fascinating, too, in this regard is Steele's concluding discussion of the relation of the church, as a spiritual force and institutional structure, both to the East German state authority and to the largely unchurched public that demanded a revolutionary change of regime (pp. 139-43).

It is the history of this inclination to think of "the church" as meaning only or primarily its hierarchical leadership that we will examine in this last excursion through the full two-millennia experience of the Christian community.

The First Eight Centuries

This is a long period to bite off, and we have to treat it as one of development of new forms rather than as of one piece. But in the one respect that will most interest us, there was a consistency through this whole span of time: the Christian community, centered then on the Mediterranean countries, thought of itself as good people, the focus of God's action in the world, "the saints," happy to be members of the community.

This community, under the pressure of having to resist the doctrinal divisiveness of early heresies, had acquired its hierarchical order: the local church of each city organized under the monarchical government of its bishop. And it had cultivated unity of faith and communion among its bishops and their local churches by emphasizing links of the local communities with "apostolic sees" ("sees" in the sense of seats, or offices, of authority), those that could claim foundation by an apostle: Jerusalem, from which the whole mission of the apostles had gone forth; Antioch, associated with the mission of Saint Peter; Alexandria, associated (strictly mythically) with Saint Mark; and Rome, missionized by both Saint Peter and Saint Paul. These were the seats of patriarchs. And when it seemed important to make Constantinople a patriarchal see because of Constantine's establishment of the city as his capital (the "new Rome"), the story was told of the foundation of a Christian community in ancient Byzantium by Saint Andrew, brother of Saint Peter and therefore having great seniority among the apostles, making it, too, an apostolic see.

This Mediterranean church had its shocks: notably the barbarian conquest of the western part of the Roman Empire, both on the northern and the southern shores of the Mediterranean; the poor performance, in terms of witnessing to Christian faith, of the Eastern Empire, with its unvarnished authoritarianism, and a broad alienation of important segments of its population that exhibited itself partly in doctrinal divisions and heresies; and finally the loss, mainly because of disillusion with Christian performance, of the Middle Eastern and North African regions of the Christian world and, for many centuries, large parts of Spain to the new faith of Islam. But by and large the conviction remained that the Christian community of faith was a world of salvation to which it was good to belong, and in which all had a role.

This sense of the basically holy character of the community ran into a far more fundamental disruption with the conversion of the "barbarian" peoples of western Europe north of the Alps. I've put an arbitrary date on this of the eighth century. In fact, the process was necessarily more gradual than that.

The Eighth to Sixteenth Centuries: Christianity Crosses the Alps

The northern "barbarians" were converted to Christianity by a different process than the Mediterranean peoples: not the evangelization from within the community that had characterized the early church, but instead the conversion of whole peoples from the top down, by decision of their kings.

There had been some of this already, of course, as the Roman imperial system made Christianity its official religion and put anyone who didn't conform at a civil disadvantage in the empire. But those who had joined the church earlier and more clearly out of conviction had set the basic tone of Mediterranean Christianity. There had been Christianity north of the Alps earlier too, of course, especially in the Roman Province of Gaul (France and much of Belgium), where the early bishops had been active in opposing the Arian inclinations of the emperors directly after Constantine. Some of the earlier "barbarians" (as we call the horse-borne nomadic invading tribes pouring in from the Eurasian steppes and beyond), like the Lombards and Goths, had become Christian as well, feeling themselves successors to Roman rule, and had brought a wave of Arianism into Italy that was ended only with a short-lived Byzantine reconquest of Italy in the sixth century, when the Eastern Empire was again safely Orthodox. The rapid collapse of that renewed Byzantine hold had left a new instability in the city of Rome and increasingly in more of Italy. And it was because of this that the popes had taken responsibility for providing order in civil society, and the papal court in Rome had become royal — even imperial — in its trappings.

It was this picture of Christianity that the new "barbarian" powers of northern Europe encountered when their ambassadors came to Rome, and it was against this background that the Frankish king Clovis decided (on his wife Clotilda's urging) to become Christian himself and mandate the baptism of all his subjects. A similar pattern followed with the conversion of other Germanic and barbarian tribes. The decision was the king's, and a people that had accepted baptism on his fiat had to be told afterwards what that was all about.[10]

---

10. An excellent discussion of this period is given in James C. Russell, *The Germanization of Early Medieval Christianity: A Sociohistorical Approach to Religious Transformation* (Oxford: Oxford University Press, 1994). Russell approaches this from the perspective of Germanic influence on the received Christian faith, whereas this present paper looks at the same phenomena

For these kings and their ambassadors, Rome with its papal court was the model not only of Christianity but also of culture and civilization. The way to arrange the etiquette of their own courts was in imitation of the papal court. Diplomatic receptions at the court of the pope were of course in church, and the great public occasions were celebrations of the liturgy of the Mass with all the trappings of a court. Ambassadorial reports contained every detail they could glean of the procedures of these occasions, and our liturgy is marked by it to this day.

Clothing, for instance. Our Mass vestments for the priest are, today, the alb (a long white tunic, the *vestimentum album* which was the staple of late Roman formal dress), a stole (the one element that was from the start an insignia of priestly rank), and a chasuble, the large outer garment in the liturgical color of the day.

This latter was the formal attire (though the liturgical colors are a much later invention) of a gentleman from the fourth century on, the replacement of what had been the toga for the ancient Romans. The Roman name for it was *casual*, literally "little house." In its original form, it was a large, full-length semicircle of material. It could either be set on the shoulders, hanging open in front (in this form it is the "cope" which we may still occasionally see in church) or sewn down the front (with an opening for the head), in which case it formed a large cloth cone. To wear it you had to pull the sides up on your arms so that, like the ancient toga, it formed horizontal folds across the body.[11]

The priest, or the pope, was not the only person so attired. Instead, this was the formal dress of every gentleman present at this Mass, which was, effectively, a diplomatic reception at the papal court. We could describe it as a sixth-century tuxedo. But when it was imitated in northern Europe for Mass at the courts of the Germanic and Frankish kings, it became the priest's vestments, with a supposition that there must be something holy about such garments. With the modifications in its shape that have come with time, it remains so.

Imitation of what the ambassadors saw, and heard, at Rome was so much the standard of good usage that other features were all avidly imitated. Incense, for instance, known as a symbol of prayer in some texts of the Hebrew Scriptures, was carried before the pope in procession, as it was before other high-

---

from the other side: the transformation wrought in the Germanic societies and culture by the Christian missionary effort.

11. This bell-shaped garment, *paenula* in secular usage but called *planeta* in the early liturgical citations, had practically replaced the older toga in late imperial times. A good account is in Fr. Josef Jungmann, S.J., *The Mass of the Roman Rite: Its Origins and Development*, trans. Francis A. Brunner, C.SS.R., 2 vols. (Benzinger, 1950; replica ed., Dublin: Four Courts Press, 1986; German original *Missarum Sollemnia*, rev. ed. of 1949, Vienna: Herder Verlag), 1:276-77.

ranking Roman officials, to protect them from the smell of the lower-class multitudes. (The ancient Roman system had been insistent on baths for everyone, with the aqueduct an essential feature of all Roman infrastructure and the public baths the main center of entertainment and social life for the multitudes. But the system had broken down, the aqueducts didn't work anymore, and Roman high society had not gotten used to the smell of poor people.) In the northern kingdoms, the incense was imitated from Rome, but with the supposition that it was a strictly ritual usage. So the altar, the crucifix, the book of the Gospels, and all the paraphernalia of the ceremony had to be incensed.

Most important of all, the language of liturgy had to be the language of the Roman court. Latin, in fact, became the international learned language of scholarship and record. In liturgy it was seen as the right language because it was used for the Mass in Rome, where, of course, it was the vernacular. At an earlier stage the vernacular language of good society in Rome had been Greek, but by about the fifth century it had become Latin. Christian Scripture and teaching and liturgy had all gone into the vernacular Greek of the empire instead of remaining in Aramaic or Hebrew, as it had been at the start. The Eastern (Orthodox) Church has always remained faithful to the tradition that liturgy should be in the language people understand — Greek, Arabic, Russian, whatever. But in the West Latin became established because the right way was the way it was done in Rome, at the court of the pope.

What is important about all this is what it reveals of suppositions about the people for whom liturgy was celebrated this way in the northern countries. It was not regarded as necessary that they understand, merely that they be impressed.

A new faith was taught them, in many cases even imposed upon them. The suppositions of Mediterranean Christianity, that the community of faith was made up of beloved, redeemed people of God, saints (however weak), were not the suppositions taught north of the Alps. Instead people were told that they were barbarians, unfit, unworthy to receive the gifts of faith and grace put before them, that they were full of evil inclinations and actions, devil's fodder, deserving of damnation. What was required of them was repentance, contrition, acceptance of their lowly state, recognition of their unworthiness.

Sin and repentance, of course, were familiar themes that had been understood in the happier "communion of saints" from the beginning of Christianity, but this was different. This was a radical supposition of the unworthiness of the congregation: a culture of guilt.

It manifested itself in striking ways. Reception of Communion became a fearful thing, incurring danger of condemnation for eating and drinking the body and blood of Christ unworthily. Consequently Communion became the exceptional thing, something people did only once a year, and that only because they were commanded that they must make their "Easter Communion" that once. Confession of sins was a precondition for this annual approach to the Sacrament. It seemed the practical assumption that it was the normal condition of people to be in mortal sin, and that they could get out of it only briefly, just long enough to receive their Easter Communion before falling again.

The prayer formulas of the Mass began to fill up with what the liturgical historians call "apologies." These were confessions of sin, admission of unworthiness, prayer to avoid condemnation for taking part in the sacred ritual. They were particularly elaborate and lengthy around the offertory part of the Mass, but were used by the celebrating priest and all other participants in the ritual at all points of the Mass: before reading from the Scripture or the Gospel, before blessing anything, most especially before Communion (which, for the most part, only the priest himself would receive). The penitential rite at the beginning of the present-day Mass is a remnant of these "apologies."[12] They were once so frequent throughout the Mass that the priest would recite them at the same time someone else would be reading some other text.

For people so radically unworthy, the priority in life was obedience to their betters, to those less unworthy than themselves. Reverence for authority, unquestioning submission became the norm. The qualifications for hierarchical office tied easily into the breeding requirements for ruling-class status. To be made bishop of Fulda, for instance, a candidate had to show fourteen "quarterings," i.e., the coats of arms, to prove patent of nobility for fourteen generations. Few others than clergy attained literacy or were trained in such disciplines as the law, and consequently civil administration was dependent on clerics to carry out essential tasks. This led to constant power struggles between civil and ecclesiastical authority, with all its potential both for aggrandizement and corruption. The authority claims of clergy escalated constantly, building always on the concept of the unworthiness of those they shepherded.

Such an acceptance of ignorance in the general population, with an assumption that the symbolic importance and intrinsic holiness of words, gestures, clothing, or practices need not be understood, meant, over an extended period of time, an invitation to superstition and mystification. That anyone should even seek understanding of the actions and rites of the church came to seem presumptuous, the sign of a weakness of faith. A gulf opened between those who were the custodians of the mysteries and those who were to be their passive recipients.

---

12. These caught the special attention of Jungmann, 1:78-80, where he analyzes the series of these formulas.

We may speak of all these features of medieval religion as particular to regions north of the Alps. But the example itself was infectious. The same demeaning self-concept of the Christian community slipped back south to the Mediterranean regions and became characteristic for the generality of the Western Church community.

Throughout this period, we can see people striving to overcome the deficiencies of this system through popular religion, which sometimes lived on holdovers of previous pagan beliefs and practices, but often showed extraordinary penetration into a Christian faith whose meaning was so largely withheld from them. If we look at the art of the medieval period, we find images of the saints that witness to the urgency with which these people, with their supposition of their own unworthiness, aspired to the holiness that seemed denied them. In their fear of actual reception of the Eucharist, they invented what amounted to substitute sacraments for themselves: the "spiritual communion" or the cult of (safely) *looking at* the consecrated elements of the Sacrament. Their pilgrimages to places associated with the holy, ordinary people's consciousness of the needs of the poor, the effort to associate themselves and their gifts with the sacramental proceedings that were so remote from them are all efforts to supersede the limits that this kind of religion placed on them.

We can sum up the principal distorting landmarks of this self-understanding of the medieval Christian under three principal headings:

1. the guilt culture,
2. authoritarianism, and
3. mystification.

A heavy price would be paid for all of them.

From the Sixteenth-Century Reformation to the Twentieth-Century Aggiornamento

Cataclysm came in the sixteenth century when, after repeated efforts and demands for reform over several centuries, Western Catholic Christianity found its institutions and practices fundamentally challenged by the Protestant Reformation. The Reformers took aim especially at the mystification elements, which they saw as superstition, and at the authority structures that kept the whole fabric so untouchably in place. They had little sense of the damage and distortion of Christian faith brought about by the guilt culture, and so hardly challenged it at all.

With regard to *mystification,* the Protestant Reformers insisted on vernacular language and removed all the rituals, vestments, gestures, practices that were assumed to be holy without what they considered appropriate understanding. There was much extremism. Music and color were curtailed, to a grim degree for a while, though they eventually found their way back in many Protestant denominations. In some of the churches there was a savage period of iconoclasm, with the destruction of images and cult objects on a massive scale. The drawing away from ritual involved an emphasis on word and text. Bible reading and preaching became the principal vehicles of religious expression. Many things were done to such excess that there had to be a corrective action later, which was delayed in some denominations until the nineteenth or even the twentieth century, but the reaction against mystification and superstition can in general be regarded as the most successful part of the Protestant Reformation.

When it came to battling the *authoritarianism* of the medieval Catholic system, the Reformers were less successful. They struck during an unfortunately authoritarian period, when the pretensions of civil rulers were at an epochal high. The central authority of the papacy was rejected, and in most of the churches that of the bishops also disappeared. Some Reformers took this step very reluctantly, as they appreciated the long tradition of episcopal order in the church. Yet they found too much abuse and corruption associated with it.

As the old authority structures were uprooted, though, two distinct countervailing tendencies emerged. On the one hand, the civil authority of princes claimed rights over the church, which they could assert once there were no bishops or pope to compete with. The position of the Church of England, where the king was recognized as supreme authority over the church, is a conspicuous example. All over Protestant Europe, though, princes and kings claimed the right to determine the faith of their subjects, prescribing rite and creed in total detail, to such an extent that *cujus regio, ejus et religio* (whoever holds the kingship, his is also the religion) became the accepted formula, and a century and a half of endemic religious warfare began. On the other hand, the new ecclesiastical authorities tended to build up structures of loyalty tests that amounted, in many cases, to authoritarianisms more rigid than those they overthrew. The net result was, at least in too many cases, the substitution of a new authoritarianism for the old.

In the eyes of the Catholics of the time, of course, what the Reformers had done (in their rejection of what they saw as superstition) was to lose access to the sacraments of the church. Their dismissal of episcopal order was seen as a break with the apostolic succession which guaranteed legitimacy in the ministry. In their turning from the magisterial authority of bishops and the pope to the Scriptures, they were felt to have lost the essential key to the proper understanding of Christian faith. Feeling was so intense over these issues that, down to very recent times, Catholics and Protestants assumed bad faith in one another's positions on all these matters. Not until we had experienced the worst of the twentieth century, the secular tyrannies and the racist and other intolerances that could be resisted only if all Christians and others of basic decency and goodwill banded together, did we begin to discover one another as resources and to suspect that the others could in fact be acting in good faith.

But it was in the matter of the *guilt culture* that the sixteenth-century Reformation fell furthest short of its opportunities. A terrifying God of wrath underlay much of their teaching. This infected their efforts to impose discipline in an unruly time as the traditional order dissolved. The supposition of radical sinfulness and, in some areas of Reformed teaching, of a predestination to doom produced, if anything, a deep intensification of the guilt culture.

The Reformation had only very partial success, then, in meeting the crisis that had engendered it, and in part actually exacerbated it. A Catholic effort at counterreformation, crafted in large part at the Council of Trent (1545-63) and developed over succeeding centuries until it reached its high-water mark at Vatican Council I (1869) and in the early twentieth century, had similarly mixed results. Like the distortions that had torn at the fabric of Christian faith and communion from the earlier periods, these remaining or even aggravated lesions festered in the church and burst into the open after the testing experiences of the world wars and other violence and infidelity of this century. Vatican Council II was a concerted effort to meet head-on the crisis they produced, and has consequently had importance not only for the Catholic world but for all branches of Christianity.

The guilt culture is at the heart of what is questioned among contemporary Christians. At times this is seen as, and sometimes actually is, a rejection of the very concepts of sin and repentance, or of accountability for one's acts, and many traditionalists who sense this react against any such questioning. As the Christian community struggles with this syndrome, recriminations are still the order of the day, within and between denominational traditions. It is perhaps especially in this area that those of us who make an effort at faithfulness to the good news of Christ need to work for responsible reconciliation.

The whole issue is worked out against a renewed background of challenge, often rude challenge, to whatever appears to be authoritarianism in any of the various churches, made more urgent now by the indifferent success of the sixteenth-century Reformation effort in this direction. Here too we run into excess as well as timidity and outright obduracy. We are left the task, before we can expect the church to regain its stability, of studying the roots of order and accountability in the community of faith.

And as at the Reformation, the mystification element has turned out to be the most easily dealt with. Catholic practice did make its effort to crop out superstitions during the Counter-Reformation. It was a timid one compared to that of the Protestant Reformers, largely because of the excesses that had been seen in early stages of the Reformation. The work of Vatican Council II, and the efforts particularly of liturgical reform since then, has provided a very responsible restoration. It has given new access to the basic sacramental expressions of the church's life of faith and the chance of a deepened understanding of them, and has done so without often losing the sense of a revered tradition.

Obscurities (promoted by foreign or obsolete language, unintelligible symbols, or diversionary attention to devotional practices that have little to do with the central symbolism of faith) have largely been corrected with what is probably only a minimal and unavoidable measure of ham-handedness. This has become, by now, the least problematic area of Catholic practice, its worst remaining trouble being routine, or uncommunicative performance.

Protestant liturgical practice, in the meantime, has been going through a very reverent rediscovery of Catholic tradition, pursued with great care not to compromise itself with any return to mystification. As it occurs, Catholic attention has turned to the Scripture. A revised lectionary, used by many Protestant denominations as well as by Catholics, puts a great deal more of the Scripture before congregations than had been the case in the past.[13] The expectation of biblical preaching grows in Catholic congregations, where people have previously thought of the sermon as a peculiarly Protestant invention.

This convergence in the area of religious symbolism and sacramental practice creates new possibilities of recognizing, behind the controversies that have separated the churches in their contentious past, the common faith. This makes the ecumenical effort of our time something exciting. It has to be done without fakery or the compromising of genuine conviction by ambiguous formulas on any side, but with an openness to one another and a confidence that the promises of Christ, the promises that his Spirit would inform the church, are made to us all.

---

13. Among a plentiful selection of other editions, in various languages and translations, cf. *Lectionary for Mass: English Translation Approved by the National Conference of Catholic Bishops and Confirmed by the Apostolic See, Revised Standard Version, Catholic Edition* (Collegeville, Minn.: Liturgical Press, 1970).

Alienation of the Christian Community from Its Institutions

We need one further excursion into history to see the present status of church, whether Catholic or Protestant. This is a more recent phenomenon of the post-Reformation centuries, a disillusionment of Christians with the institutional church, which I attribute to the Wars of Religion in the sixteenth and seventeenth centuries.

A sense of corruption and the necessity of reform had run through all the later Middle Ages. Central authority had successfully rebuffed reform efforts such as the conciliarism of the fourteenth and fifteenth centuries, but had left a bad taste which did much to motivate the Protestant Reformation movement of the sixteenth century. None of that had the impact of the religious wars. They persuaded people that churches, Protestant and Catholic, were fomenters of violence, unfaithful to their own gospel, and not to be trusted. Atheism and agnosticism had always been about in the Christian world, but as marginal, unpopular positions. After the Wars of Religion they became commonplace, and appeared to be the rational conclusions of reasonable persons, liberated from the competing intolerance of the rival churches.

This feeling of a breach of trust in the churches coincided with the advent of what we may call "the modern world," a world outlook convinced that it represented the apogee of progress. Three elements, among the most valuable innovative insights of the period, coalesced to produce that phenomenon.

A turning, in the physical sciences, from the authority of ancient authors to empiricism came first. Copernicus foreshadowed it in the fifteenth century with his theory of a solar-centric universe whose verification could only come from observation. But once Galileo had subjected it to empirical examination in the seventeenth century, a new approach had emerged, pursued by Newton, Kepler, Harvey, and others. It transformed scientific research and produced the exponentially expanding technological revolution that has given the Western world its political power advantage ever since.

The philosophical Enlightenment of the seventeenth and eighteenth centuries provided a second facet of the "modern." All things had their purely rational explanation. This related to the empirical revolution in scientific thinking, but spread more widely through all realms of thought, discrediting any extrarational claim.

And finally, political liberalism set the capstone to modernity. Political action aimed at human betterment, beginning with the "enlightened despots" of the seventeenth and eighteenth centuries and proceeding through the English, American, French, and Russian revolutions. In hindsight we see darker sides to this otherwise humane development, in its authoritarian origins, in the eventual totalitarianism of the twentieth-century ideologies, and in the rapacious laissez-faire of nineteenth-century economic liberalism. But the impetus it gave to the development of representative institutions has been its lasting value.

Coming as they did in the wake of the vast seventeenth-century disillu-sionment of the Christian constituency with its church institutions, these three grand prizes of the modern world appeared to provide the answers to all the questions. What need or place remained for religious faith if scientific research, enlightened thought, and liberal institutions held the key to everything? To many people in the intellectual mainstream, it came to represent only obscu-rantism and superstition.

The liberation theologians of more recent years have classified together all the variety of Protestant and Catholic, liberal and conservative theologies that responded to that situation. They have labeled them "European theolo-gies" and have pointed out their common feature: all of them are fundamen-tally apologetics. What the Latin Americans call "the questioner" of a theology is, for any of them, "How can you believe these things in the modern world?" That question has dominated theology for well over three centuries.

The Latin Americans make the observation that it is an adolescent ques-tion. Either we believe these things or we don't. We ought to know which. The more serious question that determines whether we are genuine in our profession of Christian faith, "the questioner" for a more serious contemporary theology, is whether we live in accordance with that faith. Faith requires living; it is not merely to be professed. The Latin American, living in a situation of deep poverty within a society Catholic at least in its culture, will ask very specifically how we relate to the poor. In another society we will ask whether in fact we live our faith.[14]

Yet something else has happened that radically changes the outlook for faith and for church. The bloody carnage of the twentieth century has con-vinced us at last that the concatenation of science, enlightenment, and liberal-ism has not in fact given us answers to all the questions. The term "post-modernism" has acquired a variety of meanings, but must surely carry this one, that we no longer believe that these three holy things, valuable though they are, will satisfy our needs. Our hearts, it turns out, are restless until they rest in a meaning higher than that.[15]

What I have called "the intellectual mainstream" has become intensely in-terested in all the wisdom traditions, including the major religious faiths. It re-tains as much suspicion as ever of institutional authority in religion, and looks sooner for spirituality than for religious system. But the tide has turned. Faith

---

14. The most obvious scriptural reference is James 1:25–2:26.
15. *Pace* Augustine.

can no longer be dismissed as atavistic or as a throwback to less enlightened times. This shapes the context in which we can imagine, or help to construct, the future of Christianity or Catholicism in the coming century or millennium.

We surely have to be modest enough as we gaze into the crystal ball. It helps to know what sorts of options the past has opened for us, and what remaining traumas our Christian *communio* has still to deal with. To a very considerable extent we will make our own future and need to know clearly which way we want to go.

The Catholic bishops at Vatican Council II worked intently to confront what most of them felt, as did Pope John XXIII, was a creeping paralysis in the church. The presence of observers from the other Christian traditions and other religions helped them break out of the institutional introspection that might otherwise have constricted their vision. It also opened the experience of that council into the other churches and into even more general world consciousness.

Now, several decades on, the blush is off the ecumenical outreach that seemed so promising in the immediate aftermath of the council, and we face internal bickering over the results of that council that could prove damaging to the entire witness of the church. Catholics are not alone in having these internal fractures. Many other Christian churches have to address such questions of the wisdom of their course over these recent years, and overcome an ideological feuding that threatens a great deal of destruction.

The new turning toward the wisdom traditions as resource creates an opening which faith communities, Christian and other, ought not neglect. A rather similar thing happened after World War II, when a widespread renewal of religious faith followed that era of brutality. A decade later, Pope John XXIII had to reckon that this openness to faith was being squandered through the rigidity of church structures, and set about to remedy that. It is the carnage experience of the entire twentieth century, even of the bloody second millennium, that generates this new attention to faith resources, shattering the all-but-exclusive reliance that Western culture has put on its modernism for three centuries and a half.

The guilt responses that have been so heavily built into our Christian culture (and which have gone unchallenged in earlier movements of reform) come under the heaviest fire in our time. So far, the reaction to this culture of guilt has gone mainly in a negative direction, kicking over the traces of restraint in areas of sexuality and civility, and thus bringing the spirit of liberty and emancipation itself into disrepute. It needs careful redirection into the gospel ways of loving care for the other, forgiveness to enemies, a taking of responsibility for the effect of our actions on others.

A great deal of the success or failure of church as a commending of its gospel teachings will hinge on the manner of its internal discipline. The Western Church has much to learn from the East in this regard. Collegial exercise of authority and widespread consultation and reliance on the work of the Spirit in the whole community have marked the experience of the Orthodox churches, during a millennium of separation in which the Western Church, largely under the impetus of political forces, developed increasingly centralized and authoritarian ways.[16]

The Second Vatican Council did seriously address this as a problem, with its teaching on the collegiality of bishops. New practices such as periodic synod meetings of selected groups of bishops in Rome were adopted only rather timidly, and their results were heavily edited by curial bureaucrats before they were published. Many have felt that the long pontificate of Pope John Paul II represented regression from such collegial developments. And yet this same pope, in his encyclical letter *Ut Unum Sint*, on unity in the church, observes that the greatest gift that the Roman Church can give to the ecumenical movement is to reform itself so that it becomes a model of participatory hierarchy and a sacramental sign of unity. Observing how the Petrine primacy has acted as an obstacle to the full unity of the church, he asks the recommendations of all Christians "to find a way of exercising that primacy which, while in no way renouncing what is essential to its mission, is nonetheless open to a new situation."[17]

Above all, if we are to design and live out the future of our church in ways conducive to the fulfillment of its essential mission, we need to recognize and rely on the work of the Spirit, which is always alive in the church. Hearing and being open to the Spirit is a thing that we do "in the church." It is an article of Christian faith, from the earliest confessional formulas that the Holy Spirit is present in the church.

We have all heard a great deal about listening attentively and receptively to the teaching of the hierarchical magisterium. That is distinctly one way the Spirit makes himself heard in the church. His work is broader than that, though, and attentiveness to the work of the Spirit involves sensitive hearing of the faith of the entire community. It is here that we are promised that the Spirit will lead us into all truth.[18]

16. One of the best recent treatments of this subject is by Terence L. Nichols, *That All May Be One: Hierarchy and Participation in the Church* (Collegeville, Minn.: Liturgical Press, Michael Glazier, 1997).

17. *Ut Unum Sint* (Boston: Pauline Books and Media, n.d.), p. 102 n. 95. This is discussed in Nichols, p. 316.

18. John 16:13.

CHAPTER SEVEN

The Theological Is Also Personal: The "Place" of Evangelical Protestant Women in the Church

ALICE MATHEWS

The issue of women's "place" in the Christian church has been around since biblical times. In the Gospels Jesus' affirmation of women and his choice of Mary Magdalene to "go and tell my disciples" of his resurrection set up the dilemma.[1] The remainder of the New Testament portrays women teaching and evangelizing throughout the Roman Empire[2] at the same time certain apostolic statements appear to limit such activities to men.[3] The story of the spread of Christianity in the Western world is also the story of the increasing marginalization of women in church leadership.[4] While it was possible for gifted Catholic women in the medieval period to find opportunities for leadership in some of the great abbeys of Europe,[5] the Reformation (in closing the cloisters) removed women

---

1. For example, Luke 7:36-50; 8:1-3; 10:38-42; 18:1-8; and John 20:17.

2. Acts 18:18, 24-28; Rom. 16:1-12. Also see Elisabeth Schüssler Fiorenza, "Word, Spirit and Power: Women in Early Christian Communities," in *Women of Spirit: Female Leadership in the Jewish and Christian Traditions,* ed. Rosemary Ruether and Eleanor McLaughlin (New York: Simon & Schuster, 1979), chap. 1, pp. 29-70.

3. 1 Cor. 14:34-35; 1 Tim. 2:12. Also see Paige Patterson, "The Meaning of Authority in the Local Church," in *Recovering Biblical Manhood and Womanhood: A Response to Evangelical Feminism,* ed. John Piper and Wayne Grudem (Wheaton, Ill.: Crossway, 1991), chap. 14, pp. 248-59.

4. Ruether and McLaughlin, p. 17; see also Ruth A. Tucker and Walter Liefeld, *Daughters of the Church: Women and Ministry from New Testament Times to the Present* (Grand Rapids: Zondervan, 1987), chap. 3, "The Rise of the Church and the Downfall of Rome: Martyrs and Sex Objects."

5. Eleanor McLaughlin, "Women, Power and the Pursuit of Holiness in Medieval Christianity," in *Women of Spirit,* pp. 99-130. See also Mary Beth Rose, ed., *Women in the Middle Ages and the Renaissance* (Syracuse: Syracuse University Press, 1986), chap. 2, "The Heroics of Vir-

even further from church leadership.[6] By the early nineteenth century in North America, the cult of true womanhood[7] limited women to the domestic sphere, away from the public square and from leadership in the institutional church.[8]

At the same time that a doctrine of separate spheres for men and women was reaching its zenith in nineteenth-century North America, other social factors were at work pushing women in new directions on behalf of the institutional church. The newly formed republic of united states brought with it the doctrine of the separation of church and state.[9] No longer could churches rely on government support of clergy. Instead, churches and denominations were forced to compete with other groups for members and tithes.[10] Following the Revolutionary War, the heady demands of capitalism pulled men from the church, leaving mostly women in the pews.[11] The Protestant clergy was forced to recast women's role in American religion. From these social pressures there emerged near the end of the nineteenth century the new idea of woman as "the angel of the home," the one whose piety and purity would recapture men for the church.[12]

---

ginity: Brides of Christ and Sacrificial Mutilation"; also Tucker and Liefeld, chap. 4, "Medieval Catholicism: Nuns, 'Heretics,' and Mystics."

6. Barbara K. MacHaffie, *Her Story: Women in Christian Tradition* (Philadelphia: Fortress, 1986), chap. 4, "Women in an Era of Reformation." See also Tucker and Liefeld, chap. 5, "Reformation Protestantism: Daring Noblewomen and Godly Wives."

7. See Aileen Kraditor, ed., *Up from the Pedestal: Selected Writings in the History of American Feminism* (Chicago: Quadrangle Books, 1968), pp. 9-11; also Barbara Welter, *Dimity Convictions: The American Woman in the Nineteenth Century* (Athens: Ohio University Press, 1976), chap. 2, "The Cult of True Womanhood, 1820-1860."

8. Carroll Smith-Rosenberg, *Disorderly Conduct: Visions of Gender in Victorian America* (New York and Oxford: Oxford University Press, 1985), p. 323. Working from William McLoughlin's analysis, she states that in Jacksonian America "conventional evangelical churches provided women with restricted and domestic religious roles. Only in the unstructured and mystical new denominations [Shakerism, Christian Science, Wilkinson's Society of the Universal Friend] could women hope to exert power."

9. See Mark Noll, *A History of Christianity in the United States and Canada* (Grand Rapids: Eerdmans, 1992), pp. 144-51.

10. See Ann Douglas, *The Feminization of American Culture* (New York: Knopf, Avon Books, 1978), chap. 1, "Clerical Disestablishment."

11. See Welter, chap. 6, "The Feminization of American Religion, 1800-1860," pp. 83-102. While this phenomenon became more apparent in post–Revolutionary War times, it had already appeared by the mid–seventeenth century. Cotton Mather wrote in 1692, "As there were three Marys to one John, standing under the Cross of our Dying Lord, so still there are far more Godly Women in the World, than there are Godly Men; and our Church Communions give us Little Demonstration of it," quoted by Nancy Cott in *The Bonds of Womanhood: "Woman's Sphere" in New England, 1780-1835* (New Haven: Yale University Press, 1977).

12. Betty DeBerg, *Ungodly Women: Gender and the First Wave of American Fundamentalism* (Minneapolis: Fortress, 1990), chap. 3, "The Divinized Home."

Thus American Protestant churches entered the twentieth century with women filling most of the pews, though men still filled most of the pulpits.[13] By 1910 clergy alarm about this gender disproportion had grown so much that the Men and Religion Forward Movement was launched and successfully carried out in 1911 and 1912.[14] This effort did bolster male membership in many of the Protestant denominations, though the numbers of men participating in the churches never rose to a point equal to that of women.

Historians and sociologists have documented the many cultural and religious strands contributing to women's ecclesiastical marginalization.[15] The question of women's "place" in the Christian church remains unresolved in many quarters. While the mainline Protestant denominations in North America have dealt with the issue at least in principle,[16] the question is still on the table (or under the table) within most American Protestant evangelical church bodies. Central to this issue is a diversity of evangelical theological stances vis-à-vis Scripture and tradition.[17] As evangelical Protestant seminaries move into the twenty-first century, the issue of women's "place" in the church will likely remain unresolved unless the theological and sociological underpinnings of the matter are more fully addressed. David Tracy cogently observed in the first essay of this volume that "all thought exists finally for the sake of action and com-

13. Women's historians have sometimes focused on the great gains women made in public ministries during the nineteenth century. But it must be noted that at the turn of the century (1890-1910), women in the Holiness tradition had more freedom to assume public ministry roles than did women in the non-Holiness evangelical traditions (principally Presbyterian and Baptist).

14. Gail Bederman, "'The Women Have Had Charge of the Church Work Long Enough': The Men and Religion Forward Movement of 1911-1912 and the Masculinization of Middle-Class Protestantism," *American Quarterly* 41 (September 1989).

15. For example, Carl Degler, *At Odds: Women and the Family from the Revolution to the Present* (New York: Oxford University Press, 1980); Smith-Rosenberg, *Disorderly Conduct;* Janette Hassey, *No Time for Silence: Evangelical Women in Public Ministry around the Turn of the Century* (Grand Rapids: Zondervan, 1986); Colleen McDannell, *The Christian Home in Victorian America, 1840-1900* (Bloomington and Indianapolis: Indiana University Press, 1986).

16. See Paula D. Nesbitt, *Feminization of the Clergy in America: Occupational and Organizational Perspectives* (New York: Oxford University Press, 1997).

17. This diversity of theological stances is reflected in the range of books published by evangelical biblical scholars in recent decades: Piper and Grudem, *Recovering Biblical Manhood and Womanhood;* James B. Hurley, *Man and Woman in Biblical Perspective* (Grand Rapids: Zondervan, 1981); George W. Knight III, *The New Testament Teaching on the Role Relationship of Men and Women* (Grand Rapids: Baker, 1977); Gilbert Bilizekian, *Beyond Sex Roles: A Guide for the Study of Female Roles in the Bible* (Grand Rapids: Baker, 1985); Mary Evans, *Woman in the Bible* (Downers Grove, Ill.: InterVarsity, 1983); Aída Spencer, *Beyond the Curse: Women Called to Ministry* (Nashville: Nelson, 1985).

mitment. . . . [A]ll thought not somehow directed to action, concern, or commitment may be ultimately empty." So while the academy is called to address the theological and sociological issues, on the basis of that work the church is called to action, concern, and commitment.

How Women Cope with This
Unresolved Question of Their "Place"

Meanwhile, how are women coping with their sometimes conflicted relationship to the church? And how are churches coping with what is going on with women in the wider society today? What roles and activities carried out by evangelical Protestant churchwomen can churches continue to count on? In what ways have societal changes in women's attitudes to the church truncated the effectiveness of the church in the contemporary North American world?

Social historian Samuel P. Huntington charted what he called "creedal passion periods" in American history when recruitment to political movements was high.[18] A creedal passion period is one in which a doctrine (such as "democracy" or "minority rights") becomes a driving moral force for reform or social change. Huntington's macrosociological analysis of creedal passion periods, while it was developed to explain peak periods of political involvement, has ramifications for the study of women in American evangelical Protestant churches, and it provides a grid for analyzing what is going on today in women's relationship to the institutional church.

Behind my use of Huntington's analysis lies Max Stackhouse's distinction between *doctrine* and *creed*. For Stackhouse, "a *doctrine* is a teaching, claim, or assertion; a *creed* is a doctrine held to be true, embraced with commitment, celebrated in concert with others, and used as a fundamental guide for action."[19] Stackhouse asserts that "doctrines rise and fall with amazing rapidity," and only a few doctrines are adopted as creed and become institutionalized. However, when a doctrine becomes creed, it provides the basis for structuring life for those who hold it to be true and who embrace it with commitment.

Historically, women have heard the Christian gospel and have responded fervently to its call to take up Christ's cross and follow him. In short, they have embraced Christian doctrine as creed. Women as well as men have died as mar-

---

18. Samuel P. Huntington, *American Politics: The Promise of Disharmony* (Cambridge: Harvard University Press, Belknap Press, 1981), pp. 64ff.

19. Max Stackhouse, *Creeds, Society, and Human Rights: A Study in Three Cultures* (Grand Rapids: Eerdmans, 1984), p. 2.

tyrs in every period of church history, and women as well as men have gone to the ends of the earth to proclaim that gospel. In fact, the history of Christian missions in the nineteenth century cannot be written without the remarkable success story of women sending women as missionaries when the denominational boards refused to do so.[20] The explosive growth of the Christian church in China today can be traced in large measure to the thousands of women who went to China as Christian missionaries a hundred years ago.[21] We might ask, what drove women to carry the Christian story of redemption and peace with God to the ends of the earth? What for many others in the church was merely a doctrine had, for these women, become creed: the gospel was held to be true, it was embraced with commitment, and it was used as a fundamental guide for action. That creed carried them to the ends of the earth.

Huntington found that in creedal passion periods, those who sign on to work for change in society soon perceived a *gap* between the ideal and the reality.[22] He further found that how individuals act in the light of that gap depends on the intensity of their belief in the ideal. Those whose belief in the ideal is low often tolerate the gap with some cynicism. Others who believe intensely in the ideal and who clearly see the gap between the ideal and the reality will commit themselves to eliminating the gap at all costs. But what happens if this effort to reduce the tension between the ideal and the reality is unsuccessful? Huntington has found that such individuals implement the following actions:

1. The person begins to question the authority behind the social construct: "Who says so? How can I be sure that person is right?"
2. Moral passion develops as the person takes the ideal seriously and asks, "Why isn't this my experience? What needs to change?" The urgency grows to capture the ideal as reality.

20. See, for example, Helen Barrett Montgomery, *Western Women in Eastern Lands* (New York: Macmillan, 1910); R. Pierce Beaver, *American Protestant Women in World Mission: A History of the First Feminist Movement in North America* (Grand Rapids: Eerdmans, 1980). Beaver's book first appeared under the title *All Loves Excelling.*

21. Ralph D. Winter, "Editorial Comment," *Mission Frontiers,* August 1999, p. 4. He acknowledged that "it is truly embarrassing for men to review the extraordinary impact of women in Christian mission," citing statistics about women's contribution in both the nineteenth and twentieth centuries to the task of world mission. This includes the fact that of the fifty thousand house churches in China today, forty thousand of them are led by women. These women are descended from the legions of legendary Chinese "Bible women," who were taught the Scriptures at the riverside by women missionaries without benefit of seminary classroom walls.

22. Not everyone embracing the doctrine as creed has a clear perception of a gap between the ideal and the reality. Those who believe intensely in the ideal may deny any gap; others whose belief in the ideal is low will probably ignore it.

3. If the tension is not reduced by action, questioning the authority behind the social construct turns to attacking the institution backing the social construct.

4. When taken to this point, the individual begins to experiment with alternatives and also begins to question all social conventions.[23]

When we ask how gender issues affect institutions, it can be helpful to examine the "danger" of having highly committed individuals on board who have embraced the ideal with "creedal passion." It is usually assumed that people with high levels of commitment to the church are an unmitigated asset. But the story of women in and out of today's church should be told as a cautionary tale. In the light of Huntington's steps in disillusioned disengagement, much can be learned from women whose experience in the church has been characterized by a massive gap between the ideal of full participation in the church and the reality of restricted roles.[24] For many evangelical Protestants, it is unthinkable that a woman who is passionately committed to serving Christ in the church could reach a point of "questioning the authority behind the social construct," then of attacking the authorities behind that construct to the extent of experimenting with alternatives. But this process is well documented in the lives of individual women, many of whom became standard-bearers for various feminisms, and some of whom eventually became feminist theologians.[25] Evangelical Protestants have, for the most part, pointed to feminism as the personification of "secular humanism" without examining the complicity of the church in producing it.[26] The story of nineteenth-century feminism is the story of strongly committed evangelical women and men who, touched deeply by the Second Great Awakening, worked diligently for the abolition of slavery, only to awaken to the parallel issues for women. It is one of the tragedies of many mid-nineteenth-century churches that the concerns of slaves and of women were overridden by personal interests. While the Emancipation Proclamation gave at

23. Huntington, pp. 65ff.

24. It is important to note that a great many evangelical Protestant women have accepted restricted roles as the biblical model for their lives, and thus they do not struggle with this gap. This chapter discusses those women for whom the gap has become salient and whose creedal passion pushes them to find a way to cope with the resulting dissonance between ideal and reality.

25. See, for example, Carol Christ, *Laughter of Aphrodite: Reflections on a Journey to the Goddess* (San Francisco: Harper and Row, 1987), p. 29.

26. For a twentieth-century feminist reading of this complicity, see Naomi R. Goldenberg, *Changing of the Gods: Feminism and the End of Traditional Religions* (Boston: Beacon Press, 1979).

least legal sanction to the abolition of slavery, women became increasingly disillusioned and restive in the churches. Twentieth-century "second wave" feminism is largely a secular movement because nineteenth-century feminists found the churches closed to their legitimate demands for equity before the law, educational opportunities, and the franchise (finally enacted in 1920).

The genesis of the second wave of feminism is often connected to the widespread social disruption of the 1960s in American social life. The civil rights movement was sweeping the country in the march toward the historic 1964 declaration of human rights for marginalized people. Betty Friedan's *The Feminine Mystique* appeared in 1963, touching off among American housewives a firestorm of reaction against gender stratification. The war in Vietnam was accelerating and, with it, the antiwar movement. "Flower power," free sex, and the drug culture of Timothy Leary and others replaced the earlier moral values of self-discipline and self-actualization. The solid, age-old institutions of government, church, and family were challenged to the point that American society at the turn of the millennium no longer resembled its pre-1960s counterpart.[27]

The tendency in such periods of social upheaval is to hark back to more stable times, decrying the loss of values. Yet such periods of upheaval do not come unbidden. The "more stable times" need to be reexamined for the stress fractures already present but denied and ignored. Sociologist Ralph Turner took note of the major shift away from an institutional locus of the self to an impulse locus of the self that was obvious in the social disruption of the 1960s. Earlier social scientists[28] had assumed that a sense of self was firmly anchored in institutional attachments — to the nation, to the family, to the church. But Turner noted that large numbers of people were slipping the institutional anchor: "To one person . . . the true self is recognized in acts of volition, in the

27. Mary Douglas, *Natural Symbols: Explorations in Cosmology* (New York: Vintage Press, 1973), pp. 32, 37, and chaps. 12 and 16. Douglas argues that the experience of social change, in and of itself, leads to the denouncing of ritual, the praise of disorder, and the affirmation of individualism. Radical or prolonged social change destroys old institutional and hierarchical arrangements. Definitions no longer elicit cultural consensus or reinforcement. Boundaries are no longer clearly defined. The societies emerging in such times will espouse political and religious ideologies that value the individual over the community and family, youth over age, inner experience rather than conformity to social norms. It is a time to challenge revealed ideas, to encourage autonomy, to question or deny boundaries, and to reject authoritarian control and symbols of hierarchical power. In such cultures, Douglas tells us, "God has turned against ritual" (cited by Smith-Rosenberg, p. 140).

28. Robert Park defined the self as "the role we are striving to live up to — this mask is our true self, the self we would like to be," in "Human Nature and Collective Behavior," *American Journal of Sociology* 32 (March 1927).

pursuit of institutionalized goals, and not in the satisfaction of impulses outside institutional frameworks. To another person, the outburst of desire is recognized . . . as an indication that the real self is breaking out."[29]

For women with an institutional view of the self, the discovery of the self is found in self-mastery, achievement, and altruism. These are the personal goals that best serve women in institutional settings. But challenging the institutional assumption and asserting the primacy of self over role, Elizabeth Janeway asks, "Is the image [the institutional role] the self? The idea is repugnant. Are we only what we seem to be? . . . We have felt for a long time that the assigned image of woman, acted out in the role-behavior expected of us, has not offered us self-fulfillment but, rather, has functioned as mask, as screen, as armor — most of all, as *barrier* between the inner self and the world. Whatever the momentary pattern of that image, every woman who has ever lived would surely cry out, 'It is not I!'"[30]

Many women in evangelical Protestant churches struggle with the disjunction between the institutional view of the self and a personal sense of self. The call to Christian service often comes within the context of the church, so the "call" has an institutional setting. But opportunities for fully responding to that call are often limited institutionally. It is possible that the more passionate a woman is about responding to God's call in her life, the more frustration she will experience in attempting to carry out that call within an institutional setting. Her "creedal passion" drives her to work for change in order to respond fully to God's call in her life — or to begin to question the basic right of the institutional church to determine the parameters of her engagement in Christ's service.

While most mainline Protestant denominations have set for their churches policies intended to open doors to women which may be closed in evangelical churches in the free church tradition, many evangelical women are unwilling to change denominational affiliations because it may also involve embracing theological or ethical positions which they cannot accept. Thus these women struggle to stay within evangelical circles while attempting to work out their calling with as little circumscription as possible. One potential consequence of this is an alienation from the self, a sense of having sacrificed the real person within for a role that feels like a fake.[31] There is a weighing of

29. Ralph Turner, "The Real Self: From Institution to Impulse," *American Journal of Sociology* 81 (1976): 991.

30. Elizabeth Janeway, *Between Myth and Morning: Women Awakening* (New York: Morrow, 1972), p. 167.

31. Arlie Russell Hochschild, *The Managed Heart: Commercialization of Human Feeling* (Berkeley: University of California Press, 1983), pp. 35-55.

costs versus benefits: Can I serve Christ best by bowing to the strictures of my church, or will I one day wake up to realize that I could have served Christ's cause more effectively had I left this venue?

Carol Christ offers three options to women who begin to ask questions about the gap between the promise and the reality of service for Christ within the church: in her analysis such a woman can (1) stay in the tradition and keep silent, (2) leave the tradition, or (3) confront the tradition.[32] Many women choose to stay in the tradition and keep silent. Christ and others chose to leave. Still others stay in contact with the tradition, confronting it from within. Within the struggle whether to stay or leave, whether to remain silent or confront, lie three very personal, theological questions:

1. How can I discern the will of God for my life? Is it made known to me only institutionally through the church? Or are there other factors which impact my understanding of God's call in my life?
2. Is it possible that the church is not accurately interpreting Scripture in reflecting the will of God for my life? (This is the first step in Huntington's process of disillusioned disengagement.)
3. Can it be that evil forces beyond the church are using the church to keep me from realizing my calling from God?

These are not the questions usually posed by denominational or congregational leaders, but they are questions that women gripped by a "creedal passion" for God do ask. The answers they supply to their questions will in some measure determine whether they attempt to stay inside the institutional church or leave.

A Case Study of Staying and Confronting

Madeleine Saillens grew up in a parsonage as the daughter of a Protestant pastor in France. In 1905 she married Arthur Blocher, also a pastor, and worked closely with him in pastoral ministry in France. In 1928 her husband was installed as the pastor of the Eglise Baptiste du Tabernacle in Paris, the largest Baptist church in France. A year later he died quite suddenly, and the elders of the congregation convened to discuss his successor. Because he had preached a series of sermons on the ministry of women in the Bible and on the need to enlarge opportunities for women in the church, the elders eventually chose his

32. Christ, p. 29.

wife, Mme. Blocher-Saillens, to succeed him as the pastor of this prestigious church. She became the first woman pastor in France, and she carried out an effective pastoral ministry at the Eglise du Tabernacle for twenty-three years until her retirement in 1952.

The twenty-three years during which she pastored this major Protestant church in Paris included the difficult, troubled years of World War II and the German occupation of the city. She guided the growing congregation with skill while also beginning a publishing house and opening a Christian bookstore to make evangelical literature available beyond the walls of the church. She founded a mission in Africa, sending French missionaries out from the church to the Côte d'Ivoire. She also founded a children's camp, all the while teaching theology at the Nogent Bible Institute and pastoring the church in Paris.

But her pastoral ministry did not go unchallenged. Christians all over francophone Europe — France, Switzerland, and Belgium — condemned her for accepting the pastorate of the church. For twenty-three years she endured a barrage of criticism that nothing would quell. She herself settled biblically the issue of her right before God to pastor the church before accepting the post, but it was not until after she retired in 1952 that she found time to put her convictions and reflections into print.[33] In defense of her ministry, she explored all the relevant biblical passages addressing women's ministries, and she made her case for women in church leadership on the strength of both biblical exegesis and theological reflection. In the resulting book, *Liberée par Christ pour Son Service,* she began with reflections on Genesis 3. Her basic thesis is this:

> Satan, who was incarnated in the serpent, is struck [by God] in his turn [who said]: "I will put enmity between you and the woman, between her posterity and your posterity. This posterity will crush your head and you will wound the heel." Have you noticed that this enmity is first of all between the woman and Satan? Also that Satan swears to fight against her and against her descendants, the ones through whom will come the One who will vanquish him? . . . Satan declares war on the woman, and that war continues to the present time as we shall see.[34]

For Mme. Blocher-Saillens, the "god of this world," Satan, lurks behind the ongoing repression of women in the wider society and in the church. She argues that the personal devil, the archenemy of God, knows that if he can immobilize committed service to Christ on the part of one-half of the human

---

33. Madame A. Blocher-Saillens, *Liberée par Christ pour Son Service* (Paris 18eme: Les Bons Semeurs, diffusion evangelique, 1961).

34. Translation from the French by Alice Mathews.

race, he will have succeeded in cutting at least in half any efforts to reclaim humanity and the earth for God. She sees Satan behind the oppressive systems of this world which hold all marginalized people down.

For many sophisticated theologians in the twenty-first century, the idea of a personal devil, Satan, is ludicrous. But many evangelical Protestant women would agree that Mme. Blocher-Saillens is not exaggerating the situation. For them, the ongoing repression seems to be part of a genuine war against women. There are times when an "unreasonable" cosmic explanation may be the only reasonable explanation for the repeated efforts throughout two millennia to cut women off from the full exercise of their gifts in the service of Christ. Mme. Blocher-Saillens's vision is of a supernatural effort to destroy the long-term and widespread effectiveness of women on behalf of the gospel. For many Christian women, this aligns with the words of Saint Paul, "We wrestle not against flesh and blood but against principalities, against powers, against the rulers of the darkness of this age, against spiritual hosts of wickedness in the heavenly places."[35] The issue is theological. It is also sociological. And for women with creedal passion, it is deeply personal.

Mme. Blocher-Saillens chose to remain within a denomination opposed to her ministry and to confront the denomination through both her effective ministry and later her written theological apologetic for broader roles for women in ministry.

Women Defecting in Place

Not all Christian women embrace Mme. Blocher-Saillens's theological explanation nor the strength it gave her to continue for twenty-three years in a ministry her contemporaries condemned. Instead, many women choose to "defect in place";[36] that is, they choose to remain inside the tradition, creating their own alternative cultural reality while at the same time staying connected to their theological commitments.

It is not unusual for evangelical Protestant women who have at one point confronted sexism within their local congregation to retrench and settle for defecting in place. For example, three young theologically trained mothers in a Midwestern city had taught a well-attended adult church school class on gender roles in the Bible. Because the content of their course did not agree with the

---

35. Eph. 6:12.

36. Miriam Therese Winter, Adair Lummis, and Allison Stokes, *Defecting in Place: Women Claiming Responsibility for Their Own Spiritual Lives* (New York: Crossroad, 1995).

(unwritten) gender assumptions of the church leadership, they were summoned to appear before the elder board of that church. The three young women were reprimanded for being divisive and the course was shut down. The personal shock and hurt were great, but they did not feel that they could walk away from that church at that time. Their families were widely involved in the life of that congregation. Their growing children were thriving in the various church programs available to them. So the three women defected in place: they kept silent while remaining in that congregation. Within a year, however, all three families had moved to different churches. In each case, the evangelical churches to which they moved were almost as restrictive on gender roles as was the church in which they had encountered opposition.[37] Only the fact of having spiritually attuned teenage children held them in the new churches to which they moved.

Many evangelical women with family commitments choose to defect in place because the spiritual development of their spouse and children is more salient than their own personal issues. This is not without a sense of personal loss, as the gifts, training, and experience of such women are buried during this period of their lives. They must wrestle with the issue of their stewardship of these gifts and training at the same time that they subordinate their personal call to the perceived needs of their families.

Sociologist Erving Goffman has explored the rich range of secondary adjustments used by individuals whose primary adjustments to their institutional setting have created some kind of inner strain.[38] The term "adjustment" is used to denote the effort an individual makes to adapt to circumstances which may not appear to be in one's best interests. Membership or participation in any institution requires some adaptation to the requirements of that institution, because inherent in the notion of an *institution* is that some custom or law is being "institutionalized," i.e., given established status.

When that primary adjustment is given sacred legitimation, it takes on cosmic significance (as seen in Max Weber's well-known dictum, "the sacred is the uniquely unalterable").[39] When limited roles for women in the church are stamped *sacred,* they are also stamped *unalterable.* What would otherwise be merely a contingency of human existence becomes a manifestation of universal

---

37. Now, in the case of one family, the boys are in college and the parents are looking for a church which is theologically evangelical but does not restrict women to secondary roles in church leadership.

38. Erving Goffman, *Asylums: Essays on the Social Situation of Mental Patients and Other Inmates* (New York: Doubleday Anchor Books, 1961), p. 188.

39. Max Weber, *The Sociology of Religion,* trans. Ephraim Fischoff (Boston: Beacon Press, 1922, 1963), p. 9.

law. A woman who gives allegiance to the institutional church must internalize the institutional requirements as core values of her life if she wants to live with the sense that she is pleasing God.

So how does she cope with the sense of inner strain between her commitment to Christ's service and the strictures of the institution within which she has chosen to remain? Goffman suggests that some inner equilibrium is achieved by the use of secondary adjustments as a means of detaching a part of herself from this official or institutional self. A secondary adjustment can be anything a person does to stand apart from the role or from the self required by the institution.[40] This is a form of defiance-within-compliance. The individual complies on the surface with the requirements of the institution, but uses a secondary adjustment to carve out a space in which the self does not have to join in the act.[41] It is to comply and defy at the same time. Goffman observed that both compliance and defiance are required to have a complete self: "Without something to belong to, we have no stable self, and yet total commitment and attachment to any social unit implies a kind of selflessness. Our sense of being a person can come from being drawn into a wider social unit; our sense of self-hood can arise through the little ways in which we resist the pull. Our status is backed by the solid buildings of the world, while our sense of personal identity often resides in the cracks."[42] For many evangelical Protestant women, defecting in place has become the preferred means of coping with institutional strictures on women's service to Christ. It is perhaps an ambiguous place "betwixt and between," an "interstructural situation," in anthropologist Victor Turner's terms.[43] Women entering this liminality for the first time may see it as "a dangerous place" lying between primary and secondary adjustments. But "defecting in place" offers the possibility of carving out a private space for the self in the midst of institutional conformity.

---

40. The list of possible secondary adjustments is as long as human creativity is wide: they can be rudeness, silence, anger, irony, sarcasm, hostile humor, griping, unauthorized distance, stiffness, dignity, coolness, utter self-possession. A major form of secondary adjustments is passive aggression, such as unfulfilled "good" intentions, procrastination, etc. Secondary adjustments, according to Goffman, are efforts in all cases to preserve some part of the self from the grip or control of the institution.

41. In Arlie Hochschild's metaphor, this is a way to "bow from the waist while standing upright in the heart"; see Hochschild, p. 76.

42. Goffman, p. 320.

43. Victor Turner, *The Forest of Symbols: Aspects of Ndembu Ritual* (Ithaca, N.Y.: Cornell University Press, 1967), p. 93.

Women Who Leave the Tradition

When Alexis de Tocqueville wrote about slavery in mid-nineteenth-century America, he concluded that there could be no intermediate ground between slavery and complete equality.[44] A "halfway" step toward equality, according to Tocqueville, is inherently unstable and cannot endure. Carol Christ and others have concluded that the same is true for women in the church. For them the only viable alternative is to leave traditional Christianity behind. This has taken various forms, well summarized in *Womanspirit Rising*.[45]

Because the sting of "patriarchy" is fresh, many women have moved toward women-led forms of religious expression. The theology of wicca or witchcraft has been articulated by Starhawk, Goldenberg, and others.[46] Much of the symbolism incorporated into the coven meetings is a repudiation of hierarchy. Others have found a "thealogy" rooted in the Goddess and the mystical experiences that spring from the earth or nature.[47] The Re-Imagining Conferences sponsored by the World Council of Churches have brought the practice of wicca and Goddess worship to the consciousness of many laywomen in mainline churches.[48]

While some of the women who have left the church in favor of wicca or Goddess worship describe their new religious allegiance in strongly positive ways, there is a poignant sadness embedded in some of their writings. Carol Christ describes the sense of loss a woman experiences when she cannot "stay and fight" but swallows her anger at the church (and at God) and leaves:

> While women sit silent, perhaps even unaware that they are deadening themselves in order to do so, others leave the churches and synagogues, cutting off their relation with the biblical God. In both cases, women who once had

44. John Stone and Stephen Mennell, *Alexis de Tocqueville: On Democracy, Revolution, and Society* (Chicago: University of Chicago Press, 1980), pp. 338-39.

45. Carol P. Christ and Judith Plaskow, eds., *Womanspirit Rising: A Feminist Reader in Religion* (San Francisco: Harper and Row, 1979).

46. See the chapter by Starhawk, "Witchcraft and Women's Culture," in *Womanspirit Rising*, pp. 259-68; Goldenberg, pp. 85-114.

47. Christ, *Laughter of Aphrodite;* also see Christine Downing, *The Goddess: Mythological Images of the Feminine* (New York: Crossroad, 1984); Nelle Morton, *The Journey Is Home* (Boston: Beacon Press, 1986).

48. Evangelical Protestant women anchored in a biblical theology, however, cannot divorce themselves from the core affirmations of the ancient creeds or from Scripture. An evangelical Protestant response to the Re-Imagining Movement is Aída Besançon Spencer, Donna F. G. Hailson, Catherine Clark Kroeger, and William David Spencer, *The Goddess Revival* (Grand Rapids: Baker, 1995).

powerful feelings about the God of biblical tradition may be denying part of themselves. They may be deadening their religious sensibility altogether, suppressing powerful, conflicting feelings toward God that come to them, perhaps, "in the night, tinged with hatred, with remorse, but most of all with infinite yearning." A woman who swallows her anger and bitterness at God may also cut off her longing for the God who provoked her to anger.[49]

For many women, leaving the church is not without a strong sense of loss.

Conclusion

The twentieth century was the setting for profound social changes, but the disruptions associated with those changes also produced a backlash which, within certain evangelical Protestant denominations, undid the gains made by women in the church. Although for women in these groups the gains have not been realized, the world even for women within these denominations is not the same as it was a hundred years ago. This heightens women's expectations for more openness to their gifts and callings in the decades to come.

Alexis de Tocqueville, in his analysis of the French Revolution, wrote:

[I]t is not always when things are going from bad to worse that revolutions break out. On the contrary, it oftener happens that when a people which has put up with an oppressive rule over a long period without protest suddenly finds the government relaxing its pressure, it takes up arms against it. Thus the social order overthrown by the revolution is almost always better than the one immediately preceding it, and experience teaches us that, generally speaking, the more perilous moment for a bad government is one when it seeks to mend its ways. . . . Patiently endured so long as it seemed beyond redress, a grievance comes to appear intolerable once the possibility of removing it crosses men's minds. For the mere fact that certain abuses have been remedied draws attention to the others and they now appear more galling. . . . In the reign of Louis XVI the most trivial pinpricks of arbitrary power caused more resentment than the thoroughgoing despotism of Louis XIV.[50]

49. Christ, p. 30. The quote is from Elie Wiesel, *The Town beyond the Wall* (1970), p. 190. Christ goes on to observe that "[h]ad God repressed anger instead of expressing it, Israel would not have known the living God in the fullness of being. Like any other relation when anger is not expressed, the covenantal relation would have stagnated, gone dead" (p. 31).

50. Stone and Mennell, p. 230.

A gender regime differs from a political regime such as Tocqueville described, yet some of the same social-psychological dynamics are present. The issue of women's "place" in the church will not go away as long as segments of the church refuse to acknowledge God's call of women to full ministry in the name of Christ. While some women will continue to find ways to "defect in place" and others will give full commitment to working within institutional frames while also challenging those frames, still other women will leave. With them will go their gifts and their passion, weakening the churches. The task before the church in the twenty-first century is to reexamine the theologies that have kept women bound.

CHAPTER EIGHT

Public Works: Bridging the Gap between Theology and Public Ethics

WILLIAM JOHNSON EVERETT

Theologically trained ethicists groan frequently during the evening news. Announcers tell of "Muslimfundamentalists" and "Rightwingchristians" terrorizing civilians in the streets and parliamentary chambers. "Catholicantiabortionists" struggle with "prochoicehumanists" over the status of life in wombs and prisons. Billy Graham and white-robed popes float like icons through a fog of detached personal piety or collective enthusiasm. The discomfort we feel is not merely due to the liberal bias of media purveyors, but to their ignorance and virtual illiteracy about matters religious. They evince little awareness or understanding of the long history out of which religious movements and institutions develop, nor do they have any familiarity with the way theology, ethics, and religious organizations work together to shape persons, institutions, and culture. When this foggy consciousness does attend to actual religion, it is usually patronizing or nostalgic. All nuns, like Whoopi Goldberg, must wear archaic habits; all preachers must have white shoes. At its worst it is unable to understand, for instance, the religious culture out of which impeachment was brought against President Clinton. But when it shapes the way American foreign policy deals with Muslim cultures and their governments, it becomes deadly. When it doesn't grasp the religious depth of African cultures, it cannot penetrate what it relegates to ethnic and tribal warfare. This illiteracy is not merely annoying, it is dangerous. How then ought we think theologically about public affairs in a language comprehensible to a more general public?

This split between theological memory and contemporary public discourse is a fracture in a complex history. Therefore, our first step must be to heal this amnesia and try to put together again how we got here. The second step is conceptual. It requires that we think more clearly about the connections

150

among religious and political ideas as well as between religious and civil institutions. First, let us turn to the problem of memory.

Recovering Our Theological Senses

The problem of finding theological literacy in civil discourse is rooted in the successful effort to distinguish these two spheres. For fifteen hundred years Europeans carried on their political, cultural, and ethical disputes in what we call today religious and theological language. Questions of authority were traced back to theories of God, Trinity, and incarnation. Struggles over the nature of law and the limits on governing power were discussed in terms of ecclesiology, Scripture, sin, and the meaning of creation. It is impossible to understand how we received key political ideas and values without awareness of this theological matrix.

Americans inherited a pattern of relationships between religion, government, and civil society that resulted from the fifteen-hundred-year European experience of Christendom. That experience, though shaped profoundly by a distinction between the Roman Church and governing monarchs, finally produced the collective decision to separate them more clearly and cleanly. What began in the seventeenth century as an effort to end the "wars of religion" between Catholic and Protestant monarchs led eventually to the institutional "separation" of the American experiment. What we often overlook are the stages in this development. At the treaty of Westphalia (1648), which ended the Thirty Years' War (think Cambodia or Vietnam for brutality), each monarch was allowed to choose his own religious affiliation and, with that choice, the established, state religion of his people. With the end of the English Civil War of the same century, the political theorist John Locke laid out principles of religious toleration that would make possible a governmental order based on rational consent, contract, and public debate.[1] While there would be an established church to provide the cultural glue and ground for proper governance, competing religious and cultural visions would be allowed to carry on their work and witness so long as they did not attack this order itself.

A century later the Americans, influenced as much by French anticlericalism as by English toleration, took the next step and severed religious institutions from state sponsorship or control in their new federal republic, though many states maintained religious institutions until well into the nineteenth century. The institutional differentiation of religion from government was nec-

---

1. John Locke, *A Letter concerning Toleration [1689]*, ed. Mario Montuori (The Hague: Martinus Nijhoff, 1963).

essary if government was to be based on the free arguments of the people rather than on the authority of traditional leaders and customs. Personal autonomy, though secured earlier on the basis of appeals to conscience, baptism, the work of the Holy Spirit, and entry into personal covenant with God, had to be freed not only from church control but also from its theological basis if politics was to be pliant, argumentative, and pluralistic.

In this important process "disestablishment," which originally meant only withdrawal of state support for a church, increasingly took on the secularist agenda of hostility to religion in public life generally. Public life was to be cleansed of religion, whether as crèches on courthouse lawns or prayers in government-run schools. Toleration became an agenda of ignorance and amnesia as history books left out the crucial religious motivations, institutions, and intellectual currents that actually shaped Western civilization. Religion was allowed to stay public, as in the military or on dollar bills, only if it clearly supported the existing political or economic order. The political separation of institutions created a cultural amnesia about public religious discourse.

We are now experiencing a reaction against this hostility and amnesia, not just from those who would reimpose some sort of governmental or cultural orthodoxy, but from those who see in this amnesia an inability to deal with the richness of human life and the organization of other cultures in a pluralistic world. The public spaces of education, media, and public discourse are filling up again with references to religion, theology, spirituality, and ethics. Religion is back, not only in the sensationalist packages of the mass media, but in serious efforts at religiously grounded public discourse. The "naked public square"[2] is full of religious costume, both gaudy and plain. The question we now face is: How to speak within this public discourse? What is the kind of "literacy" that can guide us in recovering from the amnesia effected by the well-intentioned effort at separation?

Finding the Bridges

This question leads us to the problem of concepts for speaking theologically and ethically in the general publics we inhabit. I would like to frame our problem in terms of the construction of bridge concepts and symbols between traditional religious discourse and the discourse of our governing publics. From this perspective we can then see three important dimensions of theological lit-

2. Richard John Neuhaus, *The Naked Public Square: Religion and Democracy in America* (Grand Rapids: Eerdmans, 1984).

eracy in public life: First, we can see how these bridges function in the creation and shaping of civil *society*. That is, we can see them as institutional vocabularies for shaping how people create and maintain social structures in accord with an ethical vision. Second, we can explore how theological concepts and symbols can vitalize and transform political *culture*. In this second kind of bridge work we deal with the deep level of symbols, collective psychology, and fundamental orientations that connect individual psychology to groups and institutions. These basic symbols create crucial loyalties, habits, and customs. Third, we deal with bridge concepts that can open up the pragmatic, utilitarian, and limited concerns of ordinary public life to the wider questions of existence. We can inquire about the language with which we can open up these societies and cultures to the mysterious *transcendence* of the divine purpose and power. Laying out these three bridges in a brief article is a tall order, but at least these three points can form a framework for struggling with the problem before us.

Crossing the Bridges

In speaking of bridges between theological and civil discourse, we first of all are acknowledging the relative integrity and distinct grammar of these two vocabularies. Yet we also acknowledge that they inhabit a common geography, a common world; hence the need for bridges for those of us who live in both countries. This is not an unfamiliar idea, going back at least to Augustine's *City of God* and coursing through the whole distinction between "nature" and "supernature," between natural law and the law of Christ. However, the disparateness of the languages, their grammars, and the intellectual methods they entail require even more careful attention to the bridges between them.

Frequently what the journalists call "fundamentalists" are people who seek to replace civil discourse with religious language, along with its attendant practices. However, instead of a bridge they create a landfill or isthmus merging the two. The Constitution is overlaid by the Bible or the Qur'an, and customary marriage and contracts are replaced by religiously authoritative prescriptions. They may do so for a variety of reasons, but none of them contains a concern for maintaining the fragile pluralism, consensus, and shared constructions of the civil arena. The search for a bridge concept, however, already rests in a theological decision to treat the life of civil government as a valid part of creation and of human reason and creativity. From the civil side, of course, this implies that "secular" society itself rests on a religious conviction about the goodness and necessity of these civil constructions.

Within that perspective we can identify several clusters of religious concepts or concerns that have served as bridges in European and American civilizations. (How these might then be bridges to the other historic cultures of Africa, Asia, aboriginal America, and the Pacific Islands is yet a further question that needs development elsewhere.) I will cite only four concepts here to illustrate this dynamic: covenant, assembly, household, and nature.

The Concept of Covenant

In English and American public discourse, covenant has played an exceedingly important role. Indeed, it has been so pervasive in both religious and civil contexts that we now must explore its meaning very carefully if we are to understand its role as a bridge between the two realms. Its connection with civil life can best be understood by a brief rehearsal of its history.[3]

Since the early Hebrews and Greeks, governing publics have turned to federal forms such as leagues, confederations, and alliances to maintain themselves internally and externally. Federalism itself reaches back to the ancient Hebrew concept of covenant *(bᵉrith)*. Covenantalism was derived from ancient treaty formulas and then given its theological meanings in Hebrew culture — its first function as a bridge. From Hebrew covenant and Greek and Roman leagues came the evolving modern forms of federalism. The Latin word for covenant is *foedus,* from which we have the English word "federal." Federalism is thus not only a system for sustaining and interrelating publics, but a framework for religious thought and practice as well. It is one in which the very understanding of God in Israel was shaped by the federal orders of the ancient world. It is thus a key metaphor for bridging faith and politics.

A covenant is a set of promises among independent parties to secure the future. Like publics, covenants were historically the first step beyond kinship for establishing durable and trustworthy human relationships. That is, they began to replace the "essentialist" categories of race and tribe with those of promise and negotiated agreement — a fundamental basis for civil life in a multitribal world. In their ancient biblical form, covenants were ways of relating people to the center of their deepest commitments and of relating themselves to each other, to their governors, and to the land on which they lived. Covenantal thinking is thus a complex way of approaching a variety of relationships in terms of mutual promises. We can think of covenantal constructions in terms of the parties to these agreements.

3. See the masterful presentation of this history in Daniel J. Elazar's four-volume work, *The Covenant Tradition in Politics* (New Brunswick, N.J.: Transaction Publishers, 1994-98).

Covenantal relationships assume that there are at least two relatively in-dependent parties to the set of promises. In Israel we find that this mysterious God YHWH is one who seeks to enter into covenant. This is not merely a mode of God's activity. It is essential to who God is. God is a covenanting God. Hu-man beings do not merely flow from the divine essence but exist with freedom before the Divine. The relationship of divinity and humanity comes to focus in the ever surprising story of their promises. This means that the eyes of faith fo-cus on the expectations they have of each other, the hopes that sustain them, and the way promises are broken and renewed.

Thus there are two parties — God and the people with whom God cove-nants. This "people" itself is not an automatic unity. It too is a result of a covenantal process that is known to them through their story — not the time-less round of seasonal necessities but the unique and surprising ways they have been sustained by promises over time. Their history is the outcome of promises made and kept, broken and renewed. Thus the people are also intrinsically covenantal inasmuch as they take their historical existence seriously. Thus cove-nant making in the Bible usually begins with a recitation of the story of grace, sin, and liberation that brought Israel to that point. That is how they know who they are as a party to covenant.

Finally, there is another party, often overlooked — the land. In one sense it is the "property" of the trust between YHWH and Israel. It is the gift or trust that goes with the promises and their honoring. But in another sense it too is a party to the covenant. It cries out, it dies, it flourishes. It witnesses. It partici-pates in the covenant according to its own dynamics and integrity. It is not sim-ply at human disposal but precedes humanity as God's first covenantal partner in creation. From the covenantal perspective, it has legitimate claims and stand-ing in the web of covenant-upholding life.

God, people, land — these are the parties constituting a "full covenant" in Israel. It is among these three parties that the web of covenantal promises is spun out. It is this intricate set of obligations that supports the system of law obligating all the parties to common action. They are to be faithful to each other through this law, this Torah. In the biblical concept of covenant we find the peculiar sense of law as binding, voluntary agreement. It is law as "constitu-tional," which means that the people are bound together not simply by family, tribe, race, inheritance, or nature, but by a legal framework which "constitutes" them as a people. From this covenantal understanding of law we have gradually come to a view of a higher law that stands in judgment over the laws made by an individual nation. This has been a powerful religious factor in the genera-tion of the modern conception of human rights, which the United Nations has then spelled out in international "covenants." Since World War II, national constitutions have increasingly contained extensive Bills of Rights incorporating these claims, the most recent and extensive being the new South African Constitution.

In the interaction of these three parties, we recognize that at some points Yahweh's claims and initiatives are stressed and at other times the human parties emerge with greater equality. Sometimes even the land's claims are central, as in the prophecies of Isaiah (Isa. 49; 55). The welfare of each of the parties depends on the faithfulness of the other two. Covenant always implies some kind of mutual interdependency maintained through faithfulness to promises that secure the future. This is the heart of covenantal, or federal, theology.

Covenant making itself usually occurred within a sequence of actions that began with a narrative of the gracious history by which the people of Israel formulated their image of the God of their covenant. Covenants are historical expressions of a tested, trustworthy relationship. The second step, also incorporated in this narrative, is the concept of the "people" that emerges. A people is not strictly a category of race, ancestry, or biology, as many intoned in the nineteenth and twentieth century — with disastrous outcomes — but a binding association that emerges in historical struggle. It is in this history that an identity is forged — and the second party to covenant emerges.

The third step is the formulation of the already mentioned mutual promises about their common future. These are the "commandments" of Exodus but also the promises of Deuteronomy and Isaiah. For biblical life, the land is both trust and partner in this covenant making.

The fourth step is the calling of witnesses. Here the land also plays a part, either as the witness of which Isaiah and the Psalms speak, or as the silent proof stone of Israel's fidelity. The breaking of covenant causes the land to wither and die.

The fifth step, of blessings and curses, is the part we would rather not mention. Covenant making is serious. It is the act of entrusting our life to another or to others. Thus its failure is also a diminishment of our own life. Covenants, because they are extended entrustments, also contain obligations to future generations. Their voices and claims, yet unknown, are in some sense anticipated in the covenants of the present.

Finally, there are usually provisions for remembering the covenant and continually recalling it. This also means that it is continually reworked in light of our historic experiences and emerging understandings about who we are, who God is, and what the land says to us.

Each of these moments in covenant making can lead us to ask questions about this process in any polity. They press us to ask deeper questions about the basis for a public identity and political commitment. They ask us to probe the deep conditions that make constitutional democracies possible and viable. They push us to basic questions of political loyalty and personal sacrifice.

We see this in the fact that biblical covenants are "cut." They are sacrificial acts that end an old life and begin a new one. Even more so, the establishment of new covenantal orders has always entailed great sacrifice. This work of sacrifice is not merely the brutal murders and exterminations that have dominated our century. They have produced victims and perpetrators but not necessarily new orders. The work of building up new relations of covenantal trust has required that we become vulnerable through the extension of forgiveness, of truthfulness, of apology, and of repentance. It demands the work of reconciliation.

"Covenant" is a bridge term because it relates this rich religious history with widespread political experience. It helps us talk about the basis for law, civil relationships, free association, limited government, contracts, and social breakdown in a comprehensible way that leads us back to the religious ground for these human civil endeavors and experiences.

The vocabulary and grammar of covenantal thought has both institutional and cultural dimensions. Covenantal trust is a particular way of approaching the task of constructing institutions in a world that has usually depended on kinship, race, gender, and other biological markers to create trustworthy relationships. Thus it has an affinity with the voluntary associations, professions, corporations, and congregations that constitute civil society. Covenant making is not a dispensation from "the powers that be," but the practical expression of the life of a people who see covenantal association in their fundamental relationship to God. Their history is a lifetime of experiments in covenant making, of covenantal failure, and of the struggle for reconciliation and renewed association. Thus the covenantal work of civil association precedes, in an ethical sense, the covenantal construction of government, a key concept in the republican heritage flowing from that child of Scottish covenantalists, John Locke.

The formation of these covenanted associations has always carried with it an impulse toward federation. The little assemblies, associations, and societies of the people, if they are to live together in any semblance of wider peace and security, have sought solemn league and mutually consensual relationships with each other. This is what federalism is all about. Our world is now engaged in a massive federal struggle in order to hold together people's legitimate desire for participation and public life with their need for common action to deal with shared problems of ecology, population, and global markets. How to maintain vital publics within a federal framework lies at the heart of the human struggle today. This kind of covenant making is also for many people an expression of

157

their ultimate hopes. Covenant making and federalism are not only religiously grounded practices; they are vehicles of a more transcendent vision.

These associational and federal structures thus rest in a deeper cultural ground of commitments and orientations. The cultural paradigm of the three parties to covenant always presses us to questions about what constitutes a people, their center of ultimate loyalty and trust, and the nature of the land with which they are entrusted. The cult of covenant making, covenantal memory, and acts of repentance and reconciliation shape deep paradigms for the maintenance of constitutional orders. This mirroring of covenantal practice in the creation or repair of constitutional orders is vividly evidenced in the contemporary widespread religious and civil interest in reconciliation and restorative justice. Knowledge of the covenantal roots of these efforts can help us sort out what to do in these circumstances.

Finally, this deep work of covenant making opens us up to claims and values that transcend our everyday covenants. It provides a critical dimension for all our efforts to construct constitutional orders that respect human rights, the claims of the land, and the claims of future generations. As a bridge concept, covenant illuminates the deep presuppositions of a constitutional civil order. It can both undergird this constitutionalism and, when connected to claims of human rights and ecology, also critique our present constitutional orders. Indeed, it provides the context for relating the legal structures of our time, with their ascending hierarchy of positive statutes, constitutions, and human rights covenants, with even more expansive systems of interdependence in the natural universe and history.

Covenant is a rich bridge between religious and civil discourse at all three points of institutional structure, civic culture, and openness to transcendence, but it also has its limits. It can fall prey to legalism in spite of its sense of God's mysterious workings. It can even more frequently cultivate a narrow chauvinism that elevates the covenanted people above their neighbors, thus creating a deep incivility and hostility between them. This limit opens us up to a second bridge concept which, from the religious side, is contained in the idea of assembly.

Assembly

From its earliest times the church called itself by the Greek term *ekklēsia*, public assembly. Once again, a crucial religious term was borrowed from the life of civil governance. Ancient Israel spoke of this assembly as the קָהָל of the people. In Jesus' time, with the removal of civil autonomy, it yielded up the idea of the synagogue (those gathered together), which formed the root pattern of Christian assembly. The Greek *ekklēsia* was the assembly of those "called out" from their households and from ordinary economic life in order to appear as equals engaged in argument rather than as kinfolk obeying the elders. In the traditional household, people related to each other in a hierarchical pattern of subordination — elder over younger, men over women, parents over children and slaves — but in the *ekklēsia*, at least the male citizens had the possibility to be equal, not because they were equal in physical ways but because they were equals before the law. It took many centuries before this principle could be extended to all adult humans, a process hastened in good part by the church's adoption of this institutional model in its early self-understanding. Thus, in the very concept of a separate institutional sphere from family and monarch for the expression of fundamental loyalties, we see a critical ingredient for the institutional differentiation necessary for public life in a pluralistic world.[4] The *ekklēsia*, like covenant, created a historic departure from family relations as the means to order the way we govern ourselves. The Christian *ekklēsia* carried within it the possibility of being a kind of "protopublic," a peculiar public (in Roman terms) gathered in the Spirit of Christ.[5] Ecclesiology is simply the study of the purpose and structure of this public assembly called the church.

This dynamic of assembly, or "publicity," was intensified in the church's history through the experience of Pentecost, in which people from all over the known earth could speak out of their own culture and language and yet also be heard and understood by others — surely a paradigm of public life for today. Thus the history of the church as assembly was inextricably tied up with the origins of our modern concept of a public. The early church put proclamation — public speech — at the heart of its life. With it came appeal to individual conviction as crucial to conversion and faith. It was this activity of publicity that upset the imperial order and brought persecution upon the church.

One of the basic claims that made its way across this bridge of assembly, with its companion concept of public, was the church's often contested claim that the Holy Spirit is fully the presence of God. The Holy Spirit infuses each person and gives him or her voice in the *ekklēsia*. It almost forces people to speak, sometimes in unknown tongues going beyond their linguistic barriers.

---

4. This is a favorite theme of Talcott Parsons, "Christianity and Modern Industrial Society," in *Sociological Theory and Modern Society* (New York: Free Press, 1967), pp. 385-421, and, from a theological perspective, of James Luther Adams. See his essays in *Voluntary Associations: Socio-Cultural Analyses and Theological Interpretation,* ed. J. Ronald Engel (Chicago: Exposition Press, 1986).

5. Harmon L. Smith, *Where Two or Three Are Gathered* (Cleveland: Pilgrim Press, 1995). This work presents a whole ethical outlook rooted in this act of public assembly.

The Holy Spirit continually opens up the assembly to new voices and widens the bounds of participation. Here we see a religious ground for a life of democratic participation in public assemblies. The church's often halting struggle to manifest free assembly in Christ's Spirit resonates in complex ways with the human struggle for free assembly in civil life.

We cannot go into the rich and often highly conflicted way that disputes over the nature and form of this ecclesial life shaped political theory. One would have to go back to the writings of Augustine, Aquinas, the fifteenth-century ecclesiastical councils, John Calvin, Johannes Althusius, and then in the modern era Thomas Hobbes, John Locke, and Roger Williams, to name only a few. At almost every point theological ideas about ecclesiology struggled to stake out a sphere for the cultic and ethical enactment of ultimate claims distinct from those of family and governance, whether they be princely, statist, or corporate. Without this fundamental differentiation, as many have pointed out, there would have been little social and cultural space for a civil society independent of the state or a civil society that could transcend national boundaries. For instance, the church's provision of experimental religious groupings around a particular vocation was nurtured in the monastic life for centuries before spawning the modern university and professions. Recall of the covenants and ecclesiologies by which they developed can both revitalize and critique our professions and universities in our own time.[6] More recently, in Germany and South Africa, not to mention the civil rights movement in the United States, many churches staked out spaces of free assembly that could nurture the sparks of civil freedom.

Ecclesiological debates also contained within them critical differences over the proper ordering of not only the religious life but civil life in general.[7] Sharp debates, now forgotten, must have arisen as the synagogue assemblies of the early church soon yielded to the rise of patriarchal and monarchical forms of church governance.[8] Organic notions of the church as the body of Christ competed sharply with those of charismatic societies of the saints. Saint Paul's egalitarian notions of church membership (Gal. 3:25-28) competed even in his own writings with hierarchical images of obedience and service (1 Cor. 11:3-12). All of these disputed ecclesiological conceptions have informed and contested their secular counterparts in European (and now African or Asian) mon-

6. See the covenantal treatment of professions in Eric Mount, Jr., *Professional Ethics in Context: Institutions, Images, and Empathy* (Louisville: Westminster John Knox, 1990).

7. See, for example, Max L. Stackhouse, *Ethics and the Urban Ethos* (Boston: Beacon Press, 1972) and *Creeds, Societies, and Human Rights* (Grand Rapids: Eerdmans, 1986).

8. Elisabeth Schüssler Fiorenza, *In Memory of Her: A Feminist Theological Reconstruction of Christian Origins* (New York: Crossroad, 1984).

archies, republics, and confederations. Without knowing the language of ecclesiological debate, we cannot understand the depth of contest today between those who want to govern by personal, usually parental, rule and those who seek a government tightly governed by codes, laws, and constitutions. How general councils, federated units, and popular participation should be mixed together in civil life has rich ancestry in debates over the role of the Holy Spirit in church assemblies, the relations of councils and popes, and the role of canon law in regulating church life and worship. The struggle between radical congregationalism, with its "bottom-up" federalism, continues to contest with hierarchies of national regulation, control, and corporate administration.[9] Each brings with it deep reservoirs of historical experience in ecclesiological controversies and their associated penumbra of theological claims.

Ecclesiology has shaped both people's practical forms of association and the deep cultural orientations toward the form, relative value, and function of civil institutions. It also functions to introduce a transcendental element into these institutional and cultural debates, because it is always connected to the symbolic rehearsal, in worship, of the connection between human association and ultimately divine purposes.[10] There is a necessary connection between these symbolically envisioned ultimate relationships and how we relate to one another. A worship focused on a relationship with Jesus as our friend sustains commitment to the priority of personal relationships, often among equals. A worship permeated with themes of parental care can then undergird commitment to a government that cares, even parentally, for the welfare of the people. A worship that rehearses apocalyptic destruction can fuel incentives to the warfare of Armageddon or the delegitimation of civil life in whatever form — a pressing issue for Middle Eastern politics. All of these connections require rigorous ethical analysis and critique.

On the religious side, this connection of liturgy and governance has permeated arguments over the relation of priests, ministers, bishops, laity, and councils. On the civil side it gives rise to the development of civil religion as a means to legitimate and critique the forms of civic and governmental life. Ecclesiology, by drawing the connection between worship and organization, awakens us to the rich relationships between civic institutions and their ultimate forms of devotion.[11]

9. William Johnson Everett and Thomas Edward Frank, "Constitutional Order in United Methodism and American Culture," in *Connectionalism: Ecclesiology, Mission, and Identity*, ed. Russell E. Richey and Dennis Campbell (Nashville: Abingdon, 1997), pp. 41-73.

10. See my *The Politics of Worship* (Cleveland: United Church Press, 1999).

11. See the essays by Robert Bellah and others in *American Civil Religion*, ed. Russell Richey and Donald Jones (New York: Harper and Row, 1974).

In this discussion of ecclesiology I have, for reasons of personal (though not idiosyncratic) conviction, emphasized the connection between religious assembly and "publicity," the life of civil society and association. However, I have also indicated the contrast between those who have seen the church as a public and those who have understood it as a kind of household. The concept of household, our third bridge concept, both complements and contradicts the concept of public assembly so closely associated with governance.

Household

Numerous recent theologians have drawn on the concept of household and its Greek root word, *oikos,* to form a bridge language between ecclesiology and ethics on the one hand and general discourse on ecology, feminist theories of society, and governance on the other.[12] In the ancient Greek world the word *oikos* enabled people to move easily from household management *(oikonomia)* to questions of care for the civilized world *(oikoumenē).* Christians saw their own assemblies as gathering in the *oikos tou theou* (household of God), and later spoke of God's saving word in terms of the divine *oikonomia.* In a differentiated world we can draw on this integrating term to make connections between what have become disparate languages of faith, politics, economics, family, and ecology.

In many respects the household language contrasts sharply with that of *ekklēsia* and public, with their distinctions between private and public, autonomous citizenship under the law and caring parenthood within the family. While it resonates especially with women's experience in the household, it also can undermine the public in which they seek to exercise their public citizenship. In other respects, however, it draws attention to much of the substance of what has to be argued out in the public order — how to educate the young, how to care for the earth, and how to protect the weak. It is strong on the purposes of public policy even as it may introduce paradigms of inequality into our public discourse. Household concepts enable traditional religious concerns for care, limits to life, dependency, and the need for wisdom's guidance to inform public discourse. They raise questions about our ultimate needs and interests in the

12. For example, Lewis S. Mudge, *The Church as Moral Community: Ecclesiology and Ethics in Ecumenical Debate* (New York: Continuum; Geneva: WCC Publications, 1998); Letty M. Russell, *Household of Freedom: Authority in Feminist Theology* (Philadelphia: Westminster, 1987); Konrad Raiser, *Ecumenism in Transition,* trans. Tony Coates (Geneva: WCC Publications, 1991); and William Johnson Everett, "OIKOS: Convergence in Business Ethics," *Journal of Business Ethics* 5 (1986): 313-25.

middle of the narrow, market-driven interests of much of contemporary political life. They raise questions of enduring relationships in the midst of competing claims made by supposedly autonomous — indeed isolated — individuals. Household, with its emphasis on caring relationships, whether egalitarian or dependent, contrasts sharply with legal arrangements of adversarial truth finding, retributive punishment, and monetary compensation. The symbolism of the household points to a justice of repair, restoration, and relationship that both transcends and critiques the ordinary justice of the law. In these ways we can see institutional, cultural, and transcendent dimensions of public life that are illuminated by the household concept. It is especially important to see how household and family metaphors have shaped so much of Christian discourse and how this discourse has implications for these dimensions in public life. Theologians and ecclesiologists draw on family metaphors to speak of God, of the Trinity, of ethics, and of church authority and membership (popes, abbots, fathers and mothers, not to mention the "family of God"). But these were also contested symbolisms. Let me give one example.

The use of family symbolism to talk about authority and membership in God's assembly was already contested by Jesus in his rejection of family ties or titles (Matt. 10:34-37; 12:46-50 and parallels; 23:9). In subsequent theology, the relation of the Holy Spirit, a potent "democratic" element, to Christ and to "the Father" fostered the critical break between the Eastern and Western churches. The lack of fit between the Spirit and the two male figures in the Trinity became the symbolic matrix for arguing out the relation of paternal authority to democratic participation. In this regard we need think only of the immense controversy between the seventeenth-century Society of Friends and the church establishment of England or New England.[13]

Today we face in our public life the equally vexatious problem of how to relate the democratic processes of government not only to the problems of caring for the earth and the poor but of relating "private" corporations, with their frequently parental or authoritarian administration, to the claims of the commonweal.[14] The trinitarian struggles to hold these together with respect for their differentiation can be a helpful contribution to public debate. The household bridge concept can mediate between these two discourses.

13. John Locke's attack on patriarchy in his *Two Treatises of Government* (1689) still left household authority proper intact. It was the Quakers who took the theology of the Spirit to its democratic conclusion and were persecuted mightily for it.

14. Bob Goudzwaard and Harry de Lange, *Beyond Poverty and Affluence: Toward an Economy of Care,* trans. Mark R. Vander Vennen (Grand Rapids: Eerdmans, 1995).

Nature

Finally, we turn to a bridge concept with a rich and lengthy history, but one which is bound directly to the problems of parental care for the earth, the weak, and those deprived of a household. The concept of nature is itself contested mightily. From the religious side it is rooted in the doctrine of creation and the unity of the Creator's purpose. Questions of "fact" and "value" are inseparable in nature, for we ourselves are valuing, purposive agents. In some sense the rest of creation shares this with us. All beings live in relationship with one another and with their source — God. So-called creationists may have erred in translating these questions of unity, value, and purpose into an argument about our historical origins, but they are correct in maintaining that our nature involves questions of wholeness, value, and purpose that go far beyond the mechanical and segmentary ways of understanding us that have shaped modern medicine, technology, and education.

On the civil side, nature has often been appealed to as a stand-in for God. Our rights, our legitimate claims and interests, our proper needs — all can be traced to a publicly discernible "nature" that doesn't need a Creator behind it. Our ethics can be drawn from a "law of nature" without appeal to special revelation or claims of particular church authorities. Appeals to some kind of natural law are thus indispensable in the drive to sustain a conception of human rights that transcends the positive law of the nations. Thus natural law as a body of philosophical and ethical reflection has been one of the main bridge concepts between religion and civil life since the early years of the church's existence.[15]

This in no way implies that the civil order has a settled conviction about our nature, about the way our nature fits into nature in general, or for the way this should be translated into institutional, legal, or political forms. Merely a glimpse at the heated debates over abortion and homosexuality, not to mention genetic manipulation, shows that these questions are far from resolved. However, the point here is that the concept of nature itself is a way of introducing classic theological and ethical claims into public discourse in a way that makes them publicly arguable.

The outcomes of these debates can have important cultural and institutional consequences. Family policy based on our nature to live in families, indeed families of a certain form, can be reasoned out of theories of human nature. Ecological policy is deeply shaped by theories about the way "nature"

---

15. For the classic exposition, see Ernst Troeltsch, *The Social Teachings of the Christian Churches*, trans. Olive Wyon (New York: Harper and Row, 1960). For a current use, see Lewis Mudge, *The Church as Moral Community* (New York: Continuum, 1998).

evolves, seeks equilibriums, deals with instabilities, or manages complex interdependent relationships. Concepts of nature can reshape our basic cultural orientations in ways that put them in conversation with classic theological concerns.

Arguments from nature also provide an entrée into classic concerns of transcendence, at least in an important limited form. In placing "the human" or "nature itself" over against our settled statutes, practices, habits of thought, and parochial customs, we gain a certain transcendence over our limited place in history and the world's cultures, not to mention curbing that arrogant pride that ignores our tenuous ecological perch in the cosmos. The nature-related concept of Gaia, for instance, plays an important role in our imagination today, exercising something like God's judgment over our careless destruction of our habitat.[16] Questions about the purposes of human nature can enable us to entertain alternative notions of the good society, of possible utopias and ecological scenarios that might otherwise be dismissed by an appeal to our intractable sin.

These four bridge concepts — covenant, assembly, household, and nature — offer a way of thinking about the problem of theological literacy in public life. Not only do we need to understand how these concepts have functioned on both sides of our present cultural divide, we need to see the ethical issues they have engaged in history and in our present debates. There is, unfortunately, no quick fix or twelve steps to recover from our amnesia about these debates and to compensate for our language antagonisms. It will take practical efforts in education and in religious communities that seek to enable us to find our many voices and take up the perennial task of living together on a beautiful but wounded globe.

---

16. Rosemary Ruether, *Gaia and God: An Ecofeminist Theology of Earth Healing* (San Francisco: Harper, 1992).

CHAPTER NINE

Christian Scholarship and the Demographic Transformation of the Church

ANDREW F. WALLS

Christian Mission as Christian Scholarship

Christian scholarship follows Christian mission and derives from Christian mission. It is common enough to contrast the busy practitioner with the reflective scholar, and not too uncommon to find the reflective scholar distrusted or derided as a drag on the active exercise of Christian mission; yet a glance at Christian history shows a close connection between mission and scholarship. A lively concern for Christian living and Christian witness has repeatedly called scholarly activity into existence.

The demand for scholarship occurred as soon as the gospel crossed its first cultural frontier: that between Israel and the Hellenistic world. The business of constructing a Hellenistic Christian lifestyle, a Greek way of being Christian, was intellectually demanding. In particular, once the word about Jesus Christ was translated into Greek, and entered into a Greek thought world without the built-in controls natural to Greek-speaking Jews, all sorts of new questions (e.g., about the proper way to express the relationship between the divine Savior and the one God) were raised that were not likely to be aired while all the believers in Jesus had been Jews. As the Christian mission to the Greek world expanded, Christian theology expanded too. Christians made discoveries about Christ that were only possible when their deepest convictions about him were expressed in Greek and were pondered using Greek indigenous categories and styles of debate. Sorting through the forests of affirmation and debate and identifying the genuine discoveries among the false trails and the shortcuts needed the insight and discrimination that are fundamental to scholarship. So did the business of explaining Christian faith to people whose life

166

and thought were shaped by a Greek inheritance that had been built up over centuries. Why should they take notice of a story about a Jewish carpenter? Distortions, exaggerations, misunderstandings about Christianity abounded. Christianity, after all, was but one of a range of religious options on the market, packaged as schools of philosophy or schemes for understanding the cosmos. People who inquired about Christianity might already have been looking at other options and meant to go on looking at more. Some of those who came upon the gospel were ill educated, credulous, and superstitious; others were highly educated, skeptical, and urbane. So many opportunities meant also so many possibilities of getting things wrong. The scholarly virtues of insight based on knowledge, patient examination, and disciplined imagination were called for by the very act of proclaiming the gospel.

We can chart the development of scholarly activity through those early centuries of evangelization that preceded and made possible the debates of the age of the great councils. Three figures may stand as representative of different stages in that development.

First there is Paul, an outstandingly open, learned, and culturally sensitive Jewish missionary, who delved as deeply into Hellenistic culture as perhaps any outsider, even one born in the setting, could. He could take Hellenistic words and ideas like *mystērion* and *plērōma* and flood them with Christian meaning, and daringly use them to reinterpret Christ in Hellenistic terms. The second figure is Justin, the converted philosopher, who, having investigated all the philosophical schools, eventually chose to teach Christianity as the true philosophy. Justin uses the Scriptures as a textbook for this philosophy, by this means critiquing his own cultural past, affirming and rejecting. The third representative figure is Origen, child of Christian parents, brought up on the Scriptures but thoroughly educated in Greek learning too. This dual inheritance enabled him to reconceive Greek learning so that it presented Christ and led people to God. Origen's scholarly achievement is immense. Not only did he invent, or give new impetus to, new areas of scholarship — textual criticism, systematic theology, the biblical commentary — he brought almost every trend of existing philosophy and science into Christian service. His literary output was phenomenal, and this in the course of a life of unremitting work as a teacher. Yet this activity was not sustained in a setting of academic calm, but in one of uncertainty and insecurity. Those who responded to his teaching might have their convictions tested by the threat of execution, and in the last phase of his life Origen himself underwent imprisonment and torture. This was evangelistic theology — scholarship in mission, made necessary by mission.

This had a strange result. For all its antiquity and confidence, all was not well with the Greek cultural heritage in those centuries when Christianity was making its way in the Hellenistic world. Paul on the Areopagus in Athens is respectful, if gently ironic, when he addresses the philosophers there; his companion Luke, however, notes their lack of high seriousness. The only thing they wanted, he says, was novelty. In the next century the young Justin, seeking the vision of God that Plato had posed as the goal of the philosophic life, was shocked to find how anxious professional philosophers could be to settle the tuition fees. Philosophy, once a moral and religious discipline, a search for liberating truth, was becoming a profession, a job, a career. It was getting tired and given to recycling ideas. Its last real flourish was with Origen among the Christians and with his contemporary Plotinus among their opponents; but for all the latter's vigor and wealth of ideas, the resources of the Greek tradition were wearing thin. It was the Christians who renewed them, and by that means saved the Greek academy and prolonged its life. It was Christianity, a teaching that had at first appeared utterly irreconcilable with Greek culture, that helped to preserve it, giving new life to some of its vital and authentic elements.

Christianity, as Origen's life demonstrates, gave rise to new branches of learning, but it also revitalized some of the old ones, and especially the key discipline of philosophy. The application of traditional categories and methods to the material of Christian theology refreshed and redirected them. The process put an end to recycling age-old materials and to trivial novelty seeking and hairsplitting. Philosophy was once more centered on big themes, urgent questions, matters that were worth being tortured or killed for. And the philosopher's life was no longer a niche for the careerist. Typically it meant laborious teaching without lucrative fees, pastoral responsibility for the welfare of others, and engagement in a life of discipline and prayer. Philosophy was turned toward the issues of salvation. Ironically it was the Christians, at first the apparent enemies of Greekness, who made the philosopher's life more like Plato's view of what it ought to be. Once more it had become a liberating search for truth.

It would not be hard to point to other instances of scholarship arising out of mission. We could look eastward from the Roman Empire, where the battle for the Greek intellectual heritage was won, and observe Syriac-speaking Christians spreading the gospel through Mesopotamia and Iran and across central Asia until in A.D. 635 (about the time the king of Northumbria in northern England was hearing it) it came to the emperor of China. That long missionary trail across the largest continent is also a trail of libraries. Wherever the Christians went they took books, and the encounter with new cultures, as the Chinese evidence makes clear, caused them to translate books and to write new ones. The Chinese emperor of the day was himself a scholar, who spent half of each day in study. His first concern was to see what books the Christians had brought with them, and to get them translated, and to review them himself. It was on this basis that Christianity was permitted to spread in his empire. The surviving documents show these Christians trying to present Christianity in Chinese categories, exploring how Buddhist terminology might be used to portray Christ, beginning a Christian dialogue with Buddhist monks. Whether or not, as some have argued, their work had permanent effect within Buddhism itself, promoting the hope of a merciful savior that developed in China (so different from the original teaching of the Buddha), it is clear that they entered on an intellectual project as daring as that of Paul and Justin and Origen.

Or we could turn south and follow the early planting of the Christian faith in Africa. Early Ethiopian Christianity, while resolutely confronting the territorial spirits known to African village society, developed its own distinctive literature and tradition of scholarship, using its own distinctive writing system. In the course of its tumultuous history, the recurrent revivals of the Ethiopian church and the recovery of Ethiopian Christianity from near disaster have been accompanied by a revival of scholarship, often in forbidding conditions. Scholarship has never been an easy path in Ethiopia; the fearless evangelists of its classical period had learned to copy a manuscript while sitting on a narrow ledge above a deep precipice.

The point is equally made by the early Western Christianity that grew up among the people the Romans called barbarians. Scholars such as Isidore of Seville and Bede of England used the cultural resources of the peoples of northern and western Europe to extend Christian thinking, producing historical writing of a new type — evangelistic history, one might almost call it — that related national history to the story of salvation. Scholars reflecting on issues that arose out of linking Christian themes together with traditional law and custom, strengthened by the widespread adoption of the styles of Roman law, opened the way for a deepened understanding of sin, judgment, and atonement. The early centuries of Western Christianity are a period of unspeakable violence, with recurrent invasions, ceaseless warfare, famine, plague, and destruction — conditions we might think would make scholarship impossible, especially in societies where literacy was thinly distributed. Yet, far from being a dark age, this was a period of rich, adventurous scholarship, marked by pioneering developments (A.D. dating, for instance) that the Christian Roman Empire even in its glory had never thought of. What made this flowering of scholarship possible was a modification of some of the missionary structures of the church to embrace the task of scholarship. The monasteries, always nurseries of the devotional life, and in early northern Europe important as evangelistic bases, became centers of cooperative scholarship. By building libraries, borrowing and lending and copying books, amid all the turbulence going on around them, they established the materials for generations of scholarship. Once again Christians, by going about the task of mission, had rescued scholarship in the process, at a time when it was in mortal danger.

Or, moving to more recent times, we could consider the missionary movement from the West. When it began, Christianity had become thoroughly accommodated to Western culture, and in a process extending over centuries had penetrated deep into its thought, its customs, its laws, its art and literature. For long centuries Western Christians were largely cut off from most of the non-Western world. But from the sixteenth century onward they were massively in contact with it, and the inadequacies of the Western intellectual tradition for coping with this new world were manifest. They were particularly manifest to those who wanted to communicate the word about Christ. At first it seemed a matter mainly of language; communication of the gospel would be easy once missionaries could speak the languages of Africa and Asia. It was not long before it became plain that language is only the outer skin of the consciousness we now call culture. The gospel had to pass beyond language into the depths of a consciousness that had taken centuries to form and which now shaped the way people thought and acted.

The missionary movement introduced a new element into Western Christian experience. A very surefooted, confident Christianity with centuries of cultural interaction behind it had to make its way in other people's terms, terms that at the time were only vaguely comprehended and seemed alien, if not repellent. Western Christianity came to Asia and Africa assured about its own tradition of learning, and then found that tradition had huge gaps, vast areas where the Western academy, theological or secular, had nothing useful to say. The missionary movement, out of its essential concern to communicate the gospel, was forced into innovative scholarship. Missionaries — Catholic from the early days, Protestant afterwards — turned Western scholarship in new directions. New disciplines or fields of study were invented or made possible: in the languages and literatures of the world beyond Europe, in comparative linguistics, in anthropology, and in comparative religion and tropical medicine. The Western academy in its present secular phase has forgotten where these things came from. They arose, or were made possible, by the desire that Christ should be known in other cultures.

Here then is our starting place: that Christian history indicates that searching, fundamental scholarship arises naturally out of the exercise of Christian mission and especially from its cross-cultural expression. Mission involves moving out of one's self and one's accustomed terrain, and taking the risk of entering another world. It means living on someone else's terms, as the gospel itself is about God living on someone else's terms, the Word becoming flesh, divinity being expressed in terms of humanity. And the transmission of the gospel requires a process analogous, however distantly, to that great act on which Christian faith depends. Cross-cultural diffusion (which is the lifeblood of historic Christianity) has to go beyond language, the outer skin of culture, into the processes of thinking and choosing and all the networks of relationship that lie beneath language, turning them all toward Christ. It requires generations to accomplish, for those processes have themselves taken many generations to form. This is *deep* translation, the appropriation of the Christian gospel in terms of that culture, down to the very roots of identity. It helps not only to communicate the gospel but to enlarge and enrich the whole church's understanding of it. Such deep translation needs the sustained exercise of corporate examination (individual insights, however brilliant, are inadequate) and steady discrimination. Deep translation is necessary to deep mission. So periods of active mission need to be periods of active scholarship. The converse is also true: when the sense of mission is dulled or diverted, the death knell sounds for Christian scholarship.

Reading the Signs of the Times

The particular importance of this appears when we consider which are the critical areas of Christian mission for the twenty-first century, and who will have the principal responsibility for that mission. The answer arises from the most remarkable feature of Christian history in the twentieth century: the massive demographic and cultural shift in the composition of the Christian church. It is very simply stated in crude statistical terms. At the beginning of the twentieth century the heartlands of Christianity lay in Europe and North America. More than 80 percent of professing Christians lived there; Christianity was both a Western religion and the religion of the West. But at the beginning of the twenty-first century, well over half the world's Christians lived in Africa, Asia, Latin America, and the Pacific, and the proportion is steadily rising. Europe is no longer a Christian heartland: its Christian population has long been steadily shrinking. And now North America is becoming subject to the same pressures, and, despite the apparent buoyancy of the Christian component, it shows many of the characteristics that Europe had when its decline, so rapid in its eventual acceleration, began to take effect. Christianity began the twenty-first century as a mainly non-Western religion, and if present trends continue, will become steadily more so. By the century's end, two-thirds of the world's Christians may be living in the southern continents. In any case, Africa, Latin America, and some parts of Asia have now become the Christian heartlands. Demographically, the composition of the Christian church has shifted southward, but its thought processes and cultural awareness have not yet moved proportionately to the demographic shift. The present situation of Christianity in some ways resembles its position in the late second century, when it was engaged in a mode of interaction with Hellenistic culture that would hugely enlarge and refine Christian thinking, permanently enrich the church's understanding of who Christ was, and penetrate the thought processes of a whole civilization so that long afterwards it would have the imprint of Christ. This time it is not the Mediterranean world, nor the Western world at all, that is the scene of the interaction. The crucial activity lies in the Christian interaction with the ancient cultures of Africa and Asia. The quality of African and Asian (and Latin American) Christianity, and thus the quality of twenty-first-century Christianity as a whole, will depend on the quality of that interaction. If the quality is good, we may see something like what appeared in the third and fourth and fifth centuries. We may see a great creative development of Christian theology: new discoveries about Christ that Christians everywhere can share; mature, discriminating standards of Christian living; people and groups responding to the gospel at a deep level of understanding and personality; a long-term Christ-shaped imprint on the thinking of Africa and Asia; a new stage in the church's growth toward the full stature of Christ. If the quality is poor, we shall see distortion, confusion, uncertainty, and almost certainly hypocrisy on a large scale.

Many factors will finally determine the quality of the interaction, but one of them will certainly be the emergence or nonemergence of an adequate Christian scholarship rooted in Christian mission. It was the development of an effective Christian scholarship, in a tradition that went from Paul through Justin to Origen and beyond, that enabled the conversion of the Greek past and made it possible for Christians nourished in Hellenistic culture to relate Christ to their pre-Christian inheritance. This new tradition of scholarship began by borrowing from that inheritance (Paul), moved to critiquing it, to affirm or reject (Justin), and eventually to refiguring and reconciling the whole (Origen). The three stages made Greek theology viable. We cannot ignore our past; we are made by our past, and our past gives us our identity. To lose our past is to lose our memory; and to lose one's memory means to be unable to recognize things and people for what they are; it permanently inhibits confident, assured relationships. The past that gives us identity cannot be abandoned, nor can it be suppressed. Nor can it be left as it is, untouched by Christ's hand, anymore than our present can be left without his touch. The past has to be converted, turned to face Christ, opened up to him.

Paul, Justin, and Origen represent three stages in the conversion of the Greek past. Perhaps no theological task in the twenty-first century is more urgent than that of the conversion of the African past. Paul's part, the missionary part (the part where a sympathetic outsider can help), was done long ago. Justin's part, the convert's task of establishing a discriminating critique, has also had countless worthy representatives. Africa stands in need of Origens, of people who, brought up in the Christian faith, rooted in the Christian Scriptures, are certain of their Christian identity and yet confident of their African identity, confident enough to handle the African past as Christians and as Africans. The different cultures of Asia need their own Origens too. The special needs of Latin America would require another essay.

This is not simply a matter that affects the southern continents themselves. We have seen that in the twenty-first century Christianity has been revealed as an increasingly non-Western religion. Christianity is in recession in Western countries, and in Europe has dwindled out of recognition within the lifetime of people of my own age. The implication is that Africa and Asia and Latin America and the Pacific seem set to be the principal theaters of Christian activity in its latest phase. What happens there will determine what the Christianity of the twenty-first and twenty-second centuries will be like. What happens in Europe, and even in North America, will matter less and less. It is Africans and Asians and Latin Americans who will be the *representative* Christians: those who represent the Christian norm, the Christian mainstream of the twenty-first and twenty-second centuries. That in time means that the most significant Christian developments in theology, for instance, or ethical thinking, or the Christian impact on society, will be those that take place in the southern continents, not those that take place in the West. The development of theological and ethical thinking and action in Africa and Asia and Latin America will determine mainstream Christianity. Similar development in North America and Europe may be of mainly local importance. The quality of African and Asian theological scholarship, therefore, will not only be vital for Africans or Asians; it will help to determine the shape and quality of world Christianity. Western theological leadership of a predominantly non-Western church is an incongruity. Much will depend on the quality of the theological leadership received from the non-Western world; it will be in the non-Western world that the future of Christianity will be determined; it is there that Christian witness will be made or marred.

The primary responsibility for the determinative theological scholarship of the twenty-first century will lie with the Christian communities of Africa, Asia, and Latin America. The point is worth stressing, because it is likely that (allowing for some localized specializations) theology will be the only major field of scholarship where this is the case. In most of the scientific and medical and technological spheres, leadership will remain with the West, or with east Asia in those departments where east Asia can outstrip the West. And in the humanities and social sciences the stockpiled resources of the West will continue to give it great strength. But authentic theological scholarship must arise out of Christian mission and therefore from the principal theaters of mission. Theology is about making Christian decisions in critical situations; it is in the southern continents that those decisions will be most pressing, and the key theological developments are accordingly to be looked for. If appropriate scholarship does not emerge to give guidance and discipline to that process of decision, those key theological developments are likely to be stunted and ineffectual. In a word, if Africa and Asia and Latin America do not develop a proper capacity for leadership in theological studies, there will for practical purposes be no theological studies anywhere that will be worth caring about.

An aging Western academic is forced, against the grain, to go further. The Western academy is sick, as sick as the Greek academy was in the early days of Christianity. The university developed in the West as a product of Christian concern. The earliest universities were church institutions holding the preservation and promotion of learning and its impartation to new generations as sacred duties. Over the centuries they developed as secular institutions, but they retained the old ideals in secular form. In the European tradition, the state (in North America other expressions of civil responsibility) replaced the church in maintaining and renewing them. By the twentieth century the burden was more than any of the agencies could bear, and private finance, in effect the corporate world, was called in to make the enterprise viable. The universities thus find themselves the pensioners of global capitalism. The highest academic accolade is now to have received a fat research grant from outside sources. The purpose of the grant, or of the research it underwrites, becomes secondary. The path of most academic merit is that which brings in the most private funding to the university. Triviality jostles moral compromise: biscuit manufacturing firms fund research in dunking cookies, cigarette manufacturers sponsor an academic school of business ethics. The determinative funding for medical research comes from drug companies whose priorities are best served from the afflictions of the affluent world, and charitable foundations whose consciousness is of suffering are also concentrated there. Yet the big killer diseases wreak their havoc outside the affluent world. While human life is devastated across Africa and Asia, sponsors can be found to research the most effective way of dunking cookies in tea, and universities will take the money and provide the laboratory space. This is not the purpose of universities as originally conceived, the promotion of learning for the glory of God; nor is it the best ideal of universities in their earlier secular phase, the disinterested search for truth. Our universities are coming into bondage to Mammon, and the altars of Mammon are more sanguinary than those of Moloch.

Another danger afflicts the Western academy, particularly noticeable in the United States. Professors have become a guild, a profession, and the academy a career. Increasingly that career is becoming analogous to careers in the business world. It is competitive; professors are in competition with other professors. It is individualistic; professors are expected to strive to advance their own name and reputation. Originally the university was a company, a fellowship of scholars; it has become an assemblage of workshops where individual scholars work individually. Research in the humanities, including religion, is dominated by a number of foundations, and prestigious achievement is reflected in a large grant from one of them. So professors become adept at watching for and interpreting the smiles and frowns of the foundations, and in seeking out projects that will please them. Some words of a major American publisher are burned into my heart: that in his experience research projects were mainly about the advancement of professional careers. And he was speaking about *theological* projects and their literary outcome. We need a cleansing of theological scholarship, a reorientation of academic theology to Christian mission, a return to the ideal of scholarship for the glory of God, a return to the ideal of the academic life as a liberating search for truth. How can this come about? The Western academy is corrupted; in some areas it is absolutely corrupted. Perhaps it will be in the non-Western world that the scholarly vocation will begin anew and a new breed of scholars arise who, working in community, will break the chains of Mammon and throw off the impedimenta of careerism.

Theological Tasks for the Twenty-first Century

We have already spoken of the theological enterprise of the twenty-first century being parallel in scope and extent to that of Christians in the Greek world of the third century and beyond. It will include thinking Christ into the entire cultural framework of Africa and the Asian countries, so that they really are, as the Epistle to the Ephesians puts it, summed up in him; so that the Lord of All really rules past and present. This alone would be sufficient to indicate that the great theological frontiers of the coming centuries will be those of the southern continents. The issues are too vast for even the most cursory discussion here, so it is necessary to isolate one or two tasks as illustrative of a larger undertaking. It is convenient — because the issues there are so stark — to choose some tasks that will belong particularly to Africa. And the first of these is startling enough to begin with: it is *rethinking the framework of theology.*

This is not as pretentious as it may seem. For good historical reasons, most African theological thinking necessarily started within the particular

Western framework that belonged to those from whom the Christian message was transmitted to much of Africa. Neither party was conscious of how far that framework was the product of a particular period of Western cultural history. It is not that the doctrines of Trinity and incarnation and atonement and so on are Western ideas; but rather that the framework which holds them together comes out of Western experience. One element of that experience is crucial to the way the framework has been constituted in modern times, and African experience has not been symmetrical with it.

The complex series of intellectual movements which we designate collectively as the Enlightenment presented the greatest challenge to the Christianity of the West since the rise of Islam. Its exaltation of reason and of the autonomous individual self battered the supports that had upheld Western Christianity since the barbarian conversion: revelation and the corporate consciousness as expressed in Christendom. The flurry of scientific activity and discovery assisted in refocusing the view of the universe so that it concentrated on the empirical world that we can see and feel.

The Enlightenment turned much of traditional thought upside down; and that traditional thought had known centuries of penetration by Christian teaching. The Enlightenment could have strangled Western Christianity; in France it nearly succeeded in doing so. But Christianity recovered. It accommodated many Enlightenment themes and methods, and modified or redirected others. It set about penetrating Enlightenment thought as it had penetrated the traditional pre-Enlightenment thought of Europe. The Evangelical Revival made a special contribution to the new synthesis, since it demonstrated that Christianity, formerly expressed essentially corporately within the concept of Christendom, could be reconciled with the individual consciousness and the new primacy of the autonomous self. There remained a stream of Enlightenment thinking that was hostile, or at least unfavorable, to Christianity, and that stream was to broaden in the twentieth century. But a Christianized form of the Enlightenment developed, a Christianity shaped to the Enlightenment worldview, and this became the dominant Western expression of Christianity. Modern Western theology is Enlightenment theology.

The modern missionary movement, child as it was of the evangelical and pietist movements, was deeply influenced by the Enlightenment. Its concern with education and health care, its confidence in science and technology, its ideas about civilization as the fruit of evangelization, and many more of its features, good and bad, came out of the Enlightenment. And generations of missionaries, as they set forth the gospel, also set forth that Enlightenment worldview which had given shape to their theology. They belonged to the Enlightenment tamed and conquered in the name of Christ.

Fundamental to the Enlightenment view was a demarcated frontier between the empirical world — the world of what we can see and touch, the realm in which "repeatability" can reasonably be looked for — and the other world, the world of spirit. Natural could, and must, be distinguished from supernatural. The non-Christian and anti-Christian wing of the Enlightenment argued that there is nothing on the other side of the frontier of the empirical world, or, if there is, we can know nothing about it. The greater part of the Western secular academy now works on that assumption, though it does not always make the assumption clear. It brackets out the whole of the "other" world, the world of spirit, even in the study of religion.

Of course, the Christian Enlightenment could not leave the matter there. It accepted the frontier between the worlds but asserted that there were identifiable crossing places: the incarnation, the resurrection, revelation, prayer, perhaps miracles. But these were recognized crossing points of a frontier that was generally closed, and theological activity was sometimes a matter of deciding where the bona fide crossing points were to be found. Theology, in effect, policed the frontier. Even the reading of the Bible became subject to frontier policing. So much of the Old Testament could not be accommodated within an Enlightenment universe that Enlightenment Christians developed ways of reading it at a certain distance; and even some features of the New Testament and the apostolic church — prophecy, for instance, healing, and other works of power — were designated as frontier crossings formerly in use but no longer available.

It was in such a framework that the gospel came to Africa, and the gospel was accepted and appropriated by Africans. Missionary education regularly expounded an Enlightenment worldview. One American missionary in Sierra Leone early in the twentieth century writes home after a science lesson of the privilege it is to reveal a law of nature when his pupils "expect a witch." The scientific worldview and Christian conviction intermingled and seemed equally opposed to the magical.

But African visions of the world were different. The frontier between the empirical world and the spiritual world was being crossed and recrossed every day in both directions. Africans responded to the gospel in multitudes, but they could not easily lose the vision of that open frontier. As a result, the theology they inherited, and the church practice based upon it, frequently did not seem to fit the facts of daily experience.

The problem was that Western theology is pared-down theology, cut and shaved to fit a small-scale universe. Most Africans, even when they were participating in Enlightenment activities (for science and technology readily found a home in Africa), lived in a larger universe where the frontier was still open. The distinction between natural and supernatural was not easy to preserve. Some of the most devastating aspects of life — witchcraft, for instance — were beyond the reach of mission theology, beyond the reach of Western theology. In an Enlightenment universe, witchcraft does not exist: it is an imaginary crime. As the Enlightenment took hold, legislation against witchcraft was struck from the statute books of Christendom; for similar reasons and generally with missionary approval, legislation against certain activities to neutralize witchcraft, such as ordeals, was established by colonial authorities. Missionaries, acting from Christian charity, could protect unfortunate people accused by their neighbors of witchcraft; what they generally could not cope with was the entity itself. The Enlightenment worldview blurred the line between the activity of witchcraft and the belief in the existence of witchcraft. Enlightenment Christianity swept witch and witch doctor together, along with every form of magic and divination and most forms of traditional healing, into a single pile of refuse designated "superstition." The resultant gap between worldview and theology, between what people see the world to be and the resources the church supplies for coping with it in a Christian way, has been incalculably damaging. Multitudes of Christians have not known what to do in emergencies for which traditional Africa had traditional remedies. They sincerely wish to live as Christians, but they live in a larger, more populated world than the one which supplied the theology and practice of their churches. They see things that church theology and practice does not envisage. So they go to the diviner, but secretly, and with a bad conscience. It is an act not of apostasy, but of desperation.

The people who first explored the gap between worldview and theology were often semi-educated people. More highly educated people could hope to find the missing key as their knowledge increased; those with no such hope had to make provision for the world as they saw it, for the strains of living in two worlds could be intolerable. They could see that, for Christians, God in Christ ought to fill the whole world and relate to everything in it, but the theological framework they inherited left huge areas of the world as they saw it untouched by Christ. It had nothing to say on matters of high importance to ordinary people, matters that belonged to common experience. And as they read the New Testament themselves, they saw those stretches of material that Enlightenment-influenced theology had bracketed out. The Old Testament, too, is not a foreign book in Africa; it needs no special spectacles. They put two and two together and did some theological reconstruction. There is evidence of creative informal theology all over Africa, carried out by people who did not realize they were theologians; the songs of the Ghanaian Afua Kuma, a traditional midwife by calling, are a good example. Among those informal theologians were some of the founders of the early African-instituted, or "Spiritual," churches, and the problem they addressed was essentially the gap between theology and worldview. At the time they were commonly seen as on the margins of Christianity on account of the extent to which they reflected traditional worldviews. In fact, many of them were at heart radically Christian: they were seeking to actualize the saving activity of God in Christ in the world as large numbers of Africans saw the world.

Much has happened since those early days. Africa is now one of the Christian heartlands, and the missionary episode there may be nearing its close; at least, it no longer determines the course of events. The missionary movement brought the gospel to Africa, and brought the Enlightenment with it. Africans took the gospel, and took something from the Enlightenment too; and the extent to which Africa shares in the Enlightenment is to a large extent due to the missionary contribution. But as we look at the continent, with its burgeoning Christian communities, at the beginning of the twenty-first century, we must conclude that part of the strength of Christianity in Africa today is due to the fact that it is independent of the Enlightenment.

The evidence is plentiful that in country after country African Christian practice now recognizes the need for Christ to fill the world as Africans see the world, to be applied to entities and areas of life to which old theology never had anything convincing to say, to cope with the open frontier between the empirical and spiritual worlds, with its consistent crossings and recrossings. No longer is it the African-instituted, or Spiritual, churches who take the lead in this; they have been quite outflanked by the charismatic movement, which now finds a firm base of support in the old denominational churches as well as in countless new churches and "ministries." In effect, all these use the same maps of the spiritual universe. Pastoral and evangelistic practice is in process of transformation. But there is still no adequate theology to express the change. The framework of theology inherited from the West, and still the staple of the seminaries, cannot cope: it is not big enough for the universe that most Africans live in. There is now plenty of church practice that takes that universe seriously and seeks to demonstrate the power and love of Christ within it. But there is also a great deal of confusion and ambiguity. Some of the confusion comes from imported aspects of the charismatic movement that can have a baleful effect when applied near the African open frontier. Alongside the proclamation and demonstration of Christ's deliverance from the entire range of evil powers is another message, that prosperity and health is the normal state of the true Christian life. What is the outcome when prosperity does not closely ensue? Concern leads to anxiety, and anxiety to suspicion. If I have not received the blessing I should, who is responsible? I mentally go through the list of people who may be impeding me. Suspicion is the very seedbed of witchcraft accusation, and hatred the very essence of witchcraft itself. And so, what brought delighted liberation turns back again to bondage.

The context in which the new ministries have arisen has also produced a tendency to deal with the demonic solely in terms of individual pathology. This can mask its presence in the way societies (including the church) are organized (what Paul calls the principalities and powers) not to speak of the mystery of iniquity. It could inhibit African Christian thinking from grappling with the massive irruptions of evil that appear — such as genocide. Western Christian theology is still wrestling with the fact of the Holocaust, the systematic murder of millions of Jews and the attempt to exterminate the Jewish race. African theology must not fail to deal with the genocide in Rwanda and, above all, how this happened in our own day in what by most calculations was the most Christian country in Africa. A coherent theology of the open frontier between the empirical and spiritual worlds could develop immeasurably the ecumenical understanding of the nature of evil.

Other things that African theology must do for the sake of African Christianity would equally be of wider ecumenical benefit. Enlightenment soteriology was necessarily focused on the salvation of the individual, because the intellectual matrix was the Cartesian autonomy of the self. The anxiety level in its controversies — over predestination, for instance — was due to this focus. But the African intellectual matrix is likely to call for a theology of relationships, a theology of belonging. This in turn could lead to a new approach to the doctrine of the state. The classical doctrines of church and state as developed in the West are of little use in Africa; they have no place for the various layers of loyalty and identity that Africa knows. The doctrine of the family, too, needs a new framework, for in its Western development no one thought of the ancestors, "the living dead" in John Mbiti's phrase, as part of the family.

There is more at stake here than the development of particular doctrines or their local application. There is a need for reconception of the framework of theological thinking to cope with a larger universe, and to bring coherence and confidence into areas where preaching and practice have already instinctively begun to move.

And in all this, we have spoken only of Africa. The theological vigor that will be needed in the twenty-first century becomes evident when we consider the work which interaction with the cultures of Asia will bring: in India, for instance, perhaps the most testing environment in which the Christian faith has yet had to survive; or the other Christian discourses such as those of China and of that line of Christian communities that stretches from the Himalayas through Southeast Asia, and which has appeared only in the last century. There has never been such a call for devout minds with a mastery of Scripture, an awareness of earlier Christian thinking, and as confident an apprehension of the cultural traditions and realities of life of the southern continents as was once brought to those of Hellenistic Roman civilization.

It need hardly be said that one of the areas of revision will be theological education. Generally speaking, the theological curricula across Africa and Asia have followed Western models, simply making some additions for local relevance. But Western curricula in church history, for instance, do not present some universal model; they reflect a careful process of selection that makes the West the special focus of the church's life. And biblical studies are dominated by the results of a chapter of Western intellectual history, and essentially by Enlightenment methods. There are other traditions of needing sacred and classical texts which minds conditioned by Confucian and Buddhist approaches may profitably apply to Scripture. Paul, after all, is hardly a model for the historical-critical method of exegesis. The field of the study of religions, too, is dominated by models developed for a European Enlightenment understanding of religion. For African theology and church history, the old religions of Africa are the substructure of Christianity, the materials which, in converted, or unconverted, or partly converted form, lie beneath the beliefs and practices of the Christian church in Africa.

Some Ingredients of Christian Scholarship

Only a small fraction of the theological tasks has been mentioned, but it is evident that much of the work can only be done in Africa, in Asia, in Latin America. If the churches of these continents do not produce theological leadership, the principal theaters of Christian mission in the century now opening will languish in confusion.

The ingredients required for the theological revolution will include:

1. *A renewal of the sense of Christian vocation to scholarship, with the anchoring of Christian scholarship in Christian mission.* To meet the demands envisaged here may require quite a costly form of service. It needs long training, constant self-discipline, intense labor without being much noticed. There is a peril in certain contexts of identifying scholarship with holding an academic post. We have seen that the Greek academy declined when it became a career, and that the Western academy faces the same peril. Christian scholarship in the new situation is going to require the sort of vocational sense that in one age of the church called people to be monks and in another age called them to be missionaries.

181

2. *A research climate.* The southern continents are packed with the most amazing resources for research: historical, biblical, theological, phenomenological. But their institutions, often demoralized by the lack of funding and resources of other kinds, are not always aware of the gold mines within their reach. They have the capacity to collect and preserve research materials, to foster a sense of inquiry, to develop forums for discussion and scholarly investigation. The Western university has become an ivory tower, and the economic realities of Africa and south Asia make it clear that the ivory tower is unattainable there. But there are other traditions of scholarship, and one belonging to India may have particular relevance for Christians. The ashram was, and is, a community of people living a simple life of worship and study together. Some Christian ashrams have already come into being specially for this scholarly purpose — there are splendid examples in various parts of Africa, Asia, and Latin America. But equally the Christian ashram could arise in a preexisting institution (a seminary or a university department, for instance) if it maintains the devout spirit, the active, cooperative fellowship, and the research climate.

3. *Exacting standards.* These are of the nature of scholarship. One of the frequent utterances of J. E. K. Aggrey, that pioneer of African education, was "only the best is good enough for Africa." These words were remembered in his native Ghana in the 1950s when the University of Ghana was established with sumptuous accommodations. But exacting standards can be achieved without grand surroundings.

4. *Collegial attitudes.* The Western academy is suffering from rampant individualism and built-in competitiveness. The ashram model is of scholarly cooperation, of sharing resources and corporate responsibility (remember those monasteries in eighth-century Europe borrowing and lending and copying).

5. *Pioneering spirit.* The new scholarship needs Origens: innovators who both open up new fields and develop ways of exploring them adequately. And, as Origen's own career makes clear, such experimental scholarship is risky.

6. *Dual education.* The effectiveness of scholarship will depend on its depths of understanding in two areas. One is the biblical and Christian material; the other is local society (be it African or Indian or whatever) in all its aspects. It will need people with Origen's dual education, where the Greek interpenetrated with the Christian, so that they could be most Christian when most Greek and most Greek when most Christian.

7. *A catholic attitude to knowledge.* Specialization is inevitable in scholar-

ship, but it can also inhibit it. Large theological institutions in the West no longer look for church historians but for early church historians, Reformation historians, American church historians. The new situation needs scholars who, while maintaining and developing their own expertise, are willing to listen, and learn, and absorb Christian learning from every discipline, sacred and secular.

8. *A lively interactive sense of world Christianity.* Perhaps the largest issue for the church of Christ in the twenty-first century will be ecumenical. Africa, Asia, and Latin America will be the leading theaters of mission and, it is to be hoped, of theological activity. But does this mean each of them will develop along its own local lines through its own local resources, so that in the end there are a welter of local Christianities with no fellow feeling? Will Western Christianity be one more such local Christianity meeting only local needs?

It would fit the postmodern fashion to say that each local Christian discourse is valid and sufficient in itself. But the church is Christ's body, and the picture we are given in the Epistle to the Ephesians of the relation of different cultural presences in the body is neither of uniformity nor of separated diversity but of mutual possession. And the fullness of Christ's stature is achieved only as Hellenistic and Jewish cultures come together in the one body.

The theological activity of Africa and Asia is not a matter of indifference to the church in the West. We are one body, and the health of the whole is involved. Cooperation, even in the preparation for assumption of leadership in Christian scholarship by Africa, Asia, and Latin America, could have an effect on the process. But it must genuinely be cooperation; the age of dependence (and the assumption of Western leadership) is at an end. In any case, many Western institutions are not well placed to assist in the development of theological leadership outside the West; they have neither the experience nor the expertise, and there is a sad trail of Ph.D.s across the world whose long years of study in the West have left them no better, and perhaps worse, equipped for their task than before. Perhaps the single most valuable enterprise would be the harnessing of technology to bring about a genuine sharing of library resources. True sharing of academic resources would be a small step toward the enjoyment of the riches that will be available in the body of Christ as his people from all over the world grow up in him. And the discoveries about Christ that are made in the African, Asian, and Latin American heartlands will belong to us all.

PART III

HERMENEUTICS: HOW WE UNDERSTAND
AND INTERPRET THE BIBLE

RODNEY L. PETERSEN

Theological literacy shapes the church. A theme that ran through the preface to Part II was the interplay between alienation and institutionalism. As alienation has contributed to different forms of institutional formation, it has drawn upon different readings of constitutive texts. How we read a text is the art of hermeneutics. Hermeneutics is the discipline of reading and understanding, or interpretation.[1] It involves, minimally, language, reflection on how language is used, and interpretation. Additionally, how we understand the world is a way of "reading" the world. Medieval theology drew a distinction between the two books of God, the revealed text of Scripture and the "book" of nature, the *liber naturae.*

The term "hermeneutics" means systematic exegesis. It comes from the Greek, reminding us of the god Hermes who mediated between the divine world of the gods and mundane reality. Hermeneutics has played and plays a central role in shaping an educational system.[2] Augustine takes us to the question of

---

1. Shaun Gallagher offers a helpful introduction and historical overview to the topic of hermeneutics in *Hermeneutics and Education* (Albany: State University of New York Press, 1992). Gallagher summarizes the different definitions of hermeneutics offered by Friedrich Schleiermacher, Richard Palmer, Paul Ricoeur, Wilhelm Dilthey, Martin Heidegger, Hans-Georg Gadamer, Josef Bleicher, and Jürgen Habermas (pp. 3-4).

2. There are many different accounts of the rise of hermeneutics; see Hans-Georg Gadamer, *Truth and Method,* revised translation of Joel Weinscheimer and Donald G. Marshall, 2nd ed. (New York: Crossroad, 1989), originally published as *Wahrheit und Methode* (1960); Wilhelm Dilthey, "The Rise of Hermeneutics," trans. Fredric Jameson, *New Literary History* 3 (1972): 234; and Richard E. Palmer, *Hermeneutics: Interpretation Theory in Schleiermacher, Dilthey, Heidegger, and Gadamer* (Evanston, Ill.: Northwestern University Press, 1969).

how we interpret the Bible in book 3 of *On Christian Doctrine.*[3] He raises issues that continue to shape contemporary hermeneutics — for example, the meaning of language as literal or symbolic and figurative symbol, the social location of an author, and the morality of the text as defined by or understood in different periods of time or culture. The chapters in this section are set together here in relation to Augustine's reflection. Each takes up different aspects of interpretation: the object of theology as it stands open to interpretation, interpretation as a means for penetrating false consciousness and promoting emancipation, interpretation as shaped by cultural location, and Christian theology itself in light of global religious traditions. These four issues shape us and are a part of the formative process that is shaping the global church. They constitute aspects of theological literacy with respect to ways in which we read the Bible.

Hermeneutics, or interpretation, focuses upon authoritative texts or the world understood as a "text." As texts become defined and are given authoritative status by a community, they can be referred to as a "canon," the Greek term for a measuring reed. This term has long been applied to the canon of Scripture, or the Bible. The importance of a canon and of its interpretation is seen in the early church when Jerome reveals in a letter how he awoke in a cold sweat one night, having had a nightmare in which he was ridden with guilt over whether his canon was that of the old dispensation, as defined by the works of Plato, Aristotle, and Cicero, or whether his life was really being shaped in the new dispensation by a new canon, the works of the Prophets, the Gospels, and Letters of Paul. For Christians living in the new dispensation of grace inaugurated in the life and work of Jesus as Messiah, this is the Bible, or *biblia,* "the books." Wilfrid Cantwell Smith reminds us of the additional conceptual difficulties we face today when, in the public arena, we refer to Scripture. He illustrates a movement through Christian history whereby the *Scriptures* — meaning the Hebrew Bible or Torah and New Testament writings — became thought of as *Scripture* under the impulse of the Enlightenment, then became referred to again as *Scriptures* in the plural in the contemporary period. The term, however, now bears ambiguity in public settings as the Christian Scriptures may be confused with the authoritative books of other religious traditions.[4]

---

3. Augustine, *On Christian Doctrine,* trans. D. W. Robertson, Jr. (Indianapolis: Bobbs-Merrill Educational Publishing, 1983). Book 3 (pp. 78-117) considers such issues as literal and figurative interpretation; how to understand the "immoralities" of the patriarchs, a topic taken up in Augustine's day by Jerome. On Tyconius's "Rules" for interpretation as a guide for how to read the Bible and other matters, see Pamela Bright and Charles Kannengiesser, *The Book of Rules of Tyconius: Its Purpose and Inner Logic* (Notre Dame, Ind.: University of Notre Dame Press, 2001).

4. Wilfrid Cantwell Smith, *What Is Scripture? A Comparative Approach* (Minneapolis:

Recognizing this conceptual transposition of the term "Scripture," we can no longer simply ask to have the Scriptures interpreted. Instead, we are thrown into a world of comparative religion that is shaped by at least four questions as they pertain to a canon and its interpretation. First, what, in act, is revelation? Second, how does inspiration happen? Third, who decides what "Scriptures" are the result of revelation and inspiration? Finally, in what sense are the Scriptures true?[5] Thankfully, we are not without precedents in dealing with these questions. The rich epistolary exchange between Jerome and Augustine in the fourth and fifth centuries offers us helpful guidance.[6] This discussion, and the ideas it elicited about the nature of truth and deception, continues to shape our thinking.[7] Questions about the authenticity of the documents, about interpretation, and about the nature of truth again became paramount in the sixteenth century in the context of intense religious debate subsequent to the philosophical emphasis of the Renaissance and new technologies that permitted the more rapid printing of books. The publication of Desiderius Erasmus's epoch-making Greek New Testament (Basel, 1516) with a classical Latin translation is illustrative of the hope that authentic documents could spark church and social renewal. In Erasmus's case, a return to the original sources (*veritas Hebraica,*

Fortress, 1993). See also Harold Coward, ed., *Experiencing Scripture in World Religions* (Maryknoll, N.Y.: Orbis Books, 2000). See also John Goldingay, *Models for Scripture* (Grand Rapids: Eerdmans, 1994).

5. In order to think doctrinally about Scripture, theologians have commonly used terms such as "revelation," "inspiration," "authority," and "inerrancy." As applied to Augustine, see Rodney L. Petersen, "To Behold and Inhabit the Blessed Country: Revelation, Inspiration, Scripture and Infallibility," *Trinity Journal* 4, no. 2 (autumn 1983): 28-81. For many today, the doctrine of Scripture is in disarray. Theologians such as James Barr and Edward Farley have questioned its appropriateness. See Barr's *The Bible in the Modern World* (New York: Harper, 1973) and Farley's *Ecclesial Reflection: An Anatomy of Theological Method* (Philadelphia: Fortress, 1982); and note references to others.

6. Most letters are easily accessed through *Nicene and Post-Nicene Fathers of the Christian Church,* ed. Philip Schaff, vols. 1, 3, 4 (Grand Rapids: Eerdmans, 1974). For reference, see B. Altaner, *Patrologie* (Freiberg: Herder and Herder, 1966).

7. Augustine wrote two books against lying — *On Lying* (A.D. 395) and *Against Lying* (A.D. 420). The occasion for each was Jerome's belief that Peter and Paul had used edifying lies to instruct people, that they were only pretending to differ during a conflict between them at Antioch (Gal. 2:11-14). In both works Augustine attacks any form of holy dissemblance, arguing that if we cannot trust Scripture in the smallest of details, we have no confidence in our salvation. For Augustine, difficulties in Scripture become matters of interpretation, not error. See Peter Brown, *Augustine of Hippo* (Berkeley: University of California Press, 1967), and J. N. D. Kelly, *Jerome* (New York: Harper and Row, 1975), pp. 64-65 and passim. In more recent literature, Sissela Bok drew upon Augustine's work on deception; see *Lying: Moral Choice in Public and Private Life* (New York: Knopf, 1999).

Greek, and Latin) would freshen the air of theological understanding and church life. However, even when we do get the category of a canon straight, there remains the question of interpretation. Writing with such questions in mind, Moisés Silva, committed as he is to the inerrancy of the Christian text of Scripture, has noted that the concept of inerrancy solves nothing if we do not know how to interpret Scripture.[8]

Interpretation begins with language. The importance of languages, the heritage of Jerome, and the reform of theological study in the sixteenth century are raised up as a part of theological literacy for the twenty-first century in the chapter by Walter Kaiser, "Theological Literacy for the Twenty-first Century." He takes us to the first of our four hermeneutical concerns, the object of theology as it stands open to interpretation. His chapter takes up the importance of languages together with ideas about how to interact with culture as seen earlier in the chapter by Andrew Walls. Noting the formative impact of the Enlightenment upon Christian belief, interpretation, and practice, Kaiser affirms the value of the study of original biblical languages as it became a part of the curricula at Cambridge University and Harvard College. This is a discipline and aspect of interpretation that is still maintained at some seminaries. Frequently an aspect of conservative hermeneutics, such knowledge of the biblical languages is felt to be helpful for an immediacy in interpretation. This hermeneutic allows for the possibility of objective knowledge about God. Kaiser goes on to argue for an appreciation of literary criticism. He values the way this takes us beyond language skills and historical perspective to the world of cultures. However, he stops short of more radical hermeneutical positions.[9]

Kaiser's intent is not only academic but also pastoral. Christian faith and cultural perspective are important since the pastor, or priest, speaks God's word into a specific time. Too often one may subordinate faith to culture or culture to faith. Instead, Kaiser argues for the importance of cultivating and consecrating the humanities, the arts and sciences, nature and culture, in the service of

---

8. Moisés Silva, *Has the Church Misread the Bible?* (Grand Rapids: Zondervan, 1987), pp. 2-4.

9. Shaun Gallagher defines four hermeneutical approaches: (1) conservative hermeneutics (defined by Schleiermacher and Dilthey) that posits an ability to know the truth of an author; (2) moderate hermeneutics (defined by Gadamer and Ricoeur) that finds meaning in the interplay of reader and author; (3) radical hermeneutics (inspired by Nietzsche and Heidegger and practiced by Derrida and Foucault) that finds original meaning elusive and all constructions contingent and relative; and (4) critical hermeneutics (developed by Habermas and Apel with inspiration from Marx, Freud, and the Frankfurt School of social criticism), a means of penetrating false consciousness and promoting a liberating consensus. See his *Hermeneutics and Education,* pp. 5-11.

God. In addition to valuing a deep cultural recognition, again something beyond the skin of language, extending to a deeper translation of culture as argued by Walls, Kaiser writes of the value of conscious hermeneutical theory. This offers an orienting perspective as one becomes familiar with different hermeneutical questions as posed by different cultural eras, that of the Enlightenment, of romanticism, and of today's postmodernism which, Kaiser feels, often bears affinities with romanticism.

Kaiser's point becomes more particular as he highlights the work of a variety of authors who mark out different aspects of hermeneutical theory. For example, W. K. Wimsatt and Monroe Beardsley are associated with the idea of "intentional fallacy," whereby a completed literary work becomes autonomous in meaning from that of its author. Another perspective is that of Hans-Georg Gadamer, for whom prejudice (German: *Vorurteil*) cannot be avoided in the interpretive process. Such preunderstanding is from ourselves, not from the text, which is indeterminate in its meaning. This means that it is not the author but the subject that determines the meaning of a text. At best, interpretation is a "fusion of horizons" (German: *Horizontverschmellzung*). Paul Ricoeur supplies another persuasive perspective on understanding when he argues that the text means whatever it says to its readers (*Interpretation Theory: Discourse and the Surplus of Meaning*, 1965). Finally, E. D. Hirsch's conservative hermeneutic is noted, whereby the meaning of a text is determined by its author and does not change with interpreters, although its significance can and does change (*Validity and Interpretation*, 1967).

In the end, Kaiser argues, the impact of these four theorists on culture and interpretation has been and remains significant. According to Kaiser, there is little place left for truth, and the incentive to study the Bible in the original languages is diminished. This disincentive then has a debilitating effect on other areas of theological study. And, Kaiser concludes, the problem of meaning has become a problem in our seminaries. It has contributed to biblical and theological illiteracy. "Meaning" can now be construed as different things: referent, value, entailment, significance, assertion, and intention. Kaiser's implication is that biblical and theological studies are at present overwhelmed by criteria that are governed by almost every other discipline than theology. The "theo" of theology is becoming lost. Theological studies must assert their own identity with their own method.[10] This is a typical Orthodox concern, as raised in the

10. In what is often seen as the classical period of foundational theology in the early modern period, theological studies were less oriented to the content of theology than to the principle of revelation underlying faith. Foundation theology sought first to establish the formal principle for the existence of revelation or the authority of the church, and only then an exposition of Christian faith. A recognition of this aspect of Protestant or Tridentine scholasti-

second chapter of this book by Alkiviadis Calivas. The meaning of the questions as put by the representatives of academic theology cited by Kaiser are also put into context by the cultural shifts in Christianity noted by Andrew Walls in Part II. Nevertheless, Kaiser points to a formidable task that faces theological education and literacy in the twenty-first century, particularly as theology is shaped by wider cultural experiences not derivative of the Enlightenment and such reactions to it as various forms of postmodernism.

Elisabeth Schüssler Fiorenza, in "The Ethos of Interpretation: Biblical Studies in a Postmodern and Postcolonial Context," offers a radical hermeneutical perspective as a means for penetrating false consciousness and promoting emancipation.[11] Although a leading voice of feminist biblical criticism, Schüssler Fiorenza was unwilling to join Mary Daly and other post-Christian feminists in a categorical rejection of Scripture and history as irretrievable, if painfully patriarchal in character.[12] She has also been critical of the "neo-orthodox" feminist theology associated with Letty Russell and Rosemary Radford Ruether for their failure to see clearly the androcentric perspective of the Bible. She has felt their attempt to separate out a more equalitarian content from a patriarchal form of the text to be faulted. Instead, Schüssler Fiorenza has sought to reconstitute historical memory so as to empower women for liberation,[13] a project that has been taken up more pointedly in identity-oriented womanist theology, spirituality, and politics.[14]

---

cism must be factored into the relation between hermeneutics and the evolution of theological studies. See Francis Schüssler Fiorenza, "Foundational Theology and Theological Education," *Theological Education* 20, no. 2 (spring 1984): 107-24. Fiorenza's own formulation (following David Tracy) is to begin with the doctrine of God, not revelation. He would place foundational theology at the completion of theological education, not at its beginning (following Gerhard Ebeling). Further, the starting point and method of foundational theology would follow an exposition of faith, or the conversion experience, and social location (following Johann Baptist Metz).

11. The public power and emancipatory significance of her work is taken up for all peoples in *Rhetoric and Ethic: The Politics of Biblical Studies* (Minneapolis: Fortress, 1999).

12. Her book, *In Memory of Her* (1983), sought to recover within and behind the texts of the New Testament the suppressed memory of an early Christianity in which women played a significant role as leaders. This was followed by *Bread Not Stone* (1984), a collection of essays elaborating the feminist hermeneutical strategies used in *In Memory of Her.* These two books became foundational to the critical study of women in the New Testament.

13. Richard B. Hays, *The Moral Vision of the New Testament: A Contemporary Introduction to New Testament Ethics* (San Francisco: Harper San Francisco, 1996), pp. 266-82.

14. Alice Walker defined "womanist" as moving beyond cultural boundaries, communal, grounded in love, and yet willing to press consciousness of injustice; see her book, *In Search of Our Mothers' Gardens: Womanist Prose* (San Diego: Harcourt Brace Jovanovich, 1983). Patricia Hill Collins articulates an Afrocentric feminist epistemology to shape such consciousness, taken

Her chapter makes the point that theological literacy requires more than exegetical-historical literacy. It is important to be able to reflect critically and to analyze the presuppositions, methods, mind-sets, and contexts that determine biblical readings. In this she goes beyond Kaiser in her criticism of the text. As she puts it, there is a need for hermeneutical and ideology-critical competence so as to enable critical reflection. The conscientization of readers to particular sociopolitical contexts is important. She draws our attention to two contexts of biblical interpretation that constitute the preunderstandings of biblical readers and provide the "eyeglasses" or lenses for reading texts, postmodernity and postcolonialism. These make possible an emerging emancipatory reading of the Bible, one that is essential to biblical literacy in a globalizing world. Here, and more fully in her latest publications, Schüssler Fiorenza keeps her woman-church challenge but broadens out her understanding of the political challenge to embrace a world of exclusion.[15]

A postmodern reading adds a number of correctives to how we read texts: an *aesthetic* corrective that stresses experiential concreteness and intuitive imagination over rationalist abstraction, a *cultural* corrective that insists on cultural autonomy and tradition as the wisdom of a particular community over against universalizing tendencies, and a *political* corrective that insists that there is no pure reason. This last point reminds us of Andrew Walls's move beyond modernity simply understood and with respect to global culture. For Schüssler Fiorenza this happens without loss to the emancipatory achievements of the Enlightenment. A postcolonial reading contests and resists the colonial moment itself with its ideology of domination. She argues that the form of biblical interpretation most closely associated with colonialism is that of an individualist theology, a form of literalist fundamentalism oriented to the salvation of the soul. A discussion between Andrew Walls and Schüssler Fiorenza on this point would be of interest, particularly in light of the common affirmations Walls finds in widely different cultural forms of Christianity.[16] By contrast,

---

into the domain of theology and spirituality by Emilie M. Townes. See Collins, *Black Feminist Thought* (New York: Routledge, Chapman, and Hall, 1991), and Townes, *In a Blaze of Glory: Womanist Spirituality as Social Witness* (Nashville: Abingdon, 1995).

15. Elisabeth Schüssler Fiorenza, *Jesus and the Politics of Interpretation* (New York: Continuum, 2000). Fernando Segovia explores these points from an Hispanic/Latino perspective, exploring principles that underlie all contextual readings of Scripture — his own, black feminist, and Two-Thirds World, in *Decolonizing Biblical Sudies: A View from the Margins* (Maryknoll, N.Y.: Orbis Books, 2000).

16. Andrew Walls, *The Missionary Movement in Christian History: Studies in the Transmission of Faith* (Maryknoll, N.Y.: Orbis Books, 1996). See the early chapters in this book as well as Walls's chapter in our volume.

Schüssler Fiorenza argues, critical biblical study seems to be aligned explicitly with Western colonialism and academic elites.

In the face of this, Schüssler Fiorenza seeks a "Kuhnian" shift in how we read the Bible based around four "paradigm shifts," one that relates to the doctrinal literalist reading, another to the "scientific" positivist perspective, another to a postmodern hermeneutic, and a last that affirms an emancipatory "postcolonial" paradigm.[17] Such a critical theory of rhetoric, she argues, seeks to de-center the objectivist and de-politicized ethos that surrounds biblical studies. This "ethics" of interpretation becomes uniquely able to engage in the formation of a critical historical and religious consciousness. It enables one to talk explicitly of social interests, to understand the social centeredness and "constructedness" of meaning. Such theological literacy fosters "an ethics of critical reading and an ethics of accountability." Schüssler Fiorenza's reading of the text, particularly as shaped by the experience of women as she expresses it, presupposes violence, whether physical or more subtly expressed, that is carried into wider social experience. As such her work on the book of Revelation has loomed large in her research; at issue still is needed reflection on the "the Lamb that was slain." This motif from the Apocalypse is one that might animate a conversation between Schüssler Fiorenza and Alice Mathews, whose chapter on women and ministry appeared earlier in this volume.[18] It also calls to mind two thrusts in the work of Robert Schreiter. The first deals with the violence that reconciliation often entails.[19] The second raises concerns about how local theologies become written and ways by which they connect with the trajectory of Christian experience.[20] Apart from dealing directly with the experience of women or other social groups that experience marginalization, the hard work of reconciliation among those bitterly divided, or even the writing of theologies particular to different cultural groups who might see life quite differently from

17. On this point, see Segovia, p. 7. He develops this in relation to "A Easthope," meaning a grouping of values and practices at a certain level of abstraction; see *Literary into Cultural Studies* (New York: Routledge, 1991), pp. 3-21.

18. Such a discussion brings us to the centrality of Pauline studies, as Paul on the one hand affirms Christian equality and freedom opening up an independent lifestyle for women, yet subordinates women's behavior in marriage and in worship to husbands and men in the interests of Christian mission.

19. Robert Schreiter, *In Water and in Blood: A Spirituality of Solidarity and Hope* (New York: Crossroad, 1988). Bridging social cleavages and the conflicts that are endemic to our period often necessitates the depth of sacrifice illustrated here. See also Schreiter's (edited) book, *Mission in the Third Millennium* (New York: Orbis Books, 2001).

20. Robert J. Schreiter, *Constructing Local Theologies* (Maryknoll, N.Y.: Orbis Books, 1985). Schreiter recognizes the necessity of linking particular, local theologies with essential aspects of Christian tradition (pp. 95-121). This is also a concern of Andrew Walls.

one another, there remains the difficult political issue of how far to extend the social enfranchisement extended to all in contemporary political rhetoric but denied to most in historical and contemporary experience.[21]

The issue of how our identity shapes our reading of a text, whether that might be our gender, social location, or other cultural marker — and hence theological literacy — is not only of concern to Kaiser and Schüssler Fiorenza, but it comes out pointedly in the chapter by Alvin Padilla, "Living in the Hyphen: Theological Literacy from an Hispanic American Perspective." However, Padilla's point of departure is not the academy or a given political community per se, but the local church.[22] Furthermore, he writes as a Hispanic person in the local church. This is reflected through the story Padilla tells of a young local pastor who, despite his theological "literacy" and training, finds that his work is less effective than that of other, less educated pastors in the work of church growth. In other words, a person might be theologically *trained* but theologically *illiterate* in the opinion of his or her congregation. Padilla takes his cue from W. E. B. Du Bois's "double consciousness" as an understanding of the African American reality.[23] Outlined by Eldin Villafañe, among others, for the Hispanic community, the theological vision Padilla argues for is articulated in terms of the life experience of Hispanic Americans.[24]

21. This point is raised by Mark Lilla, "The Politics of Jacques Derrida," *New York Review of Books*, 25 June 1998, pp. 36-41. Perhaps one of the reasons the works of C. S. Lewis continue to be so attractive is that they present a welcome "fusion of metaphysical affirmation and epistemological humility," as argued by David C. Downing, "C. S. Lewis among the Postmodernists," *Books and Culture* (November/December 1998): 36-38.

22. Manuel Jesús Mejido makes the point that increasing Hispanic population in the United States alerts us to the need for greater recruitment of Latino students and faculty and for programs that are more sensitive to the needs of this population; see his "U.S. Hispanic/Latinos and the Field of Graduate Theological Education," *Theological Education* 34, no. 2 (spring 1998): 51-71.

23. W. E. B. Du Bois, *The Souls of Black Folk* (New York: Signet Classics, 1995). James H. Cone writes of three contexts that have helped to promote black theology: the civil rights movement of the 1950s and 1960s, often associated with Martin Luther King, Jr.; the publication of Joseph Washington's book, *Black Religion* (1964); and the rise of the Black Power movement, strongly influenced by Malcolm X's philosophy of black nationalism. See Cone's *For My People: Black Theology and the Black Church: Where Have We Been and Where Are We Going?* (Maryknoll, N.Y.: Orbis Books, 1988).

24. The complexity of the Hispanic experience arises not only from contemporary tension with North American Anglo-American culture, but also from its own complex past. A great deal of the Hispanic Christian experience is pre-Tridentine in origin, often a blend of medieval, baroque, and indigenous practice. See Allen Figueroa Deck, S.J., *The Second Wave: Hispanic Ministry and the Evangelization of Cultures* (New York and Mahwah, N.J.: Paulist, 1989).

Padilla lifts up for consideration the ways in which theological literacy is culturally and communally defined. This marks out ways in which some theological training might be misdirecting those considered to be either "insiders" or "outsiders" in terms of different ethnic groups. For Hispanic Americans, when their bicultural, bilingual worldview is not part and parcel of the theologizing process, efforts at theological "literacy" may in fact promote dysfunctionality rather than literacy. In other words, mere knowledge of the theological disciplines does not guarantee theological literacy. The community always plays a part in determining the nature of literacy. One needs to be understood. Basic anthropology implies first learning the "language" — and this may not be Hebrew, Greek, and Latin. Places of continuity must be found between the classical theological disciplines as presently understood and, in Padilla's case, the Latino community where one serves. Padilla goes on to propose a number of characteristics of Hispanic American theological literacy and how that would impact the North American church. This is a useful exercise and might be replicated for other groups. The challenge is, in the face of diversity, to find ways to bring this back to a common theological understanding. This is something that Paul wrestles with in Galatians as the gospel is carried beyond the Jewish ethnic community to that of the Greek. As Christian theology enters a new phase of history that is defined, as in the chapter by Andrew Walls, this work will take on both greater cogency as well as ambiguity until a new "Kuhnian" paradigm emerges.

The tension over identity, whether social, gender-based, or ethnic, takes on greater social significance as we move into the area of world religions. Many authors are writing on this topic.[25] It is one that not only shapes our conception of theological literacy, but has had continuing political implications for Christianity, most obviously in the formation of Carolingian Europe, in the contours of Europe and the North Atlantic world in the early modern period, and again

---

25. A variety of projects that attempt to describe fairly an array of religious traditions in our world can be noted. These include the Pluralism Project at Harvard University, largely the effort of Diana L. Eck. See her book, *Encountering God: A Spiritual Journey from Bozeman to Banares* (Boston: Beacon Press, 1993), and *World Religions in Boston: A Guide to Communities and Resources*, edited with introductions by Diana L. Eck (Cambridge: Harvard University Press, 1994). See the work of the Comparative Religious Ideas Project, *The Human Condition: Ultimate Realities: Religious Truth*, ed. Robert Cummings Neville, 3 vols. (Albany: State University of New York Press, 2000). Peter L. Berger, codirector of the project, writes in the introduction to *The Human Condition* that religious pluralism need not result in either fanaticism or relativism but can lead to honest dialogue on the basis of "natural reason." Our concern picks up from there and is with theology, in this case a "comparative theology" that can value and assess the different ideas of God, ideal religious representatives, and conceptions of salvation as they are found in different religious traditions.

today.[26] Frank X. Clooney, S.J., our next author, writes his chapter, "Reading the World Religiously: Literate Christianity in a World of Many Religions," in light of these realities. Religion, whether universal or particular in its ethnic or cultural associations, has been central to questions of identity.[27] Clooney notes, first, the reality of religious pluralism around us today. In this he takes up a theme of several authors of this volume. Clooney notes the necessity of studying the wisdom of the world, not just of the West. The religious diversity of the world is present particularly in the United States, where recent demographic trends have highlighted this pluralism. This religious diversity affects ministries and our workplaces. It is increasingly a matter of conscious choice to belong to any religion. It is precisely here, in the area of encouraging informed choice, that education matters.[28]

Clooney goes on to note that interreligious literacy is a specifically Christian virtue required by both those interested directly in mission and those more conscious of the need for interreligious dialogue for purposes of inter-

26. The place of religion in shaping the contours of Europe is explored by different authors; see, e.g., Richard Hodges et al., *Mohammed, Charlemagne, and the Origins of Europe: The Pirenne Thesis in the Light of Archeology* (Ithaca, N.Y.: Cornell University Press, 1983). For early modern Europe, see, e.g., Menna Prestwich, ed., *International Calvinism, 1541-1715* (New York: Oxford University Press, 1985); and for early modern Catholicism, John W. O'Malley, *Trent and All That* (Cambridge: Harvard University Press, 2000); and see George H. Williams, "Erasmus and the Reformers on Non-Christian Religions and *Salus Extra Ecclesiam*," in *Action and Conviction in Early Modern Europe,* ed. Theodore K. Rabb and Jerrold E. Seigel (Princeton: Princeton University Press, 1969), pp. 319-70. On Pope John Paul II and the European Parliament, see in George Weigel, *Witness to Hope* (New York: Cliff Street Books, 1999); themes such as these contribute to themes lifted up by Samuel P. Huntington, *The Clash of Civilizations and the Remaking of World Order* (New York: Simon & Schuster, 1996).

27. Donna Hicks, "Issues of Identity and Protracted Conflict," in *Forgiveness and Reconciliation: Religion, Public Policy, and Conflict Transformation,* ed. Rodney L. Petersen and Raymond G. Helmick, S.J. (Philadelphia: Templeton Press, 2001).

28. The mark of this change in religious identity can be traced from a largely Protestant heritage at the nation's founding to the mid–twentieth century with the appearance of the sociological study by Will Herberg, *Protestant, Catholic, Jew* (Garden City, N.Y.: Doubleday, 1955), equating these three faiths with establishment status. The work of the Pluralism Project (n. 25 above) illustrates an expanding religious variety in the United States. Philip E. Hammond contends that recent social revolutions have yielded an increased emphasis on personal autonomy and have removed the churches from their traditional role as institutions mediating accepted values in American life; see his *Religion and Personal Autonomy: The Third Disestablishment* (Columbia: University of South Carolina Press, 1992). To this must be added the effects of recent patterns of immigration. Whatever the validity of Hammond's argument, a growing complexity in religious demography is found across the American landscape that makes a common moral voice more difficult to discern, a fact and theme discerned in John Berthrong, *The Divine Deli: Religious Identity in the North American Cultural Mosaic* (Maryknoll, N.Y.: Orbis Books, 1999).

communal relationships and peace. In either context, Christians have been shaped by a belief in one God, an understanding of creation that affirms the goodness of the world, the doctrine of the incarnation which defines a conception of salvation, and a high valuation of reason and understanding. For Clooney, these points shape theological literacy. Such literacy is further enhanced by a comparative understanding of religion that is different from the history of religions but shares in the theology of religions in relation to historical understanding.[29] Interreligious literacy, an aspect of theological literacy, is required in relation to an array of human problems that confront humanity. It recognizes that there are not separate solutions to global problems for Christians, Muslims, and Hindus (etc.). The study of other religions affects how we understand our own beliefs. This should affect how we understand and practice our own faith. In this light, Clooney recognizes the need for a dialogue of life, of action, of religious experience, and of theology. Clooney's interests are practical. They focus on something that must be done cooperatively, with those of other faiths and on an equal footing.

One of the areas where this has become a reality is in the domain of environmental thought in relation to religion. Reflection on Scripture, or Scriptures, and alternative theologies has inevitably led to discussion about other worldviews or living religious traditions in relation to ecology, a topic of increasing study.[30] As a part of contemporary postmodernism, a deepening interest has developed into what wisdom other religions have to offer about how to live in harmony with nature.[31] There is a growing consensus that our environmental crisis is so complex that no one religious tradition or philosophical per-

29. Clooney's work illustrates a deep commitment to religious understanding and comparative theology. It is work marked by the effort to understand a religion within its own terms, to take those ideas and reflect back critically upon his own tradition, and with hermeneutical sensitivity not to make unwarranted syntheses. See his contribution to the SUNY series, Toward a Comparative Philosophy of Religions: *Theology after Vedanta: An Experiment in Comparative Theology* (Albany: State University of New York Press, 1993); see also his *Seeing through Texts: Doing Theology among the Srivaisnavas of South India* (Albany: State University of New York Press, 1996), and *Hindu Wisdom for All God's Children* (Maryknoll, N.Y.: Orbis Books, 1998).

30. See the series Religions of the World and Ecology, facilitated by the Center for the Study of World Religions at Harvard University, Cambridge, Mass., and edited by Mary Evelyn Tucker, Bucknell University. A summary of ecological reflection among Christian and other religious communities and dialogue with the relevant sciences and educational policy is carried on in the book by Donald C. Conroy and Rodney L. Petersen, eds., *Earth at Risk: An Environmental Dialogue between Religion and Science* (Amherst, N.Y.: Humanity Books, 2000).

31. The literature in this field is rich and growing. On the different ways in which the major world religions view issues of population and resource consumption, see Harold Coward, ed., *Population, Consumption, and the Environment* (Albany: State University of New York Press, 1995), and the footnotes in Conroy and Petersen, *Earth at Risk*.

spective has the solution to it.[32] Tu Wei-ming argues for a post-Enlightenment mentality that mobilizes the spiritual resources of the ethico-religious traditions (Greek philosophy, Judaism, Christianity), non-Western axial-age civilizations (Hinduism, Jainism, Buddhism, Confucianism, Taoism, Islam), and primal traditions.[33] There is a wide field for discussion here to which Clooney is pointing, one that includes how we live together in one world holding different worldviews, reminding us of William Everett's stress on finding "bridges" between traditions for the discussion of common problems.[34]

Common problems for the plurality of religious expression do not imply that religion will supply only the emotive energy for issues that require scientific and secular solution. Theological literacy adds an analytic edge to comparative religion. If we put even the one question of environmental concern in merely Christian terms, the environmental crisis presents us with the question of a "green grace," nature as mediator of God's goodness and salvation, or a "red grace," the sacrifice of Jesus Christ as revelation of God's goodness and agent of salvation — raising the question of the extent to which religion itself is a product of culture or of nature.[35] The universality of religion in historical time and geographical space seems evident today from anthropology. But is religion a subset of culture[36] or of nature?[37] Or does religion stand in tension between the two, a natural impulse made manifest in culture?[38] And then, what

32. This is the premise of the book edited by Mary Evelyn Tucker and John A. Grim, *Worldviews and Ecology: Religion, Philosophy, and the Environment* (Maryknoll, N.Y.: Orbis Books, 1994).

33. Tu Wei-ming, "Beyond the Enlightenment Mentality," in *Worldviews and Ecology,* pp. 19-29.

34. Huntington, pp. 64-66, 47-48. George H. Williams explores the term "mercy" and its linguistic roots in a number of different cultures with the view of finding a cross-cultural basis for environmental ethics, in "Mercy in the Grounding of a Non-Elitist Ecological Ethic," in *Festschrift in Honor of Charles Speel,* ed. J. Sienkiwicz and James Betts (Monmouth, Ill.: Monmouth College, 1996). The works of John Hick, Paul Knitter, and Gavin D'Costa mark out different positions in the debate about the unique nature of Christian salvation. Special attention should be given to the ongoing discussion on gospel and culture facilitated by the World Council of Churches. See S. Wesley Ariarajah, *Gospel and Culture: An Ongoing Discussion within the Ecumenical Movement* (Geneva: WCC, 1994).

35. Walter Burkert, *Creation of the Sacred: Tracks of Biology in Early Religions* (Cambridge: Harvard University Press, 1996), pp. 1-33.

36. Clifford Geertz, *The Interpretation of Cultures* (New York, 1973). The perspective largely follows from the work of sociologist Émile Durkheim, *The Elementary Forms of Religious Life* (1918), and his idea of "collective representations." The continuing impact of the primacy given culture is seen in contemporary semiotics, structuralism, and poststructuralism.

37. See Burkert's discussion and general characteristics of religion, pp. 5-8.

38. Unresolved here is whether religious symbols are instrumental, with the implication

do we do with theology, the science of an understanding of God? If the answer to the question posed by the tension between nurture and nature is on the side of culture, then positing the existence of religion is to affirm a dualism such that the phenomenon of religion cannot be treated as an aspect of nature. This opens up a set of questions with respect to environmental issues and how they are approached. If the answer to the second question is in the affirmative, however, then epistemology is more foundational and culture less subject to reification. When dealing with environmental issues, the phenomenon of religion is more embedded and areas for discussion are clearly cross-cultural. A breach has been made for such debate as revolves around and opens up a place for natural and revealed theology.[39] However, it is not the purpose of this book to answer that question. It is sufficient to have raised the issue of nurture and nature as it applies to religion.

We come back to the question of hermeneutics, or how we read the Scriptures — and in particular for this volume, how we read and understand the Christian Scriptures, or the Bible. Even the question of how we live together in a common environment becomes, finally, a question of understanding: Certainly for the Christian, and also for adherents of many other faiths, the issue of salvation in light of the environmental crisis is neither red grace nor green grace alone. Indeed, it is to learn to live "between the flood and the rainbow."[40] As marked out in the beginning of this section introduction by reference to the work of Wilfrid Cantwell Smith, and then exemplified in articles by Kaiser, Schüssler Fiorenza, Padilla, and Clooney, there is a need for a new paradigm in our understanding of Scripture, or the Scriptures, and then in interpretation. Despite the growth of the Christian movement worldwide as noted by Andrew Walls, and the use of the Bible as a resource for social criticism, a truly universal church demands a hermeneutic framed for the social realities encountered by people in the twenty-first century.

The search for a common paradigm to conceptualize the significance of Scripture is something of a counterpart in theology to the search for a unified approach to material reality in physics. Models exist, but as Goldingay has ar-

---

of transcendence, or pragmatic with respect to divinity (Charles Peirce) or to religious forms of life (Ludwig Wittgenstein and Derrida). See Robert Cummings Neville, *The Truth of Broken Symbols* (Albany: State University of New York Press, 1996), chaps. 2–3.

39. In the Christian theological tradition, this question touches on the debate over natural theology between Emil Brunner and Karl Barth. See Rom. 1.

40. This is the title of the book compiled by D. Preman Niles, *Between the Flood and the Rainbow: Interpreting the Conciliar Process of Mutual Commitment (Covenant) to Justice, Peace, and the Integrity of Creation* (Geneva: WCC, 1992). See also James A. Nash, *Loving Nature: Ecological Integrity and Christian Responsibility* (Nashville: Abingdon, 1991).

gued, they have become overstretched in the face of alternative explanations so as to bring discredit to the study of theology. Many of the church's inherited models of Scripture can be traced to its own institutional evolution, whether parallel to Roman law and governance,[41] derivative of larger problems surrounding authority in Western culture,[42] or as categories related to ecclesial, political, and philosophical debate in the early modern and modern periods.[43] Within the world of Christian interpretation there is a need for a more nuanced understanding of Scripture together with its careful interpretation. If models for understanding the Bible exist within the scriptural material itself, these need to be more carefully conceived in relation to themselves and as against other revelations.[44] Goldingay refers to Walter Kaiser's comment that discussion concerning topics such as inspiration and revelation without reconsidering the biblical material seems strange. Finding a coalescing perspective among some "liberal" and some "conservative" scholars to look more carefully at the differences inherent to biblical literature, Goldingay outlines four models for reconsidering the nature of biblical material: a witnessing tradition with special reference to biblical narrative, an authoritative canon with reference to the Pentateuch, Scripture as inspired word with special reference to prophecy, and Scripture as experienced revelation whether in the poetic books, epistles, or apocalyptic material.[45] Without moving toward a standard model for unifying the diversity of material in Scripture, this perspective opens the text for comparative human experience, for the diversity of identities that we encounter today, and for discussion with the plurality of religious expression as we encounter it in the twenty-first century.

41. D. Brown, "Struggle till Daybreak: On the Nature of Authority in Theology," *Journal of Religion* 65 (1985): 15-32.

42. Eberhard Jüngel, G. Krodel, R. Marlé, and John D. Zizioulas, "Four Preliminary Considerations on the Concept of Authority," *Ecumenical Review* 21 (1969): 150-66.

43. Henning Graf Reventlow, *The Authority of the Bible and the Rise of the Modern World* (Philadelphia: Fortress, 1985). See, e.g., Benjamin B. Warfield, *The Inspiration and Authority of the Bible* (Philadelphia: Presbyterian and Reformed Publishing Co., 1948).

44. Christian Scriptures are clearly different from some other forms of scripture, e.g., as in Islam. See I. Glaser, "Towards a Mutual Understanding of Christian and Islamic Concepts of Revelation," *Themelios* 7, no. 3 (1982): 16-22.

45. Goldingay, p. 18.

CHAPTER TEN

Theological Literacy for the Twenty-first Century

WALTER C. KAISER, JR.

At the heart of a theological education, according to some of the leading centers on the Continent at the time of the Reformation, was the study of the Greek and Hebrew languages. For prior to the revival of the study of Hebrew among Christians of the fifteenth century, it was assumed that language study would be one of the givens for an educated person, including those involved in theology. Thus Hebrew had been required for an MA degree at the University of Cambridge since 1549.

Since the founders of Harvard College were graduates of Cambridge, they followed in the steps of their alma mater in stressing the importance of Hebrew in the preparation of ministers of the gospel. The motivating forces that led the founders of Harvard College to such an action were clearly stated: "After God had carried us safe to New England, and we had builded our houses, provided necessities for our livelihood, rear'd convenient places for God's worship, and settled the civil government: One of the next things we longed for and looked after was to advance learning and perpetuate it to posterity, dreading to leave an illiterate ministry to the churches, when our present ministers shall lie in the dust."[1]

The values described here still serve as the motivating force for a classical theological education. It is quite clear from the early literature of this period when Harvard College was being founded, that reading the Bible in the original languages of the Old Testament Hebrew and Aramaic and the New Testament Greek was seen as a prerequisite for the ministry.[2]

These same values are still espoused by a large number of seminaries, especially a number within the evangelical tradition, though not by all. Where the

1. *New England's First Fruits* (London, 1643).
2. See, for example, the article by Robert H. Pfeiffer, "The Teaching of Hebrew in Colonial America," *Jewish Quarterly Review* 45 (1954-55): 363-73.

languages have had a long history of being incorporated into the curriculum of the seminary, they have sometimes produced in recent years a countermovement which argued for dropping the study of these languages in favor of other matters thought to be more needful for our times. The hope in those who chose to drop Greek and Hebrew was to make these graduate studies less time-consuming. It was thought that the low-yielding outcomes in the study of languages should be exchanged for the more practical needs of the students, who, it was judged, were already hard pressed to gain a theological education.

The experience of those who chose to stick with the languages, despite the inordinate amount of time they consumed in the traditional three-year graduate program of most seminaries, is that language training often pays handsome dividends once a person was on his/her own in the pastorate. A certain amount of independence and freedom from relying only on secondary sources and ideas of others was preserved, for each could now extract from the biblical text fresh impressions and challenges from the inscripturated word of God.

Here, then, was the foundation stone upon which the key values of a theological program were built. The languages became the most foundational tool by which the developing theologian and exegete was able to get a handle on all the other necessary disciplines that come along with this skill.

But language skills alone, along with a theological and historical perspective, offered only one aspect of the world that full theological literacy demanded. One had to know the world of culture almost as well as the worlds of Bible and theology. The fully equipped pastor would need to stand between these two worlds in order to minister effectively. This called for another kind of literacy.

Christianity and Culture

No matter how well honed the tools of the theologian were, these tools were not to be used in abstraction, isolation, or independently of the times and settings in which the user lived. Accordingly, it becomes most necessary to cast the case for theological literacy over against the prevailing cultural norms of the day. The future pastor was not called to speak God's word into a vacuum, but into a specific culture in a specific situation at a specific time.

The academician who felt or expressed a rude indifference to the dire needs of humanity and society exhibited a faith that was vapid and with very little social application. Thus the question of Christ and culture, or, as others put it, faith and learning, theory and practice, deserves the best that theological studies had to offer. Culture must serve as the catalyst from which all learning and praxis were to be carried out. But how was this to be done?

Too often the problem has been settled by adopting one of two opposite extremes. The one extreme was to subordinate Christian faith to culture and virtually eliminate the supernatural from all serious consideration and conversation. In this case Christian faith became merely another product that was the work of our own hands. The other solution at the opposite end of the spectrum was no more acceptable, for it either denied or destroyed culture in order to raise the fortunes of Christian faith and to give it a clear platform with no competitors acknowledged. But this was no solution either, for it destroyed itself as it sought to close its eyes to all else that surrounded that faith.

A much saner approach was one that deliberately sought to cultivate and consecrate the humanities, arts, sciences, nature, and human culture in the service of God. If the claims of Christian faith were to be used even as the basis for initial assumptions and as starting points from which to view the world, it was clear that its universalistic claims must be legitimate game for all comers to investigate and judge. The invitation was for all to put everything on the board: no holds were to be barred. In fact, Christianity could not stand in its claims as long as there was any disconnect between any field of human endeavor or thought and the radical claims that Christianity made. It was impossible, then, for indifference to any branch of human research, creativity, or feeling to remain for anyone who took up ministry in the name of Christianity. The whole range of human experience must potentially be the scope for continual experiencing, thinking, and assessing.

Christianity rested its case on the finality of Jesus as the promised Christ. Therefore it was vulnerable to the charge that it posed the incomparability of its God over all other gods and all other claimants to sovereignty. To opt out of the intellectual and cultural foray after making such high claims, and making them with such extravagant assertions, as some have customarily done, is unthinkable. Vigorous and healthy Christianity must stay to either face the dissolution of such high beliefs or assist in forming adequate bases for the same in the light of all that the academy and the world have been able to garner in the meantime. Dedicating human powers to the glory of God will never destroy either the human gifts or one's Christian faith; instead, it will heighten them.

Some might object that any subjection of cultural gifts to an external authority would be fatal to both the culture's independence and to the art or science involved. But this could only happen when that cultural gift was subjected to human power; subjection to God could not result in such bondage. The reason is straightforward: it was God himself who gave each of these so-called secular gifts in the first place. He would have to move in destruction against his own creative and sustaining work.

Nor must it be thought that better Christians, or more adequately educated clergy, are produced by reducing the sphere of their studies to the Bible or theology, without any attention to the contributions of the secular society. Such a confinement may for the moment appear less cumbersome and a shorter route to a desired end, but the real task of the church would be left undone. Who then would undertake the task of penetrating the whole of culture with the gospel? Will God's kingdom be declared to be sovereign over all only to abandon the field for fear that the tensions were ultimately without resolution? It is precisely at this very point that the effectiveness of the church and the work of her seminaries are most needed.

These matters have not changed the alignment of issues that have occupied much of this century, despite the enormous shift from the Enlightenment mentality left over from the seventeenth and eighteenth centuries to the postmodern revision at the conclusion of the twentieth century. In fact, at the opening of the 101st session of Princeton Theological Seminary on 20 September 1912, J. Gresham Machen took his audience through just this type of thinking in an address entitled "The Scientific Preparation of the Minister."[3] Machen warned that modern culture has tremendous force in that it affects all of society and thought. The church, he insisted, must not simply occupy the back eddies of the current of the day, hoping thereby to avoid the torrent of ideas, creativity, and the problems for Christian thought some of these issues raised. He continued:

> If the Church is satisfied with that alone, let her give up the scientific education of her ministry. Let her assume the truth of her message and learn simply how it may be applied in detail to modern industrial and social conditions. Let her give up the scientific study of Greek and Hebrew. Let her abandon the scientific study of history to the men of the world. In a day of increased scientific interest, let the Church go on becoming less scientific. In a day of increased specialization, of renewed interest in philology and in history, of more rigorous scientific method, let the Church go on abandoning her Bible to her enemies. They will study it scientifically, rest assured, if the Church does not. Let her substitute sociology altogether for Hebrew, practical expertness for the proof of her gospel. Let her shorten the preparation of her ministry, let her permit it to be interrupted yet more and more by premature practical activity. By doing so she will win a straggler here

---

3. The substance of this address had been given previously at a meeting of the Presbyterian Ministers' Association of Philadelphia, 20 May 1912. The revised work was published in the *Princeton Theological Review* 11 (January 1913) under the title "Christianity and Culture" and then reprinted as a separate monograph under the same title. This section of my thought is beholden to the line of argumentation Machen used there.

and there. But her winnings will be but temporary. The great currents of modern culture will sooner or later engulf her puny eddy. God will save her somehow — out of the depths. But the labor of the centuries will have been swept away. God grant that the Church may not resign herself to that. God grant that she may face her problem squarely and bravely.[4]

Except for some overly optimistic statements about the ability of reason, rationality, and the supposed scientific method to solve some of these matters, the statement is just as pertinent today as it was then.

Hermeneutical Theory as an Orienting Perspective

However, Europe and America underwent an enormous intellectual development in the eighteenth century. This age of enlightenment, or Age of Reason, as it was known, affirmed its belief in a human autonomy and a sovereign reason that would replace previous authority and tradition. Without totally abandoning religion (despite a few exceptions such as skeptics like Voltaire), the emphasis of this age "was often placed on empirical observation, apart from divine revelation. As nature was their church, so reason was their bible."[5]

The central goals of the Enlightenment were: (1) to replace authority with reason and (2) to free the individual from bondage to tradition. Thus it was that rationalism (exhibited best in René Descartes) and empiricism (best seen in Francis Bacon) relied on the "self" or the "individual" to lead in the discovery of truth. Truth was available, for it was out there in the world. It was the prerogative of reason to discover it and to announce its presence in prescriptions that were absolute, universal, and unchanging. As a result of this individual work, the whole group would find those universal truths that corresponded to reality.

A countermovement grew up toward the end of the eighteenth century (approximately from 1780 to 1830). It was the advent of romanticism. The romantics reacted to the rational categories of the Enlightenment, for they believed that the Age of Reason had distorted the spiritual dimension of life. The romantics agreed with the empiricists on one common principle: the principle of autonomy. But they sought to provide a place for religion in life that could be discovered within the self as it brought out truth hidden within nature.

Though romanticism and empiricism disagreed on the means for arriving at their aspirations, both shared one major element: the celebrated "self." In

---

4. J. Gresham Machen, *Christianity and Culture,* pp. 11-12.

5. Michael Horton, *Made in America: The Shaping of Modern American Evangelicalism* (Grand Rapids: Baker, 1991), p. 94.

romantic terms, this "inner self" could uncover moral and spiritual truths. So strong was this current that Emerson told the students of Harvard Divinity School in the summer of 1838 that revelation was not to be found in a transcendent God who revealed himself through an ancient people Israel or a first-century carpenter. Revelation, Emerson opined, had its source in the inspired self filled with the "sentiment of virtues."[6] This led to various utopian constructions as well.

The interesting aspect of this brief but well-traveled survey is that human thought often tends to be cyclical in its pattern. As that would-be philosopher Yogi Berra said: "What goes around comes around." The late twentieth century has worked hard to shed itself of the Enlightenment and the rationalistic orientation that dominated the first half to first two-thirds of the previous century. It has partially succeeded in doing so, it would appear, as postmodernism has practically replaced these remnants of the eighteenth and early nineteenth centuries.

But today's postmodernism has strong affinities to the romanticists of yesterday. Once again, nature is supreme and the inner self has overthrown reason as the bar before which all must pass. However, unlike romanticism, postmodernism no longer seeks to discover "absolute principles," "universal truths," or the like. It is not as if there were ideals out there to pursue; instead, it is a pragmatic "whatever will work" that now supplies the new directive for the "self." The self is directed in postmodernism by its desires (its psychological gratification), and its individual choices determine what is ethical and moral. The self reigns supreme. Its religion is a belief in one's own self.

The two main options offered by secular culture in the past three centuries were not all that different. The self would take the place that had heretofore been occupied by God. Either the autonomous self by use of its rational powers of reason would discover reality as presented in nature, or the spiritual inner self would uncover those ideals and principles that were resident within the inner person.

The most dramatic way this whole interplay between empiricism/rationalism and romanticism came to affect the work of theological literacy in our day was in the problem of meaning. The literary shot heard around the world came from two literary critics named W. K. Wimsatt and Monroe Beardsley in 1946.[7] Most of the distinctions these two men made are now swallowed up in the popular version of the doctrine of "intentional fallacy." As now used, this

---

6. Emerson, "The Divinity School Address," in *Emerson Essays and Lectures,* ed. Joel Porte (New York: Library of America, 1983), pp. 75-76.

7. W. K. Wimsatt and Monroe Beardsley, "The Intentional Fallacy," *Sewanee Review* 54 (1946), reprinted in William K. Wimsatt, Jr., *The Verbal Icon: Studies in the Meaning of Poetry* (New York: Farrar, Straus, 1958), pp. 3-18.

fallacy is that meaning should be connected solely with what an author meant or intended to assert by his or her words. But that is judged to be mainly irrelevant for ascertaining the meaning of a passage today. Accordingly, the new dogma asserts that when a literary work is finished and delivered to its readers, it becomes autonomous from its author so far as its meaning for others is concerned. It was a fallacy for previous generations to rely on the author to determine what was meant or said. This, to my mind, was the most revolutionary concept of the twentieth century.

Theological literacy received another jolt in 1960 when Hans-Georg Gadamer published in Germany his book *Truth and Method*.[8] According to Gadamer, truth could not reside in the reader's attempt to get back to the author's meaning, since every interpreter brought a new and different knowledge to the text from the reader's own historical moment and background. Therefore, prejudice (German: *Vorurteil*) could not be avoided in the interpretive process, but was to be encouraged if it enabled us to grasp the whole of a work. Such a preunderstanding came from ourselves and not from the text, because the text was indeterminate in its meaning. The meaning of a text, Gadamer argued, always went beyond what its author meant; thus, it could not be reproduced. Instead of the author setting the meaning, the subject would be the determiner of meaning. Accordingly, any explanation of a text was wholly dependent neither upon the original historical situation of the text nor the interpreter's perspective; it was instead a result of a "fusion of horizons" (German: *Horizontverschmellzung*). The two perspectives were subsumed into a third, new, alternative meaning.

In 1965 Paul Ricoeur published in French a work entitled *Interpretation Theory: Discourse and the Surplus of Meaning*.[9] He too argued that a text is semantically independent of the assertions the author was making, for a text now could mean whatever it was saying to its readers, not necessarily what its author had intended it to mean. Once a text was written, its meaning was no longer to be determined by the understanding of the original audience or writer. Each subsequent audience must now read its own situation into the text. These new readings were no less valid than the author's meanings so long as they were not completely contradictory to that of the original audience. Thus the new meanings could be different, richer, or even more impoverished, but they were not required now to be the same as that of the original assertions of the author!

---

8. Hans-Georg Gadamer, *Truth and Method: Elements of Philosophical Hermeneutics* (New York: Seabury Press, 1975; reprint, Crossroad, 1982).

9. Paul Ricoeur, *Interpretation Theory: Discourse and the Surplus of Meaning* (College Station, Tex.: Texas University Press, 1976).

The only American to exert a major influence on this debate on the hermeneutical perspective of the art of interpreting during this epochal era of the sixties was E. D. Hirsch, Jr., an English professor at the University of Virginia. Hirsch ran counter to the trends set by Wimsatt and Beardsley, or those of Gadamer and Ricoeur. In his magisterial work of 1967 called *Validity in Interpretation*,[10] he acknowledged his indebtedness to the Italian law historian Emilio Betti, who had founded an institute for interpretation of theory in Rome in 1955. What Hirsch popularized was the view that the meaning of a text, once committed to writing, could not change, for it was determinate. However, significance could and did change. For Hirsch, meaning was that which was represented by a text and what the author had intended to assert by the linguistic signs used in the text. Significance, on the other hand, named a relationship between that meaning and another person, concept, situation, or any possible number of things. Thus the only way to validate a meaning, if anyone was still interested in the truthfulness of what was being asserted as the meaning or interpretation of any text, was to return to those linguistic signs as the conveyors of the author's assertions.

The impact of this debate in the 1960s on our culture, not to mention the major impact that such interpretive theory had on biblical and theological studies, is hard to overemphasize or exaggerate. Little place was left for the search for truth, for now there were an infinite number of meanings that could be attached to any text, including the texts of Scripture. What was the sense of trying to get back to the so-called original meaning of the author or situation in which those words were cast at one time in the past? Such an exercise would only tell us if we were completely contradictory to the original meaning. But the incentive to study the Hebrew, Aramaic, or Greek texts of the Bible was by now gone. These studies possessed only heuristic value at best, but they had little to do with validating or determining the true sense of an author. Eventually this would also imply that historical studies were just as passé and defunct for biblical and theological literacy of the present generation. Why expend all the effort needed to arrive at what the original audience understood by these words if there were an instant "open sesame" that was available to every reader, even if it were diverse, different, richer or poorer than the original meaning? The reader, on this view, had only to assert his or her own meaning, and instantly that rivaled anything that previously had come through the hard labor of grammatical-historical exegesis that attempted to get back to what the author had meant to assert.

The problem of meaning, then, is no small part of our current dilemma

---

10. E. D. Hirsch, Jr., *Validity in Interpretation* (New Haven: Yale University Press, 1967).

in the seminaries and the often heard laments about biblical and theological illiteracy. Part of the problem, of course, is with the meaning of the word "meaning." As G. B. Caird pointed out in 1980,[11] "meaning" is used in English to signify many different ideas. This may account for part of our confusion. For
example, meaning can point to the proper *referent.* Who or what are we talking
about? Meaning can also refer to the concept of *value,* as in "this course means
more to me than I can tell you." Or meaning can refer to *entailment,* as in someone statedly declaring, "This means war." Meaning may be used to indicate the
significance of an idea or concept as a relationship is named between what the
author asserted and another person, situation, or the like. Finally, meaning can
refer to the *assertion* or *intention* that the author is trying to get across. Is it any
wonder that the subject is so confusing when everyone is using the idea of
meaning with so many different concepts to which this one term can point?

For our part, we would urge that the debate be settled more in the direction traced by E. D. Hirsch in his earlier works.[12] If our search for meaning is to
be successful to any degree, we will have to return to some validating principles
that can be agreed upon by all. And if that principle is not to allow the author to
first state his or her own assertions before we apply them or state some significance that may exist between those statements and our own day, then communication itself will be at risk. Civilization as we know it must be surrendered, for
how will we be able to make each other understand what we are trying to get
across if automatically we assign any meaning that strikes our own fancy to the
words of those speaking to us? Not only will God be dead, but in the end so will
all persons have suffered extinction in a solipsism where only me, myself, and I
exist.

The Present Impasse

If the view that every reading has the potential for an infinite number of meanings was the only problem on the scene, perhaps we could still cope and find
ways to overcome the gap in theological illiteracy. But more has happened to
theological studies than the alternative hermeneutical perspective we have just
traced. Biblical and theological studies have been overwhelmed by criteria that

11. G. B. Caird, "The Meaning of Meaning," chap. 2 in *The Language and Imagery of the
Bible* (Philadelphia: Westminster, 1980), pp. 37-61.

12. See Walter C. Kaiser, Jr., and Moisés Silva, *An Introduction to Biblical Hermeneutics:
The Search for Meaning* (Grand Rapids: Zondervan, 1994). Also, Walter C. Kaiser, Jr., "The Nature and Criteria of Theological Scholarship: An Evangelical Critique and Plan," *Theological Education* 32, no. 1 (1995): 57-70.

are governed by almost every other discipline except theology. These criteria are often judged to be more historical, critical, and meaningful than those proposed in the history of the discipline. Such was the charge made by Thomas C. Oden: "Each discipline of theological education, now awash in dated Enlightenment assumptions, finds itself desperately seeking an alternative to the premises of Triune reasoning, incarnation, resurrection, and scriptural revelation. . . . [T]he pattern of so-called scientific study of religion has gradually flooded the seminary, discipline by discipline. . . . Here is where the reductionistic empirical and rational methods of enlightenment modernity have infested the sanctuaries of theological education."[13]

So homogenized are the methods of theological study that even the main object of its inquiry — the study of God — can hardly be recognized by some accounts. As Oden complained, much that comes under the heading of theology has little to do with God, either in God's revelation of himself to the world or in the worship of God. The "theo" part of theology is fast becoming a lost piece of theological reflection and study under the liberated rules of much current thinking.[14]

It is time, as Oden observes, for modern theology to come to terms with the fact that theology is a unique academic enterprise with its own distinctive subject matter — God; its own theological premise — revelation; its own method of inquiry — exegesis of the revealed word of God; its own criteria of accountability — responsible handling of the biblical text within the context of the witness of the Holy Spirit; and the conciliar work of the church through the ages.

For too long now, many "shirttail" subjects have been masquerading as legitimate substitutes for the study of theology. This has not helped theological literacy, but has only deflected it from its main objective.

This state of affairs must be reversed by a return to the unique demands of biblical and theological studies. More is at stake here than definitions. There is an absence of even a minimal understanding or a historic appreciation for ecclesiastical or theological concepts prior to enrollment in graduate studies in the seminary. This vacuum or absence of even a minimalist understanding hardly sets the basis for formative studies that will set the pattern for a lifelong calling in the ministry or the theological academy.

Theological study must first assert who she is on her own terms. The drive for scholarly excellence, a goal that is not to be denied in and of itself, must not be determined by canons derived from the social, historical, psycho-

---

13. Thomas C. Oden, *Requiem: A Lament in Three Movements* (Nashville: Abingdon, 1995), p. 63.

14. Oden, p. 44.

logical sciences, or any other area. Why not let theology base her enterprise on her own terms and criteria, just as one would allow mathematicians to talk about theorems and equations without demanding that they talk about social criticism or the arts? At least we are now able to talk openly about this issue that is causing us so much concern; perhaps that is a sign of progress.

There is an alternative methodology to the crisis we have briefly traced. Evangelicalism in these recent times of postmodernism has continued to build on the classical examples of John Calvin, Martin Luther, Charles and John Wesley, Jonathan Edwards, and others. This type of reinvigorated evangelicalism has been willing to enter the present disarray of the theological academy and speak from the position that Scripture provides us with a normative canon that can be interpreted according to the plain sense of the assertions of the authors of Scripture. It has shown that it is willing to enter many of the current critical debates and, as Tom Oden has commented, say in some of them, where necessary, that the emperor has no clothes!

Therefore, we conclude that the present state of biblical and theological illiteracy will be relieved when theology is given its own distinctive subject matter — God; its own distinctive starting point and source of subject matter — revelation; its own unique method of examining its subject matter — exegesis of Scripture in light of all the evidences, historical, cultural, scientific, as viewed along with the inner testimony of the Holy Spirit; and its own criteria of scholarly excellence — accountability to the canonical text and the work of the conciliar councils in the history of the church.

CHAPTER ELEVEN

The Ethos of Interpretation: Biblical Studies in a Postmodern and Postcolonial Context

ELISABETH SCHÜSSLER FIORENZA

The title of this chapter suggests that the categories postmodern and post-colonial equally characterize the present intellectual context of theology. How-ever, the "post" in both terms connotes something different if one understands the meaning of the prefix "post" in its original sense. The general English meaning communicates that one has moved beyond the situation characterized by the word prefixed with "post." For instance, postdoctoral studies means further studies *beyond* the doctoral degree. Such a reflection on the lexical meaning of the qualifier "post" makes it obvious that the expressions "postmodern" and "postcolonial" have two different implications. Whereas it is possible for a feminist liberation theology to understand itself as postmodern, that is, as having moved beyond modernity and its ethos, and at the same time to affirm that it presupposes and builds on the emancipatory elements of modernity, it is hardly possible for it to use "postcolonial" in the sense that we have moved beyond colonialism and still build on it.

Postmodern

Just as postdoctoral studies affirm and build on doctoral studies, so the postmodern ethos and process of scholarship is still determined by and based on its modern predecessors. Just as in postdoctoral studies one moves beyond the doctoral stage, so in postmodern studies one moves beyond the ethos and mind-set of modernity, not in order to abolish the achievements of modernity but in order to deepen and enhance them. Modernity, as a deeply European event, is all about the massive changes that took place at many levels from the mid-sixteenth century onwards. . . . Modernity questions all conventional ways of doing things substituting authorities of its own based in science, economic growth, democracy, or law. And it unsettles the self; if identity is given in traditional society, in modernity it is constructed. Modernity started out to conquer the world in the name of Reason; certainty and social order would be founded on new bases. . . . The achievement of modernity is astonishing. In the space of a few decades a transformation began in Europe that would alter the world in unprecedented and irreversible ways.[1]

Modern "scientific" studies have promoted in the name of "pure reason" a mode of inquiry that denies its own rhetorical character and masks its own historicity in order to claim historical certainty and value-detached objectivity.[2] This modern posture of value-detached inquiry in the interest of pure reason and its claims to universality has been thoroughly challenged by diverse (post)modern discourses such as philosophical hermeneutics, the sociology of knowledge, ideology critique, and critical theory.[3]

Allow me to clarify this point further with reference to the conceptualization of critical inquiry in the Western Enlightenment tradition. The ideal of the European-American Enlightenment was critically accomplished knowledge in the interest of human freedom, equality, and justice under the guidance of pure and abstract reason. Its principle of unqualified critical inquiry and assessment did not exempt any given reality, authority, tradition, or institution. Knowledge is not a given but culturally and historically embodied language, and therefore is always open to probing inquiry and relentless criticism.

This scientific principle of the Enlightenment was institutionalized in the modern university as the empiricist paradigm of knowledge that gives primary import to evidence, data, and empirical inquiry, that is, to the "logic of facts." This modern logic relies on abstraction for the sake of rigor, evidence, and precision. At the same time, this scientific principle has also engendered three major correctives that underscore the complexity, particularity, and corruption of reality. The aesthetic corrective stresses experiential concreteness and intuitive

---

1. David Lyon, *Postmodernity* (Minneapolis: University of Minnesota Press, 1994), p. 21.

2. David Tracy, *Plurality and Ambiguity: Hermeneutics, Religion, and Hope* (New York: Harper and Row, 1987), p. 31.

3. See also Jürgen Habermas, *Moral Consciousness and Communicative Action* (Cambridge: MIT Press, 1995), p. 4: "Modernity is characterized by the rejection of substantive rationality typical of the religious and metaphysical world-views and by a belief in a procedural rationality and its ability to give credence to our views in the three areas of objective knowledge, moral-practical insight, and aesthetic judgment."

imagination over rationalist abstraction; the cultural corrective insists, over and against the universalizing tendencies of the Enlightenment, on cultural autonomy and on tradition as wisdom and heritage of a particular community; and the political corrective asserts that there is no pure reason as instrument of knowledge that could lead to a just society. In the beginning was not pure reason but power. The institutions of so-called pure reason — the sciences, scholarship, and the university — hide from themselves their own complicity in societal agendas of power.

These three correctives seek to move scholarly discourses beyond Western modernity without relinquishing its emancipatory achievements. Most importantly, by critically demonstrating that the standard for the Enlightenment's claims about selfhood, reason, and universality was elite Western man, feminist postmodern thinkers have shown that the rights and knowledge of the modern elite male subject were underwritten by the negation of such rights and reason for his devalued others, such as wife, children and slave, alien, native, disenfranchised wo/men. (I want here to underscore that I always use "wo/men" as *inclusive* of disenfranchised men.) The accomplishments of the Enlightenment and its transformation of European society were achieved in the interest of the "man of reason" (Genevieve Lloyd) and at the cost of his devalued others. At this crossing point postmodern emancipatory and postcolonial analyses meet in their critique of modernity, whose achievements have been bought at the price of colonialism.

Postcolonial

If one uses the term "postcolonial" in the more commonplace sense, it does not connote the same or a similar meaning and reality as the expression "postmodern." The *American Heritage Dictionary* defines "colonialism" as a "policy by which a nation maintains or extends its control over foreign dependencies" that are called "colonies." Although colonialism is mostly associated with European or American expansionism and imperialism, it is not restricted to the West, as a brief glance at the history of Korea indicates.

Does "postcolonial" mean that the global situation has moved "beyond" colonialism by building on and affirming colonialism? Does it mean that the First World extends beyond colonialism its political rule and cultural control over the "others" of the "man of reason" or the Two-Thirds World, thereby refining and enhancing it? Would this not be neocolonialism rather than postcolonialism? Or does "postcolonial" mean that the global situation is no longer colonial and we have moved toward a utopian situation in which economic exploitation, cultural hegemony, and political domination are overcome and replaced by relationships of radical equality, independence, and well-being?

A critical feminist sociopolitical analysis of liberation as I have developed it understands Western classical and modern society and church as determined by the tension between, on the one hand, "kyriarchal" (i.e., *Lord/Master/Father/ Husband ruled*), exploitative structures of domination and exclusion, and, on the other hand, radical democratic visions of equality and well-being for all, which have been partially realized in history by emancipatory struggles and movements.[4] Such an analysis indicates that there are no postcolonial spaces which are free of exploitation, domination, and dehumanization. The "post" must therefore be understood differently in "postcolonial."

"Postcoloniality" is best understood, I suggest, as "a condition that exists within, and thus contests and resists the colonial moment itself with its ideology of domination."[5] The Bible and biblical studies are clearly associated with Western colonialism. This is aptly expressed in the pithy saying ascribed to Bishop Tutu, among others: "When the missionaries arrived they had the bible and we had the land. Now we have the bible and they have the land." Missionaries came to Asia or Africa not only in order to preach the gospel and to make converts, but also to civilize and educate the heathens. As the authors of *Sentimental Imperialists: The American Experience in East Asia* point out, along with commerce, a second persistent characterization of the American–East Asian relationship has been evangelism in its search for making converts, and the export of Western culture and learning. Missionaries were conscious agents of change. They came to Asia to reshape foreign societies.[6] Moreover, missionaries played a crucial role in the shaping of American views of Asia. They provided "a model for later American governmental efforts to reshape developing societies on a worldwide basis under secular auspices."[7]

Thus the form of biblical interpretation most closely associated with colonialism has been otherworldly evangelism and literalist fundamentalism that

---

4. For the development of such an analytic, see my books *Discipleship of Equals: A Feminist Ekklesialogy of Liberation* (New York: Crossroad, 1993); *But She Said: Feminist Practices of Biblical Interpretation* (Boston: Beacon Press, 1992); *Rhetoric and Ethic* (Minneapolis: Fortress, 1999); and *Wisdom Ways* (Maryknoll, N.Y.: Orbis Books, 2001). For an analysis of the Japanese "kyriarchal" or emperor system, see H. Kinukawa, *Women and Jesus in Mark: A Japanese Feminist Perspective* (Maryknoll, N.Y.: Orbis Books, 1994).

5. Francoise Lionnet, *Postcolonial Representations: Wo/men, Literature, Identity* (Ithaca, N.Y.: Cornell University Press, 1995), p. 4.

6. J. C. Thompson, P. W. Stanley, and J. C. Perry, *Sentimental Imperialists: The American Experience in East Asia* (New York: Harper Torchbooks, 1981), pp. 44-45.

7. Thompson, Stanley, and Perry, p. 59.

is oriented toward the salvation of the soul and professes an individualistic theology preaching the primacy of faith and personal loyalty to Scripture. In contrast, critical biblical studies seem not to be aligned explicitly with Western colonialism because they allegedly are driven by scientific rationality and objectivity. Yet, anyone studying the history of biblical interpretation from the perspective of emancipatory movements will recognize that biblical interpretation has been articulated for the most part not only by elite Western-educated clergymen but also in the interest of Western culture and interests. Anyone joining a doctoral program in biblical studies soon will learn that the only legitimate questions to ask are those of the discipline which disciplines all its members[8] to adopt a modern doctrinal exclusivist or scientific, allegedly value-free mind-set that covertly functions in the interest of kyriarchal relations.

Thomas Kuhn's categories of scientific paradigm and heuristic model provide a theoretical framework for comprehending the theoretical shifts in the discipline.[9] A paradigm articulates a common ethos and constitutes a community of scholars that are formed by its institutions and systems of knowledge. A shift in scientific paradigm can only take place if and when the institutional conditions of knowledge production change. Moreover, paradigms are not necessarily exclusive of each other but can exist alongside and in corrective interaction with each other until they are replaced by a new paradigm. In the discipline of biblical studies, one can chart four such paradigm shifts.

The Doctrinal Literalist Paradigm

For centuries the prevalent paradigm of biblical interpretation has been the dogmatic or doctrinal paradigm which understands the biblical record as sacred Scripture that is divinely revealed. But while the premodern hermeneutics of the dogmatic paradigm knows of a fourfold sense of Scripture, the modern doctrinal articulation of this paradigm insists on a literalist reading of Scripture as factual truth.

Those who quote the Bible most often are neoconservative Christians who read the Bible in the context of proliferating fundamentalist movements

---

8. See the article by W. H. Myers, "The Hermeneutical Dilemma of the African American Biblical Student," in C. H. Felder, *Stony the Road We Trod* (Minneapolis: Augsburg Fortress, 1991), pp. 40-56.

9. For a similar periodization of biblical studies, see now also Fernando F. Segovia, "'And They Began to Speak in Other Tongues': Competing Modes of Discourse in Contemporary Biblical Criticism," in *Reading from This Place: Social Location and Biblical Interpretation in the United States*, ed. Fernando F. Segovia and Mary Ann Tolbert (Minneapolis: Fortress, 1995), pp. 1-34.

and their spiritualization of the global crisis of injustice. Many people in the world experience the impact of neocolonialism that results in the increasing globalization of inequality and the complexity of their situation not only as very confusing but also as very threatening. Growing job insecurity and economic impoverishment, erosion of traditional values and loss of a familiar world, and steady news about ecological disasters, nuclear accidents, civil wars, starvation, refugees, daily murder, and the decay of neighborhoods fuel the desire for unambiguous solutions, eternal truth, and moral certainty.

Fundamentalist discourses address this global postmodern anxiety by promising certainty in a sea of change, by delineating exclusivist group boundaries and clear-cut identities, and by fabricating emotional stability in an ever more complex and changing world. To that end they not only project a spiritualized vision of the world but also manipulate symbols of evil, stereotype the "others" as deviant, and rigidly defend "orthodox" tradition. By identifying "the enemy" and by scapegoating the deviant "others," they seek both to alleviate people's helplessness in a world that seems to come to an end and to promise salvation and success to those who have a claim to righteousness.

Although these modern "fundamentalist" movements are religiously and ethnically quite different, they share common traits. In an ever changing and conflictive world, they promise religious security, certainty of faith, and a determined identity. Whether fundamentalist Christians, Muslims, or ultraorthodox Jews, they do so both by maintaining a literalist understanding of Scripture or tradition as the will of G*d and by insisting on the subordination of women as natural and as ordained by G*d. At the same time, they employ modern media technology in very sophisticated ways to advocate nationalist or religious exclusivism.

Yet while right-wing fundamentalists embrace modern technological science as well as modern nationalism, they reject many of the political and ethical values of modern democracy, such as basic individual rights; religious pluralism; freedom of speech; equal rights for women; the right to housing, health care, and work; equal compensation for equal work; social market measures; a democratic ethos; sharing of power; and political responsibility. Despite their ideological differences, they come together in their vehement demand for women's actual and symbolic subordination.

Christian fundamentalism claims that the biblical message belongs to a totally different world and does not affect societal or political structures. Christians who suffer in this world as Christ has suffered will receive their just reward in heaven. The *basileia* — the reign of G*d — is "not of this world." Or it insists that kyriarchal theocracy is the revealed order of society. In its more recent expressions, such a fundamentalist rhetoric constructs a religious world of righteousness and contrasts it with secularized, depraved, modern society. As

216

the keeper and protector of traditional values, it stereotypes those who do not agree and scapegoats homosexuals, secular humanists, feminists, and liberals as enemies of the moral order.

Literalist fundamentalism vehemently rejects modern religious tolerance and pluralism but insists that the biblical message proclaims universal moral values and truth. Like modern science, it claims that this truth can be positively established and proven. To that end it promulgates philological, historical, or theological literalism which stresses verbal inspiration that understands the Bible as the direct inerrant Word of G*d which Christians must accept without question. This emphasis on verbal inerrancy asserts that the Bible and its interpretation transcends ideology and particularity. It obscures the interests at work in biblical texts and interpretations and reduces faith to intellectual assent rather than to a way of life. Such revelatory positivism promotes believe in the Bible rather than faith in G*d.

Biblicist fundamentalism does not only read the Bible with the theological lenses of individualized and privatized bourgeois religion, but also asserts militantly that its approach is the only legitimate Christian way to do so. It thereby not only obscures that different Christian communities and churches use the Bible differently but also ignores that, throughout the centuries, different models of biblical interpretation have been and still are developed by Christians. Although such spiritualized biblicism berates mainline churches for succumbing to modernity and secularization, it itself has adopted a particular modern rationalist understanding of religion and the Bible as the only approach that is truly Christian. Even though it stands in opposition to Western modernity, it nevertheless shares some of its basic ideological structures. In spite of the fact that fundamentalism combats modern liberal religion, it is itself a modern phenomenon. It seeks to re-create inside the religious world all that is no longer viable in the outside world. To that end it offers a modernist integrative meaning system and the certainty of revealed Truth in the process of increasing market globalization that dislocates traditional worldviews and meaning systems.

The "Scientific" Positivist Paradigm

This situation of the increasing globalization of inequality and the fundamentalist response to it cries out for alternative liberating religious visions. Are Christian theology and biblical scholarship able to step into the increasing vacuum of meaning and hope generated by the transnational globalization process? Because the "scientific" ethos of biblical studies was shaped by the struggle of religious scholarship to free itself from dogmatic and ecclesiastical controls, it insists on value-free inquiry and the deep chasm between the past and the present. Hence it is not able to engage this question.

The scientific paradigm strives to establish a single true meaning of the text in order to claim universality for its interpretations. It does so, however, not on theological but on methodological scientific grounds. Although it avows objectivity, disinterestedness, and value neutrality in order to control what constitutes the legitimate scientifically established true meaning of the text, it is patently Eurocentric. Just as European and American history as an academic discipline sought in the last quarter of the nineteenth century to prove itself as an objective science in analogy to the natural sciences, so also did biblical studies. Scientific historiography ostensibly sought to establish "facts" and "data" objectively, free from philosophical considerations or political interests. It was determined to hold strictly to facts and evidence, not to sermonize or to moralize but to tell the simple truth — in short, to narrate things as they really happened. Historical science is seen as a technique that applied critical methods to the evaluation of sources which in turn are then understood as data and evidence. The mandate to avoid theoretical considerations and normative concepts in the immediate encounter with the text is to assure that the resulting historical accounts would be accurate and objective, free from any ideology.

Since biblical scholarship has developed in the political context of several heresy trials at the turn to the twentieth century, its rhetoric of disinterested objectivity continues to reject all overt religious, sociopolitical, or theological engagement as unscientific. The aspiration of biblical studies in particular (and religious studies in general) to "scientific" status in the academy and their claim to universal, unbiased modes of inquiry deny their hermeneutical-rhetorical character and mask their sociohistorical location as well as their sociopolitical or ecclesiastical interests.

Because they are rooted in the individualistic and relativistic discourses of modernity[10] and share with fundamentalism its positivist and technological character, liberal biblical discourses also are not equipped to address the crisis of well-being brought about by the globalization of inequality. In spite of their critical posture, academic biblical studies are akin to fundamentalism insofar as they insist that scholars are able to produce a single scientific, true, reliable, and nonideological reading of the Bible. They can achieve scientific certainty as long as they silence their own interests and abstract from their own sociopolitical situation.

---

10. For these characterizations of bourgeois biblical readings, see Johannes Thiele, "Bibelauslegung im gesellschaftlich-politischen Kontext," in *Handbuch der Bibelarbeit,* ed. W. Langer (Munich: Kösel Verlag, 1987), pp. 106-14.

Insofar as modern biblical scholarship insists that it is able to isolate the facts or the universal "truth" from the Bible's multivalent and often contradictory meanings, it denies its own particular Eurocentric perspectives and kyriarchal rhetorical aims that are indebted to the European Enlightenment. By objectifying, antiquating, and privatizing Scripture, it is in danger of playing into the hands of fundamentalist biblicism, which also claims that it can identify with certainty the univocal "word of G*d" in the Bible as a provable fact.

The Hermeneutical (Post)Modern Paradigm

Today this modern scientist paradigm seems to be in the process of decentering and to be replaced by a (post)modern hermeneutical paradigm. Whereas a decade ago the historical positivist and literary formalist paradigms of interpretation were still reigning, today postmodern epistemological and hermeneutical discussions that are critical of the positivist scientific paradigm abound. Their theoretical and practical force has destabilized the foundations of the field. Even the critical theory of the Frankfurt school and ideological criticism have arrived on the program of biblical congresses. Critical theory, semiotics, reader response criticism, and poststructuralist literary analyses, among others,[11] have engendered the recognition of the linguisticality of all interpretation and historiography and generated postmodern elaborations of the pluralism of meaning and the diversity of reading approaches.[12]

Such a postmodern hermeneutic does not assume that the text is a given

---

11. For bringing together the insights of this paper, I have found especially helpful the works of feminist literary and cultural criticism. See, e.g., S. Benhabib and D. Cornell, eds., *Feminism as Critique* (Minneapolis: University of Minnesota Press, 1987); Gayatri Chakravorty Spivak, *In Other Worlds: Essays in Cultural Politics* (New York: Methuen, 1987); Teresa de Lauretis, ed., *Feminist Studies/Critical Studies* (Bloomington: University of Indiana Press, 1986); E. A. Flynn and P. P. Schweickart, eds., *Gender and Reading: Essays on Reader, Texts, and Contexts* (Baltimore: Johns Hopkins University Press, 1986); G. Greene and C. Kaplan, eds., *Making a Difference: Feminist Literary Criticism* (New York: Methuen, 1983); Elizabeth A. Meese, *Crossing the Double Cross: The Practice of Feminist Criticism* (Chapel Hill: University of North Carolina Press, 1986); J. Newton and D. Rosenfelt, eds., *Feminist Criticism and Social Change* (New York: Methuen, 1985); M. Pyrse and Hortense J. Spillers, eds., *Conjuring: Black Women, Fiction, and Literary Tradition* (Bloomington: University of Indiana Press, 1985); Chris Weedon, *Feminist Practice and Poststructuralist Theory* (London: Blackwell, 1987).

12. Amos N. Wilder articulated this literary-aesthetic paradigm as rhetorical. See his Society of Biblical Literature presidential address, "Scholar, Theologians, and Ancient Rhetoric," *Journal of Biblical Literature* 75 (1956): 1-11, and his book *Early Christian Rhetoric: The Language of the Gospel* (Cambridge: Harvard University Press, 1971).

divine revelation or a window to historical reality, nor does it operate with a correspondence theory of truth. It does not understand historical sources as data and evidence but sees them as perspectival discourse constructing a range of symbolic universes.[13] Since alternative symbolic universes engender competing definitions of the world, they cannot be reduced to a single, definitive meaning. Therefore competing interpretations are not simply either right or wrong,[14] but they constitute different ways of reading and constructing historical and religious meaning. Texts have a surplus of meaning that can never be fully mined.

In short, this third hermeneutical paradigm underscores the rhetoricity of historical knowledge,[15] symbolic power, and the multidimensional character of texts. It ascribes personified status to the text in order to construe it as a dialogue partner or sees the text as a multicolored tapestry of meaning. This third cultural paradigm likens the reading of the Bible to the reading of the "great books" or classics, whose greatness does not consist in their accuracy as records of facts, but depends chiefly on their symbolic power to transfigure human experience and symbolic systems of meaning.

Feminist and liberation theological interpretation have played a great part in this postmodern hermeneutical transformation of academic biblical scholarship. Nevertheless, even a cursory glance at the literature can show that the hermeneutical contributions of critical feminist scholarship are rarely recognized and much less acknowledged by male-stream biblical studies. While the postmodern hermeneutical paradigm has successfully destabilized the certitude of the scientific objectivist paradigm in biblical studies, it still asserts its own scientific and atheological character. Hence it tends to result in a playful proliferation of textual meanings and rejects any attempt to move from the kyriocentric text to the sociohistorical situation of struggle that has generated the text. Hence, this third hermeneutical-postmodern paradigm of biblical studies also cannot address the increasing insecurities of globalized inequality nor accept the constraints which the ethical imperative of emancipatory movements places on the relativizing proliferation of meaning. Therefore a fourth rhetorical-political paradigm that inaugurates a rhetorical-ethical turn is called for.

13. See the discussion of scientific theory choice by Linda Alcoff, "Justifying Feminist Social Science," *Hypatia* 2 (1987): 107-27.

14. Maurice Mandelbaum, *The Anatomy of Historical Knowledge* (Baltimore: Johns Hopkins University Press, 1977), p. 150.

15. See my article "The Rhetoricity of Historical Knowledge: Pauline Discourse and Its Contextualizations," in *Religious Propaganda Missionary Competition in the New Testament World: Essays Honoring Dieter Georgi*, ed. Lukas Bormann, Kelly Del Tredici, and Angela Standartinger (Leiden: E. J. Brill, 1994), pp. 443-70.

The Emancipatory "Postcolonial" Paradigm

I would suggest that such a fourth paradigm is in the process of being articulated today, insofar as in interaction with postmodern critical theory emancipatory postcolonial feminist discourses have problematized the Enlightenment's notion of the universal transcendental subject as the disembodied voice of reason and at the same time insisted that the excluded others must be included.[16] These discourses have elaborated that the political-social and intellectual-ideological creation of the devalued others goes hand in hand with the creation of the man of reason as the rational subject outside of time and space.[17] He is the abstract knower and disembodied speaker of Enlightenment science who arrogates to himself a "G*d's-eye view" of the world.

But in distinction to postmodern criticism, the voices from the margins of biblical studies insist that the colonialized others cannot afford to abandon the notion of the subject and the possibility of knowing the world. Rather, the subordinated others need to engage in a political and theoretical process of constituting ourselves as subjects of knowledge and history. Those previously excluded from the academy have to use what we know about the world and our lives to critique the dominant culture and to construct a heterogeneous public that allows for the recognition of particular voices and fosters appreciation of difference.

This fourth paradigm utilizes the analytical and practical tradition of ideology critique and rhetorical inquiry. Since language does not only create a polysemy of meaning but also transmits values and reinscribes social systems and semantic patterns of behavior, it calls for a critical sociopolitical interpretation of the Bible. This paradigm understands biblical texts as rhetorical discourses that must be investigated as to their persuasive power and argumentative functions in particular historical situations. It rejects the Enlightenment typecasting of rhetoric as stylistic ornament, technical skills, or linguistic manipulation, and maintains not only "that rhetoric is epistemic but also that

16. Brian K. Blount, *Cultural Interpretation: Reorienting New Testament Criticism* (Minneapolis: Fortress, 1995), p. 3, correctly argues "that if one wants to achieve a non-ideological method of biblical interpretation, the perspectives of the societal marginal must be included." Such an inclusion will result in a multicolored rainbow of biblical interpretation. However, insofar as he positions his new approach as "cultural" interpretation which has as its explicit goal to produce a nonideological reading, he remains within the third paradigm of biblical interpretation.

17. See my article "The Politics of Otherness: Biblical Interpretation as a Critical Praxis for Liberation," in *The Future of Liberation Theology: In Honor of G. Gutiérrez*, ed. Marc H. Ellis and Otto Maduro (Maryknoll, N.Y.: Orbis Books, 1989), pp. 311-25.

epistemology and ontology are themselves rhetorical."[18] Thus it seeks to utilize both theories of rhetoric and the rhetoric of theories in order to display how as political and religious discursive practices biblical texts and their contemporary interpretations involve authorial aims and strategies, as well as audience perceptions and constructions.

Since the sociohistorical location of rhetoric is the public of the polis, the rhetorical paradigm shift situates biblical scholarship in such a way that its public character and political responsibility become an integral part of its contemporary readings and historical reconstructions. It insists on the ethical radical democratic imperative that biblical scholarship must contribute to the bringing about of a society and church that is free from all forms of kyriarchal inequality and oppression. Hence, as a feminist scholar, I have been concerned not just with exploring the conditions and possibilities of understanding and appreciating androcentric biblical texts, but also with the problem as to how in the interest of wo/men's liberation one can critically assess and dismantle their power of persuasion. For that reason I have argued that critical biblical scholarship must construct a theoretical model and epistemological framework that would move toward the articulation of a critical ethics and rhetorics of inquiry.

The "turn to rhetoric" that has engendered critical theory in literary, historical, political, and social studies fashions a theoretical context for such a paradigm shift in biblical studies.[19] The critical theory of rhetoric or of discursive practices, as developed in literary, political, and historical studies, seeks to decenter the objectivist and depoliticized ethos of biblical studies with an ethos of rhetorical inquiry that could engage in the formation of a critical historical and religious consciousness. The conceptualization of biblical studies in rhetorical emancipatory rather than scientist value-free terms would provide a research framework not only for integrating historical, archaeological, sociological, literary, and theological approaches as perspectival readings of texts, but also for raising ethical-political and religious-theological questions as constitutive of the interpretive process. Not detached value-neutrality, but an explicit articulation of one's rhetorical strategies, interested perspectives, ethical criteria, theoretical frameworks, religious presuppositions, and sociopolitical locations for critical public discussion is appropriate in such a rhetorical paradigm of biblical scholarship.

18. Richard Harvey Brown, *Society as Text: Essays on Rhetoric, Reason, and Reality* (Chicago: University of Chicago Press, 1987), p. 85. See also John S. Nelson, "Political Theory as Political Rhetoric," in *What Should Political Theory Be Now?* ed. J. S. Nelson (Albany: State University of New York Press, 1983), pp. 169-240.

19. See my article "Rhetorical Situation and Historical Reconstruction in I Corinthians," *New Testament Studies* 33 (1987): 386-403, and Wilhelm Wuellner, "Where Is Rhetorical Criticism Taking Us?" *Catholic Biblical Quarterly* 49 (1987): 448-63, for further literature.

The Ethics of Interpretation

The rhetorical understanding of discourse as creating a world of pluriform meanings and a pluralism of symbolic universes does not necessarily end up in ludic proliferation[20] if it raises the question of power. How is meaning constructed? Whose interests are served? What kinds of worlds are envisioned? What roles, duties, and values are advocated? Which social-political practices are legitimated? Or which communities of discourse sign-responsible? Such and similar questions become central to the interpretive task. Once biblical scholarship begins to talk explicitly of social interests, whether of race, gender, culture, class, or religion, and once it begins to recognize the need for a sophisticated and pluralistic reading of texts that questions the fixity of meaning and understands the social constructedness of meaning, then a doubled ethics is called for: an ethics of critical reading and an ethics of accountability.

An *ethics of reading* changes the task of interpretation from finding out "what the text meant" to the question of what kinds of reading models and methods can do justice to the text in its ancient and contemporary socio-rhetorical contexts. Although such an ethics is aware of the pluralism of historical- and literary-critical methods as well as of the pluralism of interpretations appropriate to the text, it nevertheless insists that the range of meaning and the number of interpretations that can legitimately be given to a text are limited by the text's social context. Since biblical texts are religious texts articulated in a definite moment of history, their possible meanings are historically, politically, and contextually circumscribed.

Such an ethics of reading seeks to give to the text its due by asserting its grammatically and historically limited possible meanings over and against later dogmatic usurpation or scientist reduction. It makes the assimilation of the text to our own experience and interests more difficult and thereby keeps alive the rhetorical "irritation" of the original text by challenging our own assumptions, worldviews, and practices. By reading "against the grain," it seeks to reconstruct the submerged and marginalized voices of the historically silenced who have engaged in emancipatory struggles.[21] Hence, over and against feminist polysemic textualist approaches that deny any feasibility of historical reading, I continue not only to argue for the possibility of sociohistorical recon-

---

20. See Teresa L. Ebert, *Ludic Feminism and After: Postmodern Desire and Labor in Late Capitalism* (Ann Arbor: University of Michigan Press, 1996).

21. See the introduction to the tenth anniversary edition of *In Memory of Her* (New York: Crossroad, 1994) and my article "Text and Reality — Reality as Text: The Problem of a Feminist Historical and Social Reconstruction Based on Texts," *Studia Theologica* 40 (1989): 19-34.

struction but also to insist on the importance of reclaiming subjugated historical knowledges as memory and heritage for feminist liberation struggles.

In short, the methods of historical- and literary-critical scholarship and its diachronic reconstructions distance us in such a way from biblical texts and their historical symbolic worlds that they relativize not only them but also us. Yet, they can only do so if our critical choices of interpretive methods and models allow for their reading in terms of the emancipatory historical struggles of the oppressed and marginalized for liberation and well-being. By illuminating the ethical-political dimensions of biblical texts and their sociohistorical contexts, such an ethics of historical reading allows one not only to relativize the values and authority claims of biblical texts through contextualization, but also to assess and critically evaluate them.

The rhetorical character of biblical interpretations and historical reconstructions requires an *ethics of accountability* that stands responsible not only for the choice of theoretical frameworks and interpretive models and methods but also for the ethical implications of biblical texts and their meanings.[22] If scriptural texts have served not only noble causes but also to legitimate war, to nurture anti-Judaism and misogyny, to justify the exploitation of slavery, and to promote colonial dehumanization, then biblical scholarship must take the re-

---

22. Daniel Patte, *The Ethics of Biblical Interpretation: A Reevaluation* (Louisville: Westminster John Knox, 1995), p. 7, does not understand my theoretical approach at all when he claims that in my Society of Biblical Literature presidential address, "The Ethics of Biblical Interpretation: Decentering Biblical Scholarship" (*Journal of Biblical Literature* 107 [1988]: 3-17), I argue that the "issue of critical reading must be resolved before one can meaningfully raise the issue of accountability . . . and that critical exegesis is an undertaking prior to and distinct from ethical accountability, viewed as an evaluation of how people are affected by the results of the critical exegesis." By prioritizing "critical exegesis as exempt from the ethics of responsibility," he restricts an ethics of accountability to advocacy scholars, among whom he would count himself as representing "white Euro-American male scholars." He can accommodate it as long as "critical exegesis" itself remains untouched by such an ethics of accountability. He forthrightly states: "Adopting such an androcritical attitude means that we should reject or abandon *neither* our male European-American perspective *nor* our vocation which finds expression in our critical exegetical methods. Yet our *practices* of these methods, and thus our conception of what 'critical' exegetical practices entail, should be completely reoriented: They must allow us to affirm the legitimacy of a plurality of interpretations — both our own and those of various groups. If we do so our interpretations will no longer be androcentric or Eurocentric" (p. 27). Not only does Patte arrogate to himself the power of renaming my proposal, but he also co-opts it in terms of liberal pluralism that keeps the power of naming firmly in the hands of male-stream Euro-American biblical scholarship and eschews its accountability by claiming that a truly "critical" practice of reading does not resolve the rhetorical contradictions and tensions inscribed in biblical texts but transposes them into a multiplicity of equally legitimate readings. Hence an ethics of reading is restricted to legitimating all readings utilizing critical methods.

sponsibility not only to interpret biblical texts in their historical contexts but also to evaluate the construction of their sociohistorical worlds and political-symbolic universes in terms of an emancipatory scale of values.[23] If the Bible has legitimated kyriarchal relations of inequality and has become a tool of Western cultural colonization, then the responsibility of the biblical scholar cannot be restricted to giving "the readers of our time clear access to the original intentions" of the biblical writers.[24] It must also include the elucidation of the ethical consequences and political functions of biblical texts in their historical as well as contemporary sociopolitical contexts of meaning.

Just as literary critics have called for a critical evaluation of classic works of art in terms of justice, so students of the Bible must examine both the rhetorical aims of biblical texts and the rhetorical interests emerging in the history of interpretation or in contemporary scholarship. This requires that biblical studies revive a responsible ethical and political criticism which recognizes the ideological distortions of Scripture. The task of such an emancipatory biblical criticism is not just to evaluate the ideas or propositions of a work but also to determine whether its very language and composition promote stereotypical images and linguistic violence. What does the language of a biblical text "do" to a reader who submits to its world of vision?[25]

In order to answer this question, a careful rhetorical reading of biblical texts and the appropriate reconstruction of their historical worlds and symbolic universes need to be complemented by a theo-ethical discussion of the contemporary religious power of biblical texts which claim scriptural authority today in biblical communities of faith. To open up biblical texts and the historical reconstructions of their worlds for public reflection and discussion requires that interpreters learn to traverse not only the boundaries of the diverse theological disciplines but also those of other intellectual discourses.[26]

23. For a concrete instance of such a critical emancipatory ethics of interpretation, see my book *Jesus: Miriam's Child, Sophia's Prophet: Critical Issues in Feminist Christology* (New York: Continuum, 1994).

24. Krister Stendahl, "The Bible as a Classic and the Bible as Holy Scripture," *Journal of Biblical Literature* 103 (1984): 10.

25. See Wayne C. Booth, "Freedom of Interpretation: Bakhtin and the Challenge of the Feminist Criticism," in *The Politics of Interpretation,* ed. J. T. Mitchell (Chicago: University of Chicago Press, 1983), pp. 51-82.

26. See Francis Schüssler Fiorenza, "Theory and Practice: Theological Education as a Reconstructive, Hermeneutical and Practical Task," *Theological Education* 23 (1987): 113-41.

Goal and Process of Emancipatory Interpretation

This fourth emancipatory paradigm shift in biblical studies thus articulates a change in the aims and goals of critical exegesis and biblical interpretation. The task of interpretation is *not just to understand* biblical texts and traditions *but* to analyze *their power of persuasion* in order *to change* Western hermeneutical male-stream frameworks, individualistic apolitical practices, and sociopolitical relations of cultural colonization. Thereby it seeks to engender a self-understanding of biblical scholarship as a critical communicative postcolonial praxis. Biblical interpretation, like all scholarly inquiry, is a communicative practice that involves interests, values, and visions.

Only in such a paradigm of biblical studies will liberation theologies of all colors have the possibility to engage the discourses of biblical studies on their own terms and on equal terms with Eurocentric male-stream scholarship. By beginning with the religious experiences and articulations of the marginalized and colonized, of those wo/men traditionally excluded from interpreting the Bible, articulating theology, and shaping communal Christian self-understanding, they change the starting point of traditional biblical interpretation. Liberation theologies of all colors do not only recognize the perspectival and contextual nature of theological knowledge and biblical interpretation, but also assert that biblical scholarship and theology are — knowingly or not — always engaged for or against the oppressed. Intellectual neutrality is not possible in a historical world of exploitation and oppression. At the same time, they must be careful not to romanticize the Minjung,[27] for — as the Brazilian educator Paolo Freire has pointed out a long time ago — the oppressed have also internalized their own dehumanization and oppression as the will of G*d. Thus the Minjung are divided within and among themselves. "The oppressed, having internalized the image of the oppressor and adopted his [*sic*] guidelines, are fearful of freedom. Freedom would require them to eject this image and replace it with autonomy and responsibility. Freedom . . . must be pursued constantly and responsibly."[28]

Since both the oppressed and their oppressors are "manifestations of dehumanization,"[29] the methodological starting point of liberation theologies

27. However, Kim Yong-Bok, *Messiah and Minjung: Christ's Solidarity with the People for New Life* (Hong Kong: Christian Conference of Asia, 1992), p. 8, claims that this "question often arises among those who despise and discriminate against the Minjung." In my experience, any movement that idealizes its agents is bound to lose its emancipatory impetus whenever it realizes how much they are divided in and among themselves.

28. Paolo Freire, *Pedagogy of the Oppressed* (New York: Seabury Press, 1973), p. 31.

29. Freire, p. 33.

cannot be simply "commonsense" experience but rather must be systemically analyzed and critically reflected experience. Since wo/men have internalized and are shaped by kyriarchal "commonsense" mind-sets and values, the hermeneutical starting point of feminist interpretation cannot simply be experience of wo/men but must be experience that has been critically explored in the process of "conscientization."

In short, liberation theologies of all colors derive their lenses of interpretation and criteria of evaluation not from the modern individualistic understanding of religion and the Bible. Rather they shift attention to the politics of biblical interpretation and its sociopolitical contexts. They claim the hermeneutical privilege of the oppressed and marginalized for reading and evaluating the Bible. In distinction to modern liberal theologies that address the questions and ideas of the "nonbeliever," liberation theologies of all colors focus on the experiences and struggles for survival and liberation of the "nobodies" who have been marginalized and dehumanized. For instance, whereas Schleiermacher, the "father of hermeneutics," addressed the cultured critics of religion, Gustavo Gutiérrez argues that liberation theologians take up the questions of the "nonpersons."[30]

Liberationist biblical readings seek to give dignity and value to the life of the nonperson as the presence and image of G*d in our midst. Therefore they do not restrict salvation to the individual soul but aim to promote the well-being and radical equality of all. Their goal is to inspire biblical readers to engage in the struggle for transforming internalized cultural-religious kyriocentric mind-sets and sociopolitical kyriarchal structures of domination.

Christian identity that is shaped by the Bible must in ever new readings be deconstructed and reconstructed in terms of a global praxis for the liberation of all wo/men. Hence, a critical feminist theology of liberation seeks to reconceptualize the traditional spiritual practice of discerning the spirits as a critical theo-ethical practice. As theological subjects, Christian feminists claim their spiritual authority to assess both the oppressive and the liberating imagination of particular biblical texts and their interpretations. By deconstructing the kyriarchal rhetorics and politics of inequality and subordination which are inscribed in the Bible, they are able to generate new possibilities for the ever new articulation of Christian identities and emancipatory practices.

In order to do so, a critical feminist reading does not subscribe to a single

---

30. See also Sharon Welch, *Communities of Resistance and Solidarity* (Maryknoll, N.Y.: Orbis Books, 1985), p. 7: "[T]he referent of the phrase 'liberating God' is not primarily God but liberation. That is, the language here is true not because it corresponds with something in the divine nature but because it leads to actual liberation in history. The truth of God language and of all theological claims is measured . . . by the fulfillment of its claims in history."

reading strategy and method but employs a variety of theoretical insights and methods for interpreting the Bible. Hence it does not understand biblical interpretation in doctrinal-scientific positivist or relativist terms, but rather in rhetorical-ethical terms. Such a critical rhetorical understanding of interpretation investigates and reconstructs the discursive arguments of a text, its socioreligious location, and its diverse interpretations in order to underscore the text's oppressive as well as liberative performative actions, values, and possibilities in ever changing historical situations. It understands the Bible and biblical interpretation as a site of struggle over authority and meaning.

Such an emancipatory process of biblical interpretation has as its "doubled" reference point the contemporary present and the biblical past. It engages seven *rhetorical* strategies or movements in the process or "dance" of interpretation. Crucial moves in such a critical process of interpretation are *conscientization, critical sociocultural analysis, suspicion, reconstruction, evaluation, reimagination, and action for change.* These practices of an emancipatory ethics of interpretation, however, are not to be construed simply as successive independent steps of inquiry or as methodological rules, but they must be understood as interpretive strategies that interact with each other simultaneously in the process of reading a particular biblical or any other cultural text in light of the globalization of inequality.

These strategies of an ethics of liberation have as their doubled reference point the language systems, ideological frameworks, and socio-political-religious location of contemporary readers in kyriarchal systems of domination on the one hand, and those linguistic and sociohistorical systems of biblical texts and their effective histories of interpretation on the other. An ethics of interpretation engages these hermeneutical strategies as rhetorical discursive practices in order to *displace* literalist doctrinal, positivist scientific, and relativist free-for-all depoliticized academic and popular practices of reading. Such a complex interactive model of a critical interpretation for liberation challenges both the modern male-stream ethos of biblical studies and its rhetorics of inquiry in order to transform them in the interest of all nonpersons struggling in neocolonial situations for human dignity, justice, and well-being.

CHAPTER 12

Living in the Hyphen:
Theological Literacy from
an Hispanic American Perspective

ALVIN PADILLA

It would be relatively safe to assume that every reader of this volume would identify him/herself as a theologically literate person. How each individual reader would define theological literacy, however, would not yield the same unanimity. At best, we would agree that to be theologically literate a person must have "at least a passing knowledge of apologetics, dogmatic and systematic theology, religion and history, biblical and exegetical studies, and worship."[1] Just how much weight is given to each of these vis-à-vis the others would vary with each reader and his/her particular area(s) of expertise. The "passing knowledge" of these various disciplines, it should be immediately noted, does not include the practical application of the disciplines at the local, congregational level. How the theologically literate individual communicates his/her competency in theology and applies it to the common life of his/her faith community should be considered as we seek to understand theological literacy. Moreover, when we look at our various theological seminaries/graduate schools and glance at our statements of purpose, we will find some kind of sentence declaring that the institution's purpose is "to prepare men and women for ministry in the local church." That is our declared statement of mission; it is in most cases[2] our reason for being. It must be conceded, therefore, that "the real

---

1. Raymond Van De Moortell, "Theological Literacy: What Is It?" in *On Theological Literacy: Articles Published in the 1997-98 BTI Newsletter,* ed. Forrest Clingerman (Newton Centre, Mass.: Boston Theological Institute, 1998), p. 27.

2. Excluding, I might point out, those institutions which are primarily if not exclusively graduate schools preparing men and women for academia.

significance of theological literacy is made evident in the ministry of the local church,"[3] and thus one must add that criterion to our working definition. We must, therefore, link theological literacy with congregational competency. It is, if I am permitted a cultural bias, a community affair.[4] The final grade for theological literacy is not to be given by the seminary/graduate school; that grade is merely the midterm. The final comes as the emerging theologian stands before his/her community and interprets life for them. Theology, therefore, cannot be developed in isolation from the believing and practicing community, for the community of faith determines whether the individual theologian is truly theologically literate or not.

This is, of course, very disturbing for those of us raised and educated in the highly individualistic, atomistic mentality of North Atlantic civilization. We are taught early on that we hold our own destiny within ourselves and are directed to be our own selves, depending on no one else. Therefore the understanding of theological literacy as a communal act is unsettling to many of us, for it takes control away from us and puts it in the hands of those who (as we are taught even in seminary) depend upon us for survival. According to many, it takes the objective out of the equation since now the criteria are removed from the sterility of the classroom into the sin-infested streets of our communities, inviting subjectivity. We prefer the former; and when we apparently fail in the latter, we blame not our illiteracy but the incompetence of communities. A communal assessment of theological literacy is, however, how many other cultures, including Hispanic American culture, seek to understand their immediate social environment.

Locating the practice of local congregational ministry alongside a "passing knowledge" of essential theological disciplines in order to define theological literacy is not intended to be a purely academic exercise. Rather it is to highlight a very distinctive and pragmatic goal in our theological training: we seek to prepare women and men for congregational ministries who are experts in theology while at the same time being experts in daily life. For our purposes, therefore, theological literacy is to be defined as "a passing knowledge of apologetics, dogmatic and systematic theology, religion and history, biblical and exegetical studies, and worship as well as the articulation of this knowledge in the common life of our communities of faith." The local church is a hermeneutical community

---

3. Leslie H. Stobbe, "Achieving Biblical and Theological Literacy at the Congregational Level," in *On Theological Literacy* (Newton Centre: Boston Theological Institute, 1998), p. 7.

4. "The end of all education should surely be service to others. We cannot seek achievement for ourselves and forget about the progress and prosperity for our community. Our ambitions must be broad enough to include the aspirations and needs of others for their sake and for our own." Cesar Chavez, *Americanos*, p. 38.

which daily hears the words of the leading community theologian and seeks to interpret and apply the insights into the common life of that community. Theological illiteracy could, then, be defined as the inability to effectively communicate theological insights for the daily life of the congregants. This is most often seen in superficial preaching — sermonic rumblings that often fail to connect the life and traditions of the people addressed with the faith found in Scripture, thus failing to meet the real needs of the community of faith.

Communal theological literacy is seriously compromised, however, in that expertise in daily life is not a course of study to be pursued at a particular juncture in the M.Div. curriculum. This is "taught" by the ministerial ethos of the particular theological institution. It is that which students at our theological schools are able to "soak up" from their surroundings: the life experience of women and men who constitute the faculty and staff of the seminary community. A purely academic understanding of the theological disciplines, evident far too often in many of our professorial colleagues whose experience as leading contributors at the local congregational level is seriously limited, distances the theologian in residence from true *locus theologicus:* the local community of faith.[5]

Since the racial/ethnic composition of the vast majority of our seminary communities (faculty, staff, and students) is white, it should readily be seen that to be "theologically literate" is commonly defined and presented from that ethno-cultural perspective.[6] Thus theological literacy is understood by most from an Anglo-white perspective. It may be argued by some that theological literacy as defined above is acultural and nonethnic, but that argument accepts the myth of objectivity often associated with an Anglo-white, male perspective. This myth can be observed when academia labels some forms of exegetical investigations as "ideological criticism" simply because their proponents openly confess their ideological framework whereas other investigations are branded simply as critical scholarship. The myth basically implies that Anglo-whites are

5. A problem in many seminaries nowadays is the number of men and women who have swiftly moved from college to seminary to graduate school and then secured a teaching position in seminary. See John H. Leith, *Crisis in the Church: The Plight of Theological Education* (Louisville: Westminster John Knox, 1997).

6. Many years ago I mailed my *curriculum vitae* to a seminary for faculty consideration. A week or so later I received a well-crafted letter from the academic dean explaining why I would not be given further consideration for the position. The letter plainly stated that given my cultural background and my ecclesiastical experience, my gifts would not be properly utilized at the school. I was incompatible with the seminary's ethos. I have always wondered since then: Would that seminary's office of admissions respond with similar candidness to its non-white prospective students?

nonethnic in their interpretation of the world around them, and therefore their theological perspective is purely objective.[7] We must admit that as a result, we are in effect training men and women for service only in those communities represented by the dominant culture, and far too often from a monocultural perspective.[8]

It is my conviction and my thesis in this brief essay that to be theologically literate in a Hispanic American setting is different than in other sociocultural settings.[9] It means filtering the "passing knowledge" of the theological disciplines through the life experiences of the Hispanic American community, and it also means that the theological disciplines give understanding and significance to the particulars of the Hispanic American experience. A Hispanic-American theological perspective is one born out of our painful encounter between the Word of God and our personal experiences in society; it is part and parcel of learning to live in the hyphen of our existence.[10] In other words, we are to understand theology from an Hispanic American perspective, and we are to articulate our theology for Hispanic Americans. It is important that we maintain this dynamic two-way flow (from the academic disciplines to the daily life and vice versa); without it true theological literacy is seriously compromised, and, in most cases, compromised in favor of the dominant culture's understanding.

This refinement in our understanding of theological literacy is important as we usher in the twenty-first century and our increasingly multicultural society. This increased multiculturalism is particularly evident in the tremendous growth of the Hispanic American population. In the 1980s the U.S. Hispanic American population was commonly referred to as a "sleeping giant," due to its potential for future impact on our society.[11] The increasing presence of Hispanics in many aspects of the social, economic, political, and cultural life of our nation gave advance notice of what might lie ahead for the U.S. demographic outlook in the twenty-first century. Whenever possible, U.S. Census data was used to support this claim, more often than not with the characteristic undercount phenomenon cited as a caveat. As we enter the twenty-first century, the

7. Cf. Randall C. Bailey, "Race, Class and the Politics of Bible Translation," *Semeia* 76 (1996): 1-6.

8. And this, even when we allegedly prepare men and women for cross-cultural ministry.

9. The same would be true, of course, of other ethnic, cultural groups.

10. The hyphen in Hispanic-American, though currently out of vogue in proper English grammar, is purposely inserted in this sentence. For an insightful understanding of life in the hyphen, see Illan Stavans, *The Hispanic Condition: Reflections on Culture and Identity in America* (New York: Harper Collins, 1995), pp. 7-30.

11. Mostly by its constituency, i.e., those who would be inherently interested.

sleeping giant no longer appears to be slumbering, and more than the interested few are taking note. Census projections indicate that by 2010, Hispanic
Americans will become the single largest ethnic group in the United States,[12]
with the result that one out of every six U.S. residents will be of Hispanic origin.
Hispanic Americans have so infiltrated American culture that in many ways we
fail to note their presence: they are the doctors, teachers, business owners,
cooks, politicians, farm workers, baseball players, astronauts, CEOs, etc., who
daily contribute to this society. Presently we may even speak of the Latinization
of U.S. culture! For example, Ricky Martin is at the top of the charts and on the
cover of *Time* magazine; candidates for the presidency display their "fluency" in
Spanish, and some even look for Hispanic roots; the MVPs[13] in the major
leagues in 1998 were Sammy Sosa and Juan Gonzalez; and so on. Hispanic
Americans have moved from rejects to fashion setters, from outcasts to inside
traders. It has become "chic" to be Hispanic, and Montezuma's revenge appears
eminent![14]

The church in North America's main street is finally (alas!) taking note of
this immediate future and is beginning to make plans for the incorporation of
this group of people into their pews, pulpits, and positions of authority. Denominational leaders across our nation make bold claims and projections concerning membership of Hispanic Americans in their local congregations and
the number of these congregations that are predominantly Hispanic.[15] As a result, efforts are under way in our theological seminaries to significantly add to
the relatively low number of Hispanic students in our hallowed halls.[16] But will

12. In Massachusetts, where most of the writers of these essays lead and teach, this is al-
ready a fact. See Ralph Rivera, *Latinos in Massachusetts and the 1990 U.S. Census: Growth and
Geographic Distribution* (Mauricio Gastón Institute for Latino Community Development and
Public Policy, 1990).

13. For those who are not baseball literate, the MVP (most valuable player) award is
given to the best player in each of the major leagues.

14. "Montezuma's revenge" serves as an excellent illustration of the current culture wars
and differences in perspective between Hispanics and the dominant culture. For most in our society, it is a somewhat polite way of referring to the physical discomfort associated with travel
abroad by North American tourists. For Hispanic Americans, it is a reference to the conquering
of North America by the infiltration of Hispanics and the eventual Latinization of our society.

15. In my own denomination, for example, we have projected an increase of fifty or so
predominantly Hispanic American congregations for the next decade. This is a bold projection
to make since at present 40 percent of Hispanic American congregations are without permanent ministerial leadership. Where will these leaders come from? Obviously they must come
from our theological seminaries, which must then improve their recruitment efforts and effectiveness in training Hispanic American ministers.

16. The 1998 Association of Theological Schools Fact Book indicated that 2.9 percent of
total school enrollment was of Hispanic origin. This should alarm us since Hispanics constitute

theological literacy among U.S. Hispanics be significantly and positively affected simply by increasing the number of Hispanic students? Yes and no.

It seems obvious that augmenting the number of Hispanic Americans who graduate with theological degrees will increase the number who could converse in theological jargon, i.e., have a passing knowledge of the theological disciplines as academic exercises. However, if the literacy of these experts in the theological disciplines is not evident in the ecclesiastical life of their ethnic communities, then the answer must be no. Allow me an anecdotal illustration which many of us have seen repeated often enough.

In the mid 1980s Jose graduates from a high-profile seminary located somewhere in suburbia. He is an excellent student. His instructors think he will make a significant impact in the church. He receives a call to serve in a Hispanic American church in the Bronx, New York. Feeling a sense of call and purpose, and openly confessing that one must go and preach the gospel where it is needed the most, he accepts the call. Three years into his tenure at the church he reflects upon his ministerial effectiveness. He realizes that the church has not really experienced any "growth."[17] He had arrived with high hopes and great potential. His theological literacy was unquestioned by the seminary faculty and staff. However, it seemed obvious that he was unable to project that theological literacy to the congregants that listened to him weekly and to the community which surrounded them. He "discovers," to his surprise and horror, that other churches in the area have experienced "growth," and this despite the fact that the men/women who lead these congregations are not, in his understanding, as theologically literate as he is.[18] Jose himself therefore questions his theological literacy.

Jose's predicament clearly illustrates my point: a person can be theologically trained and yet be theologically illiterate in the eyes of his/her congregants. The failure lies in not bringing academic theology to the streets of ministry and not allowing the life experience of the streets to inform the theological disciplines. Jose has been unable to marry his theological competency (acquired in seminary) with the painful reality of the ethnic community he is sin-

---

about 10 percent of the total U.S. population, are described as a highly religious people, and account for a significant percentage of church growth in North America (and in Boston in particular). See Douglas Hall, Rudy Mitchell, and Jeffrey Bass, eds., *Christianity in Boston: A Series of Monographs and Case Studies on the Vitality of the Church in Boston* (Boston: Emmanuel Gospel Center, 1993).

17. However one may choose to define growth: numerically, spiritually, in terms of community involvement, etc.

18. An assessment, by the way, that most of us in theological education would concur with!

cerely serving. It might well be that seminary/graduate school did not help Jose in his own understanding of life in the hyphen. Surrounded mostly by students, faculty, and staff who represent only half his self-identity and not the identity of his future congregation, he naturally comes to understand reality only from that perspective ("American") and loses touch with the "Hispanic" in Hispanic American.

What Jose needed was a seminary experience that would have prepared him for his particular theological task: the articulation of theological convictions in the life experience of a Hispanic American congregation. Jose's education needed a theological perspective that incorporated his sociocultural experience into all aspects of its theological curriculum. As Hispanic Americans, we live between the hyphen of two cultures, in many cases personally ambivalent as to which side of the hyphen we truly belong; we find ourselves unaccepted by those on either side of the hyphen. Eldin Villafañe's triple-consciousness paradigm aptly describes the sociocultural dilemma. Taking a lead from W. E. B. Du Bois's "double consciousness" as a way of understanding African American reality, Villafañe's paradigm depicts the psychosocial reality of Hispanic Americans: they are identified as "insiders" and "outsiders" of society by *both* identifying ethnic groups, while being effectively disassociated from both.[19] Living with a hyphenated identity, we find that we do not fit into the single history of norms for testing and identifying individuals. Neither group claims us wholly as its own; daily we live with that tension. We are denied complete acceptance by the dominant culture and are similarly rejected by Latin Americans. Any attempt to convey theological truths and their implications for living in the modern world to Hispanic Americans that does not take into consideration this struggle for identity is bound to miss the mark widely. Thus seminaries, like all educational institutions that seek to prepare men and women for service in a Hispanic American context, must facilitate the student's own understanding of life in the hyphen.[20] These days we as a society speak a great deal of becoming multicultural. Seminaries, like many other educational institutions, strive toward this goal. However, more often than not, the institutional commitment to multiculturalism is relegated to mere formality — evenings dedicated to the singing/hearing of foreign/cultural songs, tasting of exotic foods, the commemoration of Martin Luther King Day, Hispanic Heritage Week, etc. Beyond these

19. Eldin Villafañe, *The Liberating Spirit: Toward an Hispanic American Pentecostal Social Ethic* (Grand Rapids: Eerdmans, 1993), p. 22.

20. We would be utter failures as theological institutions if we were to say that we do not seek the student's self-identity. Whether evangelical or mainstream liberal, all of us attempt to shape our students' theological understanding and social identity in light of our theological framework.

public and sterilized events, little is done to realistically promote a multicultural understanding of theology. Truly, a genuinely inclusive theological seminary, one committed to a multicultural perspective, is further off than we thought! What is needed for a truly multicultural theological educational experience is theologizing in culturally different perspectives and even entertaining other theological traditions than our own. This task may even reconsider traditions from a distinctive Hispanic American perspective, such as the Reformed tradition from a Hispanic American perspective.[21]

What characterizes theological literacy from a Hispanic American perspective? There are many elements that could be cited as indicative of the Hispanic American Christian experience (music and worship, preaching and teaching, views of Scripture, etc.). Allow me to highlight a few that should be incorporated into the theological training of those wishing to serve the growing Hispanic American church and theological seminaries that aggressively recruit Hispanic American students.

First of all, theological literacy means doing theology in the complex reality that comprises our world: a reality that encompasses social, economic, cultural, pastoral, and spiritual issues which are caused and informed by our bicultural, bilingual existence. In this theological perspective, *mestizaje*, the physical, religious, and cultural confluence of the Spaniards, Amerindians, and Africans in the Americas, provides the ideological framework for our theological task.[22] As Hispanic Americans, we do not make mistakes as to our own ethno-racial consciousness. We know quite well that as an ethnic group we emerged as a result of man's violence against Amerindian women. Thus we confront ourselves — and our society at large — with a noninnocent view of history without glossing over our shameful past.[23] It must be noted that despite the efforts of the dominant culture to uniformly depict us, we are a complex social/cultural/ethnic group. That complex reality is clearly evident even at the superficial level as we debate whether we should be classified as "Hispanics," "Hispanic Americans," "Latin Americans," or "Latinos." This debate alerts every reader to the fact that we are a varied people with quite varied experiences. Socioeconomically we are also quite diverse. Culturally some are very "Hispanic" in that English is not spoken in the home, while others are so distant that flu-

---

21. Or Methodism from an Hispanic American perspective — see Edwin E. Sylvest, Jr., "Wesley desde el margen Hispano," in *Voces: Voices from the Hispanic Church*, ed. Justo L. González (Nashville: Abingdon, 1992), pp. 50-54.

22. Arturo J. Bañuelas, introduction to *Mestizo Christianity: Theology from the Latino Perspective*, ed. Arturo Bañuelas (Maryknoll, N.Y.: Orbis Books, 1995), p. 1.

23. Justo Gonzalez, *Mañana: Christian Theology from a Hispanic Perspective* (Nashville: Abingdon, 1990), pp. 75ff.

ency in Spanish has faded with previous generations. Each of these varied groups has particular needs and issues that must be addressed by theological reflection. At the same time, these groups have a lot in common. The common values shared by Hispanic Americans include family, pride, courage, passion, compassion, language assets, loyalty, cultural sensitivity, adaptability — strengths and values that are the keys to success in today's world. Both the newly arrived immigrant from Latin America and the fourth-generation Hispanic American who traces his/her ancestry to the nineteenth century trace their ethnicity and culture to Hispanic or Latin elements. Members of the dominant culture have exploited them. Both attempt to find worth, significance, in a shared past. The implication of this for the young Hispanic American theologian in training is that his/her academic theology must come to grips with that complex reality. He/she must accept this mestizo identity.

Given the complex ethnic/cultural reality of Hispanic Americans, we propose that Hispanic American theological literacy must incorporate the *mestizaje* (miscegenation) concept into its theological dictionary. *Mestizaje* is a dynamic reality: it is the creation of a new race. It contributes to God's designs for a new humanity and thus is a *locus theologicus,* particularly when, from the Latino peoples' struggles for survival, *mestizaje* is rooted in resistance against assimilationist tendencies by any oppressive, dominant culture. For this reason Latino theology affirms *mestizaje* in the Latino's struggles for self-identity and self-determination, and links with God's plans for a new world order.[24] Thus *mestizaje* provides us with a theologically rich approach for understanding the importance of the historical experience of U.S. Hispanic Americans.[25]

Secondly, an Hispanic American theological perspective must also have popular religiosity as a *locus theologicus:* an implicit theological method that takes the anthropological concept of culture very seriously.[26] A theology which purports to be of the people and for the people cannot take seriously only or mainly the socioeconomic and political factors; it must attend to the people's

---

24. Bañuelas, p. 1.

25. This idea is put into verse by Trinidad Sanchez, Jr.: "A question Chicanitas sometimes ask / while others wonder: Why is the sky blue / or the grass so green? / Why am I so Brown / God made you brown, mi'ja / color bronce — color of your raza / connecting to your raíces, / your story / historia / as you begin moving towards your future / . . . God wants you to understand . . . brown / is not a color . . . it is: / a state of being, a very human texture / alive and full of song, celebrating — / dancing to the new world / which is for everyone. . . ." Lori M. Carlson, ed., *Cool Salsa: Bilingual Poems on Growing Up Latino in the United States* (New York: Fawcett Juniper, 1994), pp. 109-10.

26. Generally speaking, popular religiosity is a term associated with Hispanic Roman Catholicism. Those of us familiar with Hispanic American Protestantism in its various forms can cite numerous examples of popular religiosity within our Protestant practices.

religion, to their devotions, rituals, and customs. This characteristic blossoms in all of us from an early age — from the time our parents introduce us to *Papacito Dios, Jesus, Maria, y los santos,* incorporating them into our immediate family, making them part of our everyday life. They were not simply dogmas to be believed and debated. Rather they were personal friends, *familia,* to converse with, even argue with. As Hispanic American Protestants, we invoke the name of Jesus with such familiarity that many use the nickname associated with the common use of Jesus in our culture. Nothing was to be accomplished without invoking (in a positive, reverential manner, not as a curse!) their names and inviting their collaboration. Even those of us who have moved from the Catholic to the Protestant expression of Christianity continue to invoke that presence without compromising our evangelical views.[27] This has, in fact, often shocked my evangelical, particularly Calvinist, colleagues!

Similarly, this popular religiosity enables us to carry our crucified Lord, the embodiment of our own crucified lives, wherever our earthly pilgrimage takes us. It enables us by the transference of his own unlimited power to endure the pain for the sake of others. They could kill his body — but could not destroy him. So it is with us. Others may humiliate us, exploit us, kill us, but they cannot destroy us. He truly becomes *mi Jesús!*

This popular religiosity is expressed in our way of being church. Life sacredness is part and parcel of daily existence. The Roman Catholic Hispanic asks the priest to bless the newly purchased home; the Protestant holds a community prayer meeting to consecrate the same; both reflect our ancestors' request to have the priest bless the fields they labored on.

Thirdly, life in the hyphen demands that Hispanic American theological literacy be committed to the social struggle of our people. It is an advocacy theology. It is to embrace the *lucha,* the struggle for survival, if we are to remain faithful to our brothers and sisters and to our emerging self-image. Once again, *mestizaje* enables us to articulate that perspective both for others and ourselves. Biologically speaking, through this mixture of different human groups new groups emerge and the human genetic makeup is strengthened. At this level *mestizaje* is quite easy to comprehend and would appear to be welcomed by most. Culturally speaking, however, *mestizaje* is normally feared and perceived as threatening. The very idea of miscegenation, moreover, suggests the disintegration of each of the previously self-affirming cultural groups. This new human being understands that he/she is born out of two conflicting histories (conquerors and conquered), and in them a new history begins. The symbolic worlds of both cultures are intermingled in the mestizo so that a new symbolic

---

27. *¡Ay bendito!, ¡Ave Maria!, ¡Dios mío!* are all part of our daily speech.

world is born. Elements of this symbolic world are meaningful to the Hispanic American, but are incomprehensible to persons who try to understand them through the meanings and symbols of either of the previous cultures alone.[28] This is precisely what caused Jose's theological illiteracy as illustrated above. Having been theologically nurtured in only one of his two histories, he proceeded to articulate his theology and interpret life for his bilingual, bicultural community of faith only from that one perspective. His theologizing proved inadequate given the circumstances of the community. Jose needed to come to grips with his dual identity.

Coming to grips with this social identity, however, is a long and painful process for the individual. Unfortunately for many, their true self-identity remains undefined for life. The mestizo struggles to belong to either of the two selves seeking expression in his/her being. He/she struggles with the extreme expressions of each identity. On the one hand, he/she attempts to become like the dominant group. Only the culture, language, and worldviews of the dominant culture appear to be legitimate. The way of the conquered is rejected, for it is presented as inferior. Assimilation into the dominant group is enthusiastically pursued — at the expense of half of his/her identity. At the other extreme is the attempt to identify solely with the conquered and reject totally the dominant culture — seeing nothing worth saving from that worldview. He/she so identifies with the conquered self that he/she utterly hates the way of the conqueror. The individual alienates him/herself from the dominant culture, in effect denying, once again, his/her true identity. Out of this struggle there emerges a radically new identity. This new identity does not try to become like someone else, but it struggles to form its own unique self.

The new identity accepts from both parent cultures without seeking to duplicate either one in its entirety. This new human group has come to terms with its own hyphenated existence and continues to discern throughout life what to keep and what to leave in both cultures. It will neither romanticize nor marginalize either culture in toto. This emerging self-image of who we are as Hispanic American Christians eventually leads us to critically evaluate our own identity. We begin to conceptualize, verbalize, and communicate our way of being a particular community of faith.

When viewed from this perspective, the figure of the historical Jesus, for example, takes on added meaning. We see Jesus not as depicted in the stained glass windows of our Western European ecclesial traditions, but as the New Testament presents him: a member of an oppressed ethnic minority from an unimportant corner of the known world. In other words, Jesus appears as a marginal-

---

28. Villafañe, p. 22.

ized, shamed, and rejected member of his society. And we see that his vision for a new humanity is begun among the most segregated and impure of Jewish society. Certainly what is peripheral to human society is central to God.[29]

Since census projections indicate that Hispanic Americans will continue to increase in the twenty-first century, the incorporation of Hispanic Americans into U.S. religious life would be of benefit to our society at large and not just this ethnic group. Immediately there come to mind two significant contributions that U.S. Hispanics can make to the religious life of our nation. First, given the current demographic trends, particularly in large urban centers, the future of American denominations depends greatly on how they adapt to and assimilate Hispanics into their church life. Take, for example, the present situation in Boston. Looking at the church landscape from a mainline perspective, we see a church in steady decline with very little hope for the greatness and influence of yesteryear. Denominational reports indicate the decrease in the number of congregants and the number of congregations in the last thirty years. However, if we look beyond mainline congregations, we see that the number of congregations in Boston has increased, not decreased, and the number of persons attending churches regularly has actually increased overall. What is different is that this increase is within ethnic churches of various traditions, a significant number of which are Hispanic.[30] The survival of many of these mainline churches in our urban centers is directly tied with the Hispanic communities which surround them. As mainline denominations seek to survive in the twenty-first century, they must be sensitive to the needs of Hispanic Americans simply because of who they are. They ought not simply attempt to assimilate them into the dominant culture. For example, forcing church structure and theological traditions which are purely expressions of Western European cultural and theological reflections tends to deny the particulars of Hispanic American culture which the church is trying to attract.

29. Virgil Elizondo, "*Mestizaje* as a Locus of Theological Reflection," in *Mestizo Christianity*, p. 17.

30. Interesting and very telling is a recent experience by the author. I was at a retreat where the present and future of the church in New England was the subject of much discussion. It was one of the most depressing presentations I have ever heard of the church and its lack of vitality for the future. It was generally concluded that the church was declining and there was no slowing this down; the church had lost its influence in our New England society. The vitality and growth of the ethnic churches was not brought into the picture. When pressed to explain why African American and Hispanic congregations were not discussed, one of the speakers simply replied that he was speaking of his personal experience and what he personally knew. That satisfied the participating audience. Had I presented the presence and future of Hispanic American congregations in New England as being indicative of the situation in New England generally, I doubt that the audience would have been satisfied with my evaluations. They would have demanded the inclusion of other people groups, notably whites, and rightly so.

Secondly, theological discourse itself would benefit greatly from a bicultural, bilingual perspective that allows the North American church to continue dialogue with Christians throughout the world. It is well known that in the twenty-first century the Christian church, particularly the evangelical church, will become predominantly nonwhite. The North American church, including its theological institutions, will lose touch with the Christian mainstream unless it can find a way of bridging the cultural distance that will soon become evident. Each world is different, socioeconomically and culturally speaking — they are even antagonistic. Hispanic American Christians, because of our dual identity, stand with one foot in each of these two worlds. We are not tourists passing through; we are here to stay and we will retain our dual cultural identity. Thus we represent both the North American church and the emerging church in developing countries. Our understanding of the Christian faith, as a result of our bicultural, bilingual nature, is thus dual (but not dualistic!).[31]

---

31. Allen Figueroa Deck, introduction to *Frontiers of Hispanic Theology in the United States,* ed. Allen Figueroa Deck (Maryknoll, N.Y.: Orbis Books, 1992), p. x.

CHAPTER THIRTEEN

Reading the World Religiously: Literate Christianity in a World of Many Religions

FRANCIS X. CLOONEY, S.J.

Pluralism Is Here

When I was in college, I was excited by the study of philosophy and found it a field to which I could imagine devoting my life. It opened me to things I could not then imagine, but the implicit boundaries of our courses puzzled me. Studying in a context where we read only the great books of the European intellectual tradition ("from the Greeks to the Germans," so to speak), I found it increasingly hard to understand how we could draw an invisible line separating ourselves, intellectually at least, from the rest of the world, contenting ourselves to study parts of it while overlooking the rest. It made no sense to me — what about China, Japan, India, Africa, the traditions of Native Americans? After college I went off to Kathmandu to teach and learn, and since then I have always found it helpful, even necessary, to look more widely and understand my faith, theology, and view of the world in that wider context. Now I find that the wider world has come home; it surrounds me here in the USA.

To preach the gospel in a diverse world, we need to be able to understand that world, to be able to read it religiously; and to read the world is in part to learn the languages of the religions which flourish around us today, even here in the United States.[1] In the past it may have been sufficient to see the encounter of re-

---

1. Throughout I use the word "religion" in a nontechnical fashion to refer to "the world religions," "the other religions," and to Christianity as a "religion." In doing so, however, I do

242

ligions as a phenomenon relevant to encounters occurring elsewhere in the world, far off in Asia and Africa, and therefore also to see knowledge about religions to be an optional or very specialized topic, but today we must realize that pluralism is a religious and cultural reality closer to home, a facet of life here in the United States, and an important, ongoing event which sheds new light on our ministries in educational institutions, churches, and local communities, and on our research and writing.

Today the United States is one of the most religiously diverse countries in the world, a land where all the world religions have now found a home and to a greater or lesser extent grow and flourish. Due to the arrival of new immigrants, particularly from Asia and the Middle East, due to conversions by people of Christian and Jewish backgrounds to other religions, and due also to the ways in which disparate elements of other religions have gained currency in our society and thus influence the thinking and spirituality of American Christians, the so-called world religions are now also "American religions." Pluralism — the simple fact of religious diversity, but also the cultural and religious climate in which diversity subtly changes the way we think about every religious topic — is a fact of life, an opportunity, and a challenge, right here where we live, work, worship.

This pluralism deeply affects all our ministries, especially if we admit that we ought not reserve our service only for those who are Christian and Catholic. We must keep on broadening our horizons and opening ourselves to include people of other faiths among those we help, those who help us, and those with whom we collaborate. Many of us are already in regular contact with people of other religious traditions, even if we do not think of ourselves as officially engaged in "interreligious dialogue." Examples abound: some of us work in schools where a significant number of students belong to other religions, some work in urban areas where there may be a large number of immigrant Muslims or African Americans who have become Muslim. Some work with Asian refugees, others have real but less regular contact with people of other faiths in hospitals or jails, on college campuses, in retreat centers or parishes — and, of course, such encounters are even more likely in business, law and medicine, government service, etc. Some have chosen to become adept in non-Christian meditation practices as a part of their pastoral ministries. Some who are involved in ecumenical relations with other Christian communities may see value in connecting this Christian ecumenism with the wider encounter of religions.

A very good reason for working with people of other faith traditions is

---

not wish to enter into the important but technical debates about how to characterize these traditions. Indeed, this is the kind of problem that demands the literacy of which I speak in this essay.

that we actually need one another's help. Natural and social problems affect us all and are not sorted out according to religion. The needs of American society call us into conversation with these other faith communities, to converse and work together with teachers and scholars, and also religious leaders and parents, on issues which concern us all — for example, ways of fostering religious faith in American culture, transmitting moral values to children, weaving together religious knowledge with other kinds of academic and broader cultural learning, making sure that ethical values have a healthy role in public discourse, etc. These are issues about which religious people of all faith traditions share concern. Indeed, the most solid foundation for dialogue may be the natural, increasingly prominent dialogue of families. Once we start to work together, a certain logic becomes operative: if we work with Hindus and Muslims and Buddhists and others too, cooperating in common tasks, we will all be better off. If we all believe that our religious commitments inspire us in that work, we must also admit that our faiths will play a role in our common projects; if so, each of does well to understand something of what the other believes and how it affects her or his work in the community. It is therefore of practical value to become interreligiously literate.

Religions thrive in their concrete details, and we are at our best when we can speak vividly, concretely, with heartfelt and particular specificity and not in terms of an imagined least common denominator acceptable to everyone in the public and hence the interreligious environment in which we live. Nor ought we to be concrete and richly particular about our own traditions but vague and abstract about everyone else's. We can never know other religions in the way we know our own, but by way of analogy our understanding of the religions around us should likewise be concrete, integral, and subtle. To be professional and concrete requires education, both information and adequate ways of thinking and expressing what we learn. All of this is interreligious literacy.

Many of us are by occupation also professional representatives of our own Christian denominations, and many people in the churches and in the wider culture expect us to have something intelligent to say about how other people believe and live their religious traditions. Physicians may specialize, but they need also to know a great amount of general information about the human body; we may have deep commitments solely to our Christian faith, but we need also to know something about different religions in their many different forms. As priests and religious, ministers of the gospel, preachers and teachers, we need to be responsible and well-informed interpreters and analysts of the living religious values already present in American culture, and so be able to speak for our churches and to our culture in ways that recognize today's pluralism. Even to preach the gospel confidently in American culture, we need to be able to communicate it in terms that are intelligible to the people around us, not only to those who are Catholic or Christian or those who are secularized and "postreligious," but also to people who belong to other faith traditions or are exploring multiple religious possibilities.

Mastering some basic information about the religions of the people around us is also important for the simple reason that it cannot be avoided. Religion permeates our culture in all kinds of ways and affects what we can say and what others understand when we speak. Whether we like it or not, the very terms in which we present our faith — "faith," "revelation," "Scripture," "God," "wisdom," "love" — are living words in American culture which cannot be stipulated to have purely Christian meanings. Young people especially are already and almost instinctively aware of resonances of such terms beyond the Christian tradition. If I say "prayer," someone may think "meditation" and "mantra"; if I speak of salvation, someone may think of "nirvana"; if I appeal for surrender to God, pilgrimage to Mecca may come to mind in those who hear me; if I say "God has come among us in Jesus," someone may agree but also think, "God always comes, in Jesus, Krishna, Rama . . . ," or may wonder, "What is the spiritual difference between 'incarnation' and *avatara?*" If this cultural flow is not to mean relativism, we must explain why it is not, and our position is more likely to be persuasive if we speak intelligently and of things we know. The more public the sphere in which we speak, the more we need to understand the current interreligious multivalence of most religious language, and how the connections people make are out of our control — even if we may then feel required to correct misunderstandings and make clear what we do *not* mean.

We are Christians in a culture where it is increasingly a matter of choice that one be or remain a Christian, instead of choosing to join some other tradition. To convert is a choice, but to remain a Christian is also a choice. Nobody, really, is exempted from the new possibilities current in our pluralistic culture, and there are probably very few "traditional Christians" untouched by pluralism to whom we might minister without attention to the broader religious climate. Other people often know and consider possibilities we haven't even thought of. Many are subtly influenced by new religious and spiritual ideas; even if they have decided not to pursue such learning to the point of conversion to another religion, they may still bring eclectic, new elements into their Christian piety or belief. We need to be able to help Christians learn from other religions in a way that is properly Christian, so that we can all make better sense of our decisions to remain Christian, yet without mythologizing or belittling others.

The experience of religious pluralism is likely to be an important feature of our own identities as ministers of the gospel and theologians in the new millennium. It would be very peculiar (albeit not impossible) to discover ourselves

untouched by religious pluralism. Pluralism, a sense of alternatives, and particular positive and negative influences of other ways of thinking and acting religiously all influence our identities today even if we think of ourselves as "not
involved" with other religions. Our sense of "Christian" is already imbued with
some sense of other religious traditions, and we are better off if we can do more
than use vague terms such as "Christian" and "non-Christian" to characterize
who we are and who "they" are. To offer a clearer and more inviting religious
presence in America today, we do well to pay attention to how we have been reshaping our own identities as Christians in the midst of religious diversity.
Spiritually, too, we ourselves must be willing to learn from other religious traditions in our encounters with God. As Pope John Paul II has put it, "By dialogue
we let God be present in our midst, for as we open ourselves to one another, we
open ourselves to God" (Madras, 1986).[2]

Interreligious Literacy as a Specifically Christian Virtue

*Many of us instinctively think of evangelization (along with a stead-
fast commitment to and retrieval of the Christian tradition as
enduringly true) as a mission prized by conservatives while dialogue
(along with the range of interreligious issues and literacies) is a favorite of the liberals, a friendly alternative to evangelization. But it never
made sense to me to think that some of us were to witness to Christ
and preach the gospel while others were to learn from people of other
faith traditions — as if preaching the gospel were a kind of monologue
where we talk but never listen and dialogue were conversation from-
and-to-nowhere: Christian lite. But how can you talk and not listen?
How can you converse if you have nothing to say? Surely we do not believe that it is conservative to talk and liberal to listen! I have found
that dialogue and evangelization are necessarily interconnected. This
is why dialogue — and the required interreligious literacy — is no less
a Christian value and duty than is evangelization.*

There is much in our Christian tradition which enables and encourages us to
respond positively to other religious traditions. The following four points draw
on this heritage, with special attention to my own Roman Catholic tradition.

---

2. An address by Pope John Paul II during his visit to Chennai (Madras), India, in 1986,
as cited in Francesco Gioia, ed., *Interreligious Dialogue: The Official Teaching of the Catholic
Church* (Boston: Pauline Books and Media, 1997), p. 326.

First, we believe that there is only one God. The Christian tradition, sharing a common heritage with the Jewish and Muslim traditions but also sharing values with important Hindu traditions, is monotheistic. There is only one all-powerful and all-knowing God, and everything is in the hands of this God. The world is not chaos or conflict, nor a permanent mix of good and evil. Nor is there anything merely outside of God's plan, for that plan has no outside. Everything human, including human religious striving, can be seen as included in God's sovereign plan for the world. It would be ironic if our religious views were in practice polytheistic, as if other gods were working in places where the church is not in charge, or if we were tribal (in a pejorative sense), as if our God works only where people address God with Christian words.

Second, according to the Christian doctrine of creation, all that God has made is good. At our best, we are willing to believe the world is good and humans too are good, even in their sinfulness. Sin cannot ever succeed in entirely corrupting human nature, which is God's enduring gift. This is true inside and outside the Christian community. In a proper way, we must believe and insist that it is good that there are other religions, even if we cannot and should not indulge in optimism without further learning and scrutiny.

Third, the incarnation is the truly divine and human event of God's coming into the world; it enhances and renders more deeply meaningful our appreciation of the world and human experiencing and human doing. The natural and the human constitute the place where God is to be found, and these are, in Christ, divinized, made God's own. This incarnationalism itself is in turn enhanced and supported by a rich sense of sacrament, in a formal liturgical sense (with reference to the seven sacraments), but also in terms of the value and sacramental power even of the things of everyday life. Normatively at least, there is no sense that God can be better found outside our world, beyond the things that humans are and humans do.

Fourth, in taking seriously the intellectual character of interreligious literacy, we do well to remember the long Christian tradition which values reasoning and the essential soundness of various ways in which life can be reasonably understood. The history of European Christianity has in important ways also been a history of the embracing of Greek thought by the church, particularly in the classic achievements of the patristic period and in grand syntheses such as the *Summae* of Thomas Aquinas. Reason is a great and distinctive gift given by God to human beings, and it is typically Catholic to be disposed to trust the products of human reasoning as sound, good, universal, and to believe that we can get quite far by thinking seriously about things. Ideas, honestly expressed and simply understood, can serve as bridges across even the widest of gaps. It is Christian to think and to understand, and the ideas developed in

Hinduism, Buddhism, Islam, and other traditions are worth understanding; such is the intellectual opportunity designated by "interreligious literacy."

These four factors by no means resolve all the issues we need to take into account when we ponder the pluralism of American society, but they do indicate a strong disposition to receive positively what we encounter around us; it is worthwhile for us to learn from our neighbors, for good religious reasons.[3]

Literacy as Comparative Theology

When I talk with colleagues and students about this interreligious literacy, some seem to think I mean the discipline commonly known as "the history of religions," but this discipline, structured by its own methods and goals, does not necessarily fit well with Christian theology; in any case, studies focused on the phenomenon or history of religion mark just one of the ways one can learn about people of other faiths. Other people I talk to seem to think that the Christian literacy in religions is simply a mastery of the discipline known as "the theology of religions." But although theologians with this specialty may achieve a great deal, they do not necessarily know anything about any religion in particular, so even the best theology of religions will not replace the required interreligious literacy. To clarify what I mean, and don't mean: about ten years ago I started calling the literacy and skills at issue here "comparative theology" — a kind of Christian theology which is neither a history of religions nor a theology of religions, but which shares some of the concerns and skills of each.

If we consider together the situation of pluralism and the four reasons I have put forward which favor a Christian literacy in the religions that flourish in America, we have a profile of the learning we need to acquire, and the motivations for it. Our Christian tradition fosters an intellectual openness which favors and fosters inquiry in all fields, including those related to religion and other peoples' religions. The concrete, particular kind of study entailed in learning the details (in text or ritual or image, etc.) of two or more religious traditions with a clear Christian consciousness, memory, and reflective intent is

---

3. I have explained these four features, and the concomitant reverse tendencies toward a nonacceptance of other religions, in "Openness and Limit in the Catholic Encounter with Other Faith Traditions," in *Examining the Catholic Faith Tradition,* ed. Anthony J. Cernera and Oliver M. Moran, S.J. (Fairfield, Conn.: Sacred Heart University Press, 2000).

what I prefer to call "comparative theology," a true venture in Christian faith seeking understanding; this can in part take the form of a history of religions, but even this is undertaken in a way that allows this knowledge to become a real part of Christian reflection on Christian beliefs. It is a Christian theological literacy, just as it is a comparative literacy.

This theology is distinguished by its attention to other religions within a context that remains thoroughly Christian, although it may also involve "unlearning" various generalizations about the "non-Christians" and likewise demythologizing various confusions of the Christian truth with some older or current cultural expressions of it. By introducing what is new and unsettling the familiar, it rearticulates the meaning of one or more aspects of Christian faith in light of this new learning and then, as appropriate, engages in a new moment in dialogue with people in other traditions. This is neither the history of religions nor area studies (both of which prescind from theological concerns) nor the theology of religions (which looks inward rather than outward, scrutinizing the Christian traditions for resources for understanding other traditions), but a way of Christian thinking (and hence believing, practicing) which is both comparative and faithfully Christian, in the dialectic of the same moment, so to speak.

As should be the case when theologically sensitive comparative work is carried forward, the process of interreligious learning instigates us to review the whole of theology, our religious commitments and practices freshly, in a subtly different light. Comparative study clears our minds of useless and harmful preconceptions — about them and about us — and helps us to confront more honestly the implications of preaching the gospel in a world where the good news is very much needed but where we also have very much to learn from our non-Christian brothers and sisters.[4]

I make the preceding points about what we need to know, our inspirations, and the promise of comparative theology without being unduly optimistic, without forgetting "the other side(s)" of the Christian tradition — not only our uneven and somewhat tainted history of intolerance and disrespect for others, but also and more importantly the necessary and proper rootedness of our faith in God's action, in Jesus who died and rose, in the need for every human to make a choice in encountering God. It would do no good to argue for a new religious literacy which entails amnesia about our full identities as Christians, as sinners and as believers. Nevertheless, knowledge of other religious tra-

---

4. I have explored the meaning of "comparative theology" and surveyed recent relevant literature on the topic in "The Emerging Field of Comparative Theology: A Bibliographical Review (1989-95)," *Theological Studies* 56, no. 3 (September 1995): 521-50.

ditions does not detract from Christian faith. I do not see how a commitment to Jesus of Nazareth could possibly serve as an excuse for interreligious illiteracy, ignorance about the religiously diverse world in which we live. Interreligious literacy, not ignorance about our neighbors, is a Christian virtue. Nevertheless, one can ask: Isn't this literacy actually in competition with other things we need to know? Where does it fit in with respect to other pressing needs? To these important questions we now turn.

Interreligious Literacy and Other Literacies

As much as I have always been excited and energized by my own areas of research and teaching, mostly related to the interface of classical Hindu theologies and Christian theologies, I am glad that I have never been free of the shadow of an anxiety: Does this kind of comparative study really deserve a niche in the overpacked curriculum? Who does it help? To study Hinduism we go to India, and there we encounter not only beautiful temples, astonishing piety, and impressive theological learning, but also poverty, suffering, an eloquent struggle for justice and respect for all that is shared by Indians of all religious traditions. Closer to home, I can see how people may feel that the needs of the poor and homeless, the rights of women, the roles of ethnic minorities within the still largely Anglo churches (and many more such concerns) are all more compelling than learning the beliefs and values of other religions. But a divide-and-choose mentality — pay attention to religious pluralism or to justice issues or to traditional values — is a friend only of a status quo, which maintains itself by playing legitimate new concerns off against one another. But they are not in competition, and we are better off if we have the imagination and determination to see and enact our reality as a whole.

I mentioned earlier the array of human problems which confront us, and how it does not make sense to imagine that there are separate solutions for Christians and Hindus and Muslims. So too in theology itself: disciplines do not flourish alone, apart from others, and what is learned in one discipline influences and is influenced by other areas of learning. After the study of religions in their rich specificity has become a secure part of theological education, we will then be able to revisit disciplines such as the theology of religions and missiology, asking how knowledge of other religions affects our Christian self-understanding in these areas. The study of other religions also impacts our thinking about the very bases of Christian theology — revelation, the saving work of Christ, the Trinity, ecclesiology — even by simply reminding us that, at least intellectually, quite comparable doctrines have developed in contexts having nothing to do with the Christian tradition. Once we understand this by gaining some literacy in the doctrines of other traditions, we will be able to integrate this awareness into our study and teaching of the most basic areas of Christian theology.

Still, however important interreligious literacy may be, obviously the goal should not be to overthrow some other theological monopoly and install interreligious issues in its place. The values put forward here are not meant to be in competition with the values put forward in other essays in this volume. Learning from religious traditions need not be in competition with learning from diverse Christian communities, or from science, or from hitherto silenced or neglected voices within the churches. One need not have to decide between taking feminist concerns seriously and taking religions seriously. All these concerns stimulate, correct, and reinforce one another, as our ways of thinking, acting, and living as Christians adapt and grow in this world in which we in fact live. Indeed, keeping a balance is the whole point behind integrating the theological study of other religions into a wider theological education alongside other subjects, instead of settling for an elective system which is only a compromise, a pluralism with no center.

What can this integration be like? In 1995 representatives of Jesuits from all over the world came together in Rome for the Thirty-fourth General Congregation of the Society of Jesus. In statements published by the congregation, the gathered Jesuits offered timely advice by highlighting the integration of dialogue with other crucial Christian commitments.[5] The congregation vigorously emphasized interreligious dialogue, but also insisted on calling for the integration of this dialogue with concerns for faith, justice, and inculturation. The value of the encounter with religious people and their traditions should infuse the whole of what we do and who we are as Christians. For our work is complex and comprised of interconnected concerns. The interlocking pattern recommended by the congregation is striking: the *service of faith* requires *the promotion of justice,* true cultural engagement, and openness to other religious traditions; the *promotion of justice* requires communicating the faith, transforming cultures, and collaborating with people in other religious traditions; *inculturation* asks us to communicate the faith in terms people can understand, to

---

5. *Our Mission and Interreligious Dialogue,* n. 4. Here and below the documents are cited according to paragraph numbers in the standard English version, *The Documents of the Thirty-fourth General Congregation of the Society of Jesus* (St. Louis: Institute of Jesuit Sources, 1985).

dialogue with people who seek God in other ways, and work for justice in all we do; *interreligious dialogue* requires that we share our faith with others, evaluate cultures from a distinctively religious perspective, and show concern for the justice which makes our living faiths credible today.[6] Literacy is ultimately a richly complex human accomplishment — created, graced — in which the wide array of issues of society, art and music and literature, justice, the environment, human rights, and so on all converge into what is at least potentially one integral human conversation. Similarly, a solid academic curriculum need not merely choose one concern over another, but should be able to integrate comparative study with the wider set of concerns which inspire our whole project in theological literacy.

Interreligious literacy also functions on different levels, and education for it can be planned according to the needs of different students with different plans for the future. The Jesuits in Rome highlighted four signal aspects of ministry which can, in different ways, be shared with people from other religious traditions: the *dialogue of life* (we all share one world, we live and live together), the *dialogue of action* (we share the many tasks of life and must respond to common needs), the *dialogue of religious experience* (our traditions have deeply spiritual aspects rooted in worship, prayer, meditation, and these can be shared), and the *dialogue of theological exchange* (wherein scholars well versed in their rich theological traditions become literate, able to understand their own traditions and articulate them in words that scholars in other traditions can receive profitably).[7] The congregation recommends each level of dialogue as important, pertinent according to the various interests and needs of various persons in their individual ministries. Therefore no apostolate or expertise and training serves to excuse any of us from interreligious encounter and dialogue, no more than we might be excused from concerning ourselves with faith and justice because those are not "our specialization." Only the status quo profits if we treat urgent, emerging questions as competitive, incompatible with one another, or if we designate interreligious literacy the domain of a few specialists, unrelated to the rest of the theology we do. If we are interreligiously and theologically literate, all these concerns begin to make sense to us — we begin to read them all into a unified text of responsible ministry.

---

6. *Servants of Christ's Mission,* n. 19.
7. *Our Mission and Interreligious Dialogue,* n. 4.

Getting Practical

Much of my teaching at Boston College has been aimed at inviting students into a reflection on their faith and theology by way of thinking through specific examples from the Hindu and Buddhist religious traditions. The content of such courses varies, but in preparing them I am always mindful of beginning with some identifiable theme or concern from the Christian tradition, giving students a few well-developed Hindu or Buddhist examples with enough context and variety that they can begin to make some informed judgments about what they are reading and develop a sense of the links between their (largely) Christian backgrounds and the new things they are learning, so that eventually they are able to rethink the themes and concerns, appreciate Hindu and Buddhist ideas, and see their own Christian traditions in a new light.

To be reflective, to communicate our values, to preach the gospel, and to help in the education of our own American people in the midst of this pluralism, we need to pay more attention to the beliefs and practices of the large world religions but also small traditions, and even new sectarian groups, as these develop in the United States today. There are many ways to encounter the ideas, beliefs, practices, and faith communities of other religions, and however exciting the possibilities, it is best to set modest expectations for ourselves and our students and focus on practically feasible steps. We will never be able to learn all that needs to be known about even the "major" religions; sociological surveys are important but do not suffice for theological education; we cannot finesse the question of so much to learn by an appeal to methodology, or by substituting a general theory about religions for actual interreligious literacy. Just as one sensibly chooses to learn just one foreign language at a time, so too one can make a reasonable choice to study one religion in depth rather than learning a little about many.

In the classroom, a course on Christ and the world religions, for instance, surely serves valuable purposes, but it will not inculcate the requisite skills for dealing with other traditions any more than a course in hermeneutics might replace the actual study of Scripture. The best approach, I suggest, is to focus on particular examples — one text or set of texts, one culture, one time period perhaps, no more than several specific issues. One does better to resist the allure of "oriental mysticism" or "Asian spirituality" and instead immerse oneself for a semester in south Indian Jainism or in the fifteenth-century vernacular *Ramayana* of Tulsidas — vastly popular today, and available in English too —

or in the spiritual practices of the monks of the Ramakrishna Order of Bengal. Better to know a few things reflectively and well than too much, poorly. Students can learn a great deal by a kind of case-study method, by focused courses which open up new ways of thinking even if they do not cover a comprehensive range of data.

The primary pedagogical value of a few well-presented examples should not be underestimated. A sophisticated course on one aspect of one religious tradition can uncover the concrete problems which invariably arise, more widely and in general, when Christians try to understand other religions without neglecting their own. Generalizations will still have to be made on the basis of the cases, but these generalizations will be practically valuable if they help us to gain insight into how we learn religiously and what we do with what we learn. I can imagine, for instance, courses such as "Family Ethics in Traditional China," "Images of God in Traditional African Cultures," "Islam in Contemporary America," and even more specific courses such as "Love of God in South Indian Vernacular Hinduism" — all taught within the explicit and conscious context of the governing theological question, "How does what we are learning here affect what we know and believe as Christians?" Such courses, if reasonably proportioned and modestly designed, work reasonably well, serving multiple needs despite their very specialized initial appearance. They inform students about another religion, they suggest skills useful in processing and evaluating that information, and they enable students to reflect anew on their own tradition in light of what they have learned about another.

But let us get more practical. The goal of interreligious literacy can be approached in many ways, but it still requires some expertise in some other religions, and expertise is not cheap. Few schools have the resources to hire experts in various religious traditions, and some cannot do this at all; most often, faculty with other areas of expertise will end up teaching the world religions courses if these are to be taught at all. Faculty may rightly be reluctant to teach outside their specialization, yet intelligent amateurism is honorable and viable if the new learning and new teaching are integrated with the professor's own established areas of expertise, content, and methods. Courses such as those suggested above can be tailored to the interests and capabilities of specific faculty, taught in one way by an exegete, in another by a systematic theologian, and in yet another by an ethicist or historian or pastoral theologian. There is no reason why the ways of thinking about religions theologically should be less varied than are the other areas of theology: classical or contemporary, textual or field-based, historical or constructive. Inventive syntheses can take place: a Scripture scholar might introduce a comparative element into the New Testament introduction by taking a look at rabbinic and Qur'anic methods of exegesis; a historian could highlight how missionary work in China affected the self-understanding of European Christians in the seventeenth and eighteenth centuries; and a systematician might illuminate a Christian understanding of grace by examining how grace is explained in one or another school of Buddhism. Faculty who are willing to study another religious tradition in a specific way that is conformed to the interests and methods of their own professional training can achieve a great deal even in one summer.[8]

If established professors undertake even modest efforts to incorporate these perspectives into their teaching and writing, then the new generation of leaders — ministers, preachers, administrators, teachers, scholars — will be able to imbue their studies with a sense of the new American pluralism, and a sense of how to articulate Christian identity vis-à-vis the realities of other religions and the lively presence in our midst of faithful believers in those religions. Interreligious literacy is normal, American, and very deeply Christian.

Interreligious Literacy as Something We Do Together

I began to teach better when I realized, as I'm sure most of my readers have, that good teaching wasn't simply a question of how well prepared I was or how clearly I had set my expectations regarding what my students should have learned. Things went much better when I started seeing learning as a cooperative venture, me and my students, but then too me and my colleagues who would be teaching some of these same students in other courses. Planning for interreligious literacy, in a way that makes sense to individuals, classes, faculties, and institutions, is a shared project, not a task delegated to just one person, to be accomplished in just one course.

Interreligious literacy is a shared project. It won't work until enough of us have been persuaded that it can and should be part of the curriculum in a way that respects and enriches our other important values. However creative individuals may be, the values I have indicated here cannot be accomplished or safeguarded by one or two individuals working in isolation. Educational institutions must be more than the sum of their parts, and, with regard for every emerging area

---

8. Like the rest of this essay, these paragraphs remain rather abstract even in suggesting, almost randomly, a few possible topics and course titles. The best way for the reader to overcome this abstraction, necessary in so short an essay, is to do something concrete — read the Bhagavad Gita, or listen to a taped recitation of some *suras* of the Qur'an, or go for a daylong Zen session, or visit a local synagogue for Sabbath worship — and then reread this essay.

of literacy, the whole must be enriched by the innovations in the various parts. No one profits if a school or department is simply an aggregate of private agendas. Since, as I have stressed, interreligious literacy ought not be considered in competition with important traditional areas of learning or other emerging cultural and aesthetic and moral concerns, cooperative reform of the curriculum is all the more sensible. Integral education is not merely the sum of all legitimate concerns, just as literacy is not merely knowledge of a large number of words.

We know that we have to work together in each generation to revise and renew and restore the thoughts, words, and deeds of our Christian faith. So, too, we need to work together in fashioning a Christian way to read our American culture and to speak intelligibly in our religiously pluralistic environment, mindful of this religious diversity as a contemporary God-given reality. We need to attend to hitherto undeciphered claims made upon us — the interreligious, to be sure, but not only those — so that we can renew our ways of theological education in keeping with the vital energies and challenges of this world in which we happen to live, now.

But if all of this is true, then in the long run interreligious literacy can't be a project undertaken only by Christians working alone. Someday we will be sharing our religious learning more systematically with interested Hindus and Buddhists, Muslims and Jews, people in native traditions and even practitioners of New Age communities — certainly not merely to agree, nor to level differences, but to create a sufficiently common vocabulary and sense of one another that we can even know what we share, where we disagree, and what we are to do next. In a seemingly secularized world, we need to create possibilities which bring us together for religious learning, conversing, arguing, stating and defending the religious truths people live and die for. Interreligious literacy requires a community, and does its share to help create one.

PART IV

THE RHETORIC OF THEOLOGY

RODNEY L. PETERSEN

Rhetoric has always been a part of literacy. Augustine takes this up in book 4 of *On Christian Doctrine*.[1] He scores the importance of teaching, of portraying with truth the message of truth. And the manner of exposition should be worthy of the message being conveyed. If rhetoric is interpreted as the art of speaking or writing effectively, i.e., the study of the principles and rules of composition that enable this to happen, we also know how easy it is for good rhetoric to spill over into insincere and grandiloquent language. Transparency, good rhetorical resonance, is a prerequisite for ministers, priests, and prophets.[2] This section is about six different facets of ministry that compose good ministerial rhetoric in the twenty-first century.

Ministry is, first of all, a ministry of forgiveness and reconciliation. It is also ministry characterized by restorative justice, a transformative process that enables meaningful reconciliation to occur. It is a ministry of pastoral care. Persons, and not abstract justice, are at the heart of ministry. Good ministry is concerned about the spiritual formation of persons. Ministry is characterized by a prophetic realism that will not stray from the truth. Finally, in good Augus-

---

1. Augustine, *On Christian Doctrine*, bk. 4, pp. 117-69. He opens the section by writing: "This work of ours entitled On Christian Doctrine was at the beginning divided into two parts. For after the Prologue . . . I wrote, 'There are two things necessary to the treatment of the Scriptures: a way of discovering those things which are to be understood, and a way of teaching what we have learned. We shall speak first of discovery and second of teaching.' Since we have already said much concerning discovery and devoted three books to that one part, with the help of God we shall say a few things concerning teaching . . ." (4.1; pp. 117-18).

2. Bernard Häring writes, "Since the role of the priest is primarily that of a credible witness, it is of the utmost importance that all Church structures, all basic relationships within the Church, and the whole of moral formation promote and encourage absolute sincerity and transparency." See his *Priesthood Imperiled: A Critical Examination of Ministry in the Catholic Church* (Ligouri, Mo.: Ligouri Books, 1996).

tinian fashion, the minister is an educator. The apostle Paul writes of equipping the saints "for the work of ministry, for the building up of the body of Christ" (Eph. 4:11-15).[3] All the minister's efforts are bent toward human maturation, the rhetorical resonance of the human with the divine.[4]

A ministry of forgiveness and reconciliation is central to the concerns raised by Ruth Bersin in the opening chapter of this section, "Healing Traumatic Memories: A Spiritual Journey." Bersin suggests that the church provides unique resources in aiding post-traumatic stress disorder (PTSD) victims, especially refugees and others who have been victims of torture or other traumas. She writes of the connection between spirituality and healing, that religion is mindful of human suffering in its historical context.[5] She surveys current medical research and the resources of faith communities such as community life, prayer, dreams, art, and retreat. The strength of her article is in sketching the healing process, conceived of as a journey that follows steps of safety, remembrance, forgiveness, restoration and reclamation, reconciliation, regeneration and reintegration.

Bersin's work reminds us of the central role played by forgiveness in the Christian life. The quality of our relationship with our neighbor is assumed in Christian theology to be a mirror of that between ourselves and God, or ultimate reality. Christianity assumes a deep need for neighbor, a need that is symmetrical to our need for God. This is seen in the structure of the Ten Commandments and in their dominical summary (Matt. 22:36-40). Writing about this relationship, the theologian Karl Barth includes the forgiveness of neighbor as a central feature of his material on "The Praise of God."[6] The neighbor is not

3. Paul's conception of Jesus as the Christ implies that union with Christ through faith imparts the divine nature upon the believer as a member of Christ's body and involves abiding in him for growth in grace and service (cf. Col. 1:15-29). Thomas F. O'Meara, O.P., writes of ministry as "(1) doing something, (2) for the advent and presence of the kingdom, (3) in public, (4) on behalf of a Christian community, (5) as a gift received in faith, baptism and ordination, (6) and as an activity with its own limits and identity existing within a diversity of ministerial actions." While the cultural ramifications of ministry may be wider than O'Meara appears to allow, he makes room for a cooperative model of ministry through the enabling work of the Holy Spirit, in *Theology of Ministry* (New York: Paulist Press, 1999).

4. James E. Loder compassionately sets different models of maturation in context with analysis from theologians like Barth and Pannenberg in *The Logic of the Spirit: Human Development in Theological Perspective* (San Francisco: Jossey-Bass, 1998).

5. André Jacques reminds us that throughout the Bible, the experience of exile and the treatment of strangers are used as tests of faithfulness to God; see *The Stranger within Your Gates: Uprooted People in the World Today* (Geneva: World Council of Churches Publications, 1986; French ed., 1985).

6. Karl Barth, *Church Dogmatics*, ed. G. W. Bromiley and T. F. Torrance, trans. G. T. Thomson and H. Knight (Edinburgh: T. & T. Clark, 1970), II.2, #18.3 (pp. 401ff.). Barth writes, "In the

the abstract "other" but God in our own image facing us in the other. Taking up the biblical challenge to "love my neighbor as I love myself," Barth writes that to love my neighbor means accepting the future that is shaped by the reality of my neighbor. We are, in fact, given to one another in order to benefit from each other, to find the restoration that is only possible because of each other, and to find our respective identities through each other.[7] It is this sense of neighbor that becomes so central when dealing with abuse.

How can the abuser be seen as my neighbor? How am I to break a cycle of victim and victimizer into which I have been drawn despite my best intentions?[8] These questions are as central to Bersin's reflections as are the larger issues of political abuse and social conflict in which they are often embedded. Trauma, brokenness, and violence shape many lives in the twenty-first century. The twentieth century was one of the most consciously violent in human history, marked by such social trauma as the Armenian genocide and the First World War, highlighted at midcentury by the Second World War and the Jewish holocaust, and ending with continuing ethnic genocide, holocaust, and violence in such places as Southeast Asia, Rwanda, the Balkans, and Palestine. How to speak into human realities shaped by such experiences becomes a central task of theological literacy in the twenty-first century. The benefit to local church life from Bersin's work is such as to form "trauma-resilient" communities. This is important whether dealing with PTSD as experienced by individuals or considering the plight of political victims and refugees to our communities.

Christian ministry is characterized by forgiveness and reconciliation, but this becomes meaningful insofar as such attitudes open out into practices of restorative justice. Restorative justice is a transformative process that enables meaningful reconciliation to occur.[9] These themes run through the chapter by

---

biblical sense of the concept my neighbor is not each of my fellow-men as such . . . as such consists of mere individuals. . . . My neighbor is an event, which takes place in the existence of a definite man definitely marked off from all other men. My neighbor is my fellow-man acting toward me as a benefactor" (pp. 419-20).

7. Barth, II.2, p. 430.

8. Working in southeast Europe, Olga Botcharova has developed models for group counseling with diagrams of steps toward revenge and steps toward reconciliation. See "Implementation of Track II Diplomacy: Developing a Model of Forgiveness," in Raymond Helmick, S.J., and Rodney Petersen, *Forgiveness and Reconciliation: Religion, Public Policy, and Conflict Transformation* (Philadelphia: Templeton Foundation Press, 2001). This is not to be negligent of what psychiatrist Judith Herman has termed "the forgiveness bypass," enabling victimizers to fail to deal with the realities of their violence and aggression, in *Trauma and Recovery: The Aftermath of Violence — from Domestic Abuse to Political Terror* (New York: Basic Books, 1992). The same point is implied in *Impunity: An Ethical Perspective,* ed. Charles Harper (Geneva: World Council of Churches Publications, 1996).

9. Howard Zehr writes that our criminal justice system ignores many of the needs of crime

Fred Smith, "A Prophetic Religious Education for Y2K and Beyond: And Black Boys Shall See Visions." Smith takes us on a personal journey that is fraught with pathos and social significance for the world that we are creating for our youth, and in particular for black youth and others perceived as apart from the mainstream. Through his experience as "Uncle Junior," Smith surveys the role of the black church, contexts of violence, and the pathology of deviated transcendence. This is the fruit of racism and the consequences of slavery.[10] We are brought to see the alarming rate of deaths by violence among young black men and boys and something of the nature of black-on-black violence. Smith's article reminds us of the role played by black theology and spirituality in American cultural life — and of the deeper background against which this experience is being articulated.[11] This also reminds us that theological literacy requires sensitivity to the disparities and inequities of life and to our need to be part of a community or sharing of all God's resources, a practice that leads not only to the liberation of others but to our own spiritual freedom.[12] Christians have often used the term "Jubilee" to express the fact that we are, at our best, stewards of God's good gifts. As such, the Jubilee refrain resounds with themes of forgiveness, liberty, and justice (Lev. 25:10; Isa. 61; and Luke 4).[13] Smith's poignant

victims and fails to deal with the accountability, closure, and healing of offenders, in *Changing Lenses: A New Focus for Crime and Justice* (Scottdale, Pa.: Herald, 1995). The need for churches and faith-based communities to stay connected with the criminal justice system is addressed by Michael L. Hadley, ed., *The Spiritual Roots of Restorative Justice* (Albany: State University of New York Press, 2001). T. Richard Snyder finds a skewed Christian ontology behind a retributive justice system in *The Protestant Ethic and the Spirit of Punishment* (Grand Rapids: Eerdmans, 2000).

10. Orlando Patterson examines the cultural consequences of slavery in America affecting male-female relations, sacrificial barbarism, and contorted, idealized images in the media in *Rituals of Blood: Consequences of Slavery in Two American Centuries* (Washington, D.C.: Civitas Counterpoint, 1998). The history of slavery in New England theology and its consequences are explored by Paul R. Griffin in *Seeds of Racism in the Soul of America* (Cleveland: Pilgrim Press, 1999). See also C. Eric Lincoln, *Race, Religion, and the Continuing American Dilemma* (New York: Hill and Wang, 1984).

11. Atron A. Gentry, *Learning to Survive: Black Youth Look for Education and Hope* (Westport, Conn.: Greenwood Publishing Group, 1996), and Charles Foster, *Working the Black Youth: Opportunities for Christian Ministry* (Nashville: Abingdon, 1989).

12. Dwight N. Hopkins outlines the pedagogy involved, in "Black Theology on Theological Education," *Theological Education* 34, no. 2 (spring 1998): 73-84.

13. A helpful perspective on Jubilee from the experience of African Americans is given in the introductory essays in *Holy Bible: The African American Jubilee Edition,* various versions, by Jubilee Staff (New York: American Bible Society, 2000). With respect to the African American experience, see James McGregor Burns and Stewart Burns, *A People's Charter: The Pursuit of Rights in America* (New York: Knopf, 1991), and Joseph Donders, *Non-Bourgeois Theology, an African Experience of Jesus* (Maryknoll, N.Y.: Orbis Books, 1985).

story calls us to a ministry of healing the wounds of America, experiences that are never merely in the abstract.[14]

Structurally, the focus of this chapter is on a specific population as reflected in a series of letters composed for a young nephew at the loss of a family member. The letter excerpts continue to draw the reader back to the intimacy of the relationship and to the human stakes involved. The central metaphor is vision. This is what is needed by young black youth in order to ensure survival. It is available through prophetic religious education, perhaps explaining, in part, the popularity of charismatic forms of Christianity and Islam among young, capable black youth.[15] Writing about the pathology of "deviated transcendence," the trap of deferring and waiting for "pie-in-the-sky, by-and-by," and the myth of redemptive violence as it can be seen in the heroes that are offered to young black men and boys by popular culture, Smith draws us instead to a set of specific and useful theological emphases and figures that can be used to promote constructive vision, such as Christ the "hope-bringer" or the "trickster Christ." Through such envisioning we are brought directly to issues of life and death. By way of creative insight and solid theological reasoning, we come to see the forcefulness of the need for Jesus Christ to be employed in today's context.[16]

Theological literacy implies the ability to minister to the wounded, hurt, and marginalized.[17] It is a ministry of pastoral care. Insofar as it is "pastoral" in nature, it is carried out as a part of a community of faith and as a representative

14. John Dawson looks at human conflict from a global perspective, then, listing what he calls "the wounds of the world," encourages a process of confession, repentance, reconciliation, and restitution, in *Healing America's Wounds* (Ventura, Calif.: Regal, 1994). A similar, spiritual approach is in Robert Schreiter, *On Reconciliation* (Maryknoll, N.Y.: Orbis Books, 1991); and note the work of Moral Rearmament that is more consciously interreligious in its work: Frank Buchman, *Remaking the World* (London, 1961).

15. A helpful perspective is offered in the introductory essays in *Holy Bible: The African American Jubilee Edition*. Franz Fanon was one of the first to bring to consciousness in the larger culture the experience of "blackness" in his books *The Wretched of the Earth,* trans. Constance Farrington (New York: Grove Press, 1963; French, 1961), and *Black Skin, White Masks,* trans. Charles Lam Markmann (New York: Grove Press, 1967; French, 1952). Apart from contemporary Islam, one of the most popular "alternative" visions of Christianity is in Jamaican Rastafarianism; see William David Spencer, *Dread Jesus* (London: SPCK, 1999).

16. A phenomenology of redemption has been most forcefully brought forward by René Girard. This work stands behind much of Smith's constructive theology. See Girard's *I See Satan Fall Like Lightning* (Maryknoll, N.Y.: Orbis Books, 2001), and earlier works on scapegoats and mimetic violence. George H. Williams offers a helpful overview of Christian typological approaches to violence: "Four Modalities of Violence, with Special Reference to the Writings of Georges Sorel," *Journal of Church and State* 16, no. 1 (1974): 11-30; 16, no. 2 (1974): 237-61.

17. J. Earl Thompson, "Theological Education as Pastoral Care," *Theological Education* 33, no. 2 (spring 1997): 29-38.

embodiment of our deepest understanding of reality. Persons, and not abstract justice, are at the heart of ministry. Carrie Doehring writes of the challenges to pastoral ministry in her chapter, "Theological Literacy and Fluency in a New Millennium: A Pastoral Theological Perspective." She outlines the challenges that have arisen in the culture to the practice of pastoral care in light of the revolution in psychology in the twentieth century. She notes the need in pastoral practice for both theological literacy and fluency. By these she means the ways in which a theoretical knowledge, or literacy, needs to be integrated with the actual living out of our faith or understanding. The tension between "head" and "life" skills can form a kind of bridge. Working to develop this bridge can be an act of healing in itself.

Doehring traces the historical development of three traditions of theological fluency and offers some critical analysis of each. Persons such as Anton Boisen, Seward Hiltner, and Wayne Oates have laid the foundation for a liberal pastoral theology, a theology that emphasizes patterns of correlation in psychology and pastoral care and offers a way of reading and interpreting Scripture that is critical, contextual, and emancipatory. For some, this line of fluency, or interpretation, has tended to overwhelm a biblical understanding of the human psyche. A second line of theological fluency is that which follows the work of Jay Adams. Defined as biblical counseling, this form, in Doehring's opinion, has tended to overwhelm the language of psychology with that of biblical narrative. Finally, Doehring defines an integrationist tradition associated with Bernard Spilka, Richard Gorsuch, and Larry Crabb that has consciously worked to develop an approach that allows each voice, biblical narrative and psychology, to remain in the conversation.

In the letters between the Swiss Reformed pastor Oskar Pfister and Sigmund Freud, the early dimensions of the cultural and theological tendencies that would define the discipline of pastoral care from Freud's day to our own are drawn out.[18] Ways in which Freud's influence have further shaped the practice of ministry in the twentieth century are illustrated by Allison Stokes. As soul guides, pastors and priests had for centuries drawn upon their intuitive gifts, scriptural guidance, and the inherited memory of spiritual guidebooks often finding their origin in medieval monastic theology. Stokes details the crisis in pastoral care that existed at the beginning of the twentieth century as ministers began to encounter and then make reference to concepts drawn from dynamic psychology — the un-

---

18. See Ernst L. Freud, ed., *Psychoanalysis and Faith: The Letters of Sigmund Freud and Oskar Pfister* (New York: Basic Books, 1954); Oskar Pfister, "The Illusion of a Future: A Friendly Disagreement with Professor Sigmund Freud," *Imago* 14, no. 2-3 (1928): 1-40. See Hans Küng, *Freud and the Problem of God* (New Haven: Yale University Press, 1990).

conscious, repression, transference, aggression, projection, and so forth — for insight into the human psyche. Stokes provides a helpful matrix into which Doehring's analysis can be set.[19] If anything, the cultural context for pastoral care is even more complex than it was a century ago, and Doehring's typology of positions might now be conceived of as different languages to describe the travail of the soul. The challenge for pastoral care — and for theological literacy — is to find the way to balance the perspectives on the psyche, or soul, found in forms of Christian spirituality with the conflicting demands of culture and scientific endeavor. Each of these, culture, contemporary reasoning and perspective, and Christian understanding, threatens to overwhelm the other.[20]

But good ministry is also about the spiritual formation of persons. This is the end toward which pastoral care tends. Brian O. McDermott, S.J., develops this point in his chapter, "Theological Literacy: Some Catholic Reflections." He lays out the importance of spirituality to the formation of persons, focusing primarily on the process of drawing youth to maturity.[21] If spirituality can be defined as "a growing intimacy with God experienced through persons, places, events, and things in everyday life," as Nicki Vandergrift puts it, McDermott adds to this an emphasis upon the transformation of consciousness.[22] Related to Vandergrift's concept of "solidarity,"[23] it is clear that McDermott moves the

19. Allison Stokes, *Ministry after Freud* (New York: Pilgrim Press, 1985).

20. Alvin Dueck, *Between Jerusalem and Athens: Ethical Perspectives on Culture, Religion, and Psychotherapy* (Grand Rapids: Baker, 1995).

21. For Ignatius of Loyola (1491/95–1556), this began with the *Spiritual Exercises,* a series of meditations and rules designed to lead souls to conquer their passions and give themselves to God. On the history of the Jesuit Order, see John W. O'Malley, *The First Jesuits* (Cambridge: Harvard University Press, 1995). The nature of spirituality, as well as Christian spirituality, a topic of contemporary cultural interest, was given a troubling analysis with respect to theological education by Paul Wilkes, "The Hands That Would Shape Our Souls," *Atlantic Monthly,* December 1990, pp. 59-88. Since then, greater attention has been given to the topic in Protestant, Roman Catholic, and Orthodox seminaries and schools of theology. See articles in *Ministerial Formation,* a quarterly journal of the WCC and its Programme on Ecumenical Theological Education, as well as in *Theological Education.* See Gordon T. Smith, "Spiritual Formation in the Academy: A Unifying Model," *Theological Education* 33, no. 1 (autumn 1996): 83-91. Smith affirms (1) the priority of spiritual maturity; (2) education as a means to this end; (3) that commitment, prayer, and the whole person are also a part of the classroom; (4) the value of formative activities to complement academic work; (5) the central place of liturgy in the life of a school; (6) opportunities to develop spiritual discipline; (7) a spiritual heritage; and (8) the responsibility of the student.

22. See the ways McDermott expresses this transformation in *What Are They Saying about the Grace of Christ?* (Mahweh, N.J.: Paulist, 1984).

23. Nicki Verploegen Vandergrift, *Organic Spirituality: A Sixfold Path for Contemplative Living* (Maryknoll, N.Y.: Orbis Books, 2000). She sketches steps of slowing down, sharing our stories, stillness, solitude, surrender, and solidarity.

concept toward an emphasis on action and participation. He even suggests that theological literacy might better be conceived of as spiritual practice.

Thanks to the work of Paulo Freire, McDermott writes, we have come to see literacy as more than learning how to read and write. It is also self-emancipation with sociopolitical consequences. Writing from a Roman Catholic perspective, McDermott develops this concept by using ideas drawn from the history of Christian spirituality, *lectio divina, meditatio, oratio, contemplatio,* and finally *actio.* Theological literacy, or "the process of becoming theologically literate about one's own faith tradition," is emancipatory. The conscience of a mature Catholic, he writes, is characterized by three features that result from this process. It is well informed by outside norms and values, self-responsible, and open to and dependent on the mercy of God. Citing Robert Kegan, McDermott adds that until recently it was not necessary for many individuals to develop their own adult or "modern" consciousness. For many, particularly those living in integrated cultures characterized by a high level of religious and political synthesis, the cultural environment often carried the complexity of consciousness. Their embeddedness guaranteed that they could function well at an adolescent level. Today, however, the world for each of us is full of options, and these include religious options as outlined by a number of our authors. McDermott continues by writing that theological literacy is more than academic competence. It comprises the schooling of the religious imagination. It is a spiritual practice, a form of the *lectio divina* as appropriate for modern cultural consciousness, contemporary generational issues, imagination, desires, and faith.[24]

Ministry can be characterized not only by work toward forgiveness and reconciliation, efforts at restorative justice, pastoral care, and spiritual formation, but also by its passion for truth, even a prophetic realism that will not stray from the truth, however difficult it may appear to be. Wesley Wildman's chapter, "Theological Literacy: Problem and Promise," values the need to struggle against using our understanding of God prematurely — even when it might bring a sense of personal stability and security.[25] Wildman defines theological

---

24. The idea of Christian spirituality can be set into a wide cultural matrix, as is done by Gerhart B. Ladner, *The Idea of Reform: Its Impact on Christian Thought and Action in the Age of the Fathers* (Cambridge: Harvard University Press, 1959). The field of Christian spiritualities moves in many directions; for an overview, see Urban T. Holmes, *A History of Christian Spirituality: An Analytical Introduction* (New York: Seabury Press, 1980); Kenneth Leech, *Soul Friend: An Invitation to Spiritual Direction* (San Francisco: Harper Collins, 1992); Glenn E. Hinson, *Spirituality in Ecumenical Perspective* (Louisville: Westminster John Knox, 1993).

25. Wildman's methodology can be seen in *Fidelity with Plausibility: Modest Christologies in the Twentieth Century* (Albany: State University of New York, 1998); see also *Religion and Science: History, Method, Dialogue,* ed. Wildman and Mark Richardson (New York: Routledge, 1996).

literacy in two ways. First of all, it is found in coming to know the language of one's beliefs so as to be able to clearly share one's understandings and clarify ideas with others.[26] It is, secondly, marked by the ability to think theologically. For Wildman, an example of the latter is the chapter by David Tracy that opens this volume.[27] Knowing how to think theologically is a form of literacy that promotes understanding, transformation, intellectual honesty, spiritual realism, and moral responsibility. But such thinking is hard to cultivate. It can even lead, at times, to distress and alienation from one's religious community.[28] But it also has the power to create community.[29]

The difficulty with theological literacy is that it often appears irrelevant to many, and even seems unattractive for some. Such literacy is a problem because it raises consciousness and disrupts the silent and relatively effective functioning of religion as a support structure in individual and corporate life. Theological literacy may represent the loss of a certain naïveté. It is less prophetic in this guise and more supportive of embedded culture. It may undermine community solidarity and societal integralism, as argued by theologian Paul Ricoeur, and as seen in cultures undergoing social transition. Theological literacy poses an even greater personal problem when our own patterns of thought and assumptions are challenged. Nevertheless, it is in this way that our dearest "idols" are challenged. Learning to think theologically, not just the ability to defend our beliefs but to internalize this way of thinking, becomes like science literacy — hard to

26. Lucretia Bailey Yaghjian stresses how writing serves not only to strengthen innate skills in this regard but can enhance our understanding of what we mean to say and find the common ground for saying it. See "Teaching Writing in a Theological Context," *Theological Education* 33, no. 2 (spring 1997): 39-68. In other words, the very effort at theological literacy begins a conversation and takes us out of ourselves and brings us to our neighbor.

27. See David Tracy's *The Analogical Imagination: Christian Theology and the Culture of Pluralism* (New York: Crossroad, 1981); also Richard Grigg, *Theology as a Way of Thinking* (Atlanta: Scholars Press, 1990).

28. Drawing upon arguments from omnipotence, philosophy in relation to revelation, and a breadth of understanding summarized in Pascal's wager ("The heart has its reasons that reason does not know"), Mortimer J. Adler writes helpfully about thinking about God in *How to Think about God* (New York: Macmillan, 1980); drawing widely, but simply and eloquently, is Dominique Morin, *How to Understand God,* translated from the French by John Bowden (London: SCM Press, 1990); and for Christian theology, Alister E. McGrath, *Christian Theology: An Introduction* (Oxford: Blackwell, 1994); additional references can be found in Part I of this book.

29. Drawing upon theologians Roger Height and David Bartholmae, Lucretia Bailey Yaghjian sees theology as a discipline that implies a community with a grammar and rhetoric. Theological literacy implies learning to speak the language so that a community can understand it; see her "Teaching Writing in a Theological Context," *Theological Education* 33, no. 2 (spring 1997): 39-68, citing Roger Haight, S.J., *Dynamics of Theology* (Mahwah, N.J.: Paulist, 1990).

achieve. However, as in mathematics, the real consequences of serious theology often do take time to manifest themselves — and they are real.

The problem of theological literacy, its sometimes difficult and obtuse nature, even as practiced as theodicy (a way to explain one's place amidst the challenges of life), is contrasted with the promise of theological literacy. Developing his ideas in relation to a sermon on the Columbine High School shootings, Wildman contends that we often invent images of God to make ourselves feel better. Suffering, however, unmasks religion, its useful fictions and comforting distractions. It is at times like this that the promise of theology can make itself felt. Theology can speak the truth that life is at the mercy of God. For Wildman this is often a "Jobian" experience: "Though he slay me, yet will I trust in him." Wildman writes, "When only the truth will do, nothing has the potential to unmask, to transform, and to evoke responsibility like theology." This is the point where, for the sake of rhetorical transparency, the prophetic model of ministry may for a time appear to erode the supportive dimension of pastoral care but in the end creates a lasting foundation for faith.

The consequences of this problem — and its promise — for theological education is to provide the training and preparation for the knowledge that theology discloses a God who undoes our pretensions even to divine knowledge and defies our convenient systems of ideas. It follows that theological literacy requires that three conditions be met. Knowledge must be coupled with consistent inquiry. Theological resources must be continually joined to new problems so as to be constructive. Theological literacy, a known language to articulate belief — or as a way of critical thinking — should evoke spiritual alertness. Finally, theological literacy leads us to recognize the social construction of reality.[30] In this, the work of the professional theologian has parallels to that of the "philosophers of suspicion" (Nietzsche, Marx, and Freud). Wildman draws us to the horizon of Ludwig Feuerbach's cultural criticism of religion's apparent veil over life's deeper currents.[31] In light of this collapse of knowledge into nihilism, radical orthodoxy might be seen to pick up where the deconstruction of many contemporary theological trends seems to move through the recognition that if nothing can really be known, one might find in God the radically unknowable.[32]

---

30. Peter L. Berger and Thomas Luckmann, *The Social Construction of Reality: A Treatise in the Sociology of Knowledge* (New York: Doubleday, 1967).

31. Ludwig Feuerbach, *The Essence of Christianity,* trans. George Eliot (Amherst, N.Y.: Prometheus Books, 1989).

32. Radical orthodoxy might be said to follow the lead of Rowan Williams and Hans Urs von Balthasar, and is defined in the work of John Milbank, who reaches beyond the dichotomies of late twentieth-century theology, finding premodern and postmodern theology to be parallel developments. Milbank articulates a position that finds all knowledge grounded in theology but

The minister is also an educator. This is clear in Wildman's work, but it is the point of the chapter by Thomas Groome, "Wisdom for Life: The Horizon of Theological Literacy." It has also been the focus of his work through his books, *Christian Religious Education* (1980) and *Sharing Faith* (1991), and in other publications focused on parish life.[33] He entitles his method "shared praxis," and, shaped through his search for a better way of doing Christian — and religious — education, there is much that is accessible to all educational programs.[34] The controlling motif of "shared praxis" is "an educational program that measures our present in light of God's Word, with a vision of God's kingdom in mind, and for which we are called to be co-creators." Groome has tried to develop a method that is open to religious as well as, more specifically, Christian educators. By "shared praxis" he means "a group of Christians (as fellow pilgrims) sharing in *dialogue* their *critical reflection* on *present action* in light of the *Christian story* and its *vision* toward the end of lived Christian faith."[35] Noting his own social location and that of the public with whom he works,

---

evolving in history. See his *Theology and Social Theory: Beyond Secular Reason* (London: Blackwell, 1990). In *The Word Made Strange: Theology, Language, Culture* (London: Blackwell, 1997), Milbank implies that church practice is often empty and rote, and in a book by former student and colleague Catherine Pickstock, *After Writing: On the Liturgical Consummation of Philosophy* (London: Blackwell, 1998), increasing focus on the liturgy and Eucharist as model for a participatory community has been articulated. See further Graham Ward, *The Postmodern God: A Theological Reader* (London: Blackwell, 1997), and Milbank, Pickstock, and Ward, *Radical Orthodoxy: A New Theology* (London: Routledge, 1999). The extent to which "radical orthodoxy" is different from historic Orthodoxy as identified with the churches of the East has yet to be clearly shown. See also William C. Placher, *The Domestification of Transcendence: How Modern Thinking about God Went Wrong* (Philadelphia: Westminster John Knox, 1996). See also the writing of Alexander Men, *Christianity for the Twenty-first Century: The Prophetic Writings of Alexander Men,* ed. Elizabeth Roberts and Ann Shukman (New York: Continuum, 1996).

33. Thomas H. Groome, *Christian Religious Education: Sharing Our Story and Vision* (San Francisco: Jossy-Bass, 1999; 1st ed., 1980), and *Sharing Faith: A Comprehensive Approach to Religious Education and Pastoral Ministry: The Way of Shared Praxis,* 1st ed. (San Francisco: Harper San Francisco, 1991).

34. Vic Lehman summarizes Groome's search for a better method of Christian education through the influence of a more learner-focused and dialogic approach laid down by Paulo Friere and through the connections made between a self-reflective critique and action, as in the work of Jürgen Habermas. See Lehman's "Renewal in Christian Education," *Journal of Christian Education* 35, no. 1 (April 1992): 7-17. Lehman goes on to write that Groome found John Westerhoff's idea of "intentional religious socialization" as bound to maintaining the status quo and the "social science approach" of James Michael Lee as "controlling and manipulative."

35. Groome, *Christian Religious Education* (1980), p. 184. Subject to critique, see the positive assessment of Groome's work by evangelical educator Barbara J. Bjelland, "A Response to Jackie Smallbones' Assessment of Thomas Groome's Christian Religious Education," *Christian Education Journal* 10, no. 2 (winter 1990): 107-10.

Groome raises up four perspectives in this chapter that flow naturally from his conception of "shared praxis." They define aspects of theological literacy: the importance of symbols, a public perception of the irrelevance of theology, the need for theology to be structured and taught so as to engage lives and social reality. Furthermore, the existential consequences for theological literacy should be life-giving for persons and societies.

Groome's assumption is that theology ought to be concerned with its public image, not in the sense of losing its character but by being concerned about becoming, and being consciously willing to appear, more relevant. Theology is a way of perceiving and putting words to the transformative power of God. A pressing question for Groome is, "Why is there so little public interest in theology?" This is not merely a rhetorical point. Groome offers some concrete pedagogical insight. First, the Enlightenment, as a legacy celebrating reason, political liberalism, and the objectivity of the scientific enterprise, has been a mixed blessing for theological education. In this, Groome highlights several of the separations noted by Tracy early in this volume. Groome emphasizes the separation of knowing from being, one that has become a focal point in the alienation of Generation X and a possible search for connections among Millennials.[36] Although the Enlightenment did bring certain assets — liberty, equality, fraternity — here agreeing with our authors Schüssler Fiorenza and Helmick, it also bore certain liabilities. It valued knowing more than wisdom, disparaged everyday experience, removed theological thinking to the domain of specialists, and fostered the separation of the theoretical from the practical.

Groome goes on to ask us to think of theological literacy as wisdom for life. As with McDermott, Groome takes his cue from Paulo Freire, finding him the exponent of modern-day literacy education. Groome writes of how people need to "read" their lives into the world as well as read books, with critical reflection on their social and political contexts. This is especially important if religion, and theology, is to be seen as a serious endeavor. The wisdom cited by Groome can demystify the powers and forces that shape our lives, giving us a more critical edge on the debilitating psychologies, consumerist orientations, and other idolatries that shape our lives.[37] This empowers people as historical

---

36. Tom Beaudoin writes of the ways Generation X holds all institutions suspect of hypocrisy, celebrates personal experience, but acknowledges the value of a suffering Jesus as a locus for meaning; see his book *Virtual Faith: The Irreverent Spiritual Quest of Generation X* (San Francisco: Jossey-Bass, 1998); and note the work of Andy Crouch, editor-in-chief, *re:generation magazine* (Cambridge, Mass.). Millennials, those born after 1982, are characterized by Neil Howe and William Strauss as more upbeat and engaged. See their book, *Millennials Rising: The Next American Generation* (New York: Vintage Books, 2000).

37. Many similar themes are raised in popular literature but are related to historic

agents. Finally, Groome advocates a wisdom pedagogy which is at the same time a "conversation pedagogy."

Recognizing theological literacy as a collective enterprise reminds us of the structure of this book and brings us back to David Tracy's opening chapter. Groome concludes by noting the seven charisms of this pedagogy. They are gifts that ask us to be engaging, attending, expressing, reflecting, accessing, appropriating, and deciding. These, he argues, express the very nature of the incarnate Christ. They express Christ's very nature, beyond us and different from us, yet one with us and engaging our reality. "Theology," Groome writes, "being one of the great liberal arts, its purpose could be stated philosophically as humanization; that theological literacy should enable people's efforts to make and keep life human for self and others. Or, in more theological terms, being literate in theology should have salvific effects for persons and societies. Echoing such sentiments, I summarize in a pithy phrase that the intent of theological literacy should be 'life for all.'"

The chapters that compose this section, summarizing concerns that theological literacy be built around a ministry of forgiveness and reconciliation, by restorative justice, a concern for persons and their spiritual formation, shaped by prophetic realism and good pedagogical practice, are the elements of good rhetoric. If much of the educational enterprise in North America today is characterized by a sense of meaninglessness that finds its way into the excessive substance abuse in much of American society, an indolence that finds its focus in hollow and belittling entertainment, or a careerism that has little room for the central importance of relationships, then the kind of theological literacy spelled out in this section can help to bring renewal not only to churches but to civil society as well.[38]

Reformed Catholic concerns about the role of idolatry in life; for example, on a psychology of victimhood, see Charles J. Sykes, *A Nation of Victims: The Decay of American Character* (New York: St. Martin's Press, 1992); on consumerism, see Richard A. Horsley and James Tracy, eds., *Christmas Unwrapped: Consumerism, Celluloid, Christ, and Culture* (Philadelphia: Trinity Press International, 2001); and on the impact of contemporary life, see Robert Reich, *The Future of Success* (New York: Knopf, 2001).

38. William H. Willimon and Thomas H. Naylor write of a disconcerting picture of American higher education and sketch a strategy for change that calls for focus on central educational objectives, teachers who lead by word and moral example, a curriculum that offers skills and insight into meaning, and a renewed focus as a learning community. See their book *The Abandoned Generation: Rethinking Higher Education* (Grand Rapids: Eerdmans, 1995).

CHAPTER FOURTEEN

Healing Traumatic Memories:
A Spiritual Journey

RUTH H. BERSIN

The twentieth century was a time of great technological achievement. We extended our vision to witness distant and ancient cosmic events, and we traveled beyond the earth's gravitational pull to gaze back at ourselves. We conquered life-threatening diseases, but we did not arrest violence. We expanded the capacity for communication and yet did not find peace. The conflict, strife, and violence left many persons, indeed whole communities, traumatized. It was a "secular age," a time when religious skepticism was praised as scientific detachment and intellectual objectivity. All too often church life slid into preoccupation with institutional maintenance, which rendered it insipid and irrelevant in a world hurting and spiritually hungry. Notwithstanding all of this, at the dawn of a new millennium we are witnessing anthropocentric arrogance giving way to a more responsible and ecologically sound perspective in government and in nascent industrial inquiry. Awareness is emerging among the religious faithful and secularists alike that a mature spirituality is critical for resilience in the face of life's most devastating experiences.

It is important for the religious community to affirm the valuable resources it offers and to look at new ways of fostering an ancient and universally observable spiritual journey which leads to maturity[1] and marks a path for trauma recovery. Spiritual formation must become the heart of each congregation's life and the center from which outreach extends to those who are hurting. This chapter will examine the current scientific knowledge in the mental health field and the resources of faith in the healing process following trauma; describe a process that people seem to travel in their recov-

---

1. Joseph Campbell, *The Power of Myth* (New York: Doubleday, 1988).

ery; and address the role of religious leaders and their congregations in the process.

Contributions from Current Medical Research

In this secular, scientific age, the medical profession has carried the major responsibility for defining traumatic response and has made numerous and important contributions to the understanding of trauma treatment which can and should be instructive for religious leaders in their work with traumatized communities and congregations. At the same time, there is growing respect for the value of spiritual resources in the treatment of trauma, as evidenced by this recent comment by Dr. Bessel van der Kolk, an international leader in the psychobiology of trauma: "The critical thing after exposure to trauma is to get the body to calm down. . . . Religious ceremonies get it: sit down, hold each other, mourn with each other. . . ."[2]

While most clergy would not describe themselves as trauma specialists, they often are the first people to whom traumatized persons turn.[3] Religious leaders are as likely as mental health specialists to provide frontline mental health services within the community for traumatized individuals and families.[4] In many communities, especially in ethnic and linguistic minority communities, religious leaders are the only source of mental health services.[5] Yet

2. Quoted in an article by Judy Form, "Instant Grief Therapy May Be No Quick Fix," *Boston Globe*, 31 May 1999, p. D5.

3. "Religious communities are one of the principal gateways for those seeking relief from human suffering including mental and emotional illness, drug and alcohol abuse, family conflict, depression and suicide, child and spousal abuse, juvenile delinquency and other societal problems of our day." American Association of Pastoral Counselors, "Executive Summary," at http://www.metanoia.org/aapc/nmhr01.htm. "Research studies are remarkably consistent in their findings that approximately four out of ten Americans seek assistance from members of the clergy in times of personal distress." G. Gurin, J. Veroff, and S. Feld, *Americans View Their Mental Health: A National Survey* (New York: Wiley, 1960); J. Veroff, R. A. Kulka, and E. Douvan, *Mental Health in America: Patterns of Help-Seeking from 1957-1976* (New York: Basic Books, 1981); H. P. Chalfant, P. L. Heller, A. Roberts, D. Briones, S. Aquirre Hochbaum, and W. Farr, "The Clergy as a Resource for Those Encountering Psychological Distress," *Review of Religious Research* 31, no. 3 (1990): 305-13.

4. A. A. Hohmann and D. B. Larson, "Psychiatric Factors Predicting Use of Clergy," in *Psychotherapy and Religious Values*, ed. E. L. Worthington, Jr. (Grand Rapids: Baker, 1993), pp. 7-84. "Each year more abuse victims, perpetrators, and family members seek help from clergy and religious leaders than from all the helping professions combined." A. L. Horton and J. Williamson, *Abuse and Religion* (San Francisco: Jossey-Bass, n.d.), preface.

5. Chalfant et al., "The Clergy as a Resource for Those Encountering Psychological Dis-

studies have repeatedly shown that parish clergy lack adequate preparation for handling pastoral issues with traumatized persons,[6] and especially with victims of crime.[7]

Traumatized individuals also testify to the importance of faith in their recovery:

A young police officer brushes off the pain of a partner's death, but he nonchalantly stops by to see his priest one day and shares his anguish.

A navy chaplain points out that many returned from Vietnam without posttraumatic stress disorder (PTSD) and is certain this is due to the work of many chaplains.

A psychiatrist from Rwanda recalls how few mental health resources they have and how they rely on churches to meet the extensive needs.

South African mothers of Soweta who lost their sons in the apartheid resistance recall: "It was faith, music and humor that kept us going."

A World War II veteran whispers, "I went to the VA for many sessions, but the deepest wounds could only be healed by God."

"The only way I could calm myself in the courtroom," an abused wife relates, "was to write prayers."

"Because my own father was so abusive, it was reassuring to me that I was a child of God and that I had a heavenly father who would never abuse me."

"I prayed," was the answer of a woman explaining how she withstood being stuffed in the trunk of her car by hijackers who drove her car around trying to use her ATM card.

Due to the research of recent decades, there is emerging support within

---

tress"; Mollica, Streets, Booscarion, and Redlich (1986), and Veroff, Kulka, and Douvan (1981), referenced by Andrew J. Weaver, Harold G. Koenig, and Frank M. Ochbert, "Posttraumatic Stress, Mental Health Professionals, and the Clergy: A Need for Collaboration, Training and Research," *Journal of Traumatic Stress* 9, no. 4 (October 1996) (New York: Plenum, 1996).

6. "In eleven out of eleven American and Canadian research studies over a fourteen year period between 1976 and 1989, the majority of demographically diverse Protestant, Catholic and Jewish clergy reported a very significant need for additional training in counseling skills. Fifty to 80% of the clergy considered their seminary training in pastoral counseling deficient and reported being inadequately prepared." Andrew J. Weaver, "Has There Been a Failure to Prepare and Support Parish-Based Clergy in Their Role as Frontline Community Mental Health Workers? A Review," *Journal of Pastoral Care* 49, no. 2 (summer 1995): 129.

7. Weaver, Koenig, and Ochbert, "Posttraumatic Stress, Mental Health Professionals, and the Clergy."

the medical profession that the body,[8] mind, and spirit naturally function toward wholeness[9] and health.[10] Research by Dr. van der Kolk, employing neuro-imaging[11] of subjects who have been diagnosed with PTSD,[12] reveals an impaired left neuro-hemisphere[13] and a comparatively unimpaired right hemisphere, while connections between the left and right brain in the limbic system are also impaired.[14] The impairment of the left brain, which holds the capacity to think or communicate analytically, to employ syntax, or to reason,[15] seems to account for a person's inability to remember or articulate clearly what has occurred. The right brain, sensitive to emotional nuances and dominant in visual-spatial, nonverbal, and emotional memory,[16] continues to operate during a traumatic experience. While there is evidence that memories are not always mutually shared by the two neuro-hemispheres, the right brain appears to be activated during times of stress, stores nonverbal images, and has extensive connections with the limbic system.[17] This is verified by the subjective experience of traumatized individuals who report experiencing profound thoughts they cannot convey in a logical manner that others understand.

8. "We can not separate the spiritual from the physical, and our relationship with God has a profound effect on our health and well-being." Kenneth L. Bakken and Kathleen H. Hofeller, *The Journey toward Wholeness* (New York: Crossroad, 1988), p. 55.

9. "The soul is a very perfect judge of her own motions, if your mind does not dictate to her. . . . The soul's deepest will is to preserve its own integrity, against the mind and the whole mass of disintegrating forces. Soul sympathizes with soul." D. H. Lawrence, 1923, cited in Shaun McNiff, *Art as Medicine* (Boston: Shambhala, 1992).

10. Herbert Benson, *Timeless Healing: The Power and Biology of Belief* (New York: Fireside, 1996).

11. Bessel A. van der Kolk, "The Psycho-biology of Posttraumatic Stress Disorder," *Journal of Clinical Psychiatry* 58 supp. 9 (1998).

12. Van der Kolk, "Psycho-biology," introduction.

13. Van der Kolk, "Psycho-biology," p. 22.

14. "The finding of right hemispheric lateralization in subjects exposed to their personalized trauma script suggests that there is differential hemispheric involvement in the processing of traumatic memories. (. . .) Our brain scans demonstrated that during exposure to a traumatic script, there was decreased activation of the Broca's area. Since an intact Broca's area is necessary for the labeling of emotions, impairment of this area would make it difficult for the traumatized individuals to 'understand' what is going on: they experience intense emotions without being able to label their feelings." Van der Kolk, "Psycho-biology," pp. 16-24. Bessel A. van der Kolk, Alexander C. McFarlane, and Lars Weisaeth, *Traumatic Stress* (New York: Guilford Press, 1996), pp. 229-31.

15. Van der Kolk, "Psycho-biology," p. 22.

16. Rhawn Joseph, *The Right Brain and the Unconscious* (New York: Plenum, 1992), pp. 46, 120.

17. Bakken and Hofeller, p. 48.

"The world shifted into slow motion, with extraordinary clarity; I knew what to do to survive. Yet, when it was over, I could only recall bits and pieces of the event."[18] This suggests the automatic shutdown of the left brain's linguistic and logic capacities[19] and the sharpened intuitive, instinctual, nonverbal right-brain function[20] that once aided survival in the early hunting and gathering communities and still aids survival in the face of primitive, life-threatening events.[21] With the left brain's logical, systematic capacities scrambled, the right-brain resources, such as spirituality, art, and music, may play a more important role than has been assumed.

Victims of violence often describe experiencing detachment to the extent of being "out of body" and watching from "the corner of the room." This phenomenon, known as dissociation,[22] occurs automatically and appears to protect the individual from too much at once. In the aftermath, images of the event may flood the mind. Assumptions that the body operates to achieve wholeness gives even these thought intrusions and flashbacks an important role in the process, leading toward integration and the rebuilding of the personality.[23]

18. Description given by sexual assault victim — used with permission.

19. "The left half of the brain controls the ability to speak, write and comprehend spoken and written language and to perform arithmetical operations. It is responsible for naming, spelling, writing, and counting. It also controls the right hand as well as the ability to perform skillful sequential movements such as those involved in manual tool making, typing and the ability to communicate via sign language. In contrast the right half of the brain controls the left hand, is good at manipulating and constructing complex shapes, puzzles, and block designs. It also controls the perception of visual spatial and geometric relationships such as depth, distance, location, movement and motion. It is more concerned with processing and mimicking of emotional, musical, environmental sounds than the left brain. The right brain, moreover, is responsible for non-linguistic forms of communicating, such as facial expressions, and the expression of sounds that convey emotional nuances. In fact, the right brain is associated with the capacity to sing, swear and even pray." Joseph, p. 22.

20. The right brain is also a dominant perception of movement, speed, distance, and depth as well as the geometrical analysis of gestalts, angles, and visual relationships. The right brain enables us to maneuver successfully about in space without getting lost, to detect and analyze the movements of others, and to determine how these actions and motions are interrelated. In this regard, the right brain was no doubt critically important in the survival of our ancient hunting ancestors, enabling them to detect, stalk, and dispatch various prey with alacrity and then to find their way home without the aid of street signs. Joseph, p. 34.

21. "The right brain is extremely well equipped for enabling us to live among the elements as our hunting, scavenging, and gathering ancestors did so well for over a million years." Joseph, p. 24.

22. Van der Kolk, McFarlane, and Weisaeth, p. 307.

23. John Sanford, *Dreams and Healing* (New York: Paulist, 1978), p. 11. Jung felt that man's energies could go in many directions — into sexuality, art, creative endeavors of all kinds, or destructive directions — but that the basic drive behind man's energy was the drive to wholeness.

Art,[24] music,[25] dance, sports, myth, ritual, meditation, and community seem to serve as means for expression of feelings and images that cannot quite be put into words. The right-brain methods of communicating the experience may well be the basis for reintegration of the psyche. Clinebell, as a pastoral counselor, has long pointed to the value of a holistic approach,[26] which integrates functions of right and left brain in the service of whole-person transformation.[27] "Human transformation is most likely to occur if counseling involves the whole brain of both the counselor and of the persons receiving care and counseling."[28] Mind-body research has repeatedly shown the connection between spirituality[29] and healing.[30] Dr. van der Kolk, in noting that religion has been mindful of human suffering in its historical context, acknowledges the long-standing antidote available within faith communities.[31] Anthropological studies reveal fifty thousand years of humanity's instinctual embracing of spirituality.[32]

24. For example, what cannot be put in words may be put into drawings. "Art has the capacity to express that which can not be spoken. It is virtually universally accepted that the artistic image has the ability to expand communication and offer insight outside the scope of the reasoning mind. The attitudes toward the images once they appear range from approaching them as graphic signs for evaluating the mental conditions of artists, to greeting them as angels who come to offer assistance." McNiff, *Art as Medicine*.

25. Ruth Ann (Bersin) Hargrave, "The Use of Music in Ministry to Disturbed Children" (master's thesis, Colgate Rochester Divinity School, 1965).

26. Howard Clinebell, *Basic Types of Pastoral Care and Counseling* (Nashville: Abingdon, 1966), pp. 26-28; Howard Clinebell, *Contemporary Growth Therapies* (Nashville: Abingdon, 1981).

27. Clinebell, *Basic Types*, pp. 27, 36-37.

28. Clinebell, *Basic Types*, p. 37.

29. Clinebell, *Basic Types of Pastoral Care and Counseling.*

30. Bakken and Hofeller, p. 48; Benson, *Timeless Healing.*

31. Van der Kolk has stated that the introduction of PTSD diagnosis has opened a door to the scientific investigation of the nature of human suffering. Although much of human art and religion has always focused on expressing and understanding man's afflictions, science has paid scant attention to suffering as an objective study. Van der Kolk, McFarlane, and Weisaeth, p. 5.

32. "Human beings have demonstrated a belief in an after life for well over 50 thousand years; our Homo Sapiens cousins, the Neanderthals, during the last ten thousand years of their reign began to bury their dead in a fetal position, sprinkle the bodies with flowers and even to leave meat; presumably in the case the dead became hungry on the trip to the hereafter. Hence, they, too, appear to have believed in the existence of some sort of soul or spirit." Joseph, p. 12.

Faith Resources

Many persons who have been traumatized report turning to their faith for resources to regain trust, meaning, and wholeness. Viktor Frankl, in writing about his Holocaust experience, defines the issue of meaning as a spiritual concern.[33] Mircea Eliade points to the universality of the search for meaning in the face of suffering.[34] These witnesses, supported by the work of Carl G. Jung,[35] demonstrate the efficacy of trusting the unconscious and natural processes in recovery.

The world's great religions (differing culturally, dogmatically, in practice and in specifics of myth and history) hold vast resources to support that recovery process. Each faith tradition has defined academically respectful and respectable left-brain theologies. Each also carries symbolic activities which utilize right-brain capacities. The interrelationship between these capacities models the integration of a healthy psyche and is essential for healthy spirituality. Each faith rests upon a foundation of myth[36] which carries profound archetypal representations[37] that mirror the human psyche and facilitate healing as well as maturation.[38] Each acknowledges history and its remembrance in rites, such as the Eucharist and Seder,[39] that define and unify community.[40] Each responds to suffering through funerals and healing rituals. Each has rituals which sanctify life, time, and space[41] that also initiate, contain, and restore the people. There are

---

33. Viktor E. Frankl, *Man's Search for Meaning* (Boston: Beacon Press, 1959).

34. "In general, it may be said that suffering is regarded as the consequence of a deviation in respect to the 'norm.' That this norm differs from people to people, and from civilization to civilization, goes without saying. But the important point is that nowhere — within the frame of the archaic civilizations — are suffering and pain regarded as 'blind' and without meaning." Mircea Eliade, *The Myth of the Eternal Return* (Princeton: Princeton University Press, 1954), p. 98.

35. Bakken and Hofeller, p. 40.

36. In 1974 Morton Kelsey made the following points about Jung's position on myth: "There is a realm of objective nonphysical reality which we come to know through strange experiences of the psyche. We come to know this reality through the dream, the vision, the fantasy, the religious experience, the intuition and the myth. It is the function of myth and ritual to help us confront this realm of reality and deal creatively with it and find in this way direction towards greater maturity, wholeness and meaning."

37. Emmett Early, *The Raven's Return* (Wilmette, Ill.: Chiron Publications, 1993).

38. Joseph Campbell, *The Hero with a Thousand Faces* (Princeton: Princeton University Press, 1949), p. 11.

39. The Eucharist, the Passover meal, the Shabis Meal, the observation of Muhammad's death at Ramadan, Good Friday, and Easter.

40. René Girard, *The Girard Reader* (New York: Crossroad, 1996); Marion Hatchett, *Sanctifying Life, Time, and Space* (New York: Seabury Press, 1976).

41. Hatchett, *Sanctifying Life, Time, and Space.*

rites of passage for major life transitions: birth, maturation, marriage, birth of one's child, mourning, and death. There are rites which define membership by initiation and restoration.

The ritual and myth of the world's great religions have for centuries allowed members to regress in a safe space with community support for the purpose of healing.[42] Rituals, by formalization of the process in specific and general issues, allow an individual to see his or her own healing journey reflected in the wider experience of humanity. Rituals, by their repetition, prepare human beings to endure traumatic experiences and indicate a method of integration of the experiences. Rituals provide a holding environment[43] for a person as he or she reintegrates the fragmented aspects of himself or herself.

Following a healing service, one woman who had been sexually assaulted two days earlier stated: "I had a long way to go to heal, but the service seemed to be a moment when the infliction of further injury stopped. When I realized my friends and family were feeling the need for healing along with me, I felt less alone." Ritual allows traumatic experience to be reframed and allows a transcendent view in which one may understand his or her own suffering as part of the human condition.

Community

Faith communities have a built-in capacity to support the healing, diminish the isolation, and in the process experience redemptive healing for themselves. With community support one is able to transfer the transcendent benevolence into human relationships where the pain is shared and one is "grounded."

42. Erik H. Erikson, *Childhood and Society* (New York: Norton, 1950). The parental faith which supports the trust emerging in the newborn has throughout history sought its institutional safeguard in organized religion. Trust born of care is, in fact, the touchstone of the actuality of a given religion. All religions have in common the periodical childlike surrender to a Provider or providers who dispense earthly fortune as well as spiritual health; some demonstration of man's smallness by way of reduced posture and humble gesture; the admission in prayer and song of misdeeds, of misthoughts, and of evil intentions; fervent appeal for inner unification by divine guidance; and finally the insight that individual trust must become common faith, individual mistrust a commonly formulated evil, while the individual's restoration must become part of the ritual practice of many, and must become a song of trustworthiness in the community.

43. The idea of ritual as a holding environment was introduced to me in private conversation by Dr. Stephen Fisher, who presented this concept in the keynote address at the First Annual Bereavement Conference, 5 October 1996. He is the executive director of the Greater Lowell Pastoral Counseling Center in Lowell, Mass.

On the other hand, the community itself may remain unhealed, indulging in denial or blame of the victim, who serves for them as a reminder that it could happen to them as well. Religious leadership needs to understand the group dynamics in order to successfully mold a congregation into a safe space that is trauma-resilient. Those who have recovered will assist, for they call the whole community to a moral accounting. For if suffering is part of the human condition, the root causes of violence are certainly the human community's moral responsibility, and so they issue a clarion call for justice.[44] Interfaith cooperation in addressing public policy issues[45] related to trauma may result in pooling resources for healing and sharing in dialogue.[46]

There are many resources within the faith community which use the right brain's intuitive capacity to express outwardly that which cannot be logically explained. In addition to ritual, they include prayer, dream analysis, art, music, and retreat.

Prayer

Often people who have been traumatized demonstrate an intuitive need for prayer and meditation. The meditative process and forms of prayer in each tradition help devotees center, focus, calm, and contain themselves. Meditation includes intuitive, emotional, and restorative activity that is dependent upon right-brain functioning where the unconscious does not distinguish between real and symbolic events.[47] Entry into the right brain's messages and unconscious configurations can enhance healing as new insights are claimed and integrated.

Thomas Keating speaks of the unloading of the unconscious as "a kind of divine psychotherapy, organically designed for each of us, to empty out our unconscious and free us from the obstacles of the free flow of grace in our minds, emotions, and bodies."[48]

44. Jeffery Jay, "Terrible Knowledge: The Trauma Survivor's Story Threatens Our Illusions of Safety and Control," *Family Networker* 15, no. 6 (November-December 1991).

45. Ewert Cousins, *Christ of the Twenty-first Century* (Rockport, Mass.: Element, 1992).

46. Huston Smith, *The World's Religions* (New York: Harper, 1991), p. 390.

47. Robert A. Johnson, *Owning Your Own Shadow* (San Francisco: Harper San Francisco, 1991).

48. Thomas Keating, *Open Mind, Open Heart — The Contemplative Dimension of the Gospel* (Rockport, Mass.: Element, 1986).

Dreams

Meditative traditions tend to be holistic. Part of meditative practice may involve attention to dreams as guides in the process.[49] Dreams[50] have a long-standing tradition within the church as a means by which God has spoken to us.[51] Taking a serious look at dreams may enhance the healing process and help reintegrate the psyche.

Art

Each faith utilizes artistic expression in worship and meditation. Great painters and sculptors as well as poets and writers have expressed for all the faithful healing power and the capacity to brings one's own story into the larger story of humanity.

Retreat

Retreat and renewal are often part of religious practice. A three- to five-day retreat using ritual, the arts, and a sense of community to assist a traumatized person to express or tell the trauma story in a safe way can be helpful in the reintegration of the psyche. It might include the simulation of a heroic journey with stages of recovery identified. The importance of self-care would be taught, and opportunities for ritual cleansing and renewal offered. Accompanying psych-education could predict and prepare persons who have experienced trauma recently to manage the symptoms, emotions, fatigue, and sense of isolation which may follow. At this time meditation and activities with arts, symbolic acts, and body work could be combined to create a process for healing that one could revisit again and again.[52]

49. Morton T. Kelsey, *God, Dreams, and Revelation* (Minneapolis: Augsburg, 1996); Wayne Rollins, *Jung and the Bible* (Atlanta: John Knox, 1983).

50. John A. Sanford, *Dreams and Healing* (New York: Paulist, 1978).

51. Tertullian, "A Treatise on the Soul," chap. 47, "Beyond a doubt the greater part of mankind derive their knowledge of God from their dreams."

52. Several sponsors of refugees have expressed the idea, "Now I know what it means to see the face of Christ in a stranger."

Ruth H. Bersin

The Healing Process as a Journey

For many, healing from trauma appears to parallel the process of human development,[53] including the initial step of (re)establishing trust. Because each person's journey is unique, there is not necessarily a straight linear pathway; it seems more to be a process of moving back and forth and weaving in and out as one passes through the healing journey.[54] Some steps may take a short while and others may require months or years to achieve. It is not unusual for a person to make significant progress and then seem to move backward. Even this regression may be needed as an opportunity for one to integrate more fully all that has happened.

Trauma shatters[55] one's whole world and destroys trust.[56] As trust is the first task of personality development,[57] its loss compromises the personality's building blocks which rest upon it.[58] Erikson has outlined the developmental tasks that humans must accomplish: trust rather than mistrust, autonomy rather than shame and doubt, initiative rather than guilt, industry rather than inferiority, identity rather than role confusion, intimacy rather than isolation, generativity rather than stagnation, and ego integrity rather than despair. With the trust damaged,[59] it is not surprising that autonomy, initiative,[60] capacity for intimacy,[61] and capacity to be in the community[62] and to set and maintain boundaries[63] are weakened. It is not difficult to understand that a resulting loss of identity may follow along with a sense of isolation, stagnation, or despair.[64]

---

53. Erikson, *Childhood and Society.*

54. Judith Herman, *Trauma and Recovery* (New York: Basic Books, 1992), p. 155. Dr. Herman describes three stages of recovery and cautions that they not be taken too literally. She defines the steps as safety, remembrance and mourning, and finally reconnecting.

55. Richard B. Ulman and Doris Brothers, *The Shattered Self* (Hillsdale, N.J.: Analytic Press, 1988), p. 3.

56. Ronnie Janoff-Bulman, *Shattered Assumptions* (New York: Free Press, 1992), p. 63.

57. Erik Erikson, *Childhood and Society* (New York: Norton, 1993).

58. James Fowler, *Faith Development and Pastoral Care* (Philadelphia: Fortress, 1987), p. 60.

59. Janoff-Bulman, p. 63.

60. American Psychiatric Association, *Diagnostic and Statistical Manual of Mental Disorders,* 4th ed. (*DSM*-IV)/(1989).

61. Bessel A. van der Kolk, *Trauma Center News,* December 1997. "Research also consistently identifies deep feelings of helplessness and alienation as major problems of traumatized individuals."

62. Van der Kolk, *Trauma Center News,* December 1997. "Traumatized people need help to reestablish a sense of safety and community."

63. Steven Prior, *Object Relations in Severe Trauma* (Northvale, N.J.: Aaronson, 1996).

64. Issues raised by extreme traumatization include affective disregulation (inability to be in the present emotionally), difficulty with anger modulation, self-preservation/destruction,

Most traumatized individuals can place themselves on this continuum and recognize where they are in their journey. This suggests that different methods of support may be needed at various stages of the process. In addition, each person has a unique journey and reliance on the natural healing properties of the human mind and body; thus we can trust each person to define his or her own needs along the way. With individual variation, the following stages can be observed in the recovery process: safety, remembrance, forgiveness, restoration, reclamation, reconciliation, regeneration, reintegration.

Safety

First, the assurance of safety, which may require significant time to achieve. One cannot move beyond survival until one is safe. Reestablishing safety involves finding someone to trust. This is difficult because trust is the first casualty of the trauma.

Only when safety is established can a person begin to heal. Usually he or she will begin to recall the events that were painful and will need to talk about them. There seems to be a need for another person to be able to witness what has happened and to bear and contain it with the person who is recovering. If this remembering can be done in the sacred context of remembrance, it is lifted out of the personal and into the corporate, historical perspective which allows a person to identify with others and reclaim his or her autonomy.

Remembrance

Remembrance is much more than mere memory. It is a reenactment of the events, an entering into the events as if they were happening again in the present. Through the process of corporate reenactment we transcend history in a sacramental way that promotes integration of the psyche. Remembrance is fos-

---

suicidal preoccupation, difficulty modulating sexual behavior, excessive risk taking. Alterations in self-perception may include ineffectiveness, permanent damage to the self-image, guilt and responsibility, shame, isolation — "no one can understand" — or minimization of the trauma — perhaps as a form of denial. Alterations in relationships with others will reflect an inability to trust, a capacity to be revictimized or to victimize others. For some, somatization of the "unfelt" horror is revealed in digestive symptoms, chronic pain, cardiopulmonary symptoms, conversion symptoms, or sexual symptoms. Finally, despair, hopelessness, and loss of previously sustained beliefs also occur. From *SIDES — Self-Reporting Index of Symptoms Used at the Trauma Center* (unpublished ms., Allston, MA).

tered and ritualized in religious traditions such as Ramadan, Passover,[65] and the Eucharist.

Bible stories which recall negative experiences without apology testify to the importance of truth telling and story sharing. Examples are Cain's killing of his own brother, the exile of Hagar, the selling of Joseph by his brothers, Moses' killing of the slave, and the rape of Tamar.

Reenactment seems to be required after devastating trauma. Rituals allow a process of reenactment which is safe within ceremony, and acknowledgment within community that negates the need for a victim to reenact the trauma by becoming a perpetrator.

The best-known example of the healing power of ritual is the funeral. Grief is brought into the community, where sacred time and space is provided within which one may be dangerously close to the world of the dead and to the eternal power of the universe. There it is possible to "let go of the dead," allowing a new relationship to form while recognizing the separate worlds of life and death. In the Jewish tradition, the ritual prayer for one who has died "binds the bereaved to the one who is lost but also to the cadence of community response, thereby lifting the bereaved from the isolation of grief into the history and presence of the community."[66] For Christians the burial service is a practice of letting go of the loved one to the abiding care of God and the benevolence of the universe.[67]

The ravenous persistence of the psyche to relive the moments of horror over and over indicates the need to spend time with the images. We are reminded of the image of Jacob, who stole his brother's birthright and ran from home; now returning and about to meet Esau for the first time in years, he finds himself wrestling until dawn with the angel until it gives him a blessing.[68] Fac-

---

65. From work presented in lectures by Dr. James A. Sanders, professor of Old Testament studies at Colgate Rochester Divinity School, in 1962-63.

66. Jeffrey Jay, "Walls for Wailing," *Common Boundary* 12, no. 3 (May/June 1994): 33.

67. "Depart, O Christian soul, out of this world: In the Name of God the Father Almighty who created you; In the name of Jesus Christ who redeemed you; In the Name of the Holy Spirit who sanctifies you. May your rest be this day in peace, and your dwelling place in the Paradise of God. Into your hands, O merciful Savior, we commend your servant. Acknowledge, we beseech you, a sheep of your own fold, a lamb of your own flock, a sinner of your own redeeming. Receive him into the arms of your mercy, into the blessed rest of everlasting peace and into the glorious company of the saints in light. Amen." *Book of Common Prayer* (New York: Oxford University Press, 1979), p. 464.

68. "Jacob refused to part with his experience until he knew its meaning, and this marked him as a man of spiritual greatness. Everyone who wrestles with his spiritual and psychological experience and, no matter how dark or frightening it is, refuses to let it go until he discovers its meaning, is having something of the Jacob experience. Such a person can come

ing into the traumatic experiences within a safe space that allows remembrance can be effective as one confronts the archetypal, demonic intrusion of night-mares and flashbacks. Our rituals can help a survivor to reframe and integrate experiences by remembering that God suffers with us. Remembrance, because it takes place in community, focuses the outrage into action and breaks through the isolation trauma imposes. One begins to see one's trauma as part of the hu-man condition, and this makes it possible to consider forgiveness.

Forgiveness

Forgiveness is a sensitive word for those who have worked with victims of vio-lence because all too often it has been suggested as a remedy, a way to "get rid of the problem" at the expense of the victim's well-being. Forgiveness, if confused with excusing, "making up," "letting the perpetrator off the hook," or "just for-getting it," underscores injustice and inflicts further pain on the victim. Re-membrance and justice are integral to healing forgiveness. The idea of "forgive and forget" is as inappropriate as the idea that forgiveness can absolve or re-move accountability from the perpetrator. Forgiveness is to heal the victim; it is not for the benefit of the perpetrator. Forgiveness asserts one's identity in the midst of horrific agony. In so doing it reestablishes a boundary between the vic-tim and the perpetrator. It allows the victim to be freed of the captor.[69] Forgive-ness is returning to the heart of God the burden that violence, abuse, or be-trayal has put into the heart of the victim.[70] Often forgiveness is difficult because the violence has stirred memories within the victim's own psyche or because it has filled the victim with violence, rage, hate, and hurtfulness. But vi-olence against a fellow human is violence against God, and therefore we can do no other than to place the pain, the rage, and the sense of shame into the heart of God, where we can be certain justice reigns. In doing this, trust, which has been shattered by trauma, is reestablished; but now it is in God, where the promise that "nothing can ever separate us"[71] can be embraced. As one's pain

---

through his dark struggle to the other side reborn." John Sanford, *The Man Who Wrestled with God* (Maryknoll, N.Y.: Paulist Press, 1974), p. 40.

69. "One ex-prisoner of war asked another, 'Have you forgiven your captors yet?' The second one replied, 'No, never,' and the other turned and said, 'Then it seems like they still have you in prison don't they?'" *Spirituality and Health* 1, special issue on forgiveness, Trinity Wall Street.

70. Luke 23:34.

71. There is nothing in death, or life, in the realm of spirits or superhuman powers, in the world as it is or the world as it shall be, in the forces of the universe, in heights or depths —

and trauma are placed in the heart of God, one is brought deeper into forgiveness by experiencing a cleansing of his or her self.[72]

Forgiveness[73] cleanses one's own soul.[74] One client, in speaking about forgiveness, concluded: "You know, forgiveness is so freeing. I don't have to carry her with me anymore." One of the most wounding aspects of being victimized is the loss of personal space and power. Should forgiveness reinforce that imbalance, it would do further injury. Any attempts at mediation must be on the victim's terms, or the tyranny of the perpetrator is reinforced. We also cannot make forgiveness dependent upon the remorse of the perpetrator, who may never feel remorse.[75]

If the perpetrators seek forgiveness and the victims can grant it, both can be redeemed in the process. Equality is reestablished as the offering of forgiveness reclaims the position of authority and the seeking of it claims the posture of vulnerability. When these opposite sides are experienced, balance is restored and relief can be achieved for each. However, it is not to be assumed that reconciliation is an automatic sequence to forgiveness. For if one is truly remorseful and feels deeply forgiven, one will make restitution. This may simply mean ceasing the victimization, or it may mean making amends in whatever way is possible.

Sometimes if others have died, the victim is plagued with survivor guilt. This is an added burden to those nearest the tragedy. Often survivor guilt thrives when the person has not had time to adequately grieve. Opportunities for such grief can be offered by religious communities, and in the process the truth embedded within survivor guilt can be heard: "We are responsible for one another." Survivor guilt must be replaced by corporate accountability.

Sometimes a victim needs to forgive himself or herself. Often one needs to let go of the second-guessing, of assuming responsibility, of feeling guilty for the loss of control. Sometimes the insidiousness of trauma's invasive power is displayed as it scatters defenses and stirs sleeping issues. Whirling images tap into layers of significant subconscious debris. When one has been traumatized by titanic evil, it is uncomfortable to realize that evil is also within one's own self. Part of the healing process is facing one's own shadow wherein lie those

---

nothing in all creation that can separate us from the love of God in Christ Jesus our Lord. See Rom. 8:38-39.

72. Isa. 6:1-8.

73. Geiko Muller-Fahrenholz, *The Art of Forgiveness* (Geneva: WCC Publications, 1996).

74. Said Bishop Tutu: "Without forgiveness, resentment builds in us, a resentment which turns into hostility and anger."

75. Rom. 8.

qualities of self which have been discarded or ignored.[76] This is a difficult task which rewards the effort as it leads to integration and wholeness.

Evil is within the experience and knowledge of each of us, as is acknowledged in the baptismal and eucharistic rites. Assigning all good to one's self and all evil to the perpetrator is often encouraged, but it is dangerous. It fosters dissociation and denial, which impede remembrance. The curious paradox in trauma recovery is this: the more one attempts to handle one's confrontation with evil by holding on to the dissociation (splitting), the more one becomes like the perpetrator. Failure to integrate the anger and hate enhances the risk of absorbing it and may cause the victim to become like the perpetrator: dissociated, angry, emotionally aloof, and dangerous.

Religious ceremony holds these dichotomies in tension: balance of good in consciousness and the shadow's evil. Robert Johnson has shown that "ceremonies the world over consist mostly of destruction. This is a safeguard of the culture to play out the shadow in a symbolic way."[77]

It is in the interest of purifying one's own soul[78] that healing requires forgiveness of self and of the enemy. Forgiveness may include "forgiving God." Instead of the anger at God for failing to execute justice and the resentment at God's abandonment, one gains a sense of awe in the discovery that God was there all along, weeping. This leads to reclamation of one's self and to the possibility of living at a more profound level.

Once the survivor has achieved this level of healing, the return to community is needed. Often the community itself is not healed, and this is where restorative justice in the community is essential to personal and private healing. A community needs to move through the denial into a renewal as it makes a claim on justice and restoration. Without providing excuses in the form of cheap grace to those who act on evil impulses, a sane society must ask itself in relation to a violent act: "Why are some people so clearly alienated from the community?" How can our societies move from injustice to justice and find common ground for all? The common ground is a call to justice, to stewardship of resources, and to respect for the dignity of every human being.

76. Johnson, pp. 10-14.

77. Johnson, pp. 52-53.

78. Larry R. Decker, "The Role of Trauma in Spiritual Development," *Journal of Humanistic Psychology* 33, no. 4 (1993): 38.

Restoration and Reclamation

As a person gradually heals in the context of remembrance and forgiveness, the traumatic event is no longer the central defining factor in his or her life. It is no longer the date around which all of life is either before or after. It becomes a part of the story. Restoration is a time when energy is released and a person is ready to "get back to work" or "get on with life." At this time one may learn new skills, take on new interests, find new friends. The old life may no longer fit; a new life may be emerging. The person may have varied levels of comfort with this. It is easy at this time to assume that the healing is completed. However, there will continue to be a cycling back over issues; sometimes memories will invade — but not for as long as before, and the person, no longer willing to talk about the trauma to everyone, may have a sense of being someone who is not fully known. For when one was about his or her life before, there was no terrible secret. This may result in a sense of feeling phony or inadequate. It is helpful to encourage a person to take on tasks if he or she is comfortable. Successful attempts can assist in overcoming the sense of inferiority.

One also learns to respect one's limits. For example, one may experience some difficulties in returning "to life," such as a lessened ability to concentrate. One may need to make space to have time alone, to organize and prepare more thoroughly. One will learn at this time to compensate for and overcome the issues which continue. One is wise not to get into rescuing others prematurely. Self-care is an important focus. Moses, following the trauma of being driven from the Egyptian courts as a young man, spent time alone, tending flocks in Midian.[79] Likewise, when the Israelites finally escaped from Egyptian tyranny, they needed to wander for a whole generation before they could settle down.

As healing occurs, the victim begins to realize that much has been gained through the experience[80] and can embrace it within his or her total life experience. This is reclamation.[81] One learns that gaining from the trauma does not mean one would have willed it; but rather that one can embrace the good which comes from the experience, for good can come from even the worst evils. To embrace that good as God's redemption action does not imply an embracing of the evil. The demanding work of examining oneself to the very core results in a deeper integration that allows one to reclaim one's gifts. This is promised by Ernest Hemingway's declaration at the end of *Farewell to Arms:* "Life breaks ev-

---

79. Exod. 2:15.
80. Rom. 5:3-5.
81. Rom. 5.

eryone a bit. But some people get stronger at the broken places."[82] Discernment is a gift of healing, and a deepened assurance of one's place in the world is developed as one recovers. This healing process allows one again to trust in God's providence.[83]

Trust[84] has to be rebuilt upon honesty and assurance which transcends the trauma. One must rebuild one's sense of security with an acknowledgment that such evil exists.[85] This is a faith issue. Dietrich Bonhoeffer,[86] who made his Nazi prison cell a world pulpit, prayed as the time of his death approached with a trusting dependence upon God.[87] Reconciliation with God is possible, based upon one's sure knowledge of God's protection. That makes trust, and therefore faith, possible again.

Reconciliation

Bishop Peter Storey has pointed out that "reconciliation is a process, a journey; not an event!"[88] Letting go of the trauma is possible because truth has been faced, as grief and denial have been overcome. Forgiveness has replaced bitterness. Trust has been reestablished. The blessing comes when reconciliation is possible: not necessarily with the enemy, but with God and one's community. "Reconciliation does not mean that we surrender rights and conditions, but rather that we use love in all of our negotiations. It means that we see ourselves in the opponent — for what is the opponent but a being in ignorance, and we ourselves are also ignorant of many things."[89]

Reconciliation cannot take place between two forces without justice and without restoration to whatever extent is possible of the harm done.

---

82. Ernest Hemingway, *A Farewell to Arms* (New York: Scribner's, 1978).

83. Uwe Siemon-Netto, *The Acquittal of God* (New York: Pilgrim Press, 1990).

84. John McDargh develops the position that "Faith is that human dynamic of trusting, relying upon, and reposing confidence in, which (1) is foundational to the life-long process of becoming a self, and (2) is fulfilled in the progressively enlarged capacity of that self for love and self-commitment." John McDargh, *Psychoanalytic Object Relations Theory and the Study of Religion* (Lanham, Md.: University Press of America, 1983), p. 71.

85. Ps. 139:7-12 RSV.

86. Dietrich Bonhoeffer, *Letters and Papers from Prison* (New York: Macmillan, 1953), p. 89.

87. Melvin R. Jacob, "A Pastoral Response of the Troubled Vietnam Veteran," in *Post-Traumatic Stress Disorders: A Handbook for Clinicians,* by Tom Williams (published by Disabled American Veterans), p. 57.

88. Peter Storey, chairman of Truth and Reconciliation Commission in South Africa.

89. Ghosananda, p. 69.

Regeneration and Reintegration

As one is restored, one knows that God alone can heal the final wound, like the person who looks back and sees only one pair of footprints in the sand. The Vietnam veterans have gradually realized that God carried them through and was never, never "absent without leave."[90] But once traumatized people have reached these insights, the reentry into the community is difficult. They need a community that is willing to foster the spirituality they have worked so hard to achieve. They intuitively know who has done his or her own journey and who has not. Religious leaders are needed who can stand in the chaos, offer pastoral leadership that encourages all the people to work for spiritual maturity, and recognize in those who have recovered from their trauma a fellow traveler. Siemon-Netto has suggested that Vietnam veterans and others who have been wounded and have recovered, have had years of preparation to fulfill the role of the new prophets.[91] With their presence the church may become the healing place it is called to be in spite of its declines and inner divisions. Like that of the survivor of trauma, the church's future will be on God's terms. As he is called to stand on holy ground before the burning bush, Moses says, "Who am I that I should go to Pharaoh, and bring the sons of Israel out of Egypt?" and God's answer is: "But I will be with you."[92] It does not matter who Moses is, what matters is that God is with Moses.

There is power in completing the tasks of rebuilding one's psyche and in the church taking a new look at its purpose. The promise is the possibility of movement to a higher level of integration. Jeffrey Jay has observed that "Most certainly things never return to 'the way they were.' All that was sham seemed to be discarded. All that previously allowed one to settle for less tends to be rendered impotent. The secrets which could not be told find the energy to break forth as a sacred knowledge belonging to the whole community."[93]

Arising from this broader cosmic sense of one's self and the universe is a deep sense of meaning in the suffering which often makes one emerge with a strong sense of justice and desire for peace in the world.[94] This is the promised possibility for the individual and for the church as well. Meaning is given to the long, difficult process of healing and reintegration when one is able to become a witness for justice and for wholeness, and to be able to offer sanctuary within the walls of the religious institutions.

90. Siemon-Netto, p. 96.
91. Siemon-Netto, p. 96.
92. Exod. 3 RSV.
93. Jay, "Terrible Knowledge," pp. 18-29.
94. Rom. 5:3-5.

Standing with one who has suffered profoundly allows one a glimpse of God's love in a renewed relationship. The task of the survivor is to ask: "How do I integrate this event into my life, so that I may become more and by so doing achieve recovery?" This is a question for the community as well as for the individual.

Recovery from PTSD is not a matter of simply getting over the event and the painful aftermath. It is a call to become more.

The journey outlined here also parallels the journey of the hero tale.[95] Creating congregations which foster such a journey would follow ancient practices of spiritual development and involve participation of everyone in his or her journey in a mutually supportive environment. Such an inner journey that integrates left-brain logical, academic learning with right-brain intuitive learning mirrors the integration needed in our world of tomorrow, and is required for trauma recovery. The pastor who has found first the safety and then the courage to travel this road will be prepared to foster such an environment in his/her parish life. We cannot travel with others any roads that we have not taken ourselves.

Just as safety is necessary for a trauma victim to begin the process, seminarians concerned about acceptance in the ordination process need a safety zone where they can, through spiritual direction, navigate their own journeys. Failure to integrate the maturation process with the scholarly tasks is often tragically revealed in a lack of authenticity that is impossible to hide. Those who have been forced by their own traumatic experience to make the journey of recovery will need pastors who have traveled their own journey, faced the vestiges of mistrust, shame, guilt, inferiority, confusion, isolation, stagnation, and despair that remain in each of us even if we have basically mastered the stages of human development.

Clinical pastoral education has offered this space and support for decades to pastors in formation. The basic three-month experience is not necessarily enough, however. Ongoing spiritual direction, pastoral counseling, and reflection seminars are important in the formation process. Our need to take the inner journey, a right-brain task, must be integrated with the left-brain study which is necessary for seminary education. We have great technological achievements, but we have yet to come to terms with the heroic endeavor of understanding one's own inner resources. There is nowhere else in the society that

95. Examples of the hero journey which parallel this journey may be found in the *Odyssey,* the *Aeneid,* Dante's *Inferno,* the descent of Christ into hell, and hero myths found worldwide that seem to symbolize the maturation process. Joseph Campbell, Jean Houston, Mircea Eliade, Huston Smith, and others have documented this pattern.

can foster this process better than the religious community. The goal for the religious community must be to build strong enough support that people do not need to deny violence, blame victims, and scapegoat the weak, but rather can be gracious and loving islands of safety and healing which are sanctuary in the troubled and spiritually hungry world.

Sharing the journey with another is a privilege, and, like love itself, the more you give the more you receive. This journey takes one onto holy ground, and as one witnesses the journey, one stands awed by the unfolding strength. In venturing into the journey with a survivor, one does not go ahead of, instead of, or move away from a pilgrim on that road. To minister, one quietly walks alongside; never interfering lest the survivor fail to gain needed strength, never leading lest the real issue be overlooked, never controlling lest fragile trust be crushed. Through this process of reclaiming his or her capacity to generate and create, to be intimate and to be alone to let go of dark emotions, and to forgive and love again, a survivor achieves a higher integration which is in touch with a cosmic reality and which is committed to justice and peacemaking. By sharing the journey, one knows God is real and that God does not abandon us, that God suffers with us.

Conclusion

Through study, reflection, spiritual direction, and pastoral caregiving, the leader of the future must be prepared to embrace his or her own journey as a lifetime process, to continue to study and learn the newest insights of other related professions, and to approach each person as a fellow pilgrim on the road. This is the leadership that, by encouraging each parishioner on his or her journey, can create trauma-resilient parishes that support and sustain those who are hurting. We fear descending into sheol until we must, and then we discover Christ is with us and learn that there is nothing to fear, for if Christ be there, then nothing can possibly separate us from the love of God.[96] This is the message the hurting and spiritually hungry world is waiting to hear. It is the message of the gospel. Just as the trauma victim is no longer innocent, so our world, racked by war, genocide, hunger, slavery, and economic and political exploitation, can no longer be innocent, and neither are the religious communities that have been in conflict and are at the root of so many wars and so much genocidal madness.

The new paradigm is for a saner, safer, cleaner world; along with relevant,

96. Rom. 8.

vital, and inspiring faith communities is the recovered trauma survivor who has faced the demons, traveled through the underworld, arisen with new wisdom, new energy, and new commitment. This new paradigm draws upon ancient strengths and centuries of human resilience, and it uses the best that modern scientific progress has given us. This process uses the power of both right- and left-brain processing. It is unifying and values all the resources we have because they are all needed, to be taken from the rich faith traditions of the world's great religions, the research and healing power of medicine, the compassion of the social service community, the wealth and resources of industry, and the power of the political community. In our congregations and through interfaith cooperation, we can face our lost innocence and move toward the wisdom that maturity promises as these resources are brought together to nurture and support those in each walk of life who are called to participate in building a safer and saner world for tomorrow.

CHAPTER FIFTEEN

A Prophetic Religious Education for Y2K and Beyond: And Black Boys Shall See Visions

FRED SMITH

Letter to a Black Boy (and All His Cousins): The Problem of Acquisitive Mimetic Desire

The Bible asks the question, "What causes fights and quarrels among you? Don't they come from your (acquisitive mimetic)[1] desires that battle within you? You want something but don't get it. You kill and covet, but you cannot have what you want. You quarrel and fight" (James 4:1-2a). Violence is not something that youth do or what happens to youth, it is the nature of our world. What then could I have told Hasaan or tell you now? That you should not want what society says makes you "the man"? That you must love one another? It sounds so lame, but what alternatives do you have?

We, your fathers and uncles, don't speak of Hasaan very much, but he is always on our minds. Each time I look at you and your cousins, I see his face and grow afraid. All I know of Hasaan came in snapshots of his life that I took with my heart. My heart reached out to him each time I visited Oakland, which was only once every year or so. I have a mental snapshot of a trip to the Great America theme amusement park when Hasaan was six or seven. He and his sister

---

1. Acquisitiveness has to do with a strong desire to gain and possess — to have. Acquisitive mimetic desire can be described in this way: desire mimics (copies) another's strong desire to have something, and it can be more or less rivalrous depending on the distance between the subject (I or ego) and the mediator (model of desire). Acquisitive desire is subject to mimesis "in that fundamental desire forms and defines the total behavior of the human being," which is to be distinguished from the natural need of hunger or the need for sleep.

were so grateful because I paid their way. In my heart there is an action shot of playing basketball on the outdoor courts at Lowell Junior High when he was eleven or twelve. I still see his jump shot from deep in the corner. He was a diminutive image of his father. However, imprinted forever in my soul are his eyes — his father's eyes — and they appeared to be too large for his face. No, we don't talk about Hasaan very much, but he had a great impact on how your fathers raised you.

In the last snapshot I have of Hasaan, he was reclining in my father's favorite chair in the family's Acorn Projects apartment. He was fifteen or sixteen at the time. It was the year before he died. Mama had just been to court with him the week before and was very worried. Hasaan's room was full of new clothes, electronic gadgets. He had a car, but no job. She wanted me to talk to him. That day he looked very tired, probably because he had spent most of the night before on East Fourteenth Street with his boys, or maybe he was just high. This morning his left eye was swollen — black and purple. It was the prettiest black eye I have ever seen.

I asked him what happened, and he said that he fell down. Of course I knew differently. There was something in his eyes that I had not recognized before. He seemed cold and distant, like I was a stranger or from another world. In fact, I had become a stranger, and the recognition of this fact made me feel so helpless. There was so much that I needed and wanted to say to him, but I did not know how or what.

What was worse, I was a minister, who had just finished cum laude from seminary. I should have known what to say, but seminary did not prepare me for this. Somehow, I believed that Hasaan's life depended on me. All my Harvard education and seminary training were of no use to me now.

I talked to Hasaan about Dr. Martin Luther King, Jr., and what he stood for. I offered him a home in Atlanta with my family. He sat there, eyes turning red, looking straight ahead and saying nothing. I told him to think about it. I didn't think he would consider my proposal or ponder my message of racial pride and the struggle for freedom that was his heritage. However, later I heard from your cousin Jerry that before he was killed he had been saving money to come to Atlanta to take me up on my proposal.

Perhaps he had heard me that morning, or maybe he was running away from people who meant to do him harm. In any case, he never made it. I don't know why Hasaan had tried come to Atlanta, if he had. All I remember is that I felt totally inadequate to change the direction of his life or its final destination. If I could relive that moment again, I often wonder what I would say. I wish I had talked to him about Christ. It was discovering Christ that saved my life by bringing new hope.

Sincerely yours,
Uncle Junior

As we enter the next century, we must find new ways of sharing the gospel of Jesus Christ while engaging in social justice and service to a generation of youth in ways that empower rather than cripple. At the end of the last millennium and the turn of the new century youth are in crisis, as evidenced by young people being gunned down by their fellow students in quiet little suburban villages. There are many Hasaans in our land today, and they are multiplying. They have become nihilistic to the point that they have cast off all restraint and are perishing. This is true for all youth but is especially the case for black boys. The task for ministers in the year 2000 and beyond is to help all our children to see visions.

Where there is no vision, the people perish: they cast off restraint, they become ungovernable, they become nihilistic. Vision has to do with a sense of transcendent authority and possibilities for daily living. In the biblical tradition of Jewish and Christian commentators, vision (Hebrew: *chazon*) refers to prophecy in its widest sense. It denotes the revelation of God's will as the word, or law, that directs the course of events in human history and is intended to be coordinated with the highest secular authority. Prophets instruct the people in divine things. They are religious educators, the standing witnesses to the truth and power of God's word, teaching a higher-than-human morality.

A corresponding theme in the same biblical tradition conveys an equally powerful message. A lack of vision or apprehension of the revelation of God's will leads to confusion, disorder, rebellion, and nihilism. Nihilism is a philosophy that regards all values as baseless. It typifies the rejection of all natural certainty in moral values. Moral values become subsumed by values that are empty of transcending tenets, and people become willing to refute the finite theories of morality.

According to Stanley Hauerwas, in *Vision and Virtue*, "Actions must be based on our vision of what is most real and valuable. The ethicist's primary task is to help discover the essential metaphors through which men can best see and understand their condition."[2] For Hauerwas the understanding of moral

2. Stanley Hauerwas, *Vision and Virtue* (Notre Dame, Ind.: University of Notre Dame Press, 1981), p. 30.

behavior is an affair not primarily of choice but of vision. Metaphors are carriers of the prophetic vision revealing the world as it is. Adapting his metaphorical viewpoint, I view vision as learning to "see" the world under the model of the divine. Metaphors help us to see and understand our condition and the divine. At least one implication is significant for this discussion. Individuals do not simply "believe" certain propositions about God; they learn to attend to reality through them. This kind of learning is transforming; it is training of the whole attention (mental, affective, kinetic) and is constantly juxtaposing experience with vision. It is a prophetic religious education.

Prophetic religious education is a metaphorical mimetic praxis (to be defined later) that helps us to participate in the transformation of the world. Vision, as the actual contact between God and the human spirit, is the necessary condition of any direct revelation. The law, the recorded result of such a revelation, is passed from mouth to mouth by tradition or written permanently in a book. Indeed, where there is no living revelation, no perceived contact between humans and God, there the bonds which hold society together are relaxed and broken. Prophetic religious education is one means by which this revelation (vision) has been presented. However, it has not been able to catch the attention of a large segment of our religious society. Few African American male children experience the presentation of this revelation in the context of the black church's prophetic religious education.

Context One: The Black Church

According to C. Eric Lincoln and L. H. Mamiya's 1990 study,[3] the typical African American congregation is composed of between 66 to 80 percent women. This study of 2,150 churches found an average of 30 percent male membership. This phenomenon is not limited to the black church. Lincoln's book also cites a national survey that suggests that women attend church more than men by the percentage of 75 to 63. It is clear that, based on church attendance, women are more inclined to practice formal religion than men, and African American women practice religion to an even greater degree than African American males. The great need for the impact the church can have in shaping the spiritual lives of men is undeniable. I set forth the hypothesis that the absence of the African American males from the black church is one possible factor leading to their present spiritual, social, and physical health crisis. Further, I am proposing

---

3. C. Eric Lincoln and Lawrence H. Mamiya, *The Black Church in the African American Experience* (Durham, N.C., and London: Duke University Press, 1990).

that the black church has been unable to convey a vision powerful enough to help African American males lead healthier lives, and this has contributed to the violence in the African American community.

I am again arguing that a vision represents a sense of transcendence. A lack of a sense of transcendence (vision) inhibits the development of a strong sense of coherence necessary to cope with a racist, market-driven society. Inability of one to comprehend, manage, and find meaningful one's environment leads to a deep sense of nihilism. Nihilism pervades the lives of many African American males. Indeed, this lack of a sense of coherence (nihilism) is a major risk factor for violence and poor health in general. Without question, violence is the central health issue facing African American males today. Black boys without a vision of how their world coheres are perishing.

Context Two: Violence

By almost every measure, the health of African American males lags far behind the health of other segments of the United States population. This is especially the case with regard to the impact of violence on the health of this segment of the population. Violence is the leading cause of death for African American males between the ages of fifteen and twenty-four. According to Mark Rosenberg of the Centers for Disease Control and Prevention, "violence is a public health problem. In 1991 there were 26,513 homicides in the United States. Homicide is the leading cause of death among black males and black females 15-23 years of age. There are over 2.2 million nonfatal injuries due to violence."[4] African American males are murdered at a rate of 158 per 100,000 as compared to 37 per 100,000 for all American males and 17 per 100,000 for white males. If all Americans were shot and killed at the same rate as young African American males, 260,000 Americans would be murdered with guns each year.[5]

The lack of a vision results in the inability to comprehend the transcendent nature of their personality. Theological questions of the truly transcendent nature of the world and ourselves result in a futile search for meaning and love in places that can never satisfy either need. Nihilism, then, is a form of deviated transcendence.

---

4. Mark L. Rosenberg and Mary Ann Frenley, eds., *Violence in America: A Public Health Approach* (New York: Oxford University Press, 1991), p. 14.

5. Gary Gunderson and Fred Smith, *Not Even One: A Report on the Crisis of Children and Firearms* (Atlanta: Carter Center, 1994), p. 4.

The Pathology of Deviated Transcendence

The Triangularity of desire means that a human being is structured with reference to transcendence. Human desire is mediated desire: it gets its goal and direction from without, not from within. The state of mimetic rivalry is the pathology of a "deviated transcendence," a desire whose goal or direction should be a truly transcendent spiritual person but instead is aroused by the immanent neighbor. The biblical name for this is idolatry, and its antidote is faith in the unseen God.[6]

The goal of prophetic Christian religious education is to correct the problem of deviated transcendence. The corrective function of a prophetic religious education, in this context, is to present persons with appropriate metaphors through which they may come to see and understand their condition differently. These metaphors provide a vision by which persons can see what people should be, what they can hope for, and how they ought to act. Prophetic religious education is a metaphorical process by which persons can also see not only how they should be, but how their world should be; not just what to hope for, but how to achieve it; not just how they ought to act, but how to change action into a transforming praxis of self and the world.

The "old folks" knew something about hope and transcendence. They had a different point of reference outside their historical context. It enabled them to relativize the historical present. That is what I mean by transhistorical consciousness. It is as if they lived simultaneously in all times. They made bricks without straw. They crossed the Red Sea with Moses in the book of Exodus. At the same time, they endured North American slavery and celebrated the Emancipation Proclamation on 19 June ("Juneteenth") in Texas. They suffered the indignity and poverty of a Jim Crow South and shared the dream of Dr. Martin Luther King, Jr. The old folks hope not only for a this-worldly freedom but also for an otherworldly salvation. They had a spirit of hope. They knew with uncommon certainty that "trouble don't last always and we're so glad that trouble don't last always."

The spirit of hope provided our elders with a hope for a transhistorical or otherworldly salvation. That hope made the struggle for a this-worldly liberation not only possible but worthwhile. The religion of my grandmother and my great-auntie Lily helped them to speak of their oppression and struggle from another perspective than those of us who are trapped inside our circumstances.

---

6. Robert G. Hamerton-Kelly, *Sacred Violence: Paul's Hermeneutic of the Cross* (Minneapolis: Fortress Press, 1991), p. 134.

They were able to achieve a "heavenly" or transcendent perspective on their circumstances. This is what I have been referring to as a sense of transcendence throughout this paper.

The Christ/The Hope-Bringer

Old Massa met our hope-bringer all right, but when Old Massa met him, he was not going by his right name. He was traveling, and touristing around on the plantations as the laugh-provoking Brer Rabbit. So Old Massa and Old Miss and their young ones laugh with and at Brer Rabbit and wished him well. And all the time, there was High John de Conquer playing his tricks of making a way out of no-way. Hitting a straight lick with a crooked stick. Winning the jack pot with no other stake but a laugh. Fighting a mighty battle without outside-showing force, and winning his war from within. Really winning in a permanent way, for he was winning with the soul of the black man whole and free. So he could use it afterwards. For what shall it profit a man if he gain the whole world and lose his soul? You would have nothing but a cruel, vengeful, grasping monster come to power.[7]

I am proposing that prophetic Christian religious education become a process for the heroic repristination of the "hope-bringer" of slave folklore for black boys and the future. According to Robert Penn Warren, "To create a hero is, indeed, to create a self."[8] Warren makes the point that the hero is not just an expression of a preexisting self, nor only a projection of that self, but instead belongs primarily to the process whereby the self emerges. Prophetic Christian religious education is an educational process for creating religious heroes and heroines that can bring hope to black boys of today.

The question is not whether or not black boys will have a model of desire, but which model will serve as a model of identity formation. Models of desire that inspire imitation are called heroes. According to John W. Roberts, professor of folklore and folklife, "The heroes that we create are figures who, from our vantage point on the world, appear to possess personal traits and/or perform

---

7. Zora Neale Hurston, "Sometimes in the Mind," in *The Book of Negro Folklore*, ed. Langston Hughes and Arna Bontemps (New York: Dodd, Mead, 1958), p. 93. Quoted in Riggins R. Earl, Jr., *Dark Symbols, Obscure Signs: God, Self, and Community in the Slave Mind* (Maryknoll, N.Y.: Orbis Books, 1993), p. 133.

8. Introduction to *The Hero in America,* by Dixon Wecter (New York: Scribner, 1972), p. xiv.

actions that exemplify our conception of our ideal self, the self that our personal or group history, in the best of all possible worlds, has prepared us to become."[9] Roberts argues that a particular culture selects and promotes heroes to fit the historical needs of the group. Slaves needed to survive a system that deprived them of liberty and the most basic human needs such as food and clothing. Thus slaves retrieved from their African heritage the wily trickster. Under Jim Crow laws black boys were not only denied the protection of law, but law served as an instrument for their continued oppression. The outlaw who could beat the law became their hero. According to Roberts, figures and actions considered heroic in one historical context or by one group of people may be viewed as ordinary or even criminal in another historical context or by other groups, or even by the same groups at different times.

Most of the cultural heroes of black boys are characters in the myth of redemptive violence (scapegoating mechanism): cowboys and Indians; gangsters like "the Godfather"; hip-hop rappers like Tupac Shakur, Snoop Doggie Dog, and Natural Born Killers; cartoon characters and action heroes like Teenage Ninja Turtles and Mighty Morphin' Power Rangers; movie heroes like the Terminator and the Eraser; figures in computer games like Mortal Kombat — the list is endless. *The question for religious education is whether or not the heroes of the myth of redeeming love can induce enough mimetic desire to lead black boys to the imitation of Christ (a countermimesis to heroes of violence).*

Jesus Christ has elicited mimetic desire for centuries in the Western world and a significant portion of humankind, "because of his multiple persona as (1) cosmic lord and divine logos — the word of God by whom all things were created and subsist; (2) an earthly (Davidic) king, heir of an ancient dynasty and of a messianic destiny of imperial power and rule; and (3) a religious leader of miraculous and prophetic powers who represents and mediates divine favor and judgment, beneficence and justice, to the acclaim and prosperity of his people and all Nations."[10] Today's religious education fails to provide metaphors of Christ capable of attracting significant mimetic desire among black boys. It abandons black boys to false metaphors and models of desire ("deviated transcendence"). For mimetic desire is attracted by charisma.

Hence the first task of prophetic Christian religious education is the social construction of Christ's personal charisma for today's black boys by positing the historicity, relevance, and seriousness of Christ's metaphorical persona as trickster. The persona of this metaphor for Christ is endowed with charisma

---

9. John W. Roberts, *From Trickster to Badman: The Black Folk Hero in Slavery and Freedom* (Philadelphia: University of Pennsylvania Press, 1989), p. 1.

10. Gunderson and Smith, p. 199.

when his metaphors have historicity, relevance, and seriousness: (1) when Christ is recognized as a historical person; (2) when he plays some role in an ongoing drama in the life world of contemporary persons; (3) when he has an impact on aspects of a highly profiled group's concerns in the world of typical persons. One function of prophetic Christian religious education, then, is to be a system of charismatic legitimation of Christ for today.[11]

The second task of prophetic Christian religious education is to endow the metaphors of Christ with charisma through charismatic teachings that enlist the mimetic desire of black boys to imitate Christ. Additionally, teacher-prophets of prophetic Christian religious education should have the gift of spiritual discernment of the scapegoating mechanism and of deviated transcendence and the wisdom and skills to correct both.

I suggest that the metaphorical framework for providing a new mimetic model of transformation for black boys is the trickster Christ.[12] Christian religious education is needed for black boys because of its compelling characteristics.

The tasks of prophetic Christian religious education as they relate to deviated transcendence are to transform human depravity (marginalization) into human dignity (a sense of transcendence) in the contexts of a pathogenetic environment. Accordingly, prophetic Christian religious education is the triangulation of "transcendent desire" and involves these five tasks:

1. *The self and environment task:* to transform double consciousness to an expanded critical consciousness via a transhistorical perspective.
2. *Environmental input task:* to expose the myth of redemptive violence; to transform it into the myth of redeeming love via a hermeneutic of suspicions.
3. *Internal processing task:* to transform internalized oppression to loyalty to the cause of Christ.
4. *Output task:* to transform the nihilistic threat into a praxis of love.
5. *Feedback task:* to perform a countermimesis of acquisitive mimetic desire through an intimate mimesis of Christ.

---

11. This social construction of charisma proposal is derived from Anthony J. Blasi's book, *Making Charisma: The Social Construction of Paul's Public Image* (New Brunswick, N.J.: Transaction Publishers, 1991), pp. 11-12.

12. Cf. Robert W. Funk, "The Jesus That Was," *Fourth R* 5, no. 6 (November 1993): 1-7; Dick Eddy, "The Jesus Seminar: Work in Progress," *Fourth R* 5, no. 6 (November 1993): 12-13; Marcus J. Borg, "Jesus — A Sketch," *Fourth R* (May/June 1994): 10-15; Jeffery L. Sheler, "In Search of Jesus," *U.S. News and World Report* 5 (8 April 1996): 47-53.

These tasks of prophetic Christian religious education are efficacious for the creation of the beloved community out of a pathogenic environment, and for transforming a "slave for life"[13] into a "child of God."

Task I

Dear Pookie (Charles Jr.):

How can I make you understand that racism is real, capitalism does exploit your community, white domination is responsible for the devastation of your race, but you must love your enemies? How can I say that to you when I know that at times you find it difficult to love yourself, much less your neighbor? How could you possibly love your enemies? However, I know for sure that you can do nothing else if you really want to escape white oppression — only love can redeem you.

The first trick this society has tried to play on you is to make you think your African heritage, the color of your skin, the way you worship, the way you talk, the clothes you wear, and your whole African American culture are second-rate and nothing to be desired. It has tried to make you believe that Euro-American heritage, white skin color, "standard" English language, and white culture are not only first-rate but ideal. They taught it to you in schools and made it a requirement for participating in the American dream. The American dream which has always been and is today an African's nightmare. The fact is that you have inherited both cultures: European white American and African. In your veins runs the blood of both ancestries. This society would have you love one and despise the other. Take your pick which to love or which to hate; either way you are divided and can never be whole until you learn to love both.

Therefore, unconsciously you strike out to destroy yourself or

13. The phrase "slave for life" is derived from the Latin term *durante vita,* which comes from the colonial law making slaves of African ancestry slaves from birth to death. To prevent slaves from claiming freedom after baptism, colonial legislators passed similar laws, as in Maryland in 1664, "to draw up an Act obliging negroes to serve *durante vita* . . . for the prevencion of the dammage Masters of such Slaves must susteyne by Slaves pretending to be Christ[e]ned[;] And soe pleade the lawe of England." In Albert J. Raboteau, *Slave Religion: The "Invisible Institution" in the Antebellum South* (New York: Oxford University Press, 1978; paperback, 1980), p. 99.

those who are divided like you. You do not respect yourself, so you cannot stand to be disrespected by others like you. Your enemy is not the white man out there, with whom you rarely have any dealings; it is the white man inside of you that you hate. Your only hope is to begin to see differently, with different eyes. The only way you can learn to love both parts of you is that you see yourself through the eyes of someone who loves both parts of you. That is, you must begin to see through the eyes of God.

Sincerely yours,
Uncle Junior

The Self and Environment: A Transhistorical Perspective Transforms Double Consciousness to Expanded Consciousness

The central problem for black boys is that they are divided into unauthentic beings. They are the host of their oppressors. Black boys suffer from a duality in which, according to Paulo Freire, "to be is to be like, and to be like is to be like" those who dominate the world in which they live. I suggested that double consciousness means that the black boys are, at the same time, themselves and "the white man" whose consciousness they have internalized. The black boys have taken "the white man" as an unauthentic transcendent model of desire, as a model of agency or hero. Their hero has become the metaphorical image of the white man as a result of a socialization process (including public education, media, corporate culture, and the church) dominated by the perspectives of successful white males. In addition, there has been much debate about the prominence of the European image of Jesus Christ in most black churches. In ways too numerous to examine here, black boys are presented with images of the white man as an authentic model of desire. Thus black boys are daily tempted to commit idolatry.

Critical consciousness has to do with critical awareness of environment, self, and the historical process as causes of one's duality and oppression. Expanded consciousness provides the added dimension of eternity (transhistorical perspective). God reveals in Jesus Christ the vision of the human. Christ becomes the truly transcendent model of desire that breaks the cycle of violence. Through a nonviolent struggle he overcomes domination and idolatry for all time.

One's ability to be critical is largely shaped by one's perspective, which in turn is largely determined by one's education and/or by the culture(s) that shapes one's identity. Thus, in order to develop a critical consciousness, one must achieve a perspective outside of the domination system and the historical epoch that is shaped by the desires and interests of one's oppressors. I propose that it is the task of prophetic religious education to provide the transhistorical perspective made possible by the Spirit of hope.

Task II

Dear Rod Rod:

How can I say that violence can't save you, when all you've known all your life is violence? We raised you with violent discipline as an expression of our love for you. Violence is glorified in our nation's history and the media. How can I explain to you that the notion that violence is redemptive somehow is a myth?

Since Hasaan died I have studied at-risk youth and developed program after program for black boys like you. I have pondered your plight and the conditions that are destroying our community. Now I want to try to tell you what I have learned. Your situation is not really different from the world of your father, who was a black boy in the fifties and sixties, and your father's father, who was a black boy in the twenties and thirties, and his father, who was born a slave for life. Slavery ended, but the deception that kept us slaves then keeps us at each other's throats now. The times have changed; the modes of transportation have changed; the music has changed; but the nature of our bondage has not changed — white domination remains the same.

The trick was to steal your heroes and turn them against you. Instead of your heroes bringing hope, your heroes bring you only death and destruction. Think about it. Who are your heroes; what do they stand for? What are the stories you listen to? From the stories you hear and crave come your heroes. It used to be that those who told our children stories had something to tell. Now stories are told by people with something to sell. These stories or myths come from the television shows, movies, and music you watch and listen to. These stories help to shape your character and behaviors. Heroes represent what we most desire to become when we are young and our most noble actions when we become adults.

The stories they sell are violent stories, thus your heroes are violent. The heroes of these stories have a desire for power and possessions. The stories that people who love you tell — are stories of hope, faith, and love. The heroes of these stories have a desire to save. Rod Rod, don't let anyone steal your heroes, for when they steal your heroes they steal your only hope and finally your freedom.

Sincerely yours,
Uncle Junior

Environmental Input:
To Expose the Myth of Redemptive Violence, Transform It into the Myth of Redeeming Love via a Hermeneutic of Suspicions

The myth of redemptive violence is the religion and spirituality of the pathogenic environment. This myth makes the claim that "violence saves." This myth is the substance of the messages that black boys receive from the pathogenetic environment: violence saves, violence works, violence makes you a man, violence is America. Even God is violent: "'Vengeance is mine,' says the Lord." Black boys are constantly bombarded with these metaphorical representations from early childhood. These characters serve as metaphorical mimetic models of the myth of redemptive violence. Black boys (as well as others) mimic the desire of these metaphors of violence to create a never-ending stream of new victims.

The second task of prophetic Christian religious education is to provide a hermeneutic of suspicion that unmasks the myth of redemptive violence. The hermeneutic of suspicion is made possible by an alternative myth, the myth of a nonviolent god found in the New Testament Christian prophecy. Prophetic Christian religious education provides metaphors that furnish alternative screens through which input of the environment can be sifted. Metaphors that can serve as models of desire attract sufficient mimetic desire to change one's perception of reality from violence to nonviolence.

Prophetic Christian religious education is a praxis education that seeks to make disciples through a shared Christian mimetic praxis. It is an educational process that nurtures and develops the faith and desire of black boys to become disciples of Christ and to be loyal to the cause of Christ. The cause of Christ is to create a universal beloved community of recovering victims, victimizers, and surrogate victims.

Task III

Dear T-Boy:

We (your father and uncles) wanted for ourselves and for you the same material things and prosperity as those who have exploited our bodies and minds for centuries. We have not only internalized their values, language, and culture but also their idols of gold. The spirit of materialism and the religion of violence now rule our life, families, and communities. It has become our cause because we have internalized our own oppression.

Those of us who benefited from affirmative action, fair housing, set-asides, and other gains achieved via the civil rights movement have failed you. We have helped ourselves instead of others in our communities. We fled our communities to pursue material things and the almighty dollar. We left our brothers and sisters in poverty as bad as they have ever suffered under the oppression of white people, because we didn't want to live next door to those brothers and sisters.

Dr. King once said if man has not found a cause worth dying for, he is not fit to live. For what cause are so many of you dying for? Even more important — for what cause are you living? Is it to be respected and feared as "the man"? To have gold chains, automobiles, money, and power over the lives of others? Many have died to give you the rights that you take for granted now. What will you contribute to the next generation? Don't follow our example, for we have failed you.

I know many of the gangs and other young people of today would rather help their communities. The movies, news media, and your peers have given you a bad rap. You need heroes whose noble causes are worth dying for. There is no greater cause than freedom. Freedom not just in a political sense but also spiritual freedom that is found in Christ. The Christ whose cause it is to seek and save the lost. I know so many of your friends have been lost to drugs, sex, violence, greed, and hopelessness. So many plan their funerals and not their future. You need a cause that is worthy of you.

The cause worthy of you is the cause of Christ, whose cause it is to trick you into an eternal future. This trickster makes foolish the wisdom of this world. He has stolen the sting out of death. This trickster Christ has given hope to the hopeless for countless generations.

Sincerely yours,
Uncle Junior

Internal Processing: To Transform Internalized Oppression to Loyalty to the Cause of Christ

The internalization of oppression by black boys takes place through their socialization by a hegemonic domination system. This socialization leads to the internalized values, beliefs, and doctrines propagated by the oppressors that become the causes by which black boys act and are rewarded by the dominant culture. These internalized values and mores become the basis on which their goals and consciences, and the interest and justification of their actions toward others and themselves, are rooted. The input from this oppressive hegemonic environment contributes to a negative self-concept and low self-esteem.

The task of prophetic Christian religious education is to foster the ability of individuals to be loyal to the cause of Christ, which is the establishment of the beloved community. Prophetic Christian religious education for the beloved community requires an ethic of universal love. An ethic of universal love is necessary for the beloved community, a community of love and justice. Prophetic Christian religious education equips one to become loyal to the cause of Christ. Black boys must come to see their actions in the context of a transcendent community and the cause for Christ.

Task IV

Dear Kilian:

I am very afraid for you, because I know that many of you looked up to Hasaan and will try to follow in his path. The street Hasaan died on is the street me and my friends used to walk day and night singing the Temptations' greatest hits without fear. We made money on that street throwing papers and returning Coke bottles to the corner store. Now kids our age then are selling dope on that same corner. We fought with fists instead of guns. We planned our futures and not our funerals.

Your ancestors learned a long time ago that we are a small minority in this country, but that did not stop them from struggling for their freedom against all odds. Our forefathers struggled for freedom from physical chains enforced by whips and hunting dogs. Your father's father struggled for freedom from legal and political chains enforced by terror and the lynching tree. Your father fought for civil rights against segregation enforced by Jim Crow laws, for voting rights, equal opportunity, and affirmative action. You must fight to stay alive, to escape from bullets instead of plantations, and you must break the bonds of mind-numbing drugs instead of chains of iron.

Many black boys today believe they have no future. I've heard it said that many plan their funerals instead of their futures. Live fast, die young, and have a pretty corpse is the logic of the terminally ill. This is the greatest challenge you will face — to keep hope alive. Every day I am shocked and bewildered by the coldheartedness of killing that takes place in our neighborhoods at the hands of young brothers of eleven, twelve, and thirteen. But I guess if you don't care about your own life, why should you care about anyone else?

No one can long endure without love, so some of you turn to gangs that become your family. You are on the right track. But does your adopted family create or destroy community? Is your new family held together by love or fear? If you are to find meaning, hope, and love in your life, you must seek to live in peace with all your brothers — not just those who wear your colors. Because your fight is "not against flesh and blood, but against principalities, against powers, against the rulers of the darkness of this world, against spiritual wickedness in high places" (Ephesians 6:12 KJV). Your struggle is against — the violence itself.

Sincerely yours,
Uncle Junior

Output: To Transform the Nihilistic Threat into a Praxis of Love

A prophetic Christian religious education promotes a praxis of love which is loyal to the cause of Christ. This praxis calls individuals into a vocation in service to a vision of love. Loyalty overcomes the nihilistic threat by giving one a cause to live for. It addresses the problem of nihilism by making clear one's duty. One cannot exist in a state of nihilism and be truly loyal to the cause of Christ.

The nihilistic threat is numbing detachment from others, a self-destructive disposition and a coldhearted, mean-spirited outlook that destroys both the individual and community. The nihilism consists of a loss of hope, an absence of meaning, and a deficit of love. A loss of hope is the nullification of the future. Without hope, one reasons like the terminally ill: "live fast, die young, and have a pretty corpse." Consequently violence and death have become a reasonable option for many black boys and their neighbors. Their neighbors are transformed into objects to fulfill their lusts of the moment. A deficit of love results in coldheartedness and a mean spirit.

The task of a prophetic Christian religious education for the black church is to prepare black boys for the journey toward a universalizing Christian faith that enables individuals and communities to utilize the religious power of faith to create the beloved community. Through its pedagogy, black boys come to see a vision of a beloved community as the organizing principle for what they do. They seek the actualization of an inclusive human community, a mutually cooperative and voluntary venture of humankind where individuals take responsibility for their neighbor. In such a community, black boys can once again become their neighbor's neighbor.

Task V

Dear Tommie:

How do I tell you that each time one young black boy kills another, he is killing himself? That those who sell drugs and guns and murder another brother are reenslaving themselves and their own people? Prison has now become a rite of passage for so many of you. More of your cousins have gone to prison than to college. Not long ago I heard an old man say, "I was always afraid that we as people would stop advancing, but I never thought we would lose ground." Have you ever stepped back and asked yourself whose game you are playing? When you have answered that question, answer this one for yourself: Are you playing or are you being played?

To love your neighbor is not enough because your neighbor is just like you. Neither of you is perfect, so sooner or later you will disappoint one another. Your desires will eventually get the best of you. You will become rivals, because you are too much alike. You will want what you believe the other has, and each will become an obstacle to the other's desires. This is not idle speculation. This is human nature, and human history has validated it over and over again. But you don't have to open your history book; look at your own family and friends you love. If this is true about your family and friends — what about your enemies? I personally don't believe blacks are any better than whites. If we were in power we would probably be at least as bad as they.

First you must learn to love someone who will never fail you and who loves you, your neighbor and enemies. It also must be someone your neighbor and even your enemy can love as well. If you love someone, you want what that person wants and you love who that person loves. Only through this person can you, your neighbor, and your enemies truly love one another. This someone is God in the person of Jesus Christ. Through the love of Christ a community where everyone can experience love is formed. This is what I mean by the beloved community.

Feedback: To Perform a Countermimesis of Acquisitive Mimetic Desire through an Intimate Mimesis of Christ

The imitation of Christ (as a nonviolent transcendent model of desire, with a desire-to-save through an intimate mimetic process) makes Christ an obstacle "to our human expressions of the will-to-power and our acquisitive desire to survive and advance by means of the domination and destruction of other beings." To continue: "To exercise mastery in the world on the basis of such a model means to accede to this form of rule or else effectively repudiate the model. Acceding to the model constitutes apprenticeship to a nonviolent God. Accordingly the mimesis of rivalry between antagonized parties is displaced, first, by a mimesis with a preeminent nonviolent model and then, where effective, by a mimesis of apprenticeship to that model."[14] Christ is not only a preeminent nonviolent model but a transcendent model that inspires ultimate mimetic desire — a hero. Mimetic desire becomes an intimate mimetic desire when it is shared with others in a community of victims, surrogate victims, and victimizers.

The task of prophetic Christian religious education is to promote a discipling mimesis or "apprenticeship" to Jesus Christ as rival to the human expression of acquisitive mimetic desire. A prophetic Christian religious education seeks to transform acquisitive (to grasp) mimetic desire into intimate (to be) mimetic desire via discipleship to a nonviolent transcendent hero — Jesus Christ.

To mimic Christ is to be loyal to the cause of Christ. The key is the imitation of Christ's desire or cause. Christ's desire can be expressed in terms of a universal love ethic illustrated by the Good Samaritan story: to love God with all your mind, heart, and strength, and your neighbor as yourself (Luke 10:27). This love ethic, as illustrated by the triangle of faith, can be expressed as being

14. Smith, p. 202.

your neighbor's neighbor. The aim here is to replace acquisitive mimetic desire with a form of nonacquisitive desire which is analogous to replacing rivalry with loyalty. To mimic Christ is to imitate his praxis by being loyal to his cause, which means metaphorically to save, not to create, victims. This appropriation of Christ is personalized and internalized as one's "ultimate myth" of meaning and ethic of life, thereby reshaping one's identity and agency in the world. My own hope and prayer is that such a prophetic Christian religious education may transform self and world not only for black boys but for all youth by means of a sense of transcendence (mimesis of Christ) in Y2K and beyond.

CHAPTER SIXTEEN

Theological Literacy and Fluency in a New Millennium: A Pastoral Theological Perspective

CARRIE DOEHRING

In this essay I will draw a distinction between theological literacy (being able to read and write about theological ideas) and theological fluency (using theological ideals as a basis for practice). I suggest that we become fluent when we "inhabit" our theology as a faith perspective that we use to understand and respond to spiritual and psychological needs. Whereas becoming theologically literate is part of learning how to think critically, becoming theologically fluent involves formation. Theological educators that teach critical thinking and form men and women as religious professionals bring feeling and thought, form and content, and theory and practice together, healing what Tracy, in the opening chapter of this volume, calls fatal separations. Hodgson describes this kind of education: "As I understand it, this entire cyclic, rhythmic process [of learning] is what constitutes paideia in the sense of the formation of human personality. It is important to stress that paideia includes the element of disciplined, critical thinking as well as the element of imagination and wonder, and that the two come together to form a kind of thinking called 'wisdom,' which construes the wholeness of things, their 'being' or 'truth,' and learns how to apply principles of value and goodness in concrete situations."[1]

In Part 1 I describe and illustrate the differences between theological literacy and fluency. In Part 2 I describe three traditions in my discipline of pastoral theology (pastoral theology as practical theology, biblical counseling, and integration counseling). I use these traditions to describe three ways of being theologically fluent and literate: contextual, propositional, and pre-

---

1. Peter C. Hodgson, *God's Wisdom: Toward a Theology of Education* (Louisville: Westminster John Knox, 1999), p. 63.

servationist.[2] I conclude that contextual and preservationist theological literacy and fluency need to be less polarized from each other and that both are viable forms of theological fluency for the twenty-first century.

Theological Literacy and Fluency

As a pastoral theologian, I understand theology as a way to talk about the big questions of life and death, questions like why people suffer. These questions are big because they make me aware of the limits of my horizons of meaning. For example, I recently saw a photograph in my local newspaper of a colleague, Cecil Rice, who was accompanied by his wife. They were in a courtroom where a man was being tried for the murder of their only daughter and two grandsons. I looked at their faces and wondered how they could live with such a brutal loss. The atrocity of the violent deaths of their daughter and grandchildren makes me reach beyond the ways in which I usually make sense of things. I can't just use psychological perspectives to live with such violence. I need theological perspectives; that is, I need ways to help me think about good and evil. I also need to put into practice these theological ways of thinking, using the religious symbols and stories of communities of faith. I need the movement back and forth, between the conversations about evil among theologians (literacy) and the lived theologies of communities of faith (fluency).

In describing what I need when I face violence, I articulate the need for both theological literacy and fluency. I would like to illustrate the need for both literacy and fluency using David Lodge's novel, *Paradise News*.[3] In the novel Bernard is a former priest and a self-described skeptical theologian who teaches at a nondenominational British theological college where "anybody could study almost anything that could be brought under the umbrella of religion."[4] In leaving the priesthood, Bernard also left behind the Catholic beliefs that car-

---

2. There are several typologies of pastoral theology, notably Brian E. Eck, "Integrating the Integrators: An Organizing Framework for a Multifaceted Process of Integration," *Journal of Psychology and Christianity* 15, no. 2 (1996): 101-13; and James N. Poling and Donald E. Miller, *Foundations for a Practical Theology of Ministry* (Nashville: Abingdon, 1985). Typologies of practical theology are also helpful in understanding pastoral theology, such as H. Richard Niebuhr's (*Christ and Culture* [New York: Harper and Brothers, 1951]) discussion of the relationships between Christ and culture, and Rebecca Chopp's (*Saving Work: Feminist Practices of Theological Reflection* [Louisville: Westminster John Knox, 1995]) description of three types of practical theology.

3. David Lodge, *Paradise News* (New York: Penguin Books, 1991).

4. Lodge, p. 28.

ried him through the first half of his life. When his aunt Ursula faces death, she seeks out Bernard as someone who can answer her questions about Roman Catholic faith. Bernard admits that he's not sure if he believes in God. His aunt persists with her questions, and Bernard tries to answer as best he can. She is troubled, for example, by a visit to a folk mass where she saw the priest chewing on the host. She remembers being told as a girl that she must never bite the host. Bernard assures her that this is an old superstition. "I gave her a brief rundown on modern eucharistic theology: the importance of the shared meal in Jewish culture, the place of the *agape* or love-feast in the lives of early Christians, the misguided Scholastic efforts to provide an Aristotelian rationale for the eucharist, leading to the doctrine of transubstantiation and the superstitious reification of the consecrated host."[5]

Bernard knows he is lecturing his aunt but cannot "shift into a more appropriate register."[6] Bernard is theologically literate in that he can read, understand, and teach theological ideas. In this conversation with his aunt, he falls short of being fluent. He is not able to use theological ideas to converse more fully with his aunt about her faith and her death.

In this example Bernard could probably become fluent if he were able to step into his aunt's shoes and use his theological concepts to experience vicariously her needs and losses. In Bernard's case fluency seems to depend upon this kind of theological empathy; that is, his ability to use theological concepts to imagine what his aunt is trying to ask of God, and how God can be present to Ursula in the sacrament of Communion.

Looking more closely at Bernard and his difficulties with theological fluency, I wonder whether his fluency also depends upon being able to describe his own needs in terms of theological concepts. When Bernard left the priesthood and his "orthodox" approach to Roman Catholic beliefs, he became skeptical. He was no longer able to inhabit[7] a religious faith of his own. He could use his theological literacy to tear down theological meanings, but was not able to build upon any meanings that he could call home. He surmises that others share his difficulty: "It often seemed to Bernard that the discourse of much modern radical theology was just as implausible and unfounded as the orthodoxy it replaced, but nobody had noticed because nobody read it except those with a professional stake in its continuation."[8] For Bernard, there is no community of faith that puts

---

5. Lodge, p. 135.

6. Lodge, p. 135.

7. Edward Farley, *Theologia: The Fragmentation and Unity of Theological Education* (Philadelphia: Fortress, 1983).

8. Lodge, p. 29.

into practice modern radical theology. A few experts are literate, but there are no communities where members are fluent in this kind of theology.

Bernard muses upon his lack of faith by having a conversation with himself in the question-and-answer format of the Penny Catechism:

> How could you go on teaching theology to candidates for the priesthood if you no longer believed in God?
> You can teach theology perfectly well without believing in the God of the Penny Catechism. In fact, there are very few reputable modern theologians who do.
>
> So what God do they believe in?
> God as "the ground of our being," God as "ultimate concern," God as "the Beyond in the Midst."
>
> And how does one pray to that kind of God?
> A good question. There are, of course, answers: for instance, that prayer expresses symbolically our desire to be religious — to be virtuous, disinterested, unselfish, ego-less, free from desire.
>
> But why should one wish to be religious if there is no personal God to reward him for being so?
> For its own sake.
>
> Are you religious in that sense?
> No, I would like to be. I thought I was, once. I was wrong.[9]

Bernard is an example of someone whose religious symbols have been broken.[10] He has not been able to reconstruct and inhabit new symbols using radical modern theology. He cannot pray and practice faith using radical modern theology because he cannot experience a connection with a transcendent being or reality. He is also not part of a community that prays or practices in this way. Bernard seems unaware of the importance of such a community, and assumes that it is up to him as an individual to rebuild and put into practice his religious faith.

Near the end of Lodge's novel, after many conversations in which Bernard is theologically literate but not fluent, Bernard and Ursula have their last conversation about God. Ursula asks Bernard to help her remember the Epistle lesson that Father Luke said when he anointed her. Bernard recites the reading

---

9. Lodge, p. 48.

10. Robert C. Neville, *The Truth of Broken Symbols* (Albany: SUNY Press, 1996).

from the Epistle of Saint James from memory: "Is there any of you sick? Let her call for the elders of the Church, and let them pray over her, anointing her with oil in the name of the Lord; and the prayer of faith will save the sick woman, and the Lord will raise her up; and if she has sinned, she will be forgiven."[11]

Ursula comments on how beautifully Bernard says the words. Then, puzzled, she asks if Father Luke said "woman" when he read the text. Bernard says no; he changed it for her. In this conversation Bernard becomes theologically fluent. He can empathize with Ursula's need for pastoral care. His tone of voice and change of pronouns is a way he can use religious faith to care for her.

I've chosen to illustrate what happens when someone is theologically literate and not fluent. I could have illustrated a more common scenario of people who have a lived theology but are not literate. The following is a brief example of fluency without literacy. A large Protestant congregation is part of a denomination that does not ordain women. A few of the women in the congregation are remarkable leaders who can speak articulately about their religious beliefs. They do this in every allowable context except preaching at the worship services. They struggle to understand why they cannot preach. To begin a conversation with those who maintain their denomination's practice of not allowing women to preach, they need to become theologically literate. In many ways they are fluent in putting into practice the beliefs about their ministry that have come from their lived theology. However, they are not familiar with theological arguments that would support their argument for the right to preach. They need to become theologically literate.

In the second part of this essay I want to describe three traditions in pastoral theology. Each tradition attempts to be theologically literate and fluent by bringing theological perspectives to bear upon life experience, like Ursula's experience of facing death and the women's experience of being called to the role of preacher. I will assess and draw conclusions about these three attempts at literacy and fluency.

Three Traditions of Theological Fluency

Pastoral theology[12] is a discipline in which theology and the social sciences (primarily psychology) are related to pastoral practice.[13] There are probably as

---

11. Lodge, p. 255.

12. I am using the term "pastoral theology" to refer to a practical theological method, not the area of theological studies that encompasses the "arts" of ministry, like liturgy, music, pastoral care, homiletics, and so on.

13. The most everyday kind of pastoral practice is the pastoral care offered by lay and or-

many ways of using theology and psychology to care for people as there are caregivers.[14] I will describe the three methods of pastoral theology that are most represented in North American literature on pastoral theology in the last quarter of last century. I'll begin with a brief history describing how these three traditions formed out of the infusion of psychology into pastoral care and the study of religious experience in the first half of that century.

The First Half of the Twentieth Century

In the first half of the twentieth century pastoral care practitioners and theorists encountered the establishment of psychology as a science, the depth psychologies of Freud and Jung, and the formation of mental health professions. Psychologists studied religious experiences. Clergy studied the ideas of Freud and Jung, relating them to pastoral practice and religious experience. Anton Boisen used his own experience of mental illness to develop a training program called clinical pastoral education for clergy, chaplains, and religious professionals set within institutions like hospitals and prisons. These years provided many opportunities for the rapid developments in psychological studies and clinical practice that endeavored to enrich the care of souls and study of religious experience.

In the 1950s several important developments helped to create new traditions in pastoral theology. The first was the establishment of doctoral programs in pastoral psychology and faculty appointments of several pastoral theologians who became spokespersons for a tradition of liberal Protestant pastoral theology: Seward Hiltner, Wayne Oates, Paul Johnson, and Carroll Wise. They proposed methods of relating psychological and theological studies, and the practice of pastoral care and counseling.[15] Another development was the professionalization of pastoral counseling in the 1950s' establishment of the American Association of Pastoral Counseling and several training centers, like the Danielsen Institute at Boston University and the Blanton-Peale Institute in New York City.

---

dained representatives of faith communities. Pastoral care can take the form of supportive care and crisis intervention. Pastoral counseling and psychotherapy are more specialized forms of pastoral care, involving specialized studies and training in theological and psychological studies and explicit treatment contracts.

14. For a historical survey of this variety, see William A. Clebsch and Charles R. Jaekle, *Pastoral Care in Historical Perspective: An Essay with Exhibits* (Englewood Cliffs, N.J.: Prentice-Hall, 1964). For a contemporary global sampling, see Robert J. Wicks and Barry K. Estadt, eds., *Pastoral Counseling in a Global Church: Voices from the Field* (Maryknoll, N.Y.: Orbis Books, 1993).

15. E.g., Seward Hiltner, *Preface to Pastoral Theology* (Nashville: Abingdon, 1958).

In the 1960s there was a great deal of interest in the practice of pastoral counseling. Much of the literature focused on therapeutic techniques and how these could be understood psychologically and theologically.[16] This 1960s' "toolbox"[17] approach to pastoral theology used a therapeutic paradigm[18] that emphasized one-on-one pastoral counseling relationships in which psychological concepts and techniques dominated.[19] Many pastoral counselors and theologians became dissatisfied with the dominance of psychological studies over theological studies, and also counseling (especially in secular settings) over pastoral care; some wanted to use more conservative theological approaches as well. The pastoral theological tradition is the most direct continuation of the history I have described, and its proponents distinguished themselves from the 1960s' toolbox approach by redefining themselves as engaged in a practical theological endeavor. I'll describe this tradition of pastoral theology first.

Liberal Pastoral Theology

Protestant, Catholic, and evangelical pastoral theologians who see themselves as practical theologians relate psychological studies and liberal theological studies to the practice of pastoral care, counseling, and psychotherapy.[20] In the 1980s and 1990s, liberal pastoral theologians redefined pastoral psychology as a subdiscipline of pastoral theology, which was in turn understood as a form of practical theology. In many ways, using the larger frame of practical theology was a reinvestment in the legacy of Seward Hiltner, a legacy set aside during the 1960s and 1970s when interest in psychological techniques dominated pastoral theological literature.

These pastoral theologians of the 1980s and 1990s also shifted from a

16. For example, Howard Clinebell, *Basic Types of Pastoral Counseling* (Nashville: Abingdon, 1966).

17. Charles V. Gerkin, *Introduction to Pastoral Care* (Nashville: Abingdon, 1997).

18. Rodney J. Hunter, "The Therapeutic Tradition of Pastoral Care and Counseling," in *Pastoral Care and Social Conflict*, ed. Pamela D. Couture and Rodney J. Hunter (Nashville: Abingdon, 1995), pp. 17-31.

19. Rodney J. Hunter and John Patton, "The Therapeutic Tradition's Theological and Ethical Commitments Viewed through Its Pedagogical Practices: A Tradition in Transition," in *Pastoral Care and Social Conflict*, pp. 32-43.

20. The mission statement of the Society for Pastoral Theology provides a fuller description of pastoral theology. Liberal pastoral theology can be described as "a constructive practical theological enterprise focused on the religious care of persons, families and communities" (Society for Pastoral Theology, "The Mission Statement of the Society for Pastoral Theology," 1998). Information about the mission statement can be obtained by contacting the author.

therapeutic or clinical paradigm to a communal contextual paradigm[21] which emphasized the pastoral care offered by *communities of faith,* and the *contextual* nature of pastoral care. By attending to context, pastoral theologians could draw upon theological and social scientific perspectives that were most relevant to particular persons and communities. Pastoral theologians recognized the need for diverse contextual pastoral theologies.[22] Pastoral theologians also became more explicit about the extent to which their own allegiances made their pastoral theology contextual.[23]

Several words can be used to describe the method of many contemporary pastoral theologies: correlational, hermeneutical, critical, contextual, and emancipatory. Many pastoral theologians *correlate* social scientific studies, theological studies, cultural studies, and feminist studies in order to understand detailed descriptions of practice. The method is correlational because each perspective maintains its integrity as it is brought into dialogue with other perspectives. To use a musical analogy, the pastoral theologian listens for the degrees of resonance and dissonance among theoretical perspectives and also between theoretical perspectives and the phenomenological richness of practice. Dissonance can help the listener hear more clearly the sharp differences between perspectives. For example, I may use in-depth interviews to gather rich descriptions of how some people of religious faith put into practice a theology of sexual intimacy. I may elaborate these operational theologies using pastoral theologian Elaine Graham's understanding of practice as an enactment of the-

21. John Patton, *Pastoral Care in Context: An Introduction to Pastoral Care* (Louisville: Westminster John Knox, 1993).

22. For example, Edward Wimberly (*African American Pastoral Care* [Nashville: Abingdon, 1991]) brings narrative theology and African American family systems theory to his pastoral practice with African American families. James Newton Poling, in *Deliver Us from Evil: Resisting Racial and Gender Oppression* (Minneapolis: Fortress, 1996), has explored historical documents on racism and relied upon feminist and womanist theologians for his study of racism and evil. Pamela Couture, in *Blessed Are the Poor? Women's Poverty, Family Policy, and Practical Theology* (Nashville: Abingdon, 1991), has used Lutheran and Wesleyan theologies and socioeconomic perspectives to understand the cultural phenomenon of single mothers and poverty in the United States. Don Browning and his colleagues (Donald S. Browning, Bonnie J. Miller-McLemore, Pamela D. Couture, K. Brynolf Lyon, and Robert M. Franklin, *From Culture Wars to Common Ground: Religion and the American Family Debate* [Louisville: Westminster John Knox, 1997]) review New Testament studies on shame and honor and construct a theological understanding of the equal-regard marriage. They have brought this theological understanding of marriage and family to the American family debate. Browning and his colleagues have proposed strategies for implementing this theology.

23. See Carrie Doehring, "A Method of Feminist Pastoral Theology," in *Feminist Pastoral Theology,* ed. Bonnie Miller-McLemore and Brita Gill-Austern (Nashville: Abingdon, 1999), for a discussion of such accountability.

ology.[24] She may help me listen for the ways in which these operational theologies are at odds with denominational standards that carry forward their historical theologies concerning sexuality. If I had only brought historical theological perspectives to understanding my interviewees' sexual practices, I might have listened only for traditional denominational themes. Using both Graham's and historical theological perspectives, I can listen for the resonance and dissonance between historical and reconstructed operational theologies of sexuality among my interviewees.

The method of many pastoral theologies is also *hermeneutical* and *critical:* hermeneutical in its emphasis on the role of interpretation in all knowledge, and critical in its desire to challenge its own methods and truth claims.

Many pastoral theologies are also *contextual,* in that they use theological and psychological perspectives that are most meaningful for particular contexts. They acknowledge that there is no single theological or psychological perspective that is universally true, and that many combinations of a variety of theological and psychological perspectives are needed to reflect upon the diversity of religious practices.

Finally, the method for many pastoral theologians is ultimately *emancipatory.*[25] They want to develop multidimensional strategies for transforming oppressive meaning systems and practices, especially those based upon hierarchical binary opposites (male/female; white/nonwhite; young/old; straight/gay; Christian/non-Christian). These strategies are based upon truth claims (sometimes described as provisional)[26] arrived at through the correlation of various theoretical perspectives on people's practices, particularly their religious practices.

These pastoral theologies can be broadly described as using contextual theological fluency and literacy. In the final illustration from Lodge's novel, Bernard inhabits his Roman Catholic tradition and offers Ursula his reading of the Epistle passage used in the rite of anointing the sick. He takes into account

24. Elaine Graham, *Transforming Practice: Pastoral Theology in an Age of Uncertainty* (London: Mowbray, 1996).

25. For example, Couture, *Blessed Are the Poor?;* Doehring, "A Method of Feminist Pastoral Theology"; Elaine Graham, *Transforming Practice;* Larry Kent Graham, *Care of Person, Care of World: A Psychosystems Approach to Pastoral Care and Counseling* (Nashville: Abingdon, 1992); Larry Kent Graham, *Discovering Images of God: Narratives of Care among Lesbians and Gays* (Louisville: Westminster John Knox, 1997); Bonnie J. Miller-McLemore, *Also a Mother: Work and Family as Theological Dilemma* (Nashville: Abingdon, 1994); Christie Cozad Neuger and James Newton Poling, eds., *The Care of Men* (Nashville: Abingdon, 1997); James Newton Poling, *The Abuse of Power: A Theological Problem* (Nashville: Abingdon, 1991).

26. Elaine Graham, *Transforming Practice.*

Ursula's gender and also her impending death as he interprets the biblical passage so that it becomes more relevant to her.

Contextual theological fluency allows for the possibility that theological perspectives may be reconstructed. The integrity of theological perspectives is important, and this integrity will set limits upon how much reconstruction can be done. For example, Bernard needs to maintain the integrity of the biblical and theological perspectives he would use to elaborate his reading of the Epistle. This correlational method ensures that the dissonance generated by the use of various perspectives will be valued and, indeed, protected. One theoretical perspective cannot be subsumed into another perspective as a way of eliminating dissonance.

Having described pastoral theology and its contextual theological fluency, I turn now to describing briefly two other pastoral theological methods: biblical counseling and integrationist.[27] These are not traditions I have experienced in practice. Indeed, I know these traditions only through some of their literature. Being partially literate and not fluent in their methods, I am at risk of stereotyping these approaches. In spite of this risk, I do want to acknowledge both the biblical counseling and integrationist traditions, because to ignore them is to act is if my tradition is all that there is to pastoral theology. These traditions represent important ways of being theologically fluent and literate. I hope to engage pastoral theologians and indeed people of faith who are different from me as I outline biblical counseling and integrationist methods.

Biblical Counseling

Jay Adams can be named as the founder of biblical counseling.[28] Adams was trained in the 1960s' methods of pastoral counseling and soon became dissatisfied with its nondirective stance (exemplified by psychotherapist Carl Rodgers) and also its limited use of Hebrew and Christian Scriptures. Adams returned to what he described as historical Calvinist forms of pastoral care that guided pastoral care seekers. He rejected clinical and counseling psychology as a source and norm of authority, and wanted to rely solely upon the Bible as a source of authority, using literalist norms.

27. For a full description of biblical counseling, and a comparison of its method with theological and integrationist traditions, see Elizabeth Susan Only, "'Rescue the Perishing, Care for the Dying': An Assessment of Jay E. Adams' Argument against the Use of Psychological Theory in Pastoral Counseling" (Th.D. diss., Boston University, 1999).

28. This tradition is represented in various journals: the *Journal of Biblical Counseling,* the *Journal of Pastoral Practice,* and the *Master's Seminary Journal.*

Adams describes the first concern of a biblical counselor as the salvation of the care seeker.[29] A biblical counselor must first be an evangelist. Biblical counseling can only be done with those who fully embrace the biblical counselor's religious beliefs. The second concern of the biblical counselor is the sanctification of care seekers. He confronts care seekers with their sinfulness and uses biblical texts literally to prescribe what God wants them to do.[30] As Adams says, "One Christian helps another to put off old, sinful life patterns and to put on the new biblical responses required by God."[31]

According to Adams, he relies upon the Bible as his only source of authority. He uses a literal interpretation of Scripture as his norm of authority. In fact, as Only concludes, "While he appeals to biblical authority to support his claims, doctrinal authority [specifically, the doctrine of plenary verbal inspiration] sets the parameters for his biblical interpretations."[32]

Adams not only rejects the social sciences as a source of authority, he sees psychological perspectives as heretical. For example, he rejects using drugs to treat mental illness because drugs are used instead of "biblical solutions," that is, the prescriptive use of a biblical text to confront the person's denial of his or her sin.[33] Drugs mask the problem, which is sin and not illness.

Biblical counseling uses a form of theological fluency that can be described as propositional.[34] Doctrines, such as the inerrancy of Scripture, are accepted as absolutely true. These doctrines provide the answers to questions raised in religious practices. These doctrines cannot be reconstructed using the experiences of people. For example, the belief that only men can be ordained cannot be called into question by the experience of women's leadership.

From my perspective, biblical counseling is not a viable form of theological fluency for the twenty-first century because it cannot be used in cross-disciplinary dialogues that draw upon current social scientific and cultural

29. Jay E. Adams, *How to Help People Change: The Four-Step Biblical Process* (Grand Rapids: Ministry Resources Library, 1986).

30. Adams, *Help People Change*, p. 37.

31. Jay E. Adams, "Reflections on the History of Biblical Counseling, 1952-1984," in *Practical Theology and the Ministry of the Church*, ed. Harvie M. Conn (Phillipsburg, N.J.: Presbyterian and Reformed Publishing, 1990), p. 214.

32. Only, p. 170.

33. Adams, *Help People Change*, p. 158.

34. I am borrowing two of George Lindbeck's approaches (*The Nature of Doctrine: Religion and Theology in a Postliberal Age* [Philadelphia: Westminster, 1984]) for describing how doctrine is used: the propositional, a term I use to describe biblical counseling, and the cultural-linguistic, which I call a preservationist approach. His third approach to doctrine (the experiential-expressivist approach) could be used to describe pastoral theologies of the 1960s but not contemporary liberal pastoral theology.

studies for perspectives on suffering. Not to use these perspectives in caring for those who suffer seems unethical to me. Biblical counselors remain isolated not only from medical and social scientific studies but also from ongoing conversations about the role of sexism, heterosexism, racism, and classism in suffering. Without being part of these critical conversations, biblical counselors are more likely to use religious traditions and practices uncritically in oppressive ways.

The Integrationist Tradition

Integration approaches to pastoral theology also became fully articulated in the 1970s. These approaches are represented in the *Journal of Psychology and Theology*, particularly in its twenty-fifth anniversary volume of 1997. There are a variety of integrationist methods (Eck identifies five).[35] Overall, integrationists identify themselves as "Christians in the field of psychology" who integrate conservative and/or evangelical Christian beliefs with their practice of the discipline of psychology. They share a belief that "all truth is God's truth":[36] "[This] ancient approach to the relation of faith/Scripture/theology to philosophy and other disciplines has emphasized the oneness of God's word in creation and Scripture, the dependence of all theoretical thought on issues of faith, and the ultimate unity of human thought in the mind of God. This position maintains that one's ultimate faith-beliefs form a special class of knowledge — beliefs that logically precede and provide the foundations for all other knowledge."[37] Psychology is "kingdom activity, activity that is an expression of God's reign on earth."[38]

Like pastoral theologians and unlike biblical counselors, integrationists accept both theological and psychological studies as legitimate. Some integrationists give precedence to either psychology or theology by filtering out data that is at odds with the dominant discipline. For example, empirical psychologists of religion — like Spilka, Hood, and Gorsuch[39] — use a scientific approach to bracket the supernatural; counselors like Crabb[40] use Scripture as a filter for

---

35. Eck, "Integrating the Integrators."

36. Eck, p. 101.

37. Eric L. Johnson, "Christ, the Lord of Psychology," *Journal of Psychology and Theology* 25, no. 1 (1997): 18.

38. Johnson, p. 15.

39. B. Spilka, R. Hood, Jr., and R. L. Gorsuch, *The Psychology of Religion: An Empirical Approach* (Englewood Cliffs, N.J.: Prentice-Hall, 1985).

40. Lawrence J. Crabb, *Effective Biblical Counseling: A Model for Helping Caring Christians Become Capable Counselors* (Grand Rapids: Zondervan, 1977).

psychological concepts that won't fit their faith perspectives. Other integrationists, like their counterparts, give equal weight to theological and psychological perspectives, and correlate these perspectives. The important differences between integrationists and pastoral theologians are that:

- Many integrationists understand Christian perspectives as the truest religious tradition; many pastoral theologians, while believing their religious tradition to be true for them, also acknowledge that other world religions can make their own truth claims.
- Integrationists are seeking links or unifying concepts between psychology and Christian theology (believing as they do that all truth is God's truth), while pastoral theologians value both the resonance and the dissonance among psychological and theological perspectives and phenomenological descriptions of practice.
- Integrationists seek unifying religious themes; pastoral theologians seek the particularities evident in various contexts and they also elaborate differences.
- Integrationists want psychological theory and practice to reaffirm the tenets of Christianity (see, e.g., the work of Thomas Oden);[41] pastoral theologians allow for the possibility that psychological theory and practice may challenge theological suppositions, and even prompt reconstruction of theological concepts.

Many integrationists work as licensed psychologists. They can most fully practice their method in care facilities that are explicitly Christian. When they practice in secular settings, they often use their religious faith privately, as an ultimate and absolute source of authority.

Integrationists seek to preserve what they see as core or essential Christian doctrine. Many of them understand their shared theological concepts as absolutely, universally, and ontologically true. They want their practice to remain true to these core concepts.

Conclusions

Both contextual and preservationist approaches are viable forms of theological fluency and literacy for the twenty-first century. Both contextual and preserva-

---

41. Thomas C. Oden, "The Historic Pastoral Care Tradition: A Resource for Christian Psychologists," *Journal of Psychology and Theology* 20 (1992): 137-46.

tionist theological fluency allow us to maintain the integrity of the various theoretical perspectives we bring to the phenomenological complexities of practice. In its purest form, preservationist fluency values consonance as creative and uses its Christian truth claims as absolute horizons of meaning that can hold the complexity of life. Religious symbols, while not likely to be broken and reconstructed, become relevant the more they are made to bear the weight of and be consonant with life experience. Contextual fluency values dissonance as creative and makes its truth claims provisional, allowing for their reconstruction. Contextual theological fluency is more likely to break and reconstruct religious symbols so that they will be relevant within the contexts of care. Such reconstruction is in dialogue with historical and biblical theologies.

These two forms of theological fluency can be seen as two poles on a spectrum, and both could benefit from not being so polarized. For example, preservationist fluency could value some levels of dissonance and difference among its psychological and theological perspectives and its practices, while contextual fluency could value some levels of consonance and commonality, particularly in terms of seeking shared religious beliefs across various contexts.

The challenge for those who are preservationist in their theological fluency is to live with their religious symbols amidst life in all its complexity. The danger is that aspects of life experience at odds with religious symbols may be muted. The challenge for those who are contextually theologically fluent is to seek out shared religious symbols, and look for commonalities across various contextual and preservationist practical theologies.

Those who are theologically fluent in the new millennium will walk a fine line, balancing, on the one hand, contextual theologies and their provisional truths and, on the other hand, preservationist theologies and their absolute truths. Perhaps such bipolar fluency cannot be achieved within single persons and communities of faith. The balancing act involved in such bipolar fluency is certainly evident in many denominations that allow a variety of subcultures to coexist within the boundaries that define these denominations. Such fluency is, in the end, a result of dialogue and tolerance: processes that certainly ought to be at the heart of theological literacy and fluency in the new millennium.

CHAPTER SEVENTEEN

Theological Literacy: Some Catholic Reflections

BRIAN O. McDERMOTT, S.J.

In this brief essay I would like first to reflect on theological literacy understood formally as the transformation of a religious person's consciousness from a preadult level of development to that of an adult. Next, I will outline the portrait of a mature conscience that mainstream Catholic moral theologians paint, the kind of conscience necessary for true moral discernment. This portrait can help us to recognize, in a broader way, the features of the psychologically adult religious consciousness at which all efforts of developing theological literacy in the Catholic tradition must aim. I then consider the schooling of the religious imagination as an essential aspect of Catholic (catholic) theological literacy and raise the question of how we might approach members of the so-called Generation X, given their culture's saturation in imagination ("virtual reality") and their stunning challenge to ordinary understandings of "literacy."

Theological Literacy as the Transformation of Consciousness

Thanks to pioneering educators such as Paulo Freire, we have come to see that literacy is much more than a matter of learning how to read and write; it is also an act of self-emancipation, fraught with sociopolitical and economic consequences.[1] Learning to read not only the letters of the alphabet but also the sociopolitical environment, in which I have up until now been embedded, constitutes one of the most momentous passages that I as an individual or my community can undertake. In this liberationist perspective, the Brazilian peasant farmer living in the impoverished northeast region of his country learns through this "alphabetization" process how to move from being an oppressed

---

1. Paulo Freire, *Pedagogy of the Oppressed* (New York: Seabury Press, 1973).

object (the image is of a heavy weight bearing down upon the individual) to a "suffering" agent. By the latter expression, I mean someone who begins to carry from below *(sub-ferro)* his situation, learning how actively to relate to it by drawing on resources in the form of shared faith, community solidarity, and, yes, the newfound ability to read and write.[2]

Understood as an emancipatory process, theological literacy, or, better, the process of becoming theologically literate about one's own faith tradition, has everything to do with learning new ways to learn; with developing a new, more complex form of consciousness; and with taking responsibility for, and trusting, what one has come to know. In the Roman Catholic tradition, with its strong emphasis on the role of the church's magisterium and the need for the "faithful" to heed that magisterium and take it as their doctrinal and moral guide, it is instructive to attend to what mainline Catholic moral theologians have to say about what a healthy adult Christian conscience looks like for clues as to what, in more general terms, a mature Christian's consciousness would look like in the Catholic context.[3]

The conscience of a mature Christian adult in the Catholic communion is supposed to be one characterized by at least the following three features: it must be well informed by outside norms and values, it must be self-responsible, and it must be open to and dependent on the mercy of God.

1. A well-informed conscience. The mature Christian is supposed to learn — given the constraints of talent, time, and circumstance — as much as possible about what revelation, witnessed to by the church in its scriptural and postscriptural tradition, has to say about the particular issues facing the individual or community. The individual is also supposed to be well informed about the specifics of his or her own situation with whatever uniqueness may be involved in it. Finally, the person needs to seek counsel with wise persons who can offer advice from a position that is different from that of the decision maker and who would be expected to bring some objectivity to the process.

2. A self-responsible conscience. Given an honest effort to be well informed within the constraints of talent, time, and circumstance, the decision maker must choose what is right and good for him or her in those circumstances, calling on God's grace and attending to the inner cognitive and affective movements to forestall any self-centered and distorting bias in the decision-making process. The buck finally stops at the individual who must decide,

---

2. Helen M. Luke, "Suffering," chap. 11 in *The Voice Within: Love and Virtue in the Age of the Spirit* (New York: Crossroad, 1987).

3. Here I am indebted to Richard M. Gula, *Moral Discernment* (Mahwah, N.J.: Paulist, 1997).

in an act of moral judgment, what course of action in the circumstances appears to be the right one. The decision maker must assume responsibility for how the decision-making process was conducted, what data received greater weight, what "wise figures" were consulted, how conflicting values were prioritized, and whether he or she was truly open to God's grace and honest in confronting biases and the extraordinary human capacity for self-deception.

3. A conscience open to and dependent on God's grace. A mature Christian needs to place the judgment before God, believing that God, who desires to bring the decision maker to Godself infinitely more than the moral agent wants it, has helped the decision maker in and through his or her best honest efforts to decide rightfully, within the amount of time the situation allows and with the capacities and resources available. Then he or she needs the courage to act, trusting God to bring good out of his or her best (graced) efforts, and remaining open to reassessment of the decision as new data and new circumstances provide new insights in the course of the implementation of the moral decision.

From a psychological-developmental perspective, the Catholic moral tradition calls on adult members of the Catholic community to think about and decide moral matters with a structure of consciousness that Robert Kegan calls "adult" or "modernist."[4] On this level one decides moral matters *for* oneself, but not *all by* oneself (i.e., in isolation). In order to be able to function within this order of consciousness, momentous transformations have had to be traversed before these capacities could emerge: from infancy to childhood to a preadult or "traditionalist" form of consciousness (the latter being, according to some research, precisely where more than half the chronologically adult American population is ensconced). Comparing the mainline Roman Catholic understanding of the mature conscience to Kegan's cognitive-affective developmental theory, it is clear that mature Christian decision making presupposes the transition from adolescent to adult ("modernist") consciousness.

What are the contours of this transition? Following Kegan, I would say it is a transition of our consciousness from one particular configuration or structure or cognitive-affective horizon to another, more complex one. Specifically, the adolescent level of consciousness consists of an embeddedness in one's loyalties and affiliations to persons, communities, and values outside the self. At this stage, the self's identity consists of those relationships to the outside world. These relationships "have" the adolescent rather than the adoles-

---

4. See Robert Kegan, *The Evolving Self: Problem and Process in Human Development* (Cambridge: Harvard University Press, 1982), and his *In over Our Heads: The Mental Demands of Modern Life* (Cambridge: Harvard University Press, 1994). What follows is derived from Kegan's work. Also very relevant here is James W. Fowler's *Stages of Faith: The Psychology of Human Development and the Quest for Meaning* (San Francisco: Harper and Row, 1981).

cent "having" them. On the adult level, those very loyalties and affiliations shift to being objects of explicit awareness. At this new level of complexity of consciousness, the very processes by which I invested my surroundings with value become the object of my awareness. I now recognize — for the first time — that *I* am the constructor of my loyalties, *I* am the constructor of my commitment to these values rather than those, and *I* am the one who "makes up" my own mind about what counts and does not count, or what counts less. The source of my commitments and allegiances is I myself, not the surroundings, which, to be sure, continue to provide me with many of the objects of my commitment and allegiance but are no longer the source of their being *my* commitments.

I have not spent much time on the development of adult moral consciousness (conscience) because I am not a moral theologian. Yet, as a systematic theologian who is interested in issues of adult spirituality, authority, and leadership, I see implications in this foundational moral theology for the perspective it offers regarding theological literacy in one of its more formal dimensions.

In his seminal work, *In over Our Heads: The Mental Demands of Modern Life,* Robert Kegan makes an intriguing statement about the times in which we live.[5] Until recently, he writes, it was not necessary for many individuals to develop their own adult or "modern" consciousness. The cultural environment in which they dwelt carried the complexity of consciousness for them. Their embeddedness in that environment guaranteed that as individuals they could function well on an adolescent level. The uniformity of the "surround," that is, the absence of significant cultural diversity, permitted a rather snug fit between individual and group.

It is a cliché to observe that today, in North America, all this is very different. We live in a heterogeneous world, full of options, full of *Weltanschauungen,* full of conflicting values about the most fundamental issues of human life.

The shift from one level of consciousness to another occurs when we are sufficiently challenged and supported by our environment (both factors are needed!) to move to a more comprehensive level because we experience the one we now inhabit as painfully inadequate to the new realities hitting us. People do not give up a long-standing form of consciousness unless they are both encouraged and required to do so.

A basic, and perhaps rather obvious, principle regarding theological literacy is this: a believing Christian's appropriation of his or her faith needs to be on a level and at a complexity comparable to the rest of his or her conscious

---

5. Kegan, *In over Our Heads,* pp. 103-6.

functioning. If the individual is functioning usually at the level of modernity or psychological adulthood, then it is crucial that he or she function that way in the personal theological appropriation of his or her faith as well. This level of complexity requires that the individual be able to objectify to a large extent the commitments entailed in the discipleship relationship to God through Jesus Christ in the power of the Holy Spirit. These commitments are capable of objectification to the degree that they involve concepts and judgments and feelings with which the individual is able to enter into an explicitly conscious relationship.[6] *From* embeddedness *to* responsible relationship: such a shift in one's connection to the religious tradition to which one belongs can feel at first alienating and uncomfortable. The sense of loss can be great indeed, as one enters into a new territory where the older markers and monuments, including one's older approach to texts and rules, no longer "work" as they once did.[7] But theological literacy as a transformative process of consciousness calls for this loss while promising significant gain.

Theological Literacy as the Schooling of the Religious Imagination

A second feature of theological literacy that I now want to highlight has to do with our religious imaginations. Written texts so often serve as the focus of discussions about literacy that it might be helpful to raise up for some reflection the role of the imagination and its schooling as one becomes more "literate" regarding one's religious tradition.

For the Catholic (but not exclusively for the Catholic), the God revealed in Jesus Christ loves to dwell within the world and among human beings in olfactory, tangible, audible, visible, and tasty ways: the animal smells of a manger, the healing touch of a parent, the challenging voice of a prophet, the gorgeous

---

6. In Kegan's schema, this transformation involves a shift from preadult or traditionalist consciousness (level 3) to an adult or modernist consciousness (level 4). For Fowler, this change consists of a development from synthetic-conventional faith (stage 3) to individuative-reflective faith (stage 4).

7. The transformative process of becoming theologically literate hardly ends with development to the adult or "modernist" level of religious and theological consciousness. There remains at least one more stage, that of "postmodernity" in its deconstructive and reconstructive phases. (See Kegan, *In over Our Heads,* chap. 9.) Kegan has persuaded me that much of the postmodern curriculum (in this term's literal and metaphorical senses) actually represents a challenge to its students to move from a traditionalist or preadult to a modernist or adult form of consciousness. See Kegan's final chapter in *In over Our Heads.*

vestments of Easter liturgy, the taste (mediocre or vintage!) of altar wine. Incarnation and sacramentality shape the body and soul of Catholic Christianity. Literacy for a Catholic must mean more than texts and doctrines. There is texture and feel, a religious imagination that can appreciate the times and places God loves to frequent: the honeymooners' marriage bed, that gathering place called the kitchen, the office and its tired politics, the fun times of recreation and sweat times of mental and physical labor.

For Catholics God's saving deed in Jesus was one enormous act of friendship, of divine "courtesy" (Julian of Norwich) extended to God's own created universe. The incarnation of the divine Word amounts to a supreme act of fidelity to the original creation, distorted and abused by sinners but still God's good (while sinned-against) creation. In incarnation God reveals that God intends creation to return to its divine source as a creation redeemed by Christ and transformed and consummated by God's Spirit. God's kinship with God's created universe, a kinship wrought by God, the transcendently immanent One, is disclosed most poignantly in the story of Jesus, the incarnation of God's own Word of truthful self-presentation, and in the pouring out of God's own Spirit of love in church and world.

The Catholic instinct probably opts more immediately for the sacramental synthesis over the prophetic-apocalyptic dialectic. This instinct has its problem, its insufficiency, and its potentiality for abuse, but it also makes its own irreplaceable contribution to a proper appreciation of the Christian "take" on life.

In theological language, this Catholic mind appreciates sacramental causality, the recognition that God's grace (which is, ultimately, God's *self*-communication as truth and love) comes to be present and available for human acceptance and cooperation in and through symbols. When that symbol is a sacramental symbol, then the tradition affirms that *"sacramentum efficit gratiam significando eam."* In the vernacular, the causality peculiar to a sacramental symbol vis-à-vis grace is precisely that proper to the process of symbolization because the symbol renders the grace present in a humanly accessible way. The providing of the symbol is, in the final analysis, grace's doing; the acceptance of the grace thus symbolized — that, too, is grace's doing. Indeed, all is grace; still, symbols have their extraordinary and gracious role to play so that grace might reach us and we might reach grace.

The Catholic imagination is an imagination that finds God in the finite (not by making end runs around the limits of this world in some magical way but in and through those very limits, compassionately and carefully negotiated). It finds God in the concrete and bodily (marriage is a sacrament; the vowed religious life is not); and it even finds God in the grotesque (whether it be the obscene cross of Golgotha or the weird characters of Flannery O'Connor's short stories).[8]

To be literate in a Catholic — and catholic — way, one needs to have an appreciation for creation's goodness; to feel for it when it is despoiled, twisted, and maimed for greed's purposes; to identify with its sinned-against goodness and thus understand, with the instinct of faith, the true horror and destructive power of sin.

An integral theological literacy in the Catholic tradition would therefore call for a schooling of the person's imagination, a development of his or her sense of and feel for the beauty and goodness of God as revealed in the world and all creation. Appreciation of the narrative forms of the Old and New Testament, of the poetry of the Song of Songs, is a part of this. Savoring the beauty of a forest, or the austere forms of some modern architecture, and developing a contemplative attitude that permits one to be drawn in by the beauty of the other and to find God there: this is the contribution of the Christian imagination, an imagination that God, who cannot be contained in the greatest infinities, is also findable in the most minuscule of entities.[9]

Theological Literacy as Spiritual Practice

So far I have reflected, in a very initial way, on two dimensions of theological literacy considered as a process of growth: the transformation of consciousness underlying it and the schooling of the imagination that helps do justice to the incarnational character of the good news.

At this point I would like to make my essay more challenging — or, better put, I want to challenge myself, the essayist, a bit more. Let's consider the situation of so-called Generation X, that is, those young adults who were born in the 1960s and 1970s and therefore in 1999 can be in their late thirties.

I am only beginning to become acquainted with these folks, much less understand them. But there are aspects of many of this cohort that pose very serious challenges to anyone who wants to write about theological literacy in the United States at the turn of the millennium. Literacy in the most ordinary sense of the word, dealing with reality through the written word, is not their métier. The literacy that characterizes them (if literacy is the appropriate term

---

8. See Gerald J. Bednar, *Faith as Imagination: The Contribution of William F. Lynch, S.J.* (Kansas City, Mo.: Sheed and Ward, 1996).

9. This is an expression found on Saint Ignatius Loyola's tombstone: "Non coerceri maximo, contineri tamen a minimo, divinum est."

here) has everything to do with TV and MTV, the computer, the Internet, virtual reality, and a most irreverent and ironic approach to life and culture.[10]

Students of Generation X note the way these young people have grown up in the America of the 1980s and 1990s. Many were latchkey children, and their minds and sensibilities have been saturated with television, videos, and other forms of electronic communication. Their imaginations are wired. The images they indwell change incessantly (watch MTV for easy confirmation of this), and their sense of life is that of a terribly disappointing and thoroughly disorienting show of which they are involuntary participants. They know much about the imagination, in a visceral sort of way. They may not have much truck with literacy in the more classical sense of the term, however. Books, articles, and texts in general are not what their mental umbilical cords are attached to. But no one has to persuade them of the power of the imagination and its power to shape a world, indeed, to shape multiple worlds for the multiple selves that constitute many a GenXer.

There are some assumptions underlying a usual theory of literacy that Generation X (or students of the phenomenon) challenges. For example, that there is a constant self, unitary in constitution, who can grow, develop, and be transformed over time. If it is correct to interpret literacy in formal, developmental terms as a transformation of consciousness from a preadult to an adult level of affective-cognitive consciousness (even if this stage is not itself a final one), where do the members of Generation X belong? I would hesitate to say. No doubt many of them are preadult, as are so many chronologically adult members of the American population. Some are no doubt adult. But the move from being embedded in the external world of TV and the Internet to taking responsibility for one's relation to these media would appear to be a major step for any member of Generation X.

How might one more classically educated in Christian and Catholic theological literacy approach someone in Generation X? Since the relation to texts that is taken for granted by the classically educated is often missing in members of this generation, it might be better if the latter were invited to consider a different approach to the Christian tradition. The approach I suggest is that of a Christian spiritual practice.

Spiritual practice has features that mirror aspects of classically understood literacy, but differs significantly as well. As Robert Wuthnow observes,

---

10. I have been greatly aided here by Tom Beaudoin, *Virtual Faith: The Irreverent Spiritual Quest of Generation X* (San Francisco: Jossey-Bass, 1998). The author is careful to state that his observations about members of this generation are not meant to apply to all, but he would argue that his depictions are accurate for a significant number of GenXers.

spiritual practice is personal and social, it has a moral dimension, it is reward-ing, it relates one to a tradition, and it fosters healthy self-possession for the sake of healthy self-giving. In his recent book, *After Heaven: Spirituality in America Since the 1950s,* Wuthnow explores the dimensions of spiritual practice as a contribution to the discussion of how people disaffected with religious in-stitutions might still deepen their spiritual journeys by staying open to the mys-tery to which religious traditions bear witness.[11]

A practice such as *lectio divina* (to choose just one example of a signifi-cant spiritual practice) could be accessible to a number of members of Genera-tion X, provided they find in themselves a hunger for the more, the healthy more that is God's work in them. *Lectio divina,* or "holy reading," is an ancient and very contemporary practice, rooted in the Benedictine tradition.[12] In this prayerful sequence one begins in the imagination, precisely the place where GenXers must begin. One starts with a text of scripture, or a picture, image, or icon, and reads *(lectio)* the text aloud several times or gives careful attention to the details of the visual image; then one meditates *(meditatio)* on the text or image, thinking about it, letting features strike home and then savoring them for their meaning. Following that, the individual moves to *oratio,* asking God for what the individual desires from God; then one passes on to *contemplatio,* where the person rests in God and waits on God, in all simplicity. Finally, there is *actio,* where the person seeks to be and to act toward and with others in a way that is shaped by this encounter with God.

Lectio divina invites a person to relate to God first through images, thoughts, and feelings; then through desires; next in simple faith, without at-tachment to ideas, feelings, or images; and finally in concrete, daily actions.

I am not suggesting that a practice such as *lectio divina* compensate for theological literacy in the classical sense — far from it. But the challenge to clas-sically oriented advocates of theological literacy is a real one: how to help spiri-tual seekers among GenXers find a way to begin to access theological literacy. One approach encourages them to choose a spiritual practice or set of practices that is, as mentioned above, personal and social, possessing a moral dimension, that is rewarding and challenging and roots them in a particular tradition. Such a practice can provide the holding environment needed for those who wish to begin to develop a spiritual identity before the holy mystery we call God. From the point of view of literacy in the usual sense, such a practice is not the end

---

11. *After Heaven: Spirituality in America Since the 1950s* (Berkeley: University of Califor-nia Press, 1998), pp. 178-98.

12. For a fine treatment of *lectio divina,* see William H. Shannon's *Seeking the Face of God* (New York: Crossroad, 1992). Shannon, who is an authority in Thomas Merton studies, has added *actio* to the steps of the process of "holy reading."

point; rather it is a beginning. But it is a beginning that the development of ordinary theological literacy, were it to develop in GenXers, would not render superfluous since, ultimately, the point of all religious texts is to bring the person or community into deeper communion with God and fuller participation in God's project in the world.

Theological literacy, as traditionally understood, may not get very far with many GenXers, but for the ones who are spiritual seekers and who are making the psychological transition from preadulthood to adulthood, helping them connect with a fundamental spiritual practice may provide the window of accessibility they need in order to develop, over time, a hunger for the texts of this religion of the Book.

CHAPTER EIGHTEEN

Theological Literacy: Problem and Promise

WESLEY J. WILDMAN

For our purposes we can divide theological literacy into two types. On the one hand, theological literacy can mean knowing enough theological terminology to express one's beliefs. This kind of literacy can promote discussion among believers, clarify what is at stake in arguments, and deepen the sense of belonging to a religious tradition. It is valuable for all these reasons, especially for religious people interested in beginning to think about their faith. I will call this "theological literacy A," but this type of literacy is not my concern here. On the other hand, theological literacy can mean knowing how to *think* theologically. This skill is rarer, harder to achieve, more disturbing (since such thinking often interferes with existing convictions), and less obviously valuable for most people. This is the sort of theological literacy of which David Tracy speaks in this volume and of which I mean to speak here. I will call it "theological literacy B," using the phrase "theological literacy" for this second type unless the context demands clarification.

Theological literacy of this second type is promising because it promotes understanding, transformation, intellectual honesty, spiritual realism, and moral responsibility. It is also a problem, however, because it is hard to cultivate and because having it can cause distress and lead to alienation from one's religious community. I shall describe both sides of the theological literacy coin on the way to fleshing out this description in terms of suggestions both for the theological training of religious leaders and for professional theological work. I turn first to the problematic wing, beginning with an argument about the relevance and attractiveness of theological literacy.

Wesley J. Wildman

The Problem of Theological Literacy

There are lots of ways to get from A to Z in life, and on our many and various paths, most of us human beings manage. Our problems have mostly to do with love, resources, safety, justice, microorganisms, misfiring immune systems, and neurochemical imbalances. These problems take most of our attention. Being theologically literate is, on a first approximation, a luxury that is irrelevant to the vast majority of human lives. It is not that theological literacy leads to terrible mistakes; on the contrary, it can produce genuine insight. It is rather that life for most people is not about understanding but about coping, and theological literacy offers too little in the way of coping power to compensate for the time and trouble that acquiring it involves. To be clear: I am not saying that most people *perceive* theological literacy as an irrelevant luxury; I am saying that it *really is* an irrelevant luxury for most people. Thus we are faced not merely with a public relations challenge to increase interest in theological literacy, but also with a reasonably accurate judgment of the masses: theological literacy is irrelevant to them. Sure, a cultural elite needs to keep theological literacy alive or else public discourse would be awash in the sort of stupid superficiality that dominates any public debate in the absence of sharp, confusion-free clarity for which cultural elites strive. It follows that we need *some* theological experts to keep the flame of thought burning beneath the essentially religious, existentially potent questions that keep coming up in human experience. But that is as far as the relevance of theological literacy goes for most people. As long as we know that someone is holding down the theological fort, the literature fort, the science fort, the economics fort, and so on, we can safely get on with our lives, reasonably confident that we can leave complicated questions to experts.

So much for relevance; now to attractiveness. Theological literacy is arguably no boon but a bane, directing people's attention to the true yet disturbing underbelly of life that is, frankly, better handled for most by religion's relatively gracious and effective soothings and distractions. Religious acts, from communal worship to centering meditation, get people back on track, keep them moving through life with dignity and forbearance. Social work and simple caring for others grease the creaky joints of the social body and keep alive the flickering prophetic flame for times when disasters of justice require it. Religious ways of understanding and acting provide orientation and comfort and thereby silently legitimate many unconsciously held assumptions that are crucial for the stability of societies and for individual happiness. All these beneficial effects of religion are strongest when we are both unaware of the social and cognitive mechanisms that produce them and unlearned about the world as it is that requires religion for that production process. Theological literacy is a problem because it raises consciousness, disrupting the silent and relatively effective functioning of religion in individual and corporate life. It is, in short, unattractive as well as irrelevant for most people. Of course, the elites who turn their attention to theological matters find the object of their attentions utterly attractive, sometimes to the point of obsession. That is understandable; theological thought systems at their best are majestic cultural achievements, powerfully synthetic and directly applicable to the many agonizing struggles of human life — a fact that would surprise many people, though no competent theologian. Knowing all that, however, makes theological literacy not one whit more attractive to most people. It is enough for most people to know that someone will dance with the theological wallflower; we each have our own romances with life under way that demand our energy and devotion.

There is one exquisitely painful aspect of this unattractiveness that is understood only by those who dabble in theology. To have one's hearing attuned by theological literacy and the study of religion to the point that the silent orienting and legitimating function of religion becomes persistently audible is to deconstruct some of the enjoyable and even precious processes in one's own spiritual life. Like a never ending stage whisper, it seriously disrupts the ability of religious practices to weave a mood of wonder. Of course, the loss of first naïveté in this way is not the tragedy; Paul Ricoeur was correct that a second naïveté can be achieved in which one draws the everlasting stage whisper of criticism into one's participation in the activity of the play. The tragedy is the loss of corporate fluency associated with first naïveté, which is never recovered in the usually highly individualistic second naïveté. Many who pass through the mysterious archway of theological literacy shrink from pressing farther into its wondrous halls for exactly this reason. This occurs in beginning seminary students, for example, whose theological fears are due not merely to a lack of seriousness about spiritual matters — though it is sometimes partly that — but also to a prescient intuition that loss of social fluency and then alienation might be some of the fruits of their striving to become theologically literate. It is a healthy reaction. I would look upon people who did not shrink from such a prospect with a suspicious curiosity and wager that they can be so cavalier about social alienation only because social fluency was never a notable feature of their lives, leaving them little to lose.

There is a general cultural need for specialists in theology (along with literature and sociology and all other special studies). This need is focused especially by the fact that certain religious or academic groups have a special interest in supporting the study of things theological, furnishing resources and communities with which to do it. Accordingly, none of what I have said

337

amounts to a case against theological literacy per se. It does, however, constitute a strong argument both against conceiving of theological literacy as a desirable goal for most people and against a policy of theological literacy for everyone. Islam understands that theological literacy is a luxury most people can ill afford because it is mostly irrelevant and unattractive. A relatively unhierarchical religion, Islam expresses its strong interest in supporting the lives of believers when it accords its relatively few theologians lowly status and instead throws its intellectual energy into the cultivation of intricate systems of law that help keep social life flowing smoothly, or at least justly.

So much for the relation between theological literacy and the general public, including most practicing religious people. But what about those church or synagogue folk who turn out for an adult education series on some theological topic (a small percentage of the membership)? What about the people who seek out books on religious topics because they want to educate themselves? Well, we takes what we can gets, as Popeye used to say. Such people range on a continuum from those having a passing interest in theological matters or feeling an urgent need to sort out theologically a crisis in their lives, to those who are curious enough to make theological literacy an avocation or even a profession. Supporting such interests makes good sense. If we give up the vain illusion that theological literacy should be for everyone in exchange for the more modest goal that means of achieving theological literacy should be available for anyone who wants to cultivate it, we are, I think, on firmer ground.

With this relatively relaxed approach to theological literacy in mind, it is interesting to note that there are many opportunities for cultivating theological literacy in simple ways. For example, common religious practices from pastoral care to sharing groups or Bible studies, though they do not in themselves necessarily involve much theological reflection, can sometimes lead into serious theological territory. Yet there is a problem here that needs to be brought into the open: full advantage can rarely be taken of such opportunities because good theological reflection is quite tricky. Consider the Bible study that usually involves relating texts read to personal life situations, an environment ideal for spiritual growth and building a sense of group cohesion. Such practices presuppose an enormous amount of theologically loaded connective material, without which it would be impossible to move so freely from an ancient text to people's living concerns in a very different cultural context. Actually being able to identify those theological assumptions usually is not important; the vital point is that they are shared by the group, thereby making possible higher-level corporate processes that build a sense of mutual belonging and help to establish or confirm each individual's beliefs. People who are too curious or argumentative about those assumptions are correctly felt to disrupt the group's optimal function and understandably are regarded affectionately as mavericks or — in extreme cases — even shunned. Occasionally, though, some theological assumptions are flushed into the open and become the topic of discussion.

If such a group reads the book of Job together, for instance, it would be understandable if the conversation turned to suffering or even to the nature of God — bona fide theological topics. But then there is a problem. Few will notice the contradiction between the God of literary convenience at the beginning and the God that defies description at the end of Job. The concluding portrayal of the abysmal, unapproachable divine discloses the literary fiction of a God who makes deals and plays with lives as a self-righteous, amoral being, worthy only of guarded respect and no love. Fewer will know enough about competing interpretations of suffering in human intellectual history to be able to assess Job's portrayal. And very few indeed will be interested in discerning that their own views of God and suffering are probably diagnosed in this book as inadequate, failing to register the dark, chaotic underside of the divine, trimming off the nasty bits that a Calvin or an Edwards understood in order to make God more palatable to current tastes. Serious theology always plays havoc with our deepest convictions, leaving no stone of concept or motivation unturned; it is a spiritually draining, intellectually demanding activity requiring learning and devotion that is capable of taking one past the pain of cognitive disruption. In spite of all these limitations of experience and insight, all in our hypothetical group will be fascinated. The conversation will be passionate; most will have something to say about how these momentous questions bear on their lives; and many will be left with a longing for more exploration of their fundamental assumptions, though simultaneously probably in dismay over their lack of resources to do that. Somehow, the people in this not-so-imaginary example are able to experience theological reflection as intriguing, yet the properly disturbing effects of ordinary theological reflection remain mostly unencountered and probably undesired.

Theological literacy, like science literacy or literacy in any complex subject, is hard to achieve. So why do the real consequences of serious theology take so long to manifest themselves? Why do novices think they are further along in theology than they really are? In this respect, the situation is quite unlike science literacy. A good science journalist can set a reader more or less on the right track fairly quickly without having to get into the amazingly complex details, yet the novice reader knows full well how far he or she is from being expert. The situation in theology is more akin to mathematics perhaps, in which serious work has almost nothing to do with the arithmetic and geometry with which one begins and in which there is almost no possibility of conveying the meaning of a specialized theorem for a general audience. Even before the beginning of a serious effort to become theologically literate, interested people probably already have had many theological thoughts and have tried to educate themselves with ready-at-hand resources. Their thoughts probably will have been disorganized and superficial from a theologically sophisticated point of view, yet their questions may have been the profound ones asked by seasoned theologians. It takes most theological students some time to discern both the senses in which their questions are truly profound and the superficiality of their former thinking. For sometime at the beginning, theological terminology and ways of thinking serve only to reattire existing convictions — that is partly what theological literacy A is about. The weight of theological wisdom takes time to be felt; it is like cultivating the continual awareness of one's own breath. It is not uncommon to hear advanced seminary students or even seasoned ministers offer theological reflections that extend little further, apart from terminological reclothing, than their poorly informed novice speculations would have taken them. Typically, many years of work are required before a novice's theological thinking passes over from the merely inspirational and confirmatory into being a potent force for transformation of one's deepest assumptions about reality. Moreover, though the novice theological learner may soundly intuit that a kind of alienation from the religious community awaits, the true difficulty of gaining theological literacy is not appreciated at all by beginners.

This point goes not to the unattractiveness of theological literacy but rather to the question of its feasibility as a goal for any but those aiming for a high level of competence. It also bears on the pedagogical challenge of making resources available to those who are interested in cultivating theological literacy. Both of these issues lead directly to the "Why bother?" question. Why bother to make available resources for cultivating theological literacy B at the basic level? Helping people merely to reexpress and then to confirm their existing beliefs through speaking about them differently — the most common consequence — is of dubious value. Perhaps we should not bother with theological education unless those who undertake it intend to go all the way, as it were. Or perhaps there is so-far-undiagnosed promise in theological literacy at the elementary level, the problems I have described notwithstanding. I think there is promise in theological literacy, though I believe it has challenging implications for theological and educational practice, as I hope to show.

The Promise of Theological Literacy

While worshiping recently in a mainline Protestant congregation, I heard a sermon that catalyzed for me the problem and promise of theological literacy. The preacher was working with the Acts account of the murder of Stephen. The wider context was the Colorado school shooting in April 1999 that so many within and beyond this congregation had found extremely disturbing. The Eucharist was to follow the sermon. It was a dramatic moment, at least for those attuned to the dynamic counterpoint of liturgy. One way or another, this sermon was going to lead us from dismay and anxiety to the eucharistic meal. What would the preacher say?

The message of the sermon was simple enough. We were encouraged to be more active sustainers of our own spiritual lives, thereby making ourselves both more resistant to the rancorous infighting (it *was* infighting, relatively speaking) that led to Stephen's death and better placed to heal a nation in uncomprehending dismay over its own children slaughtering each other. A lively spiritual depth is the key to love and healing, and the precondition for unity in religion and harmony in society. And the Eucharist is the place at which we are loved and healed, the source of the courage needed to love and heal in less safe territory.

I was grateful for the message. Upon reflection, I thought it probably comforted people in that congregation and gave them a constructive way of thinking about what might be done differently, albeit indirectly, to make a difference in the United States. It proclaimed an aspect of the Eucharist's meaning, held out the possibility of love and healing, and reminded congregants to take full and serious responsibility for what they could, beginning with their own lives.

Though the issues at stake are pregnant with both social and theological implications, the sermon contained no significant social or theological analysis. And why should it? The papers and pundits were full of social analyses, mostly insightful, that comforted no one. Those analyses in themselves changed nothing and had little impact on decisions made by schools and communities in the aftermath of the Columbine shootings; people's anxiety determined most of those policy adjustments. Why go through social analyses in a sermon? I think the preacher's judgment on that score was right on target, at least as far as meeting the needs of listeners on that occasion is concerned.

Theology might be even less promising territory for explicit sermonic exploration in this instance. Where do you turn? To Psalm-like complaints about the absence of divine intervention as the trigger squeezes? To Job-like accusations of mysterious divine standoffishness while children plunge into insane violence and social life screams down the cliff of culture wars and teenage disillusionment? To desperately wry observations of the late, safe divine arrival in the speeches of condemnation and the comforting of bereft parents in the arms of friends and siblings of the dead? To cheap speechifying about an ideal Christian social order? To the intransigence of sin and the uncontrollable emergence within complex societies of unintended effects? Or if we throw safety to the winds, refusing to immunize God from actual human suffering, should we turn instead to easy analogies with the murder of Jesus — Colorado sacrifices for the raising of consciousness? To divine judgment on societies rife with heartless overconsumption and cultural arrogance conjoined with video-game brain training in the ways of killing from an early age? Or do we forget divine action and theodicy and travel the routes of nonstandard theologies? We could deny that God is a living force who wants and acts in particular ways, which then necessarily leaves us in control of our own affairs. We could proclaim the gospel of deism wherein God creates a natural and moral order once and then leaves us to it, wondrous creatures threading our way through a glorious maze. We could promote God the great persuader, who is so impotent that divine inspiration is about the best we can expect.

My bet is that few in that congregation wanted to hear any of this. Everyone wanted to be comforted, everyone wanted to fix things, everyone wanted to understand why it happened, and everyone wanted to understand how God fitted into that tragic picture. But no one wanted actually to discover what is found by all theologians who keep working on the how-God-fits-into-the-picture question; namely, that we invent images of God to make ourselves feel better about our lives and that no one really knows much about the answer to the how-God-fits-into-the-picture question. We are left with acts of worshipful surrender, the strange world of the Bible (including David's psalmic complaining to God and Job's abandonment), and our own sweetly agonizing personal journeys through life's suffering, joys, and accidents. God is present as absence, as the blissful source of love, as the abysmal undoing of us all, as the fecund depths from which every chaotic and creative force emerges. Most people don't want decisive confirmation of their deep suspicions about how little we control, how noisily we cover our lack of knowledge, and how vainly we struggle against the limits on our existence. Nothing drives home those uncomfortable realizations more effectively than serious theology. It doesn't matter what the tradition or religion; when we think deeply and systematically about our situation and what it must mean about its fundamental nature, including divinity — in short, when we do serious theology — we always end up at roughly the same family of insights under various descriptions: we don't know much, we can't control much, we make things up to comfort ourselves, and we deny it all in amazingly sophisticated ways. How do you preach that? Who can blame the preacher for focusing the Columbine message on spiritual growth and change and bypassing social and theological analysis?

The problem with comforting sermons that challenge us in desirably limited ways is that most people know, deep down, not to believe them completely.

The reason for this is the same reason that theology consistently leads to a wilder, more unspeakably wondrous conception of God: our experience demands it. We might not want to know the truth but, when reality bites and we are face-to-face with the unmanageability of untamed divinity, only the comfort of truth will do. Suffering unmasks religion, its useful fictions and its comforting distractions, but it also drives us to the deep power of religion, to the secret it treasures and protects, to the fragile heart of human togetherness that is always at some level a blessed huddling-around-the-fire-against-the-dark companionship. At those moments when our hearts are laid bare, only two things matter, and in a very important order. First, we need to survive, to get through it. For that, nothing is better than the loving support of friends and family. Second, we need to understand, and to understand differently than we are given to understand in the usual course of events. Our questions are the same as ever but kaleidoscopically rearranged by the absolute conviction of the futility of simply comforting answers; only the searing heat of truth can comfort when normalcy is unmasked. Once touched by this curiosity, I think, few are satisfied ever again with the soothing comfort of religious distractions, and they learn to see the deeper truths to which religious practices point.

Here we come, then, to the promise of theological literacy. Far beyond merely giving people new words to strengthen their defenses against life's translucency to divine power, theology can speak the truth that life is at the mercy of the divine. Theology introduces its serious students to traditions of thought in which the unspeakable mystery is only ever named in anticipation of the collapse of all words, to traditions of poetry and disciplined argumentation, to careful distinctions and brilliant metaphors that express the unending wonders of the divine. Those students are invited to engage this mystery with every ounce of heart, soul, mind, and strength, not merely for the comfort of simple, confirming insights, but for the sake of the love of life's greatest enigma, God — though he slay me, yet will I trust in him. When only the truth will do, nothing has the potential to unmask, to transform, and to evoke responsibility like theology.

Consequences for Theological Education

The parent bereft of a young teenage child meets with the rabbi. The rabbi is skillful. Knowing how to listen and speak in time with the cross-rhythms of grief and fury, the rabbi wins trust, and there is nothing more sacred in such moments. The grieving parent wants to understand — not to know why, as if life's contingencies answer to our demands, but to know how to live in a world with such proportions, and to know how to love and trust a creator God whose own character must be configured in the world's. This parent needs to know and so implicitly entrusts the rabbi with longings and despair, with suspicions about a social fabric full of constructed comforts and valuable distractions, with a simple plea for understanding supported by an instinctive confidence that an offer of evasive comfort will be easy to detect and spurn. Heart in hand, this parent wants to know if it is really so, if the world really is as he or she now thinks it must be. The rabbi has a choice: comfort with half-truths or earn the trust that has been offered.

The question for those interested in theological literacy is whether the rabbi is ready to let the truth be seen unmasked for a moment, configured in the shape of this tragic loss. If survival of the parent were the only goal, it wouldn't matter much what the rabbi did so long as love that binds was able to flow between these two people. But understanding is also the goal in this case, and no amount of communal support can cause understanding to come forth. Only serious theology will do. A rabbi who is not seriously theologically literate will fail both to earn the trust already won with pastoral skills and to diagnose the reason for this failure. In fact, such a rabbi will probably fail even to notice that trust has been squandered in the name of conventional comforts, not least because the grieving parent will doubtless be somewhat comforted by conventional answers even as, with an elusive feeling of confusion, he or she realizes that something is wrong. Of course something is wrong: theological dullness at best and personal betrayal at worst. Without theological literacy — serious theological literacy — moments of trust like this can never be earned. With it, however, the rabbi has the chance to bring the greatest comfort of all, to let the glory of God be glimpsed in this moment as from the cleft of a rock. Such a vision immeasurably deepens the perception of the grieving parent through confirming the unspoken instincts that drive the urge to know the truth.

The rabbi, the pastor, the priest, the cleric, the monk, the guru — will they be ready? Have they been freed by serious theology from their own intoxication with being professional religious gatekeepers, released from their entrapment in endless circles of sophisticated denial and ritual comforts, liberated from the chains of vain God-concepts and ready answers that soothe the answerer as much as the answered? Theological literacy by itself cannot cause such wisdom and readiness, but without serious immersion in theology it is almost impossible to achieve. The goal of making theological literacy available to those who seek it requires religious leaders who are themselves seriously theologically literate — local theologians who know that theology discloses a God who undoes our pretensions to divine knowledge and patiently defies our convenient systems of ideas. At least three conditions need to be met in theological education if religious leaders are to have such readiness.

First, theological education of religious leaders must aim for more than mere knowledge of theological terminology and history, which is the bread and butter of theological literacy A. The ability to think theologically — theological literacy B — presupposes such knowledge but requires in addition the curiosity and persistence of determined inquiry. Every presupposition must be called into question as needed, and arguments must be constructed to support new configurations of assumptions. The guidance of tradition should be just that, guidance, and no pretense should be made that a historical formulation of doctrine is somehow timeless; all historical-cultural formulations are necessarily limited, and even more so when the topic is the divine.

Second, theological education of religious leaders must aim to be constructive, applying theological resources to new problems and also to familiar problems in new contexts. Each person must think for himself or herself, making a unique path through the complex theological terrain, checked along the way by all the well-known landmarks by which all theological adventurers travel. In so journeying, careful attention must be paid to context, which conditions both which formulations count as relevant and what conceptual and cultural resources are available for theological reflection.

Third, theological education of religious leaders must aim to evoke spiritual alertness. The skills of inquiry and independent, context-sensitive thinking are not enough by themselves to make a religious leader ready to open up the truth for people when those extraordinary moments of trust occur. It is necessary also to sense what matters, to detect the heart of an issue, to be revolted or delighted by the unexpected. Spiritual alertness conjoined with theological literacy causes everything in life and ministry to be seen differently. The toothpaste section of the typical Western supermarket aisle with its unending varieties might induce sudden nausea, and the deformed child at play, a blast of joy — experiences supported immediately by the capacity to analyze those reactions in theological terms. There is so much hiding from our dependence on nature in that excessive display of toothpaste (or hair colors or bread varieties or breakfast cereals), and the blessed triumph of simple fun in the face of limitations sings through the child at play. Spiritual alertness is, for the theologically literate, the prospector's metal detector and the bloodhound's nose.

Consequences for Theological Work

A member of the general public does not expect to be able to read with much understanding any specialized academic work. Such works are highly conventional, conditioned and actually enabled by densely elaborated semiotic codes

345

into which novices must initiate themselves for years before they can make a contribution at the cutting edge of debate. This is as true in theology as in the humanities or the social and natural sciences. Yet there is wonder in these specialized academic studies, springs of delight that would remain more or less secret were it not for a breed of communicators who spread the word as journalists or as the authors of popular and semipopular books. The largest and most adept group of popular communicators presents the secrets of the natural sciences to the general public, but there are smaller groups working with medicine, archaeology, psychology, religion, and so on. The group of popular writers trying to present theology and the Bible for the general public, especially Christians, is actually very large. Specialized Christian bookstores exist to promote and distribute such books, and many magazines and other periodicals do the same.

This body of popular work has several notable features, on average — though this is the result of my own impressions and not of a scientifically thorough survey. Most material is written by and for conservative evangelical or fundamentalist Christians. Much of it is intended to help people relate Christian insights to everyday matters of life and faith. Most of it is colorfully opinionated — a great virtue in my view — and closely related to the interpretation of biblical wisdom on each subject discussed. It is quite rare to see much at all about theology in these works. When theology does appear, it is very definitely aimed to help people acquire theological literacy of type A by introducing key episodes in the history of Christian doctrine or important contemporary debates about issues such as the authority of Scripture or denominational identity. This body of literature is aimed well, I would say: these books correctly assume that most readers are not interested in theology per se, but in making use of Christian faith and the Bible to cope better and to be happier, more productive, and more loving people.

It is extremely unusual to find popular books promoting theological literacy of type B in any bookstore, whether religious or secular. Certain periodicals such as *Christian Century* and *Christianity Today* do a little of that, but these tend to be aimed more at religious professionals and highly educated Christian thinkers than at a general audience; I have never known an ordinary church person to read them, though such readers must exist. From what I have said about the problem of theological literacy B, this dearth of books disclosing the secret wonders of profound theological reflection is far from surprising; in fact, it is completely predictable. Yet I wonder if there is not a market niche that might be filled with introductory presentations of some of the subtler joys of profound theology. It may well be a market niche having little to do with church people and better suited to religiously alienated or spiritually curious folk, people who have perhaps been too appalled by religious protectiveness about the realities of life to be able to remain in regular attendance at worship services.

With this, then, I join my voice to those of others who, in recent years, have urged theologians to commit themselves to more openness with the general public about the wonders of theology. True, most people may not be interested and some might even have an allergic reaction to the unsettling dimensions of serious theology, but there are people interested in subtler, more penetrating ways of thinking about the ultimate concerns of their lives and of existence generally.

That such serious theological work has been so little comprehended and even encountered by potentially interested people raises some thought-provoking questions. The situation is not much like that of mathematics, in which there is an almost insurmountable communication problem associated with conveying esoteric results. It is rather the twofold problem of people not wanting to know conjoined with people not wanting to tell. Well, we can dismiss the first part of this problem as intractable because the audience for serious theology conveyed in a popular style would be self-selecting anyway. But why are theologians so reluctant to spill the beans about, for instance, a God so far beyond human comprehension that religion, as Karl Barth rightly said, is a mere striving after the divine? Is it to protect religious people from the blinding reality of God? Is this reticence for the sake of the protection of religious communions, groups assumed by secretive theologians to be so fragile that self-knowledge would threaten or dissolve them?

The silence of the theologians most certainly is *not* because they do not know what is going on; all serious theologians know these basic insights from the domain of theology and ponder them as they write and teach. To attempt an explanation of why they stay quiet, I shall describe briefly what theologians know about just one of the issues mentioned a couple of times above — the social construction of reality. Subsequently, I shall mention a few other secrets that theologians seem reluctant to bring out into the open, a reluctance that blocks the general public's chances of developing theological literacy of type B.

The sociology of knowledge has made it abundantly clear through the work of scholars such as Peter Berger and Thomas Luckmann that humans construct their social reality. A theological interpretation of this basic result can be developed by likening cultural constructions to the earth's ozone layer. As the fragile ozone shields the earth from harmful high-energy radiation while allowing safer light to warm and power the ecosphere, so do the social constructions of human beings protect both individuals and corporate life from the harsher dimensions of reality while simultaneously allowing enough truth through to illumine and power personal and cultural creativity. Moreover, formal religions and informal religious or spiritual activities are key components in the construction of this protective cultural ozone layer. They promote engagement with the divine reality out of which emerges the complex wonder of our lives even as they protect us from the full glory of this reality. When the chaotic or the awesome breaks through into our lives, as it does often enough, the ozone thins and the socially constructed world becomes more translucent to the bright glory of God, at least for some. Such light sears and, in pain and awe, we blessedly never forget. This is as clear a fact of life as any other. I speak of this bright mystery on the other side of our protective social constructions as God, but for present purposes I could live happily enough with many accounts of it — as nature's fecund depths, as the mystic's unspeakable mystery, as the power of being itself — so long as they were properly empirical about explaining this fundamental feature of human experience. Any such account allows theology room to move, though not necessarily a particular religion's version of theology.

This theological interpretation of the socially constructed character of human social and religious life is well understood by theologians. Ludwig Feuerbach knew it and registered with Karl Marx the aspect of G. W. F. Hegel's thought — as Hegel resonated with the aspects of Immanuel Kant's thought — in which this awareness exists. Sigmund Freud, Max Weber, and Émile Durkheim knew it with complete conviction, as has every psychologist and sociologist since. Theologians who have paid attention to the development of human intellectual life since the Enlightenment have seen and understood all of this, beginning with Friedrich Schleiermacher. Barth was the great trailblazer of this awareness in twentieth-century theology, as well as the advocate of a solution that captured the imagination of a generation of theologians precisely because his followers felt such desperate need for a wholehearted solution. Barth's solution proved too unrealistic about the need to connect theology and culture in mutually critical correlation (to use the phrase David Tracy introduced to enhance Paul Tillich's account of this relation). Since Barth's time, however, all serious theologians know about the social construction of reality and religion's role in that; they think their theological thoughts with this intellectual heritage as a vital conditioning factor.

Despite these thoughts being well understood among theologians, it is hardly surprising, in view of the challenging conceptual content, that theologians have felt the need to harbor this knowledge as a secret. Religious groups find it intensely disturbing to become aware of their own psychic processes at work in the social realm, and doubly so when this awareness is extended to the religious domain. As I have said, such self-knowledge disturbs valuable processes that function better when we remain unaware of them. Yet the pretense becomes futile after a while, at least for the growing numbers who sense these dynamics within the ordinary processes of religious groups. Western children are educated under these assumptions about human psychology and group life, and for most, such insights become reflexively automatic aspects of their youthful self-interpretation. It is pitiful to watch young men and women, as I have often done, plead for honesty from their religious leaders without really knowing that this is what they are doing. Though they don't want to read complex theological treatises, they do long to know that their precious religious experiences can be coordinated intelligibly with what they know otherwise about the world they inhabit. This also enrages me; the churches and synagogues can never do better with their young people so long as they insist on blocking the youthful urge to synthesize the apparently conflicting insights their experiences have brought them. The same goes for those upon whom life has visited special tragedy: comfort only works with such souls when it is as deep as the truth that divides between bone and marrow.

Well, so much for theological secretiveness about the social construction of reality and why I think it is a bad idea. But there are other theological secrets, too, whose disclosure to the general public would dramatically change the odds of ordinary people developing theological literacy B when the circumstances of life provoke that interest.

First, the hermeneutical complexity associated with interpreting the Bible is well understood by all thoughtful theologians. Almost all books specifically on the Bible published for the general public tackle refined debates about the inspiration and inerrancy of Scripture and mention only in passing the hermeneutical complexities taken for granted by all mainstream theologians, whether liberal or conservative, Jewish or Christian. This is a scandal as far as public communication is concerned. Any person studying high school literature in any language already knows much of this complex hermeneutical terrain, and it is worse than absurd that serious Christian theologians are unable to be both frank and helpful about this. Fundamentalists battling over esoteric details of the doctrine of biblical inerrancy amount to little more than shrill whining when we notice how useless those debates are for actually helping people to interpret the Bible responsibly. Theologians for the most part have abdicated this territory to the effete but noisy debates of a cultural backwater.

Second, the history of the development of religious doctrines is also well understood by all serious mainstream theologians. In relation to Christianity, the trailblazers in this regard are John Henry Cardinal Newman and Adolf von Harnack. Despite their profound disagreements about the truth of certain doctrines, they firmly agreed that Christian doctrine develops and that this devel-

349

opment cannot be explained as a mere logical outworking of already established doctrines. Their explanations differed — Newman stressed the regulative role of the supernaturally authorized teaching office of the pope, whereas Harnack emphasized the contingencies of historical circumstance — but both knew, as all theologians know, that there is historical dynamism in the development of Christian doctrine. Now, thoughtful people intuitively know that historical contingencies and balancing competing interests must be involved in giving official expression to the beliefs of a religious group. Yet doctrines are typically presented simply as given, once for all, as if from heaven, unmediated by any of the usual factors involved in messy social transactions. The risk theologians would take by speaking frankly of this knowledge might be the stimulation of questions about the teaching authority of the church. But the risk they take by staying silent is convincing thoughtful people that Christian intellectual life is divorced from common sense.

Third, serious theology has almost always had a constructive and appreciative relationship with the natural sciences. This secret is deeply buried beneath the noisy, media-sustained rhetoric of conflict inspired by a few extreme instances of real conflict such as the Christian church versus Galileo on the solar system and various biblical literalists versus biologists on evolutionary theory. However, as patient scholarship has shown, the Roman Catholic Church's handling of the Galileo affair was far more gracious and reasonable than is usually assumed. Moreover, Christian theologians came around fairly quickly on the solar system issue. Even the recent Roman Catholic apology for the Galileo affair too often is received cynically. Commentators usually fail to note that, years before the official apology, the Vatican established a world-class observatory and trained excellent cosmologists, astronomers, and astrophysicists as a way of indicating its seriousness about setting matters right. With regard to evolution, biblical literalists to the contrary notwithstanding, historical analysis has shown that most theologians adjusted fairly well to the arrival of evolutionary biology, being well acquainted already with concepts of historical and cultural development from other fields. Some greeted Darwin with enthusiasm, quickly developing theologies that simply presumed evolutionary biology. Most saw no problem imagining that God could create through the evolutionary process. Yet most in the general public simply are not aware of this, nor that theology in all religious traditions has worked in close alliance with natural science since the very beginning. A few theologians are trying to get this secret out to the general public's attention, but greater effort is needed to break through popular habits of thought on this question.

Finally, the greatest theological secret of all is the impossibility of an exhaustively rational description of the divine. Virtually all theologians in all religious traditions hold this view, which is not one whit different from the view of great poets and artists in every time and place. The general public senses it for themselves, the more so when they venture to the art gallery, read their favorite poems, or find themselves utterly incapable of giving expression to their most profound experiences. Yet theologians are most often thought of as people who brashly, presumptuously, and obscurely dare to speak of the unspeakable, without any misgivings or self-restraint. And theologians are thought of this way because religious groups, especially Christian churches, are filled with God-talk that is usually more confident than it has reason to be. Such confident speech has a profound influence on the average religious believer, who adopts formulations offered with little awareness of their limitations. Islam does better in this regard, speaking bluntly about the imagination-defying richness of the divine, centralizing the ninety-nine names in religious practice so as to keep the mind from settling overconfidently on a single image of God. Judaism's reticence about the divine nature is differently effective in disrupting the grasping tendency of human imagination. Taoism, Buddhism, and mysticism in all traditions explicitly deconstruct concepts of ultimate reality. Christian theologians know much more about the impossibility of conceptually tying down the divine than their silence in the public domain indicates. The complex theological systems used by theologians are not developed in defiance of the ultimate futility of the God-talk task. Rather, they are developed to say what might be said as well as possible, but all serious theologians know that human theologies are born hovering above, and always eventually collapse into, the divine abyss beneath human existence. I do not see why this cannot be spoken of more frankly among the general public, not merely by novelists and poets but by theologians themselves.

I conclude that theologians' reticence to speak more frankly about theology for the general public is wrongheaded. The desire among many theologians not to disrupt important social processes within religious groups is commendable. But protecting the identity of a religious group is shortsighted when the cost involves its leaders' inability to be ready to speak the truth when needed and its members' inability to imagine the cloth of their lives as of one piece. Of course, it is hard to do serious theology knowing what theologians know, and it is difficult to convey religious truth when real caveats and complications are involved. But that's no excuse. Theologians have to speak clearly, with no obfuscation and no presumptuous protectiveness, if religious leaders and all interested people are to have a chance of becoming theologically literate in the type B way. Such clarity of purpose and frankness about the challenging complexities of serious theology is long overdue.

CHAPTER NINETEEN

Wisdom for Life:
The Horizon of Theological Literacy

THOMAS GROOME

I take it that the concern prompting this volume is more for public theological literacy than for the training of professional theologians, for reaching beyond the guild to make more literate the general populace in matters theological. With this most public of "publics" in mind, I begin by placing in the foreground some perspectives that shape my own view of theological education. Gadamer, who advises such foregrounding of one's preunderstanding, might call them "prejudices" — though he uses the term in a positive sense; my perspectives certainly prompt some strong convictions. By making them explicit at the outset, I will have "shown my hand" for what follows; among other things, this is more honest to the reader than feigning an objective view. And such an issue makes patent that there is "no view from no where."[1]

First, my alleged expertise is at the interface of theology and education. Some of my friends call me a "religious educator," others a "pastoral theologian" — and others use unrepeatable appellations. Whatever the title, I have a passionate concern for *what* and *how* and *why* religious communities educate in their traditions of faith — in their theologies. So, my defining interest can be stated well as public theological education. However, my concern leads me to pay more attention to the noun "education" than I find typical among theologians (reflecting how they themselves were educated). The reigning paradigm of theological education pays intense attention to the content of theology but little to how or why to educate therein. This neglect of pedagogy is at least ironic in that theology is inherently educational — its nature and purpose im-

---

1. I take this phrase from Lorraine Code, "Taking Subjectivity into Account," in *Feminist Epistemologies*, ed. Linda Alcoff and Elizabeth Potter (New York: Routledge, 1993).

pel that it be taught — and surely diminishes the effectiveness of all theological education. More on this below; for now, it is enough to alert the reader that by existential condition as well as by invitation of the editors, I write about theological literacy from the perspective of a religious *educator.*

Second, I am sadly convinced that theology holds scant if any interest for the public at large and fares little better among "people in the pews." In fact, may I submit that the editors of this volume have understated an urgent issue with the theme of *theological literacy — its content and horizons?* The pressing question is not, in what should people be theologically informed? — literate — but rather, why is there so little public interest in theology? or even, why might the public give more than a whit about theology? To focus on the content of theological literacy — overlooking the pervasive disinterest — might be "to fiddle while Rome burns" (again).

Humankind is clearly as much in need as ever of religious symbols, concepts, and commitments to find meaning and purpose in life, and to figure out "who is my neighbor." Yet theology is increasingly viewed as irrelevant by people of postmodern cultures — even as a bit of a joke. Why is theology sent to the margins — if not off the page entirely — while many sciences (from anthropology to zoology) have been mainstreamed into popular consciousness and language? Of course, we theologians are convinced that it should be otherwise, but meanwhile, except for a rarefied few, the public of society and even the public of the church find us anachronous to everyday life.

Now, I will cite no empirical surveys to support my claim: my sense of the public disinterest comes more from "straw in the wind" experiences and impressions. For example, on planes or trains or at neighborhood gatherings when a stranger asks, "What do you do?" and I say, "I'm a theologian," their response is invariably awkward, as if I'm somehow out of place and they didn't expect to find me "here." Often they intimate some surprise that such a creature still exists, or that theology could be considered a scholarly profession. When I offer the apologia, "Actually, it's a very exciting and creative field," the typical response — when polite — is the kind of sentiment one might have for a quaint but dying species. They say, "How interesting," but you suspect they mean ". . . as paper clips."

Or walk the aisles of a mall bookstore. You will find there the most advanced scholarship of the human, social, and natural sciences, written in language accessible to the nonspecialist, and obviously selling well (the book chains return what is not "moving" within a month). It seems that other scientists have learned to communicate beyond their specialized discourses and scholarly journals, to reach out to a broad public. But alas, little or no theology is to be found in Barnes & Noble or Borders. A reliable rumor is that publishers now estimate the total sale of a theology book in North America — a best-seller — at 13,000 copies, a pittance compared to the population.

Oh, indeed, according to Wall Street, *spirituality* is now considered a "growth industry" in the United States (with annual sales reaching $10 billion), and the bookstores are laden with its texts. This only attests that what theologians "do" might still be of interest to the public; clearly we are not engaging people's spiritual needs and religious appetites.[2] So my second perspective is that theology is now perceived as irrelevant to contemporary public life. However, rather than filing for endangered species protection, we must address why, and imagine and forge a better possibility.

My third perspective — following from the second — is that for theology to warrant public interest and significance, it must be structured and taught in ways that engage people's lives and the social reality of their time and place. It must represent itself in the context of what matters to people living in today's world, addressing its themes to the questions of the human condition, communicating, as Aquinas would advise, "according to the mode of the receiver." And I'm likely committing a tautology by stating that this is not how theology is typically taught nor how theologians have been prepared to teach it.

For people to learn in ways that affect their "being" — as noun and verb, who they are and how they live — they must personally appropriate the knowledge at hand, and this, in turn, requires that they be interested (and "the emperor has no clothes"). Many of the great educational reformers have emphasized the necessity of "student interest" for effective learning, but none more forcefully than Johann Herbart (1776-1841); both Dewey and Montessori noted their indebtedness to Herbart on this point. Paulo Freire, likely the most influential educator of the latter part of the twentieth century, echoed the same sentiment, insisting that all education — if it is to humanize and be socially significant — must engage the "generative themes" of people's lives.

And there are surely a thousand empirically based dissertations on education attesting that people learn most effectively what is of real interest to them. This truism may be even truer in the pragmatic ethos of our own time. Oh, we can lament the dominance of a technical rationality, so concerned with "what works," or the triumph of a "free-market economy" and its sole interest in "cash value." Meanwhile, the fact remains that pedants intent on learning for its own

---

2. Apparently, theology was symbiotic with spirituality for the first thousand years or so of the Christian era. Then, when theology shifted its primary locus from the monastery to the university, it divorced itself from spirituality — in the interest of greater scholarship. Though I will not develop the point here, there is surely need for rapprochement — for the sake of both.

sake are indeed few and far between. Theologians certainly cannot count on them to amount to a public.

To address theology to people's interests need not and should not mean the reductionism of teaching only what people are interested in. As Dewey cautioned on this point, the educator must maintain a dialectic between addressing the personal interests of the learners and arousing their interest in what should be taught. The theological curriculum I ought to teach (to honor the texts, to represent the tradition, etc.) is often, at first, "not that interesting" to my students — especially to undergraduate theologians — but I work mightily to engender their interest, knowing that without it they will learn very little.

How does one generate lively interest in theological themes and topics that could otherwise sound esoteric or irrelevant? To reiterate my third perspective: by presenting theology as addressing people's lives in their time and place. For example, the christological concept of *homoousios* could be taught simply as a theoretical concept to be understood with some rational clarity; and I sense that most theological educators would settle for as much. On the other hand, it could also be represented as an issue of great existential import — which its original protagonists realized, with the butcher and baker debating it in the marketplace. The notion could hold powerful significance for what it means to live humanly; it could be a life-giving antidote in a society that demeans the human condition and is bereft of a humanizing eschatology. To say that this Jesus, who was truly one of ourselves, was also "true God from true God, one in being with the Father" is surely significant and magnificent for who *we are* and *can become* by God's grace in Jesus. Why, it holds the portent of our own *theosis* — growing in divine likeness. If not presented within the ambit of some such existential human interest, then *homoousios* becomes an impressive term to drop at a cocktail party; but such is no longer, if it ever was, sufficient motivation to theological literacy.

Following on, my fourth perspective is that the existential consequences of theological literacy should be life-giving for persons and societies. Here we reach far beyond the intent of "faith seeking *understanding*," as Anselm would have it, and later I propose the intended learning outcome of theology as "wisdom for life." For now I note that *understanding* is simply not enough, and certainly not the rational clarity championed by the Enlightenment. In Lonergan's terms, the dynamics of theological education must push beyond attending and understanding, prompting people to judgment and inviting their decisions as well. The guiding intent throughout its dynamics of cognition should be life-enhancing for persons and society.

Theology being one of the great liberal arts, its purpose could be stated philosophically as humanization: that theological literacy should enable people's efforts to make and keep life human for self and others. Or, in more theological terms, being literate in theology should have salvific effects for persons and societies. Echoing such sentiments, I summarize in a pithy phrase that the intent of theological literacy should be "for life for all." Any lesser purpose will be unfaithful to theology's religious traditions and unworthy of people's interest. Again at the risk of a tautology, with the notable exception of the liberation theologies, such life-giving intent — personal and social — is not now identified as the raison d'être of theology.

Let us now move toward the topic as posed: (a) What content would constitute theological literacy for the twenty-first century? and (b) what horizon does this present for theological education? I respond with reflections on why theology seems irrelevant to postmodernity, focusing on the ambivalent legacy of the Enlightenment for theological education; then, moving toward a new horizon, I propose "wisdom for life" as the defining content of theology; I conclude by outlining a pedagogy that might enhance the likelihood of such theological literacy.

The Enlightenment Legacy:
A Mixed Bag for Theological Education

There is some irony that the Enlightenment legacy of critical reason has turned its guns upon the Enlightenment itself — and not with "friendly fire." Let me avoid, however, joining the fashionable chorus of strident critique of the whole movement and the "modernity" that it spawned. I affirm the values of the Enlightenment era — liberty, equality, fraternity — and its intellectual assets; it laid the foundation of the academic freedom that makes possible the whole enterprise of contemporary theology and critical biblical scholarship. It fueled the egalitarian sentiment that theology be open to all and function as a public discourse subject to the canons of reason. And not least, the Enlightenment put in place the intellectual conditions for the science and technology we now enjoy so much — including this word processor on which I'm writing.

We also do well to avoid a nostalgic postmodernism which pretends that all would be well — as in some "good old days" — if we would but erase the Enlightenment. On the other hand, there was an underside to the Enlightenment/modernity project, now so forcefully raised up by postmodern critics — its idolatry of reason alone, its canonizing of the subject, its mechanizing of nature, its myth of inevitable progress, and more. For our interest here, however, I confine myself to its negative legacy for education in general and for theological education in particular. For all of the Enlightenment's educational assets, for example, "dare to think," it bequeathed some severe limitations; they explain, at least in part, why the public is not much interested in theology and why present theological education is not likely to arouse their interest.

In sum, *the Enlightenment's problematic for education was its severing of knowledge and the processes of knowing from the historical contexts of life.* The Enlightenment championed knowledge that was abstract; it aspired to transcendentals above the fray of history; it presumed that knowledge is scholarly and scientific precisely to the degree that it does not consider the social context, involve the feelings, or affect the character of the knowers. It assumed that critical reason could provide "objective" knowledge, lending clear and distinct ideas, and with an aura of rational certainty. In fact, the Enlightenment considered its severing of "knowledge" from "knower" and "world known" — the epistemic from the ontic and social — as one of its great achievements.

There was a time in Western philosophy when human "knowing" and "being" were considered symbiotic, that knowledge was to arise from and reflect life, and likewise to guide and influence people in living humanly. Plato insisted passionately that all knowing should serve human well-being, that knowledge ought to promote happiness by helping people to realize what is true, choose what is good, and create what is beautiful. He insisted that what people know should shape how they live, and that their lives in the world stimulate their knowledge.

Aristotle, star pupil of Plato, also insisted that knowledge should enhance the human condition and promote happiness. Though his emphasis was on life leading to knowledge in contrast to Plato's emphasis on knowledge as guide for living, Aristotle agreed with his teacher on the symbiosis between knowledge and life in the world. For Aristotle, people's lives in their social context are their first source of knowledge, and what they know should shape their very being and the whole body politic.[3]

The ancient integration of life and knowledge held together, at least tenuously, throughout subsequent centuries but eventually ran aground on the shores of Enlightenment rationality. Then emerged what the philosopher William Barrett has called "the triumph of reason," and he meant reason as functioning by its own dynamic, apart from the existential life of the knower or the context of history. The move was to trust only in the mind, excluding feelings, experiences, or social considerations. Further, the Enlightenment narrowed mind to reason alone, depreciating memory and imagination as untrustworthy.

The French philosopher René Descartes (1596-1650), with his founda-

---

3. It is worth noting that both Plato and Aristotle wrote about education within the category of politics.

tional dictum "I think, therefore I am," epitomized such narrow rationalism. This one great "absolutely certain idea" was to serve as "an unshakable foundation" from which to deduce all knowledge, to solve human problems, and to conquer nature. Thereafter, reason standing alone — separated from memory and imagination, from the body and feelings, from human experience and the social context, from tradition and community, claiming to be objective, and neutral as in value-free — became the reigning epistemology.

At first theology was wary of canonizing such rationality; its sense of tradition and community as authorities of truth was counter to the ahistorical and disconnected epistemology of the Enlightenment. Eventually, however, theology embraced the Enlightenment project for the assets it could lend to critical scholarship. And, as noted, it has such assets, but it has at least four unfortunate liabilities as well; my following points are cumulative.

First, theology began to see itself as a theoretical science seeking rational and universal knowledge about God — transcendental verities through critical reason. It became abstract in the sense that its truths were considered removed from life, neither arising from nor necessarily concerned about the everyday. Perhaps theology's findings might be "applied," but from the outside in, having been derived above the frenzy of social interest or human experience. Theology's intent was clarity of ideas to be presented with an air of intellectual certainty rather than as wisdom for life to be lived in faith.[4]

Second, and following on, everyday experience was disparaged as a source of theological knowledge, as unreliable because unscholarly and nontheoretical. Reflecting a Cartesian methodology, the starting premise was great ideas that had been revealed, one way or another, and then the theologian deducing from them and rippling out into more ideas. Note: this is why the emerging praxis-based theologies — liberationist, feminist, womanist — are, among other things, a major shift in theological method: they begin with reflection on life and social praxis.

Third, as might be expected, such theology presented itself and was experienced by ordinary people as the domain of experts, of scholars. The training and expertise of the latter conferred on them an epistemic privilege over the nonscholars — who depended on the experts for reliable theological knowledge. There was little inkling that spiritual wisdom could arise from people's common sense or that God's Spirit was present in everyday lives and ordinary places — nor even that such would be of interest to theology.

Fourth, within the functional specialties of theology itself, systematics,

---

4. This would be in stark contrast to Christian theology throughout its first thousand years; then the primary intent was spiritual wisdom.

the Bible, and history were viewed as truly scholarly endeavors, whereas the function of pastoral or practical theology was simply to apply the truths derived from the more theoretical disciplines. Reflecting Kant's separating of theoretical from practical reason, the scholarly instances of theology presumed methodologically that they must be free of pastoral interest, whereas pastoral theology — without scholarship in its own right — came to be viewed as a skill at delivery. This dichotomy and hierarchical ordering between the theoretical and practical has been debilitating for all theology, diminishing its ability to engage people's lives with any sense of relevance.

Nowhere were these negative legacies felt more intensely than in the practice of theological education; though they influenced theological method, they especially shaped how it was taught. In gist, the paradigm became one of teachers "delivering" lectures as summaries of ideas to be absorbed by students — imparting and receiving — with no intentional dynamic of active student participation, personal engagement, or appropriation to one's life or society. In terms of Lonergan's schema of the dynamics of cognition, theological education settled for understanding — and a very intellectualized version thereof — and though judgment and existential decision might be desirable, the latter were not integral to the pedagogy. The upshot was a "learning about" theology rather than learning from it for life, without intentional formation in the habitus of "doing theology" in an ecclesial and social context.[5] Such pedagogy was a significant diminishment from previous eras.[6]

The negative legacies of the Enlightenment — and thus the theological education they encouraged — have received devastating critique from postmodernist authors and from many who would refuse this designation. In fact, there is now a broad consensus in Western consciousness that the Enlightenment's claim to an object, i.e., value-free, privileged, and ahistorical rationality, was at least naive, and its separating of theoretical from practical reason was downright dangerous in that it left scholarship without responsibility, science

---

5. Here I am echoing a lament of Edward Farley; see *Theologia* (Philadelphia: Fortress, 1983).

6. The teacher-centered and monologue style of teaching around ideas was in contrast to the more conversational and student-participative mode that marked how theology was taught in the first universities. The *quaestio* method of the Scholastic era — taking a controversial or complex issue and having the students debate it — was said to cause near riots at the University of Paris. Elements of such pedagogy have been retained and developed in medical and legal education — which, with theology, were the three great professional faculties of the early universities. Perhaps it is not too late for theology to learn something from its old partners. And being "lectured at" was distinctly different from the Socratic methods favored by the Carolingian schools of the ninth century, and a world away from the prayerful and personal engagement demanded by the *lectio divina* of the monasteries.

without an ethic. It is widely recognized that: instead of being objective, all knowledge is perspectival, permeated by the personal interest and social ideology of the knowers; instead of being value-free, no knowledge is "innocent" but intertwines with systems of power, favoring some to the neglect of others; instead of a privileged group or starting point for knowledge, anyone can know from anywhere;[7] instead of being ahistorical, knowledge always reflects its sociocultural site in time and place.

Further, there are mighty efforts afoot to reunite the theoretical and practical, knowledge with historical responsibility. In this regard, I have already drawn upon Lonergan's work, but the literature I find most compelling on the responsibilities of knowledge and an antidote to all false dualisms comes from feminist epistemologists.[8] On another front, Gadamer has led the argument that hermeneutics — interpretation and explanation of texts and of life — should have the interest of "application" from the beginning and throughout if we are to nurture *phronesis* as wisdom for life.

And let us recognize that there always were voices and communities of resistance within theology to the Enlightenment agenda; such reserve has recently flourished. Now there is hopeful evidence that the ideational paradigm is being replaced by an approach that dialectically unites theory and praxis and prioritizes the historical responsibilities of all Christian theology. This invites theologians, regardless of their specialty, to consciously engage their sociocultural context, to be aware of its influence on their theologizing, to be intentional about what their scholarship means for life and the world. However, though this paradigm shift is taking place at a noetic level, it is yet to be reflected in the dynamics of theological education — in its pedagogy. And surely what is taught as theology, and how and why it is taught, is the nub of the whole issue of theological literacy.

Theological Literacy as Wisdom for Life

Paulo Freire (1927-97) is identified as the great exponent of modern-day literacy education. Freire mounted a devastating critique of traditional methods of teaching literacy. In sum, he claimed that they give people the skill of reading, but in a mechanical, nonreflective, and nonhumanizing way. Instead, he proposed a mode of literacy that enables people to "read" their lives in the world as

---

7. This is what prompts Foucault's call for "an insurrection of subjugated knowledges."

8. For introductory reading, see the fine collection of essays — with contributions by many of the leading feminist scholars — Alcoff and Potter, *Feminist Epistemologies.*

well as to read books, to think for themselves with critical reflection on their social and political context, thus empowering people as historical agents.[9] Without going any further afield into his thought, I cite Freire to make the point that
theological literacy, if it is to seem worthwhile to the public at large, needs the
kind of transformation that Freire is proposing for literacy in general. Instead
of learning simply to "talk the talk" of theology, people must experience it as a
worthwhile resource for living humanly.

I propose that we educate for a theological literacy (a) that informs and
forms people to think theologically for themselves and in the context of their
own lives; (b) that enables them to correlate "life" and "faith," reflecting critically on both and integrating the two into personal conviction and commitment — into "lived faith"; (c) that is humanizing and transforming for the person and for society; it should be an influence "for life for all" in the world.

What theological *content* and what *pedagogy* would be likely to inform,
form, and transform people to realize a life-giving theology in the world? Let
me first propose a rule of thumb for the content, and then move to suggestions
for the pedagogical process.

For wisdom: I propose that theological educators approach the texts
(written and symbolic) of Christian faith — and indeed of all religious traditions — as sources of spiritual wisdom, and that they teach their Scriptures and
traditions as if people are *to learn from them* for their lives and *be disposed to live
their wisdom* in the world. In a nutshell, the *content* of theological education
should be fashioned and taught as *wisdom for life.*

In ancient Greek philosophy, the uniting of what we might now call theoretical and practical reason resulted in *phronesis*. This term is usually translated
as "prudence" but, given its present connotation of caution, prudence is an
undertranslation. Aristotle described *phronesis* as the disposition for ethical
conduct according to right reason — note the uniting of theory and practice.
To cite him precisely, *phronesis* is "a truth-attaining rational quality concerned
with action in relation to things that are good and bad for human beings."[10]
This description resonates readily with an overarching view of wisdom from
the biblical tradition.

In the Bible, the notion of wisdom evolves from a craft (Exod. 31:6) to the
very Craftsperson in the work of creation (Prov. 8:30). In its overall meaning,
biblical wisdom calls people to be reflectively faithful to the covenant in every-

---

9. For the classic statement of Freire's thought, see *Pedagogy of the Oppressed* (New York:
Seabury Press, 1970).

10. Aristotle, *Nicomachean Ethics* 6.5.4. Later, Aristotle explained that for *phronesis*,
"right judgment is the same as right understanding" (6.10.3).

day life. Wisdom is *holistic,* engaging the total person — head, heart, and hands; it is *realized* — done more than talked about; it is located — in the sociocultural context of life; it is *ethical* — it seeks what is true and does what is good. People who are wise in the biblical sense embody and live their wisdom. No wonder, then, that Jesus presented himself as the incarnation of divine wisdom: "I am the way, the truth, and the life" (John 14:6). And Paul so fittingly referred to him as "the wisdom of God" (1 Cor. 1:24). Jesus is *Sophia.*[11]

Approaching Christian faith as a wisdom for life should not weaken the academic rigor of theologians; let us reject, once and for all, the Enlightenment myth that explicit historical interest compromises scholarship. Rather, it simply encourages theological educators to allow a wisdom intent to shape their hermeneutics throughout their scholarly interpretation and explanation of Christian faith.

A wisdom hermeneutics will also dispose theologians to represent religious traditions in the context of people's lives. It will prompt them to attend to what this tradition means for now — the meaning in front of the text as well as the meaning of and behind it (Ricoeur). Likewise, a wisdom hermeneutics will allow the interest in application to be consciously present throughout theological discourse (Gadamer), not tagged on as an afterthought and a question only of technique — as in the theory-to-practice paradigm.

A Wisdom Pedagogy

To educate for wisdom, I propose that we shift theological education from a "lecture delivery" paradigm to "a community of conversation" one. Here I echo Gadamer's metaphor for reading texts — the to-and-fro, give-and-take dialectic of a good conversation. For the theological educator, creating the ethos and dynamic of "a community of conversation" means encouraging the active participation of all in the teaching/learning dynamic, welcoming the contributions of each person, approaching theology as a collaborative venture. The conversation would enable participants to speak their own word out of their life context and to listen to each other; it would give ready access to traditions and encourage participants to see for themselves what theology might mean for their lives. The conversation would be between and among participants, of the teacher

11. For a fine treatment of biblical wisdom and what it might mean to "educate for wisdom," see Charles Melchert, *Wise Teaching* (Valley Forge, Pa.: Trinity Press International, 1998). Also, for further elaboration on my proposal here, see chap. 6 of my book, *Educating for Life* (New York: Crossroads, 2001).

with students, of teacher and students with their own lives in the world and with the texts of tradition.

The overarching dynamic would be a conversation between "life" and "faith," enabling participants to bring their lives in the world to studying and appropriating religious traditions, and discerning what and why and how to bring theological traditions to life in their lives — a repeating and circular dynamic of "bringing life to faith, and faith to life."

Teaching as a conversation does not mean that teachers cannot lecture, only that monologue not be the defining mode of teaching. And when lecturing would be appropriate (a lecture can be very effective for some learning tasks),[12] it can and should be done within the general style of a conversation. This means presenting in ways that invite people to think for themselves in contrast to telling them what to think, that disclose new possibilities rather than closing down imagination, that encourage active engagement with the content instead of passive reception.

A "community of conversation" approach to theological education could be realized in many ways; it is a general style, broad enough to welcome a variety of teaching methods and to be used by teachers with different charisms. Although the teaching methods may vary greatly, yet there are commitments to be reflected in a conversation pedagogy. I can think of at least seven: *engaging, attending, expressing, reflecting, accessing, appropriating,* and *deciding.*

None of these commitments can function alone; they all overlap and coalesce. To *engage* people is to have them begin *attending, expressing* merges with *reflecting,* and so on. Although they have a logical pattern as I lay them out — e.g., *engagement* should mark the beginning and *decision* is more likely toward the end — in a real-life teaching event, these commitments would never be realized in any fixed sequence or be confined to one moment; *engagement* is needed throughout, *decision* should be intended from the beginning, and *reflection* is necessary to each. These commitments can also be honored across a variety of time frames; one class might focus on giving access to a theological tradition, and the next to appropriation and decision making.

These, then, are *pedagogical* commitments *to be honored consistently throughout an event of theological education or across a number of meetings, and*

---

12. There is significant field research which indicates that lecturing is most effective for providing conceptual structures, giving a sense of the big picture and clarifying complex issues, providing up-to-date information and summarizing scattered sources, challenging implicit or fixed ideas. On the other hand, lecturing is not very effective for presenting information that could be read; promoting recall; connecting new information to prior knowledge; developing higher-order thinking skills; changing attitudes, beliefs, or values; changing habits of mind, hand, or heart.

not a lockstep process to be followed in sequence. From my own praxis of teaching over the years, and from the experience of others with similar commitments, they are likely to promote theological literacy as "wisdom for life" and "for life for all."

Each commitment, of course, could be honored in a thousand different ways, and much depends on the context, the participants' background, and a host of other variables. After describing each one briefly, I will intimate how they might be realized in an undergraduate theology course. When an example might help, I will use the one already cited — teaching the christological notion of *homoousios.*

Engaging

The educator needs to draw students into active participation from the beginning and to maintain their "interest" throughout. As proposed earlier, little of significance can be learned unless people are personally engaged in the educational process. On the other hand, when the pedagogy reaches into the core of people's lives and hearts, when it gets them really interested and involved — engaged — then learning is almost inevitable and the outcome more likely to be of wisdom. As also suggested, interest is most likely aroused and maintained when theology is represented in the context of people's lives, when its themes engage what matters to them. This takes imagination and preparation, with the educator pausing often to wonder: "How can I engage learners' lives so that I teach what they are interested in and they become interested in what I teach?"

Personal engagement with *homoousios* by undergraduates may seem unlikely at first blush, unless one begins with some teaching strategy that says, in effect, "Hey, this is about your life — it could be interesting," then turns them to look at some aspect of their own lives in the world for which this teaching might be relevant. For example, I have begun such a unit with a story or symbol or some instance that gets them to focus on "my best hopes for myself and humankind" (the "I Have a Dream" speech of M. L. King seems invariably effective). The key is to invite them to turn to an aspect of their own life-praxis that is resonant with the theological theme to be taught.

Attending

It is a truism that teachers must get students to "pay attention" but not, as that old phrase implies, to the teacher and at a cost; rather, they are more to attend to everything that comes into their experience, initiative, and consciousness. One function of educators is to be troubadours who awaken people to "take a look" and "have a listen" to life as active participants; to recognize, to become consciously aware, mindful of, to really notice what is going on in their world — within and without. They must encourage students to attend to the data of their own lives, to the world around them, and to the world of meaning mediated through the texts and symbols of religious traditions. Attending can also merge into a contemplative stance; in fact, contemplation is likely the deepest mode of attention.[13]

Good questions that require students to draw upon their own resources are effective to encourage their attending. Regarding *homoousios,* the teacher might ask, "As you look intensely at other people and yourself, what do you recognize as some of our best possibilities?" "What do you perceive as the ultimate horizon — the highest potential — for the human person?" or, "When you go to the mountaintop, what is your own best dream for all?"

Expressing

As theological educators, let us abandon the stereotype that "teaching is telling" and instead encourage students to express themselves as integral to the learning process. *What* learners express can be their thoughts, feelings, and doings from their world within and without; their naming of what is "going on" around them; or what emerges from their encounter with the texts and symbols of religious traditions. *How* learners express themselves can be by any mode of human communication. The readiest is speaking, but imaginative educators will encourage all modes of expression: writing, composing, drawing, painting, creating, physical signs, on-line, and more.

Bringing undergraduates to expression is never easy, and yet I have found it possible — though with my share of dismal failures. What seems to "work" best is (a) that they have an effective and well-focused question around an engaging issue — this is in contrast to assigning students to "discuss"; and (b) that they experience the context as a safe one in which their expressions will be respected and never forced. Undergraduates do well when I pose a question (as in *attending* above) and then give them some silent time to write their responses. Thereafter, I usually invite them into groups of two or three to "share as they

---

13. It is interesting to note that contemplation was an integral aspect of the *lectio divina* approach to theology throughout the first millennium of the Christian church. One wonders why it was banished so completely from theological method.

feel comfortable," and only then invite conversation in the whole group. Note, too, that most often I combine expressing with reflecting, the next commitment.

Reflecting

Theological education worthy of the name encourages people to reflect critically for themselves, to reason rigorously and questioningly, to remember and imagine about their lives in the world and the theological traditions they encounter. Note that theological reflection should enlist people's "whole mind" — their reason, memory, and imagination. Reflection becomes "critical" in the discerning and creative sense as people take serious account of their historical context and how it influences — positively and negatively — their reflections. Personal critical reflection uncovers one's own wisdom and blindness, interests and biases, and the sources of the same. Social critical reflection analyzes one's public world, sees its linkages and systems, recognizes its sins and graces, gets a sense of the "whole picture," and imagines new communal possibilities.

Reflection, like all of these teaching commitments, should permeate the entire educational event; it cannot be limited to any one moment. Yet I find it helpful to invite a very deliberate moment of critical reflection — usually combined with or just after people's own expressions. In our example, the educator could ask, "What are some of the influences or experiences that have brought you to your dreams for humanity?" "What are some social factors that impede your dream? That advance it? Why?" "Are there aspects of your dream you would want to change or deepen?" I would most often pose such questions for written response immediately after my question(s) that invites their expressions. In the general conversation, after the small groups, I often frame the invitation as, "What wisdom have you gleaned from your reflections and conversation thus far?" or simply "What is beginning to emerge as significant?"

Accessing

People are always entitled to have access to "the storehouse" (Matt. 13:52) of the Scriptures and traditions of their own faith community and then, according to interest, to that of other faith communities as well. I use the term "access" because it has a gentle connotation that would avoid indoctrination and respect people's freedom, that would enable participants to personally encounter the tradition rather than having it "poured in" or "delivered." Educators can give access in a myriad of ways: lectures of various kinds, crafted with different dynamics to maintain interest;[14] handouts; readings; research projects and reports; group hermeneutics and discussion of a common text; demonstrations; direct experiences; panel discussions; colloquies and symposium dialogues; audio, video, and film media and artistic presentations; resource people from outside; field trips; and a host of other modes. This is especially the moment when the educator brings a wisdom hermeneutic to theological texts and symbols, and represents them to students as potential sources of spiritual wisdom for their lives.

In our example, this is eminently the moment when the educator gives access to the "whole story" of the christological debate and doctrine in which *homoousios* was/is a core concept. I say "story" because it is most often engaging to situate theology within its historical narrative, and I say "whole story" to signal that the educator should represent the best of scholarship, a comprehensive picture as appropriate to age level, background, and time available. This would include how and why the controversy emerged, the historical context that surrounded it, what was at issue, the leading protagonists and their positions, and then the outcome and creedal statements that emerged. Throughout such representation, it will help to correlate with the prior and life-centered comments of participants and, anticipating the next commitment, to often ask "what this might mean for us now" — not just for a confession of faith but for existential lives.

Appropriating

The abiding intent of the theological educator throughout must be for people to come to their own knowledge and wisdom, to appropriate from life and theological tradition what *they* see, understand, judge, and decide. Appropriation is learners coming to knowledge and wisdom as embraced rather than known about, with one's own conviction instead of one accepted on outside authority. The teacher promotes appropriation more by questioning than telling, more by inviting than expecting, more by resourcing than directing. Appropriation often entails waiting for learners to come to see for themselves, to make something their own. Here I have found no shortcut.

14. For review and orientation to a variety of lecture styles, see Bruce Joyce and Marsha Weil, *Information Processing Models of Teaching* (Englewood Cliffs, N.J.: Prentice Hall, 1978). Over my years of teaching theology and religious education, I have found the Advance Organizer Model (reviewed by Joyce and Weil) helpful in that it encourages clarity and logical sequence of presentation.

Questions or questioning activities that encourage appropriation can be posed throughout; I find it helpful with undergrads to often ask, "What sense — if any — is this making to you?" "Are you finding something here that seems significant to the everyday?" "What do you agree with, disagree with, or add?" "What are you coming to see for yourself around this theme — what might it mean?" "What judgments are you reaching?" It helps to have a specific moment when such questions are posed, again, allowing time for writing and then some conversation; they can also be posed in a take-home paper assignment, which would likely invite decision as well.

Deciding

Lonergan insisted that for existential subjects to reach authentic knowing — to complete the process that continues on — they must come to a decision. I agree, and this is eminently true for theological education. Inviting participants to choices and decisions should be integral to its pedagogy. In general, the decisions invited can be cognitive, affective, or behavioral, or some combination thereof. Of course, the educator must exercise good prudence here, taking account of the context, occasion, group, background, etc., to discern how best to invite people to decision. And prompting students to decision should be an invitation — not an expectation — respecting both their privacy and freedom.[15]

In the context of undergraduate theology, it is not appropriate to invite students to express their personal decisions by way of faith conviction or commitment, though this might be done with an adult faith-sharing group in a parish or congregation. However, one can often pose cognitive decision-making questions that are noninvasive, as in, "Take a position on the debate between x and y, and indicate your reasons." I also find it effective to pose a generic-type question like, "If people were to truly believe the Christian doctrine concerning the divinity and humanity of Jesus, what might be the implications for their daily lives? For the church? For society?" Even if students don't reach a decision in the class context, the pedagogy should leave them with questions likely to invite as much.

15. See my book *Sharing Faith* (San Francisco: Harper San Francisco, 1990), chaps. 4 to 10, for a complete description — with many examples — of the pedagogical approach I am recommending here.

Conclusion

In his poem "A Prayer for Old Age," the poet W. B. Yeats wrote:

> God guard me from those thoughts men think,
> In the mind alone;
> They that sing a lasting song,
> Think in a marrow bone.

My proposal here is that theological education must shift from addressing "the mind alone" to engaging the "marrow bone" of people's lives. This, I'm convinced, is our horizon as theological educators. We need to represent our content and devise pedagogies likely to move us toward it. To do less will be to ignore the elephant in the living room.

PART V

THEOLOGICAL LITERACY IN
SEMINARY AND UNIVERSITY

RODNEY L. PETERSEN

Theological literacy is about conversation. It is a collective enterprise. It is not done by oneself or in isolation from others. As Augustine raises this point in his day in *On Christian Doctrine,* so might we in ours. Theological literacy is referenced with respect to Scripture and tradition, the community of faith that has left its testimony to us. It is also carried on with respect to the reason and experience of immediate community. Regardless of how the Holy Spirit has spoken to any one of us, many things can be learned from each other, and should be learned without pride or envy.[1] This diachronic and synchronic dimension of theological literacy shapes spirituality, our understanding of relationships encompassing the grandeur of all that is. If Christian spirituality is, in part, coming to know God through an array of relationships, then theological literacy understood in this sense is a profoundly spiritual endeavor.[2] God, named by analogy and metaphor, is the organic interconnectedness in the comprehensive totality of these relationships, but is never limited by our horizon. Everything seen, heard, tasted, touched, and experienced, if followed far enough and deep enough, brings us into the presence of God (Acts 17:22-31).

The inclusive nature of this conversation implies a relational aspect to theological literacy that encompasses human development and maturation. This engagement, the result of interaction with other persons and larger envi-

---

1. Augustine, *On Christian Doctrine,* trans. D. W. Robertson, Jr. (Indianapolis: Bobbs-Merrill Educational Publishing, 1983), prologue, pp. 5-6; Wisd. 7:13; 1 Cor. 11:23; and 2 Cor 12:2, 4 are referenced.

2. Gordon Mursell summarizes an array of Christian spiritualities that surely must include theological literacy in his edited volume, *The Story of Christian Spirituality: Two Thousand Years from East to West* (Minneapolis: Augsburg Fortress, 2001).

ronments, fosters stages of development, from the intuitive and imitative to an increasingly independent, universalizing, and self-transcending faith that is often said to characterize full maturity.[3] But even these conversations and this engagement are not the largest parts of our life. Implicit in the apostle Paul's Athenian argument, referenced above, is the point that if we walk far enough and deep enough, we enter into something larger. This is the identity of God and implies a conversation between our self and God. As we listen to our inner self, we might ask, where is God in all of that which I am encountering? As God becomes more defined, the task of theology, we learn who we are. This methodology does not deny the array of sciences that define human nature, but it is to recognize that all knowledge is embedded in a larger framework. One theologian has said that there is no knowledge of God apart from that of ourselves and no knowledge of ourselves apart from God.[4] Such bipolarity implies the value of an approach to human identity that is bottom-up and top-down.[5]

This is a conversation that leads somewhere. It leads to our maturity and toward fostering healthy relationships. As we learn language, we discover not only what is there in the wider world but also what we are in relation to our world and that which we believe brought it into being, a parallel between the unfolding of intelligence and the unfolding of the history of science, between intel-

---

3. Building on the research of Piaget, Erikson, and Kohlberg, James Fowler writes of the stages through which we go to make sense of life, Fowler's understanding of faith, in *Stages of Faith: The Psychology of Human Development* (San Francisco: Harper San Francisco, 1995).

4. John Calvin, *Institutes of the Christian Religion*, in 2 vols., Library of Christian Classics, vol. 20, ed. John T. McNeill, trans. Ford Lewis Battles (Philadelphia: Westminster, 1960), 1.1.1 (p. 35).

5. James Loder offers an account of the human spirit that draws perspective "from below" in "exocentricity," or openness to the world and self-transcendence, marked by analogical relationships (order in the universe and in the human mind, the relation of entropy and death, transformation and new order, relationality as ontologically prior to rationality), and "from above" in a created and contingent order grounded beyond itself. This relational unity is developed in *The Logic of the Spirit: Human Development in Theological Perspective* (San Francisco: Jossey-Bass, 1998), pp. 5-12. He adds, "By looking at development theologically, through the lenses of the Creator Spirit, we will eventually see that the dynamics of development, down to the particulars of language, thought, patterns of affect, and moral judgment, as well as the more global moves from stage to stage in ego development, are compelled forward according to a transformational pattern that reflects on a human level the same pattern as that which characterizes the Creator Spirit" (p. 17). Loder draws theories of human development from key interactions in (1) the personal unconscious and ego development (Sigmund Freud, Anna Freud, Erikson, and the psychoanalytic tradition), (2) the conscious mind and cognitive development (Piaget, Kohlberg, Gilligan, and the structuralist tradition), and (3) the collective unconsciousness (Jung, Ulanov, and the analytic tradition) (pp. 20-26).

ligibility and ultimate order.[6] We are finding the words to connect ourselves with that which is beyond our self, with what and who is there. In his *Confessions*, Augustine marks the history of Christian spirituality with a journey toward a God who is there and who is not silent.[7] God is always at work in conditions. And we are learning in this process that there are things that make a difference. Character develops. Decisions are made. Habits are nurtured. Attention is trained. Commandments are obeyed. Sins are confessed. All of this happens as we come to see and understand more fully. From the perspective of theological literacy, relationships that demand such nurturing precede rationality. God does not reveal reality so that we can stand around and look on it as spectators, but so that we can enter into it and become cocreators toward love of God and neighbor.

Conversation may be related to growth, but it does not imply agreement. Some of our best conversations, and growth, occur as we begin to see difference and yet maintain relationship. Difference, and even disagreement, can lead to meaningful deliberation or repression and even suppression. It may lead to conflict. Maintaining dialogue in the face of difference and disagreement implies recognizing the other as neighbor. In Christian theology the neighbor is not the abstract "other" but God in our own image facing us in the other. To continue in dialogue with my neighbor, even through disagreement, is to love my neighbor and to accept the future that is shaped by the reality of my neighbor. It is to foster civil society in the face of mistrust and despair.[8] We are, in fact, given to one another in order to benefit from each other and to find the restoration that is only possible because of each other, and to find our respective identities through each other.[9] This is theological literacy.

Maintaining relationship through deliberation in the face of difference enables growth. Difference may be consensual or dissensual in nature. If it is the former, the means forward is often framed by broad underlying agreement and so is more susceptible to solution. If it is the latter, differences are deeper but all

6. Loder finds this parallel central to Piaget's work; see Loder, pp. 24-26.

7. Augustine, *The Confessions*, trans. Henry Chadwick (New York: Oxford University Press, 1991); cf. Charles Williams, *Descent of the Dove* (Grand Rapids: Eerdmans, 1939).

8. Jean Bethke Elshtain writes of "democracy's precarious present" and offers her own antidote through "citizens in their plurality," the civil rights promise, the duties of human rights, personal responsibility, and engagement with tradition, in *Democracy on Trial* (New York: Basic Books, 1995). Her definition of civil society is, "the many forms of community and association that dot the landscape of a democratic culture, from families to churches to neighborhood groups to trade unions to self-help movements to volunteer assistance to the needy" (p. 5).

9. Karl Barth, *Church Dogmatics*, ed. G. W. Bromiley and T. F. Torrance, trans. G. T. Thomson and H. Knight (Edinburgh: T. & T. Clark, 1970), II.2, 18.3 (pp. 401ff.), pp. 419-20, 430.

the more valuable for resolution.[10] Conversation at this level draws us to the realm of politics, the science of allowing for difference while holding together as community.[11] Politics has been of concern to people driven by religion, and theological literacy has been important to people concerned about politics.[12] Theological literacy allows for community to remain intact through deliberation in the face of moral disagreement because it makes the effort to understand motivation at its deepest level.[13] Such understanding also permits social dynamism and the evolution of new ministries, institutions, and the fluidity of civil society.[14] Politics is the means toward an evolution in social expression, not with the limitations of narrow utilitarianism, but with a vision of the good located in human maturation or the ability to serve God and neighbor.[15] This is

10. Louis Kriesberg draws out these distinctions and offers helpful sociological insight on the emergence of conflict, its escalation, de-escalation, and methodologies toward resolution, in *Constructive Conflicts: From Escalation to Resolution* (New York: Rowman and Littlefield, 1998). In *Difficult Conversations,* authors Douglas Stone and others from the Harvard Negotiation Project share stories and strategies for conducting tough conversations (New York: Viking Penguin Books, 2000).

11. See Jean Bethke Elshtain on "the politics of difference" (pp. 65-90). The concept of "deliberative democracy," meaning a social order with a politics regulated by reciprocity, publicity, and accountability and policies shaped by basic liberty, basic opportunity, and fair opportunity, is discussed by Amy Gutmann and Dennis Thompson, *Democracy and Disagreement* (Cambridge: Harvard University Press, Belknap Press, 1996), p. 12. According to the authors, basic human rights, such as liberty and opportunity, have priority over deliberation itself, the latter given priority by Jürgen Habermas and other discourse theorists (cf. Habermas, "Discourse Ethics," in *Moral Consciousness and Communicative Action,* trans. Christian Lenhardt and Shierry Weber Nicholsen [Cambridge: MIT Press, 1993], p. 94).

12. A point made by J. Philip Wogaman, *Christian Perspectives on Politics* (Louisville: Westminster John Knox, 2000), pp. 5-10. Anglo-American political parties find an origin in the Puritan Revolution and Commonwealth Period in England, 1642-59. See William Haller, *Tracts on Liberty in the Puritan Revolution, 1638-1647,* 3 vols. (New York: Hippocrene Books, 1965); also David Little, *Religion, Order, and Law: A Study in Pre-Revolutionary England* (New York: Harper and Row, 1969).

13. Sources of moral conflict are located in scarcity and limited generosity (as with David Hume), as well as in the added areas of incompatible values and incomplete understanding. Gutmann and Thompson posit deliberative democracy, allowing for the fluid interplay of procedural and constitutional constraints on outcomes, as the means to come together on moral and political issues (pp. 41-43). The authors discuss the limitations of utilitarianism as a goal in politics, ignoring citizen preferences and processes (pp. 165-98).

14. James Luther Adams, *Voluntary Associations: Socio-cultural Analyses and Theological Interpretation,* ed. J. Ronald Engel (Chicago: Exploration Press, 1986).

15. This ideal, taken from Jesus' summary of the Decalogue (Matt. 22:34-40), might be compared with Sigmund Freud's ideal of maturation in the ability to love and to work *(leiben und arbeiten).* See Freud's *Three Contributions to a Theory of Sex* (New York: Dutton, 1962) and *Complete Psychological Works of Sigmund Freud* (London: Hogarth Press, 1956).

good politics. It is open to universalizing principles[16] and to public reasoning.[17] It is a politics that finds moral agreement as able but allows for mutual respect when such agreement is not forthcoming. Theological literacy allows for informed politics. It can restore a moral voice without apology[18] because the dynamism of the gospel propels a universalism that is nevertheless mindful of cultural difference.[19]

Theological literacy is necessary for the well-being of the church.[20] It is also necessary for the well-being of civil society insofar as humanity is defined religiously.[21] This is a conversation that is nurtured in two locations that are intimately bound up in history, the seminary and the university — but also in other bridging institutions that have emerged through time.[22] Despite pres-

16. Brian Barry, *Culture and Equality: An Egalitarian Critique of Multiculturalism* (Cambridge: Harvard University Press, 2001).

17. Kent Greenawalt, *Private Consciences and Public Reasons* (New York: Oxford University Press, 1995).

18. The problem of the absence of this voice is raised in *Missing Connections: Public Perceptions of Theological Education and Religious Leadership,* a report by Elizabeth Lynn and Barbara G. Wheeler, Auburn Studies, bulletin no. 6 (September 1999).

19. See Jean Bethke Elshtain's point that "it is only incorporation within a single body that makes meaningful diversity possible" (p. 65). See the work of the Common Ground Initiative, *Catholic Common Ground Initiative: Foundational Documents,* ed. Joseph Cardinal Bernardin with Oscar H. Lipscomb (New York: Crossroad, 1997). An effort is made to promote the common good through discerning the role of the law as teacher while recognizing the limits of law as a moral tool. An integrated jurisprudence toward a "culture of life" (as defined by Pope John Paul II in his encyclical letter *The Gospel of Life*) might be seen in the Civil Rights Act or the Americans with Disabilities Act.

20. Theology schools are derivative of the church. Theological literacy is set within the context of expectation. David Wells writes that the pastoral vocation today is in crisis. Ministers have become, in Wells's words, "dislodged from the network of what is meaningful and valuable in society." Theological literacy has lost its meaning as it has become divorced from communities of faith and expectation. See Wells's *No Place for Truth; or, Whatever Happened to Evangelical Theology?* (Grand Rapids: Eerdmans, 1993). See D. G. Hart and R. Albert Mohler, Jr., *Theological Education in the Evangelical Tradition* (Grand Rapids: Baker, 1996), a volume that highlights evangelical assumptions in the training of ministers as different from the wider Protestant tradition and Roman Catholicism. This might be contrasted with recent books dealing with theological education and the church by liberals and mainliners: *Theological Perspectives on Christian Formation,* ed. Jeff Astley, Leslie J. Francis, and Colin Crowder (Grand Rapids: Eerdmans, 1997); and *Changing the Ways Seminaries Teach* (Hartford Seminary Center for Social and Religious Research/Plowshares Institute, 1997).

21. The significance of this is increasingly evident in global politics, a topic taken up by Natan Lerner, *Religion, Beliefs, and International Human Rights* (Maryknoll, N.Y.: Orbis Books, 2000); and see Raymond Helmick, S.J., and Rodney Petersen, eds., *Forgiveness and Reconciliation: Religion, Public Policy, and Conflict Transformation* (Philadelphia: Templeton Press, 2001).

22. A variation on these locations because of its nurturing context is that of church and

sures that periodically emerge to push for their separation, seminary and university have seldom remained separate.[23] There are reasons for this bound up in the identity of each as well as in their value to church and civic leadership. In the West this has had a particular history subsequent to the Reformation for both Roman Catholicism[24] and Protestantism.[25]

John E. MacInnis writes about the seminary in "Theological Education as Formation for Ministry," a chapter that helps to close this volume. His argu-

---

school. See Merrimon Cuninggim, *Uneasy Partners: The College and the Church* (Nashville: Abingdon, 1994). On deeper patterns of relationship, see the work of Ernst Kantorowicz on the European background and George H. Williams, who carries this into the American setting, in *"Translatio Studii:* The Puritans' Conception of Their First University in New England, 1636," *Archiv für Reformationsgeschichte* 57, no. ½ (1966): 152-81. See also Robert S. Shephard, *God's People in the Ivory Tower: Religion in the Early American University* (New York: Carlson Publishing, 1991).

23. The contemporary debate surrounding Catholic higher education illustrates this tension, which is also found in other Christian churches and schools. Propelled by discussion of the U.S. bishops document (November 1999), *"Ex Corde Ecclesiae:* An Application to the United States," the question is raised to what extent teaching in higher education is independent of church authority or derivative of it. The historical background for this discussion is lodged in *Sapientia Christiana,* promulgated by Pope John Paul II, a set of regulations for church-chartered universities and faculties of theology.

24. As a part of the reforms instituted by the Council of Trent, the shape of theological education was addressed on an institutional level by encouraging the development of seminaries. Such schools were to be formed by drawing upon models provided in the medieval cathedral school, the Jesuit college, and the Verona acolyte school. The seminary was to be an institution for instruction like the medieval cathedral school or other universities they had evolved into at Bologna, the Sorbonne, Oxford, and elsewhere. It was to be like the Jesuit college in that it was to be a place that fostered a communal lifestyle with its own instructors, unlike the university college, which only provided living accommodations. Like the Verona acolyte school, it had spiritual directors, was supervised by a local bishop, and excluded lay students. See James A. O'Donohoe, *Tridentine Seminary Legislation: Its Sources and Its Formation* (Louvain: University Press, 1957); see also Hubert Jedin, "Domschule und Kolleg. Zum Ursprung der Idee der Trienter Priesterseminars," *Trierer Theologische Zeitschrift* 67 (1958): 210-23.

25. Within Protestantism, among the Reformed, the beginning of the theological college in Zürich can be traced to the Zürich Prophezei, seen as the beginning of the University of Zürich. See G. R. Potter, *Zwingli* (Cambridge: University Press, 1976), pp. 211-24; and Philippe Denis, "La Prophétie dans les églises de la Réforme au XVI siècle," *Revue d'histoire ecclésiastique* 72 (1977): 289-316, on how to define prophecy and ways in which prophecy played a role in early education. Begun in 1525, "prophesying" took the form of public lectures in the *Grossmünster,* replacing the former canonical hours of Prime, Terce, and Sext. After prayer and the reading of the text for the day in Latin, Hebrew, and Greek, the gathered ministers, canons, and students listened to a sermon in Latin. Then, as further citizens from the city gathered, a sermon was delivered in German. On Lutheranism, see Robert Kolb, *Reformers Define the Church, 1530-1580* (St. Louis: Concordia, 1991).

ment lays out a formation for ministry that follows the steps of personal conversion, historical confession, and ecclesial communion. These are steps seen in the life of Augustine, whose guide to theological education, *On Christian Doctrine*, has been so important in the structure of this volume.[26] These steps outline what MacInnis consciously terms "formation" so as to signify intentionally the broader scope of education as it relates to ministry, "the shaping of thought, critical reflection, attitudes, outlook, and eventually commitment to a life of service." We have seen aspects of this in the last section of this book. The knowledge that people who come to a school of theology seek is that which can provide them with more than a facility with the language and methods of religious discourse. It is a knowledge that should affect them in ways of conversion, identity, and communion.

MacInnis adds three lessons for theological educators in the course of his discussion. Theological formation for church ministry takes seriously the significance of faith and virtue in the lives of students. It considers the necessity of relating the truths found in biblical texts to historical confessions of faith. And finally, it understands the reality of the church as a communication of faith and the community where education, especially for ministry, finds its point of departure and its point of arrival. Religious communities work out values in practice. Like many universities, they transcend the ecosystem in their membership and commitment.[27] Universities themselves can be viewed as a subset of religious communities, as questions unresolved in worship are wrestled through in rhetoric and dialectic in schools birthed for such purposes. This argument rejects the perspective that sees religious communities as cultural backwaters.[28] It also rejects those views of religion as ministering only to the needs of its adherents.[29] Rather, it follows Charles A. Taylor's idea, one followed in this volume,

---

26. See the essays in Duane W. H. Arnold and Pamela Bright, eds., *De Doctrina Christiana: A Classic of Western Culture* (Notre Dame, Ind.: University of Notre Dame Press, 1995).

27. Ninan Koshy, *Churches in the World of Nations: International Politics and the Mission and Ministry of the Church* (Geneva: WCC Publications, 1994); also see Paul Wapner, *Environmental Activism and World Civic Politics* (Albany: State University of New York Press, 1996). Wapner gives detailed attention to the role of transnational environmental activist groups such as Greenpeace, the World Wildlife Fund, and Friends of the Earth. The church finds its parallel to this in Konrad Raiser, *To Be the Church: Challenges and Hopes for a New Millennium* (Geneva: World Council of Churches Publications, 1997).

28. A point of view associated with Jürgen Habermas. See Don S. Browning and Francis Schüssler Fiorenza, eds., *Habermas, Modernity, and Public Theology* (New York: Crossroad, 1992).

29. See this position as variously represented in the theologies of George Lindbeck, Stanley Hauerwas, and John Milbank. See in Robert N. Bellah, "How to Understand the Church in

that individuals work out their identities in communities of discourse.[30] Just as our ecosystem cannot be nurtured apart from its biotic diversity, so society needs its communities of faith for nurturing the larger civil society.[31] Only a hope that is stronger than the earth can save the earth. Religious commitments have the ability to foster creativity and the potential to be expressive of a higher maturity.[32] They promote transformation and can be the most powerful forces in development.[33]

Another place where theological literacy is fostered is the university.[34] In his chapter, "The Classic Idea of the University: Its Relevance in the Twenty-first Century," Jan Milič Lochman structures his ideas around the phrases that frame the purpose of his university, the University of Basel. The "idea of the university" is that it is a communicative entity. Lochman writes, "The 'living spirit' of the university is demonstrated in communication. . . . Every breakdown in communication, every refusal of dialogue, is a sin against the spirit of university, . . . the communicative character of truth."[35]

---

an Individualistic Society," in *Christianity and Civil Society: Theological Education for Public Life,* ed. R. L. Petersen (Maryknoll, N.Y.: Orbis Books, 1995), pp. 1-14.

30. Charles A. Taylor, *Sources of the Self: The Making of the Modern Identity* (Cambridge: Harvard University Press, 1989) and *The Ethics of Authenticity* (Cambridge: Harvard University Press, 1992).

31. Just as a hope grounded in transcendence and brought to bear upon the environmental crisis begins to turn Lynn White's argument on its head, so such is true for social ecology. On the argument with respect to the environment, see the report by Leslie Lang, *Religion's Role in Preserving the Environment,* a Nationwide Leadership Conference for Catholic, Jewish, and Protestant Seminaries, April 1994 (American Jewish Committee, Skirball Institute on American Values); and cf. Al Gore, *Earth in the Balance: Ecology and the Human Spirit* (Boston: Houghton Mifflin, 1992).

32. Howard Gardner suggests that religious commitments may foster creativity through enhancing a sense of ultimacy, independence from convention, and depth of spirituality, in *Creating Minds: An Anatomy of Creativity Seen through the Lives of Freud, Einstein, Picasso, Stravinsky, Eliot, Grah, and Gandhi* (New York: Basic Books, 1994).

33. The history of "Great Awakening" literature makes this point. See Robert W. Fogel, *The Fourth Great Awakening and the Future of Equalitarianism: The Political Realignment of the 1990s and the Fate of Equalitarianism* (Chicago: University of Chicago Press, 2000).

34. Merrimon Cuninggim writes about the historic connections between churches and colleges and the confusion that has set in on the part of both concerning the nature of this relationship, in *Uneasy Partners;* cf. Claude Welch, *Graduate Education in Religion: A Critical Appraisal* (Missoula: University of Montana Press, 1971).

35. While it might be said that every university is founded with this ideal, this spirit has continued to animate the underlying motivations of Harvard College and its subsequent university. The historical perspective of Samuel Eliot Morison supported widening patterns of conversation, in *Three Centuries of Harvard* (Cambridge: Belknap Press, 1964). The fourth university in the Western Hemisphere, Harvard set forth in a Reformed rather than medieval Catholic

Conversation, or communication, promotes the integration of knowledge and life, individually as well as socially. While knowing — and the search for truth itself — is a gift, duty, and necessity, Lochman writes, it is not an end in itself; "it is not a *scientia pro scientia,* unconnected with other fundamental concerns of human life. . . . It is connected with the whole of life, wherein it has its special yet at the same time ministerial role." Knowledge ought to serve the contextual needs of humanity. "By naming the name of God, the university introduces a liberating dimension and a horizon of meaning which encompasses every success and failure: it introduces the perspective of the 'nevertheless.'" Here we find the hope that keeps it all going.

All of this is not without controversy.[36] Religion is often both the force for stability and the source of prophetic change in society.[37] It is also a field that has undergone tremendous change in the modern period,[38] but it has also engen-

---

cadence, struggled through its early history between adherence to Reformed Christian ideals and the challenges of the Enlightenment. An invitation was explored in 1641 between Increase Mather (president of Harvard, 1685-1701) and John Amos Comenius (1592-1670), Calvinist-educated Bohemian pedagogue and Moravian minister, to become president of Harvard College, the presidency given to Henry Dunster (1640-54). It was hoped that something of the spirit of the Reformed schools of Europe might be brought to the English colonies of North America through the possible presidency of Comenius. Jan Milič Lochman's closing chapter is not only appropriate because of the subject matter, but in his own person and name he represents something of this early spirit.

36. Donald Wiebe, *The Politics of Religious Studies: The Continuing Conflict with Theology in the Academy* (New York: St. Martin's Press, 1999). See also D. G. Hart, "American Learning and the Problem of Religious Studies," in *The Secularization of the Academy,* ed. G. M. Marsden and B. J. Longfield (New York: Oxford University Press, 1992), pp. 195-233; Ray Hart, "Religious and Theological Studies in American Higher Education," *Journal of the American Academy of Religion* 69 (2001): 715-827; and Joseph M. Kitagawa, "The History of Religions in America," in *The History of Religions: Essays in Methodology,* ed. M. Eliade and J. M. Kitagawa (Chicago: University of Chicago Press, 1959), pp. 1-30; "Humanistic and Theological History of Religion with Special Reference to the North American Scene," in *Traditions in Contact and Change,* ed. Peter Slater and Donald Wiebe (Waterloo, Ont.: Wilfrid Laurier University Press, 1983), pp. 553-63.

37. Harold Berman recognizes five revolutions in which religion has played a role in shaping the modern legal tradition, in *Law and Revolution: The Formation of the Western Legal Tradition* (Cambridge: Harvard University Press, 1983) and *Faith and Order: The Reconciliation of Law and Religion* (Atlanta: Scholars Press, 1993); see essays edited by John Witte, Jr., and Frank S. Alexander, *The Weightier Matters of the Law: Essays on Law and Religion* (Atlanta: Scholars Press, 1988). Jacques Ellul offers the insight of a sociologist on these matters brought to bear upon persons and incidents in the Bible, in *The Politics of God and the Politics of Man,* trans. and ed. Geoffrey W. Bromiley (Grand Rapids: Eerdmans, 1972).

38. Samuel Preus, *Explaining Religion: Criticism and Theory from Bodin to Freud* (New Haven: Yale University Press, 1987).

dered change. This is clearly evident in the preceding essays. Because of this, and in the face of this, conversation is all the more necessary for being more difficult. The thesis that provides the coherence for this volume, particularly in light of essays that move as differently as these do, is that conversation both promotes theological literacy and defines theological literacy. Who are you, Augustine wrote, to think that the Spirit speaks only to you?

The challenge brought to the church by the university, representing the universalizing tendencies of Christian theology as well as its own potential parochialism, is one that draws us to wider concentric circles of conversation.[39] But the church, and its seminaries, also challenge the university to overcome its tendency toward nihilism, or the nihilism implicit in the multiplicity of political corrections, and the need for the findings of science, or knowledge, to be located in a larger framework only temporarily lodged in utility. A symmetry can be found in the two, shaped from below and from above, as in Lochman's analogy. This is a symmetry that promotes personal responsibility with its possibilities for public and private decency. It is a responsibility born of humility as democratic citizens refuse to give way to despair, *accidie* (Ps. 119:28; Isa. 61:3), or the inordinate blandishments of narcissism (Obad. 1:3).[40]

Our challenge in the twenty-first century is to develop a language that permits individual and community expression within the confines of a larger public order, a language that allows for public consensus without abuse to minority rights. Several of the essays and Part introductions in this volume have suggested possibilities toward this end.[41] This can happen as we learn to support the iden-

---

39. I am following Jones, *Embodying Forgiveness* (Grand Rapids: Eerdmans, 1995), p. 220 n. 21. See Karl Barth's discussion in *Church Dogmatics* IV/3/1, trans. G. W. Bromiley (Edinburgh: T. & T. Clark, 1961), pp. 38-165. Similarly, see Paul Hiebert's analysis of the term "Christian," drawn upon the mathematical categories of "bounded sets," "fuzzy sets," and "centered sets," as he seeks to bring clarity to the meaning of the term. Opting for the latter category, he writes that a line of demarcation exists but the focus should be on "reaffirming the center" and not on "maintaining the boundary." See his article, "The Category 'Christian' in the Mission Task," *International Review of Mission* 72 (1983): 421-27, 424.

40. Despair and pride serve as two of the traditional Seven Deadly Sins. On life crafted through personal responsibility that does not give way to these deficiencies of the spirit, see "Politics and Conscience," in Václav Havel, *Living in Truth* (London: Faber and Faber, 1987), p. 151.

41. See the discussion in the introduction to Part II. The value of finding a common language for the common good is a supposition that might be taken from Robert Bellah's collaborative work (with Richard Madsen, William M. Sullivan, Ann Swidler, and Steven M. Tipton), *Habits of the Heart: Individualism and Commitment in American Life* (Berkeley and Los Angeles: University of California Press, 1985). Bellah's comment about the coequal participation of church, sect, and mysticism, each playing a role in shaping American public culture, might be extended to all religious partners (p. 246).

tity of one another.[42] As we listen and value each other's story, we allow the other to be different and yet to be neighbor. Without sacrificing our story and our identity, we give ourselves the psychological space to find the way through conflict. This is what the apostle Paul calls the ministry of reconciliation (2 Cor. 5:16-21). It may require the ability to learn to forgive one another, and our self. That forgiveness is recognized, given, and received by all people is an aspect of our common identity. That it happens through God's grace and the work of the Spirit through Christ as we are drawn into the mystery of the church is a sign of the restoration and reconciliation of all things (Col. 1:15-20).

Our challenge is also to foster ways that promote community development in which individual and group maturity can take place. If, as some have suggested, there are levels and degrees of forgiveness,[43] perhaps there are also levels and degrees of community.[44] It may be that there is a symmetry here worth uncovering.[45] Surely the ecumenical and interreligious task today embraces the discovery of what this means. Theological literacy, as nurtured by the seminary, or theological school, and university, is the means to making this possible.

---

42. In his extensive work of mediation, my colleague and friend Raymond Helmick, S.J., frequently cites the *praesupponendum* of the *Spiritual Exercises* of Saint Ignatius, founder of the Jesuit Order. Here the author makes the point about not to undo the other by taking away his or her primary point of identity. This is a valuable lesson for all would-be evangelists, negotiators, mediators, and counselors. See *The Spiritual Exercises of Saint Ignatius: A New Translation from the Authorized Latin Text,* trans. Pierri Wolff (Liguori, Mo.: Liguori Publications, 1997).

43. Michelle Nelson identifies at least three degrees of forgiveness that build on one another: detached forgiveness, a reduction in negative feeling but no reconciliation; limited forgiveness, adding the restoration of partial relationship and a decrease in emotional investment; and full forgiveness, adding a total cessation of negative feelings and restoration and growth in relationship. See Beverly Flanigan, "Forgivers and the Unforgivable," in *Exploring Forgiveness,* ed. Robert D. Enright and Joanna North (Madison: University of Wisconsin Press, 1998), pp. 95-105.

44. M. Scott Peck outlines stages of pseudocommunity, chaos, emptiness, and community as stages in development. Note should be made of how the virtues of honesty, openness, and forgiveness function in Peck's progression toward full community. See *The Different Drum: Community Making and Peace* (New York: Simon & Schuster, 1987), pp. 86-106.

45. I owe this suggestion to Donna Hicks, director of the Program in International Conflict Analysis and Resolution (PICAR), Harvard University. See her article, "The Role of Identity Reconstruction in Promoting Reconciliation," in Helmick and Petersen, *Forgiveness and Reconciliation,* pp. 129-50.

CHAPTER TWENTY

Theological Education
as Formation for Ministry

JOHN E. MacINNIS

Theological Education as Formation for Ministry:
Lessons from Augustine's *De Doctrina Christiana*

This essay takes the form of a reexamination of Augustine's classic, *De doctrina Christiana,* in light of the question: How does theological education shape future ministers? Reading that ancient text with this twenty-first-century concern in mind leads me to affirm David Tracy's insight in chapter 1 and to draw out some implications from these words:

> [A]ll thought exists finally for the sake of action and commitment. It is true that mere action without thought is blind. It is equally true that all thought not somehow directed to action, concern, or commitment may be ultimately empty. The ancients still have much to teach us on the coherence of a true education as uniting a vision of life and a way of life.
>
> Of all the disciplines, theology is that one where action and thought, academy and church, faith and reason, the community of inquiry and the community of commitment and faith are most explicitly and systematically brought together.

Theology in service to ministry is not a recent discovery or a new development in history. For Augustine, the preparation of competent pastors gives a particular shape to the enterprise of theological education. Theological literacy meant competence in reading and interpreting sacred texts, but it was intended to accomplish something more. Theological education should draw students into a reflective process which assists them in the quest for a deeper personal faith, for a well-grounded confession of that faith, and for life within a community of faith.

Writing as one for whom the work of theological formation and pastoral ministry have been closely intertwined for the past twenty-five years, I propose three lessons from that fifth-century theologian and pastor who perhaps more than any figure of that period left his mark on theology and the church of the past millennium and a half. While my perspective undoubtedly reflects my experience in a Roman Catholic seminary, I suggest that convictions which Augustine brought to theological education in the ancient church have relevance for teachers and administrators in many theology schools today. I have chosen to use the word "formation" intentionally, to signify the broader scope of education as it relates to ministry: the shaping of thought, critical reflection, attitudes, outlook, and eventually commitment to a life of service.

Formation of Church Ministers as a Goal of Theological Education

A significant number of men and women enroll at a school or institute of theology with the goal in mind of serving individuals and communities of faith. Many of those who may initially enter studies to satisfy a curiosity about religion or religious questions eventually confront the question: What do I intend to do with this knowledge? In one way or another, what affects their life as well as their learning is the pursuit of a vocation, in both the professional and the religious senses of that word. By their teaching and preaching, by worship and pastoral care, they will one day act as guides and healers to people in search of answers to life's most important questions, questions about the meaning of life and death, of work and love, of suffering and justice.

How does theological learning become a source of sustaining wisdom for minister and congregant? It does so when it enables the human mind and heart to be confronted with assertions about God, before whom no person stands indifferent or neutral. As John Courtney Murray once wrote in his exquisitely succinct survey *The Problem of God:*

> The problem of God is primary among the fateful human questions that, as Pascal said, "take us by the throat." The whole man — as intelligent and free, as a body, a psychic apparatus, and a soul — is profoundly engaged both in the position of the problem and in its solution. In fact, he is in a real sense a datum of the problem itself, and his solution of it has personal consequences that touch every aspect of his conduct, character, and conscious-

ness. Moreover, the problem of God is unique in that no man can say of it, "It is not my problem."[1]

Whether their vocation will eventually be realized in religious education, pastoral ministry, or another form of service to the church or society, men and women come to a school of theology with the need for theology to provide them with a kind of knowledge that is more than a facility with the language and methods of religious discourse. Such a knowledge should affect them in three ways related to their present life and to the future exercise of ministry. It should stir up and build upon a vibrant, personal faith. It should illumine and be illumined by the Scriptures along with an ecclesial confession of faith. It should foster a commitment to a community in which one lives out one's own faith and serves the faith needs of others. Reading Augustine's *De doctrina Christiana* with these goals in view, I will refer to these as three aims of theological formation for ministry: (1) personal conversion, (2) historical confession, and (3) ecclesial communion.

De Doctrina Christiana: Theological Formation for Pastors and Preachers

Augustine began composing *De doctrina Christiana* around the year 396, not long after being ordained bishop of Hippo.[2] It appears possible, if not quite likely, that he wrote it in response to a need in the ranks of the clergy in North Africa to be educated for good preaching, a need brought to his attention by Bishop Aurelius, primate of all Africa.[3] Augustine himself clearly states in the concluding sentence of the work: ". . . in these four books I have set out to the best of my poor ability, not what sort of pastor I am myself, lacking many of the necessary qualities as I do, but what sort the pastor should be who is eager to toil away, not only for his own sake but for others, in the teaching of sound, that

---

1. John Courtney Murray, S.J., *The Problem of God* (New Haven, Conn.: Yale University Press, 1965), p. 4.

2. Edmund Hill, O.P., introduction to his translation: *Teaching Christianity: "De Doctrina Christiana,"* ed. John C. Rotelle, in *The Works of Saint Augustine,* vol. I (New York, 1996), p. 11. Hill's recent and excellent translation provides the English text cited throughout this article.

3. Cf. Hill, translator's note, p. 95. Hill concludes his argument that Augustine intended *De doctrina Christiana* for ministers, not just students, of Christianity, in this way: "If then there is any educational establishment which the *De Doctrina Christiana* prophetically envisions, I would say it is the seminary or ecclesiastical college, not the university. And seminaries could do very much worse than use it as a textbook, even today" (p. 97).

is of Christian, doctrine."[4] In point of fact, the text he started to write and had substantially drafted early on in his episcopate was only completed some thirty years later.[5]

Within the prologue and four books of *De doctrina Christiana,* Augustine moves from a summary of the divine truth itself, to the ways we can open up the texts in which that truth is found, to the manner in which that truth can best be expressed. A short summary here will be helpful. At the very outset he affirms the need for rules by which one can grasp the meaning of the Scriptures so that a person may advance "not only by reading others who have opened up the hidden secrets of the divine literature, but also by themselves opening them up to yet others again" (prologue 1). In book 1 he sets forth the twofold aim of a learning process: "a way to discover what needs to be understood (in the scriptures) and a way to put across to others what has been understood." Here he distinguishes the "things" or content of faith from the "signs." Augustine argues that the Scriptures present us with the triune God, whose Wisdom incarnate enables us to love God, our ultimate "enjoyment" or happiness, and love rightly his creatures. Books 2 and 3 provide hermeneutical principles and rules for both an accurate and a fruitful study of the Scriptures. Finally, book 4 offers Augustine's development of rhetorical conventions suited to help preachers and teachers communicate persuasively the truth they have uncovered.

Throughout this work the bishop of Hippo frames the task of theological study as a project in which students, future pastors, enter into the text of the Scriptures and follow a challenging path. The route to insight and learning he sets forth is not a simple or easy walk, but a complex and demanding journey through the Scriptures. It is a strenuous pilgrimage that continually and profoundly engages the learner.

Invoking this image of "journey" for theological formation, what could we describe as the signposts marking the path Augustine lays out for one who would aspire to be a leader, not merely a follower, along this road? As I read the text from the perspective of men and women investing themselves in the future of church ministry, I find three realities that stand out as part of that journey. (a) It confronts them with their own need to be formed and reformed by a personal faith in God. Students need to face their own *personal conversion.* (b) It guides them in the careful, thoughtful uncovering of the mystery of God and God's plan found in Scripture. But readers and interpreters of the sacred text will need to sharpen their understanding of its content by reference to a *histori-*

---

4. Hill, p. 241 (4.31.64). Texts will be cited in this article following Hill's translation with citation of the original books and paragraphs.

5. Hill, p. 96.

cal confession of faith. (c) It enables them to draw others to God, and to be drawn along with others within the body of Christ, the community of the faithful. This is the ultimate mission of the gospel minister as true spiritual leader: *ecclesial communion,* the linking of each person's own quest for and achievement of meaning and salvation with that of others.

Theological Formation and Personal Conversion

From out of his own experience Augustine realized that the mind does not ascend swiftly or easily to what can be known about God. Rather, "our minds have to be purified, to enable them to perceive that light (the truth of God), and to cling to it once perceived. We should think of this purification process as being a kind of walk, a kind of voyage toward our home country" (1.10.10). The mind cannot grasp the message it ponders unless it has been turned to God in faith, hope, and charity. Throughout his program of theological formation, Augustine returns to this conviction: that to read the Scriptures, "what is needed above all else . . . is to be converted by the fear of God to wishing to know his will, what he bids us seek and shun" (2.7.9). He describes the various steps along which a pilgrim reader will travel: from fear to piety, to knowledge, to fortitude, to counsel, to purgation of the eyes of the heart, to single-mindedness, to wisdom (2.7.9-11).

For Augustine, attitudes of piety and docility are what we might call today preconditions for approaching sacred texts (3.1.1). Besides the help that technical rules of interpretation provide, the hearer of God's word needs criteria for uncovering meanings, even those beyond the intention of the human author, which are the work of the Spirit behind the text (3.27.38). A personal posture of faith, which shows itself in prayer, is indispensable for approaching the inspired word. "Much more important than that [i.e., familiarity with the diverse modes of expression in the Bible] and supremely necessary, is that they should pray for understanding. After all, in this very literature which they are eager to study, they read that the Lord gives wisdom, and from his face, come knowledge and understanding (Prov. 2:6)" (3.37.56). Depth of understanding comes when one approaches the words of Scripture not simply to commit words to memory but to "see into the heart of them with the eyes of their own heart" (4.5.7).

Motivating the learner must be a genuine desire for truth, not just an appreciation of words per se: "It is indeed the characteristic trait of good minds and dispositions to love in words what is true, not the words themselves" (4.11.26). Likewise, what makes for effective preaching, more so than a facility with oratory, is the minister's own prayer both for himself and for those who listen. Making a clever play on the Latin word for speaker, *orator*, with its closeness to the word for prayer *(oratio)*, Augustine insists this about the preacher: "let him be a pray-er before being a speaker" (4.15.32).

Nor is a conversion of mind and heart enough. Augustine insists that the preacher's "manner of life can itself be a kind of eloquent sermon" (4.29.61). People will not listen or give credence to one who has not taken to heart the words he preaches; rather, they will despise both the preacher and the word of God (4.27.60).

Theological Formation and Historical Confession

An attitude of piety, the practice of prayer, and a life of integrity, as indispensable as these are, do not exhaust the requirements of the person who would lead others to God. Such an individual must know the sacred Scripture. To come to the truth contained in Scripture, the minister needs to pursue an understanding of these texts using skills which allow the message contained in the inspired words to be known as they were written. Augustine, the rhetorician, appreciated the genius of human language: "Words, after all, are far and away the principal means used by human beings to signify the thoughts they have in their minds, whenever anyone wishes to express them. . . . [T]he verbal signs with which human beings express their thoughts are almost infinite in number" (2.3.4).

Given that there are many languages and not one, Scripture has had to be translated so that all peoples would come to the knowledge of salvation. Whoever reads Scripture must do so with the intention "to discover the thoughts and will of the authors it was written by, and through them to discover the will of God, which we believe directed what such human writers had to say" (2.5.6).

The meaning of a given message may not be obvious to the reader at first glance. To open up the meaning of texts, Augustine recommends certain human skills: the knowledge of languages in which they were written, namely, Hebrew and Greek. Augustine was well aware of the presence of a variety of versions of the Bible in the Latin world. He also realized that to translate a text, one needs to be sufficiently familiar with the context in which that text was written and to employ a knowledge of things derived from the people, even nonbelieving people, of various times. Most useful of all is history. All of these can serve the truth because there is but one truth and "all good and true Christians should understand that truth, wherever they may find it belongs to their Lord" (2.18.28).

But even when well equipped with such linguistic and other skills, the reader of Scripture will confront ambiguities in the sacred text. Augustine refers the preacher to what he calls "the rule of faith" which comes from "the plainer passages of scripture and from the authority of the church" (3.2.2). This phrase, "the rule of faith," appears in several instances where Augustine confronts or alludes to the need for a point of reference beyond the Scripture itself. As a bishop, Augustine preached and taught with an eye not only to the biblical text but to the words of the church's confession of faith which arose over time when one or another truth of faith was disputed. For instance, when he recognized that a heretical phrasing of the prologue of the Gospel according to John could connote a lack of equality of the Word, Jesus, with God, Augustine refuted such an interpretation by referring to "the rule of faith, which prescribes for us the equality of the three divine persons" (3.2.3). This "rule of faith" consists of the core beliefs of the church. It guides the preacher to the full and correct understanding of a biblical passage. When there is a question, for example, as to whether a text is to be understood figuratively or literally, reference is to be made to "the truth of the faith" (3.10.14). "The only thing," Augustine declares, "which it [Scripture] ever asserts is Catholic faith" (3.10.15). He reiterates this point later: the eloquence of the preacher must accord ultimately to "the rule of faith" (4.3.4).

Augustine insists that even when a variety of meanings may be found in Scripture, there is not a loss of true faith.

> But when from the same words of scripture not just one, but two or more meanings may be extracted, even if you cannot tell which of them the writer intended, there is no risk if they can all be shown from other places of the holy scriptures to correspond with the truth. However, those who are engaged in searching the divine utterances must make every effort to arrive at the intention of the author through whom the Holy Spirit produced that portion of scripture. But as I say, there is nothing risky about it, whether they do get at this, or whether they carve out another meaning from those words which does not clash with *right faith*, and is supported by any other passage of the divine utterances. (3.27.38, emphasis mine)

Such references to a norm outside of Scripture itself reflect the reality of the church in Augustine's time: a time of divisions within the church over doctrine and the practice of the faith. A pastor or church leader had not only to communicate the truth but also to dissuade people from erroneous teaching. The minister's command of an understanding of Scripture had to be guided by authoritative expressions of orthodox faith like the creeds. To unearth the truth of Scripture articulated by writers steeped in their own history, language, and culture, a fifth-century preacher needed to reference the faith of the church as found in its confessions of the faith, formulated within the context of the church's own life and history.

Theological Formation and Ecclesial Communion

Augustine revered the church as the true spiritual home of the Christian. He affirmed vigorously the unity of the church with Christ: "The Church is, after all, his body, as the teaching of the apostle confirms, and it is also called his wife. So while his body consists of many parts, having different functions, he binds it together with the knot of unity and love, as its proper kind of health. But during this age he trains and purges it with various kinds of salutary vexations and distress, so that once it has been snatched from this world, he may bind his wife the Church to himself forever" (1.16.15).

The bishop of Hippo understood that Christ and the church were bound together: "head and body, that is Christ and Church, constitute one person." He draws out the implication that "we should not let it baffle us when a text passes from head to body and from body to head, and yet still refers to one and the same person" (3.31.44).

Augustine did not idealize the nature of the church but recognized that the church consists of a mixture of both what is true and lasting and what is imperfect and only temporary. He speaks of the church as the Israel of the Spirit. The church, which is Christ, is the spiritual Israel "distinguished from that Israel of the flesh, which is one nation, by newness of grace, not by privilege of race, and by attitude of mind rather than by nationality of any kind" (3.34.49). This same church is "gathered together out of all the nations and destined to reign with Christ forever, is itself the land of the blessed, the land of the living (Psalm 27:13) and is to be understood as what was given to the fathers, when it was promised them by the sure and immutable will of God" (3.34.49).

Writing at a time when communities differed regarding the precise canon of Scripture, Augustine insisted on the importance of recognizing the authority of the church for making a final determination of what authority a particular book might carry. The faithful reader should "follow the authority of the majority of the Catholic Churches, among which, of course, are those that have the privilege of being apostolic sees and having received letters from the apostles" (2.8.12). Nor does one read the Scriptures in isolation from the church and its acknowledged leaders. Augustine cites Cyprian and Ambrose as "authors who by reading these [passages of the apostle] have made advances in the knowledge of matters pertaining to divinity and salvation, and have ministered that knowledge to the Church" (4.21.45).

Toward the end of his work, when reflecting on the importance of the preacher and teacher being a person aware of and attuned to God, "who can ensure that we say what is needed and in the way it is needed," Augustine urges a kind of learning and proficiency in speech "as befits a man of the Church" (4.15.32). Those who are "charged with the role of teacher in the Church" must be given "rules about what or how they should teach, if the Holy Spirit is making them teachers" (4.16.33).

Three Lessons for Theological Educators

Theological formation for church ministry takes seriously the significance of faith and virtue in the lives of students.
Augustine took advantage of what competencies in history, literature, and language could offer him in opening up the Scriptures. But he also quite clearly conceived of the goal of theological study as the formation of moral and religious persons. To be sure, not every student comes to the study of theology aware that its questions are ultimately questions that have, to recall Murray's words above, "personal consequences that touch every aspect of his conduct, character, and consciousness." The planning and programming of theological studies will not be complete if it does not take into account this personal dimension of theological education: the need and the opportunity for students to examine the truth claims of religion with a view toward their own growth in faith and in the Christian life.

If Augustine's concept of teaching Christianity were to shape the teaching of theology, it would set before teachers and administrators the goal of leading students not only to critical thinking about matters of faith and ethics but to critical living in the light of an informed and deepened faith and moral life.

Theological formation takes seriously the necessity of relating the truths found in biblical texts to historical confessions of faith.
Augustine did not elaborate upon a hermeneutic which would step-by-step guide the student of sacred Scripture through competing truth claims when conflicting interpretations of biblical texts arose. He simply affirmed the need to take into account normative expressions of faith which arose in the community along with the inspired word. His references to the "rule of faith" testify to the understanding that words are not truths that stand by themselves but are bearers of truths which abide in a community of faith.

How does this apply to the situation of teaching theology in the twenty-first century? In their approach to Scripture, today's theology students find themselves on the horns of a dilemma, caught between the simplistic claims of biblical fundamentalism on the one side and the elusive appeal of historical relativism on the other. Teachers of theology need to instill in their students a clear, coherent understanding of the relationship between the enduring and indeed normative revelation in Scripture and the content of faith expressed in creedal statements as these have arisen in the church in response to new questions and new insights.

Theological formation takes seriously the reality of the church as a communion of faith and the community where education, especially for ministry, finds its points of departure and arrival.

Augustine's own journey into the church and his subsequent dedication to its service witness to an ecclesiology that was operative in his life, even as it illuminated the path he laid out for the teaching of Christian doctrine. For him it would be inconceivable to explore the teachings of Christian faith outside of a community which nurtured faith and a true understanding of it. Theology and theological education are both communal exercises, not only because one belongs to a company of scholars or teachers, but all the more so because the pilgrimage to religious truth and Christian living is a path of accompaniment with fellow disciples.

In the context of a very individualistic culture which manifests itself even in the Christian churches of the United States across denominational lines, theological formation faces a twofold challenge. The first is to draw students of theology into theology and formation as the work of a community of faith and not merely individuals working out their own needs. The second is to expand the theological enterprise beyond denominational lines to attend, as Augustine did, to the church as called to unity. This is the ecumenical challenge of theological formation today. Just as theology forms one within a faith community, so too it forms the community to become one in faith and love. Such a vision of theology's purpose inspired Augustine as pastor and as theologian. A similar vision would serve well the pastors and theologians of tomorrow.

CHAPTER TWENTY-ONE

The Classic Idea of the University: Its Relevance in the Twenty-first Century

JAN MILIČ LOCHMAN

The Common Ground

Our universities are complex and dynamic institutions. This is evident both from their past and present history. To give an autobiographical illustration: when one who was a student and a professor in Prague comes to Basel via Saint Andrews and New York, he encounters along the way an astonishing and in some respects bewildering wealth of academic life, diverse in both form and content. This is not to be explained simply by the various ways in which university life has been influenced by different social, economic, and political conditions. There is also the particular *genius loci* which in each case leaves its distinctive imprint on the tradition and ethos of the various universities. In these circumstances, does it make sense to speak of an "idea of the university"?

Certainly not, if we insist on interpreting this "idea" as something timeless and preestablished, an abstraction which must be accepted and striven for always, everywhere, and by all. A rich diversity of ideas is represented by our universities, and it would be quite ridiculous to try to make them all fit a Procrustean bed of a single ideal model.

There are nevertheless common elements. They are suggested by the very name: *universitas*. That name is no empty convention, no meaningless *flatus vocis*. This name suggests important implications: *universitas magistrorum et scholarium — universitas literarum — universitas civium*. These expressions in-

---

This lecture was originally given at the conference on "The Role of the University at the Threshold of the Twenty-first Century: Commemorating the 650 Years of the Charles University," in Prague on 4 April 1998.

dicate a common direction, one which seems to me vitally important for a closer understanding of the classic idea of the university. In the light of its very name, the university sees itself as a *communicative entity*. The "living spirit" of the university is demonstrated in communication: between teachers and students, between representatives of different disciplines and faculties, between members of the academy and the citizens of its society at large. Every breakdown in communication, every refusal of dialogue, is a sin against the spirit of university.

Our past and present history is full of such sins, of such breakdowns in communication. Charles University, which celebrated its 650th anniversary in 1998, cannot forget what happened just before it celebrated its 600th anniversary in 1948: disruption of the communicative spirit by totalitarian ideology. In another way, academic life in the West also suffered sometimes from disruptive conflicts in recent times (when it was not always only students who refused dialogue). Yet precisely in the face of these discouraging experiences the classic idea of university could gain its fresh relevance and orienting value. To reflect on that idea is not an anachronistic luxury or a sign of a spiritual nostalgia but a task which will still confront us even in the year 2002 — and beyond.

Genius Loci

I would like to begin my own contribution to this theme from my own vantage point, namely, the University of Basel. It is perhaps particularly appropriate for this purpose, in a way which transcends its purely local and contingent features. In the first place, in its historical roots the University of Basel is a foundation which is still medieval in origin (as is its older sister, the Charles University), one, moreover, which is fairly conscious of being close to its classic source. In the second place, it is a school which, despite all the tensions experienced in its history, was largely spared the violent assaults and breaks in tradition suffered by some other universities, particularly in central and eastern Europe.

Some of Basel's outstanding scholars were fully aware of the significance of this tradition. Two examples will suffice: firstly, from the last century, Jakob Burckhardt, the acute interpreter of the history of European culture and, at the same time, a realistic analyst of political developments down into the twentieth century, bore impressive witness to the abiding value of the classic European university, declaring it to be not only "desirable in earthly terms but also metaphysically indispensable."[1] Secondly, in our own times

---

1. Quoted by Werner Kägi, *Über das Prophetische bei Jacob Burckhardt* (Basel: J. W. Goeth-Stiftung, 1971), p. 18.

philosopher Karl Jaspers, in particular, made with unmatched intensity repeated attempts to develop the "idea of the university (as) the idea of our intellectual existence."[2]

How to understand the classic idea of the university?

Chiseled in stone on the main entrance to the University of Basel are some Latin words which greet members of the university as they enter its building each day: "Mortalis homo ex dono Dei per assiduum studium adipisci vale scientiae margari tam quae eum ad mundi arcana cognoscenda dilucide introducit et in infimo loco natos evehit in sublimes." This is an abbreviated version of the preamble to the papal bull of Pope Pius II of 12 November 1459 founding the University of Basel. In this preamble, the founder sets before his university the lofty aim of *"obtaining by God's gift and assiduous study the pearl of knowledge."* This knowledge *"leads to a good and happy life. It makes him who acquires it like God, leading him to a clear understanding of the world's mysteries. . . . It uplifts to the very heights those born in humblest estate."*

These words were not freshly minted by the pious humanist Aeneas Silvius Piccolomini, though the Basel papal bull clothes them with particular beauty. Parallels can be found for most of the thoughts expressed, for example, in the foundation charters of such sister universities as Prague, Cologne, and Greifswald. What we find reflected in the foundation charter of the Basel university, therefore, can be considered the basic consensus of the classic European university.

Do these words, so plainly medieval in provenance and spirit, still have any message for our orientation today? Has the classic idea of the university, one of the important cultural achievements of the second Christian millennium, some validity for the third millennium? One can have respectable grounds for doubting this. The modern way — especially the modern scientific way — was largely shaped in conscious opposition to the spirituality and the world picture which lies behind the Magna Charta of our university. The terms of this foundation cannot be applied *in globo,* just as they stand, to our contemporary situation, still less to our plans for the future. In certain fundamental respects, however, they strike me as, *mutatis mutandis,* still considerably relevant to us today despite the abyss of time separating us from them historically. Every community lives through the ideals articulated in its classics. Our reflections on the mission of the university for the twenty-first century may be stimulated by

2. See Karl Jaspers, *Die Idee der Universität* (Berlin: Springer-Verla, 1980); *Vom lebendigen Geist der Universität* (Munich: Rechenschaft und Ausblick, R. Piper & Co., 1951), pp. 159-85; *Wahrheit und Wissenschaft* (Basel: Basler Universitatsreden, Helbing & Lichtenhahn, 1960).

recalling the original motivation as reflected in this preamble. As I see it, there are three emphases which deserve our attention here.

The Commendation of Scientific Knowledge

The confidence with which the preamble to the Basel foundation charter commends scientific knowledge is impressive. It assumes that knowing is basic to human nature: for human beings, the search for truth is a gift, a duty, a necessity. This is our need and our privilege. It is our need, since we cannot survive in the world at all unless we make an effort to understand it. Unlike our fellow creatures, we are by nature rather ill equipped to survive. Our possibilities of life have first to be secured, and for this, knowledge is indispensable. This is our problem. At the same time, however, it is also our privilege. In the search for knowledge and in our acquisition of knowledge, we tower above other creatures; we are "closer to the angels than to the animals," equipped as we are to become autonomous and responsible agents of life.

The conviction that inquiry and knowledge are supremely important anthropologically is deeply rooted in the heart and mind of European humanity in both its constituent sources: in the philosophy of antiquity, with its intense concern for a carefully thought-out methodical program of knowledge and research, and in the Bible, with its emphasis on the special mission and task of humanity within the creation as a whole.

To describe humane research, its nature and its method, the preamble employs two particularly memorable phrases: it speaks of *"assiduous study"* but also of the gift of *"the pearl of knowledge."* These two poles establish the magnetic field of scientific activity. In the first place, science is *assiduum studium:* patient, concentrated, unremitting labor, in rigorous thinking and rigorous living. The true scientist is distinguished from the dilettante by disciplined method and from the intellectual "playboy" by his acceptance of the need for "asceticism" (once again, both in his thinking and in his living). It is no accident that the forerunner of the modern-style researcher is to be found in the medieval monasteries, in the ranks of those who, in a life of deliberate and intense discipline, devoted themselves unreservedly to the quest for truth and, in doing so, discovered and made accessible to others the springs of intellectual concentration. For every science, *assiduum studium* is a vital necessity.

But there is another vital necessity, too. This is indicated by the reference in the preamble to *"the gift of God"* and the image of *"the pearl of knowledge."* The reference here to both theological and aesthetic motifs may strike us at first as rather surprising. Yet these motifs, too, are part and parcel of the self-understanding of Western science. I think of Plato and his insistence that the discovery of truth also proceeds in acts of enthusiasm and delight in the beautiful, delight in the beauty of truth, and that it therefore includes aesthetic and even erotic dimensions. I am also thinking of the biblical insight that fundamental human truths, human self-discovery, are imparted to us "as in a dream," as an unearned bonus and gift. These motifs, too, have their proper place in our reflections on humane research. Not, of course, as a substitute for *assiduum studium* or in competition with it, but as a reminder of its sobering and yet liberating limits. Without the life breath of creative delight and grace, even the best-intentioned scientific enterprise can all too easily become a fruitless, cheerless, and therefore unconvincing business. Our universities and scientific institutions will be well advised to remember and accept both recommendations of the preamble: to become places of *assiduum studium* and of delight in the *margarita scientiae.*

The commendation of scientific research is no longer automatic today. In the last century, especially in positivistically inclined cultural currents, people still looked to scientific progress for the solution — even the final solution — of almost all human problems. Our mood has become much more skeptical today. We are keenly aware of the *ambivalence* of science, of natural science especially. To be sure, the development of science in the modern era constitutes one of the most impressive chapters in the history of human liberation. The proofs of its success in extending our human possibilities speak for themselves. Today, however, we are constantly confronted with the debit side of the balance sheet: namely, with the destructive potentialities of scientific advance. Increasingly today the complaint is heard, especially among young people, that this modern science (which, with its development to global dimensions, is also in part dependent on and in the service of political, economic, and military lobbies representing a growing threat to our daily life by the damage it does to our environment) is both potentially and in fact a destructive force.

General and radical distrust of this kind should be countered patiently and persistently. *Abusus non tollit usum.* This is already true on economic grounds — though there is more to it than that — and, quite concretely, in respect of our continent. Rather sparingly equipped by nature as far as its resources of raw materials are concerned, Europe's prospects of survival largely depend on its research and industry. Our political leaders would be sawing off the branch on which we are all sitting if they were to cut off our scientific research, our universities and other research institutions. But we are not at liberty to ignore the grounds for mistrust. These must be critically considered and analyzed. The ambivalence of scientific development is an undeniable fact. Not everything which *can* be researched automatically *ought* to be researched. In both planning and carrying out research, discrimination must be exercised, especially in the matter of priorities for research. In more concrete terms, what we must strive for and promote is a research which is in *benefit to humanity* and the whole order of created life.

Toward the Good Life in Solidarity

The foundation bull of the University of Basel is not content to sing the praises of scientific research; it also raises and answers the question of *the aim and purpose of science and knowledge.* Two points here seem to me especially relevant. The splendid image of *"the pearl of knowledge"* is followed immediately, almost in the same breath as it were, by the qualifying clause: *quae bene beateque vivendi viam prebet.* This *margarita scientiae* "points the way to the good and happy life." Human knowledge, in other words, is not an end in itself, a static, self-contained goal; it is not a *scientia pro scientia,* unconnected with other fundamental concerns of human life. Quite the contrary: it is connected with the whole of life, wherein it has its special yet at the same time ministerial role. This role is service for life, indeed, the service of the *good* and *happy* life. It is commended only as a *humane* knowledge, a knowledge serving the sustainable needs of humanity.

This impressive phrase *bene beateque vivere* confronts the university and our science with the basic *ethical* question of the purpose and aims of scientific research and also, concretely, of its consequences and acceptance of responsibility for them. Reviewing the triumphal march of science, we find it hard to avoid the impression that this important ethical aspect of its problems has been neglected and often suppressed. Scientific research has for centuries been regarded as an enterprise "beyond good and evil." In some respects, there were understandable grounds for this: the desire, for example, to safeguard against the imposition of moralistic and even ideological "leading strings" on scientific work. Against this it was argued that the scientist's only ethic was the obligation to use impeccable methods. What is demanded of the researchers is thorough research. They are not to let themselves be bothered or sidetracked by the consideration of possible consequences. The question of a *bene beateque vivere* was deliberately left out of scientific account.

Among scientists with a sense of responsibility, this question has been coming right into the forefront of attention today — in the first place among the leading nuclear physicists, and here in a particularly dramatic way. In the fifties, the "Oppenheimer case" rightly acquired the character of an example, along with the physicist's confession that "for the first time, the scientist has known sin." Researchers in other fields, too — biologists, medical doctors, chemists, and others — are taking a lively interest in ethical questions. At most of our universities, the interdisciplinary work can hardly be imagined without the ethicists' participation. There is a growing consensus that the scientist has the obligation to ask not only the technical question as to whether something can be done, but also the ethical (and political) question as to whether it *ought* to be done. Science's capacity to do something is not ethically neutral. Science is power, and power confronts us with questions concerning our ethical and political responsibility for its use. The foundation charter is right. Only when it aims at a "good and happy life" does knowledge shine with the pristine luster of a pearl.

Another phrase in the preamble points in the same direction. The sign and the goal of the knowledge we are to seek is that it *"uplifts to the very heights those born in humblest estate."* The primary reference here, of course, is to the intellectual rank of scientists, the special dignity which "clearly distinguishes the knowledgeable person from the ignorant." At the same time, however, the intellectual rank also has a social dimension which seems to me worth noting. Did not the status conferred by knowledge sometimes make it possible already in the Middle Ages for scholars to cross the barriers of the social order determined by birth? I would like to pick this up and, following the inherent dynamic of this motif, deliberately extend its application by a further relevant emphasis. Scientific research, if it is to benefit humanity, should be directed especially to *those born in the humblest estate.*

In every age, of course, advanced research is primarily the work of the intellectual elite (the *periti* and *sublimes*); this certainly does not mean, however, that it need remain a purely elitist concern, an alliance of interest between privilege and profit. That this temptation exists cannot be denied. But to succumb to it would be a betrayal to the spirit of science as reflected in our preamble. Scientific research which is of benefit to humanity owes an obligation to those who are the worst off in any given situation. At the beginning of the twenty-first century, on the threshold of this new millennium, this focus on the *res publica* cannot halt at the city boundaries or at the frontiers of one country (or even of one continent); it must take into account the interests of the underprivileged throughout the world; it must be directed to the *populorum progressio*, the "development of the peoples" (to use the phrase made famous by one of Pius II's successors in our time).

I realize, of course, that the direction hitherto taken by Western science has never yet even adequately matched these broad objectives of a humane scientific research, despite all our democratic and social achievements. A great deal is still to be done in both science and politics. Does that mean that our preamble's standpoint is merely idealistic utopianism? I would hope not. Initial steps have been taken suggesting a change of outlook in the direction indicated. I am thinking, for example, of renewed efforts to make access to our universities easier for the disabled — access both in the broader sense and in the physical sense by at least undertaking the structural alterations required to ensure that the handicapped are not confronted with almost insuperable obstacles at every step and turn. I am also thinking of the (certainly still too slowly) growing recognition that our European centers of learning also have obligations to the developing countries and must learn to fulfill them more effectively. Following the direction indicated in our preamble, it is in this respect in particular that the dynamic inherent in the term *universitas* is to be developed in a spirit of solidarity.

At the threshold of the twenty-first century, the noticeable revival of ethical interest among the scholars of the sister faculties (particularly the faculties of medicine and science) becomes a veritable challenge to theologians within our universities. The dedication of the biblical prophets to the demands of social justice and the unconditional commitment of Jesus Christ to the underprivileged ones gain a fresh validity in universal (ecumenical!) horizon. The biblical initiatives belong to the fundamental orientation without which humankind (and its responsible research) could hardly survive the challenges of the future. Its loss would obstruct the way toward the "good life in solidarity." Theological education has to see that the "biblical salt" does not lose its ethical savor. A concentrated theological endeavor and, indeed, the resulting theological literacy are in the interest not only of the church but also of the university and society.

The Perspective of the "Nevertheless"

There is a persistent note of *confidence and hope* in the classic idea of the university as expressed in the words of the foundation charter of the Basel university. The founder is deeply persuaded of the good sense of his foundation. The overall horizon of meaning in which he sees this university set leaves him no room for doubt on this score. He is convinced that the human passion for truth and knowledge is no vain clutching at thin air. Assiduous study attains the goal; the way to the good and happy life is open; even those born in the humblest estate can achieve the heights.

Such hopeful tones are only too familiar to us in the history of modern science. From the Renaissance right down to the nineteenth century via humanism and the Enlightenment, this entire era was undoubtedly marked by an almost uninterrupted mood of optimism and belief in progress. The sun is dawning on the human race and we are on the way, finally and irresistibly, to the good and happy life. Our science and knowledge provide the keys of both heaven and earth.

Today, however, in the face of that ambivalence of the consequences of scientific progress, we have largely lost this utter confidence of earlier times. To many it now seems incredible and even suspect. Does that pervasive note of confidence, then, still have anything to say to us? I believe it has, but on one condition; namely, that we listen very carefully to what the preamble actually says and do not immediately equate it with the optimistic views of subsequent modernism. The confidence reflected in the preamble is not of a fanatical and unqualified kind but is rather a sober, realistic, and conditional confidence.

We note that the first and key adjective used in the preamble to define humanity is *mortalis*. Humanity is mortal, subject to death. Knowledge of the boundary established for us as human beings by death and by the penchant for sinful destruction "cooperating" with it in the background is assumed by the author; it is an integral part of his view of human life. *Memento mori* (Remember death!) is the watchword of the Middle Ages — in life as in science. The medievals were far more sober and realistic than we moderns in this respect. For it is surely undeniable that the reality of death and of the destructive potential universally present in us human beings has come to be repeatedly suppressed or explained away in the course of modern times. Only by this suppression did the dream of irresistible progress and the delusion of omnicompetence become possible. The foundation charter of our university indulges in no such dream, succumbs to no such delusion. Its promise is held out to *mortal* humanity.

But that is precisely the point: *the promise* is for us mortals. "In this fallible life" *(in hac labili vita)* not everything is in vain. According to the preamble, our mortal life is embedded in a broad supportive horizon of meaning. The ground underlying and supporting this horizon is *God*. The word "God" occurs twice in the preamble: at the beginning, where the foundation of the university, the human capacity for knowledge, and knowledge itself are understood as *"ex dono Dei,"* as God's gift; and at the end, where humanity is finally defined in terms of "likeness to God" *(Deo similis)*. In other words, scientific research in general and the university in particular are no fortuitous arbitrary creations. They have in God's sight a mission and a promise. This confirms the responsibility of scientists, confirms the summons to a scientific research which seeks to benefit humanity. But it also confirms and substantiates confidence and a sober hope in respect of this enterprise.

This theological background and perspective of the classic idea of the university can also throw light, perhaps, on the daily life of scientists, for their encouragement. Every science has its times of breakthrough and success but also its time of failure and frustration. Every research institute echoes sometimes to the joyful cry "Eureka!" but sighs of dejection and skepticism are also heard, as well as the question, "What's the point of it all?" How frequently has the situation of the scientist (and the teacher as well) been likened to and interpreted in terms of the situation of the mythical Sisyphus! I am thinking, for example, of Albert Camus's penetrating interpretation of *la condition humaine*. Is this not in fact the situation of the scientist many days in his or her life, the situation of the medical scientist especially: every day having to push or drag the stone a little farther up the hill of knowledge — or even the mountain of death — only in the end to find, again and again, that the stone rolls back down the hill?

I would not deny or minimize the human dignity of this Sisyphean view. It deserves our respect and admiration. However, our preamble discloses another way, a "third way" between optimism and pessimism. As we have seen, the preamble recognizes, even expressly refers to, the infirmity and fallibility of human life. By naming the name of God, however, it introduces the liberating dimension and a horizon of meaning which encompasses every success and failure: it introduces *the perspective of the "nevertheless."* Expressed pictorially: over against the stone of Sisyphus, it sets the stone of the Easter story, the stone which was rolled away from the tomb of Jesus. *Ex dono Dei*, the power of nothingness is not an ultimate power.

As is impressively clear in the foundation charter, the way taken by our culture and its scientific research has been deeply marked by this hope despite all deviations to one side or the other, whether optimistic or pessimistic. This perspective, it seems to me, is important both for our personal life and for our life in the university and society. It does not remove us to a safe distance from Sisyphus. We are not spared the backward-rolling stones. Both in science and in life, stones are more common than pearls. Yet amidst all our Sisyphean experiences, we are — *ex dono Dei* — not left without the perspective of hope.

What this might mean in practice for our daily life of research may be expressed as follows. The reference to God takes the pressure off us and at the same time encourages us. We are not the omnicompetent "fixers," the lords of life and death. Although the task of science is entrusted to our hands and heads, it is not exclusively in our control. We are not called upon to assume the part of Atlases who must bear the destiny of our cosmos on their shoulders. Once we know this, the pressure — but not the responsibility — is taken off us. At the same time, it *encourages* us: *ex dono Dei*, we are no longer fighting an eternally losing battle. Our work, our science, our life — all these are under the abiding "promise of the nevertheless." It is not pointless and futile for us, either as hu-

401

man beings or as scientists in our faculties and institutions, to push or drag our small or huge stones a few paces up the steep hill in our academic endeavor and struggle for the benefit of humanity.

Ideas and Realities

At this point at the very latest, but probably much earlier on, some of us who are accustomed to dealing with the daily life of our universities today will have begun to feel some doubts and cavils stirring within us. Surely all this is far too idealistic. Is not the classic idea of the university too grand to be true? "This is not the way things really are."

In his address on the 500th anniversary of the University of Basel, Karl Jaspers raised this very question and offered his own very realistic picture of "the way things really are": "The sciences have now been divided into compartments which take hardly any notice whatever of each other. The university is an aggregate of expert schools for specialized training. It is a department store where people can obtain the knowledge they need for their particular purposes. Concealed behind this organized system is an intellectual anarchy. The foundations of faith have either vanished or else are not admitted."[3] The somber tones of this picture reflect the situation of our university life. To some extent, the developments on which Jaspers focuses attention cannot be objected to without qualification. The shattering of the medieval consensus, for example, cannot simply be attributed to sheer willfulness. It was also in part the result of a concern for intellectual freedom. Even if it were possible, any artificial restoration of that consensus would be undesirable. We live in an age marked by the plurality of ideas, both in society and in the university. There can be no legitimate objection to that. Every ideological compulsion creates intolerable conditions. The history of the Charles University in the last fifty years provides many dismal examples. This must not be forgotten. A free exchange of ideas in mutual communication is a *conditio sine qua non*. However, a legitimate plurality of positions turns problematic when it becomes an immobilized pluralism or a chaotic lack of relationships, when mutual interrogation and the quest for agreement in thought and life are paralyzed.

Already in the seventeenth century, evaluating the developments of modern science, Jan Amos Comenius remarked with bitter irony: "For themselves only the metaphysicists sing their little songs; for themselves the physicists applaud their achievements; for themselves the agronomists perform their

3. Jaspers, *Wahrheit und Wissenschaft*, pp. 19-20.

dances; for themselves the ethicists construct their laws; for themselves the politicians formulate their schemes; for themselves the mathematicians celebrate their triumphs; for themselves rule the theologians."[4]

Facing these discouraging developments, Comenius emphasizes *the communicative character of truth.* Not only the classic idea of university, but human culture (and future) are in jeopardy if the representative scholars refuse to communicate and coordinate their endeavor. What is needed is an atmosphere of mutual respect between the members of different faculties and of different orientation, but also the common respect for the whole of the creation which transcends (and precedes!) all our specialized expertise and competence (an idea which, in our time, is of great concern to Václav Havel as well to the first postcommunist rector of the Charles University, Radim Palous).

In this sense, a realistic view of "the way things really are" is no ground for abandoning the classic idea of university and capitulating fatalistically to existing conditions. The very opposite is true. Above all, in a time when dangerous developments bring closer the physical and spiritual destruction of humanity, Jaspers speaks of a possible "deluge without surviving Noah!" — the communicative spirit inherent in the very idea of the university is desirable and valid today — and for the coming century. "If the university as originally conceived has not already come into existence, it would be necessary, today especially, to invent it."[5]

4. Jan Amos Comenius, *Prodromus pansophiae,* ed. H. Hornstein (Düsseldorf, 1963), p. 51.

5. Nikolaus Lobkowicz, *Die Zukunft der Universität* (MS, Munich, 1987).

Contributors

Ruth H. Bersin, Director
Refugee Immigration Ministry
Boston, Massachusetts
Ruth H. Bersin is an Episcopal priest who has spent many years in social service ministry and work with human migration. She was the founding director of Interfaith Refugee Ministry in Connecticut, served as Executive Director of Tokyo English Life Line, and is currently the Executive Director of Refugee Immigration Ministry in Boston. She is a pastoral pychotherapist at the Greater Lowell Pastoral Counseling Center and has given a number of papers on the subject of spirituality as a resource for healing after traumatic experiences. She holds an M.A.R. from Colgate Rochester Divinity School, an M.Div. from Yale Divinity School, and a D.Min. from the Graduate Theological Foundation.

Alkiviadis C. Calivas
Professor of Liturgics
Holy Cross Greek Orthodox School of Theology
Father Alkiviadis C. Calivas is an ordained priest of the Greek Orthodox Church. He has been teaching at Holy Cross Greek Orthodox School of Theology since 1978 and holds the title of Professor of Liturgics. In addition to his faculty position, he has served the school as dean (1980-93) and president (1996-97). He has published many articles and essays and three books, including *Great Week and Pascha in the Greek Orthodox Church*.

Francis X. Clooney, S.J.
Professor of Comparative Theology
Boston College
Francis X. Clooney, S.J., Professor of Comparative Theology, Boston College, is

also Coordinator for Interreligious Dialogue for the Society of Jesus in the United States. His most recent books are *Preaching Wisdom to the Wise: Three Treatises by Roberto de Nobili in Dialogue with the Learned Hindus of South India*, translated and introduced by Francis X. Clooney and Anand Amaladass, S.J. (St. Louis: Institute of Jesuit Sources, 2000); and *Hindu God, Christian God: How Reason Helps Faith to Cross the Boundaries between Religions* (New York: Oxford University Press, 2001).

Carrie Doehring
Professor of Pastoral Psychology
Boston University School of Theology
Carrie Doehring is an assistant professor of pastoral psychology at the School of Theology and Graduate School of Boston University. She is also a licensed psychologist and supervisor at the Danielsen Institute, a mental health clinic and pastoral counseling center at Boston University, and is ordained in the Presbyterian Church (U.S.A.). Her latest book is *Taking Care: Monitoring Power Dynamics and Relational Boundaries in Pastoral Care and Counseling.*

William Everett
Professor of Religion and Society
Andover Newton Theological School
William Johnson Everett is Herbert Gezork Professor of Christian Social Ethics at Andover Newton Theological School. He has taught and conducted research in Germany, India, and South Africa as well as in Catholic and Protestant institutions in the United States. Among his recent writings are *The Politics of Worship: Reforming the Language and Symbols of Liturgy* (United Church Press, 1999) and *Religion, Federalism, and the Struggle for Public Life: Cases from Germany, India, and America* (Oxford University Press, 1997).

Anne Foerst
Professor of Theology and Computer Science
St. Bonaventure University
Dr.theol. Anne Foerst has been visiting professor of Theology and Computer Science at St. Bonaventure University in Olean, New York, since January 2001. Previously she worked as research scientist at the Artificial Intelligence Laboratory, Massachusetts Institute of Technology, and was also affiliated with the Center for the Study of Values in Public Life of Harvard Divinity School.

At the AI-Lab she served as the theological adviser for the Cog and Kismet Projects, two attempts to develop embodied, autonomous, and social robots in analogy to human infants which might learn and develop more mature intelligences. She also initiated and directs "God and Computers," a dialogue project initially between Harvard Divinity School, the Boston Theological Institute, and MIT, and now to be continued at St. Bonaventure. In this function she has organized several public lecture series and public conferences on artificial intelligence, computer science, and concepts of personhood and dignity. She is consultant of several projects which explore the connection of new media and religion and especially the Christian churches; she has also presented various keynote addresses on the interaction between religion and science.

Her work on dialogue has been covered in numerous print and Internet media (MSNBC, *Boston Globe, Der Spiegel,* etc.), and she appeared on many radio and television shows (ABC, CNN, Odysee, etc.).

She has published papers in academic journals on the possibility for mutual enrichment between artificial intelligence, the cognitive sciences, and Jewish and Christian theologies and anthropologies. She also writes for popular media to bring the question of religion and science to a broader audience and is contributing editor for the quarterly magazine *Spirituality & Health.* Her research centers mostly on questions of embodiment and social interaction as central elements in human cognition, on questions of personhood and dignity, and on how to bring theology back into public discourse in secularized, high-tech Western cultures. She is currently working on her first book: *On Robots and Humans . . . — and God.*

Thomas Groome
Professor of Religious Education
Boston College

Thomas Groome, Professor of Theology and Religious Education at Boston College, holds a doctorate in theology and education from the joint program of Union Theological Seminary and Columbia University (1976). His first book, *Christian Religious Education: Sharing Our Story and Vision* (Harper San Francisco, 1980, now published by Jossey-Bass), introduced a "shared Christian praxis approach" to religious education. In spring 2002, Harper San Francisco published his latest work entitled *What Makes Us Catholic: Eight Gifts for Life.* Much of his writing over the years has been of children's curricula. He is the primary author of William H. Sadlier's *God with Us* curriculum, grades kindergarten to eight (1984), and of Sadlier's *Coming to Faith,* grades kindergarten to eight; the latter has had two major revisions. These texts are widely used in Catholic schools and parishes throughout the United States.

S. Mark Heim
Professor of Theology
Andover Newton Theological School

S. Mark Heim is the Samuel Abbot Professor of Christian Theology at Andover Newton Theological School in Newton Centre, Massachusetts. He has been deeply involved in issues of religious pluralism and Christian ecumenism. He is the author of *Salvations: Truth and Difference in Religion* (Orbis Books, 1995) and *The Depth of the Riches: A Trinitarian Theology of Religious Ends* (Eerdmans, 2000). He is an ordained minister in the American Baptist Churches in the United States of America and represents that denomination on the Faith and Order Commissions of the World Council of Churches and the National Council of Churches of Christ in the USA. In addition to the theology of religions and ecumenical theology, his research interests include science and theology, Baptist history, and global Christianity. He is currently working on a study of the atonement.

Raymond Helmick, S.J.
Professor of Ecumenical Theology
Boston College

Raymond G. Helmick, S.J., teaches conflict resolution in the Department of Theology at Boston College. He has mediated over the years in a number of conflicts: Northern Ireland, the Israelis and Palestinians, Lebanese, Kurdish conflicts in Iraq and Turkey, the liberation of Zimbabwe, the countries of former Yugoslavia, and so on. Founding member and executive board member of the U.S. Interreligious Committee for Peace in the Middle East, he is also a senior associate of the Center for Strategic and International Studies. In addition to his numerous monographs and articles, Helmick is coproducer of "Unexpected Openings: Northern Ireland Prisoners," and has been actively engaged as coproducer of a series of films on religion and conflict resolution.

Walter Kaiser
President and Professor of Old Testament and Marketplace Ethics
Gordon-Conwell Theological Seminary

Walter C. Kaiser, Jr., has been President and Colman M. Mockler Distinguished Professor of Old Testament at Gordon-Conwell Theological Seminary (GCTS) from 1997 to the present. He has been a Distinguished Professor at GCTS since 1993. He was previously Academic Dean and Vice President of Education at Trinity Evangelical Divinity School, Deerfield, Illinois, 1980-92.

He is the author of thirty-one books, including *Toward an Old Testament Theology, A History of Israel,* and *Toward an Exegetical Theology.*

Jan Milič Lochman
Professor Emeritus of Theology
University of Basel
Jan Milič Lochman (1922), ThDr., D.D., Dr.h.c.mult. Dr. Lochman is Czech by origin and is Professor Emeritus of Theology at the University of Basel, and was Rector of the University, 1981-83. He was moderator of the Theological Department of the World Alliance of Reformed Churches, 1970-82. He is author of *The Faith We Confess: An Ecumenical Dogmatics* (Philadelphia and Edinburgh, 1984), and of *The Lord's Prayer* (Grand Rapids, 1990).

Alice Mathews
Professor of Education and Women's Studies
Gordon-Conwell Theological Seminary
Lois W. Bennett Distinguished Associate Professor of Educational Ministries and Women's Ministries, 1999.
Dr. Mathews presently occupies a chaired professorship at Gordon-Conwell Theological Seminary as the Lois W. Bennett Distinguished Associate Professor of Educational Ministries and Women's Ministries. In addition, she participates in a daily radio program (heard throughout North America) called *Discover the Word,* in which she teams with Haddon Robinson and Mart DeHaan in exploring biblical texts through informed conversation. She regularly travels throughout the USA speaking at Christian conferences and churches on a variety of subjects related to women's lives and experience. She has authored two books of Bible studies for women, *A Woman God Can Use* and *A Woman Jesus Can Teach,* and is presently working on three new books.

John MacInnis, S.T.D.
Pastor
Saint John the Baptist Catholic Church
Rev. John E. MacInnis is currently pastor of Saint John the Baptist Catholic Church in Peabody, Massachusetts. A priest of the Archdiocese of Boston, Father MacInnis holds a Doctorate in Sacred Theology from the Pontifical Gregorian University in Rome and has served as a faculty member of the North American College, Rome, and Saint John's Seminary, Brighton, Massachusetss. For several years he held the position of Director of the Office for Ecumenical and Interreligious Affairs of the Archdiocese of Boston and, while at Saint John's Seminary, was a member of the BTI Committee on International Mission and Ecumenism.

Brian McDermott, S.J.
Rector and Professor of Theology
Georgetown University
Father Brian McDermott, S.J., a native of Brooklyn, New York, is the rector (religious superior) of the 65-member Jesuit Community at Georgetown University and teaches theology at Georgetown University. From 1973 until 2000 he was a member of the faculty of Weston Jesuit School of Theology in Cambridge, Massachusetts, one of the two schools of theology sponsored by the Society of Jesus in the U.S. From 1982 to 1988 he was rector of the 120-member Jesuit community in Cambridge. He served as Academic Dean at WJST for eight years, returning to full-time status on the faculty the summer of 1999. His teaching and writing interests are in the areas of christology, theological anthropology, Ignatian spirituality, and authority and leadership. In this last area he has collaborated with faculty at Harvard University's Kennedy School of Government. Besides engaging in the ministry of spiritual direction, he has offered workshops for men and women engaged in that service. He is tertian director for the Maryland and New York Provinces of the Jesuits. (Tertians are Jesuits who, having lived fifteen or more years in the Order, are preparing to pronounce final vows.) Fr. McDermott is in his ninth year as a member of the Georgetown University Board of Directors.

He has written numerous articles and two books: *What Are They Saying about the Grace of Christ?* (Paulist Press) and *Word Become Flesh: Dimensions of Christology* (Liturgical Press).

Robert Cummings Neville
Robert Cummings Neville is Professor of Philosophy, Religion, and Theology and Dean of the School of Theology at Boston University. The past president of the American Academy of Religion, the International Society for Chinese Philosophy, and the Metaphysical Society of America, he is the author of numerous articles and books, the most recent of which are *Boston Confucianism* and *Symbols of Jesus: A Christology of Symbolic Engagement.*

Alvin Padilla
Director of the Center for Urban Ministerial Education
Professor at Gordon-Conwell Theological Seminary
Born in Ponce, Puerto Rico, Al and his family migrated to New England when he was twelve years old. In search of jobs, his family settled in Haverhill, Massachusetts, then a thriving mill town. With the growth of the Latino community and the decline of the local mills, hard times came upon the city in general and the Latino community in particular. During these hard times Al became ac-

tively involved in the life of the community. Al's experience in community organizing and involvement led to the establishment of Latinos Unidos Inc., a community organization seeking the betterment of life for everyone in the community. It was during those years of leadership that Al felt the call to Christian ministry.

Upon graduating from Gordon-Conwell Theological Seminary in 1984, Al and his wife Cathy relocated to New York State, where they established the Spanish Eastern School of Theology. This ministry-training institute seeks to prepare Hispanic men and women for Christian ministry in a Latino context.

In 1992 Al became pastor of the Fort Washington Heights Presbyterian Church in the Washington Heights neighborhood of Manhattan. He served there for five years. At the same time, he was assistant professor of Christian studies at Nyack College in Nyack, New York.

In 1997 Al became the academic dean of Gordon-Conwell's Center for Urban Ministerial Education (CUME). The last three years have witnessed a tremendous growth in the CUME program, with near record levels in both student head count and full-time equivalency. The administrative offices have been renovated and the debt on the property has been canceled. Degree and course offerings have been expanded and the future of CUME looks bright indeed.

Al and his wife Cathy reside in Haverhill with their four children: Marta (fourteen), Ben (twelve), Luke (nine), and Jacob (five). His favorite pastime is playing and coaching baseball with his children.

Rodney L. Petersen
Executive Director, Boston Theological Institute
Adjunct in several of the BTI schools
(Rev.) Rodney L. Petersen, PhD., is Executive Director of The Boston Theological Institute (BTI), the consortium of Orthodox, Roman Catholic, and Protestant theological schools, seminaries, and university divinity schools in the Greater Boston area. In addition to this work with the BTI, Dr. Petersen teaches in both the member schools and overseas. He teaches in the areas of history and ethics, currently focusing on issues of religion and violence. His courses in Comparative Christianity take students to various regions of the world in order to understand and film ways in which faith communities are implicated in regional violence and how they can be avenues of reconciliation. He is an ordained minister in the Presbyterian Church, U.S.A., serving on several of their committees, and assists as interim pastor of the Allston Congregational Church (U.C.C.). His most recent publications include *Earth at Risk,* co-edited with Donald Conroy (Amherst: Humanity Books, 2000) and *For-*

giveness and Reconciliation: Religion, Public Policy and Conflict Transformation, co-edited with Raymond Helmick, S.J. (Philadelphia: Templeton Foundation Press, 2001).

Elisabeth Schüssler Fiorenza
Professor of New Testament
Harvard Divinity School

Elisabeth Schüssler Fiorenza is internationally recognized for her pioneering work in biblical interpretation and feminist theology and feminist studies in religion. She has taught at the University of Notre Dame, Episcopal Divinity School, Union Theological Seminary, Humboldt University in Berlin, and the Universities of Tübingen and Heidelberg. Her teaching and research focus on questions of biblical and theological epistemology, hermeneutics, rhetorics, and the politics of interpretation, as well as on issues of theological education, racial equality, and democracy. She is a cofounder and the co-editor of the *Journal of Feminist Studies in Religion* and a coeditor of *Feminist Theology, Concilium.* She was elected as the first woman president of the Society of Biblical Literature and has served on the editorial boards of the major biblical journals and societies. Her published work includes *Der vergessene Partner; Priester für Gott; In Memory of Her* (translated into twelve languages); *Bread Not Stone; Judgment and Justice: The Book of Revelation; But She Said; Discipleship of Equals; Revelation — Vision of a Just World; The Power of Naming; Searching the Scriptures; Jesus — Miriam's Child; Sharing Her Word; Rhetoric and Ethic; Jesus and the Politics of Interpretation,* and *Wisdom Ways.*

Fred Douglas Smith, Jr., Ph.D.
Associate Professor of Christian Education and Youth Ministry
Pittsburgh Theological Seminary

Rev. Dr. Fred D. Smith, Jr., is Associate Professor of Christian Education and Youth Ministry and Director of the Lilly Endowment–funded Summer Youth Institute at Pittsburgh Theological Seminary. He is also the pastor of Fellowship United Methodist Church in Ambridge, Pennsylvania. He is formerly Associate Director of the Interfaith Health Program, where he served for seven years at the Carter Presidential Center in Atlanta, Georgia. He was educated at Harvard College (BA, 1973), Perkins School of Theology of Southern Methodist University (M.Div. cum laude, 1984), and Emory University (Ph.D., 1997).

He has directed a number of national initiatives, including the Pan Methodist Coalition on Alcohol and Drug Abuse; the Carnegie Foundation's "Not Even One" — Kids and Guns Initiative; the National Volunteer Training Center's National Interfaith Alliance against Substance Abuse; the Southern Christian Leadership Conference's Stop the Killing Campaign; and the Carter Center's Whole Communities Collaborative national program.

He has authored or coauthored many articles, reports, and curricula, such as *The Revival of Hope: Faith-Based Substance Abuse Curriculum* (Cokesbury); *Not Even One: A Report on the Crisis of Children and Firearms* (Carter Center); "Violence as Public Health Issue for African American Youth" *(Caregiver Journal);* "The Role of the Faith Community" *(Community Links);* "Black-on-Black Violence" *(Contagion: Journal of Violence, Mimesis and Culture).*

He has won many honors, including the Samuel L. Davis Award for Graduate Studies (1996); the Wyle-Gaines Public Service Award (1995); the Clarence True Wilson Award for Outstanding Leadership in the Prevention of Alcohol and Substance Abuse Problems (1994); and the Leadership in Christian Education award (1990).

David Tracy
Andrew Thomas Greeley and Grace McNichols Greeley Distinguished Service Professor of Catholic Studies
Professor of Theology and of the Philosophy of Religion, the Divinity School and the Committee on Social Thought
University of Chicago
David Tracy has his S.T.L. and S.T.D. from Gregorian University. He teaches a wide variety of courses in contemporary theology. He offers classes in philosophical, systematic theology, and constructive theology and hermeneutics, and courses dealing with issues and persons in religion and modern thought. He also teaches the Greek classic texts with Professor David Greene. His publications include *The Analogical Imagination: Christian Theology and the Culture of Pluralism* and *On Naming the Present: Reflections on God, Hermeneutics, and Church.* Professor Tracy is currently writing a book on God.

Andrew Walls
Guest Professor of Ecumenics and Mission
Harvard Divinity School
Andrew Walls holds a D.D. from the University of Edinburgh. After a long and distinguished career that has spanned nearly five decades, Andrew Walls joined the Princeton Theological Seminary faculty in 1997 as a guest professor of ecumenics and mission.

Dr. Walls began his career as the librarian at Tyndale House in Cambridge in 1952. After five years of service, he joined the faculty of Fourah Bay College in Sierra Leone, West Africa, as a lecturer in theology. In 1962 he was appointed the head of the Department of Religion at the University of Nigeria. He currently serves as an honorary professor at the University of Edinburgh. He also serves as the curator of collections at the Centre for the Study of Christianity in the Non-Western World. In addition, Dr. Walls is a visiting professor at the Africa Theological Fellowship Graduate School at the University of Natal and Akrofi-Christaller Memorial Centre in Ghana.

Dr. Walls is active in several research projects, including the Scholar's Initiative in Studies of Mission and International Christianity (SISMIC) and the North Atlantic Missiology Project (NAMP).

Wesley Wildman
Professor of Theology
Boston University School of Theology
Wesley J. Wildman is Associate Professor of Theology and Ethics at Boston University, where he directs the graduate programs in systematic and comparative theology and the doctoral degree in science, philosophy, and religion. Ordained in the Uniting Church of Australia, he has served churches in Sydney and in Piedmont, California. His scholarly research involves inquiry into theological topics using resources from multiple disciplines, including the natural and social sciences. He is author of *Fidelity with Plausibility: Modest Christologies in the Twentieth Century,* and editor with W. Mark Richardson of *Science and Religion: History, Method, Dialogue.*

Index of Names and Subjects

Index of Scripture References

HEBREW BIBLE/ OLD TESTAMENT

NEW TESTAMENT

420